Model–Driven Domain Analysis and Software Development:
Architectures and Functions

Janis Osis
Riga Technical University, Latvia

Erika Asnina
Riga Technical University, Latvia

T0350437

Information Science
REFERENCE

INFORMATION SCIENCE REFERENCE

Hershey · New York

Director of Editorial Content: Kristin Klinger
Director of Book Publications: Julia Mosemann
Acquisitions Editor: Lindsay Johnston
Development Editor: Joel Gamon
Typesetter: Keith Glazewski
Production Editor: Jamie Snavely
Cover Design: Lisa Tosheff

Published in the United States of America by
Information Science Reference (an imprint of IGI Global)
701 E. Chocolate Avenue
Hershey PA 17033
Tel: 717-533-8845
Fax: 717-533-8661
E-mail: cust@igi-global.com
Web site: http://www.igi-global.com

Library of Congress Cataloging-in-Publication Data

Model-driven domain analysis and software development : architectures and
functions / Janis Osis and Erika Asnina, editors.
      p. cm.
 Includes bibliographical references and index.
 Summary: "This book displays how to effectively map and respond to the real-
world challenges and purposes which software must solve, covering domains such
as mechatronic, embedded and high risk systems, where failure could cost human
lives"--Provided by publisher.
 ISBN 978-1-61692-874-2 (hardcover) -- ISBN 978-1-61692-876-6 (ebook) 1.
Automatic control. 2. Computer simulation. 3. Computer software--
Development. I. Osis, Janis, 1929- II. Asnina, Erika, 1978-
 TJ213.M5373 2010
 005.1--dc22
                          2010043567

British Cataloguing in Publication Data
A Cataloguing in Publication record for this book is available from the British Library.

Table of Contents

Foreword xvii

Preface xix

Acknowledgment.. xxvii

Section 1
Theory-Driven Holistic Domain Modeling and Analysis in the Context of MDA

Chapter 1
Is Modeling a Treatment for the Weakness of Software Engineering?.. 1
  Janis Osis, Riga Technical University, Latvia
  Erika Asnina, Riga Technical University, Latvia

Chapter 2
Topological Modeling for Model-Driven Domain Analysis and Software Development:
Functions and Architectures.. 15
  Janis Osis, Riga Technical University, Latvia
  Erika Asnina, Riga Technical University, Latvia

Chapter 3
Topological Functioning Model as a CIM-Business Model 40
  Erika Asnina, Riga Technical University, Latvia
  Janis Osis, Riga Technical University, Latvia

Chapter 4
Derivation of Use Cases from the Topological Computation Independent Business Model................ 65
  Janis Osis, Riga Technical University, Latvia
  Erika Asnina, Riga Technical University, Latvia

Chapter 5

A Multidimensional Approach for Concurrent Model-Driven Automation Engineering 90

    Sebastian Rose, Technische Universität Darmstadt, Germany

    Marius Lauder, Technische Universität Darmstadt, Germany

    Michael Schlereth, Siemens AG, Germany

    Andy Schürr, Technische Universität Darmstadt, Germany

Section 2
Model-Driven Engineering and Model-Driven Architecture

Chapter 6

Model-Driven Configuration of Distributed Real-Time and Embedded Systems 115

    Brian Dougherty, Vanderbilt University, USA

    Jules White, Virginia Tech, USA

    Douglas C. Schmidt, Vanderbilt University, USA

Chapter 7

Model-Driven Automated Error Recovery in Cloud Computing 136

    Yu Sun, University of Alabama at Birmingham, USA

    Jules White, Virginia Tech, USA

    Jeff Gray, University of Alabama, USA

    Aniruddha Gokhale, Vanderbilt University, USA

Chapter 8

Productivity Analysis of the Distributed QoS Modeling Language 156

    Joe Hoffert, Vanderbilt University, USA

    Douglas C. Schmidt, Vanderbilt University, USA

    Aniruddha Gokhale, Vanderbilt University, USA

Chapter 9

Domain-Driven Reuse of Software Design Models 177

    Audris Kalnins, IMCS University of Latvia, Latvia

    Michał Śmiałek, Warsaw University of Technology, Poland

    Elina Kalnina, IMCS University of Latvia, Latvia

    Edgars Celms, IMCS University of Latvia, Latvia

    Wiktor Nowakowski, Warsaw University of Technology, Poland

    Tomasz Straszak, Warsaw University of Technology, Poland

Chapter 10

Quality-Driven Database System Development 201

    Iwona Dubielewicz, Wrocław University of Technology, Poland

    Bogumila Hnatkowska, Wrocław University of Technology, Poland

    Zbigniew Huzar, Wrocław University of Technology, Poland

    Lech Tuzinkiewicz, Wrocław University of Technology, Poland

Chapter 11
Exploring Business Value Models for E-Service Design...232
Jelena Zdravkovic, Stockholm University & Royal Institute of Technology, Sweden
Tharaka Ilayperuma, Stockholm University & Royal Institute of Technology, Sweden

Chapter 12
An MDA Approach for Developing Executable UML Components 254
Simona Motogna, Babeş- Bolyai University, Romania
Bazil Pârv, Babeş- Bolyai University, Romania
Ioan Lazăr, Babeş- Bolyai University, Romania

Section 3
Modeling of Product Lines and Patterns

Chapter 13
Model-Driven Impact Analysis of Software Product Lines...275
Hyun Cho, University of Alabama, USA
Jeff Gray, University of Alabama, USA
Yuanfang Cai, Drexel University, USA
Sonny Wong, Drexel University, USA
Tao Xie, North Carolina State University, USA

Chapter 14
Systematic Use of Software Development Patterns through a Multilevel and Multistage
Classification...304
Sofia Azevedo, Universidade do Minho, Portugal
Ricardo J. Machado, Universidade do Minho, Portugal
Alexandre Bragança, Instituto Superior de Engenharia do Porto, Portugal
Hugo Ribeiro, Primavera Business Software Solutions, Portugal

Chapter 15
Reducing Enterprise Product Line Architecture Deployment and Testing Costs via
Model Driven Deployment, Configuration, and Testing...334
Jules White, Virginia Tech, USA
Brian Dougherty, Vanderbilt University, USA

Chapter 16
Applying UML Extensions in Modeling Software Product Line Architecture of a Distribution
Services Platform 351
Liliana Dobrica, University Politehnica of Bucharest, Romania
Eila Ovaska, VTT Technical Research Centre of Finland, Finland

Chapter 17
Model-Driven Requirements Specification for Software Product Lines 369
Mauricio Alférez, Universidade Nova de Lisboa, Portugal
Ana Moreira, Universidade Nova de Lisboa, Portugal
Vasco Amaral, Universidade Nova de Lisboa, Portugal
João Araújo, Universidade Nova de Lisboa, Portugal

Section 4
Surveys

Chapter 18
Domain Modeling Approaches in IS Engineering 388
Marite Kirikova, Riga Technical University, Latvia

Chapter 19
Model-Driven Performance Evaluation of Web Application Portals 407
Nilabja Roy, Vanderbilt University, USA
Douglas C. Schmidt, Vanderbilt University, USA

Compilation of References 438

About the Contributors 473

Index 483

Detailed Table of Contents

Foreword xvii

Preface xix

Acknowledgment..xxvii

Section 1
Theory-Driven Holistic Domain Modeling and Analysis in the Context of MDA

Section 1 contains several discussions on application of formal theories and mechanisms for domain modeling and analysis within Model Driven Architecture. The necessity of formal theories appeared from the longstanding crisis in software engineering. Just unification of standards and use of models without proper domain analysis will be not enough to get out of the crisis, while the very beginning of software development lacks application of formal (mathematical and system) theories. Application of Model Driven Architecture will be ministerial to wide understanding of this fact.

Chapter 1
Is Modeling a Treatment for the Weakness of Software Engineering?..1
Janis Osis, Riga Technical University, Latvia
Erika Asnina, Riga Technical University, Latvia

Chapter 1, Is Modeling a Treatment for the Weakness of Software Engineering? Crisis in software engineering still is in progress. Software development was and is rather art than engineering discipline. Osis and Asnina consider causes of weakness of software development and possible ways of improvement suggested by software community. They believe that Model Driven Architecture, which put main focus on models and modeling, can become a skeleton of software engineering, but it is not enough. In order to become software engineering in its actual sense, software development requires, first, solid theory (mathematics), and, second, standardization and critical assessment of development techniques.

Chapter 2
Topological Modeling for Model-Driven Domain Analysis and Software Development:
Functions and Architectures...15
Janis Osis, Riga Technical University, Latvia
Erika Asnina, Riga Technical University, Latvia

Chapter 2, Topological Modeling for Model-Driven Domain Analysis and Software Development: Functions and Architectures. Architectural separation of concerns and model transformations provided by Model Driven Architecture is an important step towards formalization of software development, i.e., towards software engineering. However, true software engineering requires engineering models and techniques, which have solid theoretical foundations. Osis and Asnina discuss the theoretical basis of the topological functioning model and topological modeling that can be a part of those foundations. Construction of the topological functioning model promotes careful domain analysis and formal specification of the domain. In turn, this formal model can serve as a source for further activities of model-driven software development.

Chapter 3

Topological Functioning Model as a CIM-Business Model 40
     Erika Asnina, Riga Technical University, Latvia
     Janis Osis, Riga Technical University, Latvia

Chapter 3, Topological Functioning Model as a CIM-Business Model. Asnina and Osis discuss the first viewpoint, computation independent, and the corresponding model proposed by the OMG in Model Driven Architecture. Analysis of scientific publications shows that this model may include three sub-models conventionally named CIM-Knowledge Model, CIM-Business Model, and CIM-Business Requirements for the System. The first sub-model reflects a problem domain. The last one reflects a solution domain. The CIM-Business Model is a bridge between the problem and the solution. This chapter demonstrates properties of the topological functioning model as such a bridge – a formal CIM-Business Model.

Chapter 4

Derivation of Use Cases from the Topological Computation Independent Business Model 65
     Janis Osis, Riga Technical University, Latvia
     Erika Asnina, Riga Technical University, Latvia

Chapter 4, Derivation of Use Cases from the Topological Computation Independent Business Model. Osis and Asnina demonstrate derivation of use cases from the formal domain description, Topological Functioning Model. Theoretical foundations of this model ground on topology and system theory help in avoiding several limitations of use cases while keeping their simplicity, e.g. strict orientation on a solution, informal identification, conflicts and duplicates among use cases. Topological and functional properties of the topological functioning model allow establishing formal conformance between the solution domain model expressed by use cases and the problem domain model, thus increasing adequacy of the solution. In its turn, goal-based decomposition of the topological functioning model deals with conflicts and duplicates of use cases.

Chapter 5

A Multidimensional Approach for Concurrent Model-Driven Automation Engineering 90
     Sebastian Rose, Technische Universität Darmstadt, Germany
     Marius Lauder, Technische Universität Darmstadt, Germany
     Michael Schlereth, Siemens AG, Germany
     Andy Schürr, Technische Universität Darmstadt, Germany

Chapter 5, A Multidimensional Approach for Concurrent Model-Driven Automation Engineering. Rose et al. introduce a conceptual framework for the customization and integration of domain-specific modeling languages and tools in automation engineering, Concurrent Model-Driven Automation Engineering (CMDAE). CMDAE developed by Siemens AG and Technical University of Darmstadt relies on a multidimensional framework for model classification and manipulation purposes. CMDAE puts the main focus on the exchange and alignment of models needed for hardware and software development of automation devices and on the presentation of some extensions of the underlying graph grammar formalism motivated by its application to a real-world scenario. Application of this formal framework is demonstrated by the running example of High-Bay Warehouse Automation.

Section 2
Model-Driven Engineering and Model-Driven Architecture

Section 2 contains chapters which describe application of Model Driven Engineering and Model Driven Architecture for solving particular challenges in software system development. Chapters consider application of domain-specific techniques for cloud computing and distributed quality of services; and MDA for distributed real-time and embedded systems, system, and design of executable UML components, e-services and database systems. The proposed applications allow heightening quality of software development processes and products.

Chapter 6

Model-Driven Configuration of Distributed Real-Time and Embedded Systems 115
Brian Dougherty, Vanderbilt University, USA
Jules White, Virginia Tech, USA
Douglas C. Schmidt, Vanderbilt University, USA

Chapter 6, Model-Driven Configuration of Distributed Real-time and Embedded Systems. Dougherty, White and Schmidt suggest applying a paradigm of Model-Driven Architecture for ensuring that real-time quality-of-service (QoS) and resource constraints in distributed real-time and embedded systems (DRE) are satisfied. This chapter presents MDA techniques and tools that simplify and automate the configuration of COTS components for DRE systems. The authors provide an incremental methodology based on MDA principles for constructing modeling tools that can be used to create model instances of potential DRE system configurations.

Chapter 7

Model-Driven Automated Error Recovery in Cloud Computing 136
Yu Sun, University of Alabama at Birmingham, USA
Jules White, Virginia Tech, USA
Jeff Gray, University of Alabama, USA
Aniruddha Gokhale, Vanderbilt University, USA

Chapter 7, Model-Driven Automated Error Recovery in Cloud Computing. Sun et al. represent application of a Model-Driven Engineering paradigm, models and Domain Specific Modeling Languages (DSML), to automate error detection and recovery in clouds. The suggested approach is based on a run-time model specified by DSML that monitors and manages the running nodes in a cloud. Editing the models instead of using the traditional command-line interface facilitates administering changes in clouds. Besides that, the proposed approach allows semi-automation of cloud recovery - manually created recovery patterns can be used by automation infrastructure, which automatically replays the same recovery actions when an identical error state is encountered in the future.

Chapter 8

Productivity Analysis of the Distributed QoS Modeling Language 156

Joe Hoffert, Vanderbilt University, USA
Douglas C. Schmidt, Vanderbilt University, USA
Aniruddha Gokhale, Vanderbilt University, USA

Chapter 8, Productivity Analysis of the Distributed QoS Modeling Language. Hoffert, Schmidt and Gokhale discuss quantitative benefits of Distributed Quality-of-Services Modeling Language used within Model-Driven Engineering for designing valid QoS policy configurations and transforming the configurations into correct-by-construction implementations. The performed productivity analysis of DQML shows significant productivity gains compared with common alternatives, such as manual development using third-generation programming languages. The Data Distribution Service Benchmarking Environment tool suite is used as a case study to highlight the challenges of developing correct and valid QoS configurations, as well as to analyze the productivity benefits of DQML.

Chapter 9

Domain-Driven Reuse of Software Design Models 177

Audris Kalnins, IMCS University of Latvia, Latvia
Michał Śmiałek, Warsaw University of Technology, Poland
Elina Kalnina, IMCS University of Latvia, Latvia
Edgars Celms, IMCS University of Latvia, Latvia
Wiktor Nowakowski, Warsaw University of Technology, Poland
Tomasz Straszak, Warsaw University of Technology, Poland

Chapter 9, Domain-driven Reuse of Software Design Models. Kalnins et al. present an approach that combines facilities of model-driven software development and software reuse. The development process is illustrated starting from requirements specification in semiformal language. Then, the authors demonstrate composing of a platform independent model from the specified requirements by using transformations. Transformations are also applied to the platform independent model in order to get the software case, platform specific models and code. The suggested way of requirements specification supports discovering of similarities in requirements, which further can be used for reuse.

Chapter 10

Quality-Driven Database System Development 201

Iwona Dubielewicz, Wrocław University of Technology, Poland
Bogumiła Hnatkowska, Wrocław University of Technology, Poland
Zbigniew Huzar, Wrocław University of Technology, Poland
Lech Tuzinkiewicz, Wrocław University of Technology, Poland

Chapter 10, Quality-Driven Database System Development. Dubielewicz et al. discuss integration of database system development based on Mode Driven Architecture with quality models. The authors suggest using Quality-driven MDA framework that combines MDA software development and quality specification and assessment processes. The suggested framework demonstrates assessment of database system models by using external and internal quality models during the development process. The result is controlled quality of the final software product.

Chapter 11

Exploring Business Value Models for E-Service Design 232

Jelena Zdravkovic, Stockholm University & Royal Institute of Technology, Sweden
Tharaka Ilayperuma, Stockholm University & Royal Institute of Technology, Sweden

Chapter 11, Exploring Business Value Models for E-Service Design. Zdravkovic and Ilayperuma discuss challenges in efficient application of inter-organizational information systems where necessity to keep aligned business and ICT models exists. The authors suggest an MDA-based approach for design of Web services and their coordination. This approach focuses on a value-explorative analysis and modeling of business services starting from the computation independent model (CIM). Well-defined mappings and UML2 are used for transformations from computation independent to platform independent model.

Chapter 12

An MDA Approach for Developing Executable UML Components 254

Simona Motogna, Babeş- Bolyai University, Romania
Bazil Pârv, Babeş- Bolyai University, Romania
Ioan Lazăr, Babeş- Bolyai University, Romania

Chapter 12, An MDA Approach for Developing Executable UML Components. Motogna, Pârv and Lazăr discuss a use of main principles of model-driven development for applications that consist of service-oriented components. The authors suggest a framework for Software Component Definition, Validation, and Composition, COMDEVALCO. It consists of modeling (action) language, a component repository and a toolset, and supports separation of business logic and non-functional requirements. This framework can be used for developing executable service-oriented component models and in many software engineering courses as an example of applying model-driven principles in the software development process.

Section 3
Modeling of Product Lines and Patterns

Section 3 is dedicated to the development of Software Product Lines (SPLs) by using principles of Model Driven Engineering and MDA. In particular, chapter authors consider model-driven impact analysis, deployment, configuration, testing, and requirements specification of SPLs. Besides that, classification of patterns according to OMG metalevels and MDA principle of architectural separation of concerns is proposed.

Chapter 13
Model-Driven Impact Analysis of Software Product Lines... 275
Hyun Cho, University of Alabama, USA
Jeff Gray, University of Alabama, USA
Yuanfang Cai, Drexel University, USA
Sonny Wong, Drexel University, USA
Tao Xie, North Carolina State University, USA

Chapter 13, Model-Driven Impact Analysis of Software Product Lines. Cho et al. discuss how model-driven engineering can help software developers to deal with difficulties in understanding the consequences of changes in software product lines. The approach uses domain-specific modeling techniques to automate establishment of traceability relations, and impact analysis to understand the effect of changes on a product line. The domain-specific modeling makes it possible to lift the abstraction and representation of a software change such that it can be analyzed and separated from specific platform and environment details that would exist at the implementation level. The authors demonstrate the application of model-driven impact analysis by a case study in the domain of Mobile Media.

Chapter 14
Systematic Use of Software Development Patterns through a Multilevel and Multistage
Classification.. 304
Sofia Azevedo, Universidade do Minho, Portugal
Ricardo J. Machado, Universidade do Minho, Portugal
Alexandre Bragança, Instituto Superior de Engenharia do Porto, Portugal
Hugo Ribeiro, Primavera Business Software Solutions, Portugal

Chapter 14, Systematic Use of Software Development Patterns through a Multilevel and Multistage Classification. Azevedo et al. propose a systematic approach for identification of patterns that should be used in each certain stage of software development. This approach suggests multilevel and multistage pattern classification that is based on the software development process. The authors believe that leveraging patterns to metalevel M2 helps to turn the decisions on their application more objective as well as to reduce the misinterpretation of patterns from catalogues and the corruption of patterns during the pattern adaptation process. The pattern classification by type is illustrated by pattern examples.

Chapter 15

Reducing Enterprise Product Line Architecture Deployment and Testing Costs via
Model Driven Deployment, Configuration, and Testing.. 334

Jules White, Virginia Tech, USA
Brian Dougherty, Vanderbilt University, USA

Chapter 15, Reducing Enterprise Product Line Architecture Deployment and Testing Costs via Model-Driven Deployment, Configuration, and Testing. White and Dougherty discuss evaluation of the reliability of product-line architectures by using a technique supported by Model Driven Architecture. The large number of variations in product-line architectures is a challenge for developers, because only working configurations should be used. The MDA-based technique allows automation of much of the deployment, configuration, and testing of product-line architectures. The suggested approach is validated using a distributed constraint optimization system case study.

Chapter 16

Applying UML Extensions in Modeling Software Product Line Architecture of a Distribution
Services Platform 351

Liliana Dobrica, University Politehnica of Bucharest, Romania
Eila Ovaska, VTT Technical Research Centre of Finland, Finland

Chapter 16, Applying UML Extensions in Modeling Software Product Line Architecture of a Distribution Services Platform. Dobrica and Ovaska present a use of the built-in extension mechanisms of UML, namely, stereotypes, constraints and tagged values, for specification variations in software product line architectures for middleware services. The authors use two abstraction levels of design, conceptual and concrete, and three architectural views, structural, behavioral and deployment. The conceptual level means delayed design decisions concerning, e.g. technologies to be selected or details in functionality, whereas the concrete level illustrates realization of conceptual architecture. The proposed UML profile together with the design method would allow extensive and systematic using and maintaining software product line architectures in the framework of Model Driven Architecture.

Chapter 17

Model-Driven Requirements Specification for Software Product Lines 369

Mauricio Alférez, Universidade Nova de Lisboa, Portugal
Ana Moreira, Universidade Nova de Lisboa, Portugal
Vasco Amaral, Universidade Nova de Lisboa, Portugal
João Araújo, Universidade Nova de Lisboa, Portugal

Chapter 17, Model-Driven Requirements Specification for Software Product Lines. Alférez et al. disucss contribution of Model-Driven Development for requirements engineering in software product lines. The authors provide an overview of different approaches for specifying requirements models and composing models for specific products of a software product line and introduce a classification of them. One of the challenges in software product line modeling is mixing variability data into requirements specifications. The authors focus their research on exploiting a model-driven requirements specification approach, i.e. use case scenario-based techniques and feature models to model variability information in combination with specially tailored composition rules for requirements models provided by the Variability Modeling Language for Requirements (VML4RE).

Section 4
Surveys

Section 4 contains two interesting and wide surveys. The first one discusses domain modeling approaches in the field of information system engineering. This topic is very interesting because it shows fields that MDA covers at the present and should cover in future. The second one gives an overview of techniques for performance evaluation of Web application portals and analyzes advantages of the proposed model-driven approach.

Chapter 18
Domain Modeling Approaches in IS Engineering..388
    Marite Kirikova, Riga Technical University, Latvia

Chapter 18, Domain Modeling Approaches in IS Engineering. Kirikova provides an overview of domain modeling approaches and techniques used in Information System (IS) Engineering mainly in requirements engineering and enterprise modeling. This overview is interesting for users of Model-Driven Architecture (MDA), because IS Engineering has applied many different domain models long before the appearance of Model-Driven Architecture. The author demonstrates a place of MDA in the framework of cognitive engineering. Besides that the author discusses tool support for construction, maintenance and change management of the considered domain models.

Chapter 19
Model-Driven Performance Evaluation of Web Application Portals..407
    Nilabja Roy, Vanderbilt University, USA
    Douglas C. Schmidt, Vanderbilt University, USA

Chapter 19, Model-Driven Performance Evaluation of Web Application Portals. Roy and Schmidt give an overview of performance evaluation techniques. Basing on this overview, they discuss integration of Model Driven Architecture methods with performance analysis methods of Web application portals. The authors use this model-driven performance analysis and system management throughout Web application portal development lifecycles. Model-driven techniques and tools can predict web application portal performance accurately and help close the gap between domain-oriented performance problems and conventional performance modeling technologies. The proposed strategy should simplify the analysis of web application performance.

Compilation of References 438

About the Contributors 473

Index..483

Foreword

There's no question that use of MDA and other Model-Driven Software Development (MDSD) techniques is spreading rapidly. In mid-2002 BZ Research found that only 7% of software developers were using code generated from models in their applications (and even then always with some hand-tweaking). By mid-2008 a commissioned study conducted by Forrester Consulting on behalf of Unisys showed that 22% of developers claimed to be using MDD to drive development through some level of code generation.

There are several reasons for this strong growth. An obvious one is the increased productivity achieved when writing new software applications. Multiple studies over several years have shown productivity gains of around 35% when creating new code, compared to using traditional coding techniques. In spite of having to learn many new skills, software development teams nevertheless often report improved productivity from their very first MDSD project.

It's significant that these productivity gains also carry over into software maintenance. Model-driven software production would be little use if it made maintenance harder, since maintaining existing software today consumes up to 90% of all IT spending. However, laboratory studies show similar productivity improvements when maintaining model-based applications, compared to maintaining those where no precise model is available. In fact, the most spectacular MDSD benefits are often realised when moving an application to a new platform or a major revision of an exiting platform. Making changes to a code generator and re-generating a software application from source models can achieve in hours what might take months if the application code has to be modified by hand.

Another compelling reason for using MDA and other MDSD techniques is the quality of the resulting software. Buggy code that doesn't meet the its specifications costs more to own than high quality software, either because of the cost of finding and fixing the bugs, or the cost of the work-arounds required to compensate for them. Here again, empirical results are encouraging, with software generated from models having about one third the defect rate of hand-written code. As more software is found in safety-critical contexts, these improvements in code quality could literally become a matter of life and death.

It is against this background of the increasing use, importance and proven benefits of MDSD and Model-Driven Domain Analysis that Janis Osis and Erika Asnina have gathered an impressive list of international authors to describe significant new contributions to their theoretical foundations and survey how they are being applied. In this diverse collection of papers you will find contributions to several different aspects of these rapidly-growing fields. The thread that links them all, however, is a drive towards rigour and precision. While software development has traditionally been more of an empirical art than an engineering discipline, this is slowly changing as software users demand from software engineers the same levels of system reliability and predictability that are achieved by engineers in other disciplines. Several contributions to this book stem from the way that software is today increasingly embedded within complex systems that have mechanical, electronic and software components; those who build these systems quite rightly demand that the software components are built to the same levels of rigour as the non-software parts. Other contributions focus on the important but often-neglected topic of software configuration, recognising that complex software systems are often assembled from hundreds or even thousands of distinct software components, which must work together predictably and without conflict. In this, as in other aspects of Model-Driven Engineering, papers in this collection give valuable insights into the problems being addressed and make useful contributions to advancing current practice.

The closely-linked fields of Model-Driven Domain Analysis and Model-Driven Software Development are advancing rapidly as practitioners and theoreticians work together to create new techniques and extend our understanding of how and why existing methods work (and also why they sometimes fail). This impressive collection of papers makes a valuable contribution to both fields.

Andrew Watson
Vice-President and Technical Director
Object Management Group^{TM}
Cambridge, UK

Andrew Watson *has overall responsibility for OMG's technology adoption process, and also chairs the Architecture Board, the group of distinguished technical contributors from OMG member organisations which oversees the technical consistency of OMG's specifications. In previous lives Andrew researched distributed object type systems, wrote Lisp compilers and helped improve software engineering practices at large multi-nationals (but not all at the same time). He spends his spare time skiing down, gliding around or walking up mountains.*

Preface

Computer systems became a settled thing in people's life. Their application involves diverse aspects of our life from control of our family budget to solving serious scientific questions. Each domain of application or adoption of complex computer systems, a problem domain, has its own specific character. Complex computer systems, a solution domain, are intended for help in coping with this specificity and not for bringing additional hardship or constraints.

The specificity of the problem domain must be either adequately reflected in the computer system or adequately simplified, e.g. automated, optimized, modified, etc. Adequacy of the computer system to the application domain can only be provided by sufficient analysis and accurate modeling of the problem domain. Accurate means not only exact and complete, but also unambiguous for software developers who will take part in other stages of development.

Models and modeling have long history starting from times of the Ancient Near East and the Ancient Greek. People used to represent the surrounding world by using simple non-mathematical models. However, importance of mathematical models was also recognized and similar methods for building models were developed independently in China, India, and Persia. The closer to the modern times, the more complex become models and their building methods.

A model is a *simplified* representation of something that is real. In building models, the starting point is considering the real-world object, highlighting the necessary characteristics of this object and simplifying of unnecessary ones. Therefore, models describe only a part of the real-world object and are limited by their scope of application. An accurate model is a model that completely and unambiguously describes characteristics of the real-world object within the scope of application.

One of steps dedicated to increase accuracy of software development is appearance, or better to say, explicit formulation of ideas and principles of Model Driven Architecture (MDA) proposed by the Object Management Group (OMG). OMG MDA focuses developer's attention on proper design of the solution domain by using models. Undoubtedly, models as a way of reflection of the solution domain have also existed before MDA. These models were formal and informal. Formal models have been used and are used at the present mostly for process simulations. However, because of their complexity, a use of formal models is relatively narrow in the beginning of software development. In turn, informal models have wider application because of their simplicity, understandability and fast trainability. An additional factor of popularity of informal models was and stays a way of using models in software development. Models are not used as basic documentation, but as additional illustration of the solution domain, i.e., what is planned to implement. Code is that was and remains the basic documentation.

Software development uses different techniques for identification and specification of characteristics (specific or not) and requirements for a planned system. Most of them are primarily aimed at *solution domain* analysis, while the *problem domain* is regarded almost as a black box describing a number of aspects of the system. Formal mapping of knowledge about the problem domain into the software development process is a challenge until now.

The above described situation raises a few issues. The first one, which is the most important in our opinion, is a gap between the solution domain – a software system – and the real world. What domain is to be modeled at first: the domain of today's reality ("as is" or the problem domain) or the domain of customer's expected reality ("to be" or the solution domain)? If we develop software that must be used for some purposes in the real world, we must know how it will affect this world. It has especially critical importance for mechatronic, embedded and high risk systems, where failure costs could be human lives. Analysis of the problem domain is also important for complex business systems, wherein failures could lead to huge financial losses. The second issue is separation of concerns and unambiguous representation of the domains in specifications. We believe that formal mathematical methods could reduce inaccuracies and ambiguities of specifications.

Good news is that OMG MDA serves as a stimulus for changing the state of affairs. At the present, MDA puts the main focus on architectural separation of concerns in specifications, domain design, model transformation, and code generation activities. OMG MDA declares three independent but related viewpoints and corresponding models:

- Computation Independent Viewpoint and Computation Independent Model (CIM);
- Platform Independent Viewpoint and Platform Independent Model (PIM);
- Platform Specific Viewpoint and Platform Specific Model (PSM).

Models transformations are used for refinement of models. The transformation process can be performed manually, using profiles, using patterns and mappings and automatically. A mapping is a specification, including rules, output and input models, and other information, for transforming an input model in order to produce an output model. Technical choices and quality requirements can also be used as an input for transformation patterns. Models and mappings can be reused. MDA defines the following types of the mapping:

- A model type mapping, when it is specified between types described in a PIM language and a PSM language;
- A model instance mapping, where PIM elements, which are to be transformed, have to be identified and transformed in a particular way (marks can be used for identification of elements; marks may specify quality of service requirements on the implementation);
- A combined type and instance mappings;
- Templates, which are parameterized models that specify particular kinds of transformations;
- A mapping that is specified using a language to describe transformation of one model to another.

In our opinion, MDA and MDE partially address the second issue, namely, the separation of concerns. The PIM and PSM are related to customer's expected reality, the solution domain. The theoretical foundation of the CIM is quite unclear. Considering its definition, we can assume that it relates not only to customer's expected reality, but also to the domain of today's reality (the problem domain).

Domain analysis is not less important activity than design. Thus, Model-Driven Engineering (MDE) uses domain specific modeling languages (DSMLs) for domain analysis and modeling. DSMLs help in coping with domain specificity if universal modeling languages could not help. However, the issue is that models, which reflect the problem domain, usually are informal. This fact complicates application of transformation mechanisms from the beginning of software development. In order to implement transformation models must be at least formal in MDA sense, i.e. understandable by a computer, and at most they must have a formal theoretical base.

We believe that the use of formal models and approaches at the very beginning of the MDA software development life cycle addresses the both previously mentioned issues keeping and improving mechanisms of MDA. Formal mathematical methods could reduce inaccuracies and ambiguities of specifications. However, in contrast with informal methods, they usually require additional efforts in study and use. Therefore most developers of modeling languages try to avoid pure usage of those methods and suggest practice of so called semi-formal modeling languages that are formally described, but do not have any formal mathematical foundations. This book is dedicated to shift the way of developers' thinking, and to show that mathematics could be "light-weight". This means that mathematics is able to "hidden" complexity of its own mechanisms from a user, while keeping their efficiency.

AUDIENCE

The book is primarily intended for three audiences:

1. Software developers with some practical experience in development of information and software systems, who wish to acquire knowledge in applying Model Driven Architecture and Model Driven Engineering for systems such as software product lines, distributed systems, web application portals, and so on;
2. Professionals and researchers who interested in improvement of productivity of software development and quality of software products;
3. And could also be useful for computer science and information technology students who want to know more about the most advanced methods and approaches in software development.

Some prerequisite knowledge is desirable in order to benefit from the book:

1. Knowledge of the fundamental concepts of requirements engineering and object-oriented technology, such as business rules, classes, relationships, etc.;
2. Knowledge of the fundamental principles of Model Driven Architecture (and related languages such as a Unified Modeling Language) and Model Driven Engineering.

CONTENTS OF THE BOOK

The aim of this book is to give an overview of the current achievements in model-driven software development and to highlight those important things, which require deep research and efficient solutions. The necessity of efficient solutions that apply formal theories appeared from the longstanding crisis in software engineering. Just unification of standards and use of models without proper domain analysis will be not enough to get out of the crisis, while the very beginning of software development lacks application of formal (mathematical and system) theories. Application of Model Driven Architecture will be ministerial to wide understanding of this fact. Section 1 of the book, *Theory-Driven Holistic Domain Modeling and Analysis in the Context of MDA*, comprises several discussions on application of formal theories and mechanisms for domain modeling and analysis within Model Driven Architecture:

- Chapter 1, *Is Modeling a Treatment for the Weakness of Software Engineering?* Crisis in software engineering still is in progress. Software development was and is rather art than engineering discipline. Osis and Asnina consider causes of weakness of software development and possible ways of improvement suggested by software community. They believe that Model Driven Architecture, which put main focus on models and modeling, can become a skeleton of software engineering, but it is not enough. In order to become software engineering in its actual sense, software development requires, first, a solid theory that could also be presented in a form of "light mathematics"; and second, standardization and critical assessment of development techniques.

- Chapter 2, *Topological Modeling for Model-Driven Domain Analysis and Software Development: Functions and Architectures.* Architectural separation of concerns and model transformations provided by Model Driven Architecture is an important step towards formalization of software development, i.e., towards software engineering. However, true software engineering requires engineering models and techniques, which have solid theoretical foundations. Osis and Asnina discuss the theoretical basis of the topological functioning model and topological modeling that can be a part of those foundations. Construction of the topological functioning model promotes careful domain analysis and formal specification of the domain. In turn, this formal model can serve as a source for further activities of model-driven software development.

- Chapter 3, *Topological Functioning Model as a CIM-Business Model.* Asnina and Osis discuss the first viewpoint, computation independent, and the corresponding model proposed by the OMG in Model Driven Architecture. Analysis of scientific publications shows that this model may include three sub-models conventionally named CIM-Knowledge Model, CIM-Business Model, and CIM-Business Requirements for the System. The first sub-model reflects a problem domain. The last one reflects a solution domain. The CIM-Business Model is a bridge between the problem and the solution. This chapter demonstrates properties of the topological functioning model as such a bridge – a formal CIM-Business Model.

- Chapter 4, *Derivation of Use Cases from the Topological Computation Independent Business Model.* Osis and Asnina demonstrate derivation of use cases from the formal domain description, Topological Functioning Model. Theoretical foundations of this model ground on topology and system theory help in avoiding several limitations of use cases while keeping their simplicity, e.g. strict orientation on a solution, informal identification, conflicts and duplicates among use cases. Topological and functional properties of the topological functioning model allow establishing formal conformance between the solution domain model expressed by use cases and the problem domain model, thus increasing adequacy of the solution. In its turn, goal-based decomposition of the topological functioning model deals with conflicts and duplicates of use cases.

- Chapter 5, *A Multidimensional Approach for Concurrent Model-Driven Automation Engineering.* Rose et al. introduce a conceptual framework for the customization and integration of domain-specific modeling languages and tools in automation engineering, Concurrent Model-Driven Automation Engineering (CMDAE). CMDAE developed by Siemens AG and Technical University of Darmstadt relies on a multidimensional framework for model classification and manipulation purposes.

CMDAE puts the main focus on the exchange and alignment of models needed for hardware and software development of automation devices and on the presentation of some extensions of the underlying graph grammar formalism motivated by its application to a real-world scenario. Application of this formal framework is demonstrated by the running example of High-Bay Warehouse Automation.

Section 2, *Model-Driven Engineering and Model Driven Architecture*, contains chapters, which describe application of Model Driven Engineering and Model Driven Architecture for solving particular challenges in software system development. Chapters consider application of domain-specific techniques for cloud computing and distributed quality of services; and MDA for distributed real-time and embedded systems, system, and design of executable UML components, e-services and database systems. The proposed applications allow heightening quality of software development processes and products:

- Chapter 6, *Model-Driven Configuration of Distributed Real-time and Embedded Systems*. Dougherty, White and Schmidt suggest applying a paradigm of Model-Driven Architecture for ensuring that real-time quality-of-service (QoS) and resource constraints in distributed real-time and embedded systems (DRE) are satisfied. This chapter presents MDA techniques and tools that simplify and automate the configuration of COTS components for DRE systems. The authors provide an incremental methodology based on MDA principles for constructing modeling tools that can be used to create model instances of potential DRE system configurations.
- Chapter 7, *Model-Driven Automated Error Recovery in Cloud Computing*. Sun et al. represent application of a Model-Driven Engineering paradigm, models and Domain Specific Modeling Languages (DSML), to automate error detection and recovery in clouds. The suggested approach is based on a run-time model specified by DSML that monitors and manages the running nodes in a cloud. Editing the models instead of using the traditional command-line interface facilitates administering changes in clouds. Besides that, the proposed approach allows semi-automation of cloud recovery - manually created recovery patterns can be used by automation infrastructure, which automatically replays the same recovery actions when an identical error state is encountered in the future.
- Chapter 8, *Productivity Analysis of the Distributed QoS Modeling Language*. Hoffert, Schmidt and Gokhale discuss quantitative benefits of Distributed Quality-of-Services Modeling Language used within Model-Driven Engineering for designing valid QoS policy configurations and transforming the configurations into correct-by-construction implementations. The performed productivity analysis of DQML shows significant productivity gains compared with common alternatives, such as manual development using third-generation programming languages. The Data Distribution Service Benchmarking Environment tool suite is used as a case study to highlight the challenges of developing correct and valid QoS configurations, as well as to analyze the productivity benefits of DQML.
- Chapter 9, *Domain-Driven Reuse of Software Design Models*. Kalnins et al. present an approach that combines facilities of model-driven software development and software reuse. The development process is illustrated starting from requirements specification in semiformal language. Then, the authors demonstrate composing of a platform independent model from the specified requirements by using transformations. Transformations are also applied to the platform independent model in order to get the software case, platform specific models and code. The suggested way of require-

ments specification supports discovering of similarities in requirements, which further can be used for reuse.

- Chapter 10, *Quality-Driven Database System Development*. Dubielewicz et al. discuss integration of database system development based on Model Driven Architecture with quality models. The authors suggest using Quality-driven MDA framework that combines MDA software development and quality specification and assessment processes. The suggested framework demonstrates assessment of database system models by using external and internal quality models during the development process. The result is controlled quality of the final software product.

- Chapter 11, *Exploring Business Value Models for E-Service Design*. Zdravkovic and Ilayperuma discuss challenges in efficient application of inter-organizational information systems where necessity to keep aligned business and ICT models exists. The authors suggest an MDA-based approach for design of Web services and their coordination. This approach focuses on a value-explorative analysis and modeling of business services starting from the computation independent model (CIM). Well-defined mappings and UML2 are used for transformations from computation independent to platform independent model.

- Chapter 12, *An MDA Approach for Developing Executable UML Components*. Motogna, Pârv and Lazăr discuss a use of main principles of model-driven development for applications that consist of service-oriented components. The authors suggest a framework for Software Component Definition, Validation, and Composition, ComDeValCo. It consists of modeling (action) language, a component repository and a toolset, and supports separation of business logic and non-functional requirements. This framework can be used for developing executable service-oriented component models and in many software engineering courses as an example of applying model-driven principles in the software development process.

Section 3, *Modeling of Product Lines and Patterns*, is dedicated to the development of Software Product Lines (SPLs) by using principles of Model Driven Engineering and MDA. In particular, chapter authors consider model-driven impact analysis, deployment, configuration, testing, and requirements specification of SPLs. Besides that, classification of patterns according to OMG metalevels and MDA principle of architectural separation of concerns is proposed. Chapters that summarize authors' experience are the following:

- Chapter 13, *Model-Driven Impact Analysis of Software Product Lines*. Cho et al. discuss how model-driven engineering can help software developers to deal with difficulties in understanding the consequences of changes in software product lines. The approach uses domain-specific modeling techniques to automate establishment of traceability relations, and impact analysis to understand the effect of changes on a product line. The domain-specific modeling makes it possible to lift the abstraction and representation of a software change such that it can be analyzed and separated from specific platform and environment details that would exist at the implementation level. The authors demonstrate the application of model-driven impact analysis by a case study in the domain of Mobile Media.

- Chapter 14, *Systematic Use of Software Development Patterns through a Multilevel and Multistage Classification*. Azevedo et al. propose a systematic approach for identification of patterns that should be used in each certain stage of software development. This approach suggests multilevel and multistage pattern classification that is based on the software development process. The authors believe that leveraging patterns to metalevel M2 helps to turn the decisions on their application more objective as well as to reduce the misinterpretation of patterns from catalogues and the corruption of patterns during the pattern adaptation process. The pattern classification by type is illustrated by pattern examples.

- Chapter 15, Reducing Enterprise Product Line Architecture Deployment and Testing Costs via Model-Driven Deployment, Configuration, and Testing. White and Dougherty discuss evaluation of the reliability of product-line architectures by using a technique supported by Model Driven Architecture. The large number of variations in product-line architectures is a challenge for developers, because only working configurations should be used. The MDA-based technique allows automation of much of the deployment, configuration, and testing of product-line architectures. The suggested approach is validated using a distributed constraint optimization system case study.

- Chapter 16, *Applying UML Extensions in Modeling Software Product Line Architecture of a Distribution Services Platform*. Dobrica and Ovaska present a use of the built-in extension mechanisms of UML, namely, stereotypes, constraints and tagged values, for specification variations in software product line architectures for middleware services. The authors use two abstraction levels of design, conceptual and concrete, and three architectural views, structural, behavioral and deployment. The conceptual level means delayed design decisions concerning, e.g. technologies to be selected or details in functionality, whereas the concrete level illustrates realization of conceptual architecture. The proposed UML profile together with the design method would allow extensive and systematic using and maintaining software product line architectures in the framework of Model Driven Architecture.

- Chapter 17, *Model-Driven Requirements Specification for Software Product Lines*. Alférez et al. disucss contribution of Model-Driven Development for requirements engineering in software product lines. The authors provide an overview of different approaches for specifying requirements models and composing models for specific products of a software product line and introduce a classification of them. One of the challenges in software product line modeling is mixing variability data into requirements specifications. The authors focus their research on exploiting a model-driven requirements specification approach, i.e. use case scenario-based techniques and feature models to model variability information in combination with specially tailored composition rules for requirements models provided by the Variability Modeling Language for Requirements (VML4RE).

Section 4, *Surveys*, comprises two interesting, wide surveys. The first one discusses domain modeling approaches in the field of information system engineering. This topic is very interesting because it shows fields that MDA covers at the present and should cover in future. The second one gives an overview of techniques for performance evaluation of Web application portals and analyzes advantages of the proposed model-driven approach. They are the following:

- Chapter 18, *Domain Modeling Approaches in IS Engineering*. Kirikova provides an overview of domain modeling approaches and techniques used in Information System (IS) Engineering mainly in requirements engineering and enterprise modeling. This overview is interesting for users of Model-Driven Architecture (MDA), because IS Engineering has applied many different domain models long before the appearance of Model-Driven Architecture. The author demonstrates a place of MDA in the framework of cognitive engineering. Besides that the author discusses tool support for construction, maintenance and change management of the considered domain models.

- Chapter 19, *Model-Driven Performance Evaluation of Web Application Portals*. Roy and Schmidt give an overview of performance evaluation techniques. Basing on this overview, they discuss integration of Model Driven Architecture methods with performance analysis methods of Web application portals. The authors use this model-driven performance analysis and system management throughout Web application portal development lifecycles. Model-driven techniques and tools can predict web application portal performance accurately and help close the gap between domain-oriented performance problems and conventional performance modeling technologies. The proposed strategy should simplify the analysis of web application performance.

The first part of the book is special. It demonstrates application of the "light mathematics" for formalization of problem domain modeling, and hence, for advancement of software development. The book shows that application of formal models and methods as well as knowledge of system development accumulated in requirements engineering and enterprise modeling (as mentioned in the last part of the book) are ways of increasing quality of problem domain analysis and modeling in the field of MDE, in general, and MDA, in particular.

The rest of chapters of the book are dedicated to different applications of MDA and MDE in software development for increasing quality of software products (e.g. web applications, database systems, software product lines) and processes (impact analysis, performance analysis, QoS analysis). These applications demonstrate MDA and MDE power in implementing architectural separation of concerns.

Janis Osis and Erika Asnina
Riga, Latvia,
November, 2010

Acknowledgment

Many people contributed directly and indirectly to this book. First, we appreciate our colleagues from Riga Technical University for their support. We express our special gratitude to Uldis Sukovskis, who is the head of Department of Applied Computer Science, for his permission to dedicate a part of our work time for making this book.

Then, we would like to thank all chapter authors for their fast and positive reaction on call for book chapters. Quality of authors' contributions gave us confidence, because otherwise this book would not exist. We wish to express our deep gratitude to Andy Schuerr, Jeff Gray and Douglas C. Schmidt for their good advice on invitation of other authors and to Juan Trujillo for his help in inviting reviewers.

We would also like to gratitude all the reviewers and express our sincere thanks to Gundars Alksnis, Janis Silins, Jeff Gray, Marite Kirikova, Bazil Parv, Douglas C. Schmidt, Jules White, Uldis Donins, Marcela Genero Bocco, Audris Kalnins, Aniruddha Gokhale, Liliana Dobrica, Eila Ovaska, Ricardo J. Machado, Jose Norberto Mazón, Dilip Patel, Eduardo Fernández-Medina Patón, Uldis Sukovskis, Mohammad Al Saad, Sofia Azevedo, Stan Hendryx, Zbigniew Huzar, Natalya Pavlova, Juan Trujillo, and Jelena Zdravkovic. Reviewers' careful work guaranteed a high quality of each chapter and thus of the book.

We very much appreciate all Editorial Advisory Board members – Eduardo Fernandez-Medina, Jeff Gray, Stan Hendryx, Marite Kirikova, Ricardo J. Machado, Jose-Norberto Mazon, Dilip Patel, Uldis Sukovskis, and Juan Trujillo. Their obliging positive responses and help in the reviewing process fortify us. Without them, the book would not have its quality.

We wish to express our deep gratitude to the foreword author Andrew Watson for his kind agreement to describe why this book is important in the field of software development.

And last but not least, we would like to thank our families for their moral help.

Janis Osis
Erika Asnina
Editors

Section 1
Theory–Driven Holistic Domain Modeling and Analysis in the Context of MDA

Chapter 1
Is Modeling a Treatment for the Weakness of Software Engineering?

Janis Osis
Riga Technical University, Latvia

Erika Asnina
Riga Technical University, Latvia

ABSTRACT

The authors share with some other experts the opinion that the way software is built is primitive. Therefore, this chapter discusses a role of modeling as a treatment for software engineering. The role of modeling became more important after appearance of principles proposed by Model Driven Architecture (MDA). The main advantage of MDA is architectural separation of concerns that showed necessity of modeling and opened the way to software development to become engineering. However, the weakness is that this principle does not demonstrate its whole potential power in practice, because of a lack of mathematical formalism (or accuracy) in the very initial steps of software development. Therefore, the question about the sufficiency of modeling in software development is still open. The authors believe that software development in general, and modeling in particular, based on mathematical formalism in all its stages together with the implemented principle of architectural separation of concerns can become Software Engineering in its real sense. The authors introduce such mathematical formalism by means of topological modeling of system functioning.

INTRODUCTION

Software developers' community understands and forcedly accepts that software development in its current state is rather art than an engineering process. This means that qualitative software is a piece-work or a craftwork. Such an item usu-

ally is expensive, and cannot be stock-produced. However, in the modern world software users want to see and to use a qualitative and relatively cheap product. This means that software *development* must become software engineering. The word "engineering" intends a theory approved, completely realized and reused many times in practice that gives a qualitative and relatively inexpensive end product in accurately predictable timeframes.

DOI: 10.4018/978-1-61692-874-2.ch001

Software development's way to software engineering is quite long. Things that make this way long are very different. From one viewpoint, software development lacks commonly accepted theoretical foundations. From another viewpoint, software developers do not want to use "hard" theory (especially mathematical) because in order to win on the market they must provide operating software as fast as possible and even faster, but a lack of theory just slower getting an operating product. From the third viewpoint, clients do not want to pay a powerful lot of money for a product that, first, exists only as a textual document, second, includes "intellectual" work that is hard to measure and to evaluate, and third, usually it is not the same as clients wanted. Clients cannot check how work proceeds, since they cannot see the product at whole before integration of its parts and cannot evaluate (or even understand) the size of introduced efforts.

The content of this chapter is our vision of how to shorten this long way. First, we discuss effectiveness and quality of software engineering, and then differences between traditional engineering disciplines and software engineering. Next, we consider a modeling process and discuss benefits and issues, which could and could not be solved by modeling. At the end, we discuss our vision on what must be done in order to get really revolutionary improvement of software development.

BACKGROUND

Effectiveness and Quality of Software Engineering

First, let us discuss effectiveness and quality of software engineering. Our discussion is grounded on the very important results of the research performed by Capers Jones and presented in (Jones, 2009). Currently, Capers Jones is a president of Capers Jones & Associates LLC. He is also a founder and a former chairman of Software Productivity Research LLC (SPR). Jones and his

colleagues from SPR have collected historical data (since 1977 till 2007) from hundreds of corporations and more than 30 government organizations. This historical data is a key source for judging the effectiveness of software process improvement methods. This data is also widely cited in software litigation in cases where quality, productivity, and schedules are parts of the proceedings. Jones also frequently works as an expert witness in software litigation. In brief, Capers Jones is an authority in software engineering.

The main result obtained during analysis of this historical data can be expressed in one sentence - *"The way software is built remains surprisingly primitive"* (Jones, 2009, p. 1). This statement is based on the following data:

- *Budget and schedule overruns.* Even in 2008 majority of software applications are cancelled, overrun their budgets and schedules, and often have hazardously bad quality levels when released. As time passes, the global percentage of programmers performing maintenance on aging software has steadily risen, until it has become the dominant activity of the software world.

- *Product and process innovations. External product* innovations (new or improved products) and *internal process* innovations (new or improved methods for reducing development resources) are at differing levels of sophistication. Even in 2008 very sophisticated and complex pieces of software are still constructed by manual methods with extraordinary labor content (jobs from the United States to India, China, etc.) and very distressing quality levels. Yet software quality and productivity levels in 2007 are hardly different from 1977.

- *Positive and Negative Innovations.* Capers Jones and his colleagues have introduced two interesting terms, namely, positive innovations and negative innovations (Jones, 2009). Their meaning is explained on the example of agile techniques. The Agile approaches and eXtreme Programming (XP) were developed to speed up the development of small projects, where small teams in face to face contact are quite effective. Thus the Agile approaches are a positive innovation for small projects, but sometimes negative for large systems. Moreover, positive innovations tend to become negative innovations in time.

It is very hard to recognize, but there are _thirty_ Software Engineering issues that have stayed constant for 30 years (Jones, 2009, p. 23). There are four the most expensive software activities (in decreasing order): finding and fixing bugs, creating paper documents, coding, meetings and discussions. There is a big issue in the beginning of development, namely, in requirements specification, because, as Jones (2009) found, "initial requirements are seldom more than 50% complete and about 20% of them are delayed until a second release, and requirements grow at about 2% per calendar month." Moreover, there is a big issue in the end of development, namely, in testing. Causes are low testing efficiency (process as well as technique efficiency) and unsatisfying quality of test cases.

Internal innovations involve improvements in development techniques compared to prior approaches, it is necessary to have long-range precise measurements that cover both the "before" and "after" methodologies. Jones (2009) concluded that quality and reliability are hazardously bad "because most companies have not been effective in measuring software productivity and quality". And the cause is a lack of unified standards.

THE DIFFERENCE BETWEEN TRADITIONAL ENGINEERING AND SOFTWARE ENGINEERING

The way software is built remains surprisingly primitive – industry hardly accepts formal theories and looks for only fast and simple solutions for usually unforeseen problems. So, the question is why it is so?

Software development is primitive because it is *chaotic*. *Chaotic development* does not mean wrong development. This means development with low effectiveness and quality. Traditional engineering techniques are not chaotic, they are *systemic*.

What is a difference between software development and traditional engineering disciplines? In order to answer this question, let us consider civil engineering that is one of traditional engineering disciplines with long successful history.

In civil engineering, developers deal with some real situation, e.g. necessity to produce a building, and define all requirements (functional and non-functional). Then they construct a computation independent architectural project and a technology independent computation project, which are a basis for creation of a detailed construction by means of technologies. By implementing this detailed construction, developers get a final product, i.e., the building, that in most cases completely satisfies client's needs.

In traditional engineering, a project that includes documentation, calculations, drawings, and models completely specifies the corresponding product. What is a power of tradition engineering? The power is that *engineers do trust in theory, mathematics and formal methods*. Engineering sciences are based on mathematics and formal methods since the 17th century. Engineers use them without any discussions and hesitation.

Besides that, software developers helped them in using mathematics and formal methods by introducing sophisticated software products like Computer-Aided Design (CAD), Computer-Aided Manufacturing (CAM), etc. They assist manufacturing professionals in all operations including planning, design, project documentation generation, management, transportation and storage.

Returning to Capers Jones' research, he indicated that finding and fixing bugs is one of the most expensive and not so efficient software development activities. However, some of the most expensive activities in traditional engineering are exactly initial stages, while finding and fixing incompleteness is less expensive.

Software Development or Software Engineering?

The term *software engineering* (SE) was coined at NATO meeting in 1968 where ten years of the software crisis were recognized and discussed. Jones began his research in 1977. Thus, there are *twenty* years of the software crisis before Jones' research. **In total, we have *fifty* years of the software crisis. Software engineering is in permanent crisis.**

What was the first step that software engineering has done in order to overcome the crisis? It was introduction of diagrams to the development process. According to (Ralston & Reilly, 1993), dataflow-related modeling techniques proposed by Karp and Miller have been in use since 1969, flowcharts suggested by N. Chapin have found their application since 1971, and entity-relationship diagrams by Chen have been recognized in database design. The second step was creation of object-oriented methods based on diagrams, e.g. Demeter method that includes three formal models – information, state and process model (Lieberherr & Xiao, 1993) and the object-modeling technique (OMT) developed in 1991 by James Rumbaugh et al. (Rumbaugh, Blaha, Premerlani, Eddy, & Lorensen, 1990) with three main diagrams: object, dynamic, and functional. In 1997 the third step was done towards unification of diagrams by appearance of Unified Modeling Language (UML). And, the fourth and last step (at this moment) to unification of use of diagrams was done in 2001 when the first version of OMG Model Driven Architecture (MDA) Guide was published (Miller & Mukerji, 2003). The main idea is that a set of related diagrams, a model, is a cornerstone of software development – it is a

design, documentation and a way of decreasing inconsistencies and overbudget costs.

The main purpose of MDA is to separate architectural viewpoints in specifications and to strengthen the role of analysis and design in the project development. MDA suggests three viewpoints on the system that are reflected in a Computation Independent Model (CIM), a Platform Independent Model (PIM) and a Platform Specific Model (PSM) correspondingly. Transformations are the main way of MDA model refinement. MDA foresees refining transformations starting from the PIM.

So, what is MDA? At the conceptual level, MDA is a *holistic approach* for improving the entire information technology (IT) life cycle – specification, architecture, design, development, deployment, maintenance, and integration – *based on formal modeling*. More specifically, *MDA is a framework of technical standards* progressively being developed by the OMG, which is an open industry consortium supporting this approach, along with a set of usage guidelines for enabling the application of those standards with appropriate tools and processes. A quite interesting investigation of MDA industrial experience is expounded in (Guttman & Parodi, 2007).

Unfortunately, formalism of modeling within MDA is quite nominal, because a small part in standards used within MDA is supported by mathematics. Usually it is only more or less successful unification of conceptions between standards.

Therefore, unification is still considered as a potentially successful way towards *engineering*. However, classical engineering like electrical, mechanical, civil are *requirement initiated and based on theory (mathematics) driven analysis.* Traditional engineers trust in theory. *Software Engineering is based on requirements with chaotic analysis.* For software engineers theory is less of an issue. However, as a famous Austrian physicist Ludvig Boltzmann (1844 – 1906) said "There is nothing more practical as a good theory".

MDA as a Skeleton of Software Engineering

As previously mentioned, a skeleton of traditional engineering is that the product is a direct implementation of the initially developed design calculated and specified in the formal and standard documentation, calculations, drawings and models. But what a skeleton is in software engineering, and if it is absent then may MDA provide such a skeleton?

We believe that the potential power of MDA is in model transformations, because:

- Model transformations form a key part of MDA;

- Model transformations require a use of formal languages and mechanisms for description of models;
- Model transformations lead to growing up the role of mathematics for software development in the framework of MDA.

Figure 1 illustrates the main stages in software development, namely, requirements gathering, analysis, low-level design, coding, testing and deployment. Each stage produces an artifact and uses an artifact produced by the previous stage, e.g. analysis uses textual requirements and produces diagrams and text that reflect those requirements at the next level of abstraction. Therefore, when we speak about "traditional" – procedural and object-oriented – software development, all de-

Figure 1. A skeleton of software engineering

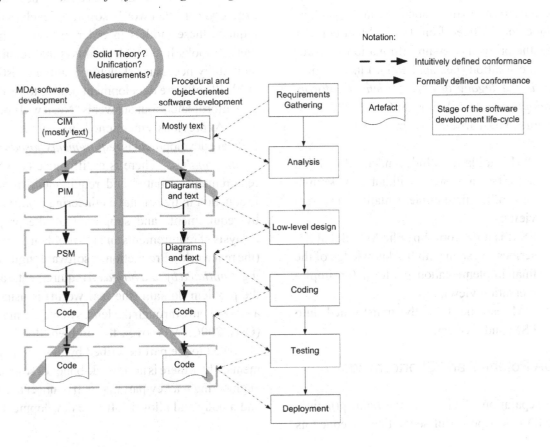

velopment artifacts are created based on intuitive understanding of the solution.

As we fairly mentioned in (Osis, Asnina, & Grave, 2007a), the beginning of MDA software development does not differ from the beginning of the traditional software development. It starts with requirements that are reflected in the CIM. Requirements engineering proposes to transform problem statements into requirements, thus to investigate a problem domain and to sketch a solution domain. The problem statements are based on goals, scenarios, expert interviews, categories, of concepts and concept relations, etc. There is a large set of requirements gathering methods developed, e.g. the KAOS approach initially presented in (Dardenne, van Lamsweerde, & Fickas, 1993), Goal Based Requirements Analysis Method, GBRAM, initially presented in (Antón, 1996), i* modeling framework developed by Eric Yu (Yu, 1997) and others. In requirements engineering, functions of the system are inferred from goals. Functions are somehow fragmentary defined from the problem domain. Thus the problem domain information is mixed with the solution (i.e., application) information. *This is the legacy of object-oriented software development* (Osis, Asnina, & Grave, 2007b).

Other MDA artifacts are more exact:

- PIM is a Platform Independent Model that describes a system without any knowledge of the final implementation (a system view);
- PSM is a Platform Specific Model that describes a system with full knowledge of the final implementation platform (an implementation view);
- PIM can be formally transformed into PSM and vice versa.

MDA Potential and Shortcomings

The separation of views as the main principle of MDA is a powerful separation of concerns

proposed by MDA. This allowed introducing formal use of artifacts starting from the analysis. A textual Computation Independent Model (CIM) that describes requirements is intuitively and manually transformed to the PIM, and then the PIM is transformed to PSMs to code by using formally defined transformation rules (Figure 1).

Code is formal, reliable, safe and executable. But is it a skeleton of software development? No, it is not. It is grabbling as in childhood or … at best, it is handicraft as in the very first days of traditional engineering. The code is rather "legs" then "skeleton" (Figure 1).

Then, maybe it is analysis and design artifacts formally conformed to each other, isn't it? In case of traditional software development such a skeleton cannot provide normal movement, it is like grabbling with additional burden. And, certainly, developers try and will try to escape this burden. In case of MDA, analysis and design artifacts – PIMs and PSMs – are vitally necessary to get code. In other words, software development requires these models in order to "get to their feet". It looks like MDA promises that required and vitally necessary skeleton. But the question is, "Will software development be able to "go"?"

Unfortunately, our answer is "No, it will not be able". As previously mentioned, in its current state software development is *requirements based with chaotic analysis*. There is a difference between requirements-initiated and requirements-based. Production in traditional engineering is *initiated* by requirements and supported by the proper analysis of requirements and the problem domain (the real world). Production in software engineering is *initiated by and based on* requirements, and the problem domain (the real world) is usually analyzed only through the lenses of requirements (Osis, 2006). Moreover, the problem domain is narrowed to the part described by those requirements. Thus, there is no a "neck-bone" of software engineering – a key part that will connect a head and a body and allows software development to "go" and really to become one of engineering disciplines (Figure 1).

The OMG says nothing essential about the computation independent view and accordingly about the CIM. The CIM could be considered as a marketing expression of the OMG. The weakness of MDA is that there is nothing well formalized and/or transformable at the beginning of the development life cycle.

It is impossible to get high efficiency with a weak beginning and a strong end of the life cycle (Osis, Asnina, & Grave, 2007b). Let us consider producing bread as an analogy. A simplified development chain is grain (CIM) → flour (PIM) → dough (PSM) → bread (code). Certainly, in order to get the high-quality bread (code) we must have high quality ingredients - flour (PIM) from high quality grain (CIM). However, it is not less important to have a proper and checked recipe (a development scheme) as well as professional staff (developers). But if quality of the grain is low, then even staff' mastership and proven recipes and tools will not help, and getting qualitative bread will be impossible.

We believe that the formal (high quality) CIM grounded on formal system analysis of the problem domain that formally specifies results of the analysis and is used as a formal base for composing a PIM is that missing neck-bone (Figure 2).

Figure 2. Formulation of software development task

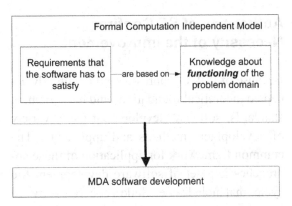

In this case, the only open question left is about a head of software engineering (Figure 1). Should the head of SE be unification of standards, measurements of end products and processes, solid theory such as formal system analysis or a union of these mechanisms? We will discuss it in the next sections.

Is Modeling and MDA a Revolutionary Innovation in Software Engineering?

Let us first discuss software modeling in its current state. What does a software developer create at the very beginning? The answer is *a business model.* Is it well defined? Is it a mathematical model? Is it well formalized? No, it is not. Now, let us get a look to the CIM that is a starting model in MDA. It is fuzzy defined, lacks mathematics and is not formalized even in MDA sense – a computer cannot understand this model. Therefore, the question is, "What will change if the business model is renamed?" What will change if another, larger or smaller, *notation* for business models is created?

OMG's MDA announced model ***transformations*** as the core innovation of software development that includes elaboration of formal transformation rules, techniques, and languages. Well, what do we have to transform in a strong formal manner in the beginning? The answer is *notations* such as Business Process Modeling Notation, BPMN (OMG, 2010a), and Unified Modeling Language, UML (OMG, 2010b), instead of formal (mathematical) models. Is it a persuasive way to high effectiveness and quality of software development? In our opinion, definitely it is not.

MDA is a positive innovation of software engineering and a certain step towards better effectiveness and quality of software development, but it remains in the line of chaotic requirement driven methods. Therefore MDA is not a crucial step. It does not solve the main problem of software engineering while there is a lack of mathematically strong models from the very beginning of software development.

Model Driven Engineering (MDE) in general also has the same shortcomings as MDA. Domain Specific Modeling (DSM) suggests solving them by gathering and managing components and languages for certain narrow domains. But the beginning of development also lacks mathematically strong models. Software factories provide a development environment but do not also provide strong mechanisms for formalization of the problem domain analysis. One MDE direction is still on the way towards unification of processes, languages, and tools; other is on the way towards their specialization. There is a lack of measurements and solid theory as well.

How to Get a Revolutionary Improvement of Software Development?

In fact, MDA is the newest branch of *Requirements* Driven Architecture. In order to satisfy high effectiveness and quality of the software development we need **TDA** – *Theory Driven Architecture* and *Scientific Software Engineering* (SSE). Is this a near future for software engineering? By our opinion, it is not. In order to achieve this fundamental goal a long time must come to pass, perhaps, another fifty years.

Our reasons for being so critical are as follows:

- Today we have mostly *practice-driven software development* or industry (software company) driven software development. There is low impact of universities to the industry. As Jones (2009) mentioned, each innovative approach or method adopted in industry stop to produce an effect in course of time. One reason is that previous and well-known practice of day by day work comes back. Software developers keep in use only those elements that do not change their work habits cardinally. Most likely

any cardinal change of practice, especially that which requires additional efforts without fast and obvious results, will be set aside of everyday work. Another reason is a lack of investments in industrial approbation of innovative methods and approaches. Measuring quality and usefulness of these innovations must be done by universities, which usually do not have an appropriate environment for such actions.

- Software engineering develops too fast. The development is quantitative. Every day a new branch is born (aspect- orientation, agile approaches, agents and so on). Tool vendors are not able to implement all innovative features on time. Industry does not have sufficient development environment, work resources and clear understanding of usefulness of these innovations in order to adopt them. Besides that the possibility that a new "better" approach will be developed soon is very high.

- Qualitative changes need authority like Isaac Newton for the traditional engineering. There aren't gurus in software engineering with such authority, wisdom and power. Nobody tries to catch the scene from scientific and system theory point of view.

However, as a Chinese philosopher Lao-tzu said "The journey of a thousand miles begins beneath one's feet."

Authorities of SE Confirm Necessity of the Improvement

Because of lack of approved and commonly accepted theoretical foundations and measurement standards, software development has a variety of development methods and approaches. The common framework for application of those approaches is a set of software development life cycles that include or exclude a concrete software development activity or activities. In other words, the present situation is that software development life cycles reflect when and how different existing methods and approaches can be used. However effectiveness of their use is rather intuitively understandable that quantitatively measured. Therefore, one aspect of improvement already recognized is to unify standards of software productivity and quality measurements.

Another aspect of improvement is proposed by the Software Engineering Method and Theory (SEMAT) group established by Ivar Jacobson, Bertrand Meyer, and Richard Soley in the end of 2009 (SEMAT, n.d.). As the main problems enumerated by the SEMAT include a lack of a solid and widely accepted theoretical basis as well as a lack of credible experimental evaluation and validation, this group supports a way that will base software engineering on a solid theory, proven principles and best practices. This way includes not only measurements, but also creation of a solid theory of software engineering. We also think that unification of standards and measurement of the end result suggested by Jones (2009) without a solid theory cannot improve the way software is built.

Hence returning to Figure 1, *the head of software engineering must be a union of the solid theoretical basis, measurements of quality of innovative technologies, and unification of standards.*

A STEP TOWARDS THEORY-BASED SOFTWARE ENGINEERING

Summarizing all the previous mentioned, in order to become real engineering, software development needs to be based on a solid theoretical base. Our proposition is based on a proven theory and holistic principles supported by functional analysis and topology. Certainly, this chapter does not provide a complete theoretical base. It just suggests a small stone that we believe must be used in these future theoretical foundations.

The Topological Functioning Model as an Engineering Model

A Topological Model of System Functioning (or a Topological Functioning Model, TFM) is a model developed by Janis Osis at Riga Technical University (RTU, former Riga Polytechnic Institute) in 1969 (Osis, 1969) and successfully applied in such complex fields as mechanics (Osis, Gefandbein, Markovitch, & Novozhilova, 1991) and medicine (Osis & Beghi, 1997). 1969 is a year when first time in the world functionality of a complex system was *mathematically* specified in a *systemic* (*holistic*) way by using a *topological model*.

The mathematical background of the TFM is its topological properties. Topological properties of the TFM are based on a branch of mathematics – topology. They include concepts of connectedness, closure, neighborhood and continuous mapping. Connectedness sets that system functional parts must be joined as a concept of system requires itself. The concepts of closure and neighborhoods allow formal identification of subsystems. The concepts of neighborhoods and continuous mappings allow transforming the system while preserving its structure and history of transformations. Besides that similarities and differences between systems can be formally identified. Summarizing, the topological properties specify only relations among objects, and hence specify system's *structure* and preserve it during modifications.

The mathematics used in the TFM is so called "lightweight" mathematics. It does not require understanding of all complex things that topologists use. It does require satisfaction of topological structure axioms. Besides that, the TFM is represented as a mathematical digraph that is widely used within software engineering, and this fact also facilitates understanding of the TFM. Although a graph is a simple combinatorial topological space, not any graph is a TFM.

The TFM specifies joined *structure (statics)* and *a process of functioning (dynamics)* and is grounded on the system theory and mathematics. The digraph that represents the TFM has system theoretical background expressed by functioning properties. Functioning properties of the TFM are based on the system theory and include concepts of inputs and outputs, cycle structure and cause-and-effect relations. The inputs and outputs relate to input and output signals the system receives, correspondingly. Input and output signals are vital for system successful interaction with its environment. The cause-and-effect relations describe causal implication between system's functional parts. Thus it is possible to introduce a chronology and follow up a process of functionality. However, here we tell about *causal* not *logical* implication. This means that it is causal chronology that may and will form cycles of cause-and-effect relations. The structure of those cycles joins functional parts of a system that are vital for its successful and long life. Summarizing, the functioning properties specify *a process of functioning* as traditional engineering does. Such formal engineering specification of a process provides satisfaction of system's goals independently of the fact either they are identified or are not.

Key properties of the TFM are described in more detail in Chapter "Topological Modeling for Model-Driven Domain Analysis and Software Development: Functions and Architectures". A use of the TFM for solution domain conforming to the corresponding problem domain is considered in Chapter "Topological Functioning Model as a CIM-Business Model" and "Derivation of Use Cases from the Topological Computation Independent Business Model".

MDA Supplemented with the TFM

In Section "MDA as a Skeleton of Software Engineering", we spoke about a lack of the "neck-bone" that does not allow MDA to be a skeleton of software engineering. We believe that the TFM is that "neck-bone". Figure 3 illustrates the place of the TFM within MDA.

Nevertheless of multiple names such as ontology, expert interviews, descriptions, concepts, business rules and goals, business models, domain models, documentation, business notation and so on, beginning of software development is one and the same – discovering and specifying experts' knowledge about the problem. The TFM specifies this knowledge in a *formal model*. This means that completeness of all models of solutions (including requirements) will be mathematically

Figure 3. The place of the TFM within MDA

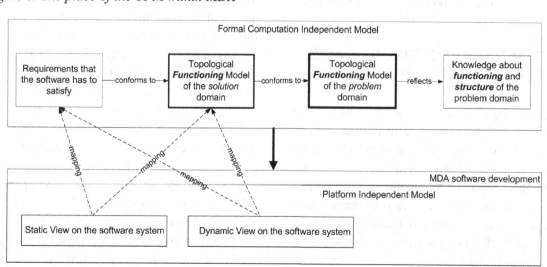

approved only if they are in conformance with the TFM of the problem (Osis, Asnina, & Grave, 2007a; Osis & Asnina, 2008b).

If a solution (software system) specified in requirements is a simple representation of the problem (information system, enterprise), then there is no need in formal modeling of the solution. However, if a solution changes the problem in some way, then it must also be specified in the TFM continuously mapped to the TFM of the problem (Figure 3). This allows preserving conformity between the solution and the problem as well as approving completeness of the solution (Osis & Asnina, 2008a; Asnina & Osis, 2010).

The topological and functioning properties of the TFM keep structural and behavioral properties of the modeled domain. Therefore, it is possible to map diagrams that specify a static view on the solution (e.g. class diagrams, object diagrams) and a dynamic view on the solution (e.g. activity diagrams, sequence diagrams and other) onto the formal topological functioning model of the solution domain. The static view on the system is based on the analysis of cause-and-effect relations among domain objects that participate in domain functioning. In its turn, the dynamic view on the system is based on the analysis of cause-and-effect relations among functional features of the domain. The main principles of the analysis are illustrated in more details in (Osis, Asnina, & Grave, 2008).

Mappings to system and software requirements are formalized, too. The reason is formally defined conformance of requirements with the TFM of the solution (Osis & Asnina, 2008a). This allows checking and supporting completeness, adequacy and traceability of requirements.

Traceability in Topology-Based Software Development

Software evolution is a permanent process that starts in requirements gathering and ends when an owner writes off his software. Besides that,

a system (businesses, enterprises) within the software works or will work has a great impact on the software. Changes may concern domain knowledge (business logic and domain vocabulary), software requirements, platform specific details, or code.

Within model-driven development, changes in domain knowledge and software requirements (i.e., in the problem and solution domains) affect a model at the highest level of abstraction, i.e. the CIM, and all consequent models, namely, PIMs and PSMs. PIMs and PSMs specify software architecture, and thus changes in the CIM also have an impact on software architecture used. Changes of platforms affect PSM and have no impact on the CIM and PIMs. Therefore, traceability support in software development that is driven by models is very important.

The TFM captures business knowledge about the problem domain, i.e. business functional characteristics and cause-and-effect relations among them, organizational units and roles and their responsibility for providing and using those functional characteristics, and domain objects and their participation in business functioning. Moreover, the TFM is a ground for checking compliance of software functional requirements to the problem domain. Hence, changes generated in the problem and solution domains must be verified at the CIM level first. Usually these changes are obtained like fragments of business system operation and may contradict, duplicate and overlap each other or miss some vital (or less vital, but still important) parts. The only existing way to find out about their incompleteness is stakeholders' and domain experts' reviews.

The TFM allows using mechanisms provided by topology and system analysis for change tracing. Careful analysis of changes in cause-and-effect relations and unique functional characteristics explicitly shows contradicted, duplicated, overlapped, or missed functionality caused by change introduction. All elements touched by modifications of relations and characteristics can be unambiguously identified in the consequent models by using mathematical continuous mapping.

FUTURE RESEARCH DIRECTIONS

We believe that the topological functioning model can be successfully used in software development. And the future research directions relate to analysis of its capabilities in formalization of software modeling, especially in model-driven engineering.

The first research direction is setting correspondence between TFM elements and elements of less abstract (and less formal by now) software analysis and design languages. One direction is decomposition of the TFM and further enhancing of parts with platform independent details. Therefore, the TFM can be used as a business model. Otherwise, composing fragments of system description by mapping them onto the TFM can be used for assessment of quality of the description.

Another very important research direction is change management and propagation. Model-driven software development enables automation of change propagation and tracing. Near fields are requirements quality and testing.

CONCLUSION

The question was, "Is modeling a treatment for the weakness of software engineering?" The answer is positive – yes, it is, but upon one important condition, namely, if and only if modeling is based on mathematical formalism from the very beginning of software development.

Software Engineering is a weak engineering. The way software is built remains surprisingly primitive (Jones, 2009). Modeling supported by MDA provides some evolution of software engineering. In other words, MDA provides a "skeleton" of software engineering. However, it does not provide a "neck-bone", a formal domain model, and a "head", scientific foundations.

The road to the *scientific* software development is still in the darkness. The main reasons are the following:

- Universities have low impact to software development;
- The software education is poor concerning theoretical issues;
- The software community isn't ready and interested in revolutionary changes.

However, on the way towards engineering, software development will not avoid such a "hard" thing as a solid theory (i.e., mathematics). The mathematics may be explicit and implicit. A well-known example of the implicit mathematics in software development is Petri nets. After solving two serious drawbacks, almost 20 years passed before they were adopted by industry as "hidden" mechanism of UML activity diagrams. The word "hidden" means that this mechanism is known for developers who implement UML, but is not evident for users of UML.

Industry requires either such implicit mathematics or "simple" one. The topological functioning model is that "simple" one. It joins "light" topology and functional analysis and was successfully used to analyze complex systems in mechanics and medicine. The TFM provides:

- Construction of Computation Independent Model (CIM) in formal and compact way;
- CIM transformation into UML diagrams;
- Classification of classes according to essential functional features;
- Handling Changes in the Model of Problem Domain Functioning.

The TFM can be a "neck-bone" of the software engineering "skeleton". The TFM can take part in filling the "head" with formalisms of topology and functional analysis. Other content of the head of software engineering is still in the darkness. However, the positive moment is that it gives wide research possibilities to the academic community.

REFERENCES

Antón, A. I. (1996). Goal-based requirements analysis. *Second IEEE International Conference on Requirements Engineering (ICRE `96), Colorado Springs, Colorado* (pp. 136-144). Washington, DC: IEEE.

Asnina, E., & Osis, J. (2010). Computation independent models: bridging problem and solution domains. In J. Osis, & O. Nikiforova (Ed.), *Proceedings of the 2nd International Workshop on Model-Driven Architecture and Modeling Theory-Driven Development MDA & MTDD 2010, In conjunction with ENASE 2010, Athens, Greece, July 2010* (pp. 23-32). Portugal: SciTePress.

Dardenne, A., van Lamsweerde, A., & Fickas, S. (1993). Goal-directed requirements acquisition. []. Amsterdam, The Netherlands: Elsevier North-Holland, Inc.]. *Science of Computer Programming, 20,* 3–50. doi:10.1016/0167-6423(93)90021-G

Guttman, M., & Parodi, J. (2007). *Real-life MDA: solving business problems with model driven architecture*. New York: Morgan Kaufmann Publishers.

Jones, C. (2009). Positive and negative innovations in software engineering. *International Journal of Software Science and Computational Intelligence, 1*(2), 20–30.

Lieberherr, K. J., & Xiao, C. (1993, April). Object-oriented software evolution. *IEEE Transactions on Software Engineering, 19*(4), 313–343. doi:10.1109/32.223802

Miller, J., & Mukerji, J. (Eds.). (2003, May 1). *MDA guide version 1.0*. Retrieved January 15, 2010, from http://www.omg.org/mda/

OMG. (2010a). *Object management group/Business process management initiative*. Retrieved January 10, 2010, from http://www.bpmn.org/

OMG. (2010b). *UML® resource page*. Retrieved January 10, 2010, from Unified Modeling Language http://www.uml.org/

Osis, J. (1969). Topological model of system functioning (in Russian). *Automatics and Computer Science, J. of Acad. of Sc.* (6), 44-50.

Osis, J. (2006). Formal computation independent model within the MDA life cycle. *International transactions on system science and applications, 1* (2), 159-166.

Osis, J., & Asnina, E. (2008a). A business model to make software development less intuitive. In *Proceedings of 2008 International Conference on Innovation in Sofware Engineering (ISE 2008). December 10-12, 2008, Vienna, Austria* (pp. 1240-1245). Washington, DC: IEEE Computer Society Publishing.

Osis, J., & Asnina, E. (2008b). Enterprise modeling for information system development within MDA. In *Proceedings of the 41st Annual Hawaii International Conference on System Sciences (HICSS 2008)*, (p. 490). Waikoloa, Hawaii, USA.

Osis, J., Asnina, E., & Grave, A. (2007a). Computation independent modeling within the MDA. In *Proceedings of IEEE International Conference on Software, Science, Technology & Engineering (SwSTE07), 30-31 October 2007, Herzlia, Israel* (pp. 22-34). Washington, DC: IEEE Computer Society, Conference Publishing Services (CPS).

Osis, J., Asnina, E., & Grave, A. (2007b). MDA oriented computation independent modeling of the problem domain. In *Proceedings of the 2nd International Conference on Evaluation of Novel Approaches to Software Engineering (ENASE 2007), Barcelona, Spain*, (pp. 66 -71).

Osis, J., Asnina, E., & Grave, A. (2008). Formal problem domain modeling within MDA. [CCIS]. *Communications in Computer and Information Science, 22*(3), 387–398.

Osis, J., & Beghi, L. (1997). Topological modelling of biological systems. In D. Linkens, & E. Carson (Ed.), *Proceedings of the third IFAC Symposium on Modelling and Control in Biomedical Systems (Including Biological Systems)* (pp. 337-342). Oxford, UK: Elsevier Science Publishing.

Osis, J., Gefandbein, J., Markovitch, Z., & Novozhilova, N. (1991). *Diagnosis based on graph models: by the examples of aircraft and automobile mechanisms*. Moscow: Transport. (in Russian)

Ralston, A., & Reilly, E. I. (Eds.). (1993). *Encyclopedia of computer science* (3 ed.). New York: Van Nostrand Reinhold Company.

Rumbaugh, J., Blaha, M., Premerlani, W., Eddy, F., & Lorensen, W. (1990). *Object-oriented modeling and design*. Upper Saddle River, NJ: Prentice Hall.

SEMAT. (n.d.). Retrieved January 20, 2010, from www.semat.org

Yu, E. (1997). Towards modelling and reasoning support for early-phase requirements engineering. In *Proceedings of the 3rd IEEE Int. Symp. on Requirements Engineering (RE'97)* (pp. 226-235). Washington, DC: IEEE.

KEY TERMS AND DEFINITIONS

Computation Independent Model: A Computation Independent Model (CIM) is a model defined within OMG Model-Driven Architecture as a primary model. This model reflects system and software knowledge from the business perspective. The CIM may contain business knowledge about system organization, roles, functions, processes and activities, documentation, constraints etc. The CIM must contain business requirements for the software system.

Domain Modeling: Analysis and specification of characteristics of the domain under the discourse.

Mathematical Formalism: The scientific direction that solves basic problems with mathematically formal axiomatic constructions.

Software Development: The practical application of computer science for commercial and industrial problems, but is based on intuitive understanding of appropriateness of the solution.

Software Engineering: The practical application of computer science for commercial and industrial problems that should be based on mathematically proven appropriateness of the solution.

Theory-Driven Development: Software development based on strong theoretical foundations.

Topological functioning model: A model based on system theory and mathematics that specifies functionality and structure of a complex system as a connected topological space of system's functional characteristics and cause-and-effect relations among them.

Chapter 2
Topological Modeling for Model–Driven Domain Analysis and Software Development:
Functions and Architectures

Janis Osis
Riga Technical University, Latvia

Erika Asnina
Riga Technical University, Latvia

ABSTRACT

Model-driven software development has all chances to turn software development into software engineering. But this requires not only mature methodologies but also engineering models. An engineering model should satisfy five key characteristics, namely, abstraction, understandability, accuracy, predictiveness and inexpensiveness. This chapter discusses capabilities of a Topological Functioning Model (TFM) as such an engineering model for the purposes of domain analysis and software development in common. The TFM has functional and topological properties. The functional properties are cause-effect relations, cycle structure, inputs, and outputs. The topological properties are connectedness, closure, neighborhood, and continuous mapping. Thanks to its formal mathematical foundations, the TFM completely satisfies the mentioned characteristics of engineering models that is illustrated in the chapter.

INTRODUCTION

There are many ways how to describe semantics. In software development during the so called problem domain analysis mostly informal approaches and languages are used. There are several causes, and one of more important is that the problem domain itself is not well determined. Thus, developers explore the problem domain by parts, at the beginning trying to understand each fragment of the problem domain and only after that trying to join those fragments together in the holistic and more formal representation.

Indeed, the question about possibility of formal description of semantics still exists. The important property of diagrams used in software development is that they must provide very precise or even formal sense. In (Diskin, Kadish, Piessens, &

DOI: 10.4018/978-1-61692-874-2.ch002

Johnson, 2000) authors wrote that if some diagram D exists, then it has some sense $M(D)$. This sense must be described in precise (it would be ideal, if mathematical) statements. This description makes some precise specification S_D that has the precise semantic $M(S_D)$. Therefore, $M(S_D)$ is abstraction of formal intuitive sense $M(D)$ and S_D may be considered as some (internal) logic specification, that is hidden in the diagram D. They pointed that this described approach is typical (or desired) for diagrams used in software engineering.

There are many intuitive worlds that can provide sense M in the real world. The authors pointed out that in spite of that when one starts to think about M formal description, this huge amount is being narrowed until several domains of mathematical constructs, e.g. set theory, type theory, high-order predicate logic or category theory, etc. All these languages are universal and expressive. Therefore, any formal semantic (some specification S_D) can be specified in any formal language of them.

But if we want to consider software development as an engineering discipline, then we need to take into account that not every formal language can be accepted for domain analysis by using models. Bran Selic (2003) enumerated five key characteristics that a useful and effective engineering model needs to satisfy. They are abstraction, understandability, accuracy, predictiveness and inexpensiveness (Selic, 2003):

- *Abstraction* is the most important characteristic. Usually, abstraction is the only available means of dealing with complex functionality and the structure of the system.
- *Understandability* makes the abstracted model expressive, reducing the amount of intellectual effort needed for model understanding.
- *Accuracy* makes the model useful. The model has to provide realistic represen-

tation of the modeled system features of interest.

- The model should be able to be used to *predict* the modeled system interesting implicit properties either through experimentation or through some formal analysis. In this case, the mathematical model is much better at predicting.
- The model should be *inexpensive*, so that it must be significantly cheaper in constructing and analysis than the modeled system.

Thus, an engineering model suitable for *model-driven engineering* is a formal mathematical model that supports abstraction and predictiveness, and at the same time it is understandable for all stakeholders (depending on the context), and cheap enough to be used for industrial tasks. As Unified Modeling Language (UML) developers' and academic practice shows, one of such models could be Petri Nets and their derivations with some limitations in using. As our practice shows (and that what we demonstrate in this chapter), another one could be topological models of systems.

The chapter is organized as follows. The next section discusses advantages and weaknesses of Petri nets, and the background of topological models. Main properties and capabilities of the topological model, which support an engineering viewpoint on system functionality and structure, are described in section "Domain analysis with topological modeling". The general framework of application of the topological model of system functioning for model-driven engineering is illustrated in section "Model-driven software development with topological modeling".

BACKGROUND

Past and Present of Petri Nets

There is one formal mathematical graphical model accepted in software development for analysis of activity flows and system states. These are Petri nets, especially Colored Petri Nets (CPNs). Basic concepts and practical use of the CPNs are discussed in (Jensen, 1997). To achieve application of Petri nets for modeling industrial tasks, their authors have combined the strength of Petri nets with the strength of programming languages. Petri nets provide the primitives for describing synchronization of concurrent processes, while a programming language provides the primitives for defining data types (color sets) and manipulating data values (Kristensen, Christensen, & Jensen, 1998). CPNs in modeling concurrency, synchronization, and communication in systems have undoubted advantages. CPNs and Petri nets are, however, also applicable more generally for modeling systems where concurrency and communication are key characteristics. Examples of this are business process/workflow modeling and manufacturing systems (Kristensen, Jurgensen, & Jensen, 2004). CPN notation is short. High-level CPNs support control and modularization of large system models. CPN models are descriptions of systems, thus they could be used as both specifications and presentation of systems. Moreover, the process of specification creation and analysis enables understanding of the modeled system. Model behavior can be analyzed by CPN model simulation or formal methods for graph analysis. And last, there are computer tools for creating, simulating and formal analyzing CPNs.

However, nevertheless development of Petri nets goes intensively during last forty years, this kind of nets have significant weaknesses. The cause is that a use of Petri nets as *self-sufficient model* is not quite convenient. In typical industrial applications, a CPN diagram consists of 10-100 pages (modules) with varying complexity (Kristensen, Christensen, & Jensen, 1998). First, a CPN model should be well-modularized, because only minor changes do not affect a structure of the CPN. However, if it is necessary to introduce large changes, then it will be quite hard work. Second, although a collection of Petri net constructs as

well CPN constructs is relatively small, the way of its visualization is very important in case of large system design, since sometimes common representation of states and transitions takes modeler's attention off one or another.

Past and Present of the Topological Model of System Functioning

Another formal mathematical model is a Topological Model of System Functioning (TFM). In this chapter we will use interchangeably several terms that defines the TFM, namely, a topological model, a topological model of [system] functioning and a topological functioning model. The TFM is completely an engineering model in Selic's sense, and it was successfully used for system analysis from 1970s. The topological modeling of system functioning (TFM) was developed at Riga Technical University. First time its theoretic foundations were represented by Janis Osis in (Osis, 1969; Osis, 1972). Its application in different areas is being developed today as well.

A large number of high-quality diagnostic algorithms and methods based on this theory were developed (Osis, Gefandbein, Markovitch, & Novozhilova, 1991). Besides that, in 1970 a new approach of creation of the system theory foundations was suggested (Osis, 1970). One perspective direction that was begun in 1973 and published in (Osis, 1973), wherein the relation to the microprogramming was affected, is software engineering.

Since 1970 topological modeling was successfully applied for medicine problem solving by Zigurds Markovitch (Markovitcha & Markovitch, 1970). His work continued with mathematical model composition from mini-models of elements (Markovitch & Rekners, 1998) and expert knowledge (Markovitch & Stalidzans, 2000). Continuing topological modeling introducing into medicine, Zigurds Markovitch and Ieva Markovitcha successfully illustrated topological modeling application for therapy selection (Markovitch & Markovitcha, 2000).

The topological modeling development was continued also by Janis Grundspenkis since the same 1970s. At the beginning his work was related to investigations in the field of cycle hierarchies for the purpose of rational diagnostic algorithm development (Grundspenkis, 1974) and (Grundspenkis & Blumbergs, 1981). The most recent interests are related to model-driven knowledge systematic acquisition and these solutions joining with knowledge management (Grundspenkis, 1996; Grundspenkis, 1997; Grundspenkis, 2004).

Besides that, the topological functioning model is being developed also in the field of the object-oriented analysis. The recent works are described in several sources: topological modeling application for business process modeling and simulation (Osis, Sukovskis, & Teilans, 1997), for the purposes of biological systems modeling (Osis & Beghi, 1997), the topological functioning model application in the software development for mechatronic and embedded systems (Osis, 2003), the topological functioning modeling application to introduce more formalism into the Model Driven Architecture framework and problem domain analysis, which grounds development of topological modeling language (Osis, 2004; Asnina, 2006a; Asnina, 2006b; Osis & Asnina, 2008; Osis, Asnina, & Grave, 2008; Asnina, 2009). We have to mention that unfortunately only publications after 1992 are available in English.

DOMAIN ANALYSIS WITH TOPOLOGICAL MODELING

The topological modeling is a modeling approach that uses a formal mathematical model to specify and analyze characteristics of a system. Before discussing what the topological modeling is, we need to refresh in minds what "topology" means.

Figure 1. Two topological axioms

$$X \in Q\,;\varnothing \in Q\,; \qquad \text{(a)}$$

$$\forall \eta \left(\bigcup_\eta A_\eta \in Q \right); \forall \varphi \left(\bigcap_{\varphi=1}^{\kappa} A_\varphi \in Q \right) \qquad \text{(b)}$$

Mathematical Foundations

Topology is a mathematical study of the properties that are preserved through deformations, twistings, and stretchings of objects. Tearing of objects is not allowed. Topology can be used to abstract the inherent connectivity of objects while ignoring their detailed form. For example, *network topology* used to describe connections of network nodes is commonly known application of topology studies in network modeling.

The "objects" of topology are often formally defined as topological spaces. A *topological space* is a set X together with a collection of open subsets A. These subsets form topology Q in the set X. In other words, topology in the set X is any system Q of open sets A of the set X. The system Q has to satisfy two topological axioms (see Figure 1) stated by Andrei N. Kolmogorov (Kolmogorov, 1999).

The axiom (a) in Figure 1 states that X is a finite closed set of elements of the system under consideration with some certain topology Q among those elements, and this topology Q is set or defined, indeed. The axiom (b) in Figure 1 states that different systems (unions and intersections) of a finite number of open sets A of the set X belongs to the defined topology Q.

In order to study problems related to topology graph theory is used. In the mathematics and computer science, graph theory studies the properties of graphs. Informally, a *graph* is a set of objects called vertices (or nodes) connected by links called arcs (or oriented edges). Usually, a graph is designed as a set of vertices connected by edges. A graph structure can be extended by assigning a weight to each edge, or by making the edges to the graph directional, technically called a *digraph*. A digraph with weighted edges is called a *network*.

Many applications of graph theory exist in the field of network analysis. They can be divided into two categories. The first is analysis for determination of structural properties of networks, and the second is analysis for discovering measurable quantities within networks.

Topological spaces in network analysis usually describe structural properties of systems, i.e., networks. However, the "subject" of the topological space may be also dynamical properties of systems, e.g. system functionality. Therefore, as theoretic foundations presented by Janis Osis (1969) state, *a topological model of system functioning* can be represented in the form of the topological space (*X, Q*), where *X* is a finite set of functional features of the system under consideration, and *Q* is topology in the form of a directed graph. This model occurs through the acquisition of experts' knowledge about the complex systems, verbal descriptions, and other documents concerning the structure and functioning.

Although the topological model of system functioning specifies functionality of the system, it also captures knowledge about the structure of the system. The topological modeling of functioning offers the formal, compact and comprehensive way to transform problem domain functioning processes (dynamics) into a structure (statics), i.e., information mapping from the model of functioning to the class diagram at the conceptual level. *The main idea is that the functionality determines the structure of the planned system.* Each system

has the purpose of its existence. It relates as to living organisms (including human beings) as to mechanical, social and business systems. Each system functions in order to fulfill its purpose. In order to function successfully, the system needs to have a proper structure. Certainly, ways towards the purpose can differ, and the system is forced to achieve different goals which can also be changed. This means that the system should be able to change (remove, add, modify) its functions. Thus the structure of the system also may be changed according to these changed functions. However, it is clear that main functions of the system should be persistent in order for this system to be able to fulfill the purpose of its existence. This means that the structure of the system depends on its functionality.

Abstract Topological Model of System Functioning

Let us assume that an abstract finite closed set *X* = *{a, b, c, ..., z}* defined in topology *Q* is given. It is known that the simplest way of representation of topology *Q* can be direct listing of those subsets, which we consider as open subsets in *X*. It is possible, for example, to set binary relations in the form of some hypothetic rules, which connect two points of the set *X*. Then for any two different points, *a* and *b*, which belong to *X*, only one of four statements of binary relations (see Figure 2) will be true.

A binary relation can be represented in the form of an arc of a directed graph (digraph). In

Figure 2. Four statements which are possible for two different elements in X

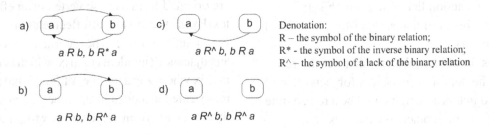

Denotation:
R – the symbol of the binary relation;
R* - the symbol of the inverse binary relation;
R^ – the symbol of a lack of the binary relation

Figure 2 digraphs that are corresponding to those four possible binary relations are illustrated above each statement.

An abstract topological model of system functioning visually can be represented as a directed graph $G(X, U)$, where X is a finite closed set of elements with some certain topology Q among them, and U is a set of arcs that illustrates this topology. The set X is a union of a subset N of features of the system itself and a subset M of features of other systems, constituting the surrounding environment interacting with the system under consideration. This theoretical statement is explained below in more detail in Subsection "Separation of a topological model of system functioning".

Elements of the Topological Model of System Functioning

Functional Features of the System

When we speak about functioning, we need to discuss what a concept "function" means. A "function" is the natural purpose (of something) or the duty (of a person). "Functional" means designed for or capable of a particular function or a use. This means that a functional feature is a characteristic of the system (in its general sense) that is *designed* and *necessary* to achieve some system's goal. Functional features must be defined in accordance with the verbs (actions) defined in the description of the system. The unique nature of each functional feature defined in (Asnina, 2006b) is extended in this chapter.

Each functional feature is a **unique tuple <A, R, O, PrCond, PostCond, Pr, Ex>**, where:

- A is an action linked with an object;
- R is a result of that action (it is an optional element);
- O is an object (objects) that get the result of the action or an object (objects) that is used in this action; it could be a role, a time period or a moment, catalogues etc.;

- *PrCond* is a set $PrCond = \{c_p, ..., c_i\}$, where c_i is a precondition or an atomic business rule (it is an optional element);
- *PostCond* is a set $PostCond = \{c_p, ..., c_i\}$, where c_i is a post-condition or an atomic business rule (it is an optional element);
- *Pr* is a set of responsible entities (systems or subsystems) that provide or suggest an action with a set of certain objects;
- *Ex* is a set of responsible entities (systems or subsystems) that enact a concrete action.

A name of the functional feature could be expressed in the following form:

<action>-ing the < result> [to, into, in, by, of, from] a(n) <object>

For example, the name of the functional feature *"evaluating the condition of a print"* contains description of the action *"evaluate"*, result *"condition"*, and object *"print"*.

In case if a result of the action cannot be evaluated, a name of the functional feature could be written down in the following form:

<action>-ing a(n) <object>

For example, a name of the functional feature *"servicing a reader"* indicates at the action *"service"* and the object of this action *"reader"*.

Topological Structure

The topology is represented by cause-and-effect relations between functional features. Graphically, the cause-and-effect relations are represented as arcs between vertices of a directed graph, which are oriented from a cause vertex to an effect vertex. By far, the cause-and-effect relations between functional features can be recorded in the form of an adjacency (incident) matrix, which is a Z by Z matrix where Z is a number of functional features represented as nodes in the topological space. If there is an arc from some vertex x to some vertex *y*, then the element $M_{x,y}$ is 1, otherwise it is 0. This makes it easier to find sub-graphs, it is vitally important for analyzing subsystems.

It is assumed in topological functioning modeling that a cause-and-effect relation between two functional features of the system exists if the appearance of one feature is caused by the appearance of the other feature without participation of any third (intermediary) feature. Since identification of cause-and-effect relations is rather intuitive work, the essence of cause-and-effect relations needs to be described.

The connection between a cause and an effect is represented by a certain conditional expression, the causal implication. It is characterized by the nature or business rules not by logic rules. They are such concepts as ontological necessity, probability etc. In causal connections "something is allowed to go wrong", whereas logical statements allow no exceptions. Using this property of the cause-and-effect relations a logical sequence, wherein the execution of the precondition guarantees the execution of the action, can be omitted; this means that even if a cause is executed, it is allowed that the corresponding effect will not be generated because of some functional damage.

Cause-and-effect relations have *a time dimension*, since a cause chronologically *precedes* and *generates* an effect. The concept of generating is necessary in order to distinguish a cause-and-effect relation from the simple consequence that is not causal. Causes may be sufficient or necessary (in other words, complete or partial) for generating an effect (Farlex Inc., 2009). A sufficient (complete) cause generates its effect ever, in any conditions. On the other hand, a necessary cause (partial) only promotes its effect generating and this effect is realized only if this partial cause joins other conditions. However, most cause-and-effect relationships involve multiple factors. Sometimes there are factors in series. Sometimes there are factors in parallel. *In case of the topological functioning model, it is assumed that a deal is always with necessary causes as the functionality of the system has its known and unknown risks at the time of analysis.* And the last, the causality is universal. This means that there is no such a problem domain without causes and effects. The person can see nothing, but a cause or an effect exists.

As already mentioned, a structure of cause-and-effect relations can form a causal chain (in series or in parallel). The causal chain begins with an initial cause and follows with series of intermediate actions or events to a final effect. Though one link may not be as important or as strong like the other ones, they are all necessary to the chain. If just one of these intermediate causes is absent, then the final effect would not be reached. As an example, the situation of payment in restaurant can be considered. A causal chain of this case can be the following: ordering in a restaurant, then eating the order, making a decision about payment, paying the bill. If the decision about payment is not made, the last action (paying the bill) will not be generated. Additionally, even if you change something, you cannot remove the effect without removing or changing the cause.

Separation of a Topological Model of System Functioning

As stated in the beginning of this section, "Abstract topological model of system functioning", a topological space of the system is represented by the expression (a) in Figure 3, where Z is a set of system functional features, N is a set of inner functional features of the system, and M is a set of functional features of other systems, constituting the environment affecting the system or that is affected by the system. Inner functional features and external affecting functional features are stated by domain experts. However, there is a way that allows checking of experts' statements. In common case, external affecting functional features should be inputs and outputs in the model. For example, in the topological space presented in Figure 3 (c) the set $Z = \{a, b, c, d, e, f, g\}$ that is a union of $M = \{a, d, f, g\}$ and $N = \{b, c, e\}$ as

Figure 3. Separation of the topological model of abstract system functioning

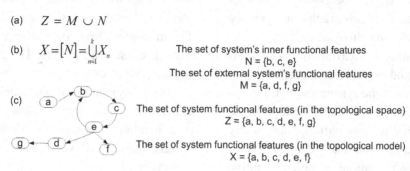

(a) $\quad Z = M \cup N$

(b) $\quad X = [N] = \bigcup_{n=1}^{k} X_n$

The set of system's inner functional features
N = {b, c, e}
The set of external system's functional features
M = {a, d, f, g}

(c)

The set of system functional features (in the topological space)
Z = {a, b, c, d, e, f, g}

The set of system functional features (in the topological model)
X = {a, b, c, d, e, f}

stated by the expression (a) in the same figure. Besides that this topological space also satisfies axioms in Figure 1.

Separation of a topological model of system functioning from the topological space, i.e., formal definition of the set X, can be done by using *the closure operation over the set N* as illustrated by the expression (b) in Figure 3, where X_n is an adherence point of the set N; and k is a number of adherence points of N, i.e. capacity of X. In order to execute this operation, definitions of neighborhood and an adherence point need to be done.

Definition 1: The *neighborhood* of the vertex x in a graph is a set of all the vertices adjacent to x and the vertex x itself. It is assumed here that all the vertices adjacent to x lie at the one step distance from x. This means that only direct successors of x are taken into accounts.

Definition 2: An *adherence point* of the set N is a point, each neighborhood of which includes at least one point from the set N.

For example, in case of the topological space in Figure 3 (c), the neighborhood of the vertex e is a set of vertices e (the vertex itself), b, d, and f. The vertex c is not included in this neighborhood, because it lies at a distance of one step back.

When we need to define the set X, we should define neighborhoods for all vertices in the topological space and then to unite those neighborhoods, which contain at least one point that belongs to

N. Taking as an example the topological space in Figure 3 (c), sets of neighborhoods are as follows:

- The neighborhood of the vertex a is a set $X_a = \{a, \boldsymbol{b}\}$;
- The neighborhood of the vertex $\boldsymbol{b}$ is a set $X_b = \{\boldsymbol{b}, \boldsymbol{c}\}$;
- The neighborhood of the vertex c is a set $X_c = \{\boldsymbol{c}, \boldsymbol{e}\}$;
- The neighborhood of the vertex d is a set $X_d = \{d, g\}$;
- The neighborhood of the vertex e is a set $X_e = \{\boldsymbol{e}, \boldsymbol{b}, d, f\}$;
- The neighborhood of the vertex f is a set $X_f = \{f\}$;
- The neighborhood of the vertex g is a set $X_g = \{g\}$.

Vertices names, which belong to the set N, are denoted with **bold.** Hence, we have four from seven neighborhoods, which contain vertices from the set N. They are neighborhoods of vertices a, b, c, and e. Therefore, the set X is a union of neighborhoods of those vertices, or in other words a union of adherence points X_a, X_b, X_c, and X_e. Note that the neighborhood of the vertex a also belongs to this union, although the vertex a itself belongs to the set M, not to the set N. The result of the union is the set $X = \{a, b, c, d, e, f\}$. Functional feature g is out of the scope of this abstract system.

In case of studying complex systems it is essential to investigate systems division into series of subsystems. Selection of the topological subspace of the subsystem from the topological space of the system also is formulated as closuring over the subset of own properties of the subsystem, thus this amounts taking into consideration the closures of subsets of *N*.

Practically, studying topological and functional properties of topological models of system functioning (discussed below) reduces to checking on those properties of the according topological digraph. The formalized statements given below provide the control of correctness in the process of model construction (Osis, 2004). Examples which illustrate topological and functional properties of topological models of system functioning are presented in the next subsection.

Common Topological and Functional Properties of Systems

A topological functioning model has topological and functional properties. According to (Osis, 1969), the topological properties are connectedness, neighborhoods, closure, and continuous mapping; and the functional properties are cause-and-effect relations, cycle structure, inputs and outputs. Statements described below formalize these model properties.

The topological and functional properties are illustrated by a few examples. One of them is a quite simplified description of the part of library's work but allows us to demonstrate the represented theory. Let us assume that we have the following description:

"The library invites people to come. The Advertising Company gives the informational support for the library. When a reader comes, he is serviced by a librarian. Each month the librarian evaluates the condition of used prints. If a print is damaged, then it is either restored by the Restoration Company or removed by the Liquidating Company. The removed prints are liquidated by the Liquidating Company, while the library continues to use the restored prints.

Library's Fund Company gives the financial support that is based on annual library's reports. The Library's Fund Company itself is credited by its partners. Library's fund gets this financial support. The library distribute the obtained income among paying salaries to employees, restoring prints, removing damaged prints and purchasing prints. Each three months the library purchases prints which are published by publishing houses in order to service their readers. Before each purchase, the library evaluates readers' requirements as well the condition of library's prints. The library gives the information support by fee."

Topological Properties

Connectedness

The first topological property is *connectedness*.

Statement 1: A topological space, which represents functioning of the business or technical system, must be connected.

Statement 1 defines that the topological space of the functioning system must be connected. This means that the digraph cannot have isolated vertices. It defines also formal semantics of concepts of subsystems and independent systems.

- Corollary 1-1: The topological digraph *G(X, U)* of functioning of the system cannot include any isolated vertices.
- Corollary 1-2: Every business and technical system is a subsystem of the environment.

As mentioned, functional features are determined from the verbal description of the system given above. Table 1 enumerates defined functional features of the topological space according with the unique tuple *<A, R, O, PrCond, PostCond, Pr, Ex>* described hereinbefore (an exception is the last column that describes to which system a functional feature belongs). They correspond to the graph vertex labels in Figure 4 (a). For example,

Table 1. Functional features of the library

Label	Name			Preconditions	Postconditions	Providers	Executors	Subordination
	action-ing	*the result*	*an object*					
	A	R	O	PrCnd	PostCond	Pr	Ex	N/M
a	Publishing		a print			PH	PH	M
b	Comng		a reader			Lb	R	N
c	Purhasing		a print			PH	Lb	N
d	Sericing		a reader		income	Lb	Lb	N
e	Evauating	the condi-tion	of a print	each month	damaged or undamaged condition	Lb	Lb	N
f	Evauating	the require-ments	of a reader		reader's require-ments	Lb	Lb	N
g	Resoring		a print	if a print is dam-aged		RC	Lb	N
h	Disributing		Income			Lb	Lb	N
i	Remving		a damaged print	if a print is dam-aged		LC	Lb	M
j	Givng		financial support	review of library's annual report	income	LF	LF	N
k	Payng	the salary	to an em-ployee			Lb	Lb	N
l	Givng		information-al support			Lb	Lb	N
m	Creting		a report	deadline of annual report submission		Lb	Lb	N
n	Liqidating		a print	if a print is removed		LC	LC	M
o	Invting		a man			AC	AC	M
p	Creiting		library's fund company			Cr	FC	M

the vertex *c* graphically denotes the functional feature "*c: Purchasing a print*". Letters used for denoting providers and executors specifies the following entities: *Lb* - the library, *Cr* – a creditor, *R* – a reader, *LF* – Library's Fund Company, *AC* – an advertising company, *RC* –a company that restores prints, *LC* – a company that liquidates prints, and *PH* – a publishing house. In the last column, *N* denotes inner (system) functional features, and *M* denotes functional features of the external environment.

Neighborhoods

According to expression (b) in Figure 3, we should identify neighborhoods of functional features of *N*. According to Table 1 the set $N = \{b, c, d, e, f, g, h, j, k, l, m\}$, and the set $M = \{a, i, o, n, p\}$. The set *X* of system properties is obtained by uniting adherence points of *N*. The list of neighborhoods is as follows:

$X_a = \{a, \mathbf{c}\}$,
$X_b = \{\mathbf{b}, \mathbf{d}\}$,
$X_c = \{\mathbf{c}, \mathbf{d}\}$,

$X_d = \{\mathbf{d}, \mathbf{f}, \mathbf{h}, \mathbf{e}\},$

$X_e = \{\mathbf{e}, \mathbf{g}, i\},$

$X_f = \{\mathbf{f}, \mathbf{c}\},$

$X_g = \{\mathbf{g}, \mathbf{d}\},$

$X_h = \{\mathbf{h}, \mathbf{c}, \mathbf{k}, \mathbf{g}, i, l, \mathbf{m}\},$

$X_i = \{i, n\},$

$X_j = \{\mathbf{j}, \mathbf{h}\},$

$X_k = \{\mathbf{k}, \mathbf{d}\},$

$X_l = \{\mathbf{l}, \mathbf{b}\},$

$X_m = \{\mathbf{m}, \mathbf{j}\},$

$X_n = \{n\},$

$X_o = \{o, \mathbf{b}\},$ and

$X_p = \{p, \mathbf{j}\}.$

Labels of vertices denoted by bold are labels of functional features which belong to the set N.

Closure

In order to get the set X we should perform closure over set N, i.e., we should unite neighborhoods X_a, X_b, X_c, X_d, X_e, X_f, X_g, X_h, X_j, X_k, X_l, X_m, X_o, and X_p. Thus, the set of system functional features is $X = \{a, b, c, d, e, f, g, h, i, j, k, l, m, o, p\}$. It includes also functionality from the set M, i.e., vertices a, i, o and p. The vertex n is out of the system's boundary. In such a way, the system boundary is formally (mathematically) defined.

Figure 4 (a) illustrates a topological model of library functioning that is constructed from the description given above. Elements that are in the external environment, for example "*n: Liquidating a print*" (the vertex n) or "*p: Crediting a fund company*" (the vertex p), do not belong to the inner system characteristics; however, they must

Figure 4. The topological model of library functioning

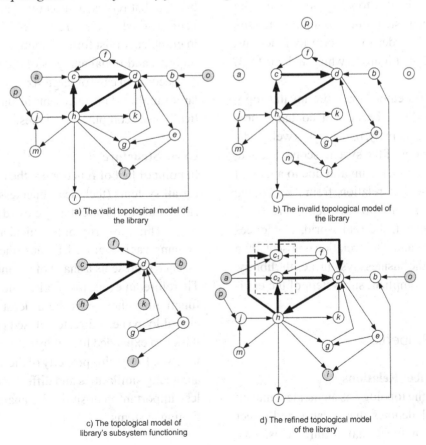

a) The valid topological model of the library

b) The invalid topological model of the library

c) The topological model of library's subsystem functioning

d) The refined topological model of the library

Table 2. The TFM represented as the incident matrix X

	a	b	c	d	e	f	g	h	i	j	k	l	m	o	p
a	0	0	1	0	0	0	0	0	0	0	0	0	0	0	0
b	0	0	0	1	0	0	0	0	0	0	0	0	0	0	0
c	0	0	0	1	0	0	0	0	0	0	0	0	0	0	0
d	0	0	0	0	1	1	0	1	0	0	0	0	0	0	0
e	0	0	0	0	0	0	1	0	1	0	0	0	0	0	0
f	0	0	1	0	0	0	0	0	0	0	0	0	0	0	0
g	0	0	0	1	0	0	0	0	0	0	0	0	0	0	0
h	0	0	1	0	0	0	1	0	1	0	1	1	1	0	0
i	0	0	0	0	0	0	0	0	0	0	0	0	0	0	0
j	0	0	0	0	0	0	0	1	0	0	0	0	0	0	0
k	0	0	0	1	0	0	0	0	0	0	0	0	0	0	0
l	0	1	0	0	0	0	0	0	0	0	0	0	0	0	0
m	0	0	0	0	0	0	0	0	0	1	0	0	0	0	0
o	0	1	0	0	0	0	0	0	0	0	0	0	0	0	0
p	0	0	0	0	0	0	0	0	0	1	0	0	0	0	0

be represented in the topological functioning model since the system must communicate with other systems in order to perform its functions. Those vertices in Figure 4 which belong to *M* are shadowed.

Figure 4 (b) demonstrates the invalid topological model. First, because it contains three isolated vertices, namely, *a, o* and *p* as well as the vertex *n* that is out of the system scope. Second, the topological model is invalid due to a lack of the cause-and-effect relation from "*k: Paying salaries to employees*" to "*Servicing a reader*". In the environment, the real world, employees work for money, and if this relation is absent, then this means that the business system, i.e., the library, is invalid or incompliant subsystem of the environment.

Functional Properties

Cause-and-Effect Relations

Table 2 shows the topology as an incident matrix $X_{a-p,a-p}$, where 1 denotes that a cause-and-effect relation between functional features exist. We believe that representation by matrix is not convenient. First, cycles are not so evident then it is in graphical or list forms. Identification of cycles requires additional analysis of the matrix.

Second, in case of large sizes of the TFM, the large number of null elements in matrices impractically uses computer resources.

Cycle Structure

In point of fact of functioning the common thing for all systems (technical, business and biological) should be an oriented cycle (a directed closed path). This similarity of technical and biological systems was recognized, because the main cycle in essence represents a shape of the main feedback. Therefore, in every topological model of system functioning there must be at least one directed closed loop (i.e. a directed closed path). Usually it is even expanded hierarchy of cycles. As stated in (Osis, 1969), this property of the model enables analyzing similarities and differences (that is not less important than similarity analysis) of functioning systems.

In Figure 4 (a) the model reflects the following cycles. The *main cycle* of the system model is *c-d-h-c,* because the system will not be able to function if it does not offer services to clients, or it has no new prints (books and magazines become unreadable as time goes by), or it has no money. The system can function without other characteristics but, perhaps, not so efficiently. This cycle represents the main feedback. The first order subsycle is a cycle that has at least one vertex shared with the main cycle. The second order subcycle is a cycle that has at least one vertex shared with the first order subcycle, and so on. Cycles can form hierarchies.

The *first order subcycles* are as follows:

- The subcycle *c-d-f-c* represents the way the system analyzes its work taking into consideration clients' desires.
- The subcycle *h-k-d-h* represents a subsystem of money relationships among the organization and its employees.
- The subcycle *h-m-j-h* represents system relationships with financial support organizations. The library needs to report information about its work in order to get some financial support from these organizations.
- The subcycle *d-e-g-d* represents functionality that is necessary to perform when the used print condition requires restoration.
- The subcycle *d-h-g-d* represents the financial support necessity when a used print needs restoration.
- The subcycle *d-h-l-b-d* describes activities that let readers know any necessary information.

For comparison, the list of incident tuples for the same topological model in Figure 4 (a) is as follows:

<a, **c**>, [<**c**, **d**>, <**d**, **h**>, <**h**, **c**>], (**cd**, <**d**, f>, <f, **c**>), (**dh**, <**h**, k>, <k, **d**>),

(**dh**, <**h**, g>, <g, **d**>), <**d**, e>, <e, g>, (**dh**, <**h**, l>, <l, b>, <b, **d**>), <o, b>, <p, j>,

(<j, **h**>, <**h**, m>, <m, j>), <e, i>, <**h**, i>, <i, n>.

Where:

- squared brackets "[sublist]" denote a sublist of arcs, which form the main functioning cycle, e.g. the cycle [<**c**, **d**>, <**d**, **h**>, <**h**, **c**>];
- simple brackets "(sublist)" denote a sublist of arcs, which form a subcyle, e.g. (**cd**, <**d**, f>, <f, **c**>);
- "**label**" denotes functional features that belong to the main functioning cycle, e.g. vertex **c**;
- "**label1 label2**"denotes an arc of the higher rang that is presented in the given subcycle, e.g. arc **cd**.

This clear representation allows tracing back a hierarchy of the cycle structure also if the TFM description is given in the list form.

Inputs and Outputs

The topological model must have input vertices as well as output vertices. This enables to identify what functionality from the external environment and inside the system generates other functional properties of the system. For example, the constructed topological model has the input vertices *{a, p, o}* and the output vertex *i*. Formal definition of the TFM by using the closuring operation over a set is considered hereinafter.

Input and output functional features can be identified by analyzing values in rows and columns. Namely, input functional features of the TFM have all nulls in columns, and output functional features of the TFM have all nulls in rows (see Table 2 row *i*, and columns *a, o,* and *p*).

Statement 2. If a vertex α of the neighborhood $X_\alpha = \{\alpha, \beta\}$ belongs to the set *M* and the neighborhood X_a contains a vertex β of the set N, then the vertex α is a TFM input vertex.

For example, the neighborhood of vertex p is $X_p = \{p,j\}$, hence p is an input vertex. For input vertex columns in the incident matrix X all values are nulls (see Table 2).

Statement 3. If a vertex w of the set M belongs to a neighborhood of some vertex of the set N, then the vertex w is a TFM output vertex.

For example, vertex i belongs to M and the neighborhoods of vertices h and e of the set N, namely, $X_e = \{e, g, i\}$ and $X_h = \{h, c, k, g, i, l, m\}$. Thus, vertex i is an output vertex.

Corollary 2/3-1. If a vertex γ that belongs to the set M can be found only in those neighborhoods, all vertices of which belong to the set M, then γ does not belong to the set X and is not reflected in the graph representing the TFM.

For example, the vertex n can be found only in the neighborhoods $X_i = \{i, n\}$ and $X_n = \{n\}$, where all vertices (here: i and n) in these neighborhoods belong to M. Therefore, n is not depicted in the topological models in Figure 4 (a) and (d).

Decomposition in Subsystems

According to Corollary 1-2, there is no difference between a system and a subsystem. Every subsystem is a system regarding to its environment. Therefore, in case of subsystems, the environment is a system that in turn is separated from the larger environment.

If we would like to separate a topological model of the subsystem, we should do the same activities. For example, if we need to create a subsystem that provides qualitative services for readers. Let us assume that an expert has defined that functionality described by functional features d and e should be included in this subsystem. Thus, the set of system inner functional features

is $N_{subsystem} = \{d, e\}$. The set of functional features $M_{subsystem}$ is the set difference of X and $N_{subsystem}$, i.e., $M_{subsystem} = X \backslash N_{subsystem} = \{a, b, c, f, g, h, i, j, k, l, m, o, p\}$. By using the closure over $N_{subsystem}$, we get the following neighborhoods:

$X_a = \{a, c\}$,
$X_b = \{b, \mathbf{d}\}$,
$X_c = \{c, \mathbf{d}\}$,
$X_d = \{\mathbf{d}, f, h, \mathbf{e}\}$,
$X_e = \{\mathbf{e}, g, i\}$,
$X_f = \{f, c\}$,
$X_g = \{g, \mathbf{d}\}$,
$X_h = \{h, c, k, g, i, l, m\}$,
$X_i = \{i\}$,
$X_j = \{j, h\}$,
$X_k = \{k, \mathbf{d}\}$,
$X_l = \{l, b\}$,
$X_m = \{m, j\}$,
$X_o = \{o, b\}$, and
$X_p = \{p, j\}$.

Labels of vertices denoted by bold are labels of functional features which belong to the set $N_{subsystem}$. In order to get the set $X_{subsystem}$ we should unite neighborhoods $X_b, X_c, X_d, X_e, X_g,$ and X_k. The set of subsystem functional features is $X_{subsystem} = \{b, c, d, e, f, g, h, i, k\}$, and the topological model of this subsystem with shadowed vertices, which denotes external functional features, is illustrated in Figure 4 (c). This model is valid, because it has not isolated vertices, and has its main functioning cycle d-e-g-d that represents functionality that is necessary to perform when the used print condition requires restoration.

According to Statement 2, input functional features of the TFM of the subsystem are b, c, g, k. The reason is neighborhoods $X_b = \{b,\mathbf{d}\}$, $X_c = \{c,\mathbf{d}\}$, $X_g = \{g,\mathbf{d}\}$, and $X_k = \{k,\mathbf{d}\}$. According to Statement 3, output functional features of the TFM of the subsystem are f, h, g and i. The reason is neighborhoods $X_d = \{\mathbf{d}, f, h, \mathbf{e}\}$, and $X_e = \{\mathbf{e}, g, i\}$. Functional feature g belongs as to inputs as to outputs, this means that it is an inner functional feature that was not recognized by the experts before and it should belong to the set N. Hence, inputs are b, c, and k, and outputs are f, h and i.

The model shows that experts' definition of subsystem functionality (functional features "*d: servicing a reader*" and "*e: evaluating the condition of a print*") was incomplete, because they did not include the functional feature "*g: Restoring a print*". However, this is one of the essential functions of the subsystem, because the bad condition of prints can be a cause of decreasing a count of readers as well as a cause of unnecessary costs for purchasing new copies of prints. Fortunately, the topological model in graph representation shows such particularities evidently in comparison with matrices or lists. The essential nature of the functional feature "*g: Restoring a print*" is evident from its belonging to the first-order functioning cycle *d-e-g-d* that is a main functioning cycle for this subsystem (if we look at this subsystem independently from the library). The subsystem cannot operate without at least one functioning cycle. Moreover, experts, matrices and lists cannot formally point to this incompleteness, only the TFM enables discovering this important feature of the subsystem-to-be during formal separation of the subsystem-to-be from its environment.

Besides that, the topological model enables us to see that such a subsystem will have multiple communication points with other subsystems, since this model has multiple inputs and outputs. Figure 4(c) illustrates that in order to service readers qualitatively the subsystem should purchase new prints or new copies of liquidated prints (functional feature "*c: purchasing a print*"), extend or at least not decrease a number of readers (functional feature "*b: coming a reader*"), satisfy employees' desires (functional feature "*k: paying the salary to an employee*"). Besides that the subsystem should provide information to the external environment about the condition of used prints (functional feature "*f: evaluating the condition of a print*"), income got by servicing readers (functional feature "*h: distributing income*"), and

damaged prints (functional feature "*i: removing a damaged print*"). These cause-and-effect relations from input to inner functional features and from inner to output functional features illustrates related functionality that extend the initial set of subsystem functions.

Certainly, subsystems should have a minimum of communication points with other systems. And our assumed subsystem is not good from the viewpoint of creating components (modules), but at the same time this example is good for illustrating the principle of creation of subsystems and discovering its incompleteness. We should note, again, that definition of subsystems is rather more evident in topological digraph representation than in matrices or lists. Graphical representation allows seeing possible subsystems straighter than matrices and lists do.

Continuous Mapping

Continuous mapping is the last *topological property* that can be presented only now – after overview of all functional properties of the TFM.

A functional feature of the system can be considered as a more detailed subset of specialized features. The model with any complexity can be abstracted to the simpler one and vice verse. This means that continuous mapping of topological models is realized. Continuous mapping states that direction of topological model arcs must be kept as in a refined as in a simplified model. Moreover, a lack of knowledge about the system can be filled up with knowledge that is obtained from the continuous mapping of the same type model to the system model under consideration. This property may be very useful for development of product lines. Because core functions of the systems in product lines are the same, optional functionality may be explicitly represented in corresponding TFMs.

- Statement 2: If some more detailed functioning system is formed by substitution of a subset of specialized properties for some functional property, then continuous mapping exists between a detailed model and a simplified parent topological model of the same system.

- *Proof*: The continuous mapping of the topological space of the detailed system T^* into the topological space of the simple parent system T will take place, if neighbourhoods of T^* will map into neighborhoods of T.

Let us assume that the contrary is the case, i.e., that neighbourhoods of T^* are not mapped into neighborhoods of T. This means that T^* possesses other essential topological properties. Therefore, either the mode of functioning of the detailed system will be different, or the detailed system will cease to exist at all. It follows that new essential functional features are being added but it contradicts to the premise of the statement. It's easy to prove also the converse statement.

- Corollary 2-1: In the topological digraph $G^*(X^*, U^*)$, the direction of arcs, which join the specialized point subset nodes with other nodes, is determined by the direction of the arcs, which join the replaced point with the corresponding nodes of the digraph $G(X, U)$.
- Corollary 2-2: A data lack that sometimes arises during the composing of a topological model of functioning can be filled up by data that are obtained, when models of the same type systems are being continuously mapped to the model of the system under study.

For example, let us consider the topological model in Figure 4 (a). This model can be continuously mapped to a more detail model, e.g., to such a model like in Figure 4 (d), where the vertex *"c: purchasing a print"* is specialized to two vertices *"c1: purchasing a book"* and *"c2: purchasing a magazine"*. In order to prove the

continuous mapping between models in Figure 4 (a) and (d), neighbourhoods of the detailed system in Figure 4 (d) must map into neighborhoods of the system in Figure 4 (a). Considering list of neighborhoods of those two models, the mapping between all neighborhoods is one-to-one except the following ones:

- $X_a^* = \{a, c_1, c_2\}$ is mapped into $X_a = \{a, c\}$, as c_1 belongs to c, and c_2 belongs to c;
- $X_{c1}^* = \{c_1, d\}$ is mapped into $X_c = \{c, d\}$, as c_1 belongs to c;
- $X_{c2}^* = \{c_2, d\}$ is mapped into $X_c = \{c, d\}$, as c_2 belongs to c;
- $X_f^* = \{f, c_1, c_2\}$ is mapped into $X_f = \{f, c\}$, as c_1 belongs to c, and c_2 belongs to c;
- $X_h^* = \{h, c_1, c_2, k, g, i, l, m\}$ is mapped into $X_h = \{h, c, k, g, i, l, m\}$, as c_1 belongs to c, and c_2 belongs to c.

But also these neighborhoods of the detailed system (denoted by "*") are mapped into the neighborhoods of the system. Thus, the topological functioning model of the detailed system is continuously mapped into the topological functioning model of the system. The continuous mapping between models means that if something changes in one model, the same changes must be taken into account in the other one. Moreover, all arcs that belong to refined vertices have the same direction as before.

The topological model in Figure 4 (d) illustrates how the main functioning cycle *c-d-h-c* is divided into two main cycles – c_1-*d-h-*c_1 and c_2-*d-h-*c_2. These are two duplicating cycles. The library can operate if it provides continuously replenished collections of magazines, books or both.

By the way, continuous mapping serves as a very useful mechanism for handling changes and discovering similarities and differences between systems.

Similarities and Differences between Systems

Speaking about analysis of similarities and differences between functionality of systems, let us consider the topological model of functioning represented in Figure 5, the meaning of its vertices is given in Table 3.

The simplified topological model of functioning shown in Figure 5 represents the basic functional features of a technical system, diesel engine, and a live organism. This model seems to be very much simplified; nevertheless it captures the most important feature of all functioning systems (technical, biological, social, etc.). All functioning systems can be characterized by their cycle structure. Every functioning is possible only if there is *at least one directed cycle* in the topological model (a closed path in the graph). In case of the digraph shown in Figure 5, there are three cycles in it: *a-b-c-d-f-g-a*, *c-d-f-c*, and *b-c-d-f-b*. We shall define the cycle *a-b-c-d-f-g-a* as a main one, in contrast to other two, which are first order sub cycles and are main cycles for subsystems.

The analogy between live systems and technical systems was noted earlier on the level of control. The feedback circuits in control systems and live organisms are similar. However, topological models permit to consider otherwise the cybernetic resemblance of functioning systems. Similarity of systems can be studied in details up

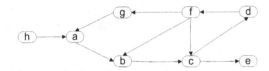

Figure 5. The topological digraph of system functioning G(X,U)

to level, which is determinate beforehand. Let us notice in particular that both resemblance and difference between live organisms and technical devices can be studied with the help of topological models.

MODEL-DRIVEN SOFTWARE DEVELOPMENT WITH TOPOLOGICAL MODELING

Organizations are complex man-made systems that deal with many concepts such as people, business processes and information systems, technology, etc. Understanding how these complex systems operate or function is very important in order to introduce software solution into organization's framework.

According to (IEEE, 2000) *architecture* is the fundamental organization of a system embodied in its components, their relationships to each other and to the environment and the principles guiding its design and evolution. The fundamental

Table 3. Basic functional features of systems

Label	Diesel engine	Live organism
a	Contacting the diesel fuel in a tank	Contacting food
b	Taking the fuel in by a pump	Swallowing food
c	Burning up fuel	Digesting food
d	Transferring energy to crankshaft	Absorbing food by cells
e	Flowing used up gases out	Throwing waste out
f	Distributing energy	Distributing energy
g	Moving to a filling station	Moving to food
h	Supplying the fuel from a tank	Procuring food from surroundings

Figure 6. Relations between the problem domain and solution domain

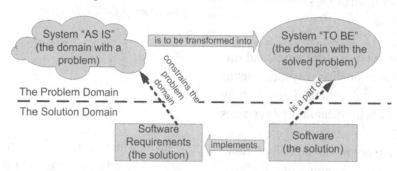

organization means essential, unifying concepts and principles of the system. The term "system" depicts applications, systems, platforms, systems of systems, enterprises, product lines, etc. And the environment depends on the context of the system – it can be developmental, operational, programmatic, and so on. Architecture is always applied to the certain universe of discourse, where a problem must be solved. Views on the system are parts of an architectural description of the system, i.e., products which document the architecture. An *architectural view* is a representation of a whole system from the perspective of a set of concerns (IEEE, 2000).

The topological functioning model is an engineering model with simple notation but solid foundations and modeling capabilities. It combines functional and structural views on the system within one formal holistic representation of the system. How these views can be used in software development is discussed hereinafter.

The initial stages of traditional software development are requirements gathering and system analysis that sometimes includes also business modeling. The objective of these initial stages is to find the solution which solves the stated problem and complies with client's *desires*, i.e. understanding of what software must do in order to satisfy client's *needs*.

Requirements are to be specified as complete as possible, describing external behavior of software to be built. Therefore after determining what

functionality of the system in the real world exists, the next step is to determine those functional parts which will benefit from automation. This means that the real world system - the system "as is" is additionally constrained by client's requirements for the software. These requirements will change the real world system, if are implemented and introduced, thus will modify the system "as is" to the system "to be", where the software is a part of the system "to be" (Figure 6).

As mentioned in the previous sections, the TFM is an engineering model that can be successfully used for domain modeling and analysis based on formal mathematical constructions and mechanisms. And this self-sufficient engineering model of the domain ("as is" and "to be") is a solid ground for further development of software.

The suggested process that relates domain analysis with the TFM and further construction of software models used in software development is illustrated in Figure 7. It starts from modeling and analyzing the problem domain with the TFM (see Figure 7-1a). At the high level of abstraction the TFM can be used as a simplified model for software developers – business and system analytics, but it has one significant advantage – it is formal and has mathematical foundations and thus may be formally refined to a more complex model (or models) of subsystems.

The TFM of the system "as is" is transformed into the system "to be" by using mappings from functional requirements as in Figure 7(2). As

Figure 7. Software development started with topological modeling of systems

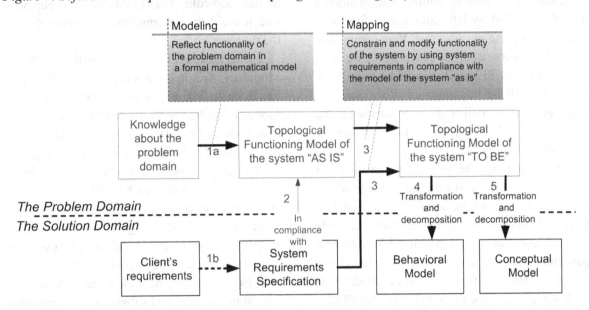

mentioned in (Osis, Asnina, & Grave, 2008), mappings describe the case of new non-existing functionality (one-to-zero), functionality that will not be implemented in the solution (zero-to-one), and functionality that exists and will be implemented in the solution (one-to-one, one-to-many, and many-to-one).

One to One is used if requirement *A* completely specifies what will be implemented in accordance with functional feature *B*.

Many to One is used if requirements (A_1, A_2,..., A_n) overlap the specification of what will be implemented in accordance with functional feature *B*. In case of the covering requirements, their specification should be refined. Another case is *a disjoint (component) relation* that is used if requirements (A_1, A_2,..., A_n) together completely specify functional feature *B* and do not overlap each other.

One to Many is used if a part of requirement *A* completely specifies some functional feature *B*. This means that requirement *A* completely specifies a set of functional features (B_1, ..., B_n). For this purpose a relation called *separating family of functions* is used. This case can occur if: a)

the requirement joins several requirements and can be split up or b) functional features are more detailed than the requirement.

One to Zero is used when one requirement specifies some new, invalid (impossible) or undefined functionality. New functionality requires definition of possible changes in the problem domain functioning. Undefined functionality forces more careful investigation of the problem and solution domains. In turn, invalid or impossible functionality requires identification of additional constraints in the problem domain. The discovered constrains can cause modifying or even removing those requirements.

Zero to One is applied if specification does not contain any requirement corresponding to the defined feature. This means that it could be a missed requirement, and therefore it could be left unimplemented in the application. Thus, it is mandatory to take a decision about the implementation of the discovered functionality together with the client.

The result of this activity is both checked requirements and TFM, which describes a needed and possible functionality of the system and the environment it operates within. The mappings modify the TFM by introducing new functions and changing the existing one, thus composing the TFM of the system "to be" as in Figure 7(3). This composed TFM will illustrates both functions that will be implemented in the solution and functions that will not be implemented in the solution but still will exist in the problem domain (manual activities).

After mapping, the TFM of the system "to be" can be transformed into the behavioral and structural models of the solution as in Figure 7 (4 and 5). These behavioral and structural models are viewpoints on the system which describe particular concerns about the role of the system and may belong to different existing architectures.

For example, wide and long known John Zachman's framework for information systems architecture (Sowa & Zachman, 1992) is a set of architectures structured according with perspectives of development. According with this framework, the topological modeling of the system is allocated in context and business model perspectives of the first dimension and answers the following questions of the second dimension: data ("what?"), function ("how?"), network ("where?"), people ("who?"), time ("when?"), and motivation ("why?"). The *data* perspective is shown as a list of objects, subsystems and external systems that are used in system functioning. The *function* perspective is shown as functional features and cause-and-effect relations among them. The *network* perspective is shown as a place where each functional feature is allocated, i.e., within the system or in the external environment. The *people* perspective is shown by an entity that provides each functional feature. The *time* perspective is shown as cause and effect sequences, because the effect may occur only if a cause generated it. The *motivation* perspective is shown by functioning cycles, inputs and outputs in the topological functioning model. Therefore, it holds all the necessary information from the business model perspective for construction of

models according to the more detailed perspective, namely, the information system model from the designer's viewpoint.

Let us take for another example the 4+1 View Model of Architecture suggested by Philippe Kruchten in1995 (Kruchten, 1995). The View Model describes software architecture by five related views. One of these views, a scenario view, is related with other four views, namely, logical, process, development and physical. The topological functioning model is a holistic representation of all possible scenarios of the system operation. It is a base for constructing the logical view that specifies design object model, the process view that specifies time and synchronization aspects, and also the development view that specifies the system by modules and subsystems and communications among them.

Therefore, these solution models will be in conformity with the problem domain, and client's requirements will be thoroughly checked and inspected. Some of those aspects are highlighted and discussed in more detail in other chapters of the book.

The Metamodel of the TFM for System Modeling

The main purpose of metamodeling is definition of modeling languages. Besides that, metamodeling is also used for defining domain specific languages and for transforming artifacts among various languages. Thus metamodeling supports conformance among tools and languages. The metamodeling language used for this purpose is a Meta-Object Facility (MOF) standard developed by the Object Management Group (2006). The MOF is implemented within several commercial and open-source tools.

The topological model of system functioning has a concrete and abstract syntax and construction rules (which we can call also as well-formedness rules). Thus, the TFM is a modeling language.

Figure 8. The standalone metamodel of the TFM

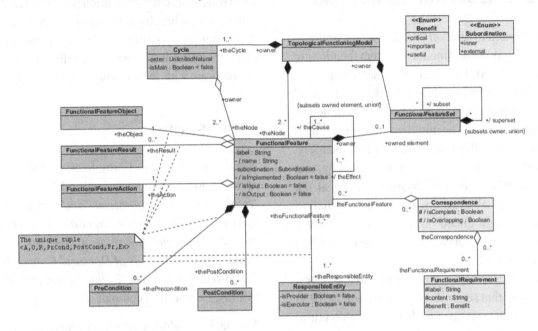

The standalone metamodel of the TFM that defines abstract syntax and construction constraints is represented in Figure 8. The metamodel is described at the MOF metalevel M2 (the level of metamodels), and represents the topological functioning model as an instance of the metaclass *TopologicalFunctioningModel* that includes at least two functional features of the metaclass *FunctionalFeature*.

Instances of functional features *Functional-Feature* can be joined in functional feature sets (the metaclass *FunctionalFeatureSet*). This means that a functional feature represented in a TFM can visualize a functional feature set. One functional feature can contain only one set and one functional feature can belong only to the one set. A functional feature can be subordinated to a system itself or to an external system (enumeration *Subordination*). Each functional feature contains an instance of the object (the metaclass *FunctionalFeatureObject*), an instance of the result (the metaclass *FunctionalFeatureResult*), and an instance of an action (the metaclass *FunctionalFeatureAction*).

The combination of these three instances together with preconditions (the metaclass *Precondition*), postconditions (the metaclass *Postconditions*) and instances of responsible entities (the metaclass *ResponsibleEntity*) associated with the functional feature must be unique within the model instance.

Functional features should form functioning cycles (the metaclass *Cycle*) of different order. Only one cycle can be the main one. Cause-and-effect relations connect functional features. A cause functional feature must have at least one effect. An effect functional feature must have at least one cause.

Functional features are related to functional requirements (the metaclass *FunctionalRequirement*) via correspondence (the metaclass *Correspondence*). The correspondence generally is many-to-many. The correspondence can be complete or incomplete, overlapping or disjoint. The corresponding functional requirements are associated with the functioning cycle, whose order establishes their benefit value (the type *Benefit*).

FUTURE RESEARCH DIRECTIONS

As mentioned in Section "Background", application of the topological model of system functioning is quite wide. At the present we research application of topological modeling for development of information systems within model-driven development paradigm. The initial results are presented in this book in the following chapters. Namely, application of the topological model of system functioning as a holistic business model at the high level of abstraction, formal determination of use cases grounded on the TFM, and formal determination of a class diagram at the conceptual level from the TFM.

Future research directions are related to developing a tool that supports construction of the TFM and its transformations to different architectural views (or dimensions) on the system, and refinement of a technique of TFM application in practice.

CONCLUSION

In this chapter we have discussed mathematical foundations of the topological model of system functioning and formalism of the modeling approach based on this model, and have explained applications of this model with examples. The topological model of systems functioning is an engineering model, i.e., it supports understandability, accuracy, predictiveness and inexpensiveness. Comparing with Petri nets, the topological functioning model can be used as a self-sufficient model for modeling functionality of businesses, mechanical systems and even living organisms. The main advantage of the topological model is its holistic representation of the system that allows analyzing the system as a whole, not by fragmental presentation of system's parts. Analysis of cause-and-effect relations allows identifying missing or weakly defined functionality as well identification of subsystems could be more evident, because the

TFM reflects all communication points of assumed subsystems. Therefore, we can start analysis and development of systems or subsystems seeing their operation in the whole together with their interactions with the external environment.

REFERENCES

Asnina, E. (2006a). Formalization aspects of problem domain modeling within Model Driven Architecture. In *Databases and Information Systems. Seventh International Baltic Conference on Databases and Information Systems. Communications, Materials of Doctoral Consortium, July 3-6, 2006, Vilnius, Lithuania* (pp. 93-104). Vilnius, Lithuania: Technika.

Asnina, E. (2006b). The formal approach to problem domain modelling within Model Driven Architecture. In *Proceedings of the 9th International Conference "Information Systems Implementation and Modelling" (ISIM'06), April 25-26, 2006, Přerov, Czech Republic, 1st edn.* (pp. 97-104). Ostrava, Czech Republic: Jan Štefan MARQ.

Asnina, E. (2009). A formal holistic outline for domain modeling. *Local Proceedings of Advances in Databases and Information Systems, 13th East-European Conference, ADBIS 2009, Associated Workshops and Doctoral Consortium, Riga, Latvia, September 7-10, 2009* (pp. 400-407). Riga Technical University.

Diskin, Z., Kadish, B., Piessens, F., & Johnson, M. (2000). Universal arrow foundations for visual modeling. In *Proc. Diagramms'2000: 1st Int. Conference on the theory and application of diagrams,* (LNAI No. 1889, pp. 345-360). Berlin: Springer.

Farlex Inc. (2009). *Causality*. Retrieved November 2009, from The Free Dictionary.Com http://encyclopedia.thefreedictionary.com/causality

Grundspenkis, J. (1974). Fault localisation based on topological feature analysis of complex system model. In *Diagnostics and Identification*, (pp. 38-48).

Grundspenkis, J. (1996). Automation of knowledge base development using model supported knowledge acquisition. In *Databases and Information Systems: Proceedings of the 2nd International Baltic Workshop, Tallinn, June 12-14, 1996, 1*, (pp. 224-233). Tallinn, Estonia: Institute of Cybernetics.

Grundspenkis, J. (1997). Causal model driven knowledge acquisition for expert diagnostic system development. In Wang, K., & Pranavicius, H. (Eds.), *Application of AI to Production Engineering. Lecture Notes of the Nordic-Baltic Summer School '97* (pp. 251–268). Kaunas, Lithuania: Kaunas University Press.

Grundspenkis, J. (2004). Automated transformation of the functional model into the diagnosis knowledge base. In *Proceedings of 5th Int. Conf. on Quality, Reliability and Maintenance, QRM2004, Oxford, April 1-2 (Ed. McNulty)* (pp. 295-298). London: Professional Engineering Publishing.

Grundspenkis, J., & Blumbergs, A. (1981). Investigation of complex system topological model structure for analysis of failures. In *Issues of Technical Diagnosis*, (pp. 41-48).

IEEE. (2000). *IEEE recommended practice for architectural description of software-intesive systems*. Washington, DC: IEEE Architecture Working Group.

Jensen, K. (1997). Coloured Petri nets. Basic concepts, analysis methods and practical use. Monographs in theoretical computer science. 2nd corrected printing: *Vol. 1. Basic Concepts*. Berlin: Springer-Verlag.

Kolmogorov, A. N. (1999). *Elements of the theory of functions and functional analysis*. New York: Dover Publications.

Kristensen, L., Christensen, S., & Jensen, K. (1998). The practitioner's guide to coloured Petri nets. *International Journal on Software Tools for Technology Transfer*, 2, 98–132. doi:10.1007/s100090050021

Kristensen, L., Jurgensen, J., & Jensen, K. (2004). Application of coloured Petri nets in system development. In J. Desel, W. Reisig, & G. Rozenberg (Eds.), *Lectures on Concurrency and Petri Nets. Advanced in Petri Nets. Proc. of 4th Advanced Course on Petri Nets* (LNCS 3098, pp. 626-685). Berlin: Springer-Verlag.

Kruchten, P. (1995, November). The 4+1 view model of architecture. *IEEE Software*, 42–50. doi:10.1109/52.469759

Markovitch, Z., & Markovitcha, I. (2000). Modelling as a tool for therapy selection. In *Proc. Of the 14th European Simulation Multiconference "Simulation and Modelling,"* (pp. 621-623), Ghent, Belgium.

Markovitch, Z., & Rekners, Y. (1998). Synthesis of systems model on basis of topological minimodels. *Automatic Control and Computer Sciences*, *32*(3), 59–66.

Markovitch, Z., & Stalidzans, E. (2000). Expert based model building using incidence matrix and topological models. In *Proc. Of the 12th European Simulation Symposium "Simulation in Industry 2000"*, (pp. 328-332), Hamburg, Germany.

Markovitcha, I., & Markovitch, Z. (1970). Mathematical model of pathogenesis of hard differentiable diseases. *Cybernetics and Diagnostics*, *4*, 21–28.

Object Management Group. (2006, January). *Meta Object Facility (MOF) core specification*. Retrieved December 2009, from http://www.omg.org/spec/MOF/2.0/PDF/

Osis, J. (1969). Topological model of system functioning. *Automatics and Computer Science. J. of Acad. of Sc, Riga, Latvia, 6*, 44–50.

Osis, J. (1970). Mathematical description of complex system functioning. [Kibernetika i Diagnostika]. *Cybernetic and Diagnosis, 4,* 7–14.

Osis, J. (1972). *Diagnostics of complex systems (Dissertation of Dr. Habil. Sc. Eng.).* Riga, Latvia: Latvian Academy of Sciences.

Osis, J. (1973). Some questions of microprogramming optimization using topological model properties. In *Cybernetic methods in the diagnosis,* (pp. 30-34).

Osis, J. (2003). Extension of software development process for mechatronic and embedded systems. In *Proceeding of the 32nd International Conference on Computer and Industrial Engineering* (pp. 305-310). Limerick, Ireland: University of Limerick.

Osis, J. (2004). Software development with topological model in the framework of MDA. In *Proceedings of the 9th CaiSE/IFIP8.1/ EUNO International Workshop on Evaluation of Modeling Methods in Systems Analysis and Design (EMMSAD'2004) in connection with the CaiSE'2004, 1,* (pp. 211–220). Riga, Lativa: RTU.

Osis, J., & Asnina, E. (2008). A business model to make software development less intuitive. In *Proceedings of 2008 International Conference on Innovation in Sofware Engineering (ISE 2008)* (pp. 1240-1245). Vienna, Austria: IEEE Computer Society Publishing.

Osis, J., Asnina, E., & Grave, A. (2008). *Formal problem domain modeling within MDA. Communications in Computer and Information Science (CCIS), 22 (III)* (pp. 387–398). Berlin: Springer.

Osis, J., & Beghi, L. (1997). Topological modelling of biological systems. *Proceedings of the third IFAC Symposium on Modelling and Control in Biomedical Systems (Including Biological Systems), D.A. Linkens, E.R. Carson (eds)* (pp. 337-342). Oxford, UK: Elsevier Science Publishing.

Osis, J., Gefandbein, J., Markovitch, Z., & Novozhilova, N. (1991). *Diagnosis based on graph models. (By the examples of aircraft and automobile mechanisms).* Moscow: Transport.

Osis, J., Sukovskis, U., & Teilans, A. (1997). Business process modeling and simulation based on topological approach. In *Proceedings of the 9th European Simulation Symposium and Exhibition,* (pp. 496-501), Passau, Germany.

Selic, B. (2003, September/October). The pragmatics of model-driven development. *IEEE Software,* 19–25. doi:10.1109/MS.2003.1231146

Sowa, J., & Zachman, J. (1992). Extending and formalizing the framework for information systems architecture. *IBM Systems Journal, 31*(3), 590–616. doi:10.1147/sj.313.0590

KEY TERMS AND DEFINITIONS

Cause-and-Effect Relation: A relation between two functional features of the system where appearance and execution of one functional feature is caused (generated) by the other functional feature without any intermediate functionality.

Continuous Mapping: A mathematical relation between two topological directed graphs that preserve their functional and structural properties.

Cycle Structure: A closed directed path that is formed by cause-and-effect relations between TFM functional features. Cycle structure describes functioning cycles of the system. The system must have at least one functioning cycle. Cycle structures may form hierarchies.

Functioning Cycle: A closed path of cause-and-effect relations among functional features in the topological functioning model. A main cycle joins functional features which are vitally important for the system operation. Functioning cycles may form hierarchies.

Metamodel: A model that specifies abstract and concrete syntax of the modeling language as well as well-formedness rules. A metamodel is specified in terms of a reflexive metametamodeling language, e.g. OMG's Meta-Object Facility.

Model of System Architecture: A set of viewpoints on behavioral and structural characteristics of the system under consideration from different dimensions and perspectives.

System's Function: The natural purpose of the system or its part.

System's Functional Feature: A functional characteristic of the system that is needed to reach system's functioning goal.

Topological Functioning Model: A model based on system theory and mathematics that specifies functionality and structure of a complex system as a connected topological space of system's functional characteristics and cause-and-effect relations among them.

Chapter 3
Topological Functioning Model as a CIM–Business Model

Erika Asnina
Riga Technical University, Latvia

Janis Osis
Riga Technical University, Latvia

ABSTRACT

The first model in Model Driven Architecture (MDA) is a Computation Independent Model (CIM) that specifies domain information. One of issues discussed in this chapter is the meaning of "computation independence". Another one is formalism of CIMs. And the last issue discussed is a use of a Topological Functioning Model (TMF) for problem domain modeling from a computation independent viewpoint. The TFM is a mathematical model that holistically and formally represents functionality of the problem domain, and does not show any details of the implementation and modeling platform. The TFM contains information from functional, information, and organizational domains of business process modeling. Construction of the TFM from the informal description of the system and guidelines for its decomposition into business processes are discussed and demonstrated by an example.

INTRODUCTION

The Object Management Group (OMG) proposed Model Driven Architecture (MDA) that architecturally separates viewpoints on specifications. MDA suggests three different models for each of the proposed viewpoints. According to MDA principles stated in (The Object Management Group, 2003), they are a Computation Independent Model (CIM), a Platform Independent Model

DOI: 10.4018/978-1-61692-874-2.ch003

(PIM), and a Platform Specific Model (PSM). The CIM describes system requirements and a way a system works within its environment, while details of the application structure and realization are hidden or as yet undetermined. This model is sometimes called a domain model (a business model) and a vocabulary. The PIM describes operation of a system. It suppresses all the details necessary for a particular platform a system works within and shows only those parts of the complete specification that do not change going from one platform to another. The PSM shows these suppressed platform-specifics details for each certain platform.

Since the CIM initially was "embedded" into the PIM, the border between these two viewpoints and, correspondingly, models is fuzzy. Besides that, the notion of platform independence is clear enough in comparison with the notion of computation independence.

The first objective of this chapter is to answer the following questions: What does the "computation independent" mean? Does the computation independent model have a single viewpoint on the system or does it have sub-viewpoints? Could it be a formal model in MDA sense? The second objective is to demonstrate how a formal mathematical model, Topological Functioning Model (TFM), complies with the notion of the CIM.

BACKGROUND

When we try to answer questions about the computation independent model asked in Introduction, it is worth to overview academic researches and results in application and understanding of this model.

As mentioned in Introduction, the CIM is a *domain model* or *a business model*. The term "business model" and related terms such as "a business fact", "a business rule" and "a business process" originated from business modeling. According to (Hendryx, 2003a, para. 2), a business model is a precise description of the business in its environment, by the business, in the language of business people, dedicated to business purposes (not necessarily IT). A model can be textual, tabular, graphic or a combination of them. If underpinnings of the business model are formal, then it is possible to handle this model by machine. Moreover, different objectives can require different models, thus it is necessary to determine purposes of construction of business models. The definition in (Hendryx, 2003b, p. 1) extends the previous one with the statement

that "A business model provides comprehensive answers to the six basic interrogatives: What? How? Where? Who? When? Why?".

Thus, a business model reflects some *business knowledge*. Usually business knowledge is expressed using words and phrases that business people know and understand, i.e. in other words by using terms. *Business facts* are constructed using these terms as foundations, and express things that business peoples know about their own businesses. *Business rules* make a use of facts in order to help in control of business operations and to ensure that business is executed in the way required by business people (Chappel, 2005). Besides that, a *business process* can be considered as a category of a business model that focuses on transforming input resources to the output in order to add value for people inside and/or outside the business (Hendryx, 2003b). Summarizing, a business model is able to reflect those parts and rules of business that are not related to computerized information systems as well as those ones that are related to computerized information systems.

Hence, the CIM is mainly oriented on the business people. However, a discussion of what is to be modeled in the CIM and how the CIM can be organized is held still. Thus first we need to understand what does it mean "computation" and "computation independent" in the context of system modeling?

The conception of "computation" comes from mathematics, where this conception means an algorithmic process that generates certain results by following an effective procedure. In turn, the poly-semantic conception "information processing" comes from the control engineering, where this means things that are transmissible (mentally or physically) using messages to the target point. As stated in (Piccinini & Scarantino, 2008), these two conceptions were separated in cybernetics at the beginning, but as the years go by, they merged.

However, when we speak about computation in the context of software development, it is necessary to understand that "computation" means rather digital computation than information processing as such. Thus, *the CIM means a model that does not show exactly information processing by digital computation means*. In other words, the CIM may reflect computation and logic without specification of participating actors or mechanisms. The CIM may specify that the computation or logical inference must be executed by a computer, but specification of a type of the computer or how the computer organizes or performs this computation or logical inference is forbidden. This thought coincides with (Hendryx, 2003a, para. 8), where the author stated that the CIM should not be defined in any way to limit what business people can say in the CIM, regardless of how much of a computational flavor it may or may not have: "Business process charts, business arithmetic, business formulae, and business decision tables... all are always fair game in the CIM, to describe business terms, business facts, business processes, business events, business organization, business locations, and business policies." If IT people think that there is too much digital computation in the CIM, then the CIM must be modified in accordance with the decision made together by business and IT people after their discussions.

By analyzing researches proposed in (Hendryx, 2003a; Hendryx, 2003c; Grangel, Chalmeta, & Campos, 2007; Che, Wang, Wen, & Ren, 2009; Jeary, Fouad, & Phalp, 2008), the CIM may include three main parts:

- CIM–Knowledge Model (called also a pre-CIM and a Global Model),
- CIM–Business Model,
- CIM–Business Requirements for the System.

The next three subsections will discuss what domain information and in what form is represented in the considered publications.

CIM-Knowledge Model

The idea of *CIM–Knowledge Model* proposed by (Grangel, Chalmeta, & Campos, 2007) relates to the highest level of the CIM model levels. This model reflects an enterprise from the holistic point of view, thus providing the general vision of the enterprise with focus on enterprise knowledge. This knowledge should be locally refined throughout sequential lower levels. The CIM–Knowledge Model may include three types of diagrams, namely, block, ontological and knowledge diagrams. We should note here that two kinds of holistic representation can exist. The first one is a single indivisible (or able to be formally refined) model. And the second one is a view on the problem on the whole from different aspects. The models proposed in this research support the latter kind.

Authors in (Che, Wang, Wen, & Ren, 2009) proposed the similar viewpoint on this level, but they called this model by Global Model. The Global Model includes a global business analysis model (G model) and a global business model (GB model). G model describes function requirements of every enterprise domain and information transmission relationships between those requirements. In turn, GB model describes the whole business logic and information transmission relationships, based on which CIMs at the detailed levels could be composed. The basic concepts included in CIMs at this level are business requirements recognized in the process of enterprise business analysis, organization requirements that describe responsible departments, a domain that reflects a set of enterprise business, requirements for information that is necessary for business processes, and required functions that indicate at work needed to be finished in order to satisfy business requirements.

Authors in (Jeary, Fouad, & Phalp, 2008) discussed a pre-CIM level, which is dedicated for business managers who take a part in system development process and who are responsible for gathering informal information about the processes involved in their departments. At this pre-CIM level business managers can create informal models of those processes. The authors stated that semi-formal languages and models are not very suitable in case of small enterprises, where those languages and models could be difficult for understanding by business managers. Thus, the authors believe, and so do we, that a model that is understandable for both domain users and business analysts should be presented at one of CIM levels, taking into account the fact that domain users usually are not familiar with software development but have deep understanding of business economics and enterprise management, and at the same time business analysts do not have this deep understanding but are able to transform domain users' knowledge into a format suitable for software developers. As the authors wrote, the pre-CIM may include organizational hierarchies, informal documentation, private process views, details of responsibilities, any requirements relevant information, very informal concept models, etc. In other word, the pre-CIM should hold business domain knowledge, while CIMs holds business process models, and only after that requirements are defined.

Authors in (Garrido, Noguera, González, Hurtado, & Rodríguez, 2006) presented a use of the CIM for modeling enterprises and developing groupware applications. The main reason was the necessity to provide conceptual and system models in the computation independent form and relate software models to these CIMs. The authors provided two kinds of CIMs. One kind of them is ontology-based CIMs "consisting of a conceptual domain model formalized through domain ontology and concretized for each particular system using application ontology" that can be considered as *CIM-Knowledge Model*. The model is presented by using the AMENITIES conceptual framework that allows establishing a common vocabulary of system knowledge. The transformation between

these two CIMs and from CIMs to PIM is done by using marks on model elements.

CIM-Business Model

The idea of *CIM–Business Model* proposed by (Grangel, Chalmeta, & Campos, 2007; Hendryx, 2003c) is a "pure" business model that is focused on the business scope and goals as well as terminology, resources, facts, roles, policies, rules, organizations, locations and events of concern to the business. However, it does not reflect software system considerations. *The scope of the Business Model in the CIM must, at a minimum, include business functions served by the software system.* According to (Archimate, n.d.) "a business function is a unit of internal behavior that groups behavior according to for instance required skills, knowledge, resources, etc., and is performed by a single role within the organization". A business function may have many-to-many relations with business processes.

Authors in (Grangel, Chalmeta, & Campos, 2007) defined three possible types of models within the CIM–Business Model. The first of them is *Organizational Model*. The Organizational Model can be described in terms of goals, organizational structure, analysis diagrams and business rule diagrams. The last two are system models – *Structural Model* and *Behavior Model*. The Structural Model includes product and resource diagrams, and the Behavior Model includes process and service diagrams.

Authors in (Kanyaru, Coles, Jeary, & Phalp, 2008) defined four kinds of CIM views: a process view, a data [object] view, an organizational view and a business rules view, which can be interconnected. These views also coincide with organizational, structural, and behavior models.

Authors in (Huang & Fan, 2007) defined the CIM for enterprise integration issues in Service Oriented Architecture (SOA). They called this model by Enterprise Integration Model, which describes business contexts and business requirements for an enterprise integration system. This model includes Organization Model, Process Model, Data Model, System Model, and Service Model. In essence, these models also can be reduced to those three models described previously.

Authors in (Garrido, Noguera, González, Hurtado, & Rodríguez, 2006) defined an UML-based system model in the form of UML Class Diagram that can be related as *CIM-Business Model*. The model is presented in the form of Cooperative Model (COMO-CIM) that allows highlighting of interaction processes between groups from the point of view of system's structure and behavior by using UML (Unified Modeling Language) State and Activity Diagrams based on the Colored Petri Nets formalism.

CIM-Business Requirements for the System

The *CIM–Business Requirements for the System* proposed in (Hendryx, 2003c) contains the contract between the business and IT about what the business people expect the system (information system) to do. These expectations are expressed in precise terms, clearly indicating what parts of the business the system will automate. This model is built on and refers to the CIM–Business Model. This model may contain functional requirements, system user interaction requirements, and environmental contracts. The *functional requirements* specify the information stored and processed by the system-to-be, the business rules and business processes that will be implemented in the system-to-be. However, there may be some information, business processes and business rules the business does not want to implement in the system. The *system user interaction requirements* describe the details of use cases, leaving out user interface technical details. It reflects data presentation and navigation requirements, and look-and-feel standards. Even though screen shots are discouraged as excessive in this model. And the *environment contracts* specify the non-functional requirements

for the system, including performance, throughput, availability, and reliability.

Authors in (Hendryx, 2005; Zachman, 1987; Sowa & Zahman, 1992) stated that in case of information systems each requirement is a system's obligation to execute a business rule or rules, i.e. system requirements are usual rules about other rules. A system requirement is simply a business rule about what business thinks of its own IT system. In other words, requirements rules are under business jurisdiction, thus they are business rules. Hence, requirements for the system must be in consistency with the environment where they will be implemented and as complete as possible.

Authors in (Cao, Miao, & Chen, 2008) proposed a use of feature models for developing CIMs and patterns for transforming CIMs to PIMs. The authors state that the feature model describes the problem of a domain while patterns describe the problem across domains. Thus, "reuse" becomes possible at requirements as well as at development levels. Models they use can be considered as *CIM-Business Requirements for the System*.

Authors in (Trujillo, Soler, Fernández-Medina, & Piattini, 2009) proposed the CIM for requirements analysis for data warehouse modeling based on an extension of the *i** framework that deals only with functional requirements at the business level. This extension could be related to *CIM-Business Requirements for the System*. The conceptual level is considered as a platform independent one by the authors and represented as a Multidimensional Secure Model based on UML Metamodel.

Formalism of CIMs

After we have defined the possible contents of CIMs, we can summarize possible representation means for them.

The simplest and the least formal means for *CIM-Knowledge Model* representation is unstructured natural language. This could be interview records, work instructions, process descriptions, etc. Another means is semi-formal languages such that business managers or domain experts are able to use.

CIM representations with the focus put on *CIM-Business Model* and *CIM-Business Requirements for the System* include more or less structured natural language models accepted by the requirements community, e.g. the Language Extended Lexicon (LEL) and scenarios used in (Debnath, Leonardi, Mauco, Montejano, & Riesco, 2008), Semantics for Business Rules and Business Vocabulary (SBVR), and use cases. Another means for CIM definitions are different languages and notations for business process modeling (Rodriguez, Fernández-Medina, & Piattini, 2007) that may include semi-formal languages, such as ARIS-Event Process Chains, Business Process Modeling Notation (BPMN) used in Business Process Modeling (BPM), Vide CIM Level Language (VCLL), UML profiles, UML Activity Diagrams, e.g. proposed in (Tekinerdogan, Aksit, & Henninger, 2007; Bragança & Machado, 2007), and so on.

The only one formal means for definition of business models is Petri nets and their extensions. However, Petri nets are too "heavy" mathematics for business people and software developers. None wants to exert himself in order to study any additional "hard" mathematics. Therefore, a trend is to use Petri nets as formal underpinnings for languages (and notations) that are more understandable for business analysts and domain experts.

TOPOLOGICAL FUNCTIONING MODEL AS A FORMAL CIM-BUSINESS MODEL

Summarizing researches in the previous sections, there are possible at least two transformations within the CIM itself: transformation from *CIM-Knowledge Model* to *CIM-Business Model*, and transformation from *CIM-Business Model* to *CIM-Business Requirements for the System*. Models used within MDA transformations should be formal (in MDA sense). The word "formal" means to be understandable by a computer machine and transformable. The MDA proposes model transformations starting from the PIM, since the CIM is considered rather informal then formal. And this point of view is valid in most cases as we can conclude from the considered researches.

We suggest not avoiding the CIM and starting transformations from this model, thus providing evident consistency of PIMs, at a minimum, with the *CIM-Business Model*, but at a maximum, consistency also with the *CIM-Knowledge Model*. This requires CIMs to be formal at least in MDA sense and mathematically formal at most.

In this chapter, we discuss our proposed transformation from *CIM-Knowledge Model*, an informal textual description of the system, to *CIM-Business Model*, a Topological Functioning Model (TFM). Additionally, we continue discussion of TFM capabilities for business modeling started in (Osis & Asnina, 2008a; Osis & Asnina, 2008b).

Guidelines for the transformation from *CIM-Business Model* (the TFM) to *CIM-Business Requirements for the System* (use cases) are described informally in (Osis, Asnina, & Grave, 2008) and refined in Chapter "Derivation of Use Cases from the Topological Computation Independent Business Model" in this book.

As previously mentioned, Petri nets, mathematically formal models, are usually hidden from users of business models. The cause is both hard mathematics and representation of domain information that is not intuitive for users. We suggest a formal mathematical means that has solid mathematical background and at the same time is intuitively understandable, the Topological Functioning Model (TFM).

Compliance with MDA Foundation Model

The Object Management Group (2005) stated that models within MDA are allowed to be described in any modeling language defined in accordance with the MDA Foundation Model. The formulated proposal shows relationships between MDA major concepts: models, metamodels, and transformations.

The main idea is that metamodels in the context of the MDA Foundation Model are expressed using the Meta-Object Facility (MOF), and therefore models are instances of the MOF metamodel. The models consist of elements, links between them, and can be represented using graphical and textual notations. This means that MDA does not require only usage of UML, but also supports the use of another modeling language with one requirement – the abstract syntax of those modeling languages must be defined in terms of the MOF.

The metamodel of the topological functioning model specified in the MOF terms is presented in this book in Chapter "Topological Modeling for Model-Driven Domain Analysis and Software Development: Functions and Architectures" and in (Osis, Asnina, & Grave, 2008).

Mathematical Formalism of the TFM

First of all let us explain the formal foundations of the TFM in brief. The more detailed description is presented in this book in Chapter "Topological Modeling for Model-Driven Domain Analysis and Software Development: Functions and Architectures".

The TFM formalism (Osis, 1969) is based on assumption that a complex system can be described in abstract terms as a topological space (X, Q), where X is a finite set of properties or functional features and Q is a topology, i.e. a collection of open subsets that satisfies Kolmogorov's axioms of topological spaces (Kolmogorov & Fomin, 1975), given in the form of a digraph (an oriented graph). The set X is the union of a subset N of properties or features of the system itself, and of a subset M of properties from other systems, constituting the environment interacting with the system under consideration.

The TFM has topological and functional properties. The topological properties are *connectedness*, *closure*, *neighborhood* and *continuous mapping*. The functional properties are *cause-and-effect relations*, *cycle structure*, *inputs* and *outputs*. These properties state the following (Osis, 1969):

- Separation of a topological model of system functioning from the topological space of an environment system works within. They define also formal semantics of concepts of subsystems and independent systems.

- In point of fact of functioning the common thing for all systems (technical, business and biological) should be at least one oriented cycle (a directed closed path). This property of the model enables analyzing similarities and differences of functioning systems.

- The model with any complexity can be abstracted to the simpler one and vice verse. This means that continuous mapping of topological models is being realized. Thanks to that a lack of knowledge about the system can be filled up with knowledge that is obtained from the continuous mapping of the same type model to the system model under consideration.

Such a formal model comes about through the acquisition of the experts' knowledge about the complex system, verbal description, and other documents concerning the structure and functioning (in documental, analytical, statistical, etc. form).

Thus adequacy of any abstract topological model of the concrete functioning system is to attain in such a way, that the sense of the content of the analyzed system is carried on abstract mathematical objects. The topological model of a problem domain is an advantage for analysis and decomposition of complex systems described in (Osis, 1997; Osis, Sukovskis, & Teilans, 1997; Osis & Beghi, 1997).

Construction of the TFM: Manual Transformation from an Informal CIM-Knowledge Model to a Formal CIM-Business Model

The formal method for construction of the topological functioning model of a complex technical or business system from its informal verbal description consists of the steps illustrated by an UML activity diagram in Figure 1:

- Define a set X of business functional characteristics of the considered system and other systems interacting with the system itself.
- Introduce in X topology Q in the form of a digraph G(X, U) indicating the cause-and-effect relations existing among elements of

X (where U is a set of directed arcs connecting elements of X). It is assumed that a cause-and-effect relation between two functional characteristics (elements of the set X) exists, if appearance of one property is caused by appearance of the other without participation of any middle property.
- Separate a topological functioning model from the constructed topological space.

All changes, which can happen, first must be checked or compared with the knowledge about the system; this means that all changes must be consistent with the existing problem domain. The adequacy of the model in describing operation of a concrete system can be then achieved by analyzing the topological and functional properties of the topological model.

Definition of Business Functional Characteristics

A formal way of physical or business characteristic (hereinafter: functional feature) definition from an

Figure 1. Transformation from an informal system description to the TFM

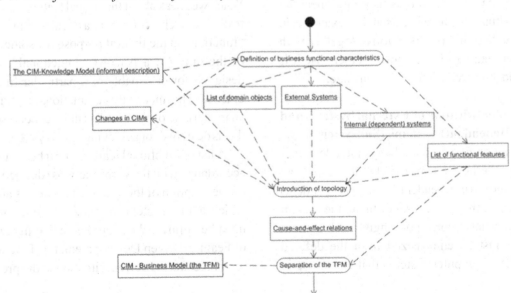

informal description of a problem domain consists of the following steps:

- Definition of actions, objects and their properties from the system description;
- Identification of external systems and internal (dependent) systems (i.e., subsystems and staff);
- Definition of functional features.

As a result of these steps, a list of domain objects, a list of functional features, and knowledge about functional features in the list must be found. Each mentioned step is explained hereafter.

Step 1: Definition of Actions, Objects and their Properties from the System Description

In an informal system description, every noun together with its direct object that is not expressed as a numeral or a pronoun is to be identified. These nouns are domain entities (objects, subsystems or systems) and their properties. For example, they can be products (e.g. a ticket, a train, a card, etc.), results of the actions (e.g. "a purchase" that is a result of the selling a ticket to a passenger), documents (a pass, a receipt), etc.

For each noun synonyms and homonyms must be analyzed as well as its proper meaning in each situation where it is used. For example, in one case "a train" is a locomotive together with a certain number of carriages, in other case it is only a locomotive without any carriage.

Step 2: Identification of External Systems and Inner (Dependent) Systems (Subsystems)

A description of a system always includes functionality of other systems or subsystems that can act as external (independent) or inner (dependent) entities, i.e., they do not subordinate the system or do it partially, correspondingly. Such domain objects must be emphasized from the defined object list. Computer systems that are in use in

an organization can be mentioned as an example of this kind of objects at that point of analysis.

Besides that, the list of defined objects can contain inner system's objects as well as objects that affect this system functionality from the external environment, or that get something from the system work, e.g. such objects as human roles, services, and organizations, etc. A company that uses by-products of functionality of the organization can be mentioned as an example. Therefore, those objects, which are not subsystems of the system under consideration and whose functionality is not directly subordinated to the system, are external systems.

Referring the mathematical definition in Section "Mathematical Formalism of the TFM", external systems enact functional features from the set of functionality of external systems, M, while inner (dependent) systems enact inner functional features of the system itself, i.e., functional features from set N.

Therefore, the result of this step is a list of external systems and inner (dependent) systems that communicate with or take a part in operation of the system under research.

Step 3: Definition of Functional Features

When we speak about functional features, we need to discuss such a concept as a business function. A "function" is the natural purpose (of something) or the duty (of a person). "Functional" means designed for or capable of a particular function or a use. This means that a functional feature is a characteristic of the system (in its general sense) that is designed for achieving some system's goal.

A list of functional features must be defined in accordance with the verbs (actions) defined from the description of the system. This means actions which help a system to realize its functionality must be defined. We should note that in contrast of Feature-Driven Development, this functionality represents the current situation in the problem domain, not desired client's requirements for the system.

The actions defined can be considered as abstracted or as specialized functional features (Osis, 1969). Specialized functional features can be abstracted, and abstracted functional features can be refined (specialized) thanks to *continuous mapping* provided by properties of the TFM (for details please see Chapter "Topological Modeling for Model-Driven Domain Analysis and Software Development: Functions and Architectures" in this book). *Abstracted* functional features are those, whose further expansion is not necessary at this stage; in their turn, *specialized* (*atomic*) functional features are those, whose further expansion is not possible at this stage. Therefore, in order to define functional features, verbs denoting actions and their preconditions, post-conditions and business rules are to be found in the same informal description of the system.

Preconditions specify a set of conditions that allows triggering a functional feature. Post-conditions specify a set of conditions that are set after a functional feature was successfully executed. According to (Desfray, 2004), a business rule usually prevents, provokes or allows triggering certain processes, and defines or constrains some business process aspects. A business rule and a business fact defined in the system description must be refined to the "atomic", i.e., it should be extended until the level, where it is not possible to break it down into sub-rules. Afterwards, each action, precondition (and post-condition) or business rule either has to introduce a new appropriate functional feature or it should be attached to the already defined one.

Besides that, a set of entities which provide the functional feature and a set of entities which enact it are defined for each identified functional feature.

A description of functional features was first defined in (Asnina, 2006), and extended in this work. Thus, each functional feature is a unique tuple

$$<A, R, O, PrCond, PostCond, Pr, Ex>,$$

Where:

- A is an action linked with an object;
- R is a result of that action (it may be empty);
- O is an object (objects) that get the result of the action or an object (objects) that is used in this action; it could be a role, a time period or a moment, catalogues etc.;
- $PrCond$ is a set $PrCond = \{c_1, ..., c_i\}$, where c_i is a precondition or an atomic business rule (it may be empty);
- $PostCond$ is a set $PostCond = \{c_1, ..., c_i\}$, where c_i is a post-condition or an atomic business rule (it may be empty);
- Pr is a set of entities (systems or subsystems) that provide or suggest an action with a set of certain objects;
- Ex is a set of entities (systems or subsystems) that enact a concrete action.

The action, result and object together constitute a name of the activity this functional feature is responsible for. The name of the functional feature could be expressed in the following form:

<action>-ing the < result> [to, into, in, by, of, from] a(n) <object>
Completing the sale of a ticket

Because functional features can be joined in a functional feature set, representing a certain business function, a set of specialized functional features can be correlated with the appropriate business function and corresponding business processes. In this case or if a result is not specified, a name of the functional feature set could be written down in the shortened form:

<action>-ing a(n) <object>
Printing a ticket

It ought to be noted that a distinction between a specialized functional feature and a functional feature set is their level of abstraction.

Introduction of Topology

After defining the list of functional features, cause-and-effect relations among them should be defined or, in other words, a topology Q should be set.

The topology described in Section "Mathematical Formalism of the TFM" is represented by cause-and-effect relations between functional features. Topological functioning modeling states that a cause-and-effect relation between two functional features of the system exists if the appearance of one feature is caused by the appearance of the other feature without participation of any third (intermediary) feature. Since identification of cause-and-effect relations is rather intuitive work, the essence of cause-and-effect relations needs to be described.

The connection between a cause and an effect is represented by a certain conditional expression, the causal implication. It is characterized by the nature or business rules not by logic rules. They are such concepts as ontological necessity, probability etc. In causal connections "something is allowed to go wrong", whereas logical statements allow no exceptions. Using this property of the cause-and-effect relations a logical sequence, wherein the execution of the precondition guarantees the execution of the action, can be omitted; this means that even if a cause is executed, it is allowed that the corresponding effect will not be generated because of some functional damage.

Cause-and-effect relations have *a time dimension*, since a cause chronologically *precedes* and *generates* an effect. The concept of generating is necessary in order to distinguish a cause-and-effect relation from the simple consequence that is not causal. Causes may be sufficient or necessary (in other words, complete or partial) for generating an effect (Farlex Inc., 2009). A sufficient (complete) cause generates its effect ever, in any

conditions. On the other hand, a necessary cause (partial) only promotes its effect generating and this effect is realized only if this partial cause joins other conditions. However, most cause-and-effect relationships involve multiple factors. Sometimes there are factors in series. Sometimes there are factors in parallel. In case of the topological functioning model, it is assumed that a deal is always with necessary causes as the functionality of the system has its known and unknown risks at the time of analysis. And the last, the causality is universal. This means that there is no such a problem domain without causes and effects. The person can see nothing, but a cause or an effect exists. This may harden a process of discovering relations between causes and effects which are not obvious at the first sight.

As already mentioned, a structure of cause-and-effect relations can form a causal chain (in series or in parallel). The causal chain begins with an initial cause and follows with series of intermediate actions or events to a final effect. Though one link may not be as important or as strong like the other ones, they are all necessary to the chain. If just one of these intermediate causes is absent, then the final effect would not be reached. As an example, the situation of payment in restaurant can be considered. A causal chain of this case can be the following: ordering in a restaurant, then eating the order, making a decision about payment, paying the bill. If the decision about payment is not made, the last action (paying the bill) will not be generated. Additionally, even if you change something, you cannot remove the effect without removing or changing the cause.

Besides that, causal chains can form causal cycles as well. In this case, an initial cause simultaneously is a final effect. In the TFM, the causal cycles represent functional cycles of the system (or its subsystems) that are vitally necessary for system (subsystem) operation. The TFM states that a valid model must have at least one functional cycle within it.

In order to identify cause-and-effect relations in a verbal text, we follow by advice suggested in many print sources for article writers and scenarists:

- Some words and phrases can signal cause-and-effect relationships, e.g., accordingly, because, effect, in order that, since, cause, for, therefore, as a result, if…then, why, consequently, due to, etc;
- Certain verbs are causative verbs, i.e., verbs that express cause-and-effect relationships (describes an effect one thing has on another), e.g. have, get, let, allow, require and so on;
- Some suffixes can indicate changes, causes and effects: "-ate" can mean to become, to cause (e.g., to update), "-ation" – the result of _ing (e.g., registration is the result of registering process), "-ize" – to make, a cause to be (e.g., finalize), etc.

Graphically, cause-and-effect relations are represented as arcs between vertices of a directed graph, which are oriented from a cause vertex to an effect vertex.

By far, cause-and-effect relations can be also recorded in the form of an adjacency matrix, which is a Y by Y matrix where Y is a number of functional features represented as nodes in the topological space. If there is an arc from some vertex i to some vertex j, then the element $Y_{i,j}$ is 1, otherwise it is 0, or in the form of a list. However, these representations have significant limitations in comparison with digraphs.

However, the most user-friendly specification is a graph. The graph is more demonstrative. It facilitates discovering functioning cycles, inputs and outputs that is necessary for analysis of the system. This is illustrated in Chapter "Topological Modeling for Model-Driven Domain Analysis and Software Development: Functions and Architectures" within this book.

Figure 2. The closure operation over the set N

(a) $Z = M \cup N$

(b) $X = [N] = \bigcup_{i=1}^{k} X_i$

Concluding all the above mentioned, the result of this stage is a "list" of cause-and-effect relations between defined functional features formally represented in form of arcs of a digraph, a list of relations between causes and effects, or a matrix.

Separation of the Topological Functioning Model

As mentioned in Section "Mathematical Formalism of the TFM", in order to define the topological functioning model that consists of the set X of functional features and the topology Q, we must divide the set Z of functional features of all systems into two subsets: M that is a set of functional features of external systems that interact with or are affected by the system under consideration, and N that is a set of inner functional features of the system (Figure 2-a).

In turn, the set M can be divided into two subsets: an input and an output subset. The input subset is formed by those functional features of external systems which do not have causes and take part in cause-and-effect relations as initial causes for system functional features or functional features of external systems. Those functional features which take part in cause-and-effect relations as final effects generated by the system functional features and are not causes for any other functional feature constitute the output subset. These input and output subsets are essential to business process identification that is discussed below.

A TFM of the system under investigation is separated by using *the closure operation over the set N* (Figure 2-b), where X_i is an adherence point of the set N; and k is a number of adherence points of N, i.e. capacity of X. In order to execute this operation, definitions of neighborhood and an adherence point need to be done.

Definition 1: The *neighborhood* of the vertex i in a graph is a set of all the vertices adjacent to i and the vertex i itself. It is assumed here that only direct successors and predecessors of i are taken into accounts.

Definition 2: An *adherence point* of the set N is a point, each neighborhood of which includes at least one point from the set N.

TFM Relations to Business Functions, Activities and Processes

As stated by Mathias Weske (2007), business process modeling assumes that an analyst will have a complete as possible picture of business processes in an organization. Business process modeling includes different integrated modeling domains, where the most important ones are function modeling, information modeling, organization modeling, and modeling of the operation information technology landscape.

A functional model specifies work units that are being initiated and performed within the business process. At the high level of aggregation work units represent *business functions* that at the lower level are organized as *business processes* and refined to *business activities* at the operational level, where each activity is enacted by a worker or an information system. Activities are functions at the finest granularity. The lower aggregation level, the more formal specifications of business functions. Functional decomposition is a technique of refinement of business values to business functions to operational business processes. Activities in operational business processes are related to each other by execution constraints.

A business process is initiated when the start event occurs; when it is completed, an end event occurs. Events reflect interrelationships between activities of the business process and business processes themselves (Weske, 2007).

The TFM can be refined and simplified thanks to its topological property, namely, *continuous mapping*. A valid topological functioning model allows substitutions of a functional feature by a subset of specialized features and vice versa. At that time, a simplified model must keep every cause-and-effect relation corresponding to them in the detailed model and vice versa. In case of a lack of data, models of the same type system may be continuously mapped into a TFM. This property is demonstrated in detail in Chapter "Topological Modeling for Model-Driven Domain Analysis and Software Development: Functions and Architectures" within this book.

At the high level of abstraction the TFM reflects cause-and-effect relations among *business functions*. At the lower level of abstraction the TFM reflects cause-and-effect relations among *business activities*. Moreover, at this level the TFM can be decomposed into *business processes*. In our case, a criterion for decomposition is organization's or organization worker's *business goal*. Correspondence between these concepts is illustrated in Figure 3 (*see below*).

In common, the TFM contains system knowledge about its business functions, organizational units (positions, rules, subsystems, units), and relations between business functions and between business functions and organizational units. The TFM can be considered as a formal "outline" that contains and holistically specifies most of those integrated modeling domains mentioned in the beginning, namely, function modeling, information modeling, and organization modeling, and provides formal identification of boarders of the system under investigation.

In order to derive business processes from the TFM, we have defined several informally described guidelines (however, by now our guidelines still requires human participation in order to state concurrency properties for execution of

Figure 3. The common vision of the TFM for modeling business processes

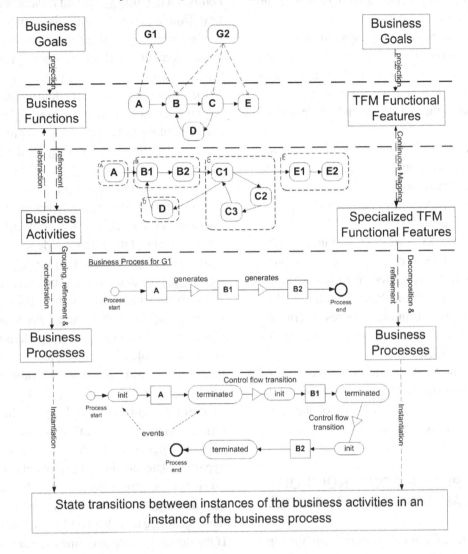

business activities within a business process) that are illustrated by an example in the next section:

- **Guideline 1:** A specialized functional feature is transformed to a business activity.
- **Guideline 2:** A functional feature (set) is transformed to a business function. Each specialized functional feature of this set is transformed to the corresponding business activity that is necessary to perform the business function.
- **Guideline 3:** A cause-and-effect relation between functional features A and B

is transformed to a control flow between corresponding business activities A and B. The direction of the control flow is the same as the direction of the cause-and-effect relation.

- **Guideline 4:** If a functional feature transformed to a business activity does not have any input cause-and-effect relation within the business process, then it is generated by the process start event.
- **Guideline 5:** If a functional feature transformed to a business activity does not have any output cause-and-effect relation within

the business process, then it generates the process end event.

- **Guideline 6:** An entity (system or subsystem) that provides a functional feature and an entity (system or subsystem) that enacts a concrete functional feature are transformed to the organizational unit/position/role.

- **Guideline 7:** A cause-and-effect relation between functional features that belong to different business processes is transformed to the sequence flow between those business processes.

- **Guideline 8:** When an instance of the functional feature transformed to a business activity is started, it raises an initial event. When the instance is completed or finishes its execution, it raises a termination event that can be successfully terminated or failed.

- **Guideline 9:** Post- and pre- conditions of the functional feature are transformed to the post- and pre- conditions of the functional activity correspondingly.

AN EXAMPLE OF CONSTRUCTION OF FORMAL CIM-BUSINESS MODEL

Let us consider a fragment of operation of the supposed organization, namely, State Railway Company (SRC) that provides local and international transportation services for private and juridical persons. The company partially implements a process of ticket selling, and provides clients with online information of train timetable, types, prices and availability of tickets for an indicated trip.

The CIM-Knowledge Model: Informal Description of the SRC Operation

The SRC *provides* a client on-line data about their train services. A client *enters* a departure station and a destination station from the suggested list,

chooses a departure date and *indicates* departure time from and till. The SRC information system *outputs* train traffic timetable for those stations: train's number, run days, transport type, carriage type, departure time, arrival time, and train route. **If** the client *chooses* the certain train, **then** the system *outputs* a count of available tickets and the corresponding ticket price. The client can *print out* an entire timetable of a trip, and a timetable of a certain train with all stops and corresponding departure time and arrival time.

In order to *purchase* a ticket on a train, the client *informs* a seller at the book office at the Central Train Station about a departure station, a destination station, a departure date and time, a carriage type and a place (optional). The seller *searches* trains for a trip by these client's data in the database. **If** at least one train *is found*, and a client *agrees to purchase* a ticket, **then** the seller *completes* a sale of the ticket and *prints out* the ticket. **If** any train *is not found*, **then** the seller *offers* a clien *t to modify* his/her data.

Once a client *purchased* a ticket, he/she *may return* it to the SRC. **In this case**, the seller *completes* the ticket return. A seller *checks* whether departure date and time of this ticket *is passed*. **If** this is true or current date *is equal* to a departure date in the ticket, **then** the seller *returns* 50% of the ticket price to a client and *prints out* a receipt. **If** the departure date and time *are not passed* and the departure date is later than the current date is, **then** the seller *returns* 80% of the ticket price to a client and *prints out* a receipt.

The CIM – Business Model

Definition of Business Functional Characteristics

By using noun and verb analysis extended with the advices mentioned before, we can define entities and functional features that take a part in operation of the system.

Definition of Actions, Objects and Their Properties from the System Description

Nouns and their objects (underlined in the description) are as follows: SRC, a client, on-line data, train services, a departure station, a destination station, a list [of stations], a departure date, departure time from, departure time till, an SRC information system (a synonym: a system), a train traffic timetable, a station, train's number, a run day, a transport type, a carriage type, departure time, arrival time, a train route, a train, a [train] ticket price, an entire timetable [of the trip], a trip, a timetable [of a train], a stop, a ticket, a seller, Central Train Station, a place, client's data, database, a sale [of the ticket], a current date, a ticket return, a receipt.

At this step, nouns could be analyzed in order to create a data vocabulary, i.e. to find synonyms, entities and their attributes, and to refine meaning of each entity. The result list of entities defined during analysis of this group of nouns is the following:

- The *SRC* is the organization in the real world;
- A *client* is a user of organization's transport services;
- A *train services* are the sale and return of tickets, and representation of information about trains' timetable and ticket prices;
- A *station* is a train stop (a synonym in the description is a stop);
- A *departure* is a place and a period of time, where from and when a client want to leave, it includes a station, date, time from and time till;
- A *destination* is a finish station of the trip;
- *Client data* includes a *departure* and a *destination*;
- The *SRC information system* is the online system that supports some of organization's train services (a synonym is a system);
- A *route* is a list of station from a start stop to a finish stop;

- A *timetable* is associated with the route and provides train departure time and arrival time for each station (a synonym is on-line data);
- A *train* is a railway engine, for each train is kept its number, run day, transport type, carriage type, place, route and timetable;
- A *ticket* is a printed document valid for travel on the train from a departure station at a departure date and time on a place of a price to an arrival station; it could be available and non-available.
- A *trip* shows routes, timetables, ticket prices from a departure station to an arrival stations at the departure date and time from and time till;
- A *seller* is an employee of the SRC who sells and takes back tickets and provides a client with timetables for a trip;
- The *Central Train Station* is a place where seller's book office is located;
- A *database* keeps data about routes, trains, tickets and is used by the SRC information system;
- The *ticket sale* is a document about selling a ticket at a concrete date;
- The *ticket return* is a document about taking back a sold ticket and returning percents of a price paid by a client;
- A *receipt* is a printed document about the ticket return;

Identification of external systems and internal dependent systems

The next step is identification of external systems and objects as well as systems and objects that act under system's business rules. The latter are the SRC information system, and a seller. The former is a client.

Definition of Functional Features

After this step, identification of functional features of the SRC is performed as well cause-and-effect relations between them. Verbs used to action identification are highlighted with *italic* in the description of the SRC.

The presented description has several levels of abstraction. They are hierarchically located by using the following numbering system: the label "FF" and numbers 1, 2 and so on (for the highest level of abstraction, i.e. abstract functional features that denote *business functions*) as well numbers 1-1, 1-2 and so on (for the lower levels of abstraction, i.e. specialized functional features that denote *business activities*), where the first number, 1, denotes a corresponding more abstract functional feature, and the second number, 1 and 2, denotes the functional feature under consideration.

Let us look at the *FF1-1 "Entering the station of a departure"*, where an action is "to enter", a result is "the station", an object is "a departure", a provider is the SRC information system, an executor is a client. There are no preconditions and postconditions. The subordination is "inner", since the SRC information system – a subsystem of the SRC itself is a provider of this functional feature. In the *FF1-2 "Entering the destination of a trip"*, a result is "the destination" and an object is "a trip". Other elements are the same as in FF1-1. So, the whole list of the functional features with indicated preconditions *Precond*, postconditions *Postcond*, a provider *Pr*, an executor *Ex*, and a subordination *S* is presented below.

FF1. Providing the data of a train service

FF1-1 "Entering the station of a departure": Pr = "SRC information system", Ex = "client", S = "inner";

FF1-2 "Entering the destination of a trip": Pr = "SRC information system", Ex = "client", S = "inner";

FF1-3 "Entering the date of a departure": Pr = "SRC information system", Ex = "client", S = "inner";

FF1-4 "Indicating the time period of a departure": Pr = "SRC information system", Ex = "client", S = "inner";

FF1-5 "Searching the timetable of a trip": Pr = "SRC information system", Ex = "SRC information system", S = "inner";

FF1-6 "Outputting the timetable of a trip": Pr = "SRC information system", Ex = "SRC information system", S = "inner";

FF1-7 "Choosing the train of a trip": Pr = "SRC information system", Ex = "client", S = "inner", Precond = "if the timetable is outputted";

FF1-8 "Outputting the count of available tickets": Pr = "SRC information system", Ex = "SRC information system", S = "inner", Precond = "if a client chooses the train";

FF1-9 "Outputting the price of a ticket": Pr = "SRC information system", Ex = "SRC information system", S = "inner", Precond = "if a client chooses the train";

FF1-10 "Printing out the timetable of a trip": Pr = "SRC information system", Ex = "client", S = "inner";

FF1-11 "Printing out the timetable of a train": Pr = "SRC information system", Ex = "client", S = "inner".

FF2. Purchasing the ticket on a train

FF2-1 "Informing the departure station of a trip": Pr = "client", Ex = "client", S = "external";

FF2-2 "Informing the destination station of a trip": Pr = "client", Ex = "client", S = "external";

FF2-3 "Informing the departure date and time of a trip": Pr = "client", Ex = "client", S = "external";

FF2-4 "Informing the carriage type of a train": Pr = "client", Ex = "client", S = "external";

FF2-5 "Informing the place in a carriage": Pr = "client", Ex = "client", S = "external";

FF2-6 "Entering the client data of a trip": Pr = "SRC information system", Ex = "seller", S = "inner";

FF2-7 "Searching the trains for a trip": Pr = "SRC information system", Ex = "seller", S = "inner";

FF2-8 "Modifying the client data of a trip": Pr = "SRC information system", Ex = "seller", S = "inner", Precond = "if the trains are not found";

FF2-9 "Committing the trains for a trip": Pr = "client", Ex = "client", S = "external";

FF2-10 "Selecting the trains for a trip": Pr = "SRC information system", Ex = "seller", S = "inner", Precond = "if at least one train is found";

FF2-11 "Completing the sale of tickets": Pr = "SRC information system", Ex = "seller", S = "inner", Precond = "if a client agrees to purchase a ticket";

FF2-12 "Printing out tickets on trains": Pr = "SRC information system", Ex = "seller", S = "inner".

FF3. Returning a ticket

FF3-1 "Returning the ticket on a train": Pr = "client", Ex = "client", S = "external";

FF3-2 "Completing the return of a ticket": Pr = "SRC information system", Ex = "seller", S = "inner";

FF3-3 "Checking the validity of a ticket": Pr = "SRC information system", Ex = "seller", S = "inner";

FF3-4 "Returning the 50% price of a ticket": Pr = "SRC information system", Ex = "seller", S = "inner", Precond = "if the ticket is invalid or its departure date is equal to the return date";

FF3-5 "Returning the 80% price of a ticket": Pr = "SRC information system", Ex = "seller", S = "inner", Precond = "if the ticket is valid and its departure date is later than the return date";

FF3-6 "Printing out the receipt of a return": Pr = "SRC information system", Ex = "seller", S = "inner".

Topology Introduction and Separation of the TFM

After definition of functional features of the SRC, cause-and-effect relations among them are defined using previously mentioned advices. Some of indicating words are highlighted with the **bold font** in the SRC description. A topological space of the SRC "as is" is illustrated in Figure 4-a.

As previously mentioned, in order to separate the TFM from a topological space, functional features of the system should be divided into two sets, a set of inner system's functional features, N, and a set of external system's functional features, M. According to the subordination of defined functional features shown in the previous subsection, these sets are as follows.

The set of system's inner functional features N = *{FF1-1, FF1-2, FF1-3, FF1-4, FF1-5, FF1-6, FF1-7, FF1-8, FF1-9, FF1-10, FF1-11, FF2-6, FF2-7, FF2-8, FF2-10, FF2-11, FF2-12, FF3-2, FF3-3, FF3-4, FF3-5, FF3-6, FF4-1, FF4-2, FF4-3, FF4-4}*.

The set of external system's functional feature M = *{FF2-1, FF2-2, FF2-3, FF2-4, FF2-5, FF2-9, FF3-1}*.

The closure of N identifies all those functional features, set X, that belong to the SRC "as is". Neighborhoods of all functional features in the topological space are the following:

X_{FF1-1} = {FF1-1, FF1-5},
X_{FF1-2} = {FF1-2, FF1-5},
X_{FF1-3} = {FF1-3, FF1-5},
X_{FF1-4} = {FF1-4, FF1-5},
X_{FF1-5} = {FF1-5, FF1-9, FF1-6},
X_{FF1-6} = {FF1-6, FF1-7},
X_{FF1-7} = {FF1-7, FF1-8},
X_{FF1-8} = {FF1-8, FF1-9},
X_{FF1-9} = {FF1-9, FF1-11},
X_{FF1-10} = {FF1-10},
X_{FF1-11} = {FF1-11},
X_{FF2-1} = {*FF2-1*, FF2-6},

Figure 4. The topological space (a), the topological functioning model (b), and the simplified topological model (c) of the SRC

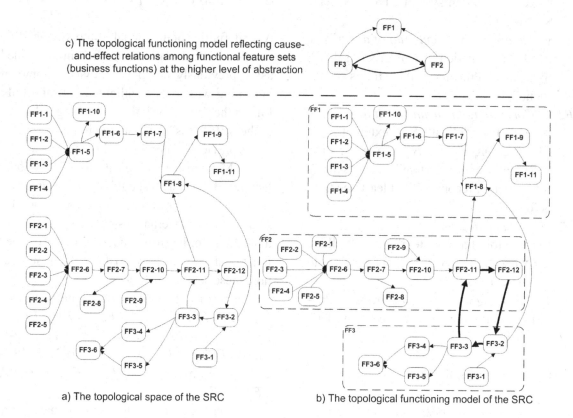

a) The topological space of the SRC

b) The topological functioning model of the SRC

$X_{FF2\text{-}2}=\{FF2\text{-}2, FF2\text{-}6\}$,
$X_{FF2\text{-}3}=\{FF2\text{-}3, FF2\text{-}6\}$,
$X_{FF2\text{-}4}=\{FF2\text{-}4, FF2\text{-}6\}$,
$X_{FF2\text{-}5}=\{FF2\text{-}5, FF2\text{-}6\}$,
$X_{FF2\text{-}6}=\{FF2\text{-}6, FF2\text{-}7\}$,
$X_{FF2\text{-}7}=\{FF2\text{-}7, FF2\text{-}8, FF2\text{-}10\}$,
$X_{FF2\text{-}8}=\{FF2\text{-}8\}$,
$X_{FF2\text{-}9}=\{FF2\text{-}9, FF2\text{-}10\}$,
$X_{FF2\text{-}10}=\{FF2\text{-}10, FF2\text{-}11\}$,
$X_{FF2\text{-}11}=\{FF2\text{-}11, FF2\text{-}12, FF1\text{-}8\}$,
$X_{FF2\text{-}12}=\{FF2\text{-}12, FF3\text{-}2\}$,
$X_{FF3\text{-}1}=\{FF3\text{-}1, FF3\text{-}2\}$,
$X_{FF3\text{-}2}=\{FF3\text{-}2, FF3\text{-}3, FF1\text{-}8\}$,
$X_{FF3\text{-}3}=\{FF3\text{-}3, FF3\text{-}4, FF3\text{-}5\}$,
$X_{FF3\text{-}4}=\{FF3\text{-}4, FF3\text{-}6\}$,
$X_{FF3\text{-}5}=\{FF3\text{-}5, FF3\text{-}6\}$,
$X_{FF3\text{-}6}=\{FF3\text{-}6\}$.

Functional features that do not belong to the set *N* are highlighted by *italic* in the neighborhoods. Thus, set $X = \{FF1\text{-}1, FF1\text{-}2, FF1\text{-}3, FF1\text{-}4, FF1\text{-}5, FF1\text{-}6, FF1\text{-}7, FF1\text{-}8, FF1\text{-}9, FF1\text{-}10, FF1\text{-}11, FF2\text{-}1, FF2\text{-}2, FF2\text{-}3, FF2\text{-}4, FF2\text{-}5, FF2\text{-}6, FF2\text{-}7, FF2\text{-}8, FF2\text{-}9, FF2\text{-}10, FF2\text{-}11, FF2\text{-}12, FF3\text{-}1, FF3\text{-}2, FF3\text{-}3, FF3\text{-}4, FF3\text{-}5, FF3\text{-}6\}$. The separated TFM of the SRC "as is" is illustrated in Figure 4-b. This means that the CIM-Business Model of the system "as is" (or of the problem domain) is obtained.

This example illustrates a simple case, where only one functional cycle exists, namely, "FF2-11→ FF2-12→ FF3-2→ FF3-3→FF2-11". From description of functional features it becomes clear that these features handle a sale and a return of train tickets. If the ticket returned is still valid, it

Figure 5. Business processes derived from the TFM of the SRC

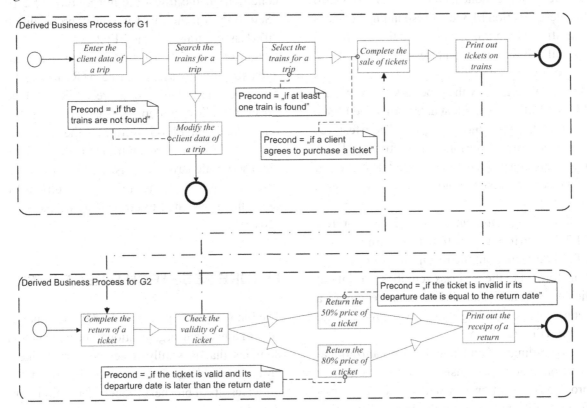

could be sold once more time, since a corresponding place in a train becomes unoccupied again.

The simplified TFM of the SRC is illustrated in Figure 4-c. It preserves the main functional cycle of the system and represents the cause-and-effect relations among defined business functions specified in the form of TFM functional feature sets.

The CIM-Business Model: Getting Business Processes from the TFM

In this section, derivation of business processes, their interrelations, and organizational units from the TFM is illustrated using the model of the SRC. Decomposition of the TFM and refinement of business processes is done according to the nine guidelines defined above Section "TFM Relations to Business Functions, Activities and Processes". The result is presented in Figure 5.

A criterion for decomposition of business processes is business goals. Let's have two business goals, namely, G1 "Sell train tickets" and G2 "Provide train ticket return". According to Guideline 2, business functions are abstract functional features FF1 "Providing the data of a train service", FF2 "Purchasing the ticket on a train", and FF3 "Returning a ticket".

In our example, all other functional features are specialized functional characteristics; therefore, we can follow Guideline 1 and transform them into business activities with the same names.

Let us assume that in order to satisfy business goal G1 functional features FF2-6, FF2-7, FF2-10, FF2-11, FF2-12 and FF2-8 should be executed. In turn, to satisfy business goal G2 functional features FF3-2, FF3-3, FF3-4, FF3-5 and FF3-6 should be executed. This means that we relate business goal G1 to business function FF2 to business activities specified by functional features just mentioned, and business goal G2 to business function FF3 to corresponding business activities which are specified by the mentioned specialized functional features.

Following Guideline 4, functional features that are generated by the process start events are FF2-6 "Entering the client data a trip" and FF3-2 "Completing the return of a ticket". These features are transformed to the functional activities "Enter the client data of a trip" and "Complete the return of a ticket" correspondingly and two start events (Figure 5).

Following Guideline 5, functional features, FF2-12 "Printing out tickets on trains" and FF3-6 "Printing out the receipt of a return", are transformed to the business activities ""Print out tickets on trains" and "Print out the receipt of a return" correspondingly, and two process end events (Figure 5).

According to Guideline 6, the organizational position that is responsible for these business processes execution is a *seller*. The seller uses functionality provided by the SRC information system.

According to Guideline 7, two sequence flows demonstrate that these business processes are interrelated, namely, the cause-and-effect relations from FF2-12 to FF3-2 and from FF3-3 to FF2-11 are transformed to these sequence flows. They state that it is not possible to return the ticket that is not sold yet, and it is not possible to sell any already sold ticket.

According to Guideline 8 all functional features which are not inputs and outputs are transformed into initial and termination events that are hidden in generation flows in Figure 5, e.g. the generation flow from activity "Enter the client data of a trip" to "Search the trains for a trip" which are specified by functional features FF2-6 and FF2-7 correspondingly.

Finishing, following Guideline 9 pre- and post-conditions are assigned to the corresponding functional activities that are specified by FF2-8 "Modifying the client data of a trip" and its pre-

condition "if the trains are not found", FF2-10 "Selecting the trains for a trip" and its precondition "if at least one train is found", FF2-11 "Completing the sale of tickets" and its precondition "if a client agrees to purchase a ticket", FF3-4 "Returning the 50% price of a ticket" and its precondition "if the ticket is invalid or its departure date is equal to the return date", and FF3-5 "Returning the 80% price of a ticket" and its precondition "if the ticket is valid and its departure date is later that the return date". Figure 5 illustrates these preconditions by using notes assigned to corresponding business activities.

FUTURE RESEARCH DIRECTIONS

The topological functioning model joins knowledge of functional, organizational and information domains that is vitally necessary for business process modeling. This chapter illustrated the initial results of business process derivation from the TFM. However, the example shown in this chapter does not address the question about concurrent execution of business activities. By now this issue is resolved by human participation in further refinement of business processes. Thus, the future research direction is tightly related to addressing this issue, namely, specification of information about concurrency that a description of the system contains in explicit or implicit form by means of the topological functioning model preserving model simplicity, and transition of this knowledge to the more detailed levels of abstraction. The related research direction is automating business process derivation, i.e., definition of TFM transformation rules in some transformation language for a concrete business process modeling language and automated execution of these rules.

Another research direction is transformation from business model to requirements model that is formal in the MDA sense, i.e., that could be used for automated derivation of the Platform

Independent Model from the computation independent one.

CONCLUSION

The overview of scientific research on MDA CIMs resulted in the fact that in general the Computation Independent Model suggested by MDA could have three main parts, namely, CIM-Knowledge Model, CIM-Business Model, and CIM-Business Requirements for the System. These models specify domain information from different interrelated perspectives.

This research illustrated that the TFM is a formal mathematical model that is capable to specify business functions and business activities from the computation independent viewpoint. The topological and functional properties of the TFM relate business goals to business functions to business activities and vice versa by using mathematical continuous mapping between graphs. Besides that, the holistic nature of the model allows defining relationships among business functions and among business activities unambiguously according to expert knowledge of the system.

The result of this research is that the TFM is able to specify information from three business modeling domains, namely, the functional domain, the organizational domain and the information domain. The information from the functional domain is business functions, business activities, and cause-and-effect relations between business functions and between business activities, results of decomposition and refinement of business processes, control flows within the processes, and relations between business processes made in compliance with the TFM cause-and-effect relations. The organizational domain is represented as organizational entities (units, subsystems, systems, work positions, roles, etc.) that provide and enact TFM functional features. The information domain is specified by objects that are used in actions of functional features. These objects are identified from knowledge of the system, and they

are verified during the construction of the TFM. It is not represented here, but these objects and topology of their use is the basis for construction of a class diagram. Thus, the TFM can be used as a formal CIM-Business Model.

However, transformation from CIM-Knowledge Model (informal description of the system) to CIM-Business Model (the topological functioning model) cannot be performed automatically. It requires human participation since information in the CIM-Knowledge Model is specified informally and used to have implicit knowledge. However, a formal CIM-Business Model gives an opportunity to make transformation to the CIM-Business Requirements for the System at least partially automated. And this issue requires further research activities.

REFERENCES

Archimate. (n.d.). *ArchiMate resource tree*. Retrieved April 8, 2010, from http://www.archimate.org/ART/

Asnina, E. (2006). The formal approach to problem domain modelling within model driven architecture. In *Proceedings of the 9th International Conference "Information Systems Implementation and Modelling" (ISIM'06), April 25-26, 2006, Přerov, Czech Republic, 1st edn.* (pp. 97-104). Ostrava, Czech Republic: Jan Štefan MARQ.

Bragança, A., & Machado, R. J. (2007). Adopting computational independent models for derivation of architectural requirements of software product lines. In *Fourth International Workshop on Model-Based Methodologies for Pervasive and Embedded Software (MOMPES'07)* (pp. 91-101). Washington, DC: IEEE.

Cao, X.-x., Miao, H.-k., & Chen, Y.-h. (2008). Transformation from computation independent model to platform independent model with pattern. [English Edition]. *Journal of Shanghai University*, *12*(6), 515–523. doi:10.1007/s11741-008-0610-2

Chappel, O. (2005, October). *Term-fact modeling, the key to successful rule-based systems*. Retrieved November 10, 2009, from Business Rules Journal / BRCommunity: http://www.BRCommunity.com/a2005/b250.html

Che, Y., Wang, G., Wen, X., & Ren, B. (2009). Research on computational independent model in the enterprise information system development model based on model driven and software component. In *International Conference on Interoperability for Enterprise Software and Applications China, 2009. IESA '09.* (pp. 85 - 89). Washington, DC: IEEE.

Debnath, N., Leonardi, M. C., Mauco, M. V., Montejano, G., & Riesco, D. (2008). Improving model driven architecture with requirements models. In *Proceedings of the Fifth International Conference on Information Technology: New Generations* (pp. 21-26). Washington, DC: IEEE.

Desfray, P. (2004). *Making a success of preliminary analysis using UML*. Retrieved November 10, 2009, from Softeam: http://www.objecteering.com/ressources_whitepapers.php

Farlex Inc. (2009). *Causality*. Retrieved November 4, 2009, from The Free Dictionary Com: http://encyclopedia.thefreedictionary.com/causality

Garrido, J. L., Noguera, M., González, M., Hurtado, M. V., & Rodríguez, M. L. (2006). Definition and use of computation independent models in an MDA-based groupware development process. *Science of Computer Programming, 66*(1), 25–43. doi:10.1016/j.scico.2006.10.008

Grangel, R., Chalmeta, R., & Campos, C. (2007). Using UML profiles for enterprise knowledge modelling. In *Proceedings of the 26th International Conference on Conceptual Modeling (ER 2007), the 3rd International Workshop on Foundations and Practices of UML (FP-UML 2007), LNCS, Computer Science, Theory & Methods* (pp. 125-132). Berlin: Springer Verlag.

Hendryx, S. (2003a, January). *A home for business models in the OMG*. Retrieved April 8, 2010, from Business Rules Journal: http://www.BRCommunity.com/b127.php

Hendryx, S. (2003b, November 14). *Architecture of business modeling*. Retrieved April 8, 2010, from http://www.semanticcore.org/white_papers.htm

Hendryx, S. (2003c). *Integrating computation independent business modeling languages into the MDA with UML 2*. Retrieved November 10, 2009, from Object Management Group: http://www.omg.org/docs/ad/03-01-32.doc

Hendryx, S. (2005, September). Are system requirements business rules? *Business Rules Journal, 6* (9). Retrieved November 10, 2009, from http://www.BRCommunity.com/a2005/b249.html

Huang, S., & Fan, Y. (2007). Model driven and service oriented enterprise integration - the method, framework and platform. In *Proceedings of the Sixth International Conference on Advanced Language Processing and Web Information Technology (ALPIT 2007)* (pp. 504-509). Washington, DC: IEEE Computer Society.

Jeary, S., Fouad, A., & Phalp, K. (2008). Extending the model driven architecture with a pre-CIM level. In *Proceedings of the 1st International Workshop on Business Support for MDA co-located with TOOLS EUROPE 2008*. Retrieved October 30, 2009, from http://ftp.informatik.rwth-aachen.de/Publications/CEUR-WS/Vol-376/

Kanyaru, J. M., Coles, M., Jeary, S., & Phalp, K. (2008). Using visualisation to elicit domain information as part of the model driven architecture (MDA) approach. In *Proceedings of the 1st International Workshop on Business Support for MDA co-located with TOOLS EUROPE 2008*. Retrieved October 30, 2009, from http://ftp.informatik.rwth-aachen.de/Publications/CEUR-WS/Vol-376/

Kolmogorov, A. N., & Fomin, S. V. (1975). *Introductory real analysis* (Silverman, R. A., Ed.). Mineola, NY: Courier Dover Publications.

Osis, J. (1969). Topological model of system functioning (in Russian). *Automatics and Computer Science. J. of Acad. of Sc.*, 6, 44–50.

Osis, J. (1997). Development of object-oriented methods for hybrid system analysis and design. In *Proceedings of the 23rd Conference of the Association of Simula Users (ASU)*, (pp. 162-170), Stara Lesna, Slovakia.

Osis, J., & Asnina, E. (2008a). A Business model to make software development less intuitive. In *Proceedings of 2008 International Conference on Innovation in Sofware Engineering (ISE 2008)* (pp. 1240-1245). Vienna, Austria: IEEE Computer Society Publishing.

Osis, J., & Asnina, E. (2008b). Enterprise modeling for information system development within MDA. In *Proceedings of the 41st Hawaii International Conference on Systems Science (HICSS-41 2008), 7-10 January 2008, Waikoloa, Big Island, HI, USA* (p. 490). Washington, DC: IEEE Computer Society.

Osis, J., Asnina, E., & Grave, A. (2008). Computation independent representation of the problem domain in MDA. *e-Informatica. Software Engineering Journal*, 2(1), 29–26. Retrieved from http://www.e-informatyka.pl/wiki/e-Informatica_-_Volume_2.

Osis, J., & Beghi, L. (1997). Topological modelling of biological systems. In D. Linkens, & E. Carson (Ed.), *Proceedings of the 3rd IFAC Symposium on Modelling and Control in Biomedical Systems, University of Warwick, 23-26 March 1997* (pp. 337-342). Oxford, UK: Elsevier Science Publishing.

Osis, J., Sukovskis, U., & Teilans, A. (1997). Business process modeling and simulation based on topological approach. In *Proceedings of the 9th European Simulation Symposium and Exhibition*, (pp. 496-501), Passau, Germany.

Piccinini, G., & Scarantino, A. (2008). *Computation vs. information processing: How they are different and why it matters*. Retrieved November 30, 2008, from Conference on Computation and Cognitive Science 2008 http://people.pwf.cam.ac.uk/mds26/cogsci/program.html

Rodriguez, A., Fernández-Medina, E., & Piattini, M. (2007). Towards CIM to PIM transformation: From secure business processes defined in BPMN to usecases. In *Proceedings of the International Conference on Business Process Management, Brisbane, Australia*, (pp. 408–415).

Sowa, J., & Zahman, J. (1992). Extending and formalizing the framework for information systems architecture. *IBM Systems Journal*, 31(3), 590–616. doi:10.1147/sj.313.0590

Tekinerdogan, B., Aksit, M., & Henninger, F. (2007). Impact of evolution of concerns in the model-driven architecture design approach. *Electronic Notes in Theoretical Computer Science*, 163, 45–64. doi:10.1016/j.entcs.2006.10.015

The Object Management Group. (2003). *MDA guide version 1.0.1.* (J. Miller, & J. Mukerji, Eds.) Retrieved November 10, 2009, from http://www.omg.org/docs/omg/03-06-01.pdf

The Object Management Group. (2005). *A proposal for an MDA foundation model, ORMSC White Paper, V00-02, ormsc/05-04-01*. Retrieved November 10, 2009, from www.omg.org/docs/ormsc/05-04-01.pdf

Trujillo, J., Soler, E., Fernández-Medina, E., & Piattini, M. (2009). A UML 2.0 profile to define security requirements for data warehouses. *Computer Standards & Interfaces*, 31, 969–983. doi:10.1016/j.csi.2008.09.040

Weske, M. (2007). *Business process management. Concepts, languages, architectures*. Berlin: Springer-Verlag.

Zachman, J. (1987). A framework for information systems architecture. *IBM Systems Journal, 26*(3), 276–292. doi:10.1147/sj.263.0276

KEY TERMS AND DEFINITIONS

Business Model: A business model is a model that specifies business knowledge in terms of business facts, rules, processes and activities. A business model can be constructed from different viewpoints, e.g. organizational, process, resource, event viewpoints and so on.

Business Requirements: Requirements for the system (and software) set by business people. The requirements contain business knowledge that must be kept and implemented in the system (and software). System requirements and software requirements are a part of the business requirements.

Cause-and-Effect Relation: A relation between two functional features of the system where appearance and execution of one functional feature is caused (generated) by the other functional feature without any intermediate functionality.

Computation Independent Model: A Computation Independent Model (CIM) is a model defined within OMG Model-Driven Architecture as a primary model. This model reflects system and software knowledge from the business perspective. The CIM may contain business knowledge about system organization, roles, functions, processes and activities, documentation, constraints etc. The CIM must contain business requirements for the system.

Continuous Mapping: A mathematical relation between two topological directed graphs that preserve their functional and structural properties.

System's Functional Feature: A functional characteristic of the system that is needed to reach system's functioning goal.

Topological Functioning Model: A model based on system theory and mathematics that specifies functionality and structure of a complex system as a connected topological space of system's functional characteristics and cause-and-effect relations among them.

Chapter 4
Derivation of Use Cases from the Topological Computation Independent Business Model

Janis Osis
Riga Technical University, Latvia

Erika Asnina
Riga Technical University, Latvia

ABSTRACT

In Model Driven Architecture (MDA), business requirements for the information system are described in a Computation Independent Model (CIM), which additionally can describe knowledge of the business, and structure and behavior of both business and supporting information system. In object-oriented software development requirements are described by use cases. Use cases and identification of them are informal and application-oriented. Goal-based approaches provide a more systematic way for discovering use cases from informal knowledge about a system. The main and very important difference of the approach suggested in this chapter is that we ground our domain analysis on a mathematical engineering model, Topological Functioning Model. It is a formal holistic computation independent business model, whose characteristics help in avoiding challenges in functional requirements caused by non-systematic approaches and fragmental nature of use cases, namely, completeness, traceability and compliance with the problem domain.

INTRODUCTION

Model-Driven Architecture (MDA) developed by the Object Management Group (OMG) proposes three (or at least two) transformable models for system specification. The first one is a Computation Independent Model or CIM. The CIM is a model that should eliminate the gap between business people and software developers. Two other models are a Platform Independent Model (PIM) and a Platform Specific Model (PSM). The last two models specify the system structure and behavior according to the object-oriented paradigm and definitely are transformable.

This chapter discusses the CIM. This model specifies domain information: business vocabulary, business rules, business knowledge, system requirements (in a broad sense), etc. This means

DOI: 10.4018/978-1-61692-874-2.ch004

it may be as transformable as non-transformable. Moreover, this model may have different users and thus may describe different domains – a problem as well as a solution.

Summarizing authors' viewpoints in (Hendryx, 2003a; Hendryx, 2003b; Grangel, Chalmeta, & Campos, 2007; Che, Wang, Wen, & Ren, 2009; Jeary, Fouad, & Phalp, 2008), the CIM can contain three parts: CIM-Knowledge Model, CIM-Business Model, and CIM-Business Requirements for the System.

The *CIM-Knowledge Model* reflects an enterprise from the holistic point of view, thus providing the general vision of the enterprise with focus on enterprise knowledge. It reflects the problem domain.

The *CIM-Business Model* focuses on the business scope and goals as well as terminology, resources, facts, roles, policies, rules, organizations, locations and events of concern to the business. It does not reflect considerations of the computerized information system. However, the scope of the Business Model in the CIM must include, at a minimum, those business functions which are planned to be served by the computerized system. Thus, this model reflects both problem domain and solution domain.

The *CIM–Business Requirements for the System* contains the contract between the business and IT about what the business people expect the computerized information system to do. It reflects functional and non-functional requirements for the computerized system. Thus it reflects the solution domain.

Thus, models used for business analysis and requirements gathering/specification may be used as the CIM within MDA. However, if we speak about the object-oriented paradigm in software development, these models usually are expressed by natural language in an informal way as somehow structured text. This means that correspondence between the solution and the problem domain is intuitive and weak. If we want to incorporate object-oriented software development (OOSD)

with MDA and all its models, greater attention to problem domain analysis should be devoted.

There are two fundamental aspects for system modeling that need to be distinguished. The first one is *analysis*, which defines *what* an application has to do with a problem domain to fit customer's requirements. The second one is *design*, which defines *how* an application will be built. This means that at the analysis stage, a developer breaks a complex system under consideration into smaller parts to gain a better understanding of it, and at the design stage he/she makes a synthesis (combines) these separated and analyzed parts into the whole to reproduce the complex system under consideration as complete as possible. Therefore, at the beginning a developer considers each part independently of others, and only then he/she looks for relationships between those parts. A line between the analysis and design is fuzzy in the OOSD. Besides that, analysis implies that a software developer should analyze client's current situation as precise as possible, gather requirements to the system planned to build and implement them in some suitable modeling language.

Usually, requirement analysis is erroneously considered as determination of what software the client *wants*. Actually, requirements should determine what software the client *needs* (Schach, 1999). And, as Michael Jackson stated in (1999; 2005), not only what software the client needs, but also within what environment this software will work.

The OOSD does not provide such a thing as an "object-oriented requirement". Therefore, requirements are gathered and then specified in the analysis phase in order to determine functionality of the planned system. Object-oriented analysis (OOA), an initial stage of the OOSD, usually is a set of semiformal specification techniques that contains in some order three core steps, which are related to each other, but at the same time they can be performed in parallel (Schach, 1999; Jacobson, Christerson, Jonsson, & Overgaard, 1992):

- Use case modeling that is largely action-oriented (elicitation of functional requirements and objects),
- Class modeling that is purely data-oriented (organization of the objects and definition of internal structure of the objects),
- Dynamic modeling that is purely action-oriented at the class level (description of how the objects interact and definition of operations of the object).

Being introduced by Ivar Jacobson, the term *use case* is widely known since 1987. Use cases have become a very popular technique of the OOA from the end of 1990s. After some elaboration, uses cases have become one of the fundamental techniques used in the OOA.

Use cases describe the solution domain at the third part of CIMs, the CIM-Business Requirements for the System. Use cases are simple and informal, and this is their main advantage. But at the same time, the informal nature of use cases and a lack of a solid background (i.e., a lack of compliance with a domain model) are causes of core limitations of use cases discussed below. Indeed, it would be wonderful to have a solid background while keeping simplicity of use cases. We propose to solve this issue by deriving the CIM-Business Requirements for the System, namely, a use case model, from the formal mathematical CIM-Business Model, namely, a Topological Functioning Model (TFM), by using mappings between these two models.

BACKGROUND

Ivar Jacobson et al. (Jacobson, Christerson, Jonsson, & Overgaard, 1992) offered use cases in a use case model as a means for requirements model representation. This model should specify all the functionality of the system and support traceability. But the use case model is only a part of the requirements model. The main aim of use case

introducing was to improve traceability between the functional requirement specification and an analysis model, because the requirements specification represented in a textual description only usually leads to missing requirements. Therefore, in order to overcome this weakness and to improve traceability the authors separated three parts of the requirements model, which applies use cases:

- A use case model that defines what exists outwards the system and what should be done by the system,
- Interface description, and
- A problem domain object model.

All these three parts of the requirements model are *solution-oriented*. This means that even when they consider knowledge about the problem domain, they do it from the perspective of the computerized system (software). As mentioned, use cases specify functionality of the system from software developer's viewpoint. In other words, the functionality is described as a set of fragments (use cases) without formally defined relations among these fragments.

Let's consider an essence of use cases, i.e., three definitions of this term in brief:

- According to Jacobson et al. (1992), a use case is "a special sequence of behaviorally related transactions performed by an actor and the system in a dialogue... This transaction consists of different actions to be performed... The set of all use case descriptions specifies the complete functionality of the system".
- In turn, according to UML 2.2 specification (OMG, 2009), use cases are a notation for capturing requirements, primary functional requirements, of a system.
- Authors in (Schneider & Winters, 2001) defined use cases as "a behavior of the system that produces a measurable result of value to an actor". From the user's view-

point a use case should represent a complete task that can be performed in a relatively short run.

We should note that transactions (and tasks) may be described for different (not only software) domains and at the different level of abstraction. This leads to the fact that use cases may be described in different levels of detail – it depends on the point of view use cases describe. Therefore, it must be clear for whom you are writing use cases – for managers, users or developers (Schneider & Winters, 2001). Therefore, in the course of time, software developers have distinguished system and business use cases. As stated in (Leffingwell & Widrig, 2003), a business use case is a stereotype of an original (i.e., of a computerized system) use case introduced for purposes of business modeling. A business use case model consists of actors and use cases. Business use cases specify the functionality of the business in order to be used to drive application development. Actors are users and systems that interact with the business. Besides that, a business object model exists. It describes the entities – departments, paychecks, systems – and their interactions in order to provide the functionality necessary to the implementation of the business use cases.

Benefits and Limitations of Use Case Techniques

Use cases *per se* are only a way of the description of a set of fragments of system's functionality. But if use cases became so popular that they were included in the standard, what benefits they have? Edward V. Berard (1998) noted use case protagonists' four primary motivations for the use case application: gaining and understanding the problem, capturing and understanding of proposed solution, identifying candidate objects, and testing of the entire system by testing the whole set of use cases. Some other advantages were enumerated in (Firesmith, 2002; Schneider & Winters, 2001):

- Use cases are user-centric. They are able to capture requirements from the system users' viewpoint, mostly functional requirements.
- Use cases are good means for communication between developers and customers/users. They use natural language and simple understandable notation.
- Complex functionality of large-scale systems can be decomposed into major functions. This means use cases can be distributed among subsystem boundaries.
- Use cases have accented the use of lower-level scenarios, and, hence, implicitly support some abstracted kind of object collaboration patterns.
- Use cases can serve as a good basis for functional requirements validation and higher-level model verification; use cases are traceable.
- Use cases can serve for project management as measurement in development process planning.

But what limitations and issues occur in practice? The first point is that use cases were accepted without some more or less significant criticism (Firesmith, 2002). Stephen Ferg (2003) even compared the use case driven technique as the single method for requirements gathering with a chocolate diet for people: it gives early satiety, but does not provide balanced nutrition. The ground of this statement is some issues caused by characteristics of use cases (Ferg, 2003; Firesmith, 2002). These issues can be separated into three relative groups as follows:

- **Information capturing.** Some developers try to capture implementation details. However, one of the principles of use cases is their independency of implementation. Another point is that use cases can be described at different levels of detail. Defining a use case at the very high level can hide information that should be described explicitly. Otherwise, use cases described at the very low level can make the business context hardly understandable. It would not be a weakness, if use cases provide a mechanism for consistent increasing and decreasing a level of abstraction. By now, the only way is a use of the "realization" relationship, which cannot specify relations between levels of abstraction accurately.

- **Limitation of Thinking.** Their simple concept tends developers to think that requirements gathering can be limited with creation of a list of use cases. Besides that, exclusion of other requirements gathering techniques and proper problem domain analysis leads to the poor quality of the system developed. Literally this means that developers get fragments of functional parts of the computerized system, but a mechanism for making a synthesis of these parts is not provided.

- **Completeness checking.** Use case application is not systematic in comparison with "traditional" requirements gathering techniques – interviewing, document analysis, requirements workshops, brainstorming, formal specification, concept maps, goal-based approaches, and so on. Although a use case model allows looking at the computerized system functions in common, this model does not allow representing relationships and dependencies among use cases. If developers want to see the whole picture of the system functioning in order to check completeness of the specification, they are forced to analyze use case specifications and keep almost all dependencies in mind. However, this is a quite difficult task, if a count of use cases is more than seven. Hence, use cases do not give any answer on questions about completeness of the specification of the system, conflicts among use cases, gaps that can be left in system requirements, and how changes can affect behavior that other use cases describe.

In order to avoid these limitations, different developers have tried to improve the formal basis of use cases or to systemize application of use cases in the software development processes. These applications are discussed hereinafter.

Approaches for Making Use Cases in Compliance with the Problem Domain

Since use cases capture functional requirements, but are not well dedicated for non-functional requirement capturing, they can be the best choice for requirements capturing when most requirements the system has are functional, the system has many types of users, and, therefore, many interfaces (Arlow & Neustadt, 2005). Some development methodologies require only a brief use case survey. Other require that use cases to be refined step by step according with the development process from business use cases to more detailed system-level use cases to highly developed complete test cases. Thus, let us discuss how several more complete use-case driven approaches manage use cases to fill in the gap between the real world system, the problem domain, and an information system, the solution domain.

Business Components

Authors in (Dubielewicz & Hnatkovska, 2005) suggested using business components based on the concept of UML 2.0 components in order to solve a granularity and completeness issues of use cases. A business component represents a business process or its part, and contains business use cases (services offered to the business actors) and their realization (how the services are provided). Then each business component that could be considered as elementary business process can be traced for the system use case, thus providing completeness of a set of use cases and the same granularity of the system use cases.

However, if use cases identification is based mainly on identification and refinement of a set of business processes of the business system, the question about completeness and interaction of those business processes still is open. The cause is unclearly (informally) specified shared and related activities in those business processes. Again, at the first a developer is forced to separate system operation into weak related or unclearly related parts, and then to synthesize them into the whole working system.

Business Object-Oriented Modeling

Another interesting approach, Business Object-Oriented Modeling (B.O.O.M.) developed by Howard Podeswa (Podeswa, 2005), is dedicated to relate business analysis documentation to the object-oriented software development. This approach distinguishes and relates business use cases and system use cases.

The main idea of the B.O.O.M. is to identify and describe business use cases that a planned application will affect, thus, analyzing possible changes in business workflows and human roles. Then each business use case is analyzed, looking for activities that the application will realize, and this information is specified as system use cases, which further will drive the whole development process.

Business use cases describe business requirements for the project, i.e. specify end-to-end business processes that the IT project will impact. Workflows they specify can be described in text or using appropriate diagrams and discussed with all stakeholders. Actor identification is done eliminating any who does not interact with the application from the business actor list and adding any role that is required because of technology.

After that, system use case packages are identified either in accordance with the main actor, who uses them, or each business use case, or placing logically related system use cases together. Then, system use cases are identified for each defined package. System use case identification processes by going back to the business use case workflow and selecting what activities in it can benefit from full or partial automation. Then identified system use cases are specified by a use case diagram within the package. A class diagram is drawing for all business classes.

However, first, this approach excludes other requirements gathering techniques except use cases. Second, identification of business use cases is IT project driven not business driven, although business use cases are checked for conformance to the existing business processes. Third, creation of use case packages in accordance with logical relation among system use cases is an intuitive and *ad hoc* approach. And fourth, if system use cases' packages are created in separation from the business use cases, then changes in business processes cannot be traceable to the system use cases in a natural way.

The Unified Process

The widely-known Unified Process (UP) (Arlow & Neustadt, 2005) positions use cases as the basis to construct different defined views of the systems, because they are dedicated to capture the basic requirements for it. In order to perform requirement tracing simpler, the functional and non-functional requirements are gathered, then prioritized and traced to use cases.

Use case modeling starts with some initial estimation (a tentative idea) about where the system boundary lies. Then actors and use cases are found, and, after some number of iterations, system boundary, use cases, and actors are stabilized. For actor identification, accessorial questions are developed. For each actor in the list, a way how the actor is going to use the application is found.

Therefore, a list of candidate use cases is obtained. Use case identification, in turn, can force additional actor identification. Accessorial questions for use case identification are also developed.

The next point is project glossary identification that is necessary, because some terms can be synonyms or homonyms. Then, use cases are detailed, namely, main, alternative and repetitive flows are identified and specified in the textual form.

Therefore, after these steps a developer has two sets of functional requirements that must be related to each other, e.g. by creating a requirements traceability matrix. Then use cases are refined.

Weak points of the UP, by our opinion, are as follows. First, use cases are requirements driven. The UP does not decline a use of business models, but does not also specify any formal relationship between the business and the application. A business model can serve as an accessory in identifying use cases and actors. Second, actors and use cases are identified using a *tentative* idea about what the system boundary is. Thus, developers do not have any formal or precise method to identify the boundary of their future project. Third, the requirement traceability to use cases is defined *ad hoc* using only developer's intuition and experience in this field. Such incompleteness as requirements covering, missing or duplicating can be discovered only in manual specification reviews. Fourth, identification of inclusion and extension use cases (in other words the shared or optional functionality) is monotonous work that requires careful investigation of all specified use cases. Although, it needs to be noticed that inclusion and extension relationships are advanced and can be not used.

Goal-Based Approaches

The next two approaches base use case identification on goals of business systems. This eliminates issues caused by fragmentary nature of a set of use cases or business processes that is obtained in *ad hoc* manner.

Eriksson-Penker Business Extension

Eriksson-Penker Business Extension (Eriksson & Penker, 2000) suggests business modeling as a primary activity in development of information systems. Business modeling deals with identification and understanding of processes, resources, rules and goals of a business system, an *enterprise*. A model of the business system should serve as a base for software system requirements.

Authors introduced an *assembly line diagram* that "is based to a large extent of the UML activity diagram". An example of the assembly line diagram is illustrated in Figure 1. It contains two parts – the above part represents a process diagram, while the below part illustrates a number of horizontal packages (assembly lines), each representing a group of objects. This diagram represents how the processes write and read objects in the packages. The reference items between these two parts represent an interface between the business system and information system. By analyzing these diagrams from a very high level, such as the system or subsystem level, to the information system level, processes and classes in the information system can be identified. Each detailed "set of references" that becomes a use case (the interface) is selected accordingly to the rules of use case identification. Therefore, thanks to work with goals and processes of the business system, it is possible to verify and validate all systems requirements.

Alistair Cockburn's Structuring Use Cases with Goals

Alistair Cockburn (Cockburn, 2000) suggested to structure use cases according with four dimensions: *purpose (*stories, requirements*), contents (*contradicting, consistent prose, and formal content*), plurality* (one, or multiple) and *structure* (unstructured, semi-formal, and formal structure). In the book, the author considered use cases, whose purpose is requirements and which are written with consistent prose, have multiple scenarios per a use case and have a semi-formal

Figure 1. Assembly Line Diagram and use cases for booking train tickets

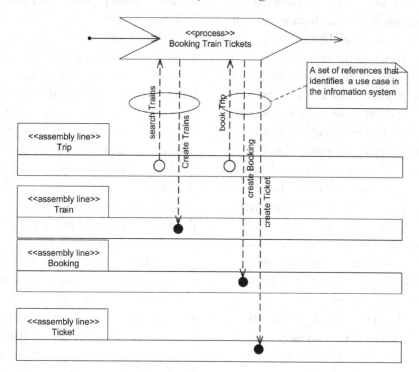

structure. The author suggested to structure use cases with goals.

According to Alistair Cockburn, the goal and use cases can be at *system scope* (in case of considering a system under design) and at *strategic scope* (in case of considering the organization). The goals themselves can consist of summary goals, user goals, and sub-functions. The user goals correspond to "a user task" or "an elementary business process". Sets of user goals form summary goals. Below a user goal are sub-functions. Talking about interaction detail, A. Cockburn pointed out that this interaction must be at the semantic interface level.

The benefits of structuring with goals are the possibility to attach non-functional requirements to goals, to manage a project by goals, to recognize subtle requirements earlier from goal failures, such a form of requirements description facilitates work with requirement specifications. But a few gaps also exist in this approach. In spite of using this approach since 1994, some confusion about the levels, goals and data variations still exist. The author regards it to the multilevel character of the technique that is not easy for everyone.

Weaknesses of the Goal-Based Requirements Gathering Approaches

As we have mentioned above, principles of goal-oriented (based) requirements engineering introduce more formalism in use case identification. They focus developers on understanding *why* a system is to be created and for what purpose, thus allow discovering conflicts among stakeholders' viewpoints already in requirements analysis (Antón, 1996).

Goals also are not a panacea. Some weaknesses common for goal-based approaches were already discussed in (Antón, 1996). The one point is the process of goal identification is not clear. Some approaches assume that developers should use existing goals of enterprises, other suggest exploring enterprise documentation. However, those goals do not always fit the real operation of enterprises.

Another point is related to goal evolution. It is necessary to trace changes in goals to requirements. The solution was proposed in Goal-Based Requirements Analysis Method (GBRAM) in the same publication. The core idea that still is evolved is to extract goals (removing redundant and synonym goals) and agents responsible for achieving them from the information about enterprises, and then to explore achievement of each identified goal by using a detailed process description (a scenario), which can be further operationalized in the computerized system.

But we consider another weakness of goal-based approaches for identification of use cases that is common also for other approaches, which try to solve limitation of use cases. This weakness is in the way of thinking about the system mentioned in Introduction. Namely, it is synthesis of separated parts of the system without clear understanding of the purpose and interrelation among them. Instead of system thinking where at first the system is investigating in the whole, and only then is separated into parts for analysis, those approaches take separated parts of the system and join them in order to simulate somehow operation of the real system.

We believe that exactly system thinking should take the adequate place in software engineering, and thus propose a use of the topological modeling in the beginning of software development.

USE CASE DERIVATION FROM THE TOPOLOGICAL FUNCTIONING MODEL

We also suggest identifying the use cases by using goals, thus we do not reject any goal-based technique. Besides that, any other more systematic technique may be also used. The main and very important difference of our approach from those described above is that we ground our analysis of domains on a *mathematical engineering model*, Topological Functioning Model (TFM), which reflects functionality of systems holistically. The holistic nature of the model helps to avoid challenges caused by fragmental modeling, namely, completeness, traceability and compliance with the problem domain.

Source Model: Topological Functioning Model in Brief

Let us remind to you in brief what a topological functioning model (TFM) is. The more extended description of the TFM is given in this book in Chapter "Topological Modeling for Model-driven Domain Analysis and Software Development: Functions and Architectures".

The Topological Functioning Model is developed at Riga Technical University. The TFM is a mathematically formal model that describes a topology among system functional features from the computation independent viewpoint. This model is independent of any modeling and implementation technique. TFM formalism is based on assumption that a complex system can be described in abstract terms as a topological space (X, Q), where X is a finite set of functional characteristics (or features) and Q is a topology, given in the form of a digraph (oriented graph). Such a model comes about through the acquisition of the experts' knowledge about the complex system, verbal description, and other documents concerning the structure and functioning. The set X is the union of a subset N of features of the system itself, and of a subset M of features from other systems, constituting the environment interacting with the system under consideration. The topological model of problem domain is the advantage for analysis and decomposition of complex systems described in (Osis, 1969).

A functional feature is a characteristic of the system (in its general sense) that is designed for achieving some system's goal. The functional features are activities that help the system to realize its functionality. These activities can be considered as (specialized) functional features (Osis, 1997), i.e., functional features, whose further expansion is not necessary at this stage. The first definition of parts of the functional feature was defined in (Asnina, 2006).

Each functional feature is a unique tuple *<A, R, O, PrCond, PostCond, Pr, Ex>*, where:

- A is an action linked with an object;
- R is a result of that action (it is an optional element);
- O is an object (objects) that get the result of the action or an object (objects) that is used in this action; it could be a role, a time period or a moment, catalogues etc.;
- PrCond is a set PrCond = $\{c_1, ..., c_i\}$, where c_i is a precondition or an atomic business rule (it is an optional element);
- PostCond is a set PostCond = $\{c_1, ..., c_i\}$, where c_i is a post-condition or an atomic business rule (it is an optional element);
- Pr is a set of entities (systems or subsystems) which provide or suggest an action with a set of certain objects;
- Ex is a set of entities (systems or subsystems) which enact a concrete action.

A name of the functional feature could be expressed in the abstract and detailed form. Functional features can be joined in a functional feature set, representing a certain business function. Therefore, a set of specialized functional features can be correlated with the appropriate business function and corresponding business process. In that case, a name of the functional feature set is written down in the abstract form.

Cause-and-effect relations among functional features (or topology) must be set. It is assumed that a cause-and-effect relation between two functional features of the system exists if the appearance of one feature is caused by the appearance of the other feature without participation of any third (intermediary) feature.

The TFM has topological and functional properties (Osis, 2003). The topological properties

are connectedness, closure, neighborhood and continuous mapping. The functional properties are cause-effect relations, cycle structure, inputs and outputs. These properties state the following:

- Separation of a topological model of system functioning from the topological space of an environment system works within. This defines that the topological space of the functioning system must be connected. This means that the digraph cannot have isolated vertices. It defines also formal semantics of concepts of subsystems and independent systems.
- In point of fact of functioning the common thing for all systems (technical, business and biological) should be an oriented cycle (a directed closed path). This similarity of technical and biological systems was recognized, because the main cycle in essence represents a shape of the main feedback. Therefore, in every topological model of system functioning there must be at least one directed closed loop (i.e. a directed closed path). Usually it is even expanded hierarchy of cycles. This property of the model enables analyzing similarities and differences (that is not less important than similarity analysis) of functioning systems.
- Some functional features of a system can be considered as a more detailed subset of specialized features. The model with any complexity can be abstracted to the simpler one and vice verse. This means that continuous mapping of topological models is being realized. It defines that direction of topological model arcs will be kept as in a refined as in a simplified model. Moreover, a lack of knowledge about the system can be filled up with knowledge that is obtained from the continuous mapping of the same type model to the system model under consideration.

Figure 2. Main elements of Use Case Diagram

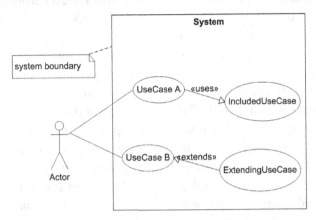

Graphical representation of the TFM and descriptions of TFM functional features will be illustrated in the section that discusses an example.

Target Model: UML Use Case Diagram and Specification

Main elements of *UML Use Case Diagram* (Figure 2) are the subject (system boundary) that defines what is a *part* of the system and what is *external* to the system; an actor that specifies a role of an external entity that interacts with the system directly; a use case itself and its steps; and relationships between use cases, between use cases and actors, and between actors.

Commonly, *Use Case Specification* contains the following items (Arlow & Neustadt, 2005): use case's name (a verb or verb phrase), identification, brief description (the goal); actors, involved in the use case; preconditions and postconditions of the use case; a main flow and alternative flows (a list of alternatives to the main flow) of the use case.

Formalized Derivation of Use Cases Based on the TFM: in General

As previously mentioned, use cases are mainly functional requirements representation used for discussions with customers. A use case model describes computerized system's behavior modeled as use cases, users of the system modeled as actors, and relationships between the users and system use cases. A use case *per se* is *not* a single scenario; it is a set of scenarios. Therefore, we agree that among other techniques separation of use cases using business goals is more effective, because it avoids representing a single scenario as a use case. This means that a use case is a complete task that has some useful or valuable result. This useful or valuable result is that goal, which must be achieved by a system.

Taking into account the considered approaches which try to eliminate the gap between the problem domain and use cases, we can summarize that these approaches discover use cases from the knowledge about the problem domain by using such *ad hoc* techniques as assisting questions, users' goals, categories of concepts and concept relations (Figure 3-a). In the more complete and rarer cases, developers use systematic requirements gathering techniques and base their analysis on a set of defined goals, business processes and business objects in order to define (textual) requirements specification and then to derive use cases intuitively. Besides that, it is hard to distinguish a domain "as is" and a domain "to be" in these artifacts, i.e., a problem and a solution. Usually, developers are focused on the solution from the very beginning, and the problem domain is analyzed by them only if the solution seems not to be adequate to the domain "as is" and only in those "weak" parts. Hence we should conclude that in general derivation of use cases still is developer's mental and intuitive work.

Our approach that is ground on a mathematical engineering model eliminates this informality. The reason is that a TFM of the system captures both structural and functional information about the system, while use cases also supports functional paradigm. This means that a TFM of the solution domain, which is based on and continuously mapped to the TFM of the problem domain, can serve as a formal basis for the use case identification (Figure 3-b).

As mentioned in Introduction and discussed in detail in this book in Chapter "Topological Functioning Model as a CIM-Business Model", three models, namely, CIM-Knowledge Model, CIM-Business Model, and CIM-Business Requirements for the System, constitute the CIM. Starting from the informal CIM-Knowledge Model, knowledge about the system-as-is and the system-to-be are extracted and reflected in corresponding TFMs in a formal way. While constructing the TFM of the system-to-be, software requirements for this system and business (and system) goals are checked on conformity to the TFM of the system-as-is. Continuous mapping between these two TFMs, two formal CIM-Business Models, is a bridge between problem and solution domains. In order to get a CIM-Business Requirements for the System in a form of use cases, we use a goal-based technique. A goal is a criterion for the use case identification and separation from the TFM. Goals are set either by users of the business system or by users of the computerized system. Incompliance or incompleteness of goals is checked by mapping all goals onto the formal TFM in accordance with the domain under consideration. At the same time, every computerized system goal must be in compliance to the corresponding business system goal (Osis, Asnina, & Grave, 2008). We will demonstrate this approach hereinafter in this chapter.

Making Requirements in Compliance with the Domain Model

When one wants to make functional requirements for the system in compliance with functional features of the system, the following five cases may occur (Osis & Asnina, 2008): a) one-to-one mapping, b) many-to-one mapping, c) one-to-many mapping, d) zero-to-one mapping, and e) one-to-zero mapping.

One-to-one mapping is the simplest and less problematic situation, when one functional requirement maps into the one functional feature. For example, if we have a requirement: "The system shall provide entering of client's data" and a functional feature "Entering client's data", then it is this case.

Many-to-one mapping is a case when several functional requirements map into the same functional feature. This can happen if they are:

- Covering (overlapping) requirements, or
- The target functional feature is an abstracted functional feature set, i.e., when functional requirements describe functionality in more detail than the functional feature does.

If functional requirements are covering, this means that they describe the same functionality reflected by the functional feature or by the same part of the abstracted functional feature. In this case the repeating functional requirements may be merged. For example, let us assume that we have two requirements "A: The system shall provide entering client's data and booking train tickets" and "B: The system shall provide entering client's data and selling train tickets", and a functional feature "Entering client's data". The client's data are the same in both cases. Hence, this is a case of two covering requirements, because they have the same part about handling client's data that maps to the given functional feature. In such a

Figure 3. Use Case Derivation in the OOA (a) and in the formalized approach with the TFM (b)

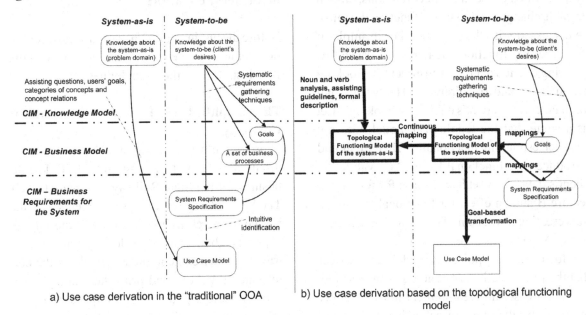

a) Use case derivation in the "traditional" OOA

b) Use case derivation based on the topological functioning model

case, it is possible to re-specify the requirements by separating this part into one new requirement.

In the second case, a more abstract functional feature can be refined. This means that it can be specialized to several functional features in correspondence with the specified requirements. For example, if we have two requirements "A: The system shall provide entering client's data" and "B: The system shall provide validating client's data" that map onto an abstract functional feature "Validating client's data", then we can refine this functional feature to two features, namely, "Entering client's data" and "Validating client's data".

But it is important to note that the rational decision about what actions must be taken can be done taking into account information of the project.

One-to-many is a case when one functional requirement maps into several functional features. The causes can be:

- The functional requirement under discussion joins several functional requirements, or

- The functional features in the topological functioning model are defined at the more detailed level of abstraction than the level the functional requirement describes.

In the first case the discovered content in the functional requirement must be split into several functional requirements in accordance with functional features in the topological functioning model. Otherwise, the corresponding functional features need to be abstracted to the necessary level. Thus, it is a reverse case of many-to-one mappings.

One-to-zero is a case when one functional requirement describes some new (previously undefined), erroneous or even impossible functionality of the system.

In case of new functionality it is necessary to define how it affects previously defined system functionality that is represented by the topological functioning model. What can be a cause or causes for generation of this functionality and what can be an effect or effects of it? The topological functioning model must be supplemented by all defined cause-and-effect relations, and all possible changes in the system functionality must be discussed with the customer. For example, if there are two functional features – a cause "A: Entering client's data" and an effect "B: Booking a train ticket" and a requirement "The system shall validate entered client's data when booking". Let us assume that the topological model does not have corresponding functionality. Then we should introduce new functional feature "C: Validating client's data", and set it as a cause for functional feature B and an effect for functional feature A, thus creating new chain of cause-and-effect relations "A generates C generates B".

However, the topological model can discover that the functionality is erroneous or impossible. In such a case, this requirement must be either modified by the client or set as impossible and removed from the requirements specification.

Zero-to-one is the last case where requirements specification does not contain any functional requirement corresponding to the defined functional feature of the system. This situation is a sub-case of the more general situation, when a topological functioning model contains more than one functional feature that does not have corresponding functional requirements. The causes can be:

- This functional feature will not be implemented in the computerized system,
- It is a missing functional requirement.

If the functional feature under consideration will not be implemented and it is connected by cause-and-effect relations with functional features that the client wants to be implemented, then information about input and output data of this functionality must be defined. Otherwise, a corresponding functional requirement must be added to the requirements specification and correspondence between this requirement and that functional feature must be set.

Illustrating Example

Before discussing guidelines for use case derivation, let us describe a small example we will use for illustration of those guidelines.

The Simplified TFM of the State Railway Company

In order to illustrate our approach along with the discussion, we will use a simplified TFM of the business of the State Railway Company (SRC). The SRC sells train tickets to its clients. A seller is able to search trains for trips by entering client's data about trips. By selecting trains for the trip, the seller can complete the sale of the corresponding tickets, and print them out. If there is no suitable trip, the system requires the seller to enter another client's data. Clients can return purchased tickets. If it is an invalid ticket or its departure date is equal to the return date, then the seller returns only 50% of the ticket price. If it is a valid ticket and its departure date is alter than the return date, then the seller returns 80% of the ticket price. When the return is completed, the seller prints out also a receipt of the return of the ticket. Besides that, the seller can create the report of made sales.

Functional Requirements for the SRC Information System

Let us assume that we have the following functional requirements for the SRC information (computerized) system, namely, for the system-to-be:

- FR1: The system shall provide booking train tickets for a trip by a client.
- FR2: The system shall provide selling train tickets for a trip by a seller.
- FR3: The system shall provide selling booked train tickets by a seller.

Table 1. SRC functional features

Label	Functional Feature	Provider	Executor	Subordination	Precondition
1	Entering the client data of a trip	SRC	seller or client	inner	
2	Searching the trains for a trip	SRC	seller or client	inner	
3	Requiring the client data of a trip	SRC	seller or client, SRC	inner	if the trains are not found
4	Selecting the trains for a trip	SRC	seller or client	inner	if at least one train is found
5	Completing the sale of tickets	SRC	seller, SRC	inner	if a client agrees to purchase a ticket
6	Printing out tickets on trains	SRC	seller, SRC	inner	
7	Checking the validity of a ticket	SRC	seller, SRC	inner	
8	Completing the return of a ticket	SRC	SRC	inner	
9	Returning the 50% price of a ticket	SRC	seller	inner	if the ticket is invalid or its departure date is equal to a return date
10	Returning the 80% price of a ticket	SRC	seller	inner	if the ticket is valid and its departure date is later than the return date
11	Printing out the receipt of a return	SRC	SRC	inner	
12	Completing the book of tickets	SRC	client, SRC	inner	if a client agree to purchase a ticket
13	Entering the number of a book	SRC	seller	inner	
14	Searching the book of tickets	SRC	seller, SRC	inner	
15	Creating the report of sales	SRC	seller	inner	

The Topological Functioning Model of the SRC Information System

Let us assume that functional requirements were mapped onto the topological functioning model of the SRC. The corresponding topological functioning model is illustrated in Figure 4. Those functional features that will be executed not only by users of the computerized system, but also by the system itself, contain the name of the system, SRC, as an executing entity. The list of functional features created according to the description (tuple) of functional features given in Section "Source Model: Topological Functioning Model in Brief" is given in Table 1.

In the TFM (Figure 4) the number of the vertex corresponds to the number of the functional feature. Vertices with the squared background (12, 13, 14) denote new functionality introduced by the information system planned to be built, ver-

tices with the solid white background (5, 6, 7, 8, 11) denote functionality that already existed in the business and that will be implemented in the information system, a vertex with the grey background (9, 10, 15) denotes functionality that exists in the business, but will not be implemented in the information system, and vertices with the white background and the squared shadow (1, 2, 3, 4) represents already existing functionality that is extended according to the new requirements. The SRC has provided selling and returning train tickets by a seller. The information system to be built is dedicated to support these functions, and to provide a client the possibility to book train tickets. Functional features 1, 2, 3 and 4 are extended in order to support two enacting entities – a seller (already existing) and a client (new introduced).

Figure 4. The TFM of the State Railway Company (SRC)

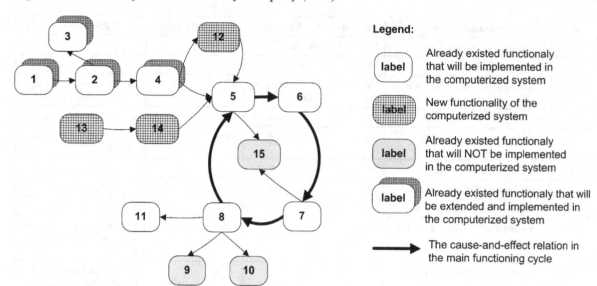

Cause-and-effect relations denoted by bold arrows form the main functioning cycle "5-6-7-8-5" of the system. The main functioning cycle relates those functional features that are vitally necessary for operation of a system; here it is a sale and a return of tickets. The detailed discussion is presented in this book in Chapter "Topological Modeling for Model-Driven Domain Analysis and Software Development: Functions and Architectures".

Guidelines for Derivation of Use Cases from the TFM

We suggest the following guidelines that should help us in getting use cases and their specification from the holistic formal TFM of the computerized system created in the formal compliance with the TFM of the business system wherein the computerized system will work.

From here, we will describe the guidelines, their explanation and illustration by the example of the TFM of the SRC.

Guideline 1: Identification of business actors. Each external system or an entity that provides or initiates a functional feature from the external environment is a business actor.

Explanation: Actors are *external* entities interacting directly with the business system that establish business goals within the business system. Actors are external entities in the TFM, where they can be represented as an external system itself (e.g., a company, a customer) or as an entity that is responsible for initiation of a functional feature from the external environment or a functional feature that describes system interaction with the external environment (in this case must be identified with whom the system interacts). Two latter cases can be realized considering information in topological space of the system and its environment functioning.

Illustration: The business actor is *a client.* A client is an external entity that initiates the functional feature "1: Entering the client data of a trip" and "13: Entering the number of a book" by contacting a seller, who is a worker within the business system and enters those data. In order to define this, we identified that executing those functional features the seller interacts directly with clients.

Guideline 2: Identification of business workers. Each partially-dependent system or an entity that initiates an inner system functional feature is a business worker.

Explanation: Workers are *inner* entities interacting directly with the business system that either establish system goals or realize some business goals. Workers are human, roles, etc. that work within the business system and can be identified from the TFM. In the TFM they can be represented as inner dependent systems that are subordinated to the system (e.g., the seller) or as inner system functional features, for whose initiation they are responsible.

Illustration: Since we consider the business system, there are two business workers. They are a seller and a client. The client is a responsible entity of functional features 1, 2, 3, 4 and 12, which allows a client to book train tickets by himself. In turn, the seller is a responsible entity of all the TFM functional features except functional features 8 and 11.

Guideline 3: Identification of business goals. Each identified business user (actor or worker) that interacts with the business system has his business goal. Business goals for each user are to be identified.

Illustration: Client's business goals are CG1"Purchase a train ticket", CG2"Book a train ticket", and CG3"Get money for an unused train ticket". Seller's business goals are SG1"Sell a train ticket", SG2"Get back a train ticket", SG3"Create a report about sales".

Guideline 4: Associating functionality with business goals. Each direct goal is to be corresponded to the functional features (one or many) of the system. For each user's goal, an input functional feature (input transaction), an output functional feature (output transaction), and a functional feature chain between them should be identified. Transaction may consist of the only one functional feature. Each TFM functional feature can be associated with more than one business goal.

Explanation: Users are initiators, or, in other words, they are a cause, of an event happened in the business (and computerized) system. Besides that TFM functional features are abstracted according to business processes and business activities. This means that this caused the events start running of the input functional feature and onward through a functional feature chain. Therefore, actors and workers help in identifying business goals.

Illustration: The 2nd and 3rd column in Table 2 illustrates user's business goals and associated chains of functional features. For example, client's goal CG1 "Purchase a train ticket" is associated with three chains of functional features, namely, "1-2-3" for the situation when client's data cannot satisfy the goal, "1-2-4-5-6" for the situation when a client satisfies the goal in case without prior booking, and "13-14-5-6" for the case of pre-booking. Analogously functional feature chains are given for all the business goals. Figure 5 illustrates all mappings from business users' (business) goals to the TFM functional features.

Guideline 5: Identification of system goals. Both actors and workers can be users of the computerized system. Functional features to be implemented that are associated with a business goal constitute functionality that is dedicated to reach a corresponding system goal. Thus, each system goal is mapped to a corresponding business goal.

Explanation: The connectedness between business goals and system goals keeps relation between the problem domain and the software domain. Moreover, the identification of system goals (that means we identify functionality that must help an application user to reach this goal) serves to additional functional requirement validation, i.e., it helps in discovering missed functional requirements. Let's consider the last point in more detail. Why the criterion for further use case separation is a goal? A business goal is a product or a service that must be produced, purchased or suggested by the business system. Otherwise, a system goal is some observable result that must be achieved by the computerized system. A busi-

Table 2. Users, goals and TFM functional features

Business User	Business Goal	Functional Feature Chains	Functional Feature Chains to be Implemented	System Goal	System User
1	2	3	4	5	6
Client (actor)	CG1	1-2-3; 1-2-4-5-6; 13-14-5-6;		SysG1	Seller
Client (worker)	CG2	1-2-3; 1-2-4-12;	1-2-3; 1-2-4-12;	SysG2	Client
Client (actor)	CG3	7-8-11; 7-8-9; 7-8-10;		SysG3	Seller
Seller (worker)	SG1	1-2-3; 1-2-4-5-6; 13-14-5-6;	1-2-3; 1-2-4-5-6; 13-14-5-6;	SysG1	Seller
Seller (worker)	SG2	7-8-11; 7-8-9; 7-8-10;	7-8-11;	SysG3	Seller
Seller (worker)	SG3	15	-------	--------	-------

ness goal is being achieved performing business processes. It is the essential principle which can show that a use case should be broken apart; the time gap cannot do it since a use case (especially a business use case) can be long running.

Another reason is that focusing on goals keeps from attempts of unnecessary use case multipli-

cation. For instance, even if someone sets two business goals "Purchasing a train ticket" and "Selling a train ticket", the TFM shows that these business goals are reached performing the same functional feature sequence. In common, business (and system) goals can be achieved using some actions or in other words performing some

Figure 5. Mappings from business and system goals onto the TFM

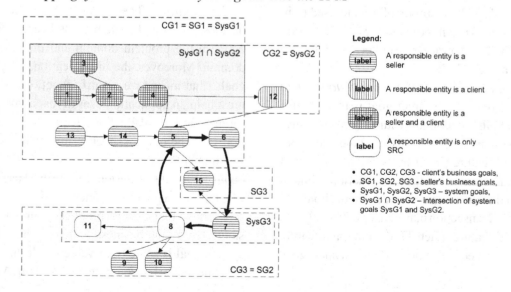

functionality. TFM functional features show all possible functionality of the business system, and functionality that must be implemented in the application. This means that at this stage of modeling we know what business logic is in the problem domain, what functionality will be implemented in order to automate this business logic in the solution domain, and what business goals must be achieved by the real world system and, correspondingly, system goals can be derived. This means that functional features that will be implemented in the solution and are associated within the same business goal are dedicated to achieve the corresponding systems goal.

Illustration: For each identified chain of functional features that helps to achieve a business goal, functional features to be implemented are identified *for each business worker*. Therefore, even the client has business goal CG1 "Purchase a train ticket", he/she will not directly use the system in order to achieve this business goals, and functional features to be implemented are not defined for him/her. This goal will be achieved by the seller while satisfying business goal SG1 "Sell a train ticket". Figure 5 shows this as overlapping of CG1 and SG1. In our example all chains of the TFM functional features will be implemented, except functional features 9, 10, and 15. The common functional feature chains are associated with the same system goal as shown in the 4th and 5th column in Table 2. Figure 5 demonstrates system goal overlapping with business users' goals. Business goals CG1 "Purchase a train ticket" and SG1 "Sell a train ticket" can be reached by reaching the same system goal SysG1 "Sell a train ticket", business goals CG3 "Get money for an unused train ticket" and SG2 "Get back a train ticket" can be reached by satisfying the system goal SysG3 "Return a train ticket" (which excludes functional features 9 and 10), and business goal CG2 "Book a train ticket" can be reached when SysG2 "Book a train ticket" is reached. Business goal SG3 "Create a report about sales" will not

be supported by the planned information system as stated in system requirements.

Guideline 6: Decomposition of the TFM to use cases. The system, whose functionality is described by the TFM, is the subject of the use case diagram. The TFM is decomposed by using system goals. The goals are objectives of use cases. Due decomposition, the main functional cycle is divided into a set of paths (or sequences). After decomposition, each decomposed part of the TFM is to be transformed into a use case and corresponding use case specification.

Illustration: According to the defined system goals SysG1 "Sell a train ticket", SysG2 "Book a train ticket" and SysG3 "Return a train ticket", the TFM will be decomposed into three fragments or three use cases, namely, UC1 "Sell a train ticket", UC2 "Book a train ticket" and UC3 "Return a train ticket" correspondingly. Thus, the main functional cycle *5-6-7-8-5* of the TFM is divided into a set of paths "5-6" and "7-8". The paths between functional features 6 and 7, and 8 and 5 are lost in the use case diagram due to its limitations in representation, but should be specified in specifications of use cases UC1 and UC3. The subject of the use case model is the name of SRC information system. The initial use case diagram is illustrated in Figure 6.

Guideline 7: Identification of actors. A system user, the owner of the system goal, is an actor that communicates with use cases defined to reach this goal. In other words, an entity that enacts the functional feature is transformed into an actor involved in the use case or its step. The fact that the entity belongs to a functional feature is transformed to the "communication" relationship between the actor and use case.

Illustration: As shown in the 6th column in Table 2, a seller is a system user for SysG1 "Sell a train ticket" and SysG3 "Return a train ticket", but a client is a system user for SysG2 "Book a train ticket". Actor "Seller" communicates with UC1 "Sell a train ticket" and UC3 "Return a train ticket". Actor "Client" communicates with UC2

Figure 6. The initial use case diagram of the SRC

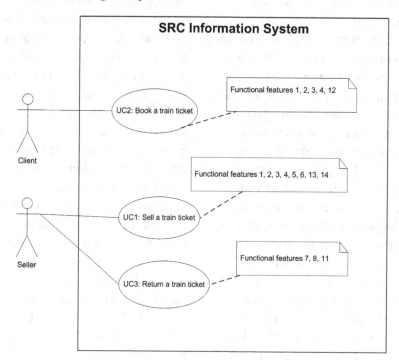

"Book a train ticket". The initial use case model is illustrated in Figure 6.

Guideline 8 (optional): Refinement of use cases. An *inclusion* use case is a common sequence for several use cases. In the TFM, it is intersection of functional feature sets of several system goals. The common functional features should be analyzed, as there can be a situation, when a common functional feature is located in an alternative workflow of the use case, i.e., in a sub-cycle or a branch in the TFM (Figure 7-a). In turn, an *extension* use case shows an alternative way of the scenarios execution. In the TFM, it is a sub-cycle or a branch, existing within the system goal. The point of branch beginning is an extending point (Figure 7-b). In case of subsystem separation from the TFM, system use cases must be defined in the associated subsystem context.

Explanation: The detailed information that is necessary for developers can be kept with a use case as a supporting subordinate, or separately as extended or included use case. A subordinate use

case is just a piece of another use case (Schneider & Winters, 2001).

Illustration: By analyzing intersections of the defined functional feature chains (Table 2, Figure 5), the common functionality of system goals SysG1 "Sell a train ticket" and SysG2 "Book a train ticket" is found. These are two chains of functional features, namely, "1-2-3" and "1-2-4". By analyzing these chains, we decided to create only one use case, although functional feature 3 represents an alternative flow for this use case. However, execution of this functional feature will not affect other functionality, thus it does not require creating any extending use case. Thus, the common part "1-2-4" may be separated as an *inclusion* use case IUC_1-2 "Select a trip" and related to UC1 and UC2 with the "include" relationship. The obtained use cases are illustrated in Figure 8.

Guideline 9: Exploration of a system use case and its specification. A functional feature is transformed into a step of a use case. A set of functional features is transformed into a use case and

Figure 7. Definition of included and extending use cases by analyzing the TFM

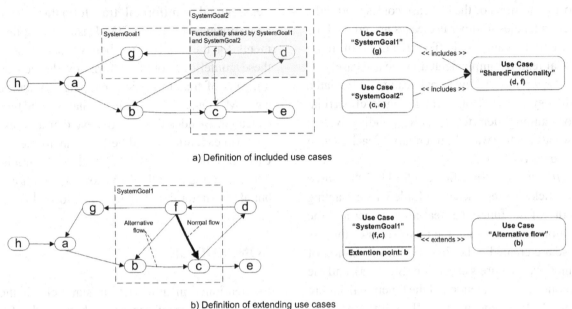

a) Definition of included use cases

b) Definition of extending use cases

Figure 8. The refined use case diagram of the SRC

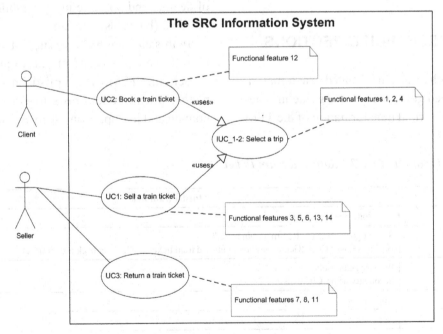

its steps. Optional execution of the step (IF condition), and cyclic execution of the steps (WHILE or FOR cycles) can be also defined. However, it is impossible to define synchronous or asynchro-

nous executions of these steps without human participation. Functional feature's object, action and result are parts of the name of the corresponding use case or step. Preconditions and postconditions are mapped to preconditions and post-conditions of the use case correspondingly. Dependencies to other use cases are created according to cause-and-effect relations of functional features implemented in the use case.

Explanation: Functional features associated with a system goal together with cause-effect relations among them form a corresponding system use case. In this way, the boundary of each system use case is defined.

Illustration: Specification for UC3 "Return a train ticket" is represented in Table 3. If an enacting entity of the functional feature is a user and the computerized system, then two steps of the use case are created – the first one for invocation of functional feature's execution (Step 2-a), and the second one for execution of the functional feature (Step 2-b). Dependency to UC1 "Sell a train ticket" is defined according to the cause-and-effect relation between functional features 6 and 7.

FUTURE RESEARCH DIRECTIONS

Future research direction is related to automation of the described guidelines. These guidelines describe manual formal transformation of the TFM to a use case model and use case specifications, i.e., manual semiformal transformation from CIM-Business Model to CIM-Business Requirements for the System. We believe that most of these guidelines could be formally defined by a means of transformation mapping languages, e.g. OMG Qurey/View/Transformation, and thus executed. Besides that, we believe that use case scenario execution could be also transformed to UML 2 Activity Diagrams and Class Diagrams, thus extracting from the TFM not only functional but also structural information in a formal way.

CONCLUSION

As mentioned in Introduction, simplicity is the main advantages of use cases, but a lack of a solid background is a cause of their weaknesses such as possible incompleteness, different levels of details, and possible incompatibility with the problem (business) domain.

In this chapter, we have suggested identification of use cases based on the formal business model, the TFM. The holistic nature of this mathematical model draws together a business domain and its supporting software, thus solving

Table 3. Specification of UC3 "Return a train ticket"

Name	Return a train ticket
Identification	Functional features 7,8,11
Brief description	System goals: SysG3 "Return a train ticket". Business goals: CG3 "Get money for an unused train ticket", SG2 "Get back a train ticket".
Actors	Primary actor: Seller Secondary actor: Client
Preconditions	None
Postconditions	None
Main flow	1. The use case begins when the Seller selects "Return a train ticket" 2-a. The Seller invokes "check the validity of a ticket" 2-b. The SRC checks the validity of a ticket 3. The SRC completes the return of a ticket 4. The SRC prints out the receipt of a return
Alternative flows	None
Dependencies	"UC1: Sell a train ticket"

an issue of use case incompatibility, validates the completeness of use cases, and allows operating with use cases at different levels of details keeping understanding of those levels in the common view on the business system. Besides that dependencies among use cases are formal and explicit, because of formal and explicit dependencies among business and system goals.

REFERENCES

Antón, A. I. (1996). Goal-Based Requirements Analysis. *Second IEEE International Conference on Requirements Engineering (ICRE '96)* (pp. 136-144). Colorado Springs, CO: IEEE.

Arlow, J., & Neustadt, I. (2005). *UML2 and the Unified Process: Practical Object-Oriented Analysis and Design*. Reading, MA: Addison-Wesley, Pearson Education.

Asnina, E. (2006). The Formal Approach to Problem Domain Modelling Within Model Driven Architecture. In *Proceedings of the 9th International Conference "Information Systems Implementation and Modelling" (ISIM'06), April 25-26, 2006, Přerov, Czech Republic, 1st edn.* (pp. 97-104). Ostrava, Czech Republic: Jan Štefan MARQ.

Berard, E. V. (1998). *Be Careful With "Use Cases"*. The Object Agency, Inc.

Che, Y., Wang, G., Wen, X., & Ren, B. (2009). Research on Computational Independent Model in the Enterprise Information System Development Mode Based on Model Driven and Software Component. *International Conference on Interoperability for Enterprise Software and Applications China, 2009. IESA '09.* (pp. 85 - 89). Washington, DC: IEEE.

Cockburn, A. (2000). *Writing Effective Use Cases*. Reading, MA: Addison-Wesley Professional.

Dubielewicz, I., & Hnatkovska, B. (2005). Structural specification of business processes. In *Proceedings of 8th Conference "Information Systems Implementation and Modeling", April 19-20, 2005, Hradec nad Moravici, Czech Republic* (pp. 111-118). Ostrava, Czech Republic: Jan Štefan MARQ.

Eriksson, H.-E., & Penker, M. (2000). *Business Modeling with UML: Business Patterns at Work*. Toronto: John Wiley & Sons, Inc.

Ferg, S. (2003, February 15). *What's Wrong with Use Cases?* Retrieved January 30, 2010, from Jackson Methods home page: http://www.jacksonworkbench.co.uk/stevefergspages/papers/ferg--whats_wrong_with_use_cases.html

Firesmith, D. G. (2002). *Use Cases: the Pros and Cons*. Retrieved November 30, 2009, from Knowledge Systems Corporation: http://www.ksc.com/article7.htm

Grangel, R., Chalmeta, R., & Campos, C. (2007). Using UML Profiles for Enterprise Knowledge Modelling. In *Proceedings of the 26th International Conference on Conceptual Modeling (ER 2007), the 3rd International Workshop on Foundations and Practices of UML (FP-UML 2007), LNCS, Computer Science, Theory & Methods* (pp. 125-132). Berlin: Springer Verlag.

Hendryx, S. (2003a, January). *A Home for Business Models in the OMG*. Retrieved November 30, 2009, from Business Rules Journal: http://www.BRCommunity.com/b127.php

Hendryx, S. (2003b). *Integrating Computation Independent Business Modeling Languages into the MDA with UML 2*. Retrieved November 30, 2009, from Object Management Group: http://www.omg.org/docs/ad/03-01-32.doc

Jackson, M. (1999). *The Real World*. Retrieved November 20, 2009, from Problem Analysis and the Problem Frames Approach. Jackson Methods Home Page: http://www.jacksonworkbench.co.uk/stevefergspages/pfa/index.html

Jackson, M. (2005). *Problem Frames and Software Engineering*. Retrieved November 30, 2009, from Problem Analysis and the Problem Frames Approach. Jackson Methods Home Page: http://www.jacksonworkbench.co.uk/stevefergspages/pfa/index.html

Jacobson, I., Christerson, M., Jonsson, P., & Overgaard, G. (1992). *Object-Oriented Software Engineering: A Use Case Driven Approach*. Reading, MA: Addison-Wesley.

Jeary, S., Fouad, A., & Phalp, K. (2008, July 3). *Extending the Model Driven Architecture with a pre-CIM level*. Retrieved January 20, 2010, from Proceedings of the 1st International Workshop on Business Support for MDA co-located with TOOLS EUROPE 2008: http://ftp.informatik.rwth-aachen.de/Publications/CEUR-WS/Vol-376/

Leffingwell, D., & Widrig, D. (2003). *Managing Software Requirements: a use case approach* (2nd ed.). Reading, MA: Addison-Wesley.

OMG. (2009, February). *UML 2.2 Superstructure*. Retrieved January 30, 2010, from http://www.omg.org/spec/UML/2.2/

Osis, J. (1969). Topological Model of System Functioning (in Russian). *Automatics and Computer Science. J. of Acad. of Sc.*, 6, 44–50.

Osis, J. (1997). Development of Object-Oriented Methods for Hybrid System Analysis and Design. In *Proc. of the 23rd Conference of the Association of Simula Users (ASU)*, (pp. 162-170). Stara Lesna, Slovakia.

Osis, J. (2003). Extension of Software Development Process for Mechatronic and Embedded Systems. In *Proceedings of the 32nd International Conference on Computers and Industrial Engineering, August 11-13, 2003* (pp. 305-310). Limerick, Ireland: University of Limerick.

Osis, J., & Asnina, E. (2008). Enterprise Modeling for Information System Development within MDA. In *Proceedings of the 41st Annual Hawaii International Conference on System Sciences (HICSS 2008)* (p. 490). USA: IEEE.

Osis, J., Asnina, E., & Grave, A. (2008). Computation Independent Representation of the Problem Domain in MDA. *e-Informatica. Software Engineering Journal*, 2(1), 29–26. Retrieved from http://www.e-informatyka.pl/wiki/e-Informatica_-_Volume_2.

Podeswa, H. (2005). *UML for the IT Business Analyst: A Practical Guide to Object-Oriented Requirements Gathering*. Boston: Thomson Course Technology PTR.

Schach, S. R. (1999). *Classical and Object-Oriented Software Engineering with UML and Java* (International edition). New York: WCB/McGraw-Hill.

Schneider, G., & Winters, J. (2001). *Applying Use Cases. A Practical Guide* (2nd ed.). Reading, MA: The Addison-Wesley.

KEY TERMS AND DEFINITIONS

Cause-and-Effect Relation: A relation between two functional features of the system where appearance and execution of one functional feature is caused (generated) by the other functional feature without any intermediate functionality.

Computation Independent Model: A Computation Independent Model (CIM) is a model defined within OMG Model-Driven Architecture as a primary model. This model reflects system and software knowledge from the business perspective. The CIM may contain business knowledge about system organization, roles, functions, processes and activities, documentation, constraints etc. The CIM must contain business requirements for the system.

Functional Feature: A functional characteristic of the system that is needed to reach system's functioning goal.

Functional Requirements: Requirements for the software set by business people, hardware and an environment where the software will operate. Functional requirements contain business and technological knowledge that must be kept and implemented in the software.

Goal: A goal is a valuable objective that a system must reach in order to satisfy its user. There are business system and software system goals that relate to the enterprise (or business) and software correspondingly. Software system goals must be set in compliance with the business system goals.

Topological Functioning Model: A model based on system theory and mathematics that specifies functionality and structure of a complex system as a connected topological space of system's functional characteristics and cause-and-effect relations among them.

Use Case: A use case is a fragment of system's functionality. Execution of this fragment must reach a goal set by system's user, i.e., must return a valuable result to the user. Use cases are related by cause-and-effect relations.

Chapter 5
A Multidimensional Approach for Concurrent Model–Driven Automation Engineering

Sebastian Rose
Technische Universität Darmstadt, Germany

Marius Lauder
Technische Universität Darmstadt, Germany

Michael Schlereth
Siemens AG, Germany

Andy Schürr
Technische Universität Darmstadt, Germany

ABSTRACT

Automation engineering heavily relies on concurrent model-driven design activities across multiple disciplines. The customization and integration of domain-specific modeling languages and tools play an important role. This contribution introduces a conceptual framework for this purpose that combines the modeling standards of the Object Management Group (OMG) with precisely defined specification techniques based on metamodeling and graph grammars. The main focus is on the development of synchronization mechanisms between modeling tools and on the presentation of some extensions of the underlying graph grammar formalism motivated by its application to a real-world scenario. These techniques are presented by a case study about the application of graph grammars within automation engineering.

INTRODUCTION

Mechatronic engineering is about integration of different engineering disciplines, mainly mechanical engineering, electrical engineering, and software engineering. Within the machine and plant engineering process, software engineering is part of automation engineering, which deals with configuration and programming of devices like programmable logic controllers (PLC), motion controllers, and human machine interface (HMI)

DOI: 10.4018/978-1-61692-874-2.ch005

panels. Additional minor engineering disciplines are pneumatic and hydraulic engineering. Each discipline follows its own design methodology and uses specific models. Within the system development process, the sub-processes of the mechatronic engineering disciplines run in parallel with their own design iterations and design workflows. Furthermore, each discipline has a set of mainstream design tools for different types of models, different design principles, and a way of thinking that has evolved over time, depending on the maturity of a specific discipline.

As a consequence, the development processes of automation engineering are – at least on a first glance – considerably more complex than the established development processes for the software engineering subdiscipline of automation engineering. Any attempt to apply the principles of model-driven development as originally defined by the Object Management Group under the trademark MDA (Model-Driven Architecture) (Object Management Group, 2009) is likely to fail for the following reasons: MDA puts its main focus on the development of a single sequence of models on different *levels of abstraction* such that models on a more concrete level are automatically derived from models on a more abstract level. Usually, models on three levels of abstraction or refinement are distinguished: Computation Independent Models (CIM), Platform Independent Models (PIM), and Platform Specific Models (PSM).

In contrast, *Concurrent Model-Driven Automation Engineering (CMDAE)* as developed by Siemens AG and TU Darmstadt relies on a multidimensional framework for model classification and manipulation purposes. The *CMDAE Hypercube* distinguishes five main model classification dimensions:

1. Concurrent Engineering Disciplines
2. Metamodeling Layers
3. Domain Customization Steps
4. Abstraction Levels
5. Evolution Timeline

The classification of a (meta-)model within these five dimensions clarifies its role in a mechatronic engineering project like the case study presented in the following section. Furthermore, the CMDAE hypercube simplifies the systematic study of all kinds of (meta-)model manipulation activities and their interdependencies in an organization. The adoption of a new modeling language version in one discipline may, for instance, require that (1) its relationships to modeling languages used in other disciplines has to be modified, (2) old models must be converted such that they are legal instances of the new language version, (3) language specializations (profiles) for different domains must be updated, and (4) language preserving transformations to higher/lower levels of abstractions have to be modified, too. Different subsets of these ranges of so-called *megamodeling* activities (Kurtev, Bézivin, Jouault, & Valduriez, 2006) are studied by many research groups around the world, but a common classification framework comparable with the CMDAE hypercube that covers all these activities was missing until now.

In the Section "Background" we discuss related work activities. Thereafter, in Section "The Running Example and the CMDAE Hypercube" we present a running example that is used for illustration purposes. In Section "The CMDAE Hypercube" we describe the CMDAE hypercube and its dimensions in more detail. Section "The Metamodeling Pyramid (Dimension M)" and "Collaboration across Engineering Disciplines (Dimension C)" then focus on the hypercube dimensions (M) and (C) and present a number of extensions of our graph-grammar-based model engineering approach that have been developed in the context a joint research project between Siemens AG and Technische Universität Darmstadt. Section "Application and evaluation of CMDAE concepts" afterwards sketches how the first version of a CMDAE prototype, which supports concurrent model-driven mechatronic engineering activities, has been developed using the meta-case tool MOFLON (Amelunxen, Königs, Rötschke,

& Schürr, 2006). Finally, open issues and future work plans are presented in Section "Future Research Directions"; whereas Section "Conclusion" contains some final thoughts.

BACKGROUND

The increasing popularity of model-driven engineering activities has the side effect that many system development projects are running into the problems sketched in the preceding section to manage thousands of modeling artefacts across different disciplines. The systematic study of models, metamodels, and all kinds of relationships between them – sometimes summarized by the term *modelware* (Institut National de Recherche en Informatique et en Automatique (INRIA), 2009) – is a relatively new research area. Research activities focused on the integration of CASE tools and their underlying modeling languages were initiated several years ago (Brown, Carney, Morris, Smith, & Zarrella, 1994), (Nagl, 1996), but a more comprehensive view including the management of modeling language definitions and model transformations was missing for a long time. Megamodeling and modeling-in-the-large research activities (Klar, Königs, & Schürr, 2007) address this problem domain: (de-)composition, abstraction, versioning, and integration of models, metamodels, and their transformations. The term megamodeling introduced in (Bézivin, Jouault, & Valduriez, 2004) addresses the management of models and metamodels. Nevertheless, a comprehensive conceptual framework for the categorization of (meta-)models and their relationships is still missing. The CMDAE hypercube presented here is a first step towards the definition of such a framework.

More specifically, management of activities related to dimension (C) of our hypercube, i.e. the concurrent development of models using quite a number of different domain-specific modelling languages and their related COTS tools, is

still a major issue from a model transformation point of view. Today, industrial solutions for the management of traceability relationships (Geensys, 2009) are available, but the development of techniques that support incremental propagation of consistency re-establishing changes is still an active research area. NAOMI (Denton, Jones, Srinivasan, Owens, & Buskens, 2008) is an experimental platform from the Lockheed Martin Advanced Technology Laboratories that addresses dependencies between models based on different domain specific modelling languages. NAOMI focuses on the implementation of a multimodel repository that supports version management and incremental propagation of changed attribute values. For an overview of other frameworks supporting the implementation of tool and model integration solutions the reader is referred to (Dörr & Schürr, 2004) due to the fact that this chapter puts a main focus on a conceptual framework for model management activities as well as on the further development of a high-level model transformation language; activities related to the development of a tool integration framework are out-of-scope here.

The special journal section (Schürr & Dörr, 2005) summarizes the state-of-the-art of modelling tool integration technologies from a model transformation point of view; for a summary and categorization of model transformation languages in general the reader is referred to (Mens, Czarnecki, & Van Gorp, 2005). This survey distinguishes between unidirectional and bidirectional transformation languages. Unidirectional languages have the major disadvantage that separate transformations have to be implemented for the three different consistency checking and re-establishing scenarios mentioned earlier. On the other hand, bidirectional transformation languages such as QVT Relational (Object Management Group, 2008) or Triple Graph Grammars (TGGs) (Schürr, 1995) as introduced here are still rather immature and lack expressiveness, when the regarded relationships between models are complex. The reader is referred to (Czarnecki, Foster, Hu, Lämmel, Schürr, & Terwilliger, 2009) for a survey of different sorts of bidirectional languages and a summary of open research problems. For a detailed description of another approach using TGGs for model transformation and synchronization the reader is referred to (Giese & Wagner, 2009).

TGGs as used in this chapter are a category of bidirectional transformation languages that are especially well-suited for the declarative and visual specification of consistency relationships between pairs of models like QVT Relational, but avoid the problems concerning the imprecise definition of the semantics of QVT. In this contribution we introduced an extended version of TGGs that solves the following problems concerning their expressiveness: (1) m-to-n relationships can now be handled properly, (2) points for user interaction are now specified explicitly as rule parameters in contrast to other TGG approaches that support user interaction implicitly (Körtgen & Mosler, 2008), (Körtgen & Heukamp, 2008) and (3) the «optional create» concept suggested in (Kindler & Wagner, 2007) is introduced for the first time with a well-defined semantics.

THE RUNNING EXAMPLE AND THE CMDAE HYPERCUBE

Concurrent Model-Driven Automation Engineering (CMDAE) introduces a new methodology for automation engineering as part of the mechatronic development process of machine or plant builders (The concepts of MDAE can be applied to machine engineering as well as to plant engineering. For reasons of simplicity we will talk in the following about machine engineering only). Within machine development, automation engineering has evolved from a standalone design activity at the end of a design process to a concurrent activity related to other design disciplines like mechanical or electrical engineering with many interdisciplinary design dependencies. Therefore, machine engineering

faces two challenges: adapt the well-established development processes of mechanical engineering to mechatronic development and establish an interdisciplinary exchange of design models between different mechatronic disciplines. Coming from the concepts of model-driven architecture in software engineering, model-driven automation engineering (CMDAE) sets the focus on the second challenge: the exchange and alignment of models needed for hardware and software development of automation devices. Model-Driven automation engineering does not claim to provide new answers to the first challenge, the definition of new mechatronic development processes, but helps to streamline existing (sub-)processes and to establish new interactions between existing processes by integrating design models from different engineering disciplines.

CMDAE captures these existing design models with the technique of metamodeling as described in Section "The Metamodeling Pyramid (Dimension M)". Within mechanical engineering, the leading engineering discipline of machine construction, the concepts of models of mechanical items and mappings between models are already established. Abstraction of models, which we will establish as dimension (A) for automation engineering within the CMDAE hypercube, is common for physical items as shown in Figure 1. Concurrent engineering within an engineering discipline and between collaborating engineering disciplines, the dimension (C) of the CMDAE hypercube, is partly established by PDM (product data management) systems (VDI-Richtlinie, VDI 2219). CMDAE will extend this document-centric approach to a model-driven engineering process which links the content of design models of different engineering disciplines to speed up development and to minimize errors due to missing interdisciplinary data alignment. These links between design models as shown in the lower part of Figure 1 are created by triple graph grammars presented in Section "Introduction to Standard Triple Graph Grammars".

Figure 1. Multiple perspectives of the High-Bay Warehouse Application Example © Siemens AG 2010 All rights reserved. Used with permission

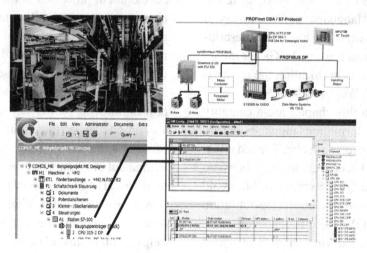

The concepts of CMDAE are demonstrated by an application example from the mechatronic engineering workflow of a machine builder as defined by (VDI-Richtlinie, VDI 2206). In this iterative design workflow, the mechanical engineering discipline defines the mechanical construction and the operating sequence of the machine. Electrical engineering is involved in the selection and wiring of sensors and actuators required for the machine operation. Automation engineering combines the expected behavior from the mechanical engineering with the specified sensors and actuators from electrical engineering to control hard- and software.

For the demonstration of the integration between concurrent engineering disciplines, the C-dimension of the MDAE hypercube, we will focus on the bi-directional integration between the design models of the electrical engineering and the automation engineering discipline with a special emphasis on exchange of information about the automation devices used. This information consists of the type of devices used and the wiring of the terminals of these devices. The design models might be changed concurrently in electrical engineering and in automation engineering. A change of the automation device due to

performance requirements must be reflected in the bill of material of the electrical cabinet. A change of the device terminals in electrical engineering for optimized cabinet layout requires a change of the input/output signals used in control functions. Change propagation is supported by links between the design models created by triple graph grammars as mentioned above.

Application Example: High-Bay Warehouse Automation

The dimensions of model transformations within the CMDAE hypercube will be explained by an application example from the logistics domain: the automation of the storage and retrieval machine of a high-bay warehouse. The storage and retrieval machine runs within the warehouse aisle and accesses the storage shelf to pick and place goods (depicted in the upper-left part of Figure 1).

The upper-right part of Figure 1 shows a typical configuration of automation devices for the storage and retrieval machine. A Siemens SIMATIC CPU315-2 DP PLC is connected by a fieldbus network to the warehouse control systems and to field devices such as distributed I/O with Siemens SIMATIC ET 200 or data matrix systems (e.g. for identification of goods). Within our application example, we will focus on the configuration of the PLC with its I/O terminals and leave out the field bus configuration for reasons of simplicity.

Integration between Concurrent Engineering Disciplines (C)

The concurrent engineering disciplines considered in this example are automation engineering and electrical engineering. The engineering tool *SIMATIC STEP 7* (Siemens AG, 2009)) is used to define the hardware configuration and programming of the automation devices within automation engineering. Within our application example, we will focus on the hardware configuration. The hardware configuration describes the type and parameters of PLC used for the I/O modules and the fieldbus configuration. The lower part of Figure 1 shows a screenshot of the STEP 7 hardware configuration on the right-hand side. The catalog of automation devices available in STEP 7 is shown on the right within the STEP 7 main window. These automation devices with their order number and parameter definition can be used on the left-hand side within the main window to build a mounting rack of an automation controller configuration that can be inserted in an electrical cabinet. Within the STEP 7 hardware configuration at the bottom of the STEP 7 main windows, this rack is filled by a PS 307 power supply unit, a CPU315-2 DP PLC and a DI16 digital input module. For the application of model synchronizations, this hardware configuration can be imported and exported in *SimaticML* file format (Siemens AG, 2006)). Within electrical engineering, the mounting rack with automation devices is part of the engineering of electrical cabinets. The placement of electrical cabinets and mounting racks is described by the location-oriented structure model according to the international standard IEC 61346-1 (International Standard, IEC 61346-1). Beside the location-oriented structure model, IEC 61346 also defines a function-oriented structure

and a product-oriented structure, which are not part of our application example. The lower part of Figure 1 shows the mounting rack with the automation devices as part of the location-oriented structure model in the electrical engineering tool Comos ET on the left-hand side (Comos Industry Solutions GmbH, 2009). Within our application example, the location-oriented structure model can be exported and imported from the electrical engineering tool in XML Metadata Interchange (XMI) format according to (International Standard, ISO/IEC 19503).

THE CMDAE HYPERCUBE

Figure 2 depicts the CMDAE hypercube as a star chart (Chambers, Cleveland, & Tukey, 1983) that is useful for the visualization of multidimensional information. The dotted and the dashed line in this diagram represent a pair of a specific SimaticML model version and its related location model version (dimension E) as introduced in the previous section with their classifications along the CMDAE dimensions.

The five CMDAE dimensions are defined as follows:

1. *Concurrent Engineering Disciplines (C)*: concurrent or simultaneous model-driven engineering introduces the principles of model-driven development in different, but related disciplines; keeping concurrently manipulated models of different (sub-) disciplines – that deal with different aspects of a mechatronic system – in a consistent state will be called *horizontal model integration* in the following.

2. *Metamodeling Layers (M)*: the OMG concept of metamodeling layers (International Standard, ISO/IEC 19502) is adopted without any modifications – except the fact that different (meta-)modeling- approaches may coexist on *each* metamodeling layer includ-

Figure 2. Dimensions of the CMDAE-Hypercube

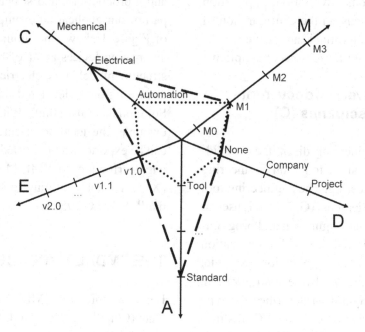

ing the layer M_3, where different technological metamodeling spaces are often used in parallel in huge projects; furthermore, different domain-specific modeling approaches are simultaneously defined and used on layer M_2 and M_1 that take the specifics of different electrical engineering tools or different implementation strategies like central or decentral automation concepts into account.

3. *Domain Customization Steps (D)*: often modeling components on layers M_1 and above must be adapted to a specific application domain and/or for the purposes of a specific project. UML profiles are an excellent example for the customization of a general purpose modeling language on layer M_2 to a specific domain, whereas the instantiation of a generic model (framework) for the development of a specific application takes place on layer M_1. Finally, the tagging mechanism of MOF supports the principle of customization on metamodeling layer M_3.

4. *Abstraction Levels (A)*: model abstraction generalizes the OMG principle of CIM, PIM,

and PSM levels across all metamodeling layers; i.e., the distinction between PIM and PSM models is not only restricted to layer M_1, but also used on layer M_2 and M_3. On layer M_3, the principle of platform abstraction allows one to replace one metamodeling technique by another one i.e., it guarantees a certain degree of independence from so-called technological metamodeling spaces (e.g., replace EMF by MOF or Step/Express by XMI). Keeping models on different levels of abstraction in a consistent state will be called *vertical model integration* in the following.

5. *Evolution Timeline (E)*: all models that are used for the development of a specific product may and will evolve over time. Incremental and iterative development processes that are specific for a regarded discipline continuously create new revisions of models; even metamodels and metametamodels change from time to time with the distribution of new releases of modeling and metamodeling languages. Activities related to the evolution

dimension are summarized under the name *model configuration management*.

The above introduced five dimensions of the CMDAE hypercube are used within our projects as a guideline for the classification, formalization, evaluation, selection, and further development of modeling and metamodeling tools and techniques. Additional dimensions that deal with the decomposition and modularization of models as well as with the definition of variants and families of models are studied and will be added in the future.

THE METAMODELING PYRAMID (DIMENSION M)

Different modeling (language) standards and a variety of related engineering tools are used in automation engineering. Unfortunately, most of these standards and their relationships are not precisely defined. As a consequence, it is difficult to exchange models between different tools as well as to keep models of different disciplines in a consistent state. As a first step out of this modeling muddle, metamodels are used to define the abstract syntax and static semantics of a modeling language precisely. A metamodel defines a language's abstract syntax collecting

and relating terms and properties of a modeling language standard or tool similar to object-oriented design using classes, attributes, and associations. Complex static semantics rules are usually defined using some kind of predicate logic formulas. The dynamic semantics of a modeling language is an optional part of a specification and specifies the behavior of model instances. Therefore, description of behavior is mandatory for executable models like statecharts or petri nets. Model transformations can be used for describing the behavior of a modeling language usually adopting an operational semantics approach (see de Lara, Jaramillo, Ermel, Taentzer, & Ehrig, 2004 and Jurack, Lambers, Mehner, & Taentzer, 2008 for a detailed example).

The OMG introduced the four-layer metadata architecture for this purpose. Figure 3 depicts the four-layer architecture based on the picture in the OMG standard using terms from our running example. On the lowest layer called information we will find instances of real-world objects. The depicted objects represent CPUs in the automation context. These real-world *CPUs* are instances of AutomationEquipment objects on the next layer, the so-called model layer. The AutomationEquipment metaobject requires that each CPU has a name as well as two attributes with name model and speed of type Attribute, respectively. The

Figure 3. Four Layer Metadata Architecture Adapted from (International Standard, ISO/IEC 19502, p. 10)

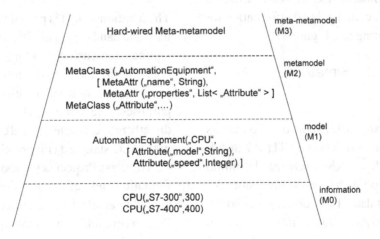

metamodel layer defines the modeling language concepts AutomationEquipment and Attribute as instances of the metametaobjects MetaClass and MetaAttr.

Briefly, elements on layer M_n have *instance-of* relationships to elements on layer M_{n-1} (Kühne, 2006). As a consequence a (meta-)model on layer M_n describes the language of all legal models on layer M_{n-1} precisely. The single metamodel on layer M_3 is an instance of itself, thereby avoiding the construction of an infinite hierarchy of metamodels. It is called Meta Object Facility (MOF) 2.0 (Object Management Group, 2006a) and represents a modeling language for the definition of modeling languages. For further details on metamodeling or the OMG architecture the reader is referred to (Object Management Group, 2006a).

Metamodeling

Metamodels belong to category M_2 within dimension M of the CMDAE hypercube. Related models are categorized as M_1, but both belong to the same category in dimension C (Collaboration). Regarding our example, we need to define a metamodel for each modeling language used in the mechatronic engineering process. Within our example automation engineering uses the SimaticML-format for exchanging hardware configuration information and the IEC 61346 (International Standard, IEC 61346-1) location model to capture location-related information for electrical engineering (cf. Figure 4).

Introduction of the SimaticML Metamodel

STEP 7 provides an XML export function for its hardware configuration data. The STEP 7 installation files include an XML schema definition (XSD) (World Wide Web Consortium, 2008) for this import/export data. This format is called SimaticML (Siemens AG, 2006). Since the relation

between the XML files and their XSD is similar to the relation of models to their metamodel, it is possible to translate an XSD into a metamodel and vice versa (International Standard, ISO/IEC 19503). The result of this (semi-automatic) translation process, the relevant part of the SimaticML metamodel, is depicted in Figure 4a).

ProjectT is the root node for an actual project. ProjectT contains a ProjectObjectListT which contains all further elements of the hardware configuration description (HW Config) of a STEP 7 project. ProjectT derives from ObjectBaseT, as all elements in the following. The ProjectObjectListT contains instances of DeviceT, which represents a controller for other devices. Each DeviceT element additionally may refer to a collection of type DeviceItemT, which are elements of a DeviceObjectListT. Thus, elements are connected via associations with names DeviceTReferencesDeviceObjectListT and DeviceObjectListTReferencesDeviceItemT. A DeviceItemT stands for all kind of automation hardware controlled by the corresponding DeviceT. Each DeviceItemT instance may include a collection of GenericAttributeT elements. GenericAttributeT elements are referred by a container element called GenericAttributeListT. This container is related to DeviceItemT by an association named DeviceItemTReferencesGenericAttributeListT.

Introduction to Location Metamodel

The location model is part of the IEC 61346 standard and can be used in different engineering disciplines (dimension C). Our example metamodel contains the location-oriented structure of IEC 61346-1 and is used for electrical engineering purposes. The metamodel of the location model directly reflects the terms and concepts introduced in the IEC standard (Figure 4b).

The class Project is the root element of all information and defines a container for everything related to an electrical engineering project. Each Project contains elements of type Location, which

Figure 4. a) SimaticML Metamodel b) Location-oriented model Metamodel

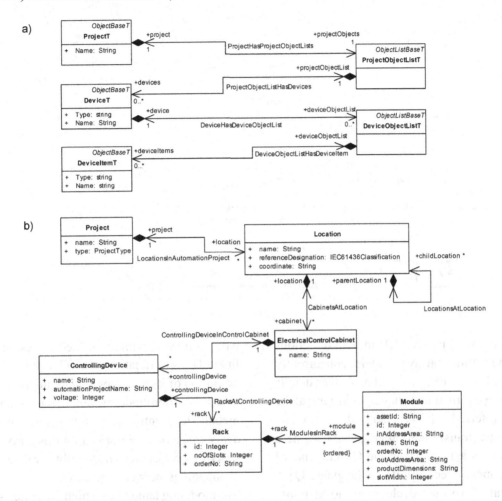

correspond to physical locations like buildings, rooms or areas. Each location may contain locations as well. Thus, an association named LocationsAtLocation points from Location to itself. Each Location can hold ElectricalControlCabinets for placing controlling devices, racks and modules inside. Only the element ControllingDevice is referenced directly by an association, because racks and modules build a hierarchy reflected by the metamodel. Each controlling device contains a number of racks. Thus, element Rack is connected to element ControllingDevice by an association named RacksAtControllingDevice. Modules like CPUs or IODevices are placed on slots within a rack. An element named Module represents these

elements and is connected via an association named ModulesInRack. The metamodel contains some additional elements, which are not relevant in the following.

COLLABORATION ACROSS ENGINEERING DISCIPLINES (DIMENSION C)

The horizontal integration of models and metamodels (dimension C) from different disciplines relies on a so-called *bidirectional model transformation language*. A single specification written in such a language can be used to propagate

Figure 5. Basic TGG metamodel for the integration of the Location model and SimaticML

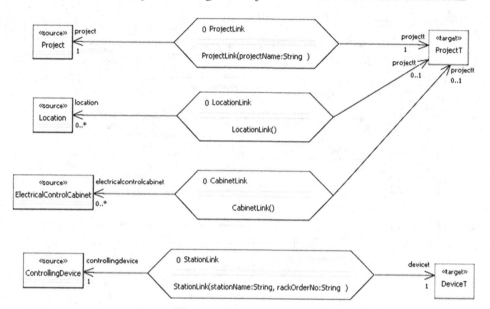

changes between two models in both directions from time to time that are otherwise concurrently evolving. For a survey as well as further details concerning bidirectional languages in general the reader is referred to (Czarnecki et al., 2009). The bidirectional transformation language used here resembles on a first glance the OMG standard QVT or, more precisely, its sublanguage QVT Relational of a visual declarative model transformation language (Object Management Group, 2008), but has a well-defined formalization based on so-called Triple Graph Grammars (TGGs).

Introduction to Standard Triple Graph Grammars

Schürr introduced in 1994 TGGs (Schürr, 1995) as an extension of Pratt's pair grammar approach from 1971 (Pratt, 1971). TGGs aim at the declarative specification of model to model integration rules and couple two graphs explicitly with correspondence links. TGGs consist of a metamodel, which integrates the metamodels of the two regarded modeling languages. In addition, TGGs consist of a set of rewriting rules that generate consistent pairs of models with associated correspondence links. The specification of a TGG starts with the definition of its metamodel that integrates in our case the location model metamodel and SimaticML metamodel. It introduces a number of *correspondence link type declarations* for this purpose that describe consistency (traceability) relationships or mappings between elements of the regarded two modeling languages which are called *source* and *target* (cf. Figure 5). Each correspondence link type (short: link type) owns a *TGG rule* that declaratively describes the simultaneous evolution of integrated models and links in between. The latest state-of-the-art of TGG theory can be found in (Schürr & Klar, 2008).

The left-hand side of Figure 5 depicts elements of the location model metamodel that are marked with the stereotype «source». Correspondingly, the right-hand side of the figure shows a simplified metamodel of SimaticML (elements labeled with «target»). Finally, the center of Figure 5 introduces the correspondence link types used in our scenario.

Figure 6 shows an excerpt of a location model and its related SimaticML model, where

Figure 6. Object diagram of simultaneously evolved models

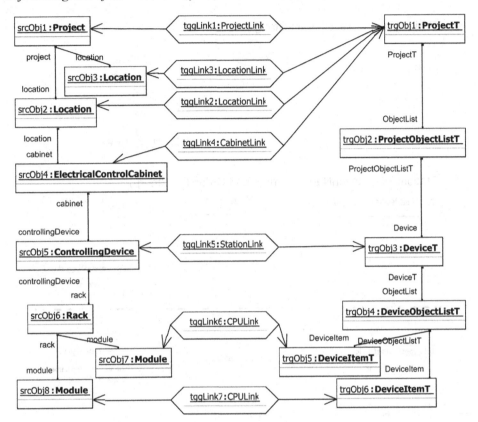

corresponding modeling elements are connected by appropriately typed correspondence links. At the top a Project object is linked to a ProjectT object. Furthermore, Location objects and the ElectricalControlCabinet objects are also linked to the ProjectT object. The bottom of the figure shows two Module objects that are linked to DeviceItemT objects.

The top of Figure 7 depicts the TGG rule for the correspondence type ProjectLink, which is used as a kind of axiom to start the parallel evolution of the integrated models of Figure 6. This rule creates a pair of linked ProjectLink and Project objects in a location model (left-hand side) and SimaticML model (right-hand side), respectively. These two elements are the so-called *primary* (source and target) *objects* of this rule. The parameter projectName of the rule is assigned to both name attributes. The value for this param-

eter has to be passed to the rule, whenever the rule ProjectLink is used to populate an empty pair of source and target models with their project root objects. Additionally, the TGG rule creates a ProjectObjectListT which is associated with ProjectT. This object is a *non-primary object* i.e., it is not directly associated with a correspondence link, but attached to a primary object of the rule.

A second TGG rule (cf. bottom of Figure 7) is responsible for creating an arbitrary number of ControllingDevice objects that correspond to DeviceT objects in the SimaticML model. Please notice that both rules depicted in Figure 7 are chosen for explanation purposes. The use-case described so far includes more rules not depicted here. The rule depicted at the bottom of Figure 7 associates a new ControllingDevice object of the source model with a new Device object of the target model. This rule is composed of two dif-

Figure 7. TGG rule of ProjectLink type (top) and TGG rule of StationLink type (bottom)

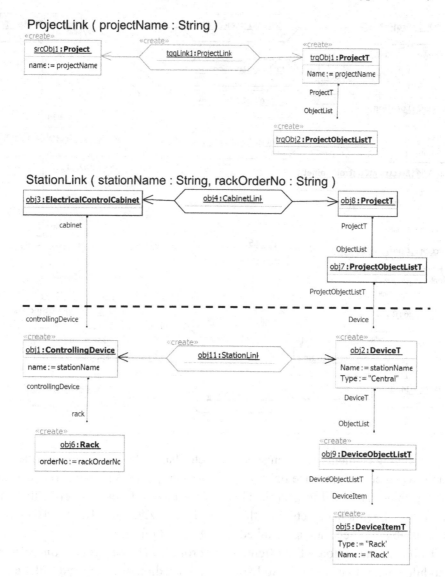

ferent sorts of elements: *context elements* above the dashed line and «create» elements below the dashed line. Furthermore, the rule assigns the value stationName to the attributes Controlling-Device.name and DeviceT.name. The value stationName is a parameter of the TGG rule itself and has to be provided by the model synchronization algorithm that triggers the rule application (or the end-user, who starts a synchronization procedure). An application of this rule to an already existing pair of location model and SimaticML

model works as follows: each context element is bound to one element of the regarded pairs of models such that links connect the bounded objects as required. In our case the context of the rule matches the top-most three objects in the lower part of Figure 7 with the associated link. The rule application then creates new object instances and links as required and connects them to the matched context elements. The rule of the lower part of Figure 7 has been applied once to create the ControllingDevice and DeviceT objects of Figure 6.

The simultaneous creation and evolution of models with TGG rules cannot be used directly in practice due to the fact that engineers usually do not manipulate models simultaneously. Therefore, TGG rules are translated into so-called *operational model transformation rules*, which are able to synchronize concurrently modified models on demand by propagating changes in both directions. The operational rules that are derived from a single TGG rule support the following application scenarios:

- Propagate changes from a source model sm to a target model tm (forward translation) such that (sm, cl', tm') is an element of the specified TGG, where tm' is a modified version of tm and cl' the resulting set of correspondence links between sm and tm'.
- Propagate changes from a target model tm to a source model sm (backward translation) such that (sm', cl', tm) is an element of the specified TGG, where sm' is a modified version of sm and cl' the resulting set of correspondence links between sm' and tm.
- Update a set of correspondence links cl between two already existing models sm and tm such that (sm, cl', tm) is an element of the specified TGG (if possible).

In (Schürr & Klar, 2008) an algorithm is presented that deals with synchronizing models consistently. Therefore, the algorithm picks element by element and checks whether the element is yet translatable or not. An element is not yet translatable if it has untranslated context elements that have to be taken into account previously. The element is scheduled and the algorithm tries to proceed with the context element. If an element cannot be translated due to incompatibilities the element and all subsequent elements remain untranslated and verbose information is passed to the user in order to support maintenance. The algorithm deals with all kind of operational rule

to be applied and, therefore, supports propagating changes from one model to another as well as updating correspondence links and associated elements. Recently, the algorithm starts at random by picking an element from the source model. In future, we are planning to evolve strategies to determine a fix translation order in before. This should result in deterministic behavior and transformation results.

Extended TGGs for Real-World Examples

Our attempts to use triple graph grammars as presented in Section "Introduction to Standard Triple Graph Grammars" for the specification of consistency relationships between Location model and SimaticML models highlighted quite a number of deficiencies:

1. Multiplicities of correspondence link types as shown in Figure 5 have already been used in the past in the TGG metamodel, but the associated TGG rules were not able to create m-to-n correspondence relationships as permitted by the specified multiplicities.
2. Furthermore, we had to realize that our TGG parameter concept was not able to handle cases, where the translation of one model into another model requires interaction with an end-user (semi-automatic creation of model elements and selection of translation options)
3. In addition, we were running into problems when we had to handle situations where some model elements have to be created only if they do not yet exist.

In the following we will sketch how the definition of TGGs can be extended to cope with the problems listed above.

Multiplicities of Correspondence Link Types: multiplicities of correspondence link types have been introduced in analogy to multiplicities of regular associations in (Klar et al., 2007). With multiplicities it is possible to express the fact that a single primary source/target model element must have a counterpart in the target/source model by applying a multiplicity of 1 to the counterpart. Otherwise, multiplicities can also express that a primary source/target model element needs not have a counterpart by applying a lower bound of 0 to the counterpart element. Note that a lower bound cannot be used without an upper bound >0. Finally, multiplicities permit to associate more than one correspondence link with a translated modeling element when using an upper bound of >1 up to n. Unfortunately, standard TGGs neither are able to associate a source/target model element with more than one target/source element nor able to ignore certain modeling elements.

Consider the following TGG metamodel excerpt for the correspondence type LocationLink as depicted in Figure 5. It states that – in general – an arbitrary number of Location objects are related to a single ProjectT object, but that some Location objects may exist on their own. In order to be able to describe such a situation with a TGG we have to introduce two new types of TGG rules that are not excluded by the TGG theory introduced in (Schürr, 1995){Schürr 1995 #958}, but have never been implemented in a TGG tool until now. First we introduce rules that create a new primary object on one side, but reuse an existing primary context object on the other side. These rules support the association of an object in one model with an arbitrary number of elements in the related model. A first derived rule for Location-Link would match a Project object-ProjectLink object-ProjectT object pattern and only create a new Location object linked to the existing Project object and a new link of type LocationLink. Furthermore, we sometimes have to introduce rules that only create elements in one model. These rules can be used to explicitly exclude elements from a model-to-model translation process if not needed e.g., when a user wants to add information by hand and preserve the data when synchronizing with

another model. Thus, the second derived rule for LocationLink would match a single Project object and only create a new associated Location object. The operational rule derivation process for both derived rules can easily be adapted to these rules by simply ignoring forward (backward) translation rules that do not match any new elements in the source (target) model. These rules are not used for the translation of a SimaticML model into a location model. Otherwise, a model synchronization process would be able to create an infinite number of Location objects.

A TGG containing both rules as previously described based on StationLink would result in a forward translation implementation that nondeterministically either associates a Location object with a ProjectT object or simply ignores it during the translation process. In practice, this kind of nondeterminism is either resolved by user interaction or by introducing additional context/attribute conditions in both rules that are somehow able to distinguish (1) isolated Location objects that are irrelevant for the regarded translation process and (2) Location objects that have a counterpart in the SimaticML model and that are needed as context objects for other translation steps.

The next TGG deficiency that was identified during the collaboration between TU Darmstadt and Siemens AG concerns the handling of rule parameters. Figure 7 (bottom) presented a TGG rule for the creation of corresponding ControllingDevice and DeviceT objects such that DeviceT objects are appended to a nondeterministically selected ElectricalControlCabinet object. In practice, a source model contains many (manually created) objects of this kind and a mechanism is needed that supports the manual or semi-automatic selection of a specific ElectricalControlCabinet object. For this purpose, object-valued rule parameters are introduced that trigger a synchronization rule application strategy that allows the user to control the selection of ElectricalControlCabinet context objects:

StationLink(stationName:string, cabinet:Electri calControlCabinet)

Furthermore, it turned out that it is sometimes convenient to be able to specify default values for rule parameters (of primitive types). Let us assume that we either want to attach a new ControllingDevice object to an ElectricalControlCabinet object with a manually specified name or to such an object with a default name. For this purpose, we introduce rule signatures with default parameter values as follows:

StationLink(stationName:string, cabinetName:s tring="DefaultName")

The use of even more complex parameter concepts, such as computing parameter values on-the-fly while transforming, is not yet introduced. It remains open to further TGG researches to establish a concept of permitting engineers to compute for example free slots in a control cabinet and place a module there. First ideas mention the introduction of an additional metamodel with modeled method behavior may be a starting point to cope with this open challenge.

Finally, it may happen that we are running into a situation during the specification of model correspondences, where we do not know whether a needed object exists. Let us assume that the rule displayed in the top of Figure 7 does not create the non-primary object ProjectObjectListT. Instead, the creation of such an object should be a side effect of the creation of the first object of type DeviceT. For this purpose, optional rule elements are needed that are labeled with «optional create». Informally, TGG rules first search for matches where optional elements are treated like context elements and bound to already existing elements of the regarded models. All optional elements for which such a match cannot be found are then treated like elements labeled with the «create» stereotype. The demand for optional create was already stated by Wagner (Kindler & Wagner,

2007), but with no precise definition of its dynamic semantics. In the following we will present such a precise definition that relies on the translation of a TGG rule with «optional create» stereotypes into a set of standard TGG rules with different rule application priorities. Reconsider the rule of CabinetLink type as depicted in Figure 7 with an «optional create» on the ProjectObjectListT. As previously described, this ProjectObjectListT would not be created by the ProjectLink rule depicted in the top of Figure 7. This modified TGG rule would use a single «optional create» object plus a number of associated links, which inherit the «create» property of their source and target objects. Such a rule has to be translated into two different standard TGG rules:

1. A rule with a high execution priority that reuses an existing context object
2. A rule with low execution priority that creates a new object.

The second rule will only be applied if the first rule fails i.e., if we do not find a matching context object.

The previous case of a rule with a single optionally created object was quite trivial. It becomes more complicated when more than one object can be created optionally within a single rule. The remainder of this section presents a derivation algorithm that translates a TGG rule with an arbitrary number of «optional create» elements into a set of standard TGG rules with priorities such that rules which create more optional elements have lower priority than rules which reuse more context elements. Due to complexity reduction we explain our algorithm using an abstract example. Consider the following excerpt of a TGG rule:

The rule contains one context object and three «optional create» labeled objects either on the source or target side. Please consider that this excerpt displays only part of the source or target pattern of a TGG rule. The algorithm works in a combinatorial way by generating in a first step all

Figure 8 Simple excerpt of a TGG Rule and all derivable standard TGG rules

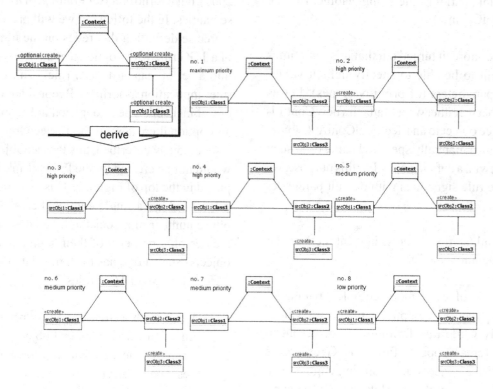

rule instances where «optional create» occurrences are either deleted or replaced by «create». Applied to the TGG rule excerpt depicted in the upper-left corner of Figure 8, our algorithm first generates the rule, where all «optional create» objects are already given and, therefore, no object has to be created. Second, the algorithm derives three rules where one object will be created. Third, the algorithm derives three rules where two objects will be created. Fourth, the algorithm derives one rule where all «optional create» labeled objects will be created.

Figure 8 depicts the whole set of derivable TGG rules with a rule number and a priority for each rule next to the original rule. In a second step some of the generated standard TGG rules have to be discarded due to the fact that they contain new context objects that are only connected to the original context elements of the TGG rule via «create» objects. Rule no. 3 is one example of this kind. It contains a new context element srcObj3 that is only associated with the «create» object srcObj2. The application of such a rule would match any Class3 object in the graph and associate it via a new Class2 object to a regarded context. We have made the experience that users don't expect such a rule behavior and restrict, therefore, the reuse of optionally existing context objects to cases, where these special context objects are already connected to normal context objects of the regarded TGG rule. Additionally, rule no. 5 is also rejected for the same reasons.

Finally, the algorithm assigns to all generated TGG rules an execution priority such that rules that create a smaller number of objects (with their associated links) have a higher priority than rules that create more objects. As a consequence, model synchronizations that are based on the generated set of TGG rules minimize the number of created objects that are needed to re-establish the consistency of a pair of regarded models. Whenever there are two options with the same number of new objects to synchronize between two models, then one of these options is either selected non-deterministically or chosen via user interaction. Please note that the actual implementation of «optional create» does not explicitly generate the set of rules which has been used here to explain the semantics of this new TGG construct. Instead, TGG rules with «optional create» labeled elements are directly translated into operational translation rules with optional create elements which are then directly translated into Java code with the appropriate behavior (cf. "Application and evaluation of CMDAE concepts").

To summarize, extended TGGs as introduced here combined with the metamodeling standards of the OMG offer the appropriate support for the metamodel-driven development of integrated engineering environments. These environments have commercial-of-the-shelf (COTS) modeling tools from different disciplines as their basic components and support the concurrent manipulation and (re-)synchronization of development artifacts as shown in the next section.

APPLICATION AND EVALUATION OF CMDAE CONCEPTS

Our metamodeling (meta-CASE) tool MOFLON (Amelunxen et al., 2006) supports the development of new COTS tools as well as the integration and extension of existing COTS tools relying on the concepts introduced in the previous sections. Based on the graph transformation tool Fujaba (University of Paderborn Software Engineering Group, 2007), it implements the complete MOF 2.0 standard for metamodel specification. In addition, in-place model transformations are expressible by *Story Driven Modeling (SDM)* (Zündorf, Schürr, & Winter, 1998). A code generator translates MOFLON metamodels and SDM diagrams into *Java Metadata Interface (JMI)*-compliant (Sun Microsystems, 07-June-2002) Java code. The generated code supports the manipulation of (meta-)

models in main memory via typed and reflective interfaces; furthermore, model transformations and checking OCL (Object Management Group, 2006b) constraints are supported. In addition the generated code is divided in an interface part and a number of implementations of this interface. Beside a standard main memory implementation, a specialized implementation for accessing the data of a specific COTS tool using its API can be chosen. The semi-automatic generation of API-specific COTS tool adapters is an ongoing research topic. The standard implementation is called *offline model repository*, the implementation of a JMI model repository interface on top of the API of a specific COTS tool is called *online adapter*.

Furthermore, MOFLON includes a module for the specification of out-place (out-place transformations create a new model from an existing model, while in-place transformations keep the transformation result within the same model) model to model transformations based on TGGs. The Java code derived from a TGG specification keeps pairs of models synchronized which are stored in any kind of repository that is JMI-compliant like the model repositories or tool adapters generated by MOFLON or Sun's Netbeans Metadata Repository (MDR) repository (Sun Microsystems, 2007).

Prototype

MOFLON is applied in different industrial corporations and research projects. The *MATLAB Simulink/Stateflow Analysen und Transformationen (MATE) (Schürr, Schäfer, Stürmer, & Legros, 2009)* project has a focus on model checking and repair actions on a single tool, Matlab/Simulink. On the other hand, our tool integration approach *Tool Integration Environment (TiE)* (Klar, Rose, & Schürr, 2009) is specialized on supporting information exchange between different COTS tools and addressing traceability issues. For TiE we have already defined a workflow (Klar, Rose,

& Schürr, 2008) for setting up integrations between different tools.

The application of MOFLON within the domain of mechatronic engineering revealed quite a number of deficiencies of MOFLON version 1.3 as well as of its related integration framework TiE. A systematic approach for the classification of *modelware* artefacts was missing which can be used to select the appropriate metamodeling and model transformation techniques for a specific purpose. Furthermore, we had to realize that our TGG approach was not yet expressive enough to cope with complex real-world scenarios, where the semi-automatic integration of rather differently structured models is an issue. As a consequence, we have developed the CMDAE hypercube as well as a number of extensions of our TGG approach. A TiE prototype of the location to SimaticML model integration scenario has already been implemented. It is a first proof-of-concept of the viability of our approach and supports the following working scenario:

1. Create an instance of a Location model
2. Transform all relevant information from this instance into an instance of SimaticML
3. Open the SimaticML document with STEP 7
4. Insert an additional I/O module
5. Export the changed project to a SimaticML document
6. Merge made changes into the Location model instance

For the Location model, our prototype does not include an integration of a COTS tool for managing data yet. As a consequence, we use a generic editor based on JMI instead (step 1 of our working scenario). The model data of STEP 7 is not accessed by an API in contrast to tools integrated in TiE so far. Instead, SimaticML model data from the import and export interface is used. As already mentioned in Section "The Metamodeling Pyramid (Dimension M)" MOFLON imports the SimaticML XSD in a semi-automatic manner. The resulting metamodel corresponds to the SimaticML XSD and generated code enables full access to the XML files of the import and export interface through JMI. As a consequence, STEP 7 still accepts the XML files (step 3, 4 and 5 of our working scenario), but access through JMI as required by the transformations is also possible (step 2 and 6).

In order to enable bi-directional transformation between Location model instances and the SimaticML models (step 2 und 6 of our working scenario), we have to identify corresponding elements within the metamodels. This process is a joint effort of experts of all involved domains. Identified relationships between both models exist for the elements: Project and ProjectT, ControllingDevice and Device, Module and DeviceItem. Furthermore, correspondence links are added which are needed for technical reasons only: Location and ProjectT; ElectricalControlCabinet and ProjectT. Technical links are used as a work around as long as we have not yet finished the implementation of the next MOFLON release that will support the here introduced new TGG concepts.

To summarize, our application prototype covers all steps defined in our working scenario which actually addresses all presented dimensions of the CMDAE hypercube. Dimension (E) is implicitly involved, because the working scenario contains a typical evolution of models in time. This evolution only has an impact on layer M1 of dimension (M).

FUTURE RESEARCH DIRECTIONS

In the mechatronic engineering domain the area of product data management (PDM) (VDI-Richtlinie, VDI 2219) or product lifecycle management (PLM) (Saaksvuori & Immonen, 2008) is strongly related to our activities. Industrial PLM systems provide a platform for model storage and related services like versioning or security on a large-scale level as well as for the definition of customized engineering processes. Therefore, we are planning to use PLM systems with their client/server architecture as one possible backend for our tool integration framework TiE. Furthermore, we are involved in research activities sponsored by the Deutsche Forschungsgemeinschaft (DFG) concerning the development of globally distributed engineering environments (Mukherjee, Kovacevic, Benz, & Schürr, 2007), where a peer to peer network of model repositories belonging to different subprojects or organizations replaces the single server solution of a PLM System (Ahmad, Yuqing, Cheng, & Jihua, 2006).

CONCLUSION

Concurrent Model-Driven Automation Engineering as introduced here is a new approach for the systematic development of concepts and tools that support the collaboration of engineers in multidisciplinary model-driven system engineering projects. The CMDAE hypercube is a first step towards a comprehensive modelware categorization framework. In this contribution we laid the main focus onto its concurrent engineering dimension and sketched the state-of-the-art of metamodel-driven language definition activities. Dimensions dealing with abstraction, domain customization, and evolution including all kinds of interaction have not been described in detail yet. It is the subject of future research activities to study how the combination of MOF 2.0 metamodeling concepts with graph grammar technology can be used to handle these additional aspects of the management of models and modeling languages.

Using our metamodeling tool MOFLON we have created an integration prototype for two different modeling tools/standards as a result of the cooperation of Siemens AG and Technische Universität Darmstadt. Due to the complexity of this case study we were running into problems concerning the expressiveness of our model integration approach based on triple graph grammars. As a consequence, we presented three extensions that allow for the specification of m-to-n traceability relationships and interaction interfaces with end-users. The implementation of all TGG extensions is in progress. Their availability is planned for a future release of MOFLON.

ACKNOWLEDGMENT

The work of Marius Lauder is supported by the 'Excellence Initiative' of the German Federal and State Governments and the Graduate School of Computational Engineering at Technische Universität Darmstadt

REFERENCES

Ahmad, R., Yuqing, F., Cheng, Z., & Jihua, Z. (2006). Closing Information Loops with Extended PLM. In *CSECS'06: Proceedings of the 5th WSEAS International Conference on Circuits, Systems, Electronics, Control & Signal Processing* (pp. 344–349). Stevens Point, WI: World Scientific and Engineering Academy and Society (WSEAS).

Amelunxen, C., Königs, A., Rötschke, T., & Schürr, A. (2006). MOFLON: A Standard-Compliant Metamodeling Framework with Graph Transformations. In A. Rensink & J. Warmer (Eds.), *Lecture Notes in Computer Science (LNCS), Model Driven Architecture - Foundations and Applications: 2nd European Conference* (pp. 361–375). Berlin: Springer Verlag.

Bézivin, J., Jouault, F., & Valduriez, P. (2004). On the Need for Megamodels. In *Proceedings of Workshop on Best Practices for Model-Driven Software Development at the 19th Annual ACM Conference on Object-Oriented Programming, Systems, Languages, and Applications,* Vancouver, British Columbia, Canada.

Brown, A. W., Carney, D. J., Morris, E. J., Smith, D. B., & Zarrella, P. F. (1994). *Principles of CASE tool integration.* New York: Oxford University Press, Inc.

Chambers, J. M., Cleveland, W. S., & Tukey, P. A. (1983). *Graphical methods for data analysis. The Wadsworth statistics/probability series.* Belmont, CA: Wadsworth.

Comos Industry Solutions Gmb, H. (2009). *Comos ET.* Retrieved June 21, 2009, from Comos Industry Solutions GmbH: http://www.comos.com/elektrotechnik.html?&L=1

Czarnecki, K., Foster, J. N., Hu, Z., Lämmel, R., Schürr, A., & Terwilliger, J. F. (2009). Bidirectional Transformations: A Cross-Discipline Perspective. GRACE Meeting notes, state of the art, and outlook. In *International Conference on Model Transformations (ICMT), Zurich, Switzerland,* (pp. 260–283).

Denton, T., Jones, E., Srinivasan, S., Owens, K., & Buskens, R. W. (2008). NAOMI – An Experimental Platform for Multi–modeling. In K. Czarnecki, I. Ober, J.-M. Bruel, A. Uhl, & M. Völter (Eds.), *Lecture Notes in Computer Science (LNCS), Model driven engineering languages and systems, 11th international conference, MoDELS 2008, Toulouse, France, September 28 - October 3, 2008; proceedings* (pp. 143–157). Berlin: Springer.

Dörr, H., & Schürr, A. (2004). Special section on tool integration applications and frameworks. *International Journal on Software Tools for Technology Transfer, 6*(3), 183–185.

Geensys. (2009). *GEENSYS Homepage.* Retrieved July 27, 2009, from Geensys http://www.geensys.com/.

Giese, H., & Wagner, R. (2009). From model transformation to incremental bidirectional model synchronization. *Software and Systems Modeling, 8*(1), 21–43. doi:10.1007/s10270-008-0089-9

Institut National de Recherche en Informatique et en Automatique (INRIA). (2009). *Model transformation at Inria.* Retrieved December 07, 2009, from Institut National de Recherche en Informatique et en Automatique (INRIA) http://modelware.inria.fr/

International Standard, ISO/IEC 19502 (2005, November 01).

International Standard, ISO/IEC 19503 (2005, November 01).

International Standard, IEC 61346-1 (1996-2003).

Jurack, S., Lambers, L., Mehner, K., & Taentzer, G. (2008). Sufficient Criteria for Consistent Behavior Modeling with Refined Activity Diagrams. In K. Czarnecki, I. Ober, J.-M. Bruel, A. Uhl, & M. Völter (Eds.), *Lecture Notes in Computer Science (LNCS), Model driven engineering languages and systems. 11th international conference, MoDELS 2008, Toulouse, France, September 28 - October 3, 2008; proceedings* (pp. 341–355). Berlin: Springer.

Kindler, E., & Wagner, R. (2007). *Triple Graph Grammars: Concepts, Extensions, Implementations, and Application Scenarios: Technical Report.* University of Paderborn, Germany. Retrieved November 27, 2008, from http://wwwcs.uni-paderborn.de/cs/ag-schaefer/Veroeffentlichungen/Quellen/Papers/2007/tr-ri-07-284.pdf.

Klar, F., Königs, A., & Schürr, A. (2007). Model transformation in the large. In *ESEC-FSE '07: Proceedings of the the 6th joint meeting of the European software engineering conference and the ACM SIGSOFT symposium on the foundations of software engineering* (pp. 285–294). New York: ACM.

Klar, F., Rose, S., & Schürr, A. (2008). A Meta-Model-Driven Tool Integration Development Process. In R. Kaschek, G. Fliedl, C. Kop, & C. Steinberger (Eds.), *Information Systems and e-Business Technologies, 2nd International United Information Systems Conference, UNISCON 2008, Klagenfurt, Austria, April 22-25, 2008. Proceedings* (LNBI Vol. 5. pp. 201–212). Berlin: Springer-Verlag.

Klar, F., Rose, S., & Schürr, A. (2009). TiE - A Tool Integration Environment. In J. Oldevik, G. K. Olsen, T. Neple, & D. S. Kolovos (Eds.), *CTIT Workshop Proceedings, Proceedings of the 5th ECMDA Traceability Workshop* (pp. 39–48).

Körtgen, A.-T., & Heukamp, S. (2008). Correspondence Analysis for Supporting Document Re-Use in Development Processes. In *Proceedings of the 11th World Conference on Integrated Design & Process Technology (IDPT 2008). Asia University Taichung, Taiwan, June 1-6, 2008* (pp. 194–205).

Körtgen, A.-T., & Mosler, C. (2008). Recovering Structural Consistency between Design and Implementation using Correspondence Relations. In D. A. Karras, D. Wei, & J. Zendulka (Eds.), *International Conference on Software Engineering Theory and Practice (SETP-08). Orlando, Florida, USA, July 7-10 2008* (pp. 53–60).

Kühne, T. (2006). Matters of (Meta-) Modeling. *Software and Systems Modeling*, (4), 369–385.

Kurtev, I., Bézivin, J., Jouault, F., & Valduriez, P. (2006). Model-based DSL frameworks. In *OOPSLA '06: Companion to the 21st ACM SIG-PLAN symposium on object-oriented programming systems, languages, and applications* (pp. 602–616). New York: ACM.

Lara, J., & de, , Jaramillo, Ermel, C., Taentzer, G., & Ehrig, K. (2004). Parallel Graph Transformation for Model Simulation applied to Timed Transition Petri Nets. *Electronic Notes in Theoretical Computer Science*, *109*, 17–29. doi:10.1016/j.entcs.2004.02.053

Mens, T., Czarnecki, K., & Van Gorp, P. (2005). A Taxonomy of Model Transformations. In Bézivin, J., & Heckel, R. (Eds.), *Language Engineering for Model-Driven Software Development*.

Mukherjee, P., Kovacevic, A., Benz, M., & Schürr, A. (2007). Towards a Peer-to-Peer Based Global Software Development Environment. In K. Herrmann & B. Bruegge (Eds.), *Vol. 121. Lecture Notes in Informatics, Software Engineering 2008. Fachtagung des GI-Fachbereichs Softwaretechnik, 18. - 22.02.2008 in München,* (pp. 204–216). Bonn, Germany: Gesellschaft für Informatik.

Nagl, M. (1996). *Building Tightly Integrated Software Development Environments: The IPSEN Approach.* (LNCS Vol. 1170). Berlin: Springer.

Object Management Group. (2006a). *Meta Object Facility (MOF) 2.0 Core Specification*. OMG Available Specification. Retrieved June 25, 2009, from Object Management Group: http://www.omg.org/cgi-bin/doc?formal/06-01-01.pdf.

Object Management Group. (2006b). *Object Constraint Language (OCL), Version 2.0*. OMG Available Specification. Retrieved June 25, 2009, from Object Management Group http://www.omg.org/cgi-bin/doc?formal/06-05-01.pdf.

Object Management Group. (2008). *Meta Object Facility (MOF) 2.0 Query/View/Transformation Specification*. OMG Available Specification. Retrieved July 27, 2009, from Object Management Group http://www.omg.org/spec/QVT/1.0/PDF/.

Object Management Group. (2009). *OMG Model Driven Architecture*. Retrieved July 21, 2009, from Object Management Group http://www.omg.org/mda/.

Pratt, T. W. (1971). Pair Grammars, Graph Languages and String-to-Graph Translations. *Journal of Computer and System Sciences*, *5*, 560–595.

Saaksvuori, A., & Immonen, A. (2008). *Product Lifecycle Management. Springer-11643 /Dig. Serial].* Berlin: Springer-Verlag.

Schürr, A. (1995). Specification of Graph Translators with Triple Graph Grammars. In E. W. Mayr, G. Schmidt, & G. Tinhofer (Eds.), *Graph-Theoretic Concepts in Computer Science, 20th International Workshop, WG '94 Herrsching, Germany, June 1618, 1994 Proceedings*, (LNCS Vol. 903, pp. 151–163). Berlin: Springer.

Schürr, A., & Dörr, H. (2005). Special Section on Model-based Tool Integration. *Software and Systems Modeling, 4*(2), 109–170.

Schürr, A., & Klar, F. (2008). 15 Years of Triple Graph Grammars - Research Challenges, New Contributions, Open Problems. In *Lecture Notes in Computer Science (LNCS), 4th International Conference on Graph Transformation* (pp. 411–425). Heidelberg: Springer Verlag.

Schürr, A., Schäfer, W., Stürmer, I., & Legros, E. (2009). MATE - A Model Analysis and Transformation Environment for MATLAB Simulink. In *Lecture Notes in Computer Science (LNCS)*. Heidelberg: Springer Verlag.

Siemens, A. G. (2006). *Configuring Hardware and Communication Connections with STEP 7: Manual*. Order number: 6ES7810-4CA08-8BW0. Retrieved June 07, 2009, from http://support.automation.siemens.com/WW/llisapi.dll/csfetch/18652631/S7hwV54_e.pdf?func=cslib.csFetch&nodeid=18653484&forcedownload=true

Siemens, A. G. (2009). *SIMATIC STEP 7 Programming Software*. Retrieved October 09, 2008, from http://www.automation.siemens.com/simatic/industriesoftware/html_76/products/step7.htm

Sun Microsystems. (2007). *mdr: netbeans.org: Metadata Repository home*. Retrieved July 27, 2009, from Sun Microsystems: http://mdr.netbeans.org/

Sun Microsystems. (07-June-2002). *Java Metadata Interface (JMI) Specification*. JSR 040 Java Community Process. Retrieved October 28, 2009, from http://jcp.org/en/jsr/detail?id=40.

University of Paderborn Software Engineering Group. (2007). *Fujaba-Homepage*. Retrieved July 27, 2009, from University of Paderborn Software Engineering Group: http://wwwcs.uni-paderborn.de/cs/fujaba/.

VDI-Richtlinie, VDI 2219 (2002, November).

VDI-Richtlinie, VDI 2206 (2004, June 01).

World Wide Web Consortium. (2008). *W3C XML Schema*. Retrieved July 27, 2009, from World Wide Web Consortium: http://www.w3.org/XML/Schema.

Zündorf, A., Schürr, A., & Winter, A. J. (1998). Story Driven Modeling. *ACM Transactions on Software Engineering and Methodology*

KEY TERMS AND DEFINITIONS

Concurrent Engineering: Engineers from different disciplines work simultaneously on models typical for their discipline; these models contain partially redundant information that have to be kept in a consistent state.

Mechatronic Engineering: Engineering which involves mechanical, electrical and automation engineering activities as known by the automation industry.

Metamodel: A model capturing abstract syntax and semantics of a modeling language.

Model Classification: A schema for grouping models by different criteria that allows for the classification of models.

Model Integration: Models of different modeling languages share redundant information. The information is kept in a consistent state by some integration technique.

Model Transformation: Model transformation allows for the automated usage of models. A transformation is defined by a rule set. In-place transformations operate on one model, which is changed during the transformation process, whereas model-to-model or model-to-text transformations create new models from a given input model.

Graph Grammar: A graph grammar consists of production rules. Each rule contains two graph patterns. The second pattern replaces occurrences of the first pattern whenever the first one matches within a given graph

Section 2
Model–Driven Engineering and Model–Driven Architecture

Chapter 6
Model–Driven Configuration of Distributed Real–Time and Embedded Systems

Brian Dougherty
Vanderbilt University, USA

Jules White
Virginia Tech, USA

Douglas C. Schmidt
Vanderbilt University, USA

ABSTRACT

Distributed real-time and embedded (DRE) systems are increasingly being constructed with commercial-off-the-shelf (COTS) components to reduce development time and effort. The configuration of these components must ensure that real-time quality-of-service (QoS) and resource constraints are satisfied. Due to the numerous QoS constraints that must be met, manual system configuration is hard. Model-Driven Architecture (MDA) is a design paradigm that incorporates models to provide visual representations of design entities. MDAs show promise for addressing many of these challenges by allowing the definition and automated enforcement of design constraints. This chapter presents MDA techniques and tools that simplify and automate the configuration of COTS components for DRE systems. First, the challenges that make manual DRE system configuration infeasible are presented. Second, the authors provide an incremental methodology for constructing modeling tools to alleviate these difficulties. Finally, the authors provide a case study describing the construction of the Ascent Modeling Platform (AMP), which is a modeling tool capable of producing near-optimal DRE system configurations.

INTRODUCTION

Emerging trends and challenges. Distributed real-time embedded (DRE) systems (such as avionics systems, satellite imaging systems, smart cars, and intelligent transportation systems) are subject to stringent requirements and quality of service (QoS) constraints. For example, timing constraints require that tasks be completed by real-time deadlines. Likewise, rigorous QoS de-

DOI: 10.4018/978-1-61692-874-2.ch006

mands (such as dependability and security), may require a system to recover and remain active in the face of multiple failures (Wang, 2003). In addition, DRE systems must satisfy domain-specific constraints, such as the need for power management in embedded systems. To cope with these complex issues, applications for DRE systems have traditionally been built from scratch using specialized, project-specific software components that are tightly coupled with specialized hardware components (Schmidt, 2002).

New DRE systems are increasingly being developed by *configuring* applications from multiple layers of commercial-off-the-shelf (COTS) hardware, operating systems, and middleware components resulting in reduced development cycle-time and cost (Voas, 1998). These types of DRE systems require the integration of 100's-1,000's of software components that provide distinct functionality, such as I/O, data manipulation, and data transfer. This functionality must work in concert with other software and hardware components to accomplish mission-critical tasks, such as self-stabilization, error notification, and power management. The software configuration of a DRE system thus directly impacts its performance, cost, and quality.

Traditionally, DRE systems have been built completely in-house from scratch. These design techniques are based on in-house proprietary construction techniques and are not designed to handle the complexities of configuring systems from existing components (Gokhale, 2002). The new generation of configuration-based approaches construct DRE systems by determining which combination of hardware/software components provide the requisite QoS (Alves, 2001; Chung, 2004; Morisio; 2002), In addition, the combined purchase cost of the components cannot exceed a predefined amount, referred to as the project budget.

A DRE system can be split into a software configuration and a hardware configuration. Valid software configuration must meet all real-time constraints, such as minimum latency and maximum throughput, provide required functionality, meet software architecture constraints, such as interface compatibility, and also satisfy all domain-specific design constraints, such as minimum power consumption. Moreover, the cost of the software configuration must not exceed the available budget for purchasing software components. Similarly, the hardware configuration must meet all constraints without exceeding the available hardware component budget. At the same time, the hardware and software configuration must be aligned so that the hardware configuration provides sufficient resources, such as RAM, for the chosen software configuration. Additional constraints may also be present based on the type and application of the DRE system being configured.

Often, there are multiple COTS components that can meet each functional requirement for a DRE system. Each individual COTS component differs in QoS provided, the amounts/types of computational resources required, and the purchase cost. Creating and maintaining error-free COTS configurations is hard due to the large number of complex configuration rules and QoS requirements. The complexity associated with examining the tradeoffs of choosing between 100's to 1,000's of COTS components makes it hard to determine a configuration that satisfies all constraints *and* is not needlessly expensive or resource intensive.

Solution approach → Model-driven automated configuration techniques. This chapter presents techniques and tools that leverage the *Model Driven Architecture* (MDA) paradigm (Mellor, 2004), which is a design approach for specifying system configuration constraints with platform-independent models (PIMs). Each PIM can be used as a blueprint for constructing platform-specific models (PSM)s (Poole, 2001). In this chapter, MDA is utilized to construct modeling tools that can be used to create model instances of potential DRE system configurations. These tools are then applied in a motivating example to determine valid DRE system configurations that fit budget limits and ensure consistency between hardware and software component selections.

To simplify the DRE system configuration process, designers can use MDA to construct modeling tools that visualize COTS component options, verify configuration validity, and compare potential DRE system configurations. In particular, PSMs can be used to determine DRE system configurations that meet budgetary constraints by representing component selections in modeling environments. Modeling tools that utilize these environments provide a domain-centric way to experiment with and explore potential system configurations. Moreover, by constructing PSMs with the aid of modeling tools, many complex constraints associated with DRE system configuration can be enforced automatically, thereby preventing designers from constructing PSMs that violate system configuration rules.

After a PSM instance of a DRE system configuration is constructed, it can be used as a blueprint to construct a DRE system that meets all design constraints specified within the metamodel (Kent, 2002). As DRE system requirements evolve and additional constraints are introduced, the metamodel can be modified and new PSMs constructed. Systems that are constructed using these PSMs can be adapted to handle additional constraints and requirements more readily than those developed manually using third-generation languages, such as C++, Java, or C#.

Chapter organization. The remainder of this chapter describes and evaluates MDA-based analyses techniques for determining high quality DRE system configurations utilizing COTS components. The background section describes the numerous challenges that make large-scale DRE system configuration extremely difficult; The section "Applying MDA to Derive System Configurations" presents an incremental methodology for applying MDA to the construction of domain specific modeling tools; The case study section provides a case study of utilizing this methodol-

ogy to construct a model-based configuration tool which can ultimately be used to produce output models that provide valid, high-quality large-scale DRE system configurations.; The future research and directions section describes future work; and the conclusion section presents concluding remarks and lessons learned.

BACKGROUND

This section describes some key constraints that DRE systems must adhere to, summarizes the challenges that make determining configurations hard, and provides a survey of current techniques and methodologies for DRE system configuration. A DRE system configuration consists of a valid hardware configuration and valid software configuration in which the computational resource needs of the software configuration are provided by the computational resources produced by the hardware configuration. DRE system software and hardware components often have complex interdependencies on the consumption and production of resources (such as processor utilization, memory usage, and power consumption). If the resource requirements of the software configuration exceed the resource production of the hardware configuration, a DRE system will not function correctly and will thus be invalid.

Challenge 1: Resource Interdependencies

Hardware components provide the computational resources that software components require to function. If the hardware does not provide an adequate amount of each computational resource, some software components cannot function. An overabundance of resources indicates that some hardware components have been purchased unnecessarily, wasting funds that could have been spent to buy superior software components or set aside for future projects.

Figure 1. Configuration options of a satellite imaging system

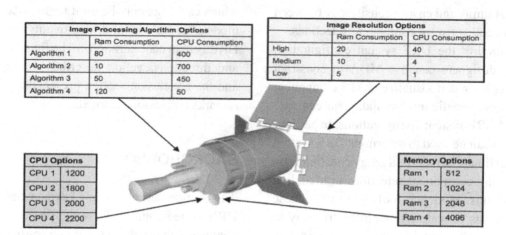

Image Processing Algorithm Options		
	Ram Consumption	CPU Consumption
Algorithm 1	80	400
Algorithm 2	10	700
Algorithm 3	50	450
Algorithm 4	120	50

Image Resolution Options		
	Ram Consumption	CPU Consumption
High	20	40
Medium	10	4
Low	5	1

CPU Options	
CPU 1	1200
CPU 2	1800
CPU 3	2000
CPU 4	2200

Memory Options	
Ram 1	512
Ram 2	1024
Ram 3	2048
Ram 4	4096

Figure 1 shows the configuration options of a satellite imaging system. This DRE system consists of an image processing algorithm and software that defines image resolution capabilities. There are multiple components that could be used to meet each functional requirement, each of which provides a different level of service. For example, there are three options for the image resolution component. The high-resolution option offers the highest level of service, but also requires dramatically more RAM and CPU to function than the medium or low-resolution options. If the resource amounts required by the high-resolution option are not supplied, then the component cannot function, preventing the system from functioning correctly. If RAM or CPU resources are scarce the medium or low-resolution option should be chosen.

Challenge 2: Component Resource Requirements Differ

Each software component requires computational resources to function. These resource requirements differ between components. Often, components offering higher levels of service require larger amounts of resources and/or cost more to purchase. Designers must therefore consider the additional resulting resource requirements when determining if a component can be included in a system configuration.

For example, the satellite system shown in Figure 1 has three options for the image resolution software component, each of which provides a different level of performance. If resources were abundant, the system with the best performance would result from selecting the high-resolution component. In most DRE systems, such as satellite systems, resources are scarce and cannot be augmented without great cost and effort. While the performance of the low-resolution component is less than that of the high-resolution component, it requires a fraction of the computational resources. If any resource requirements are not satisfied, the system configuration is considered invalid. A valid configuration is thus more likely to exist by selecting the low-resolution component.

Challenge 3: Selecting Between Differing Levels of Service

Software components provide differing levels of service. For example, a designer may have to choose between three different software components that differ in speed and throughput. In some cases, a specific level of service may be required, prohibiting the use of certain components.

Continuing with the satellite configuration example shown in Figure 1, an additional functional constraint may require that a minimum of medium image resolution. Inclusion of the low-resolution component would therefore invalidate the overall system configuration. Assuming sufficient resources for only the medium and low-resolution components, the only component that satisfies all constraints is the medium image resolution option.

Moreover, the inclusion of a component in a configuration may prohibit or require the use one or more other components. Certain software components may have compatibility problems with other components. For example, each of the image resolution components may be a product of separate vendors. As a result, the high and medium-resolution components may be compatible with any image processing component, whereas the low-resolution component may only be compatible with image processing components made by the same vendor. These compatibility issues add another level of difficulty to determining valid DRE system configurations.

Challenge 4: Configuration Cannot Exceed Project Budget

Each component has an associated purchase cost. The combined purchase cost of the components included in the configuration must not exceed the project budget. It is therefore possible for the inclusion of a component to invalidate the configuration if its additional purchase cost exceeds the project budget regardless of computational resources existing to support the component. Moreover, if two systems have roughly the same resource requirements and performance the system that carries a smaller purchase cost is considered superior.

Another challenge of meeting budgetary constraints is determining the best way to allocate the budget between hardware purchases and software purchases. Despite the presence of complex resource interdependencies, most techniques require that the selection of the software configuration and hardware configuration occur separately. For example, the hardware configuration could be determined prior to the software configuration so that the resource availability of the system is known prior to solving for a valid software configuration. Conversely, the software configuration could be determined initially so that the resource requirements of the system are known prior to solving for the hardware configuration.

To solve for a hardware or software configuration individually, the total project budget must be divided into a software budget for purchasing software components and a hardware budget for purchasing hardware components. Dividing the budget evenly between the two configuration problems may not produce a valid configuration. Uneven budget divisions, however, may result in valid system configurations. Multiple budget divisions must therefore be examined.

Challenge 5: Exponential Configuration Space

Large-scale DRE systems require hundreds of components to function. For each component there may be many components available for inclusion in the final system configuration. Due to the complex resource interdependencies, budgetary constraints, and functional constraints it is hard to determine if including a single component will invalidate the system configuration. This problem is exacerbated enormously if designers are faced with the tasks of choosing from 1,000's of available components. Even automated techniques require years or more to examine all possible system configurations for such problems.

Large-scale DRE systems often also consist of many software and hardware components with multiple options for each component, resulting in an exponential number of potential configurations. Due to the multiple functional, real-time, and resource constraints discussed earlier, arbitrarily selecting components for a configuration is ineffective. For example, if there are 100 components to choose from then there are 1.2676506×10^{30} unique potential system configurations, the vast majority of which are invalid configurations.

The huge magnitude of the solution space prohibits the use of manual techniques. Automated techniques, such as Constraint Logic Programming (CLP), use Constraint Satisfaction Problems (CSPs) to represent system configuration problems (Benavides, 2005; Sabin, 1996). These techniques are capable of determining optimal solutions for small-scale system configurations but require the examination of all potential system configurations. Techniques utilizing CSPs are ideal, however, for system configuration problems involving a small number of components as they can determine an optimal configuration—should one exist—in a short amount of time.

The exhaustive nature of conventional CSP-based techniques, however, renders them ineffective for large-scale DRE system configuration. Without tools to aid in large-scale DRE system configuration, it is hard for designers to determine *any* valid large-scale system configuration. Even if a valid configuration is determined, other valid system configurations may exist with vastly superior performance and dramatically less financial cost. Moreover, with constant development of additional technologies, legacy technologies becoming unavailable, and design objectives constantly in flux, valid configurations can quickly become invalid, requiring that new configurations be discovered rapidly. It is thus imperative that advanced design techniques, utilizing MDA, are developed to enhance and validate large-scale DRE system configurations.

Subsequent sections of this chapter demonstrate how MDA can be utilized to mitigate many difficulties of DRE system configuration that result from the challenges described in this section.

APPLYING MDA TO DERIVE SYSTEM CONFIGURATIONS

System configuration involves numerous challenges, as described in the previous section. Constructing MDA tools can help to address these challenges. The process of creating a modeling tool for determining valid DRE system configurations is shown in Figure 2.

This process is divided into four steps:

1. Devise a configuration language for capturing complex configuration rules,
2. Implement a tool for manipulating instances of configurations,
3. Construct a metamodel to formally define the modeling language used by the tool, and
4. Analyze and interpret model instances to determine a solution.

By following this methodology, robust modeling tools can be constructed and utilized to facilitate the configuration of DRE systems. The remainder of this section describes this process in detail.

Devising a Configuration Language

DRE system configuration requires the satisfaction of multiple constraints, such as resource and functional constraints. The complexity of accounting for such a large number of configuration rules makes manual DRE system configuration hard. Configuration languages exist, however, that can be utilized to represent and enforce such constraints. By selecting a configuration language that captures system configuration rules, the complexity of determining valid system configurations can be reduced significantly.

Feature models are a modeling technique that have been used to model Software Product Lines (SPLs) (Jaring, 2002), as well as system configuration problems. SPLs consist of interchangeable components that can be swapped to alter system

Figure 2. Creation process for a dre system configuration modeling tool

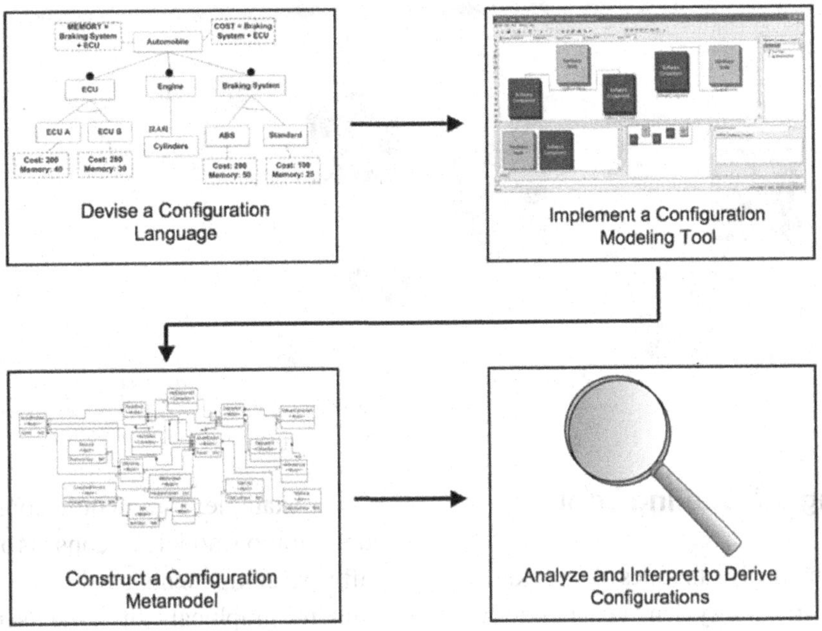

functionality. Czarnecki et al. use feature models to describe the configuration options of systems (Czarnecki, 2005). Feature models are represented using tree structures with lines (representing configuration constraints) connecting candidate components for inclusion in an SPL, known as *features*. The feature model uses configuration constraints to depict the effects that selecting one or more features has on the validity of selecting other features. The feature model serves as a mechanism to determine if the inclusion of a feature will result in an invalid system configuration. Czarnecki et al. also present staged-configuration, an incremental technique for manually determining valid feature selections. This work, however, cannot be directly applied to the configuration of large-scale DRE system configuration because it doesn't guarantee correctness or provide a way of handling resource constraints. Moreover, it takes a prohibitive amount of time to determine valid system configurations since staged-configuration is not automated.

Benavides et al. introduce the extended feature model, an augmented feature model with the ability to more articulately define features and represent additional constraints (Benavides, 2005). Additional descriptive information, called attributes, can be added to define one or more parameters of each feature. For example, the resource consumption and cost of a feature could be defined by adding attributes to the feature. Each attribute lists the type of resource and the amount consumed or provided by the feature. Additional constraints can be defined by adding extra-functional features. Extra-functional features define rules that dictate the validity of sets of attributes. For example, an extra-functional feature may require that the total cost of a set of features representing components is less than that of a feature that defines the budget. Any valid feature selection would thus satisfy the constraint that the collective cost of the components is less than the total project budget.

Figure 3. GME model of DRE system configuration

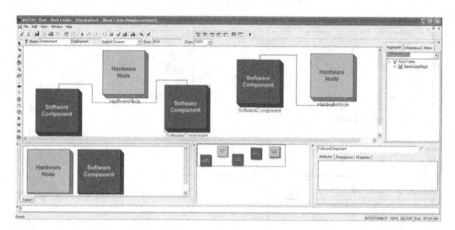

Implementing a Modeling Tool

Designers using manual techniques often unknowingly construct invalid system configurations. Even if an existing valid system configuration is known, the introduction of a single component can violate one or more of these constraints, thereby invalidating the entire configuration. Modeling tools allow designers to manipulate problem entities and compare potential solutions in an environment that ensures various design rules are enforced that are not accounted for in current third-generation programming languages, such as Java and C++. Automated correctness checking allows designers to focus on other problem dimensions, such as performance optimization or minimization of computational resource requirements.

One example of a modeling tool is the *Generic Modeling Environment* (GME) composing domain-specific design environments. (Ledeczi, 2001b) GME is modeling platform for building MDA based tools that can then be used to create model instances. The two principles components of GME are GMeta and GModel, which work together to provide this functionality. GMeta is a graphical tool for constructing metamodels, which are discussed in the following section. GModel is a graphical editor for constructing model instances that adhere to the configuration rules.

For example, a user could construct a system configuration model that consists of hardware and software components as shown in Figure 3. By using the graphical editor, the user can manually create multiple system configuration instances. If the user attempts to include a component that violates a configuration rule, GModel will disallow the inclusion of the component and explain the violation. Since GModel is responsible for enforcing all constraints, the designer can rapidly create and experiment with various models without the overhead of monitoring for constraint violations.

Constructing a Metamodel

Metamodels are used to formally define the rules that are enforced by modeling tools (Ledeczi, 2001a). This collection of rules governs the entities, relationships and constraints of model instances constructed. After constructing a metamodel, users can define modeling tools that are capable of creating model instances that enforce the rules and constraints defined by the metamodel.

Most nontrivial problems require multiple modeling entities, types of relationships between entities, and complex constraints. As a result, constructing metamodels can be a confusing, arduous task. Fortunately, metamodeling tools exist that provide a clear and simple procedure for creating metamodels. Tools for generating metamodels provide several advantages over defining them manually. For example, metamodeling tools can prevent defining rules, such as defining nameless entities, that are contradictory or inappropriate. Likewise, by using a metamodeling tool, metamodels can easily be augmented or altered should the domain or other problem parameters change. Moreover, the same complexities inherent to creating PSMs are also present in the construction of metamodels, and often amplified by the additional abstraction required for their creation. Metamodeling tools use an existing language that defines the rules for creating metamodels, thereby enforcing the complex constraints and facilitating quick, accurate metamodel design.

To create a metamodel for describing system configuration the entities that are involved in DRE system configuration must first be defined. For example, at the most basic level, DRE system configuration consists of hardware and software components. The manner in which these entities interact must then be defined. For example, it is specified that hardware components provide computational resources and that software components consume computational resources. Also, a way is needed to define the constraints that must be maintained as these entities interact for a system configuration to be valid. For example, it may be specified that a software component that interacts with a hardware component must be provided with sufficient computational resources to function by the hardware component.

After all the necessary entities for the modeling tool are created the rules that govern the relationships of these entities must be defined. For example, the relationship between hardware nodes and software components in which the software components consume resources of the hardware nodes must be defined. Before we can do this, however, an *attribute* must be defined that specifies the resource production values of the hardware nodes and the resource consumption values of the software nodes. Once attribute has

been defined and associated it with a class, we can include the attribute in the relationship definition.

A relationship between two model entities is defined by adding a *connection* to the metamodel. The connection specifies the rules for connecting entities in the resulting PSM. Within the connection, we can define additional constraints that must be satisfied for two classes to be connected. For example, for a software component to be connected to a hardware node the resource consumption attribute of the software component can not exceed the attribute of the hardware node that defines the amount of resource production.

GME provides GMeta, a graphical tool for constructing metamodels. GMeta divides metamodel design into four separate sub-metamodels: the Class Diagram, Visualization, Constraints, and Attributes. The Class Diagram defines the entities within the model, known as models, atoms, and first class objects as well as the connections that can be made between them. The Visualization sub-metamodel defines different aspects, or filters, for viewing only certain entities within a model instance. For example, if defining a metamodel for a finite state machine, an aspect could be defined in the Visualization sub-metamodel that would only display accepting states in a finite state machine model instance. The Constraints sub-metamodel allows the application of Object Constraint Language (OCL) (Richters, 1998) constraints to metamodel entities. Continuing with the finite state machine metamodel example, a constraint could be defined that only a single starting state may exist in the model. To do this, users would add a constraint in the Constraints sub-metamodel, add the appropriate OCL code to define the constraint, and then connect it to the entity to which it applies. Finally, the Attributes sub-metamodel allows additional data, known as attributes, to be defined and associated with other metamodel entities defined in the Class Diagram.

After the metamodel has been constructed using GMeta, the interpreter must be run to convert the metamodel into a GME paradigm.

This paradigm can then be loaded with GME and used to created models that adhere to the rules defined within the metamodel. User may then create model instances with the assurance that the design rules and domain specific constraints defined within the metamodel are satisfied. If at any point the domain or design constraints of the model change, the metamodel can be reloaded, altered and interpreted again to change the GME paradigm appropriately. As a result, designers can easily examine scenarios in which constraints differ, giving a broader overview of the design space.

Analyzing and Interpreting Model Instances

After a configuration language is determined, a modeling tool implemented, and a metamodel constructed, designers can rapidly construct model instances of valid DRE system configurations. There is no guarantee, however, that the configurations constructed with these tools are optimal. For example, while a configuration instance may be constructed that does not violate any design constraints, other configurations may exist that provide higher QoS, have a lower cost, or consume fewer resources. Many automated techniques, however, exist for determining system configurations that optimize these attributes.

Benavides et al. provide a methodology for mapping the extended feature models described earlier onto constraint satisfaction problems (CSPs) (Benavides, 2005). A CSP is a set of variables with multiple constraints that define the values that the variables can take. Attributes and extra-functional features, such as a project budget feature, are maintained in the mapping. As a result, solutions that satisfy all extra-functional features and basic functional constraints can be found automatically with the use of commercial CSP solvers. Moreover, these solvers can be configured to optimize one or more attributes, such as the minimization of cost. Additionally, these techniques require the examination of all potential

solutions, resulting in a system configuration that is not only valid, but also optimal. Benavides et al. present empirical results showing that CSPs made from feature models of 23 features require less than 1,800 milliseconds to solve.

While extended feature models and their associated automated techniques for deriving valid configurations by converting them to CSPs can account for resource and budget constraints, the process is not appropriate for large-scale DRE system configuration problems. The exhaustive nature of CSP solvers often require that all potential solutions to a problem are examined. Since the number of potential system configurations is exponential in regards to the number of potential components, the solution space is far too vast for the use of exhaustive techniques as they would require a prohibitive amount of time to determine a solution.

To circumvent the unrealistic time requirements of exhaustive search algorithms, White et al. have examined approximation techniques for determining valid feature selections that satisfy multiple resource constraints (White, 2008b). Approximation techniques do not require the examination of all potential configurations, allowing solutions to be determined with much greater speed. While the solutions are not guaranteed to be optimal, they are often optimal or extremely near optimal. White et al. present *Filtered Cartesian Flattening* (FCF), an approximation technique for determining valid feature selections.

FCF converts extended feature models into *Multiple-choice Multi-dimensional Knapsack Problems* (MMKP). MMKP problems, as described by Akbar et al. are an extension of the *Knapsack Problem* (KP), *Multiple-Choice Knapsack Problem* (MCKP) and *Multi-Dimensional Knapsack Problem* (MDKP) (Akbar, 2001). Akbar et al. provide multiple heuristic algorithms, such as I-HEU and M-HEU for rapidly determining near optimal solutions to MMKP Problems.

With FCF, approximation occurs in two separate steps. First, all potential configurations

Figure 4. FCF optimality with 10,000 features

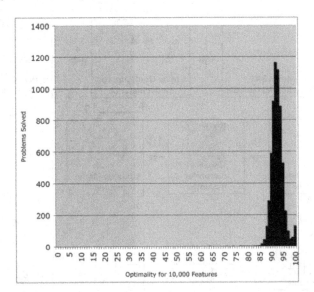

are not represented in the MMKP problems. For example, if there is an exclusive-or relationship between multiple features, then only a subset of the potentially valid relationships may be included in the MMKP problem. This pruning technique is instrumental in restricting problem size so that solving techniques can complete rapidly. Second, heuristic algorithms, such as M-HEU can be used to determine a near-optimal system configuration. M-HEU is a heuristic algorithm that does not examine all potential solutions to an MMKP problem, resulting in faster solve time, thus allowing the examination of considerably larger problems. Due to these two approximation steps, FCF can be used for problems of considerably larger size compared to methods utilizing CSPs. This scalability is shown in Figure 4 in which a feature model with 10,000 features is examined with 90% of the solutions resulting in better than 90% optimality.

While FCF is capable of determining valid large-scale DRE system configurations, it still makes many assumptions that may not be readily known by system designers. For example, FCF requires that the project budget allocation for purchasing hardware and the project budget al-

location for purchasing software components be known ahead of time. The best way to split the project budget between hardware and software purchases, however, is dictated by the configuration problem being solved. For example, if all of the hardware components is cheap and provide huge amounts of resources while the software components are expensive, it would not make sense to devote half of the project budget to hardware and half to software. A better system configuration may result from devoting 1% of the budget to hardware and 99% to software.

The *Allocation baSed Configuration ExploratioN Technique* (ASCENT) presented by White et al. is capable of determining valid system configurations while also providing DRE system designers with favorable ways to divide the project budget (White, 2008a). ASCENT takes an MMKP hardware problem, MMKP software problem and a project budget amount as input. Due to the speed and performance provided by the M-HEU algorithm, ASCENT can examine many different budget allocations for the same configuration problem. ASCENT has been used for configuration problems with 1000's of features and is over 98% optimal for problems of this magnitude, making

Figure 5. AMP workflow diagram

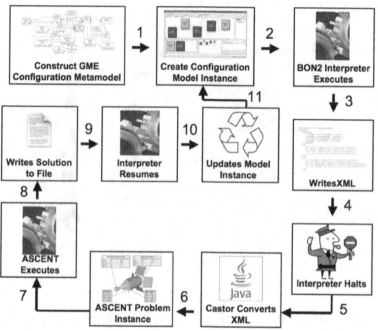

it an ideal technique for large-scale DRE system configuration.

To take advantage of these techniques, however, model instances must be converted into a form that these techniques can utilize. Interpreters are capable of parsing model instances and creating XML, source code, or other output for use with external programmatic methods. For example, GME model instances can easily be adapted to be parsed with Builder Object Network (BON2) interpreters. These interpreters are capable of examining all entities included in a model instance and converting them into C++ source code, thus allowing the application of automated analysis techniques, such as the use of CSP solvers or ASCENT (Benavides, 2005; White, 2008a).

CASE STUDY

The background section discussed the challenges of DRE system configuration. For problems of non-trivial size, these complexities proved too hard to overcome without the use of programmatic techniques. The section entitled "Devising a Configuration Language" described how configuration languages can be utilized to represent many of the constraints associated with DRE system configuration. That section also described how modeling tools can enforce complex design rules. The section entitled "Constructing a Metamodel" described the construction of a metamodel to formalize the constraints to be enforced in the modeling tool. The section entitled "Analyzing and Interpreting Model Instances" introduced several automated techniques for determining valid DRE system configurations, such as ASCENT, that provide additional design space information, such as how to allocate a project budget, which is extremely valuable to designers. This section describes the process of creating the *Ascent Modeling Platform* (AMP) to allow rapid DRE system configuration, while also addressing the challenges described in the background section. The target workflow of AMP is shown in Figure 5.

Designing a MDA Configuration Language for DRE Systems

ASCENT was originally implemented programmatically in Java, so constructing an entire configuration problem (including external resources, constraints, software components and hardware components along with their multiple unique resource requirements) required writing several hundred lines of complex code. As a result, the preparation time for a single configuration problem took a considerable amount of time and effort. Moreover, designers could not easily manipulate many of the problem parameters to examine "what if" scenarios. To address these limitations with ASCENT, *Ascent Modeling Platform* (AMP) tool was constructed that could be used to construct DRE system configuration problems for analysis with ASCENT.

Implementing a Modeling Tool

GME was selected to model DRE system configuration and used this paradigm to experiment with AMP. The following benefits were observed as a result of using GME to construct the AMP modeling tool for DRE system configuration:

- **Visualizes complex configuration rules** – AMP provides a visual representation of the hardware and software components making it significantly easier to grasp the problem, especially to users with limited experience in DRE system configuration.
- **Allows manipulation of configuration instances** – In addition to visually representing the problem, by using AMP designers are able to quickly and easily change configuration details (budget, constraints, components, resource requirements etc.) makes the analysis much more powerful.
- **Provides generational analysis** –Models produced with AMP may be fed a previous solution as input, enabling designers to ex-

amine possible upgrade paths for the next budget cycle. These upgrade paths can be tracked for multiple generations, meaning that the analysis can determine the best long-term solutions. This capability was not previously available with ASCENT and would have been considerably harder to implement without the use of GME.

- **Can easily be extended** – It is simple to add additional models and constraints to the existing AMP metamodel. As DRE system configuration domain specific constraints are introduced, the AMP metamodel can be altered to enforce these additional constraints in subsequent model instances. Since most DRE system configuration problems only slightly differ, existing metamodels can be reused and augmented.
- **Simplifies problem creation** – AMP provides a drag and drop interface that allows users to create problem instances instead of writing 300+ required lines of complex java code. The advantages of using a simple graphical user interface are (1) designers do not have to take the time to type the large amount of code that would be required and (2) in the process of typing this large amount of code designers will likely make mistakes. While the compiler may catch many of these mistakes, it is also likely domain specific constraints that the compiler may overlook will be inadvertently violated. Since GME enforces the design rules defined within the metamodel, it is not possible for the designers using AMP to unknowingly make such a mistake while constructing a problem instance.

To expand the analytical capabilities of AS-CENT, GME was utilized to provide an easily configurable, visual representation of the problem via the AMP tool. Using these new features, it is possible to see a broader, clearer picture of the

Figure 6. GME class view metamodel of ASCENT

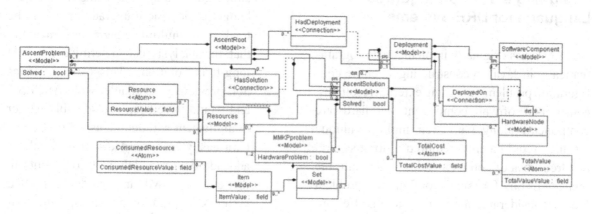

total design process as well as the global effects of even minor design decisions.

Constructing a Metamodel

A metamodel is created for DRE system configuration using MetaGME. Figure 6 shows the Class Diagram portion of the AMP metamodel. The root model is labeled as AscentRoot and contains two models: AscentProblem and AscentSolution. The configuration problems are defined within AscentProblem. The configuration determined by interpreting the AscentProblem model and applying the ASCENT technique is represented as the AscentSolution.

Within the AscentProblem, there is MMKP-problem models and a Resources model. The MMKPproblems are used to represent the components available for inclusion in the configuration. Also included in the MMKPproblem is a boolean attribute for setting whether or not an MMKPproblem is a hardware problem. A constraint is also defined that requires the definition of two MMKPproblems, one of which contains the hardware components while the other represents the software components.

The components shown in Figure 6 contain the resource amounts that they consume or produce, based on whether they are members of a hardware MMKP problem or a software MMKP

problem. The common resources model contains the Resource atoms, which represents the external resources of the problem that are common to both the hardware and software MMKPproblems, such as available project budget and power. The AscentSolution model contains a Deployment model, as well as atoms that represent the total cost and total value of the configuration determined by analyzing the AscentProblem. The Deployment model contains SoftwareComponents that represent the software components, HardwareNodes that represent the hardware components, as well as a DeployedOn connection that is used to connect the software components with the hardware components on which they are deployed.

Analyzing and Interpreting

A BON2 interpreter was written in C++ to analyze model instances. This interpreter traverses the AscentRoot model and creates an XML representation of the models, atoms and connections contained within. An XML representation of the model instance is then written to a file. This XML file matches a previously defined schema for use with the Castor XML binding libraries, a set of libraries for demarshalling XML data into Java objects. The ASCENT technique is defined within a Java jar file called ASCENTGME.jar. Once the XML data is generated, the interpreter makes a system call to execute the ASCENTGME.jar, passing in the XML file as an argument. Within ASCENTGME.jar, several things happen. First, the XML file is demarshaled into Java objects. A Java class then uses these objects to create two complex MMKPProblem instances. These two problem instances, along with a total budget value, are passed to ASCENT as input.

When ASCENT executes it returns the best DRE system configuration determined, as well as the cost and value of the configuration. A First Fit Decreasing (FFD) Bin-packer then uses these solutions along with their resource requirements to determine a valid deployment. This deployment data, along with the total cost, total value, hardware solution and software solution, is then written to a configuration file. The interpreter, having halted until the system call to execute the jar file terminates, parses this configuration file. Using this data, the ASCENT solution and deployment are written back into the model, augmenting the model instance with the system configuration.

The system configurations created by ASCENT can be examined and analyzed by designers. Designers can change problem parameters, execute the interpreter once again, and examine the effects of the changes to the problem on the system configuration generated. This iterative process allows designers to rapidly examine multiple DRE system configuration design scenarios, resulting in substantially increased knowledge of the DRE system configuration design space.

Motivating Example

AMP can be applied to determine valid configuration for the satellite imaging system shown in Figure 1. Not only should the resulting configuration be valid, but should also maximize system value. For example, a satellite imaging system that produces high-resolution images has higher inherent value than an imaging system that can only produce low-resolution images. In addition, the collective cost of the hardware and software

components of the system must not exceed the project budget.

To create an AMP problem instance representing the satellite imaging system described in Figure 1, several GME models must be created. First, an ASCENT Problem instance is added to the project. ASCENT Problem instances contain three models: A hardware MMKP Problem representing the hardware component options, a software MMKP Problem representing the software component options and Resources, representing the external resources, such as power and cost, that are consumed by both types of components.

A hardware MMKP problem instance is added to represent the hardware components. Within the hardware MMKP instance, Set model instances can be added. Each Set represents a set of hardware components that provide a common resource. For example, there are two types of hardware components, Memory and CPU available for consumption in the satellite system shown in Figure 1. To represent these two quantities, two Set instances are added with one instance representing CPU options and the other Memory Options.

Within each Set instance, the available options are represented as instances of Items. Item instances are added within the CPU option set to represent each of the available CPU options. Within each Item, a Resource instance is added to indicate the production amounts of the Item. For example, within the Item instance representing CPU 1, a Resource instance would be added that has a value of 1200, to represent the CPU production of the option. The instances representing the other CPU options and Memory options are constructed in the same manner, concluding the construction of the Hardware MMKP problem.

Now that the hardware options are represented, a software MMKP Problem instance must be prepared to represent the software component options. Continuing with the satellite imaging system shown in Figure 1, model representations of the software options for the Image Resolution component and Image Processing Algorithm must be constructed. Inside of the software MMKP instance, a Set instance is added for each set of component options, in this case a set for the Image Resolution component options and a set for the Image Processing Algorithm options. Similarly to the hardware MMKP problem, each software component option is represented as an Item. So within the Set instance of Image Resolution options, three Item models are added to represent the low-resolution, medium-resolution, and high-resolution options.

Unlike the hardware MMKP Problem, however, a value attribute must be assigned to represent the desirability of including the option. For example, it is more desirable to provide high-resolution image processing rather than medium-resolution or low-resolution image properties. Therefore, the value attribute high-resolution option would be set to a higher number than the other resolution options. Once the value is set, the resource consumption of each option can be set within each item representation of the software component options in the same manner as described for the hardware MMKP Problem. Once the hardware MMKP Problem, software MMKP Problem, and Resources are set, the model can be interpreted.

After the interpreter executes, a Deployment Plan model instance is created. Within the Deployment Plan the selected hardware components and software components can be seen. In this case, the deployment plan consists of the CPU 1, RAM 1 hardware components and Algorithm 4, high-resolution software components. Further examination shows that both of the software components can be supported by the hardware components selected.

FUTURE RESEARCH DIRECTIONS

Modeling tools can facilitate the process of DRE system configuration. The methodology described in this chapter has presented a process for constructing a modeling tool for system con-

figuration from scratch. The model instances that are created using these modeling tools require that a user manually constructs model instances. For larger model instances, this may take a large amount of time. Therefore, techniques are needed that facilitate model instance construction from existing model instances.

Typically, system designers wish to construct a single model instance from data spread out over multiple model types. For example, a system designer may have a UML diagram for describing system software architecture, excel spreadsheets listing the cost and specifications of candidate components, and a Ptolemy model providing fault tolerance requirements. To manually extract this information form multiple models would be laborious. Multi-modeling tools are applications that allow the manipulation of multiple PSMs defined by different metamodels. Multi-modeling tools could allow the automated aggregation of data from models of different types. In future work the use of multi-models to collect reliability, fault-tolerance, and performance data from multiple disparate models will be investigated and applied to the evaluation of model instances of DRE system configurations.

The migration of a model instance defined by a certain metamodel to a model instance defined by a different metamodel is known as a model transformation. Since these metamodels define different rules for constructing PSMs, the semantic meaning of the model that is migrated can be partially or entirely lost, resulting in an incomplete transformation. In future work, procedures to transform models while minimizing data loss will be researched. Using these techniques, models that contain additional system configuration data, such as Ptolemy models, could be transformed into model instances that can be used in concert with AMP (Eker, 2003). The Lockheed Martin Corporation is currently constructing NAOMI (Denton, 2008), a multi-modeling environment that can be utilized to aggregate data from multiple models of different types and perform complex multi-model transformations.

CONCLUSION

Determining valid configurations for distributed real-time and embedded (DRE) systems is hard. Designers must take into account a myriad of constraints including resource constraints, real-time constraints, QoS constraints, and other functional constraints. The difficulty of this task is exacerbated by the presence of a plethora of potential COTS components for inclusion in the configuration, with each providing varying quality of service, functionality, resource requirements and financial cost. This high availability of COTS components results in an exponential number of potential DRE system configurations. As a result, manual techniques for determining valid DRE system configurations are far too cumbersome. Even exact automated techniques, such as the use of CSPs, require a prohibitive amount of time to execute. Approximation techniques, such as ASCENT, however, do not require an exhaustive search of the vast design space allowing a much more rapid execution while often resulting in solutions with over 95% optimality.

The use of complex programmatic techniques in approximation techniques like ASCENT often have a steep learning curve and require large amounts of coding to construct a problem for execution. Due to the complex coding involved, these techniques carry the added burden of being error prone when defining problem instances. To address these challenges, an MDA-based tool called the *Ascent Modeling Platform* (AMP) that utilized GME to construct problem instances and display valid solutions for DRE system configurations was utilized. The following are lessons learned during our creation and use of AMP:

- **Modeling tools provide rapid problem construction**. Through the use of GME, problems could be constructed in a fraction of the time of using programmatic techniques.

- **Utilizing MDA reduces human error**. AMP utilizes a GME metamodel that enforces the many complex design constraints associated with DRE system configuration. As a result, users of AMP are prevented from constructing a configuration problem that is invalid.

- **Modeling tools facilitate design space exploration**. Solutions are posted directly back into the model for analysis by system designers. Designers can then change problem parameters within the model and execute the interpreter to explore multiple configuration scenarios, resulting in an increased understanding of the design space.

- **Multiple execution options still needed**. Currently ASCENT is the only technique that is executed upon interpreting models in AMP. Other techniques, such as the use of CSP solvers, should be implemented to determine solutions to problems with an appropriately reduced number of candidate components.

The current version of AMP with example code is available in open-source form at ascent-design-studio.googlecode.com.

REFERENCES

Akbar, M., Manning, E., Shoja, G., & Khan, S. (2001). Heuristic Solutions for the Multiple Choice Multi-dimension Knapsack Problem. *Lecture Notes in Computer Science*, 659–668. doi:10.1007/3-540-45718-6_71

Alves, C., & Castro, J. (2001). CRE: A systematic method for COTS components selection. In *Brazilian Symposium on Software Engineering*, (pp. 193–207).

Benavides, D., Trinidad, P., & Ruiz-Cortes, A. (2005). Automated Reasoning on Feature Models. *17th Conference on Advanced Information Systems Engineering (CAiSE05, Proceedings)*, (LNCS, 3520, pp. 491–503).

Chung, L., Cooper, K., & Courtney, S. (2004). COTS-aware requirements engineering and software architecting. In *Proceedings of the SERP*. Citeseer.

Czarnecki, K., Helsen, S., & Eisenecker, U. (2005). Staged configuration through specialization and multi-level configuration of feature models. *Software Process Improvement and Practice*, *10*(2), 143–169. doi:10.1002/spip.225

Denton, T., Jones, E., Srinivasan, S., Owens, K., & Buskens, R. (2008). NAOMI-An Experimental Platform for Multi-modeling. In *Proceedings of the 11th international conference on Model Driven Engineering Languages and Systems*, (pp. 143–157). Berlin: Springer.

Eker, J., Janneck, J., Lee, E., Liu, J., Liu, X., & Ludvig, J. (2003). Taming heterogeneity - the ptolemy approach. *Proceedings of the IEEE, 91*(1), 127–144. doi:10.1109/JPROC.2002.805829

Gokhale, A., Schmidt, D., Natarajan, B., & Wang, N. (2002). Applying model-integrated computing to component middleware and enterprise applications. *Communications of the ACM, 45*(10), 65–70. doi:10.1145/570907.570933

Jaring, M., & Bosch, J. (2002). Representing variability in software product lines: A case study. *Lecture Notes in Computer Science*, 15–36. doi:10.1007/3-540-45652-X_2

Kent, S. (2002). Model Driven Engineering. In *Proceedings of the Third International Conference on Integrated Formal Methods*, (pp. 286–298). London: Springer-Verlag.

Ledeczi, A., Maroti, M., Bakay, A., Karsai, G., Garrett, J., Thomason, C., et al. (2001b). The generic modeling environment. In *Workshop on Intelligent Signal Processing, Budapest, Hungary*, vol. 17.

Ledeczi, A., Nordstrom, G., Karsai, G., Volgyesi, P., & Maroti, M. (2001a). On metamodel composition. In *IEEE CCA*.

Mellor, S., Scott, K., Uhl, A., & Weise, D. (2004). *MDA distilled: principles of model-driven architecture*. Reading, MA: Addison-Wesley Professional.

Morisio, M., Seaman, C., Basili, V., Parra, A., Kraft, S., & Condon, S. (2002). COTS-based software development: Processes and open issues. *Journal of Systems and Software, 61*(3), 189–199. doi:10.1016/S0164-1212(01)00147-9

Poole, J. (2001). Model-driven architecture: Vision, standards and emerging technologies. In *Workshop on Metamodeling and Adaptive Object Models, ECOOP*.

Richters, M., & Gogolla, M. (1998). On formalizing the UML object constraint language OCL. *Lecture Notes in Computer Science*, 449–464.

Sabin, D., & Freuder, E. (1996). Configuration as composite constraint satisfaction. In *Proceedings of the Artificial Intelligence and Manufacturing Research Planning Workshop*, (pp. 153–161). Chesapeake, VA: AAAI Press.

Schmidt, D. (2002). Middleware for real-time and embedded systems. *Communications of the ACM, 45*(6), 43–48. doi:10.1145/508448.508472

Voas, J. (1998). Certifying off-the-shelf software components. *Computer, 31*(6), 53–59. doi:10.1109/2.683008

Wang, N., Schmidt, D., Gokhale, A., Gill, C., Natarajan, B., & Rodrigues, C. (2003). Total quality of service provisioning in middleware and applications. *Microprocessors and Microsystems, 27*(2), 45–54. doi:10.1016/S0141-9331(02)00096-0

White, J., Dougherty, B., & Schmidt, D. C. (2008a). *Ascent: An algorithmic technique for designing hardware and software in tandem.* Tech. Rep. ISIS-08-907, ISIS-Vanderbilt University.

White, J., Dougherty, B., & Schmidt, D. C. (2008b). *Selecting Highly Optimal Architecture Feature Sets with Filtered Cartesian Flattening.* Journal of Software and Systems - Special Issue on Design Decisions and Design Rationale in Software Architecture.

ADDITIONAL READING

Balasubramanian, K., Gokhale, A., Karsai, G., Sztipanovits, J., & Neema, S. (2006). Developing applications using model-driven design environments. *Computer*, *39*(2), 33–40. doi:10.1109/MC.2006.54

Batory, D., Sarvela, J., & Rauschmayer, A. (2004). Scaling step-wise refinement. *IEEE Transactions on Software Engineering*, *30*(6), 355–371. doi:10.1109/TSE.2004.23

Bosch, J., Florijn, G., Greefhorst, D., Kuusela, J., Obbink, J., & Pohl, K. (2002). Variability issues in software product lines. *Lecture Notes in Computer Science*, 13–21.

Deelstra, S., Sinnema, M., Van Gurp, J., & Bosch, J. (2003). Model driven architecture as approach to manage variability in software product families. In *Proc. of Model Driven Architecture: Foundations and Applications*, (pp. 109–114).

Fey, D., Fajta, R., & Boros, A. (2002). Feature modeling: A meta-model to enhance usability and usefulness. *Lecture Notes in Computer Science*, *2379*, 198–216. doi:10.1007/3-540-45652-X_13

France, R., & Rumpe, B. (2007). Model-driven development of complex software: A research roadmap. In *International Conference on Software Engineering*, (pp. 37–54). IEEE Computer Society Washington, DC, USA.

Freville, A. (2004). The multidimensional 0–1 knapsack problem: An overview. *European Journal of Operational Research*, *155*(1), 1–21. doi:10.1016/S0377-2217(03)00274-1

Gokhale, A., Schmidt, D., Natarajan, B., Gray, J., & Wang, N. (2003). *Model-Driven Middleware.* Middleware for Communications.

Gomaa, H., & Webber, D. (2004). Modeling adaptive and evolvable software product lines using the variation point model. In *Proceedings of the Proceedings of the 37th Annual Hawaii International Conference on System Sciences (HICSS'04)-Track*, vol. 9, (pp. 05–08).

Gu, X., Yu, P., & Nahrstedt, K. (2005). Optimal Component Composition for Scalable Stream Processing. In *Distributed Computing Systems, 2005. ICDCS 2005. Proceedings. 25th IEEE International Conference on*, (pp. 773–782).

Hein, A., Schlick, M., & Vinga-Martins, R. (2000). Applying feature models in industrial settings. In *Software Product Lines: Experience and Research Directions: Proceedings of the First Software Product Lines Conference (SPLC1), August 28-31, 2000, Denver, Colorado*, (p. 47). Kluwer Academic Publishers.

Her, J., Choi, S., Cheun, D., Bae, J., & Kim, S. (2007). A Component-Based Process for Developing Automotive ECU Software. *Lecture Notes in Computer Science*, *4589*, 358. doi:10.1007/978-3-540-73460-4_31

Hi, M., Michrafy, M., & Sbihi, A. (2006). A Reactive Local Search-Based Algorithm for the Multiple-Choice Multi-Dimensional Knapsack Problem. *Computational Optimization and Applications*, *33*(2), 271–285. doi:10.1007/s10589-005-3057-0

Hiremath, C., & Hill, R. (2007). New greedy heuristics for the Multiple-choice Multi-dimensional Knapsack Problem. *International Journal of Operational Research*, *2*(4), 495–512. doi:10.1504/IJOR.2007.014176

Kang, K., Lee, J., & Donohoe, P. (2002). Feature-oriented product line engineering. *IEEE Software*, *19*(4), 58–65. doi:10.1109/MS.2002.1020288

Kumar, V. (1992). Algorithms for Constraint-Satisfaction Problems: A Survey. *AI Magazine*, *13*(1), 32–44.

Mikic-Rakic, M., & Medvidovic, N. (2002). Architecture-Level Support for Software Component Deployment in Resource Constrained Environments. *Lecture Notes in Computer Science*, 31–50. doi:10.1007/3-540-45440-3_3

Shahriar, A., Akbar, M., Rahman, M., & Newton, M. (2008). A multiprocessor based heuristic for multi-dimensional multiple-choice knapsack problem. *The Journal of Supercomputing*, *43*(3), 257–280. doi:10.1007/s11227-007-0144-2

Slomka, F., Dorfel, M., Munzenberger, R., & Hofmann, R. (2000). Hardware/software codesign and rapid prototyping of embedded systems. *Design & Test of Computers, IEEE*, *17*(2), 28–38. doi:10.1109/54.844331

Srinivasan, S., & Jha, N. (1995). Hardware-software co-synthesis of fault-tolerant real-time distributed embedded systems. In *European Design Automation Conference: Proceedings of the conference on European design automation*, vol. 18, (pp. 334–339).

Svahnberg, M., & Bosch, J. (2000). Issues concerning variability in software product lines. *Lecture Notes in Computer Science*, 146–157. doi:10.1007/978-3-540-44542-5_17

Ulfat-Bunyadi, N., Kamsties, E., & Pohl, K. (2005). Considering Variability in a System Familys Architecture During COTS Evaluation. In *Proceedings of the 4th International Conference on COTS-Based Software Systems (ICCBSS 2005)*, *Bilbao, Spain*. Springer.

White, J., Benavides, D., Dougherty, B., & Schmidt, D. (2009). Automated Reasoning for Multi-step Configuration Problems. In *Proceedings of the Software Product Lines Conference (SPLC)*. San Francisco, USA.

White, J., Schmidt, D. C., Benavides, D., Trinidad, P., & Ruiz-Cortez, A. (2008). Automated Diagnosis of Product-line Configuration Errors in Feature Models. In *Proceedings of the Software Product Lines Conference (SPLC)*, (pp. 225–234). Limerick, Ireland.

Woeginger, G. (2003). Exact algorithms for NP-hard problems: A survey. *Lecture Notes in Computer Science*, *2570*, 185–208. doi:10.1007/3-540-36478-1_17

KEY TERMS AND DEFINITIONS

DRE System: Distributed Real-time Embedded system consisting of distributed components and subject to real-time requirements, QoS constraints, and limited resources.

COTS Components: Configurable Commerical Off The Shelf components that can be purchased and combined to construct DRE system configurations.

GME: The Generic Modeling Environment is a standalone modeling environment that allows for metamodel construction, creation of model instances, and is compatible with multiple interpreters.

ASCENT: The Allocation based Configuration Exploration Technique is an algorithmic technique that uses and MMKP problem representation of candidate components to determine valid, near-optimal DRE system configurations.

Software Component: COTS component that carries a purchase cost, provides functionality, and requires resources provided by hardware components to function.

Hardware Component: COTS component that carries a purchase cost and provides the computational resources required by software components to function.

Project Budget: The maximum amount of money that can be spent purchasing COTS components.

Chapter 7
Model–Driven Automated Error Recovery in Cloud Computing

Yu Sun
University of Alabama at Birmingham, USA

Jules White
Virginia Tech, USA

Jeff Gray
University of Alabama, USA

Aniruddha Gokhale
Vanderbilt University, USA

ABSTRACT

Cloud computing provides a platform that enables users to utilize computation, storage, and other computing resources on-demand. As the number of running nodes in the cloud increases, the potential points of failure and the complexity of recovering from error states grows correspondingly. Using the traditional cloud administrative interface to manually detect and recover from errors is tedious, time-consuming, and error prone. This chapter presents an innovative approach to automate cloud error detection and recovery based on a run-time model that monitors and manages the running nodes in a cloud. When administrators identify and correct errors in the model, an inference engine is used to identify the specific state pattern in the model to which they were reacting, and to record their recovery actions. An error detection and recovery pattern can be generated from the inference and applied automatically whenever the same error occurs again.

INTRODUCTION

With the increasing complexity of software and systems, domain analysis and modeling are becoming more important for software development and system applications. Applying domain-specific modeling languages and transformation engines is an effective approach to address platform complexity and the inability of third-generation languages to express domain concepts clearly (Schmidt, 2006). Building correct models for a specific domain can often simplify many complex tasks, particularly for distributed applications

DOI: 10.4018/978-1-61692-874-2.ch007

Figure 1. Two options to control application instances

Application Instances in Cloud

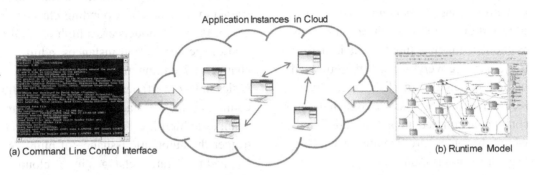

(a) Command Line Control Interface

(b) Runtime Model

based on cloud computing (Hayes, 2008) that offer several opportunities for customization and variability.

Cloud computing shifts the computation from local, individual devices to distributed, virtual, and scalable resources, thereby enabling end-users to utilize the computation, storage, and other application resources (which forms the "cloud") on-demand (Hayes, 2008). Amazon EC2 (Elastic Compute Cloud) (http://aws.amazon.com/ec2/, 2009) is an example cloud computing platform that allows users to deploy different customized applications in the cloud. A user can create, execute, and terminate the application instances as needed, and pay for the cost of time and storage that the active instances use based on a utility cost model (Rappa, 2004).

In the cloud computing paradigm, the large number of running nodes increases the number of potential points of failure and the complexity of recovering from error states. For instance, if an application terminates unexpectedly, it is necessary to search quickly through the large number of running nodes to locate the problematic nodes and states. Moreover, to avoid costly downtime, administrators must rapidly remedy the problematic node states to avoid further spread of errors.

Just like standard enterprise applications, cloud computing applications can suffer from a wide range of problems stemming from hardware failure to operator error (Oppenheimer et al., 2003). For example, Amazon EC2 provides

limited guarantees about availability or reliability of hardware or virtual machine (VM) instances. Operators must be prepared to re-launch VM instances when failures occur, transfer critical data to newly provisioned VM images, start critical services on new VM instances, join new nodes to virtual LANs or security contexts, or update load balancers and elastic IP addresses to reference newly provisioned infrastructure.

Although Amazon EC2 provides a user-friendly and simple interface to manage and control the application instances (Figure 1a), administrators must still be experienced with the administrative commands, the configuration of each application, as well as some domain knowledge about each running instance. Administrators must therefore be highly trained to effectively and efficiently handle error detection and error recovery. The complexity of managing a large cloud of nodes can increase maintenance costs, especially when personnel are replaced due to turnover or downsizing.

Even with experienced administrators, the process of error recovery involves the following challenges:

- It is hard to locate errors accurately with a large number of running application instances.
- It may take too much time to detect and locate an error, causing a long period of service termination or further error propagation.

- Error recovery becomes a time-consuming and error-prone task when it involves multiple and/or complex modification actions.
- Without a logging function, it is hard to track past recovery actions, thereby leading to a potentially unreliable recovery.
- Key error recovery knowledge may become concentrated in a few individuals, which becomes problematic when they leave the organization.

The main reason for these challenges is the lack of automated mechanisms to aid error recovery. Relying on manual actions to handle each error does not scale as the number of node instances increases.

This chapter presents a new automated approach to error recovery in cloud computing based on high-level graphical models of distributed application state to present the application status to an administrator. When administrators identify and correct errors in the model, an inference engine is used to identify the specific state pattern in the model to which they were reacting. Moreover, the administrator's recovery actions are recorded. Subsequently, the model is automatically monitored for the previously identified error state and when it is encountered, the recorded recovery actions are automatically replayed or presented to the administrator as a potential course of action.

In this approach, a domain-specific modeling language (DSML) is first developed to define the running status of a specific cloud application. A DSML is usually a graphical domain-specific language to model the various aspects of a system (Gray et al., 2007). It tends to support higher level abstractions than general-purpose languages, resulting in less effort to specify a system. A DSML can be designed to construct a runtime model that serves as a graphical monitoring interface to reflect the running nodes and states of an application. Whenever errors appear in the cloud, they are also reflected in the model (i.e., models are relevant at runtime). A causal connection is established

such that correcting errors in the runtime model triggers the same corresponding changes in the cloud. Because models are a high-level abstraction of the application instances, administering changes by editing the models (Figure 1b) is easier and more efficient than using the traditional command-line interface (Figure 1a). Moreover, changes to high-level modeling abstractions can trigger the automatic issuance of multiple low-level administrative changes in the cloud.

Recovering from errors by modifying runtime models is still a manual procedure that has similar drawbacks with respect to scalability, productivity, knowledge centralization, and repeatability. Instead of correcting erroneous model states manually for each occurrence of a fault, this chapter focuses on "Recovery by Demonstration," which is derived from the idea of Model Transformation by Demonstration (MTBD) (Sun et al., 2009). Recovery by demonstration is a process whereby an administrator manually specifies a series of recovery actions for an error state and then the automation infrastructure automatically replays the same recovery actions when an identical error state is encountered in the future. Recovery by Demonstration is facilitated by the use of domain-specific models and model transformations. Specifically, the first time that an error appears in a cloud application, a user must manually discover the problematic model elements associated with the error and manually demonstrate the recovery process by modifying the model to remove the error state.

This chapter describes an Eclipse plug-in called MT-Scribe, which integrates with a domain-specific modeling tool that can record all the recovery operations performed and then infer the error state from patterns in the model. After the first occurrence of the error, the model's state is continuously checked for the error. Whenever the error pattern is matched, the recorded recovery operations are replayed automatically to correct the error. To showcase Recovery by Demonstration, this chapter presents two case studies involving the detection and recovery of errors in a 3-tiered Enterprise Java Beans (EJB) application that is executed within the Amazon EC2 platform. By recovering from some common errors, the case study demonstrates the potential for dynamic cloud application reconfiguration through Model-Driven Engineering (MDE) (Schmidt, 2006). The goal of our approach is to manually correct once and then automatically recover anytime and anywhere from the same error.

The rest of this chapter is organized as follows. We first provide background information on cloud computing, Amazon EC2, as well as error detection and recovery problems in this field. This introduction is followed by an explanation of how to build a runtime model for the running applications in the cloud computing server and how to establish a causal relationship between the model and application. Then, model transformation by demonstration is introduced. Through two case studies, we will illustrate how to use this technique to simplify the error detection and recovery processes. Related works and some lessons learned are summarized after the case studies. Finally, we offer concluding remarks and discuss areas for future work.

BACKGROUND

Cloud computing allows businesses to build and utilize complex hardware and network configurations that would normally require a large investment in a dedicated datacenter (Buyya et al., 2009). With cloud computing services, such as Amazon EC2, computational services are purchased on an incremental basis. For example, EC2 allows businesses to purchase computation time, software licenses, networked data storage, queuing services, and database space on an hourly or per gigabyte basis.

The underlying cloud infrastructure is based on virtualization (Armbrust et al., 2009), which allows the environment to rapidly boot multiple custom operating system (OS) images on the same hardware platform while guaranteeing separation of their address spaces and security. Each instance of an OS image is booted as a separate virtual machine (VM) instance in the cloud. The most basic operation that a developer using cloud infrastructure can perform is the specification of OS images that should be booted as VM instances in the cloud.

Cloud failure recovery is normally performed at the VM level. When a failure due to misconfiguration, hardware error, or excessive load is observed, developers must manually determine which VM instances to shutdown and which new VM instances to launch. Furthermore, after the new cloud assets are launched, developers must painstakingly replicate any configuration actions (e.g., editing XML configuration files for a Java application server) that cannot be packaged into the OS image.

Most existing cloud computing recovery mechanisms are based on autoscaling (Moreno-Vozmediano et al., 2009; Fronckowiak, 2008), which is a technique whereby VM instances are continuously monitored through a programmatic framework to detect failures and new VM instances are automatically launched when failures are detected. Autoscaling has been implemented in production cloud infrastructure systems by companies, such as Amazon and RightScale.

Existing autoscaling solutions leave a number of unaddressed research challenges. These challenges stem primarily from their focus on VM-level recovery mechanisms, which cannot always handle the complex application-specific requirements of cloud applications. The shortcomings of existing autoscaling-based recovery mechanisms can be broadly categorized into the following three areas:

1. **OS images for VMs cannot always encapsulate all configuration actions that must be taken to bring a VM into the application's architecture.** Applications

may require complex startup orderings for applications, editing of configuration files, or state injection. Although many OS facilities exist for automating such actions, they require expert knowledge, extensive testing, and complex development to implement properly.

2. **VM-level monitoring cannot capture many application-specific failure conditions.** Most cloud computing autoscaling mechanisms allow developers to specify failure conditions based on VM instance availability, CPU load, or disk I/O conditions. Application-specific failure conditions, such as poor response times of specific components in the web-tier or exceptions generated from application processes, cannot be monitored. The lack of this type of application-specific fine-grained monitoring prevents developers from automatically identifying and reacting to numerous types of failures.

3. **Implementing recovery actions requires expert knowledge to perform complex analyses to identify root failure causes and design appropriate autoscaling avoidance tactics.** Although an application operator may know how to repair a failure, they may not possess the intimate understanding of autoscaling to design a future avoidance strategy.

Next, we will describe how each of these limitations of using autoscaling-based recovery mechanisms can be overcome by applying a combination of modeling and Recovery by Demonstration.

BUILDING RUNTIME CLOUD COMPUTING MODELS

In order to address Challenges 1 and 2 mentioned in the previous section, an accurate model of the application must be constructed that can precisely capture: (1) configuration details that cannot easily be embedded into an OS image, and (2) application-specific state information needed to identify failures. Furthermore, once this model is constructed, a causal link between the model and the running cloud application must be established to synchronize the model with the running application's state. The remainder of this section describes how the model and causal link are constructed.

To capture the concerns of the cloud application precisely, a DSML is constructed that is tailored specifically for the concepts and terms in the application. Because of the significant cost and development time to implement a complex graphical editor for the customized DSML, a metaprogrammable modeling environment (Balasubramanian et al., 2006), such as GME (Ledeczi et al., 2001) or GEMS (http://www.eclipse.org/gmt/gems/, 2009) can be used to build the editing environment. A metaprogrammable modeling environment provides developers with a graphical environment to specify the metamodel for the DSML.

The metamodel defines the terms, notation, and syntax of the final DSML. Moreover, in a metaprogrammable modeling environment, the metamodel specifies the visualization mechanisms for the language elements. After the metamodel is constructed, the metaprogrammable modeling environment automatically generates a graphical modeling editor for the DSML. This generative capability allows developers to rapidly construct application-specific models for capturing cloud application state. Figure 3 shows the metamodel of the DSML used for an EJB cloud application case study.

After the DSML is defined, a causal link must be established between the running application in the cloud and the model. Changes to the state of the cloud application must be communicated back to the DSML modeling tool and translated into changes in the elements of a specific model. For the case study presented in the next section, JavaScript Object Notation (JSON) (http://www.

Figure 2. DSML application model and causal link through JSON over HTTP

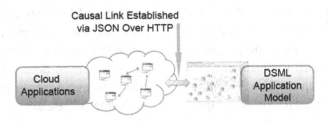

json.org/, 2009) messages sent over HTTP are used to communicate state changes from the cloud application back to the modeling tool. As shown in Figure 2, the modeling tool polls each server's control uniform resource identifier (URI) via HTTP for changes in its state. Common state events, such as the availability of a node in the cloud, can be captured using a reusable library. Application-specific events, such as the response time of a custom Java web application, require a custom implementation of the monitoring logic. The control URI is a web-based URI that can be used to receive state updates from the application and post changes that should be made to the configuration. Change messages sent in either direction are encoded as JSON messages.

To translate application state changes into corresponding changes in the modeling tool, an application-specific semantic transformation layer (STL) is used. The STL receives incoming unprocessed state change messages from the cloud application and translates these messages into equivalent changes in the modeling elements of the model to which the application is causally linked. It is possible for the STL to reside within the modeling tool or on a remote host that serves as a proxy to translate messages into native DSML semantics before they arrive at the modeling tool. Currently, our implementation of STL is built using several platforms, including: (1) the Java Jetty (http://www.mortbay.org/jetty/, 2009) embedded HTTP server to receive JSON messages, (2) the Eclipse Modeling Framework (EMF) (http://www.eclipse.org/modeling/emf/, 2009) as the model implementation platform, and (3) customized Java transformations built into the GEMS modeling tool to perform the semantic mapping.

Figure 3. Metamodel of the DSML for EJB cloud application

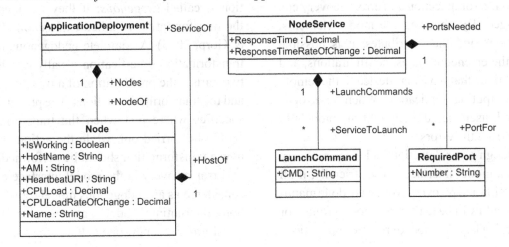

In some scenarios, a one-to-one mapping can be established between the state changes in the application and the required changes in the model. For example, each application concept can be tagged with an identifier that is directly mapped to a single model element representing the concept in the model. In more detailed scenarios, complex predicate logic using Prolog or other mechanisms can be used to synchronize the state of the application with the model (Nechypurenko et al., 2007).

Changes from the model must also be pushed back into the cloud. In each HTTP polling operation performed by the modeling tool, change messages, such as configuration actions that should be run, can be posted to the control URI. The STL is also responsible for translating changes in the model into control messages that use the proper semantics of the cloud application.

The runtime model provides a direct and clear representation of the status of applications running in the remote cloud computing server. With the established causal relationship between model instances and applications, it offers a convenient interface for users to monitor, control and manage cloud computing applications.

RECOVERY BY DEMONSTRATION

Based on the runtime model interface and the causal relationship between models and applications, both error detection and error recovery can be realized. By checking the model elements, connections and their attributes, it is possible to find the erroneous states, configurations, and combinations that have manifested in the remote cloud computing application. When an error is identified, users can directly edit the models to recover from the errors.

Although error detection and error recovery through a model interface is user-friendly, if all the detection and recovery work were done manually, it would still be tedious and error-prone. For instance, if a large number of remote applications

existed simultaneously, being reflected as thousands of model elements, relying on administrators to find any inconsistencies in the model elements would be a significant burden. In addition, some errors need to be detected and recovered immediately to avoid catastrophic failures or costly downtime. In these cases, even for a small number of applications, administrators must continually monitor and check each model element. If several errors occur simultaneously, the situation is even more difficult to rectify due to identification of the problems that are the root cause of an error. Therefore, it is important to automate both error detection and error recovery processes, rather than relying on completely manual management.

Error Recovery Automation by Model Transformation

Because the error detection and recovery involve checking and editing the model instances, it is very straightforward to translate these actions into model transformations in order to create an automated process. Model transformation (Sendall & Kozaczynski, 2003) is a core technology in MDE. A model transformation receives a source model that conforms to a given metamodel as input, and produces as output another model conforming to a given metamodel. When the source and target metamodels are different (i.e., between two different domains), the transformation is called *exogenous*; if they are identical, the transformation is called *endogenous* (Mens & Gorp, 2005). A complete endogenous model transformation specification usually consists of two parts – the precondition of a transformation and the transformation actions. The precondition specifies where and when the transformation should be carried out, while the actions define how a transformation should be performed.

Error recovery in the model interface can be considered as an endogenous model transformation - the runtime model in an erroneous state is transformed to a new one in the correct state, because in this case both the source and target models conform to the same metamodel. The precondition of this transformation specifies when and where to execute an error recovery transformation. In other words, the precondition serves as the criteria of error detection. When a model instance meets the precondition, the transformation actions will be executed, which consists of all the specific error recovery operations. Therefore, an error detection and recovery process through the model interface can be realized by a model transformation.

The main advantage of converting the error detection and recovery problems to a model transformation is that a number of automatic model transformation approaches already exist, which can be applied to automate the error detection and recovery tasks. The most common and mature approach to implement model transformations is to use an executable model transformation language, such as ATL (Jouault et al., 2008) or C-SAW (Gray et al., 2006). Most of these languages provide a high-level of abstraction, and support a declarative mechanism to simplify the specification of transformations. Each error detection and recovery process can be expressed through a model transformation. By executing these transformations whenever a change happens in the model instances, errors can be detected immediately by matching the precondition, and can be recovered by performing the associated transformation actions.

Limitations of Model Transformation Languages

Model transformation languages provide a powerful approach to automate error detection and recovery. However, they are not perfect and still present some challenges to users, particularly to those who are unfamiliar with a specific model transformation language. Although declarative expressions are supported in most model transformation languages, the transformation rules are defined at the metamodel level, which requires a

clear and deep understanding of the abstract syntax and semantic interrelationships between the source and target models. In some cases, certain domain concepts are hidden in the metamodel and difficult to unveil (Wimmer et al., 2007; Kappel et al., 2006). These implicit concepts make writing transformation rules challenging. Moreover, a model transformation language may not be at the proper level of abstraction for an end-user and could result in a steep learning curve.

For cloud computing server administrators, it is not necessary to be a programmer or model transformation expert. Therefore, the difficulty of specifying metamodel-level rules and the associated learning curve may prevent some administrators from using transformation languages to leverage their experience and contribute to the design and implementation of error detection and recovery processes.

Model Transformation by Demonstration

To assist administrators who do not posses deep knowledge of programming or model transformation languages, a simple model transformation approach is needed to support error detection and recovery. Model Transformation By Demonstration (MTBD) is an innovative approach to simplify model transformation tasks. Instead of writing the transformation rules manually, MTBD enables the inference of model transformations from the demonstration of a transformation process by end-users. Figure 4 provides an overview of the MTBD approach in the context of error recovery, which consists of five main steps.

Step 1: User demonstration and operations recording. A user-recorded demonstration provides the basis for transformation pattern analysis and inference. Whenever an error appears in the runtime model, the demonstration of an error recovery process is given by directly editing a model instance (e.g., add a new model element or connection, modify the attribute of a model

Figure 4. Error recovery using MTBD

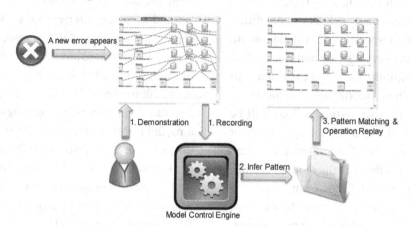

element) to fix the error. An event listener monitors the operations occurring in the model editor. For each operation that is captured, all the information about the operation is encapsulated into an object, similar to the Command pattern (Gamma et al., 1995). The final list of these command objects represents the sequence of operations needed to finish a model transformation (in this case, error recovery) task.

Step 2: Infer the transformation pattern. Based on the recorded operations, a general transformation pattern is inferred that is independent of any model transformation language. This pattern describes the precondition of a transformation (i.e., where the transformation should be performed) and the actions of a transformation (i.e., how the transformation should be realized). By analyzing the recorded operations, meta-information of model elements and connections is extracted to construct a precondition, with actions specified by an operation sequence.

Step 3: Transformation refinement. The initial precondition inferred in Step 2 is called the weakest precondition, which only specifies the minimum number of necessary model elements needed to execute the transformation actions. However, in practice, this precondition is usually insufficient, because it is often too imprecise to determine where and when to transform a model.

For instance, a transformation may only need to be applied when a specific model element attribute is set to a precise value. For example, a transformation may need only to be applied when an attribute is set to a value that indicates an exception has occurred. MTBD provides a user-friendly interface to specify the detailed restrictions on the precondition. In some other cases, the inferred transformation actions are too specific to the demonstration, and therefore not generic enough. An example is that a user deletes two elements contained in another element, intending to demonstrate deleting all elements in it. However, the initially inferred transformation actions will only delete two elements in a certain container when applied. If three or more elements existed, only two of them will be removed, not all of them. Thus, enabling generic transformation actions also requires user refinement in this step.

Step 4: Precondition matching. After a pattern is summarized, it can be reused and applied to any model instance. By selecting a pattern from the repository, the engine automatically traverses the model instance to search for all locations that match the precondition (i.e., meet the criteria of the error) in the selected pattern. A notification is given if no matching locations are found.

Step 5: Executing actions and correctness checking. When a matching location is found

Figure 5. PetStore web tier 1 node

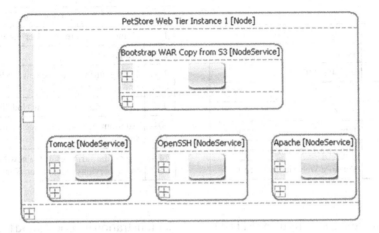

(i.e., an error is found), the transformation actions are executed to transform the current model instance (i.e., to recover the error). The precondition matching step guarantees that operations can be executed with necessary operands. However, it does not ensure that executing them will not violate the metamodel. Therefore, each action is logged and model instance correctness checking is performed after every action execution. If a certain action violates the metamodel definition, all executed actions are undone and the whole transformation is cancelled.

Based on this approach, the error recovery can be demonstrated step-by-step so that a model transformation pattern can be inferred. The inferred and refined precondition can then be used as a criterion for error detection, while the actions recover the error. A repository has been built to store all the generated patterns. When a change happens in a model instance, all the patterns in the repository will be applied one-by-one to check if certain patterns could be matched and executed, ensuring that an error could be detected and recovered in a timely manner compared with the manual detection and recovery. These patterns may serve as reusable failure identifiers that are joined with autoscaling tactics, attacking the third challenge identified in an earlier section.

Error Detection and Recovery Case Studies

In the remainder of this section, we illustrate how to apply MTBD in error detection and recovery through two examples.

Scenario 1: Restarting a Failed Node

Error description: The attribute IsWorking in a Node is used to represent its working status. If this attribute is set to false, it indicates the web server has failed and needs to be restarted immediately. For example, Figure 5 shows a Node (called PetStore Web Tier 1), which controls the web server on an EJB e-commerce site for selling pets to customers. Table 1 lists all the attributes of this Node with the associated values. The IsWorking attribute indicates that the Node has failed.

Error recovery solution: Whenever a Node fails to work, it should be replaced with a new Node that has the same structure, including any configuration actions that could not be embedded into the OS image. Therefore, the solution is to replace the failed Node with a new Node, which contains exactly the same structure and configuration as the old one except the IsWorking attribute is set to true.

Table 1. Attributes of PetStore web tier instance 1 (failed node)

Attribute Name	Value
IsWorking	False
AMI	ami-45e7002c
CPULoad	12.0
CPULoadRateOfChange	1.5
HeartbeatURI	http://ps01.aws.amazon.com/hb
HostName	http://ps01.aws.amazon.com/hb
Name	PetStore Web Tier Instance 1

Table 2. Operations demonstrated for scenario 1

No.	Operation Recorded
1	Remove PetStore Web Tier Instance 1
2	Add a new Node
3 – 8	Set the attributes of the new Node to be those in the old one (6 attributes)
9	Set IsWorking of the new Node to be true
10 – 13	Add four new NodeService elements
14 – 25	Set all the attributes of the new NodeService elements to the previous values (3 attributes)

To handle this simple scenario by using MTBD, we need to first demonstrate the desired transformation process by performing the replacement operations on a concrete Node. Thus, in step 1, we select the PetStore Web Tier Instance 1 Node for our demonstration. Then, we delete this Node, and add a new one. There are four NodeService elements in the original Node (i.e., Bootstrap WAR Copy from S3, Tomcat, OpenSSH, Apache) that indicate processes that must be launched and active on the Node. The same NodeService elements should also be added in the new Node. Finally, to keep the new Node and the original one consistent, we should set all the attributes of the newly added elements to be the same as those in the old ones. For instance, there are seven attributes in a Node: IsWorking, AMI (Amazon Machine Image), CPULoad, CPULoadRateofChange, HeartbeatURI, HostName, Name. We can set each of the attributes in the new Node to be the same as the one in the removed Node through the attribute editor, except for the IsWorking attribute. It is the same case for NodeService. In total, 12 attribute editing operations are needed to set the three attributes for the four new NodeService elements.

Table 2 shows the operations performed to replace a Node. All of these operations and related information (e.g., metamodel information and location of the operations) can be recorded in sequence. Figure 6 shows a screenshot of the demonstration in process and the operations being recorded in the view.

In step 2, when the demonstration is finished, the basic transformation pattern is inferred. This pattern consists of the list of actions (shown in Table 2), as well as the weakest precondition. This precondition means that in order to execute this transformation there must be sufficient model elements for the recorded operations to be replayed correctly. Because the recorded operations are based on specific model elements (e.g., Web Tier Instance 1, Tomcat), the precondition is generalized by extracting the metamodel information in each recorded operation, and renaming each element in sequence. As shown in Table 3, the precondition for this example is that there must be a Node, which contains at least four NodeService elements.

However, the weakest precondition is usually not sufficient to determine when and where to apply a transformation. For instance, in this scenario, we only want to replace the Node whose IsWorking attribute is false. But if the inferred precondition in step 2 is applied, all the Nodes with at least four NodeService elements will be replaced, regardless of whether they are working or not. Therefore, more specific constraints are needed to refine the inferred precondition. In this case, the precondition should be further modified to be the Node with at least four NodeService elements with the IsWorking attribute set to false.

Figure 6. Screenshot of demonstration process and operation recording view

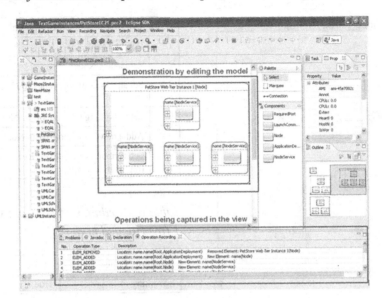

To realize this refinement, in step 3, users are asked to provide more restrictions on the generated precondition. Users can specify Node.IsWorking == false through a precondition editor dialog (Figure 7). This refinement will be integrated with the original precondition and applied in future steps.

Another problem related to the inferred precondition is that not all of the Nodes contain four NodeService elements. Consider the Data Tier Instance 1 Node as an example; only three NodeService elements are contained – MySQL, Apache, PHPMyAdmin. In this case, the inferred precondition cannot be matched even if the Data Tier Instance 1 failed to work. Therefore, we need to give some feedback information on the recorded

operations and indicate that some of them are generic and can be executed with a different number of available elements. From Table 2, it can be found that operations 10 through 13 are the same remove operations repeated, and 14 – 16, 17 – 19, 20 – 22, 23 – 25 are also four sets of repeated operations. Therefore, in step 3, we can provide a feedback result indicating that steps 9 – 12 are the same, so only one is needed, and this set can be repeated according to the number of elements available; 13 – 24 is the four same set of operations, so only one set is needed, and this set can be repeated similarly. After this step, the final operation list is shown in Table 4. The associated precondition can be seen in Table 5. All these lists are shown to illustrate the abstract representation of the pattern data stored, which are not visible to administrators. The administrators only need to demonstrate the process and refine the pattern in the user-friendly interfaces (e.g., the dialog shown in Figure 7), after which all the other following steps will be carried out automatically.

After refining the transformation precondition, a complete transformation pattern is generated

Table 3. The weakest precondition for scenario 1

Model Elements Needed
Node
Node.NodeService1
Node.NodeService2
Node.NodeService3
Node.NodeService4

Figure 7. Precondition specification dialog

Table 5. Final precondition after refinement

Model Elements Needed
Node (Node.isWorking == false)
Node.NodeService1 (repeat if needed)

Table 4. Final operation list after refinement

No.	Operation Recorded
1	Remove Node
2	Add a new Node1
3 – 8	Set attributes of the Node1 to Node (6 attributes)
9	Set IsWorking attribute of the Node1 to true
10	Add a new NodeService1 in Node1 (repeat if needed)
11 – 13	Set attributes of NodeService1 to Node.NodeService (repeat if needed)

Table 6. Attributes of PetStore web tier instance 1 (overloaded node)

Attribute Name	Value
IsWorking	True
AMI	ami-45e7002c
CPULoad	22.0
CPULoadRateOfChange	5.5
HeartbeatURI	http://ps01.aws.amazon.com/hb
HostName	http://ps01.aws.amazon.com/hb
Name	PetStore Web Tier Instance 1

and saved in the repository. This pattern has a precondition, which in this case can be used as the criteria of error detection, and a sequence of actions, which are the error recovery operations. Whenever a change happens in the model, all the saved patterns including this one will be executed one-by-one automatically. When executing a pattern, the engine will first match the precondition in the current model instance at step 4. In other words, the current model instance will be traversed and all the locations matching the precondition will be found. In this process, a back-tracking matching algorithm is applied. More details about this algorithm can be found in (Sun et al., 2009).

At the matching locations, the sequence of actions in the transformation pattern will be executed. Because the possibility of violating the metamodel definition exists when executing the transformation actions, each execution will be logged. If a violation happens, all the executed actions will be undone and the transformation will be canceled in that matching position.

Scenario 2: Overload Management

Error description: If the CPULoad of a Node exceeds 20, and CPULoadRateofChange exceeds 5, the Node is overloaded. Table 6 shows a Node in the erroneous overloaded state.

Error recovery solution: Replace the Node with two identical Nodes, and split the CPULoad equally to the two new Nodes. In other words, the task is to set the CPULoad attribute of each new Node to be half of the original Node.

Similar to Scenario 1, we first select a Node and perform the demonstration. As shown in Table 7, after adding the two new Node elements

Table 7. Operations demonstrated for scenario 2

No.	Operation Recorded
1	Remove PetStore Web Tier Instance 1
2	Add a new Node
3 – 8	Set the attributes of the new Node to be those in the old one (6 attributes)
9	Set the CPULoad attribute of the new Node to be half in the old one
10 – 13	Add four new NodeService elements
14 – 25	Set all the attributes of these NodeService to be those in the old ones (3 attributes)
26	Add a another new Node
27 – 31	Set the attributes of the new Node to be those in the old one (6 attributes)
32	Set the CPULoad attribute of the new Node to be half in the old one
33 – 36	Add four new NodeService
37 – 48	Set all the attributes of the new NodeService elements to the previous (3 attributes)

Figure 8. Attribute editing dialog

through the same set of operations in Scenario 1, the attributes are setup as usual. In order to split the original CPULoad into two equal parts, the attribute editor is applied. For example, if the original CPULoad is 25, we can set NewNode. CPULoad = 25 / 2 = 12.5 through an attribute editor dialog, which can be internally recorded as NewNode.CPULoad = PetStore Web Tier Instance 1.CPULoad / 2. The attribute editor enables users to specify the attribute computation at the instance level in a demonstration process, but infer the transformation rules at the metamodel level, so that when the value changes the next time (e.g., 50, not 25), it can still compute the correct value. As shown in Figure 8, the attribute editing dialog enables users to access all the attributes of the current model instance, and specify a complex attribute refactoring computation. In some of the other related approaches, which will be discussed in the "Related Works" section, only concept mapping is supported without considering attribute transformation, such that splitting the value into halves cannot be realized as used in this case.

The original transformation pattern inferred needs to be refined as well. In this scenario, the precondition should be all the Nodes whose CPULoad is greater than 20 and CPULoadRateofChange is greater than 5. Therefore, we added one restriction on the precondition: PetStore Web Tier Instance 1.CPULoad > 20 && PetStore Web Tier Instance 1.CPULoadRateofChange > 5. In addition, adding NodeService and attribute editing operations should be marked as generic, as in the last scenario.

Executing this transformation will automatically find all of the Nodes that have too much working load, and split the load into two new Nodes. If the load in the new Node is still over the limit, it can be split again by invoking the transformation repeatedly until the values satisfy the precondition.

RELATED WORK

Error recovery plays an important role in many aspects of computer science. A number of research efforts have investigated error recovery in fields such as compilers (Graham & Rhodes, 1973), robotics (Donald, 1989), and network applications (Carle & Biersack, 1997). Because cloud computing is a newly emerging area, the research on error recovery in this field is still limited. In (Wang et al., 2009), a schema is proposed to ensure the correctness of data storage in cloud computing. Recovering errors in the administration of cloud computing applications have not been thoroughly investigated.

In our approach, domain-specific modeling and model transformation are the foundation of the implementation. MTBD is the core technology in this work. Its original aim is to simplify implementation of model transformation tasks, following the similar direction of Model Transformation By Example (MTBE) approaches. Balogh and Varró introduced MTBE by using inductive logic programming (Balogh & Varró, 2009; Varró & Balogh, 2007). The idea is to generate graph transformation rules from a set of user-defined mappings between the source and target model instances by applying an inductive logic engine. Similarly, Strommer and Wimmer implemented an Eclipse prototype to enable generation of ATL rules from the semantic mappings between domain models (Strommer & Wimmer, 2008; Strommer et al., 2007). Both approaches provide semi-automatic generation of model transformation rules, which need further refinement by a user. Because both approaches are based on semantic mappings, they are more appropriate in the context of exogenous model transformations between two different metamodels, and may not be as conveniently applied in endogenous model transformations, as shown in this chapter. In addition, the generation of rules to transform attributes is not well-supported in most MTBE implementations, which makes MTBE insufficient to fully support error detection and recovery as discussed in this chapter.

A closely related work to MTBD is called program transformation by demonstration (Robbes & Lanza, 2008). To perform a program transformation, users first manually change a concrete program example, and all the changes are recorded by the monitoring plug-in. Then, the recorded changes are generalized into a transformation. After editing and specifying the generated transformation, it can be applied to other source code locations.

Our work involves a runtime model to reflect the status and transmit the changes of the remote applications in a cloud computing server. This is actually a typical application in the field of research known as models at runtime (Blair et al., 2009). An increasing number of works have been conducted in this field. For instance, in (Jouault et al., 2006), a method to extract runtime models to support reverse engineering and software evolution is introduced. Chitchyan and Oldevik (Chitchyan & Oldevik, 2006) presented the challenges and solutions of maintaining a multi-dimensional separation of concerns model at runtime and dynamic introspection and adaptation of concerns in such a model. A runtime model and its evolution for self-adaptation in the assisted living domain are illustrated in (Schneider & Becker, 2008).

LESSONS LEARNED

The inferred transformation pattern can be used as a valuable source for cloud application administrator training, which is an essential process in cloud computing application management. The most effective training process must contain various examples and real cases. When teaching administrators how to detect and handle errors, the inferred transformation pattern can be used to better illustrate the problems. For instance, the precondition in a transformation pattern formally specifies the conditions of an error. By executing the pattern, it shows whether a certain sample model meets the criteria of an error according to the result of pattern matching. Additionally, the transformation actions can serve as an instructional guide on how to remedy the error. By executing the transformation pattern, the final status of the model after correcting the error also can be observed easily, so that the administrator can compare the original and final state. This is especially important when a large number of complex operations are needed to fix the error. In future work, we plan to investigate the use of a transformation debugger with forward and backward stepping to help train administrators.

The recording mechanism can also be used to realize logging so that the reason for a failure can be tracked. The current operation recording mechanism can monitor and capture a wide variety of operations from the model editor. Extending the operation recording mechanism to record all operations (e.g., start / stop cloud server, open / close files, execute transformation pattern), rather than just operations in a demonstration process, can provide a complete logging mechanism. When necessary, the sequence of changes made on any model instance can be tracked, and the administrators' control on the servers is enhanced. This logging functionality may be particularly useful for post-mortem analysis of failures due to administrator error.

Another benefit to recording more generic actions, rather than only model editing operations (e.g., running a model transformation, and invoking certain applications), is that it can enhance the richness of error recovery solutions. For example, if two error recovery transformations are already inferred and available, they can be applied together if needed when solving another new error. For this new error, two operations are needed to demonstrate the process, invoke the first transformation and invoke the second transformation, which are much more efficient than solving this problem step-by-step. In addition, we can also integrate other system operations into the demonstration, such as restarting the monitoring system, closing the model editor, or even opening a web browser and sending an email.

Although this work is specific to the Amazon EC2 cloud computing system, it can serve as a useful framework for controlling and managing

runtime models with model transformations. For other areas, the only modifications required would be additional metamodels for the new domains. The current mechanism of the model and domain causal relationship can also be reused, and MTBD works for any model instances, independent of the underlying metamodel. Therefore, in a similar area where runtime monitoring and controlling is not well-supported, our approach offers a powerful and flexible framework to realize the related tasks. Additionally, our approach is not restricted to error recovery tasks. Several general administration tasks in cloud computing could also benefit from this framework, such as reconfiguration of the applications based on certain criteria, and adding and stopping application nodes. More exploration of using our approach on these general administration tasks is one of our future works.

The design of the metamodel can be either generic or specific to the individual application. In the cloud computing domain, for instance, we could build a generic metamodel which is capable of describing all kinds of applications like the one used in the case study. However, this generic metamodel can only cover similar functions among different applications, and there must be some specific aspects in certain domains that cannot be reflected through this generic metamodel. Thus, before building a metamodel, it is necessary to conduct a complete domain analysis and decide what kind of metamodel is needed. Generally, the simpler the metamodel, the easier it will be to model the application implementation.

CONCLUSION

This chapter describes a novel application of using MDE to support domain analysis by automating the error detection and error recovery processes in cloud computing servers. The implementation is based on a runtime modeling framework that reflects the real status of applications executing in remote servers and is capable of transmitting the changes made in models to the corresponding applications. This runtime modeling framework not only provides a more user-friendly interface for administrators to manage and control the cloud computing applications, but also makes automating error detection and recovery processes easier to realize. MTBD is an innovative method to simplify model transformations. It can infer the precondition and needed actions of a transformation from the user demonstrated operations. Because detecting and recovering errors in the runtime models can be regarded as endogenous model transformations, using MTBD to demonstrate an error recovery process and infer a generic model transformation including the precondition (i.e., the criteria of error detection) could improve the productivity and simplicity of the work. Based on this approach, each error must be manually corrected on the first occurrence. After that, with the inferred model transformation pattern, the same error can be automatically detected and recovered anywhere without manual intervention. From this application, it has been found that domain analysis and management could benefit from some of the model-driven technologies, and therefore could be accomplished more appropriately in the context of MDE.

Although MTBD greatly simplifies certain model transformation tasks, it is not as powerful as writing general-purpose model transformation specifications. Many of the functions and mechanisms that can be expressed by a general transformation language are difficult to demonstrate and infer with MTBD. For instance, precondition specification is still a weak part of our process. Constraints can be placed on the attributes of the model elements, but it is impossible to specify the desired model structure (e.g., a Node is connected with exactly two other Nodes). Enhancing the precondition specification in MTBD will be our main future work. To further improve MTBD, more complex operations should be supported, such as adding a specific number of certain elements, or functions such as min(), max().

ACKNOWLEDGMENT

This work is supported in part by an NSF CAREER award (CCF-1052616), NSF RAPID CNS award (CNS-1047780), and NSF CNS Core award (CNS-0915976).

REFERENCES

Amazon Elastic Compute Cloud (Amazon EC2). (n.d.) Retrieved March 2010 from http://aws.amazon.com/ec2/

Armbrust, M., Fox, A., Griffith, R., Joseph, A., Katz, R., Konwinski, A., et al. (2009). *Above the Clouds: A Berkeley View of Cloud Computing.* Technical Report 2009-28, UC Berkeley.

Balasubramanian, K., Gokhale, A., Karsai, G., Sztipanovits, J., & Neema, S. (2006). Developing Applications Using Model-Driven Design Environments. *IEEE Computer*, 39(2), 33–40.

Balogh, Z., & Varró, D. (2009). *Model Transformation by Example using Inductive Logic Programming. Software and Systems Modeling.* Berlin: Springer.

Blair, G., Bencomo, N., & France, R. (2009). Models@run.time. *IEEE Computer*, 42(10), 22–27.

Buyya, R., Yeo, C., Venugopal, S., Broberg, J., & Brandic, I. (2009). Cloud Computing and Emerging IT Platforms: Vision, Hype, and Reality for Delivering Computing as the 5th Utility. *Future Generation Computer Systems*, 25(6), 599–616. doi:10.1016/j.future.2008.12.001

Carle, G., & Biersack, E. (1997). Survey of Error Recovery Techniques for IP-based Audio-visual Multicast Applications. *IEEE Network Magazine*, 11(6), 24–36. doi:10.1109/65.642357

Chitchyan, R., & Oldevik, J. (2006). A Runtime Model for Multi-dimensional Separation of Concerns. *Models@run.time, held at MODELS 2006*, Genova, Italy, October 2006.

Donald, B. (1989). *Error Detection and Recovery in Robotics,* (LNCS 33). Berlin: Springer-Verlag.

Eclipse Modeling Format (EMF). (n.d.). Retrieved March 2010, from http://www.eclipse.org/modeling/emf/

Fronckowiak, J. (2008). Auto-scaling Web sites using Amazon EC2 and Scalr. In *Amazon EC2. Articles and Tutorials.*

Gamma, E., Helm, R., Johnson, R., & Vlissides, J. (1995). *Design Patterns: Elements of Reusable Object-oriented Software.* Retrieved from Addison-Wesley.

Generic Eclipse Modeling System (GEMS). (n.d.). Retrieved March 2010 from http://www.eclipse.org/gmt/gems/

Graham, S., & Rhodes, S. (1973). Practical Syntactic Error Recovery in Compilers. In *Symposium on Principles of Programming Languages,* (pp. 52-58), Boston.

Gray, J., Lin, Y., & Zhang, J. (2006). Automating Change Evolution in Model-Driven Engineering. *IEEE Computer. Special Issue on Model-Driven Engineering, 39*(2), 51–58.

Gray, J., Tolvanen, J., Kelly, S., Gokhale, A., Neema, S., & Sprinkle, J. (2007). Domain-specific Modeling. In Fishwick, P. (Ed.), *Handbook of Dynamic System Modeling* (pp. 7-1–7-20). Boca Raton, FL: CRC Press.

Hayes, B. (2008). Cloud Computing. *Communications of the ACM, 51*(7), 9–11. doi:10.1145/1364782.1364786

Java Jetty Server. (n.d.). Retrieved March 2010 from http://www.mortbay.org/jetty/

JavaScript Object Notation (JSON). (n.d.). Retrieved March 2010 from http://www.json.org/

Jouault, F., Allilaire, F., Bézivin, J., & Kurtev, I. (2008). ATL: A Model Transformation Tool. *Science of Computer Programming, 72*(1&2), 31–39. doi:10.1016/j.scico.2007.08.002

Jouault, F., Bezivin, J., Chevrel, R., & Gray, J. (2006). Experiments in Runtime Model Extraction. *Models@run.time, held at MODELS 2006,* Genova, Italy, October 2006.

Kappel, G., Kapsammer, E., Kargl, H., Kramler, G., Reiter, T., Retschitzegger, W., et al. (2006). Lifting Metamodels to Ontologies - A Step to the Semantic Integration of Modeling Languages. In *Proceedings of International Conference on Model Driven Engineering Languages and Systems (MoDELS),* (LNCS 4199, pp. 528–542), Genova, Italy. Berlin: Springer-Verlag.

Ledeczi, A., Bakay, A., Maroti, M., Volgyesi, P., Nordstrom, G., Sprinkle, J., & Karsai, G. (2001). Composing Domain-specific Design Environments. *IEEE Computer, 34*(11), 44–51.

Mens, T., & Gorp, P. (2005). A Taxonomy of Model Transformation. In. *Proceedings of the International Workshop on Graph and Model Transformation, 152,* 125–142.

Moreno-Vozmediano, R., Montero, R., & Llorente, I. (2009). Elastic Management of Cluster-based Services in the Cloud. In *Proceedings of the 1st Workshop on Automated Control for Datacenters and Clouds,* Barcelona, Spain, (pp. 19– 24).

Nechypurenko, A., Wuchner, E., White, J., & Schmidt, D. (2007). Application of Aspect-based Modeling and Weaving for Complexity Reduction in the Development of Automotive Distributed Realtime Embedded Systems. In *Proceedings of the 6th International Conference on Aspect-Oriented Software Development,* Vancouver, British Columbia, (pp. 10).

Oppenheimer, D., Ganapathi, A., & Patterson, D. A. (2003). Why do Internet Services Fail and What Can be Done About It? In *Proceedings of the 4th USENIX Symposium on Internet Technologies and Systems,* Seattle, WA, (pp. 1).

Rappa, M. (2004). The Utility Business Model and the Future of Computing Services. *IBM Systems Journal, 43*(1), 32–42. doi:10.1147/sj.431.0032

Robbes, R., & Lanza, M. (2008). Example-based Program Transformation. In *Proceedings of International Conference on Model Driven Engineering Languages and Systems (MoDELS),* (LNCS 5301, pp. 174–188), Toulouse, France. Berlin: Springer-Verlag.

Schmidt, D. (2006). Model-Driven Engineering. *IEEE Computer, 39*(2), 25–32.

Schneider, D., & Becker, M. (2008). Runtime Models for Self-adaptation in the Ambient Assisted Living Domain. *Models@run.time, held at MODELS 2008,* Toulouse, France, October 2008.

Sendall, S., & Kozaczynski, W. (2003). Model Transformation - The Heart and Soul of Model-driven Software Development. *IEEE Software. Special Issue on Model Driven Software Development, 20*(5), 42–45.

Strommer, M., Murzek, M., & Wimmer, M. (2007). Applying Model Transformation by-example on Business Process Modeling Languages. In *Proceedings of the 3rd International Workshop on Foundations and Practices of UML,* Auckland, New Zealand, (pp. 116–125).

Strommer, M., & Wimmer, M. (2008). A framework for model transformation by-example: Concepts and tool support. In *Proceedings of the 46th International Conference on Technology of Object-Oriented Languages and Systems,* Zurich, Switzerland, (pp. 372–391).

Sun, Y., White, J., & Gray, J. (2009). Model Transformation by Demonstration. In *Proceedings of International Conference on Model Driven Engineering Languages and Systems (MoDELS),* (LNCS 5795, pp. 712-726), Denver, CO. Berlin: Springer-Verlag.

Varro, D. (2006). Model Transformation by Example. In *Proceedings of International Conference on Model Driven Engineering Languages and Systems,* (LNCS 4199, pp. 410–424), Genova, Italy. Berlin: Springer-Verlag.

Varró, D., & Balogh, Z. (2007). Automating Model Transformation by Example using Inductive Logic Programming. In *Proceedings of the 2007 ACM Symposium on Applied Computing,* Seoul, Korea, (pp. 978–984).

Wang, C., Wang, Q., Ren, K., & Lou, W. (2009). Ensuring Data Storage Security in Cloud Computing. In *Proceedings of 17th IEEE International Workshop on Quality of Service,* Charleston, SC, (pp. 1-9).

Wimmer, M., Strommer, M., Kargl, H., & Kramler, G. (2007). Towards Model Transformation Generation By-Example. In *Proceedings of the 40th Hawaii International Conference on Systems Science,* Big Island, HI, (pp. 285).

KEY TERMS AND DEFINITIONS

Cloud Computing: Is an Internet-based computing approach, which shifts the computation from local, individual devices to distributed, virtual, and scalable resources, enabling end-users to utilize the computation, storage, and other application resources on-demand.

Model-Driven Engineering: Is a new software development methodology to increase software development productivity by raising the level of abstraction from traditional general-purpose programming languages to high-level problem domain concept models.

Domain-specific Modeling Language: Is one type of domain-specific language used to represent the various aspects of a system at a higher level of abstraction than general-purpose modeling languages, which requires fewer details and less effort to specify a system.

Error Recovery: Is focused on recovering the errors occurring in the cloud computing configuration and management processes.

Model Transformation: Is a core technology in Model-driven Engineering. It receives a source model that conforms to a given metamodel as input, and produces as output another model conforming to a given metamodel.

Model Transformation Languages: Are domain-specific languages to implement model transformation tasks.

Model Transformation by Demonstration: Is a new model transformation approach that enables general end-users to implement model transformation tasks without learning any model transformation languages or knowing the metamodel definitions.

Chapter 8
Productivity Analysis of the Distributed QoS Modeling Language

Joe Hoffert
Vanderbilt University, USA

Douglas C. Schmidt
Vanderbilt University, USA

Aniruddha Gokhale
Vanderbilt University, USA

ABSTRACT

Model-driven engineering (MDE), in general, and Domain-Specific Modeling Languages (DSMLs), in particular, are increasingly used to manage the complexity of developing applications in various domains. Although many DSML benefits are qualitative (e.g., ease of use, familiarity of domain concepts), there is a need to quantitatively demonstrate the benefits of DSMLs (e.g., quantify when DSMLs provide savings in development time) to simplify comparison and evaluation. This chapter describes how the authors conducted productivity analysis for the Distributed Quality-of-Service (QoS) Modeling Language (DQML). Their analysis shows (1) the significant productivity gain using DQML compared with alternative methods when configuring application entities and (2) the viability of quantitative productivity metrics for DSMLs.

INTRODUCTION

Model-driven engineering (MDE) helps address the problems of designing, implementing, and integrating applications (Schmidt, 2006; Hailpern, 2006; Atkinson 2003; Kent, 2002). MDE is increasingly used in domains involving modeling software components, developing embedded software systems, and configuring quality-of-service (QoS) policies. Key benefits of MDE include (1) raising the level of abstraction to alleviate accidental complexities of low-level and heterogeneous software platforms, (2) more effectively expressing designer intent for concepts in a domain, and (3) enforcing domain-specific development constraints. Many documented benefits of MDE

DOI: 10.4018/978-1-61692-874-2.ch008

are qualitative, *e.g.*, use of domain-specific entities and associations that are familiar to domain experts, and visual programming interfaces where developers can manipulate icons representing domain-specific entities to simplify development. There is a lack of documented quantitative benefits for domain-specific modeling languages (DSMLs), however, that show how developers are more productive using MDE tools and how development using DSMLs yields fewer bugs.

Conventional techniques for quantifying the benefits of MDE in general (*e.g.*, comparing user-perceived usefulness of measurements for development complexity (Abrahao and Poels, 2007, 2009)) and DSMLs in particular (*e.g.*, comparing elapsed development time for a domain expert with and without the use of the DSML (Loyall, Ye, Shapiro, Neema, Mahadevan, Abdelwahed, Koets, & Varner, 2004)) involve labor-intensive and time-consuming experiments. For example, control and experimental groups of developers may be tasked to complete a development activity during which metrics are collected (*e.g.*, number of defects, time required to complete various tasks). These metrics also often require the analysis of domain experts, who may be unavailable in many production systems.

Even though DSML developers are typically responsible for showing productivity gains, they often lack the resources to demonstrate the quantitative benefits of their tools. One way to address this issue is via *productivity analysis*, which is a lightweight approach to quantitatively evaluating DSMLs that measures how productive developers are, and quantitatively exploring factors that influence productivity (Boehm, 1987; Premraj, Shepperd, Kitchenham, & Forselius, 2005). This chapter applies quantitative productivity measurement using a case study of the *Distributed QoS Modeling Language* (DQML), which is a DSML for designing valid QoS policy configurations and transforming the configurations into correct-by-construction implementations. Our productivity analysis of DQML shows significant productivity

gains compared with common alternatives, such as manual development using third-generation programming languages. While this chapter focuses on DQML, in general the productivity gains and analysis presented are representative of DSMLs' ability to reduce accidental complexity and increase reusability.

BACKGROUND

This section presents related work in the area of metrics for MDE and domain-specific technologies. We present work on quantitative analysis for MDE technologies as well as metrics to support quantitative evaluation.

Conway and Edwards (2004) focus on measuring quantifiable code size improvements using the *NDL Device Language* (NDL), which is a domain-specific language applicable to device drivers. NDL abstracts details of the device resources and constructs used to describe common device driver operations. The creators of NDL show quantitatively that NDL reduces code size of a semantically correct device driver by more than 50% with only a slight impact on performance. While quantifiable code size improvements are shown by using NDL, the type of improvement is applicable to DSLs where a higher level language is developed to bundle or encapsulate lower level, tedious, and error prone development. The productivity analysis for a DSL is easier to quantify since common units such as lines of source code are used. Conway and Edwards present compelling evidence of productivity gains of NDL although they do not encompass all the benefits of automatic code generation found with DSMLs such as the ease of a GUI.

Bettin (2002) measures productivity for domain-specific modeling techniques within the domain of object-oriented user interfaces. Comparisons are made between (1) traditional software development where no explicit modeling is performed, (2) standard Unified Modeling

Language (UML)-based software development, where UML is interpreted as a graphical notation providing a view into the source code, and (3) domain-specific notations to UML to support a higher-level abstraction that automatically generates large parts of the implementation. While the use of the domain-specific notations show a sharp reduction in the number of manually-written lines of source code as compared to traditional software development, the addition of modeling elements comes at some cost since no models are developed in traditional software development. The trade-off of the manual coding and modeling efforts is not clear quantitatively.

Balasubramanian, Schmidt, Molnar, & Ledeczi (2007) quantitatively analyze productivity gains within the context of the *System Integration Modeling Language* (SIML). SIML is a DSML that performs metamodel composition augmenting elements of existing DSMLs or adding additional elements. The productivity analysis of SIML focuses on the reduction of development steps needed for functional integration as compared to manual integration including design and implementation using native tools. The design and implementation steps are weighted more heavily (*i.e.*, are more expensive in development resources such as time and man-power) than using SIML which provides automated DSL integration. The analysis shows a 70% reduction in the number of distinct integration steps for a particular use case.

Genero, Piattini, Abrahao, Insfran, Carsi, & Ramos (2007) qualitatively measure ease of comprehension for class diagrams generated using various transformation rules via an experimental approach. From a given requirements model UML class diagrams were generated using 3 different sets of transformation rules. Human subjects were then asked to evaluate how easy the generated diagrams were to understand. While this experimental approach gleans valuable user feedback, this approach also incurs substantial experimental resources and time by involving human subjects

and also targets the qualitative aspect of ease of understanding.

Abrahao and Poels (2007) have created OO-Method Function Points (OOmFP) which enhance function point analysis (FPA), originally designed for functional user requirements, to be applicable to object-oriented technologies. The metric generates a value related to the amount of business functionality a system provides to a user. Experimental procedures were conducted with students to compare FPA and OOmFP. The experiments showed that OOmFP consumed more time than FPA but the results were more accurate and more easily reproducible. Abrahoa and Poels (2009) then extended their OOmFP work into the area of Web applications which they termed OOmFPWeb. OOmFPWeb was designed to evaluate functionality of Web systems based on user-defined requirements encapsulated in the conceptual model of an application developed for the Web rather than based on solely on implementation artifacts created once the application had been fully developed (Cleary, 2000; Reifer, 2000).

In contrast to the work outlined above, this chapter showcases productivity metric of interpreters for DSMLs that transform models into implementation artifacts. This metric is important since interpreter developers need to understand not only the quantitative benefit of an interpreter but also the development effort for which the interpreter is justified.

OVERVIEW OF THE DISTRIBUTED QOS MODELING LANGUAGE (DQML)

The *Distributed QoS Modeling Language* (DQML) is a DSML that addresses key inherent and accidental complexities of ensuring semantically compatible QoS policy configurations for publish/subscribe (pub/sub) middleware. Semantic compatibility is accomplished when the combination and interaction of the specified

QoS policies produce the overall desired QoS for the system, *i.e.*, when the system executes with the QoS that is intended. DQML automates the analysis and synthesis of semantically compatible QoS policy configurations for the OMG *Data Distribution Service* (DDS), which is an open standard for QoS-enabled pub/sub middleware (Object Management Group, 2007). DQML was developed using the *Generic Modeling Environment* (GME) (Ledeczi, Bakay, Maroti, Volgyesi, Nordstrom, Sprinkle, & Karsai, 2001), which is a metaprogrammable environment for developing DSMLs.

This section provides an overview of DDS and the structure and functionality of DQML. Although DQML focused initially on QoS policy configurations for DDS, the approach can be applied to other pub/sub technologies, such as Web Services Brokered Notification (OASIS, 2006), Java Message Service (Sun Microsystems, 2002), CORBA Event Service (Object Management Group, 2004-1), and CORBA Notification Services (Object Management Group, 2004-2).

Overview of the OMG Data Distribution Service (DDS)

DDS defines a standard pub/sub architecture and runtime capabilities that enables applications to exchange data in event-based distributed systems. DDS provides efficient, scalable, predictable, and resource-aware data distribution via its *Data-Centric Publish/Subscribe* (DCPS) layer, which supports a global data store where publishers write and subscribers read data, respectively. Its modular structure, power, and flexibility stem from its support for (1) *location-independence*, via anonymous pub/sub, (2) *redundancy*, by allowing any numbers of readers and writers, (3) *real-time QoS*, via its 22 QoS policies, (4) *platform-independence*, by supporting a platform-independent model for data definition that can be mapped to different platform-specific models, and (5) *interoperability*, by specifying a standardized

protocol for exchanging data between distributed publishers and subscribers.

Several types of DCPS entities are specified for DDS. A *domain* represents the set of applications that communicate with each other. A domain acts likes a virtual private network so that DDS entities in different domains are completely unaware of each other even if on the same machine or in the same process. A *domain participant factory*'s sole purpose is to create and destroy domain participants. The factory is a pre-existing singleton object that can be accessed by means of the *get_instance()* class operation on the factory. A *domain participant* provides (1) a container for all DDS entities for an application within a single domain, (2) a factory for creating publisher, subscriber, and topic entities, and (3) administration services in the domain, such as allowing the application to ignore locally any information about particular DDS entities.

DDS is topic-based, which allows strongly typed data dissemination since the type of the data is known throughout the entire system. In contrast, content-based pub/sub middleware, such as Siena (Carzaniga, Rutherford, & Wolf, 2004) and the Publish/subscribe Applied to Distributed REsource Scheduling (PADRES) (Li & Jacobsen, 2005), examine events throughout the system to determine data types. A DDS *topic* describes the type and structure of the data to read or write, a *data reader* subscribes to the data of particular topics, and a *data writer* publishes data for particular topics. Various properties of these entities can be configured using combinations of the 22 QoS policies that are described in Table 1. In addition, *publishers* manage one or more data writers while *subscribers* manage one or more data readers. Publishers and subscribers can aggregate data from multiple data writers and readers for efficient transmission of data across a network.

Topic types are defined via the OMG Interface Definition Language (IDL) that enables platform-independent type definition. An IDL topic type can be mapped to platform-specific native data

Table 1. DDS QoS policies

DDS QoS Policy	Description
Deadline	*Determines rate at which periodic data should be refreshed*
Destination Order	*Determines whether data writer or data reader determines order of received data*
Durability	*Determines if data outlives the time when written or read*
Durability Service	*Details how data that can outlive a writer, process, or session is stored*
Entity Factory	*Determines enabling of DDS entities when created*
Group Data	*Attaches application data to publishers, subscribers*
History	*Sets how much data is kept for data readers*
Latency Budget	*Sets guidelines for acceptable end-to-end delays*
Lifespan	*Sets time bound for "stale" data*
Liveliness	*Sets liveness properties of topics, data readers, data writers*
Ownership	*Determines if multiple data writers can write to the same topic instance*
Ownership Strength	*Sets ownership of topic instance data*
Partition	*Controls logical partition of data dissemination*
Presentation	*Delivers data as group and/or in order*
Reader Data Lifecycle	*Controls data and data reader lifecycles*
Reliability	*Controls reliability of data dissemination*
Resource Limits	*Controls resources used to meet requirements*
Time Based Filter	*Mediates exchanges between slow consumers and fast producers*
Topic Data	*Attaches application data to topics*
Transport Priority	*Sets priority of data transport*
User Data	*Attaches application data to DDS entities*
Writer Data Lifecycle	*Controls data and data writer lifecycles*

types, such as C++ running on VxWorks or Java running on real-time Linux. Below we show an example topic definition in IDL that defines an analog sensor with a sensor id of type *string* and a value of type *float*.

```
struct AnalogSensor {
    string sensor_id; // key
    float value; // other sensor data
};
```

DDS provides a rich set of QoS policies, as illustrated in Table 1. Each QoS policy has ~2 attributes, with most attributes having an unbounded number of potential values, *e.g.*, an attribute of type character string or integer. The DDS specifi-

cation defines which QoS policies are applicable for certain entities, as well as which combinations of QoS policy values are semantically compatible. For example, if a data reader and data writer associated via a common topic want data to flow reliably, they must both specify reliable transmission via the reliability QoS policy.

The extensive QoS support of DDS and the flexibility of the QoS policies present the challenges of appropriately managing the policies to form the desired QoS configuration. These challenges not only include ensuring valid QoS parameter types and values but also ensuring valid interactions between the policies and the DDS entities. Moreover, managing semantic compatibility increases the accidental complexity of creating valid QoS configuration since not all valid combinations of QoS policies will produce the desired system behavior as outlined above with the flow of reliable data.

DSMLs can help address these challenges. DSMLs can reduce the variability complexity of managing multiple QoS policies and their parameters by presenting the QoS policies as modeling elements that are automatically checked for appropriate associations and whose parameters are automatically typed and checked for appropriate values. DSMLs can also codify constraints for semantic compatibility to ensure that data flows as intended. Moreover, DSMLs can automatically generate implementation artifacts that accurately reflect the design.

Structure of the DQML Metamodel

DDS defines 22 QoS policies shown in Table 1 that control the behavior of DDS applications. DQML models all of these DDS QoS policies, as well as the seven DDS entities (*i.e.*, *Data Reader*, *Data Writer*, *Topic*, *Publisher*, *Subscriber*, *Domain Participant*, and *Domain Participant Factory*) that can have QoS policies. Associations between the seven entities themselves and also between the entities and the 22 QoS policies can be modeled taking into account which and how many QoS policies can be associated with any one entity as defined by DDS. While other entities and constructs exist in DDS none of them directly use QoS policies and are therefore not included within the scope of DQML.

The constraints placed on QoS policies for *compatibility* and *consistency* are defined in the DDS specification. DQML uses the Object Constraint Language (OCL) (Warmer & Kleppe, 2003) implementation provided by GME to define these constraints. Compatibility constraints involve a single type of QoS policy (*e.g.*, reliability QoS policy) associated with more than one type of DDS entity (*e.g.*, data reader, data writer) whereas consistency constraints involve a single DDS

entity (*e.g.*, data reader) with more than one QoS policy (*e.g.*, deadline and latency budget QoS policies). Both types of constraints are included in DQML. The constraints are checked when explicitly prompted by the user. Programmatically checking these constraints greatly reduces the accidental complexity of creating valid QoS configurations.

Functionality of DQML

DQML allows DDS application developers to specify and control key aspects of QoS policy configuration in the following ways.

Creation of DDS entities. DQML allows developers to create the DDS entities involved with QoS policy configuration. DQML supports the seven DDS entities that can be associated with QoS policies.

Creation of DDS QoS policies. DQML allows developers to create the QoS policies involved with QoS policy configuration. DQML supports the 22 DDS policies that can be associated with entities to provide the required QoS along with the attributes, the appropriate ranges of values, and defaults. DQML ameliorates the variability complexity of specifying (1) valid associations between QoS policies and DDS entities and (2) valid QoS policy parameters, parameter types, and values (including default values).

Creation of associations between DDS entities and QoS policies. As shown in Figure 1, DQML supports the generation of associations between the entities and the QoS policies and ensures that the associations are valid. DQML's support of correct associations is important since only certain types of entities can be associated with certain other entities and only certain types of QoS policies can be associated with certain types of entities.

Checking compatibility and consistency constraints. DQML supports checking for compatible and consistent QoS policy configurations. The user initiates this checking and DQML reports

Figure 1. Modeling entities, policies, and association in DQML

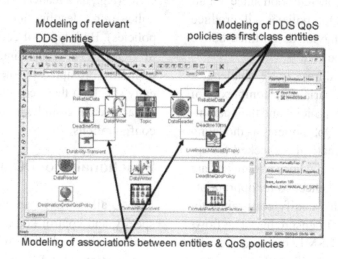

if there are any violations. Figure 2 shows DQML detecting and notifying users of incompatible reliability QoS policies.

Transforming QoS policy configurations from design to implementation. DQML transforms QoS policy configurations into implementation artifacts via application specific interpreters. Figure 3 shows a representative implementation artifact for a data reader and two data writers. At runtime the DDS middleware will then read this XML while deploying and configuring the DDS entities.

DQML CASE STUDY: DDS BENCHMARKING ENVIRONMENT (DBE)

Developing DDS applications is hard due to inherent and accidental complexities. The inherent complexities stem from determining appropriate configurations for the DDS entities. The accidental complexities stem from managing the variability, semantic compatibility, and transformation of QoS configurations. This section presents a case study highlighting development complexity to show how

Figure 2. Example of DQML QoS policy compatibility constraint checking

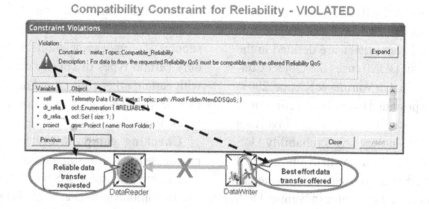

Figure 3. Example QoS policy configuration file

```
- <DQML>
  - <DataWriter name="DataWriter1">
      <deadline>period="50"</deadline>
    </DataWriter>
  - <DataReader name="DataReader1">
      <deadline>period="100"</deadline>
      <timebased_filter>min_separation="0"</timebased_filter>
    </DataReader>
  - <DataWriter name="DataWriter2">
      <reliability>kind="RELIABLE" max_blocking_time="100"</reliability>
    </DataWriter>
  </DQML>
```

DQML can be applied to improve productivity compared to manual approaches.

At least five different implementations of DDS are available each with its own set of strengths and market discriminators. A systematic benchmarking environment is needed to objectively evaluate the QoS of these implementations. Such evaluations can also help guide the addition of new features to the DDS standard as it evolves. The *DDS Benchmarking Environment* (DBE) (www.dre.vanderbilt.edu/DDS/html/dbe.html) tool suite was developed to examine and evaluate the QoS of DDS implementations (Xiong, Parsons, Edmondson, Nguyen, & Schmidt, 2007). DBE is an open-source framework for automating and managing the complexity of evaluating DDS implementations with various QoS configurations. DBE consists of a repository containing scripts, configuration files, test ids, test results, a hierarchy of Perl scripts to automate evaluation setup and execution, and a shared C++ library for collecting results and generating statistics.

We use DBE as a case study in this chapter to highlight the challenges of developing correct and valid QoS configurations, as well as to analyze the productivity benefits of DQML. Although we focus on DBE in our case study, production DDS-based applications will generally encounter the same accidental complexities when implementing QoS parameter settings, e.g., design-to-implementation transformation fidelity; valid, correct, compatible, and consistent settings. DDS QoS policy settings are typically specified for a DDS implementation programmatically by manually creating source code in a third-generation computer language, e.g., Java or C++. Manual creation can incur the same accidental complexities as the DBE case study without the integration of MDE tools like DQML.

Since DDS has a large QoS configuration space (as outlined in the DDS overview in Section 3A) there is an exponential number of testing configurations where QoS parameters can vary in several orthogonal dimensions. Manually performing evaluations for each QoS configuration, DDS implementation, and platform incurs significant accidental complexity. Moreover, the effort to manage and organize test results also grows dramatically along with the number of distinct QoS configurations.

DBE deploys a QoS policy configuration file for each data reader and data writer. The files contain simple text with a line-for-line mapping of QoS parameters to values, *e.g., datawriter. deadline.period=10*. A file is associated with a particular data reader or data writer. For DBE to function properly, QoS policy settings in the configuration files must be correct to ensure that data flows as expected. If the QoS policy configuration is invalid, incompatible, inconsistent, or not implemented as designed, the QoS evaluations will not execute properly.

The DBE configuration files have traditionally been hand-generated using a text editor, which is tedious and error-prone since the aggregate parameter settings must ensure the fidelity of the

QoS configuration design as well as the validity, correctness, compatibility, and consistency with respect to other values. Moreover, the configuration files must be managed appropriately, *e.g.*, via unique and descriptive filenames, to ensure the implemented QoS parameter settings reflect the desired QoS parameter settings. To address these issues, we developed an interpreter for DBE within DQML to automate the production of DBE QoS settings files.

When applying DQML to generate a QoS configuration for DBE we model (1) the desired DDS entities, (2) the desired QoS policies, (3) the associations among entities, and (4) the associations between entities and QoS policies. After an initial configuration is modeled, we then perform constraint checking to ensure compatible and consistent configurations. Other constraint checking is automatically enforced by the DQML metamodel as a model is constructed (*e.g.*, listing only the parameters applicable to a selected QoS when modifying values, allowing only valid values for parameter types).

We then invoke the DBE interpreter to generate the appropriate QoS settings files. These files contain the correct-by-construction parameter settings automatically generated by the interpreter as it traverses the model and transforms the QoS policies from design to implementation. Finally, we execute DBE to deploy data readers and data writers using the generated QoS settings files and run experiments to collect performance metrics.

DSML PRODUCTIVITY ANALYSIS

This section provides a lightweight taxonomy of approaches to developing quantitative productivity analysis for a DSML. It also presents a productivity analysis for DQML that evaluates implementing QoS configurations for the DBE case study from Section 4.

Productivity Analysis Approach

When analyzing productivity gains for a given DSML, analysts can employ several different types of strategies, such as

- **Design development effort,** comparing the effort (*e.g.*, time, number of design steps (Balasubramanian *et al.*, 2007), number of modeling elements (Kavimandan & Gokhale, 2008; von Pilgrim, 2007)) it takes a developer to generate a design using traditional methods (*e.g.*, manually) versus generating a design using the DSML,
- **Implementation development effort**, comparing the effort (*e.g.*, time, lines of code) it takes a developer to generate implementation artifacts using traditional methods, *i.e.*, manual generation, versus generating implementation artifacts using the DSML,
- **Design quality**, comparing the number of defects in a model or an application developed traditionally to the number of defects in a model or application developed using the DSML,
- **Required developer experience**, comparing the amount of experience a developer needs to develop a model or application using traditional methods to the amount of experience needed when using a DSML, and
- **Solution exploration**, comparing the number of viable solutions considered for a particular problem in a set period of time using the DSML as compared to traditional methods or other DSMLs.

Our focus is on the general area of quantitative productivity measurement—specifically on implementation development effort in terms of lines of code. The remainder of this section compares the lines of configuration code manually generated for DBE data readers and data writers to the lines of C++ code needed to implement the DQML DBE interpreter, which in turn generates the lines of configuration code automatically.

Metrics for DQML Productivity Analysis

Below we analyze the effect on productivity and the breakeven point of using DQML as opposed to manual implementations of QoS policy configurations for DBE. Although configurations can be *designed* using various methods as outlined in previous work (Hoffert, Schmidt, & Gokhale, 2007), manual *implementation* of configurations is applicable to these other design solutions since these solutions provide no guidance for implementation.

Within the context of DQML, we developed an interpreter specific to DBE to support DBE's requirement of correct QoS policy configurations. The interpreter generates QoS policy parameter settings files for the data readers and data writers that DBE configures and deploys. All relevant QoS policy parameter settings from a DQML model are output for the data readers and data writers including settings from default as well as explicitly assigned parameters.

As appropriate for DBE, the interpreter generates a single QoS policy parameter settings file for every data reader or data writer modeled. Care is taken to ensure that a unique filename is created since the names of the data readers and data writers modeled in DQML need not be unique. Moreover, the interpreter's generation of filenames aids in QoS settings files management (as described in Section 3) since the files are uniquely and descriptively named. The following subsections detail the scope, development effort, and productivity analysis of DQML's DBE interpreter versus manual methods.

Table 2. DDS QoS policies for data writers

QoS Policy	Number of Parameters	Parameter Type(s)
Deadline	1	Int
Destination Order	1	Enum
Durability	1	Enum
Durability Service	6	5 ints, 1 enum
History	2	1 enum, 1 int
Latency Budget	1	Int
Lifespan	1	Int
Liveliness	2	1 enum, 1 int
Ownership	1	Enum
Ownership Strength	1	Int
Reliability	2	1 enum, 1 int
Resource Limits	3	3 ints
Transport Priority	1	Int
User Data	1	String
Writer Data Lifecycle	1	Boolean
Total Parameters	25	

Scope

DBE uses DDS data readers and data writers. Our productivity analysis therefore focuses on these entities and, in particular, the QoS parameters relevant to them. In general, the same type of analysis can be performed for other DDS entities for which QoS policies can be associated. As shown in Table 2, 15 QoS policies with a total of 25 parameters can be associated with a single data writer.

Likewise, Table 3 shows 12 QoS policies with a total of 18 parameters that can be associated with a single data reader. Within the context of DBE, therefore, the total number of relevant QoS parameters is **18 + 25 = 43**. Each QoS policy parameter setting (including the parameter and its value) for a data reader or writer corresponds to a single line in the QoS parameter settings file for DBE.

Table 3. DDS QoS policies for data readers

QoS Policy	Number of Parameters	Parameter Type(s)
Deadline	1	Int
Destination Order	1	Enum
Durability	1	Enum
History	2	1 enum, 1 int
Latency Budget	1	Int
Liveliness	2	1 enum, 1 int
Ownership	1	Enum
Reader Data Lifecycle	2	2 ints
Reliability	2	1 enum, 1 int
Resource Limits	3	3 ints
Time Based Filter	1	Int
User Data	1	String
Total Parameters	**18**	

Interpreter Development

We developed the DBE interpreter for DQML using GME's Builder Object Network (BON2) framework, which provides C++ code to traverse the DQML model utilizing the Visitor pattern. When using BON2, developers of a DSML interpreter only need to modify and add a small subset of the framework code to traverse and appropriately process the particular DSML model. More specifically, the BON2 framework supplies a C++ visitor class with virtual methods (*e.g.*, visitModelImpl, visitConnectionImpl, visitAtomImpl). The interpreter developer then subclasses and overrides the applicable virtual methods.

The DDS entities relevant to DQML are referred to as *model implementations* in BON2. Therefore, the DBE interpreter only needs to override the *visitModelImpl()* method and is not concerned with other available virtual methods. When the BON2 framework invokes *visitModelImpl()* it passes a model implementation as an argument. A model implementation includes methods to (1) traverse the associations a DDS

entity has (using the *getConnEnds()* method) and specify the relevant QoS policy association as an input parameter (*e.g.*, the association between a data writer and a deadline QoS Policy), (2) retrieve the associated QoS policy, and (3) obtain the attributes of the associated QoS policy using the policy's *getAttributes()* method.

The DQML-specific code for the DBE interpreter utilizes 160 C++ statements within the BON2 framework. We stress that any interpreter development is a one-time cost; specifically there is no development cost for the DBE interpreter since it is already developed. The main challenge in using BON2 is understanding how to traverse the model and access the desired information. After interpreter developers are familiar with BON2, the interpreter development is fairly straightforward. We detail the steps of developing the DBE interpreter below.

Figure 4 outlines the visitor class that has been created for the DBE interpreter for use within the BON2 framework. This class is the only class that needs to be implemented for the DBE interpreter. Line 1 determines the class name and its derivation from the BON2 Visitor class. Lines 3 and 4 declare the default constructor and destructor respectively. Lines 7 – 9 declare the abstract methods visitAtomImpl, visitModelImpl, and visitConnectionImpl inherited from the BON2 Visitor class that need to be defined for the DBE interpreter. Lines 11 and 12 declare methods to process data readers and data writers respectively. Lines 14 – 22 declare the main method that processes the QoS properties for a data reader or data writer and writes the QoS parameters to the appropriate file. Line 25 defines the debugging output file that had been used for debugging the DBE interpreter.

As is shown in Figure 4, the structure of the DBE visitor class is fairly simple and straightforward. Moreover, of the three methods inherited from the BON2 Visitor class and declared on lines 7 – 9 only the visitModelImpl method declared on line 8 is a non-empty method. For DBE, the only DQML entities of interest are what GME

Figure 4. Visitor class for DBE interpreter

```
1   class DDSQoSVisitor : public Visitor {
2   public:
3       DDSQoSVisitor ();
4       ~DDSQoSVisitor ();
5
6   protected :
7       virtual void visitAtomImpl (const Atom& atom);
8       virtual void visitModelImpl (const Model& model);
9       virtual void visitConnectionImpl ( const Connection& connection);
10
11      void processDataReaderQos (const Model& dataReader);
12      void processDataWriterQos (const Model& dataWriter);
13
14      void outputDDSEntityQos (const Model& dds_entity,
15                              const std::string &entity_name,
16                              const std::string &entity_abbrev,
17                              const std::string &qos_connection_name,
18                              const std::string &qos_name,
19                              const std::map<std::string, std::string> &attribute_map,
20                              int entity_count,
21                              bool &file_opened,
22                              std::ofstream &out_file);
23
24  private:
25      std::ofstream out_file_;
26  };
```

terms the *model elements* which for DBE's interests are the data readers and data writers. The DBE interpreter is not concerned with traversing atom or connection elements since these elements will be addressed by processing the model elements.

We now focus on the implementations of the relevant methods particularly as they relate to complexity and required background knowledge. The default constructor and destructor simply open and close the file used for debugging which is not required functionality for the DBE interpreter. Therefore the implementations of these two methods (which total two C++ statements) are excluded to save space. The visitAtomImpl and visitConnectionImpl methods are defined (since the inherited methods are abstract) but empty (since they are not needed).

As shown in Figure 5, the visitModelImpl method determines the type of model element currently being processed and calls the appropriate method, *i.e.*, processDataReaderQos for a

Figure 5. visitModelImpl method

```
1   void DDSQoSVisitor::visitModelImpl( const Model& model )
2   {
3       if (model->getModelMeta().name() == "DataReader")
4       {
5           out_file_ << "DDS DataReader Name: " << model->getName() << std::endl;
6           processDataReaderQos(model);
7           out_file_ << "...Done DDS DataReader Name: " << model->getName() << std::endl;
8       }
9       else if (model->getModelMeta().name() == "DataWriter")
10      {
11          out_file_ << "DDS DataWriter Name: " << model->getName() << std::endl;
12          processDataWriterQos(model);
13          out_file_ << "...Done DDS DataWriter Name: " << model->getName() << std::endl;
14      }
15  }
```

Figure 6. processDataWriterQos method

```
1    void DDSQoSVisitor::processDataWriterQos( const Model& dataWriter )
2    {
3        static int dw_count = 1;
4        const std::string dw_name("DataWriter");
5        const std::string dw_prefix("DW");
6        std::ofstream output_file;
7        bool file_opened = false;
8        std::map<std::string, std::string> attrib_map;
9
10       // Handle Deadline QoS Policy
11       attrib_map.clear ();
12       attrib_map["period"] = "datawriter.deadline.period=";
13       outputDDSEntityQos (dataWriter,
14                           dw_name,
15                           dw_prefix,
16                           "dw_deadline_Connection",
17                           "Deadline",
18                           attrib_map,
19                           dw_count,
20                           file_opened,
21                           output_file);
22
23       // Handle History QoS Policy
24       attrib_map.clear ();
25       attrib_map["history_kind"] = "datawriter.history.kind=";
26       attrib_map["history_depth"] = "datawriter.history.depth=";
27       outputDDSEntityQos (dataWriter,
28                           dw_name,
29                           dw_prefix,
30                           "dw_history_Connection",
31                           "History",
32                           attrib_map,
33                           dw_count,
34                           file_opened,
35                           output_file);
                              .
                              .
                              .
```

data reader on line 6 and processDataWriterQos for a data writer on line 12. The lines written to out_file_ are simply for debugging purposes and are not required by DBE. The DBE interpreter developer required familiarity with the DQML metamodel to know the names of the model elements of interest but the model elements in the metamodel were given intuitive names to reduce accidental complexity, *e.g.*, DataReader and DataWriter on lines 3 and 9 respectively.

Figure 6 outlines the processDataWriterQos method. For each QoS policy applicable to a data writer this method sets up a mapping of DQML QoS parameter names to DBE QoS parameters names. Then the method calls outputDDSEntity-QoS method to write the QoS parameter values to the appropriate file. The interpreter developer needed to have an understanding of the QoS parameter names for DBE, the QoS parameter names in the DQML metamodel, and the names of the associations between data readers/writers and QoS policies in the DQML metamodel. However, as with the model elements in the DQML metamodel, the QoS parameters were given intuitive names to reduce accidental complexity, *e.g.*, history_kind and history_depth on lines 25 and 26 respectively, as were the connection names, *e.g.*, dw_deadline_Connection and dw_history_Connection on lines 16 and 30 respectively.

Figure 7. outputDDSEntityQos method

```
1   void DDSQoSVisitor::outputDDSEntityQos (const Model& dds_entity,
2                                           const std::string &entity_name, // e.g., "DataReader"
3                                           const std::string &entity_abbrev, // e.g., "DR"
4                                           const std::string &qos_connection_name,
5                                           const std::string &qos_name,
6                                           const std::map<std::string, std::string> &attribute_map,
7                                           int entity_count,
8                                           bool &file_opened,
9                                           std::ofstream &out_file)
10  {
11      std::multiset<ConnectionEnd> conns = dds_entity->getConnEnds(qos_connection_name);
12      if (conns.size() > 0)
13      {
14          if (conns.size() > 1){ ... }
22          else
23          {
24              std::multiset<ConnectionEnd>::const_iterator iter(conns.begin ());
25              ConnectionEnd endPt = *iter;
26              FCO fco(endPt);
27              if (fco)
28              {
29                  std::set<Attribute> attrs = fco->getAttributes ();
30                  std::set<Attribute>::const_iterator attr_iter(attrs.begin());
31                  if (!file_opened)
32                  {
33                      file_opened = true;
34                      std::string filename;
35
36                      char cnt_buf [10];
37                      ::sprintf_s (cnt_buf, "%d", entity_count);
38                      std::string cnt_str = cnt_buf;
39                      filename = entity_abbrev + cnt_str + "_" + dds_entity->getName () + ".txt";
40                      out_file.open(filename.c_str ());
41                  }
42                  for (; attr_iter != attrs.end (); ++attr_iter)
43                  {
44                      Attribute attr = *attr_iter;
45                      std::string attr_name = attr->getAttributeMeta ().name ();
46                      std::map<std::string, std::string>::const_iterator map_iter =
47                          attribute_map.find (attr_name);
48                      if (map_iter != attribute_map.end ())
49                      {
50                          out_file << map_iter->second << attr->getStringValue () << std::endl;
51                      }
52                  }
53              }
54              else{ ... }
58          }
59      }
60  }
```

Figure 6 shows the source code for processing the deadline and history QoS policies. The rest of the method which has been elided for brevity handles all the other QoS policies relevant to data writers. Finally, the method closes the QoS parameter file if one has been opened previously and increments the count of data writers processed so that unique filenames can be generated. Likewise, the processDataReaderQos method provides the same functionality for QoS policies and parameters relevant to data readers. Its source code is not included due to space constraints.

Figure 7 presents the outputDDSEntityQos method which traverses the connection that a data reader or data writer has to a particular QoS policy (e.g., connections to QoS policies for data readers or data writers) and writes the QoS parameters out to the QoS settings file for that data reader or writer. Lines 14 – 21 and 54 – 57 provide error checking for the BON2 framework and have been elided for space considerations. Line 11 retrieves the associations that the data reader or writer has with a particular QoS policy, e.g., all the associations between a data reader and the reliability

QoS policy. Lines 24-27 retrieve the endpoint of the connection which will be the associated QoS policy of the type specified as the input parameter of line 4. Lines 29 and 30 retrieve the parameters of the associated QoS policy, lines 31 – 41 open a uniquely named DBE QoS settings file if one is not currently open, and lines 42 – 52 iterate through the QoS parameters and write them out to the opened file in the required DBE format using the attribute mapping passed as an input parameter on line 6.

The C++ development effort for DQML's DBE interpreter is only needed one time. In particular, no QoS policy configuration developed via DQML for DBE incurs this development overhead since the interpreter has already been developed. The development effort metrics of 160 C++ statements are included *only* to be used in comparing manually implemented QoS policy configurations.

Comparing Manually Developing DBE Implementation Artifacts

To compare model-driven engineering approaches in general and the DQML DBE interpreter in particular, we outline the steps to generate the implementation artifacts of DBE QoS settings files given a manually generated QoS configuration design. Several areas of inherent and accidental complexity need to be addressed for manual development of DBE QoS settings files. To illustrate these complexities we follow the steps needed to transform a data reader entity associated with a reliability QoS policy from design into implementation. We assume the QoS configuration design is specified either in a text or graphics file or handwritten. We also assume that the QoS configuration design has been developed separately from the generation of implementation artifacts to separate these concerns and divide the labor.

Variability Complexity

Implementation developers must ensure the correct semantics for the association between the data reader and the reliability QoS policy. Developers cannot assume that the data reader, the reliability QoS policy, or the association between the two are valid and correctly specified since the configuration was manually generated. The data reader and reliability QoS policy must be cross-referenced with the DDS specification. This cross-referencing entails checking that (1) a data reader can be associated with a reliability QoS policy, (2) the parameter names specified for the reliability QoS policy are appropriate (e.g., only kind and max_blocking_time are valid reliability QoS parameters), and (3) the values for the parameters are valid (e.g., only RELIABLE and BEST_EFFORT are valid values for the reliability kind). Moreover, developers must manage the complexity of creating a separate QoS settings file for the data reader and ensuring a unique and descriptive filename that DBE can use.

Semantic Compatibility Complexity

Implementation developers must ensure the correct consistency semantics for the data reader's reliability QoS policy and the other QoS policies associated with the data reader. If QoS policies associated with the data reader are inconsistent then the policies cannot be used. Moreover, the developer must ensure correct semantics for the data reader's reliability QoS policy and data writers associated with the same topic. If QoS policies associated with the data reader are incompatible then the data will not be received by the data reader.

For the reliability QoS policy there are no inconsistency concerns. Developers must verify that this is the case, however, by checking the DDS specification for consistency rules. For the reliability QoS policy there are potential incompatibilities. If the reliability QoS policy kind for the data reader is specified as RELIABLE the developer must traverse the QoS configuration and check the reliability QoS policies for *all* data writers associated with the same topic. If no associated data writer has a reliability QoS kind set to RELIABLE (either explicitly or implicitly via default values) then the data reader can never receive any data thereby making the data reader superfluous. Default values for QoS parameters must therefore be known and evaluated for compatibility even if not explicitly specified. Manually traversing the QoS configuration to check for compatibility and accounting for default parameter values is tedious and error prone and greatly exacerbates the accidental complexity of generating implementation artifacts.

Faithful Transformation

Implementation developers must ensure that the QoS configuration design is accurately mapped to the implementation artifacts appropriate for DBE. As noted above, this transformation includes creating and managing a QoS settings file for each data reader and writer. Moreover, the developer must ensure that the syntax of QoS settings conform to what DBE requires. For example, the reliability's maximum blocking time of 10 ms must be specified as datareader.reliability.max_blocking_time=10 on a single line by itself in the QoS settings file for the particular data reader.

Analysis

The hardest aspect of developing DQML's DBE interpreter is traversing the model's data reader and data writer elements along with the associated QoS policy elements using the BON2 framework. Conversely, the most challenging aspects of manually implementing QoS policy configurations are (1) maintaining a global view of the model to ensure compatibility and consistency, (2) verifying the number, type, and valid values for the parameters of the applicable QoS policies, and (3) faithfully transforming the configuration design into implementation artifacts. On average, implementing a single C++ statement for the DBE interpreter is no harder than implementing a single parameter statement for the DBE QoS settings files. When implementing a non-trivial

QoS policy configuration, therefore, development of the C++ code for the DBE interpreter is no more challenging than manually ensuring that the QoS settings in settings files are valid, consistent, compatible, and correctly represent the designed configuration. Below we provide additional detail into what can be considered a non-trivial QoS policy configuration.

The development and use of the DBE interpreter for DQML is justified for a *single* QoS policy configuration when at least 160 QoS policy parameter settings are involved. These parameter settings correlate to the 160 C++ statements for DQML's DBE interpreter. Using the results for QoS parameters in Table 2 and Table 3 for data readers and data writers, Figure 8 shows the justification for interpreter development. The development is justified with ~10 data readers, ~7 data writers, or some combination of data readers and data writers where the QoS settings are greater than or equal to 160 (*e.g.*, 5 data readers and 3 data writers = 165 QoS policy parameter settings). For comparison, the breakeven point for data reader/writer pairs is **3.72** (*i.e.*, 160/43).

We also quantified the development effort needed to support topics if the DBE interpreter required that functionality. Table 4 shows the DDS QoS policies and policy parameters applicable to topics. To support topics an additional 59 C++ statements would need to be added. Conversely, for manual generation 23 more QoS parameters need to be considered for each topic. The breakeven point for data reader/writer/topic triplets becomes **3.32** (*i.e.*, (160 + 59)/(43 + 23)) which is less than the breakeven point for data reader/writers alone (*i.e.*, 3.72).

This breakeven point is less because the additional source code to support topics can leverage existing code, in particular, the outputDDSEntityQos method outlined in Figure 7. The breakeven point can be applicable for *any* interpreter that leverages the commonality of formatting regardless of the entity type (*cf.* outputDDSEntityQos method). Moreover, the complexity of

Figure 8. Metrics for manual configuration vs. DQML's interpreter

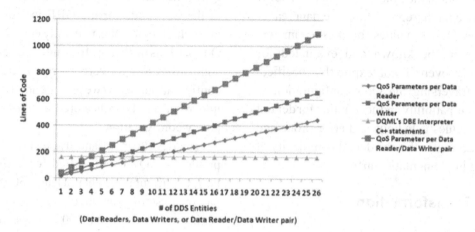

developing any DQML interpreter is lessened by having the DBE interpreter as a guide. The design and code of the DBE interpreter can be reused by another application-specific interpreter to navigate a DQML model and access the QoS policies.

Table 5 also shows productivity gains as a percentage for various numbers of data readers and data writers. The percentage gains are calculated by dividing the number of parameter values for the data readers and data writers involved by the number of interpreter C++ statements, *i.e.*, 160, and subtracting 1 to account for the baseline manual implementation (*i.e.*, ((# of data reader and writer parameters)/160)-1). The gains increase faster than the increase in the number of data readers and data writers (*e.g.*, the gain for 10 data readers and data writers is more than twice as much for 5 data readers and data writers) showing that productivity gains are greater when more entities are involved.

The interpreter justification analysis shown relates to implementing a single QoS policy configuration. The analysis includes neither the scenario of modifying an existing valid configuration nor the scenario of implementing new configurations for DBE where no modifications to the interpreter code would be required. Changes made even to an existing valid configuration require that developers (1) maintain a global view

Table 4. DDS QoS policies for topics

QoS Policy	Number of Parameters	Parameter Type(s)
Deadline	1	int
Destination Order	1	enum
Durability	1	enum
Durability Service	6	5 ints, 1 enum
History	2	1 enum, 1 int
Latency Budget	1	int
Lifespan	1	int
Liveliness	2	1 enum, 1 int
Ownership	1	enum
Reliability	2	1 enum, 1 int
Resource Limits	3	3 ints
Transport Priority	1	int
Topic Data	1	string
Total Parameters	**23**	

Table 5. Productivity gains using DQML's DBE interpreter

# of Data Readers and Data Writers (each)	Total # of Parameters	Productivity Gain
5	215	34%
10	430	169%
20	860	438%
40	1720	975%
80	3440	2050%

of the model to ensure compatibility and consistency and (2) remember the number of, and valid values for, the parameters of the various QoS policies being modified. These challenges are as applicable when changing an already valid QoS policy configuration as they are when creating an initial configuration. Moreover, the complexity for developing a new interpreter for some other application is ameliorated by having the DBE interpreter as a template for traversing a model in BON2.

In large-scale DDS systems (*e.g.*, shipboard computing, air-traffic management, and scientific space missions) there may be thousands of data readers and writers. As a point of reference with 1,000 data readers and 1,000 data writers, the number of QoS parameters to manage is *43,000* (*i.e.*, 18 * 1,000 + 25 * 1,000). This number does not include QoS parameter settings for other DDS entities such as publishers, subscribers, and topics. For such large-scale DDS systems the development cost of the DQML interpreter in terms of lines of code is amortized by more than 200 times (*i.e.*, 43,000 / 160 = **268.75**).

The productivity analysis approach taken for DQML's DBE interpreter is applicable to other DSMLs since the complexities involved will be similar. A break-even point for the development effort of an interpreter for any DSML will exist. We outline four areas that directly influence this break-even point: number of entities, complexity of the entities, complexity of associations between the entities, and level of maintainability needed.

The number of entities affects the break-even point for interpreter development since the more entities that are to be considered the less likely any one individual will be able to manage these entities appropriately. Miller (1956) has shown that humans can process up to approximately 7 items of information at a time. This guideline of 7 can be helpful in exploring the break-even point for interpreter development. If there are more than 7 entities to be considered then the accidental

complexity increases since the developer must manage the entities using some tool or device (e.g., a piece of paper, a database) external to the person. With this external management comes the possibility of introducing errors in the use of the management tool (e.g., incorrectly transcribing the entities from the developer's head to the tool).

Likewise, this same analysis holds for the complexity of entities as determined by the number of fields or parameters. If an entity contains more than 7 fields then some external tool should be used to manage this complexity. The use of a tool introduces accidental complexity (e.g., incorrectly transcribing the order, names, or types of the parameters). The same analysis can also be applied to the number of associations made between entities to determine that complexity as well as the number of times a configuration will need to be modified.

If any one of these four areas exceeds the threshold of 7 then an interpreter might be warranted. If more than one of these areas exceeds the threshold (e.g., more than 7 entities with more than 7 associations between the entities) then the break-even point for an interpreter is lowered. The exact determination for justifying interpreter development will vary according to the application but the guidelines presented can provide coarse-grained justification.

FUTURE RESEARCH DIRECTIONS

Our future work for DQML includes assembly and deployment support as well as providing domain-specific QoS profiles for ease of development. DQML is available as open-source software and is included as part of the Component Synthesis with Model Integrated Computing (CoSMIC) tool chain. Information regarding downloading, building, and installing CoSMIC can be found at www.dre.vanderbilt.edu/cosmic.

CONCLUSION

Although MDE and DSMLs have become increasingly popular, concrete evidence is needed to support the quantitative evaluation of DSMLs. This chapter described various approaches to quantitatively evaluating DSMLs via productivity analysis. We applied one of these approaches to a case study involving the *Distributed QoS Modeling Language* (DQML). The following is a summary of the lessons learned from our experience developing DQML and conducting productivity analysis using it for the DBE case study:

- **Trade-offs and the break-even point for DSMLs must be clearly understood and communicated.** There are pros and cons to any technical approach including DSMLs. The use of DSMLs may not be appropriate for every case and these cases must be evaluated to provide balanced and objective analysis. For a DSML product line the advantages of DSMLs will typically outweigh the development costs. For a one-time point solution the development of a DSML may not be justified, depending on the complexity of the domain.
- **The context for DSML productivity analysis should be well defined.** Broad generalizations of a DSML being "X" times better than some other technology is not particularly helpful for comparison and evaluation. A representative case study can be useful to provide a concrete context for productivity analysis.
- **Provide analysis for as minimal or conservative a scenario as possible.** Using a minimal scenario in productivity analysis allows developers to extrapolate to larger scenarios where the DSML use will be justified.

REFERENCES

Abrahao, S., & Poels, G. (2007). Experimental Evaluation of an Object-oriented Function Point Measurement Procedure. *Information and Software Technology*, *49*(4), 366–380. doi:10.1016/j.infsof.2006.06.001

Abrahao, S., & Poels, G. (2009). A Family of Experiments to Evaluate a Functional Size Measurement Procedure for Web Applications. *Journal of Systems and Software*, *82*(2), 253–269. doi:10.1016/j.jss.2008.06.031

Atkinson, C., & Kuhne, T. (2003). Model-driven development: a metamodeling foundation. *IEEE Software*, *20*(5), 36–41. doi:10.1109/MS.2003.1231149

Balasubramanian, K., Schmidt, D., Molnar, Z., & Ledeczi, A. (2007). Component-based system integration via (meta)model composition. In *14th Annual IEEE International Conference and Workshops on the Engineering of Computer-Based Systems* (pp. 93–102). Washington, D.C.: IEEE Computer Society.

Bettin, J. (2002, Novermber). *Measuring the potential of domain-specific modeling techniques*. Paper presented at the 17th Annual ACM Conference on Object-Oriented Programming, Systems, Languages, and Applications. Seattle, WA.

Boehm, B. (1987). Improving Software Productivity. *Computer*, *20*(9), 43–57. doi:10.1109/MC.1987.1663694

Carzaniga, A., Rutherford, M., & Wolf, A. (2004). A routing scheme for content-based networking. *INFOCOM*, *2*, 918–928.

Cleary, D. (2000). Web-*based development and functional size measurement*. Paper presented at IFPUG Annual Conference, San Diego, USA

Conway, C., & Edwards, S. (2004). Ndl: a domain-specific language for device drivers. In *Proceedings of the 2004 ACM SIGPLAN/SIGBED conference on languages, compilers, and tools for embedded systems* (pp. 30–36). New York: ACM

Genero, M., Piattini, M., Abrahao, S., Insfran, E., Carsi, J., & Ramos, I. (2007). A controlled experiment for selecting transformations based on quality attributes in the context of MDA. In *First International Symposium on Empirical Software Engineering and Measurement* (pp.498-498). Washington, DC: IEEE Computer Society

Hailpern, B., & Tarr, P. (2006). Model-driven development: the good, the bad, and the ugly. *IBM Systems Journal*, *45*(3), 451–461. doi:10.1147/sj.453.0451

Hoffert, J., Schmidt, D., & Gokhale, A. (2007). A QoS policy configuration modeling language for publish/subscribe middleware platforms. In *Proceedings of the International Conference on Distributed Event-Based Systems* (pp. 140–145). New York: ACM.

Kavimandan, A., & Gokhale, A. (2008). Automated middleware QoS configuration techniques using model transformations. In *Proceedings of the 14th IEEE Real-Time and Embedded Technology and Applications Symposium* (pp. 93–102). Washington, D.C.: IEEE Computer Society

Kent, S. (2002). Model driven engineering. In *Proceedings of the 3rd International Conference on Integrated Formal Methods* (pp. 286–298). Heidelberg: Springer

Ledeczi, A., Bakay, A., Maroti, M., Volgyesi, P., Nordstrom, G., Sprinkle, J., & Karsai, G. (2001). Composing domain-specific design environments. *Computer*, *34*(11), 44–51. doi:10.1109/2.963443

Li, G., & Jacobsen, H. (2005). Composite subscriptions in content-based publish/subscribe systems. In *Proceedings of the 6th International Middleware Conference* (pp. 249-269). New York: Springer-Verlag New York, Inc.

Loyall, J., Ye, J., Shapiro, R., Neema, S., Mahadevan, N., Abdelwahed, S., et al. (2004). A Case Study in Applying QoS Adaptation and Model-Based Design to the Design-Time Optimization of Signal Analyzer Applications. *Military Communications Conference (MILCOM)*, Monterey, California.

Miller, G. (1956). The magical number seven, plus or minus two: some limits on our capacity for processing information. *Psychological Review*, *63*(2), 81–97. doi:10.1037/h0043158

OASIS. (2006). *Web services brokered notification 1.3*. Retrieved December 11, 2009 from http://docs.oasis-open.org/wsn/wsn-ws_brokered_notification-1.3-spec-os.pdf.

Object Management Group. (2007). *Data distribution service for real-time systems, version 1.2*. Retrieved June 8, 2009, from http://www.omg.org/spec/DDS/1.2.

Object Management Group. (2004-1). *Event service specification version 1.2*. Retrieved December 11, 2009, from http://www.omg.org/cgi-bin/doc?formal/2004-10-02.

Object Management Group. (2004-2). *Notification service specification version 1.1*. Retrieved December 11, 2009, from http://www.omg.org/cgi-bin/doc?formal/2004-10-11.

Pilgrim, J. (2007). Measuring the level of abstraction and detail of models in the context of mdd. In *Second International Workshop on Model Size Metrics* (pp. 105–114). Heidelberg: Springer-Verlag

Premraj, R., Shepperd, M., Kitchenham, B., & Forselius, P. (2005). An empirical analysis of software productivity over time. In *11th IEEE International Symposium on Software Metrics* (37). Washington, DC: IEEE Computer Society.

Reifer, D. (2000). Web development: estimating quick-to-market software. *IEEE Software*, *17*(6), 57–64. doi:10.1109/52.895169

Schmidt, D. (2006). Model-driven engineering. *IEEE Computer, 39*(2), 25–31.

Sun Microsystems. (2002). *Java Message Service version 1.1*. Retrieved December 11, 2009 from http://java.sun.com/products/jms/docs.html.

Warmer, J., & Kleppe, A. (2003). *The object constraint language: getting your models ready for MDA*. Boston: Addison-Wesley Longman Publishing Co., Inc.

Xiong, M., Parsons, J., Edmondson, J., Nguyen, H., & Schmidt, D. (2007, April). *Evaluating technologies for tactical information management in net- centric systems*. Paper presented at the Defense Transformation and Net-Centric Systems conference, Orlando, Florida.

KEY TERMS AND DEFINITIONS

Pub/Sub Middleware: Middleware that supports the transmission of data anonymously from data senders to data receivers.

Event-Based Distributed System: A system that is distributed across several computing platforms that exchange information based on events rather than request and reply invocations between a client and a server.

Domain-Specific Modeling Language: A graphically-based language that represents artifacts and processes in the context of a particular domain (*e.g.*, QoS configurations).

Model-Driven Engineering: A software development methodology which focuses on producing and leveraging high-level models or abstractions for particular domain concepts.

Productivity Analysis: The process of evaluating how a system, process, or tool affects the overall development cycle.

Quantitative Productivity Analysis: Productivity analysis that utilizes objective, quantifiable metrics to determine the effect on productivity.

QoS Configuration: The combination of QoS policies and settings that are used in a system. The overall QoS of a system is determined by the aggregation of the QoS policies and settings along with their interactions.

Chapter 9
Domain–Driven Reuse of Software Design Models[1]

Audris Kalnins
IMCS University of Latvia, Latvia

Michał Śmiałek
Warsaw University of Technology, Poland

Elina Kalnina
IMCS University of Latvia, Latvia

Edgars Celms
IMCS University of Latvia, Latvia

Wiktor Nowakowski
Warsaw University of Technology, Poland

Tomasz Straszak
Warsaw University of Technology, Poland

ABSTRACT

This chapter presents an approach to software development where model driven development and software reuse facilities are combined in a natural way. The basis for all of this is a semiformal requirements language RSL. The requirements in RSL consist of use cases refined by scenarios in a simple controlled natural language and the domain vocabulary containing the domain concepts. The chapter shows how model transformations building a platform independent model (PIM) can be applied directly to the requirements specified in RSL by domain experts. Further development of the software case (PSM, code) is also supported by transformations, which in addition ensure a rich traceability within the software case. The reuse support relies on a similarity based comparison of requirements for software cases. If a similar part is found in an existing software case, a traceability link based slice of the solution can be merged into the new case. The implementation of the approach is briefly sketched.

DOI: 10.4018/978-1-61692-874-2.ch009

INTRODUCTION

Some of the most significant cornerstones for state-of-the-art software development are model driven development (MDD) and software reuse. There is a lot of success in applying them separately, but practically nothing has been done to combine them. The proposed approach provides a tight natural integration of both. The third equally important cornerstone is an adequate facility for specifying semiformal requirements to the software system being developed. All these three components together provide support for "model and requirement driven reuse". Only in this way a complete MDD life cycle can be supported, where the use of models starts from the "very beginning". Reuse can also be significantly simplified this way because requirements alone can be used to find candidates for reuse and to select system parts to be reused.

Our approach is based on a special Requirements Specification Language (RSL). This language is semiformal in the sense that it is close to a natural language and understandable to non-IT specialists, but on the other hand it has a meaning precise enough to be processed by model transformations and reuse mechanisms. Consequently, a true model driven development (MDD) is possible, where the initial version of next model in the chain is built from the previous one by model transformations. In totality, these models form a software case. Thus, there is an automatic transformation supported path from requirements to code. All these models play an important role in the reuse process.

More precisely, requirements in RSL consist of two related parts. The domain concepts to be used in the requirements are described in a domain vocabulary. This domain vocabulary serves as a semiformal easy readable equivalent of the domain class model. The meaning of domain elements can be specified by means of links to corresponding WordNet (Fellbaum, 1998) entries. The domain

model serves as the basis for the other part of requirements – the required system behaviour description. This description is centred on use cases. The distinctive feature of RSL is that a use case is refined by one or more scenarios in a simple controlled language. Each noun within a scenario sentence must be defined in the domain vocabulary, thus the whole sentence gets a precise meaning. In addition to use cases, non-functional requirements to the system can be described by natural language sentences, using hyperlinks to the same vocabulary. The precise syntax of RSL is described by a metamodel. RSL will be described in more details in next section. Requirements model in RSL can be treated as a Computation Independent Model (CIM) in the classical MDA model chain (Object Management Group, 2003).

When the software case development starts, the requirements model is transformed into the initial version of Platform Independent Model (PIM) in the selected subset of UML (Object Management Group, 2009). The static structure of this model is generated from the domain vocabulary within requirements. Consequently, the whole structure of the system, especially its business logic and data access layers, depend on this domain. Thus a true domain driven design is supported. An initial version of the behaviour is obtained by transformations analyzing the use case scenarios, thus aspects of use case driven design are also present. The precise contents of the generated PIM depend on the selected architecture style for the software system to be developed. Model transformation sets supporting several architecture styles have been developed. The obtained PIM can be manually extended, then another transformation can be applied to generate the initial version of PSM. A similar step leads to initial code for the system. More details on the transformation assisted software case development will be given in section "Definition of software cases".

One more important aspect of the approach is the strong support of traceability in the form of mapping links between the models. Since the initial version of next model is generated by transformations, a rich set of mapping links between consecutive models can be easily supported. The starting point for this traceability is always the requirements model in RSL. In particular, the domain vocabulary is the starting point for traceability to models describing the static structure of the system to be built.

The traceability is the key element for reuse of software cases in the approach. If a set of software cases has been already built using the approach, just requirement models of these cases must be compared to the requirements of a new case to be created. If a similar part is found in the requirements of an existing case, the whole chain of model parts traceable from this one can serve as the basis for reuse. This chain is called a "slice" in the approach.

In order to reuse artefacts included in a software case, requirements specifications written in RSL need to be compared through formulating a query. The query is based on the newly specified requirements specification which might be partial (requirements sketch). This "new" specification is compared with "old" specifications taken from the repository of software cases. Appropriate domain-driven similarity metrics are applied which are discussed in more detail in section "Reuse of software cases". After finding similar requirements, slices leading from these requirements are calculated. This slice can then be copied into the current software case for adaptation of the contained model elements to the current problem. Thus a true domain driven reuse of software cases is supported.

This research has been performed within the EU 6FP project ReDSeeDS (IST-2006-33596) (ReDSeeDS, n.d.). The proposed approach has been implemented in this project as the environment called ReDSeeDS Engine. The implementation and practical validation of the approach will be briefly described in section "Implementation and validation".

BACKGROUND

Model driven development of software systems has become an everyday practice nowadays. Typically this development starts from a general system model in UML – PIM model according to OMG MDA terminology (Object Management Group 2003). Both commercial and open source tools support this development to a certain degree. However there are several unsolved issues too. One of the issues addressed by this chapter is the coverage of complete MDD life cycle, starting from system requirements. Another issue to be solved is the reuse of artefacts produced by MDD life cycle. In our approach both issues are solved by introducing a semiformal requirements specification language (RSL).

Transformations from Requirements in Controlled Natural Language

The Computation Independent Model (CIM) in the classical MDA methodology (Object Management Group 2003) means requirements for the system, understandable by domain experts. Typically requirements are written as a free text (though may be, subject to various style templates – see e.g., Larman 2005), but MDD approach suggests to apply transformations to the whole development life cycle including CIM. Thus the problem arises how to process requirements by formal transformations.

Two approaches are possible here. The first one is to use an additional step to convert the informal text manually into some semiformal notation. Then this intermediate notation can be processed formally by transformations. An interesting approach of this kind is proposed in (Osis, Asnina & Grave, 2007) where the initial requirements in natural language are manually converted into a list of semiformal functional features which then can be transformed formally using the topological functioning model. The approach proposed in (Bryant et. al., 2003) also requires an initial semi-manual transformation of requirements. The approach by manual transformation is applicable to wide spectrum of requirements but is also error prone as any purely manual processing. Similarly, in (Dromey, 2005) it is proposed to convert manually textual requirements into formalized behaviour trees.

Another natural approach is to specify requirements in a controlled natural language (which can be used both as a formal and informal language), as it is proposed in this chapter. A similar kind of requirements are used as a starting point in (Leal, Pires, & Campos, 2006; Leonardi & Mauco, 2004). The approach closest to ours is (Leal, Pires, & Campos, 2006), where the Natural MDA language is proposed for behaviour description. This language uses a large set of keywords therefore it is much closer to programming languages than RSL, and the transformation based approach there is only partial. The approach in (Leonardi & Mauco, 2004) is based on the Language Extended Lexicon and does not use the behaviour description thoroughly. Thus, though the idea of using controlled natural language for requirements has been used before, the approach in this chapter (where scenarios are linked to a domain model) permits to apply formal transformations directly to the requirements specified by domain experts. The use of controlled natural language requires a well balanced approach between readability by domain experts and formality required by transformations. Experiments with RSL show that an adequate balance has been reached.

Software Reuse Based on Requirements

The importance of software reuse based on requirements has been stressed already in literature. In (Cybulski, Neal, Kram, Allen, 1998) a survey of requirements-related artefacts in the context of their reusability is made. This approach identifies the benefits that can be drawn from reuse of the early software artefacts and provides some

initial directions on how to support this reuse. In our approach to software reuse we choose a very popular type of such artefacts used in many contemporary software projects – use cases. The research on use case based reuse has been started by Jacobson et al. in their Reuse-Driven Software Engineering (Jacobson, Griss & Jonsson, 1997). In this approach, Jacobson style use cases are written in a quite rigorous language adorned with specific information that denotes potential variability of the user-system interaction. This additional information allows for extracting necessary use cases for reuse when a specific new system is being built. It can be noted that by adding variability information we define a whole family of similar systems. This notion gave rise to the idea of software product lines. Within the vast literature of this field, the works of Gomaa (see e.g. (Gomaa, 2004)) define an approach similar in some elements to ours. In this approach, use cases drive the construction of the software product lines. This approach gives detailed guidelines on how to specify use cases with variability information and how to relate them with other software artefacts (design and code). Unfortunately, the problem with these approaches is lack of automation. There were no mechanisms introduced to automate mapping between use cases and the other artefacts, moreover, there were not defined any mechanisms to retrieve use cases based on their similarity. It can be also noted that the product line approaches necessitate a significant effort to prepare the variability information.

In order to enable automation of requirements based reuse we need to introduce rigour into the requirements representations. In (Laguna, Lopez, Crespo, 2004) we can find a very interesting insight into this problem. This paper stresses the need to standardise requirements by defining precise meta-models of their representations. This significantly facilitates requirements comparison. This also enables transformation of requirements, but in contrast to the approach presented in this chapter, Laguna et al. concentrated on transformation between different variant representations of requirements. In the context of software product lines, a similar approach which advocates introducing a precise meta-model for reusable requirements is introduced in (Moon, Yeom, & Chae, 2005). Prior to these approaches, an interesting attempt to introduce rigour in functional requirements was provided in (Biddle, Noble, & Tempero, 2002). There, a precise notation (but not meta-model) for essential use case scenarios is given. This notation is suitable for reuse, but neither similarity comparison mechanisms, nor automatic transformation rules were provided. Another, analogous approach was presented in (Woo, Robinson, 2002). In this approach, the scenarios are written using UML sequence diagrams and an automatic learner is used to facilitate retrieval of such scenarios.

REQUIREMENT SPECIFICATION LANGUAGE

The Requirements Specification Language (RSL) (Śmiałek, Bojarski, Nowakowski, Ambroziewicz & Straszak, 2007; Kaindl et al., 2007) is a semi-formal language for specifying requirements to a software system.

RSL employs use cases for defining precise requirements to the system behaviour. As traditionally for requirements, a use case corresponds to a targeted interaction between an actor and the system to be specified. Related use cases can be grouped into a package. An essential difference from traditional requirement elicitation methods is that use case behaviour can be precisely defined. Each use case is detailed by one or more scenarios, one of which is the main (describes the typical behaviour of the use case) and others provide various alternatives.

A scenario in turn consists of special controlled natural language sentences. The main type of sentences is the SVO(O) sentence (Kaindl et al., 2007), which consists of subject, verb (or predicate) and direct object (optionally, also indirect object). These sentences express the actions to be

performed in the scenario, for example, **System-***reserves***facility** for **customer**. On the one hand, the SVO(O) sentences can be read informally as simple conventional natural language sentences, thus readability for non-IT professionals is maintained. On the other hand, links to domain elements (see below) permit to perform formal analysis and transformations of these sentences. SVO(O) sentences can contain also some other syntactic elements, such as modifiers (adjectives or participles) associated to a subject or object. In addition to SVO(O), there can be also conditions, rejoin sentences ("gotos" to a point in the same or another scenario) and invocation sentences (invoke another use case). The precise invocation relation between a scenario and another use case in RSL replaces the rather vague inclusion relationship between use cases in UML.

Alternatively, the set of scenarios for a use case can be visualized in a natural way as a profile of UML activity diagram. SVO(O) sentences serve as the nodes of the diagram, and conditions and rejoins as control flows (in addition to the natural "next sentence" control flow).

Another part of RSL is the domain definition which consists of actors (system users), system elements and notions. Notions correspond to elements (classes) of the conceptual domain model of the future system. It is possible to define also notion generalization and simple associations between notions. Thus the essential part of domain model can be specified in requirements. From the syntax point of view, a notion is a single noun (e.g., *facility*) or a "complex noun" (e.g., *reservable facility list*).

The behaviour and domain parts in a valid RSL requirements model must be strictly related. The subject of an SVO(O) sentence must be an actor or system element. An object (direct or indirect) must be a notion. The informal meaning of each noun and verb must be defined in a vocabulary (currently, WordNet(Fellbaum, 1998)). We remind that in WordNet each term (a noun or verb) has a set of predefined meanings. The most appropriate

Figure 1. RSL example

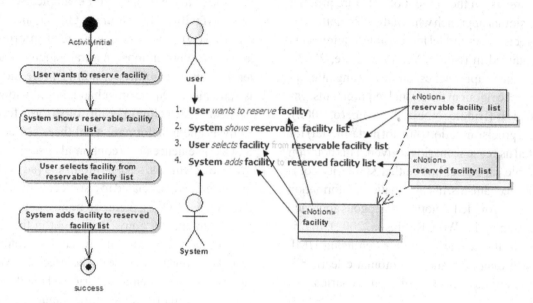

one of these meanings is selected for the given term, but if none matches, it is possible to extend the used copy of WordNet vocabulary. New complex nouns can also be added to the vocabulary.

There are also informal requirements in RSL, describing additional functional or non-functional properties of the system in plain natural language, but with hyperlinks to notions. Complete description of RSL is available in (Kaindl et al., 2007).

An RSL example is demonstrated in Figure 1. In this picture a small example from fitness club application is demonstrated. User selects facility from reservable facility list, which he wants to reserve. The scenario is shown both in the form of sentence list and activity diagram. For each element of the SVO sentences (subject or object) arrows show the corresponding domain element.

The precise syntax of RSL is defined by means of a metamodel (Kaindl et al., 2007). This metamodel has been built with the goal to provide a convenient abstract syntax specification of RSL. Another goal was an easy usability for model transformation definition and ReDSeeDS engine development.

As already mentioned, RSL is a language for requirements specification. The main class in the metamodel is RequirementsSpecification. Each specification contains a RequirementsPackage hierarchy with RSLUseCases. Each RSLUseCase is represented by one or more ConstrainedLanguageScenario. ConstrainedLanguageScenario consists of ordered sentences. The main type of sentences is SVOSentence. However there are also InvocationSentence and RejoinSentence. InvocationSentence is used to invoke another RSLUseCase. RejoinSentence is used to describe loops in sentence execution order. A SVOSentence consists of Subject and Predicate (a verb together with objects). Subject is (more precisely, is defined by) a NounPhrase, but predicate is a VerbPhrase. This part of the metamodel can be seen in the top of Figure 2.

Each *SVOSentence* is refined for further analysis by specifying links to the terminology used in this sentence. Subject must be a *Noun-Phrase* containing (more precisely, referencing uniquely) a *Noun*. Predicate is a *VerbPhrase*. There are *SimpleVerbPhrase* and *ComplexVerbPhrase*.

Figure 2. Top: RSL Use case metamodel; Bottom: Terminology metamodel

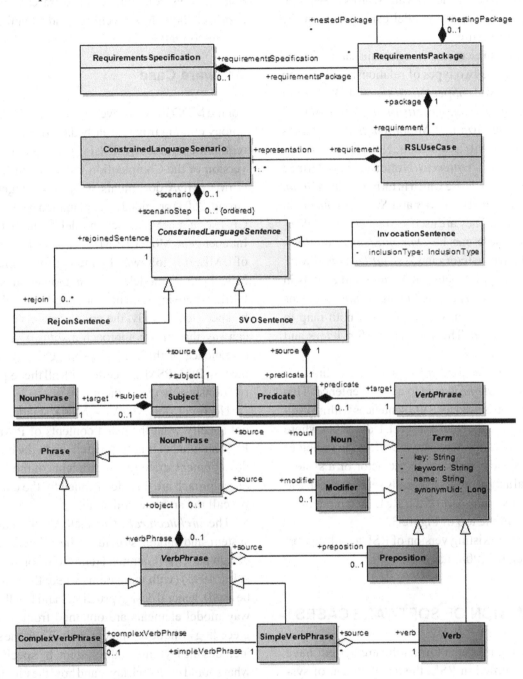

SimpleVerbPhrase contains a *Verb* and a direct object – a *NounPhrase*. *ComplexVerbPhrase* contains a *SimpleVerbPhrase* and an indirect object – also a *NounPhrase*. A *Preposition* is also contained in a *ComplexVerbPhrase*. A *Noun-Phrase* may also include a *Modifier*. For every term used a mapping to WordNet meaning is defined. It is done using the attribute *synonymUid*. The WordNet vocabulary is not directly a part of the model repository therefore this attribute is used to reference the relevant WordNet element. This part of the metamodel can be seen in the bottom of Figure 2.

The main element of the domain part is *Notion*. There can be two types of relationships between *Notions*: *NotionSpecialisation* and *NotionRelationship*. *NotionSpecalisation* corresponds to UML generalization, *NotionRelationship* corresponds to UML association. Notions are used as objects in *SVOsentences*. Notion name is defined using a *NounPhrase* which in turn contains a *Noun*.

There are also *Actors* and *SystemElements* in the domain. They are used as *subjects* of *SVOSentences*. There can be *DomainElementRelationships* between *Actors* and *SystemElements* as well.

The mapping between *Notions* and objects in *SVOSentences* is defined using *Nouns*. It means that an object maps to a *Notion* if both map to the same *Noun*. The same is true for *Actors* and *SystemElements*.

An additional *recipient* association links an *Actor* or *SystemElement* to a SVOSentence. This association is used for SVO sentences with a *SystemElement* in the role of subject. It describes where the action in the sentence is directed to (whether it is a system response to the actor or a system internal action) and is explicitly set by the scenario writer. Domain part of the RSL metamodel can be seen in the top of Figure 3.

For the existing version of RSL a tool support (Rein et al., 2008) has been built.

DEFINITION OF SOFTWARE CASES

When requirements for a software system have been specified in RSL, the development of system may start. In our approach the development is done in a model driven way. This means that a sequence of models finally leading to code is being developed. These models in totality form a software case. For all steps, automated model transformations assist in the creating of the next model in the sequence. This section explains what models constitute a software case in our approach, how they are chosen and what the role of transformations is.

Software Case

For the MDD life cycle we have chosen the terminology coming from the early days of MDA. The requirements model in RSL is treated as a concrete version of the Computation Independent Model (CIM) (MDA documents (Object Management Group, 2003) provided no explanation what in fact CIM should be). The next model is the Platform Independent Model (PIM) in a selected subset of UML. It is followed by the Platform Specific Model (PSM) model, again in another subset of UML, where implementation specific details can be specified. Finally, the code comes. Thus, we can say that in our approach a *software case* is a sequence of the corresponding CIM (requirements), PIM, PSM and code, with all the required relationships between them.

However, the MDA or MDD standards do not specify what the exact contents of PIM and PSM should be. It is completely up to the chosen development strategy. The contents of models in our approach are thus determined by the concept we call the architectural style.

The *architectural style* includes the chosen system and model structure, the related set of design patterns (Gamma, Helm, Johnson & Vlissides, 1995) (with indications where they should be used), general design principles and finally, the way model elements are obtained from models preceding in the development chain. Thus, the style includes the layering of the system, by specifying what should be in each layer and how they interact. A very important part of an architectural style is the chosen coherent set of design patterns. Patterns should be applied for all models in the chain and all layers. That is because patterns provide strict guidelines what kind of model elements should be created in each situation.

Figure 3. Top: Notion metamodel; Bottom: Traceability metamodel

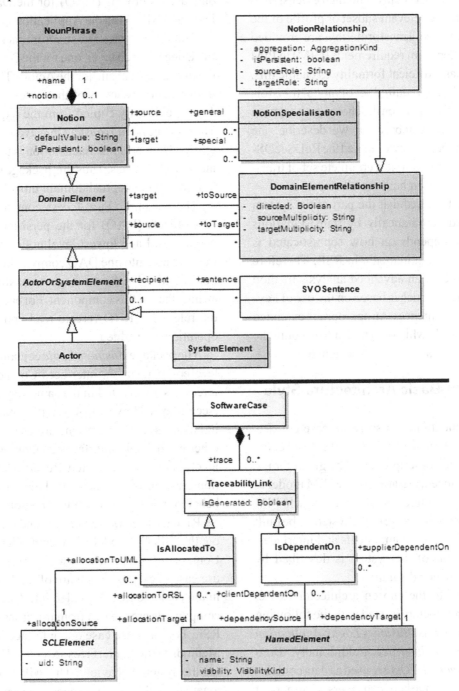

A precise definition of the architectural style is vital for creating model transformations which support the chosen development process of a software case. The style provides clear guidelines as to what elements should be created in the target model of the transformation (according to the analysis of the source model). Our goal is to ensure that transformations can create a significant part of the target model. Certainly, a manual extension of the model (in the relevant subset or profile of the UML) is then done. Transformations are provided also for the step from requirements (CIM) to PIM since RSL has sufficient formality to enable this.

Obviously, the required set of model transformations heavily depend on the chosen architectural style. In the next subsection we describe one specific architectural style, named the ReDSeeDS-Basic style. For this style a complete set of transformations has been built for all steps.

It should be noted that the part of the system to be created automatically by transformations significantly depends on how sophisticated is the analysis of requirements in RSL. Therefore we briefly sketch an advanced analysis method of requirements which is based on the use of keywords in SVO sentences. An appropriate extended architecture style which can take into account the results of this analysis is also sketched.

ReDSeeDS-Basic Architecture Style

As already mentioned, a software case consists of the Requirements model, PIM, PSM and code. A more detailed description will be given for the PIM model since its relation to the CIM model in RSL is the most interesting in our approach. PIM defines the static structure of the system to be built by means of classes, components and interfaces. Draft behaviour of the system is described by means of sequence diagrams.

According to the chosen architecture style, four-layer architecture is used with the following layers: *Data Access*, *Business Logic*, *Application Logic* and *User Interface*. Additionally, *Data Transfer Objects (DTOs)* are used as data containers for data exchange between layers. Component and interface based design style is used at all layers. Components encapsulate groups of related elements of the system. Interfaces appear as provided interfaces of the respective components. The main patterns used in this architectural style are

data access objects (DAO) for the Data Access layer and MVC for the Application Logic layer.

There are seven static structure packages in the PIM, one for each layer, one for the DTOs, one for the Interfaces and one for the Actors. The package *Actors* contains actors of the system to be built. They are directly copied from the requirements. The package *Data Transfer Objects* contains DTOs created from notions. Each notion is transformed into one DTO class. Thus this package serves also as a sort of conceptual domain model.

The package *Data Access* contains data access objects (DAO) for the persistence related operations. Each lowest level notion package is transformed into one DAO component. Each Notion contained in this package is transformed into an interface of this component. For each interface the relevant CRUD (create-read-update-delete) operations are added.

The package *Business Logic* contains business level components and interfaces. Components and interfaces are created in the same way as in Data Access layer. However, only notions participating in business level operations are used therein. In other words, only interfaces containing business level operations are created. Business level operation creation will be described together with the behaviour sequence diagram creation.

Packages *Application Logic* and *UI* are based on the MVC (model-view-controller) pattern. Components in application logic are created from use case packages which are of the lowest level in the package tree. Provided interfaces of these components are created from use cases written in RSL. For each use case one interface is created. Methods of these interfaces are created by analyzing the system behaviour. This will be described together with the sequence diagram creation. Currently, only a placeholder for the UI part is created. It could be replaced by a real UI support, but it is out of the scope of this chapter.

The above rules for generating the static structure of the system introduced in Figure 1 are illustrated in the top of Figure 4.

Figure 4. Top: Static structure example; Bottom: Behaviour example

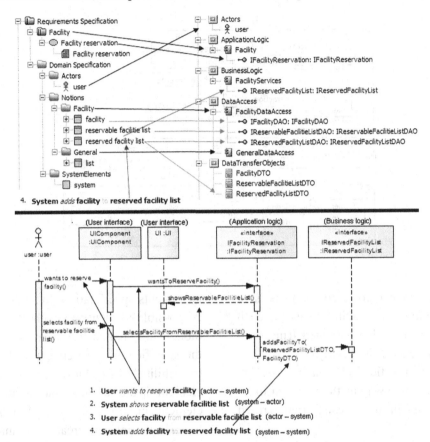

Certainly, the most complicated part is the description of system behaviour. The sequence diagrams describing system behaviour are created by analyzing scenario sentences. There can be three types of SVO sentences. The first one is an actor – system sentence. In this case the subject of SVO sentence is an actor. For two other sentence types the subject of sentence is a system element. Sentence types are distinguished using the recipient link. Recipient is an SVO sentence element; it defines where the behaviour described in the sentence is directed. The second kind of sentence is system – actor. In this case the subject is a system and the recipient is an actor. The third kind of sentence is system – system. In this case the subject and recipient is the system. It is used to describe system internal actions. The type of the particular message generated in the sequence

diagram depends on the type of sentence. The bottom of Figure 4 illustrates the behaviour sequence diagram for the previously described example. It shows that the operations in the business logic layer are created only for the system – system sentences. From actor-system sentences the application logic methods are created. From system – actor sentences UI methods are created.

The PIM can be manually extended after the initial generation. Then it is transformed to the PSM. The same four layers and DTOs are used. In this model, the factory pattern is used. It enables the management of classes and interfaces. Each component in the PIM is transformed into a package and a factory class in the PSM. Every interface is transformed into an interface and an implementing class. Classes and interfaces are located in packages created from components.

Figure 5. Transformation example

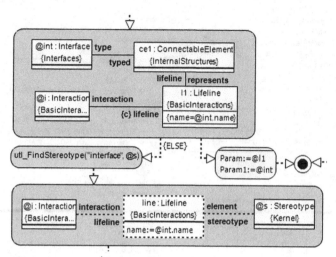

Factory classes created from components have methods for getting provided interfaces. For each layer, one more factory class is created. It manages all other factory classes in this layer.

The platform specific model can be extended manually in the same way as the platform independent one. Then this model can be transformed to code.

Transformation algorithms described above are implemented in the model transformation language MOLA (Kalnins, Barzdins & Celms, 2005; UL IMCS, n.d.). Figure 5 presents a MOLA transformation example which creates (or finds an existing) lifeline in a sequence diagram. The first rounded rectangle represents the most typical construct in MOLA – rule. Each rule contains a pattern for searching/creating/deleting model elements. This concrete rule searches for a lifeline in a sequence diagram.

Traceability

In order to support reuse, links between elements in different models within a software case are required. It must be possible to trace what elements in the PIM, PSM and code are created from which elements in the requirements. It is important, if we want to reuse parts of the re-

quirements specification. In such case it should be possible to identify which elements in other models are created from particular elements of the specifications. To ensure such possibilities, traceability links are introduced. They show which elements in the next model are created from which elements in the previous model. In our approach, traceability links are created automatically when creating models using model transformations. It ensures that traceability links are really present. If the user should create them manually, he could easily forget to create some links.

It should be noted that in our approach using the model transformation language MOLA traceability links serve also as the base for easy definition of transformation rules.

To save traceability links they should be stored in a software case. Therefore, the traceability metamodel is created. There are two types of traceability links: *IsAllocatedTo* from RSL to UML and *IsDependentOn* from UML to UML. The first type is created and used in the first transformation from RSL to PIM. The second type is used in the transformation from PIM to PSM. In the transition from PSM to code, traceability links are treated differently, because code is a text and it is not defined through a metamodel. The traceability metamodel can be seen in the bottom of Figure 3. Here *SCLElement* is the root class of RSL metamodel and *NamedElement* plays the role of root class for UML metamodel.

Keyword Based Analysis

As it was shown in previous subsections, the basic domain based analysis of RSL scenarios and the basic architecture style supports transformation based development for all steps within a software case. However, the part of business logic layer, which can be generated automatically in the PSM model (and consequently, in code), is not always sufficiently large.

More advanced solutions are available here. If we look at the SVO sentences:

System *shows* **reservable facility list**
User *selects* **facility,**

it is clear that more can be inferred from them. The first sentence clearly means displaying a form (containing reservable facility list – a list of rows showing facility data). The second one means that the user has selected a facility from this list. This intuitive reasoning can be made formal with the simple concept of keywords. We can decide that verbs *show* and *display* will mean the action of displaying a form (as it in fact always is). So we can declare them to be the syntactic forms of the keyword *show* with the above described semantics. Similarly, *select* can be defined as a keyword for a user action which means a selection of one element in a previously displayed list (not specifying exactly the technique used – be it a list-box or data grid or something else). A noun (more typically, one part of a complex noun) can also be defined as a keyword. Thus, *list* (within the complex noun "reservable facility list") should be defined as a keyword specifying that a list with elements being the notions defined by the remaining part of the complex noun (here – reservable facility) is being used. Examples of other verb keywords

are *build*, *add*, *remove*, another noun keyword could be *form*.

The use of keywords permits to perform a significantly more "semantic" analysis of SVO sentences. Thus, by means of analyzing notions together with scenario sentences, a more adequate domain model (a class diagram with appropriate stereotypes) can be created where basic (persistent) notions are distinguished from various temporary concepts such as lists and forms; nontrivial associations can also be created.

The keyword based style permits to specify detailed requirements for system behaviour in a natural and readable way. Using these detailed requirements it is possible to extract more information about the system behaviour to be used for building platform independent description of the system. For example, operations to be performed within the business logic layer frequently can be inferred without being explicitly specified as SVO sentences.

Certainly, this smarter analysis of sentences requires also an extension of the architectural style. More design patterns (manager, façade, POJO instead of DTO, abstract ORM) are used in this style. These patterns provide guidelines how data-related operations should be assigned to interfaces in a standard way during the behaviour specification in PIM by means of sequence diagrams. In the result, model transformations can be built which generate a realistic behaviour in PSM on the basis of requirements in RSL similar to those in Figure 1, but with keywords used in a consistent way.

Similarly, a more "practical" architectural style can be used for PSM. For example, patterns specific to Spring and Hibernate frameworks can be included. This way a quite realistic PSM, and even more, an executable Java code which serves as a draft prototype for the system can be built by transformations. Certainly, this created software case prototype then has to be manually extended to a real system.

Figure 6. Reuse overview

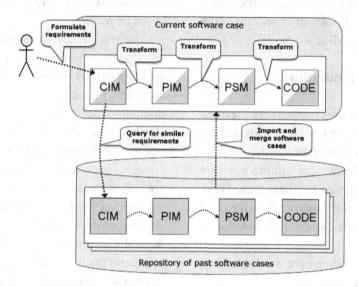

REUSE OF SOFTWARE CASES

In the previous section the process of developing software cases in the MDD way was described. This section describes activities and techniques that extend the above process in order to enable the reuse of software cases.

Figure 6 shows general overview of activities in the process of creating and reusing software cases in ReDSeeDS' approach. To enable reuse process, we need a repository that stores software cases created during past projects. The whole process begins when we formulate initial requirements model (CIM) for a new software system. This model can be transformed into PIM and PSM models and finally into code, as it was described earlier. Then we can query the repository for similar software cases. This is done by comparing the actual requirements model with requirements models of past software cases. As a result of this comparison, also design models (PIM and PSM) and code being a solution to the software problem expressed by requirements are found, thanks to the traceability links connecting all these artefacts. The whole past software case found in the repository or just selected, usually the most similar, part of it, called slice, can be then imported and merged with the current software case. The remaining part of this section provides more details of reuse-related issues.

Querying for Similar Software Cases

The initially specified requirements model for the currently built system can serve as a basis for querying a repository of past software cases in order to find solutions manifested by requirements models similar to the current one. In the ReDSeeDS' approach, the initial requirements model is the query itself. Therefore, the time consuming task of specifying separate queries can be omitted. Querying for a similar software case is performed by comparison of the two graphs – the one representing requirements specification of the prospective system and the latter, which represents requirement specification of the past software case stored in the repository. For these two graphs a special similarity measure is calculated. The similarity measure takes into account many factors as it is a combination of several measures commonly used in the processes of information retrieval, case based reasoning and description logic. These measures are described in more details further in this section.

From the point of view of the user, the query is performed by running a special query engine which takes the current requirements specification as the input parameter. As the result of a query, the query engine returns the list of similar software cases found in the repository along with the values indicating the degree of similarity. The returned values can range from 0, meaning no similarity at all, to 1, denoting that the current requirements model is completely contained in the past software case. As the result of the query, also similarities between particular requirements representations like use cases scenarios are calculated and returned.

Similarity Measures

In order to construct a similarity measure appropriate for comparing different requirements representations expressed in RSL, several local similarity measures from different research domains were combined.

Information retrieval techniques allow for texts comparison and can be applied to all representations. They provide lexicographic term matching – textual artifacts are equal if the same words occur with the same frequency. This approach does not take into account structural information. For example, when there are two scenarios using the same words but describing opposing procedures, they are considered equal. The meaning of words is also not considered – there is no distinction between homonyms.

In addition to information retrieval techniques also WordNet-based similarity measures for comparing synsets (synset in WordNet is a synonym set that groups synonymic words or sequences of words, i.e., words having the same defined meaning) are used. These measures are based mainly on path lengths between synsets defined by semantic relations. Two synsets are more similar, the shorter the distance between them there is. This approach

can handle synonyms and homonyms but cannot compare sentences or whole paragraphs of text.

Structure-based similarity measures cope with the structure of the artifacts to be compared. Two different structure-based measures were used to construct the global similarity measure: Graph-based and Description Logics. Both approaches handle the structure of artifacts. Basically, graphs are compared using both taxonomic comparison of elements and their relations to other elements. In this approach, two artifacts are considered equal when the same elements are represented with the same relations to other elements. Structure-based similarity measures give good results when comparing artifacts with a flexible structure like requirements specifications expressed in RSL and are not suitable for unstructured elements like plain text in RSL's natural language hypertext sentences.

Software Case Slicing

What is very important in the ReDSeeDS' approach to reuse is the possibility of reusing specific parts of software cases. Such a partial software case contains all the artifacts that are related with some selected elements from the requirements specification. It is illustrated in the top of Figure 7. A complete software case contains elements of requirements specification, elements of design models (PIM and PSM models) and, finally, pieces of code generated from design models. As it was described in one of the previous sections, all elements of the model on one level can be traced from elements of the model on contiguous levels, thanks to traceability links created during models transformations. In order to create a software case slice, a slicing criterion has to be chosen. A slicing criterion is a selected set of requirements (use cases) along with interlinked elements from the domain vocabulary. Following traceability links outgoing from the selected elements from requirements specification, all the artifacts from the following levels can be determined. Rephrasing

Figure 7. Top: The idea of software case slicing; Bottom: Detailed slicing example

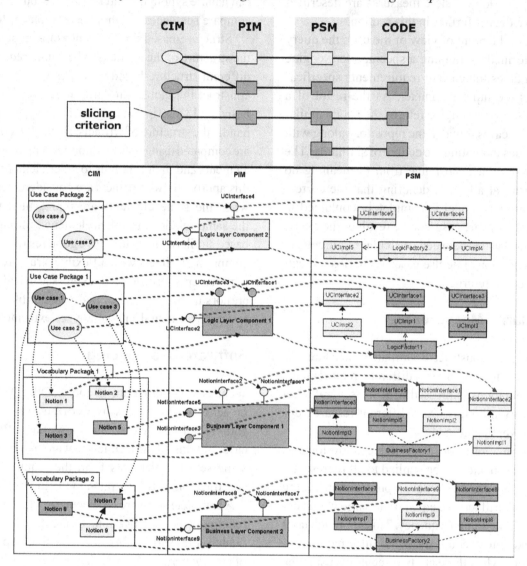

the definition of program slicing (Weiser, 1984), we can define software case slicing as follows:

Software Case slicing is a decomposition technique that extracts from a Software Case, artifacts relevant to a particular set of requirements. Informally, a slice provides the answer to the question "What artifacts realize the system behavior described by given set of functional requirements?"

For a particular software case, starting with the same slicing criterion, it is possible to create several different slices varying by the scope of elements from the source software case that will be included in the slice. The minimal slice is composed of the selected requirements, their nested elements, inter-level dependencies (i.e. traces between elements from contiguous levels, e.g. interfaces on the PIM level trace from requirements-level use cases) and intra-level dependencies (i.e. dependencies between elements from the same level, e.g. use case scenarios relate to vocabulary elements) of selected requirements. This kind of slice usually is not sufficient for reuse, as elements used by elements present in such a slice would not be selected, having the whole solution incomplete (e.g. missing some vocabulary elements). The maximal slice incorporates any elements related in any degree to the elements already present in the slice. Such a slice is, in most cases, nearly identical to the source software case (especially in case of incorrectly decomposed system). An optimal slice is a compromise between minimal and maximal slice, where dependencies among elements are broken or left untouched depending on their type and according to the advanced set of rules.

Some of the slicing principles described above are exemplified in the bottom of Figure 7. If we took Use Case 1 from Use Case Package 1 as a slicing criterion, the elements from the requirements tier to be also included in the slice would be: Use Case 3 (linked by RSL's invocation relation), Notion 3, Notion 8 (these notions are used in a scenario or description of Use Case 1). Please note that Notion 1 (related to Notion 3) would not have to be included (it is not directly linked with any of the slicing criteria). Already selected Use Case 3 has some subsequent elements: it links to Notion 7 and Notion 5. Therefore, Notion 5 and Notion 7 would also have to be included in the computed slice, but e.g. Notion 9, a child in the generalization relationship between Notion 7 and Notion 9, would not be the part of the minimal slice. The elements from other tiers that would form the minimal slice are: UCInterface1 and UCInterface3 (as linked to Use Case 1 and Use Case 3), NotionInterface3, NotionInterface5, NotionInterface7, NotionInterface8 (from Architecture layer) along with parent components Logic Layer Component 1, Business Layer Component 1 and Logic Layer Component 2 and their implementations in Detailed Design: UCInterface1, UCImpl1, UCInterface3, UCImpl3, NotionInterface3, NotionInterface5, NotionInterface7,

NotionInterface8, NotionImpl3, NotionImpl5, NotionImpl7, NotionImpl8 with LogicFactory1, BusinessFactory1 and BusinessFactory2 as parent elements. The result of such a slicing operation would be a CIM model containing the selected part of requirements specification, and elements of PIM and PSM tiers corresponding to the functionality contained in use cases selected as the slicing criterion.

Merging Slices

The selected slices from the past software cases can be reused in the currently built software case. To include the slice into the current software case, import and merge operations should be applied. The Clipboard – special temporary space is used for import operation. It is a waiting room for slices which had been selected to reuse in the current software case. A selected slice is imported into the Clipboard, but not directly into the main software case. Every import operation causes new Clipboard creation – one software case would then have many Clipboards. Although the Clipboard is an integral part of a software case, it is logically separated on the level of:

- terminology – e.g. the word "car" in the main software case and in the Clipboard have separable meanings;
- structure – both Clipboard and the main software case have CIM-PIM-PSM structure, but with separate sub-package structure;
- transformation – all Clipboards should be excluded from the transformations.

Such a separation gives the opportunity to make pre-merge changes in the imported slice as well as in the current software case in order to avoid merge conflicts. These conflicts affect names, semantics and structure. To support the user in a repetitive conflict resolution during the merge operation, simple "skip/override/auto-solve" mechanisms have been introduced. In general, each element of the software case, which is not a package, should have a unique name. Uniqueness of packages must hold on the level of the parent package. To avoid hyponym occurrence, each notion can have only one meaning.

If conflicts violating the above constraints occur, the user may decide how the conflict should be resolved (skip, override or auto-solve), and applicable operations should be applied. The skip option in the conflict resolution mechanism leaves untouched the element in the target software case. The override option erases the element's characteristics and content in the target software case and puts a new one from the imported slice. The auto-solve option adds a suffix to the requirements specification element name, equal to the name of the slice's clipboard. When the imported slice is not needed any more, it can be simply deleted.

IMPLEMENTATION AND VALIDATION

The domain-driven reuse of software design models is fully supported by a set of tools integrated in one complete environment called the ReDSeeDS Engine. The engine allows for editing and validating requirements, storing current and past software cases, querying for similar software cases, merging slices from past software cases into the current one and performing transformations.

Component based architecture, which was chosen for ReDSeeDS, gives the opportunity for replacement of particular parts of the engine according to further changes of technical requirements and needs. Considering such a style of the architecture, the Eclipse framework as the integration platform and its dynamic plug-in model that accomplish above functionalities – were chosen to build the complete ReDSeeDS environment (see top of Figure 8). The user interface, business and application logic are divided into several plug-ins, which are enclosed in the ReDSeeDS Eclipse Perspective. The layout and function of the Eclipse-based application is under fine-grained control of its developer, but also a subject to easy customisation by an end-user.

The main part of the ReDSeeDS Engine is the RSL editor. It allows for viewing and editing all elements of the requirements specification through individual editors for Requirements, Use Cases, Notions, Domain Statements, Actors and System Elements, which have similar layout and functionality. The user can edit element's description, name and relations to other requirements specification elements.

Very important feature of the software case is the central domain vocabulary, which includes all notions and their operations in the form of domain statements used in use case scenarios and other requirements definitions. Domain statements are in fact noun or verb phrases, whose descriptions can be linked to other notions. Every notion from the domain vocabulary can be edited in the Notion Editor. Beside notion details, it allows for editing domain statements. Usually, domain statements are added automatically when the user writes use case scenario sentences but, if needed, domain statements can be also added manually at any time by using the Domain Statement Editor.

For the purpose of determining similarity between different requirements specifications, notions are referred to a central terminology within the WordNet framework (i.e., the chosen software cases should rely on a common WordNet vocabulary copy). Term sense assignments can be managed in the special property view, which can be used for all term occurrences in the domain based requirements specification (see middle of Figure 8). The user has an opportunity to expand the central terminology with new terms as well as new relations (synonym, antonym, hyponym, meronym) in order to make possible further similarity measures.

The Use Case Editor is the most sophisticated editor in the ReDSeeDS Engine. It is a multipage editor, where the first page is similar to other editors, and other pages contain scenarios for the

Figure 8. Top: ReDSeeDS Engine Architecture; Middle: ReDSeeDS Perspective with Scenario Editor and Term assignment property view; Bottom: ReDSeeDS Engine perspective with multi tree view, and similarity results for use cases and scenarios

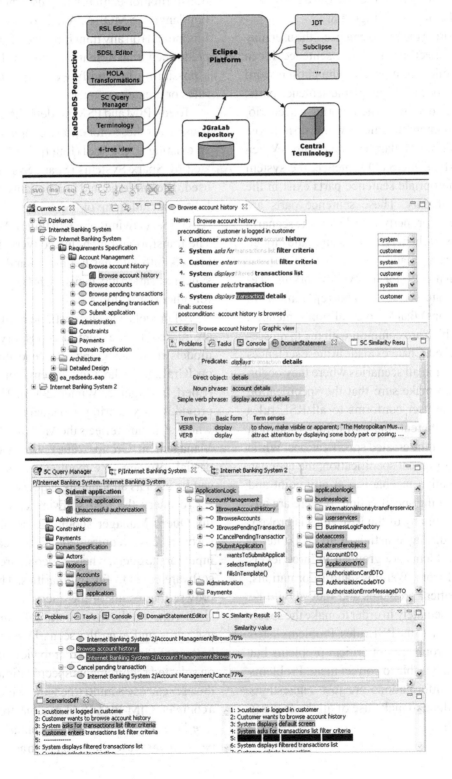

particular use case and visualisation of all scenarios in the form of an activity diagram. The Scenario Editor, which is a part of the Use Case Editor can be seen in the middle of Figure 8.

While writing the SVO sentences, the user may tag words as specific parts of the sentence. It can be done by clicking mouse on the chosen word and selecting one of the available sentence parts. As it was stated above, when writing a scenario, notions and domain statements which do not exist in the domain vocabulary can be created. When marking parts of the SVO sentence, the system checks if appropriate sentence parts exist in the domain vocabulary. These sentence parts are displayed in the property view below the scenario tab and if any of them is not present in the model, the tool suggests to add it.

The Scenario Editor allows for forking scenarios (alternate scenarios) and rejoining them (including loops) thanks to condition sentences. Sentences which are common with the main scenario are marked. Changes made in these sentences will take effect in all scenarios where they occur.

In order to make sure that the specification written by the user conforms to all RSL rules and is fully coherent, the tool offers validation mechanisms for the created specifications. While writing a requirement specification, the user can run the validation mechanism at any point and for any part of the specification. If there are any incoherencies or any of the RSL rules is broken, the tool will display a listing of all encountered problems. Problems are grouped in three levels of severity: Errors, Warnings and Informations. Errors are critical problems and they should be corrected immediately in order to make the specification conform to the RSL rules. Problems listed in Warnings group are not critical problems but it is strongly advisable to correct them. Problems classified as Informations are just suggestions what can be done to make use of all the features offered by RSL.

Transformations between models in the ReDSeeDS Engine are performed with an integrated transformation engine, which uses the transformation language MOLA. A user of the ReDSeeDS Engine can run any transformation from the list of predefined transformation profiles. There is also a possibility to modify existing transformation rules or create new ones.

To edit PIM and PSM models, the SDSL Editor is used. As these models are expressed in UML, an existing CASE tool (Enterprise Architect created by Sparx Systems (Sparx Systems, n.d)) is used. The implemented functionality of the SDSL Editor includes invoking Enterprise Architect (EA) for viewing the existing UML models. The transformation engine converts ReDSeeDS models into internal EA model and back. Such synchronisation mechanism can be easily adapted for other CASE tools.

All models, which constitute a software case, are stored in the central repository. As these models are in fact graphs, the repository is based on JGraLab – a Java implementation of TGraph (Ebert, Riediger, & Winter, 2008). This solution provides easy storing and querying of graphs, whose structure reflects the MOF models (Object Management Group, 2006). Any well defined partial software case requirements specification can be used as an input for a query.

To query the past software case repository, the Query Manager should be used. A current software case requirements specification is an input for the query, where it is compared with past software cases to find similarities. The user can browse the results of the query, view particular similarities on the level of the software case, the use cases and even the scenario sentences (see bottom of Figure 8). In order to view slices based on selected requirements specification elements, the user can use a multi tree view, which contains a complete CIM-PIM-PSM structure tree browsers (see bottom of Figure 8). To obtain a slice of a past software case, the generated traceability links are used. These traceability links lead to the PIM and PSM parts that were generated from selected requirements.

The multi tree view provides reuse of selected past software case slices in the current project. The ReDSeeDS Engine fully supports merging slices from a past software case into the current one by implementation of the import and merge functionality described in the previous section.

In order to confirm applicability of the presented ideas and usability of the tool, a comprehensive validation cycle in the industrial context is currently being conducted. This cycle is led by Fraunhofer IESE with the participation of four software development teams. The current validation outcomes show, that the whole system can be used in real industrial environments and that it reduces effort associated with formulating requirements and building complete software cases. Validation results point that requirements analysts accept the RSL. At the same time applicability of automatically generated design models was confirmed by software architects. Finally, the initial evaluation results of reuse activities prove that the effort to construct a new software case with the slices of existing ones is noticeably smaller than predicted.

FUTURE RESEARCH DIRECTIONS

The experiments have shown that a nontrivial part of a software system can be generated by transformations from appropriately defined requirements. However, this automatically generated part can be increased even more. One of the future research directions is to add more formality to requirements by means of keyword based analysis. At the same time, this extension does not compromise the understandability of requirements by domain experts. Alternatively, a formal ontology based semantic analysis could be applied to requirements sentences, then detailed behaviour could be extracted even without use of keywords. Another direction of future research is to refine the defini-

tion of similarity and building of slices, in order to provide a more targeted reuse of software case elements, with less manual adaptation required.

CONCLUSION

This chapter has shown how to combine model driven development and software reuse in a natural way. The basis for all of this is the semiformal requirements language RSL. The requirements in RSL consist of use cases refined by scenarios in a simple controlled language and the domain vocabulary containing the domain concepts. The meaning of each noun in a scenario sentence is defined in the domain vocabulary thus giving a precise meaning for the whole sentence. The requirements language is simple enough to be used directly by domain experts.

On the other hand, the specification of requirements to a system in RSL permits to apply model transformations directly to the original requirements. A non-trivial PIM model can be obtained by these transformations which after a manual extension can be transformed to PSM and further to code thus building an initial version of a complete software case. The transformations provide all necessary traceability links between the generated models.

The reuse aspect is also based on requirements in RSL. Requirements for a new software case are compared for similarity to the requirements of existing ones. Similar parts in requirements which are found this way are extended to slices on the basis of traceability links. These slices can then be imported into the current software case and adapted accordingly. Thus reuse is supported for all development artefacts.

A support tool named ReDSeeDS engine has been built for the described approach within the EU 6FP project ReDSeeDS. A validation has confirmed the usability of both the approach and the tool. The tool is now available as an open source project (SourceForge.net ReDSeeDS pages, n.d.) and can be extended and adapted for specific needs.

REFERENCES

Biddle, R., Noble, J., & Tempero, E. (2002). *Supporting reusable use cases. LNCS 2319* (pp. 210–226). Berlin: Springer.

Bryant, B. B., Lee, B. S., Cao, F., Zhao, W., Burt, C. C., & Gray, J. (2003). From Natural Language Requirements to Executable Models of Software Components. In. *Proceedings of the Monterey Workshop on Software Engineering for Embedded Systems, 2003*, 51–58.

Cybulski, J. L., Neal, R. D. B., Kram, A., & Allen, J. C. (1998). Reuse of early life-cycle artifacts: workproducts, methods and tools. *Annals of Software Engineering, 5*, 227–251. doi:10.1023/A:1018983220136

Dromey, R. G. (2006). Formalizing the Transition from Requirements to Design. In He, J., & Liu, Z. (Eds.), *Mathematical Frameworks for Component Software - Models for Analysis and Synthesis* (pp. 156–187). World Scientific Series on Component-Based Development.

Ebert, J., Riediger, V., & Winter, A. (2008). Graph Technology In Reverse Engineering, The TGraph Approach. In R. Gimnich, U. Kaiser, J. Quante, & A. Winter, (Eds.), *10th Workshop Software Reengineering (WSR 2008)*, (vol. 126 of *GI Lecture Notes in Informatics*, pp. 67-81), Bonn, Germany.

Fellbaum, C. (Ed.). (1998). *WordNet: An Electronic Lexical Database*. MIT Press.

Gamma, E., Helm, R., Johnson, R., & Vlissides, J. (1995). *Design Patterns: Elements of Reusable Object Oriented Software*. Reading, MA: Addison-Wesley.

Gomaa, H. (2004). *Designing Software Product Lines with UML: From Use Cases to Pattern-Based Software Architectures*. Reading, MA: Addison Wesley.

Jacobson, I., Griss, M., & Jonsson, P. (1997). *Software reuse: architecture process and organization for business success*. New York: ACM Press.

Kaindl, H., Smiałek, M., Svetinovic, D., Ambroziewicz, A., Bojarski, J., Nowakowski, W., et al. (2007). *Requirements specification language definition*. Project Deliverable D2.4.1, ReDSeeDS Project, Retrieved June 17, 2009 from www.redseeds.eu

Kalnins, A., Barzdins, J., & Celms, E. (2005). Model Transformation Language MOLA. In *Proceedings of MDAFA 2004,* (LNCS 3599, pp. 62-76). Berlin: Springer.

Laguna, M. A., López, O., & Crespo, Y. (2004). Reuse, Standardization, and Transformation of Requirements, (LNCS 3107, pp. 329-338). Berlin: Springer

Leal, L., Pires, P., & Campos, M. (2006). Natural MDA: Controlled Natural Language for Action Specifications on Model Driven Development. In *Proceedings of OTM 2006*, (LNCS 4275, pp. 551–568).

Leonardi, M. C., & Mauco, M. V. (2004). Integrating natural language oriented requirements models into MDA. In [WER]. *Proceedings of Workshop on Requirements Engineering, 2004*, 65–76.

Moon, M., Yeom, K., & Chae, H. S. (2005). An approach to developing domain requirements as a core asset based on commonality and variability analysis in a product line. *IEEE Transactions on Software Engineering, 31*(7), 551–569. doi:10.1109/TSE.2005.76

Object Management Group. (2003). *MDA Guide Version 1.0.1,* omg/03-06-01.

Object Management Group. (2006). *Meta Object Facility Core Specification,* version 2.0, formal/2006-01-01.

Object Management Group. (2009). *Unified Modeling Language: Superstructure,* version 2.2, formal/09-02-02.

Osis, J., Asnina, E., & Grave, A. (2007). Computation Independent Modeling within the MDA. In. *Proceedings of, ICSSTE07,* 22–34.

ReDSeeDS. (n.d.) *Requirements Driven Software Development System (ReDSeeDS) project. EU 6th framework IST project (IST-33596).* Retrieved June 17, 2009 from http://www.redseeds.eu

Rein, M., Ambroziewicz, A., Bojarski, J., Nowakowski, W., Straszak, T., Kalnins, A., et al. (2008). *Initial ReDSeeDS Prototype. Project Deliverable D5.4.1, ReDSeeDS Project.* Retrieved June 17, 2009, from www.redseeds.eu

Smiałek, M., Bojarski, J., Nowakowski, W., Ambroziewicz, A., & Straszak, T. (2007). Complementary use case scenario representations based on domain vocabularies. *Model Driven Engineering Languages and Systems,* (. *LNCS, 4735,* 544–558.

SourceForge.net ReDSeeDS pages. (n.d.) Retrieved December 11, 2009, http://sourceforge.net/apps/mediawiki/redseeds/

Sparx Systems. (n.d.). *Enterprise Architect tool.* Retrieved June 17, 2009, from http://www.sparxsystems.com.au/

UL IMCS. *MOLA pages.* (n.d.). Retrieved June 17, 2009, from http://mola.mii.lu.lv/

Weiser, M. (1984). Program Slicing. *IEEE Transactions on Software Engineering, 10,* 352–357. doi:10.1109/TSE.1984.5010248

Woo, H. G., & Robinson, W. N. (2002). Reuse of scenario specifications using an automated relational learner: a lightweight approach. In *Proceedings of IEEE Joint International Conference on Requirements Engineering,* (pp. 173-180).

KEY TERMS AND DEFINITIONS

Requirements: A description of what a software system should be. Here used mainly in the meaning of functional requirements, describing the desired functionality of a system.

RSL: Requirements Specification Language, used in the EU 6. FP project ReDSeeDS. It is a semiformal language based on a small subset of UML and controlled natural language.

MDA: Model Driven Architecture, an approach to software system development initiated by OMG. According to it a sequence of models – CIM (computation independent model), PIM (platform independent model), PSM (platform specific model) and finally code of a system – is created.

Model Transformation: The process of converting one model to another model (usually of the same system) according to the given rules. The models have to conform to the corresponding metamodels. The transformation is specified in a model transformation language.

MOLA: Model transformation LAnguage, developed by IMCS UL. It is a graphical language combining advanced pattern matching with imperative control structures.

Software Reuse: The use of existing software (and artefacts created together with it) to build a new software.

Software Case: A sequence of artefacts (models) for the development of a software system according to MDA principles. It typically contains CIM (requirements), PIM, PSM and code, with all the required relationships between them.

ENDNOTE

[1] This work is partially funded by the EU: Requirements-Driven Software Development System (ReDSeeDS) (contract no. IST-2006-33596 under 6FP). The project is coordinated by Infovide, Poland with technical lead of Warsaw University of Technology and with University of Koblenz-Landau, Vienna University of Technology, Fraunhofer IESE, University of Latvia, HITeC e.V. c/o University of Hamburg, Heriot-Watt University, PRO DV, Cybersoft and Algoritmu Sistemos.

Chapter 10
Quality–Driven Database System Development

Iwona Dubielewicz
Wrocław University of Technology, Poland

Bogumila Hnatkowska
Wrocław University of Technology, Poland

Zbigniew Huzar
Wrocław University of Technology, Poland

Lech Tuzinkiewicz
Wrocław University of Technology, Poland

ABSTRACT

The chapter presents a quality-driven, MDA-based approach for database system development. It consists of four parts. The first part gives a short presentation of quality models and basic MDA concepts. The second one discusses the specific relationships between software development and quality assessment processes. The third part presents the Q-MDA framework which combines the aforementioned processes. The framework is next tailored for database systems design. In particular the authors discuss the relationship between MDA models and data models. The last part contains an example of the framework application. The example shows how the specification and evaluation of the quality of database models can influence the process of database system development.

INTRODUCTION

As information systems become more complex and widespread, their quality becomes a more and more important concern in their development. Therefore, requirements for software product quality should be treated in the same way as functional requirements, however it involves ad-

ditional effort and extra costs. To ensure product quality two basic approaches can be considered: the first based on the evaluation of the quality of the final product, and the second based on the evaluation of the quality of the process by which the product is developed. The quality of software development process influences positively on the quality of a software product.

DOI: 10.4018/978-1-61692-874-2.ch010

Many modern approaches to software development are based on modeling paradigm and they implement the notions from Model Driven Architecture (MDA). Developers are encouraged to build a sequence of models in which the following is a refined or transformed version of the previous one. In such model-driven development approaches, the requirements to the models at the different levels of abstraction are clearly identified and specified. MDA focuses on functionality. It means that developers during building a model concentrate on the specification of its functionality, and next on the transformation that preserves functionality into a subsequent model. MDA is a very promising approach, however the quality aspect is not explicitly considered by it.

This chapter presents a quality-driven framework for model-based software development. The framework integrates two complementary processes. The first – based on the MDA approach (Miller & Mukerji, 2003) – is used for development purposes while the second – based on the quality specification and evaluation process defined by International Organization for Standardization (ISO) and the International Electrotechnical Commission (IEC) in ISO/IEC 9126 and ISO/IEC 14598 series of standards – is used for the verification and validation of the output artifacts from the former one. For this reason we call it the Quality-Driven MDA framework (Q-MDA). We are convinced that the integration of both the aforementioned processes is necessary to gain high quality software product.

The framework can be refined for specific purposes. We present its adaptation to quality-driven database system development. The adaptation forms a systematic approach to data modeling at different levels of abstraction and evaluation of their quality that adheres to MDA and ISO standards.

The chapter is organized as followed. The background part contains the basic notions relating to the MDA approach and to quality specification and evaluation models. Next, we give a brief outline of the Q-MDA framework, and next a more detailed description of using the framework for database system development is presented and illustrated by a simple example. The chapter is summarized by conclusions and an outline of future research within the Q-MDA approach.

BACKGROUND

As a software system is a kind of a product which is developed in a production process, therefore its quality may be considered in two perspectives: the product quality and the development process quality. The perspectives are strongly interrelated, for example, in shipbuilding industry, which is a more matured discipline compared to software engineering; the controlled quality over the design and building process is necessary to guarantee the quality of a ship – the final product. In software engineering, the quality of software development process also influences positively on the quality of a software product but does not guarantee the expected quality of the product. The software development process may be considered as a sequence of activities that deliver different artifacts. At the beginning of the process, software requirements are defined (usually on the basis of the business model). At the end a final software product is delivered. Other activities deliver intermediate artifacts. The quality of the intermediate artifacts influence the quality of the final software product. The chapter abstracts from the quality of the software development process, and concentrates on the quality of the software product and its relationship to the quality of the intermediate artifacts.

How to get high quality software becomes a more and more important question today. The question concerns two subquestions: how to develop software and how to control quality within the development process.

Furthermore, we consider MDA as a modern approach to the development of software systems.

OMG document (Miller & Mukerji, 2003) describes MDA as an approach to system *"development...[that]... provides a means for using models to direct the course of understanding, design, construction, deployment, operation, maintenance and modification."*

MDA provides a frame for structuring the modeling process. The frame defines models and their transformations. Three kinds of models are introduced: Computation Independent Model (CIM), Platform Independent Model (PIM), and Platform Specific Model (PSM), each representing a different viewpoint. The different viewpoints enable the separation of the specification of system's functionality from the specification of its implementation on a specific platform.

The CIM focuses on the environment of the system, and the requirements for the system; the details presenting the system structure and behavior are hidden or not yet determined. The PIM focuses on the operation of a system while hiding the details necessary for a particular platform. The PIM shows that part of the complete specification that remains unchanged for different platforms. The PSM combines the platform independent viewpoint with an additional focus on the details of a specific platform. For example, in database system design, the details are related to specific data models and the languages for their specification, e.g. relational, object, XML models.

System development is seen as a transformation of models that represent different viewpoints. In the transformation process, mainly functional requirements are taken into account. Those stated by CIM should be maintained by PIM, next by the PSM model, and finally by complete software product implemented in the selected programming language. However, the functionality of the developed system is the main but not the only requirement. Non-functional demands should also be considered. Unfortunately, up to now, the specification of the quality requirements and their transformation within modeling is not considered.

Therefore, it further shows how the quality aspect may be built into the MDA approach.

The international standard ISO/IEC 9126-1 concerning the quality of software products defines the notion as *the totality of characteristics of a software product that bears on its ability to satisfy stated and implied needs*. The quality is evaluated on the basis of the measurement of the software product attributes, i.e. measurable physical or abstract properties. Software quality attributes are classified into the quality characteristics that are further subdivided into subcharacteristics. ISO/EIC 9126 standardizes the terminology concerned with the definition of quality characteristics and subcharacteristics for the final product, as well as for intermediate artifacts that are produced in a software process development.

A quality of a software product is not defined in a unique way, it may be defined and evaluated from different perspectives. Furthermore, we will use perspectives defined in the ISO/IEC 9126-1. This standard introduces three kinds of quality models for software product: a quality-in-use model, an external quality model, and an internal quality model.

There are also other approaches, for example, Garvin (Garvin, 1984) defines five different quality views: transcendent view, product view, user view, manufacturing view, and value-based view. The ISO models could be mapped into Garvin views, e.g. in use model (ISO) could be mapped into user view. In (Wagner & Deissenboeck 2007) the authors propose a three level architecture for quality models that allows to define all (except transcendent) views in one solution. In our approach we concentrate on external and internal quality models – we build separate quality models for each of them. An in use model is not often explored in the literature as it usually uses different assessing techniques (e.g. questionnaires), and is more subjective.

The ISO/IEC 9126-1 quality-in-use model represents the perspective of a final user which uses the software product in a specified environment and a specific context of use. The external quality model represents a common perspective of a developer that delivers and a customer that acquires the software product. The external quality model should be agreed as an essential element of the contract between the developer and customer. These participants evaluate the product when it is used in simulated customer environment, usually in productive environment. The internal quality model represents the perspective of a software developer and relates to the artifacts that are produced during the software development process (e.g. data model).

The quality models representing the aforementioned perspectives are strongly interrelated. The relationships may be explained in the context of the software development process.

Explicit and implicit user needs (implicit needs are those not expressed directly, but elicited by developers) prompting a software product development are transformed into the system requirements that are the basis for quality-in-use model.

The model is used to define the users' quality expectations and it is used to assess the quality of the final software product when used in specific environment and specific context of use. It means that the quality-in-use model is strongly dependent on a specific user.

Next, the external quality model is defined with the intention that the final software product satisfaction will also satisfy the quality-in-use model. So, the external quality model is derived from the quality-in-use model. The model is separated from the direct influence of particular users.

The established external quality model is the basis for internal quality models that are used to assess the artifacts generated within the software development process. That is the decision of software developer of which artifacts to select for quality evaluation. In general, only the artifacts which influence the quality of the final software product should be considered. So, the internal quality models are a means to help the software

developer to assure the quality of the final software product.

For quality models representing the different perspectives, ISO/IEC 9126 defines two separate sets of quality characteristics: one set for quality-in-use perspective and another common set for external and internal perspectives. The scope of our further consideration is limited to the external and internal quality models. We ascertain only that the quality-in-use model relates to the capability of software product to enable specified users to achieve specific goals with effectiveness, productivity, safety and satisfaction in the specified context of use. The set of characteristics (subcharacteristics) for external and internal quality contains: *functionality* (suitability, accuracy, interoperability, security, compliance), *reliability* (maturity, fault tolerance, recoverability, functionality compliance), *usability* (understandability, learnability, operability, attractiveness, usability compliance), *efficiency* (time behaviour, resource utilisation, efficiency compliance), *maintainability* (analysability, changeability, stability, testability, maintainability compliance), and *portability* (adaptability, installability, co-existence, replaceability, portability compliance).

There are also other selections of quality characteristics, especially relating to specific information systems. For example, radar systems, medical devices, defense communication etc. have particular needs for high dependability, including such characteristics as availability, reliability, maintainability, maintenance support, and trustability. A review and discussion of quality needs for special types of systems is given in Guide to the Software Engineering Body of Knowledge (SWEBOK, 2004).

In the ISO/IEC 9126-1 the quality characteristics are defined informally. For example, efficiency is defined as "*the capability of the software product to provide appropriate performance, relative to the amount of the resources needed, under stated conditions*". The subcharacteristics of efficiency are defined in a similar way. Time behavior expresses "*the capability of the software product to provide appropriate response and processing times and throughput rates when performing its functions, under stated conditions*". Resource utilization expresses "*the capability of the software product to use appropriate amounts and types of resources when the software performs its function under specified conditions*". Efficiency compliance expresses "*the capability of the software product to adhere to standards or conventions relating to efficiency*" (ISO/IEC 9126-1, 2001).

To enable the quantitative interpretation of characteristics, the notion of a measure is introduced. Measures are functions defined over the values of measurable software attributes yielding results from a set, usually a numerical set. Many measures may be assigned to a given quality characteristic or subcharacteristic. How to define measures and to assign them to characteristics of the quality model are serious and independent research problems to be solved.

A set of selected quality characteristics and subcharacteristics together with the assigned measures forms the quality model. The quality model provides the basis for specifying quality requirements and evaluating quality.

To evaluate quality, quality assessment functions have to be defined. An assessment function rates the quality of a software artifact on the basis of its measurement. The measurement brings the values of defined measures. The assessment functions may be defined to rate the quality of whole software products, a set of selected artifacts or even separate artifacts. The functions may also be defined to give complete or partial evaluation of an artifact or set of artifacts. Complete evaluation takes into account all the characteristics and subcharacteristics of the quality model while partial evaluation takes into account only the selected quality characteristic or subcharacteristic from the quality model.

The scale rating quality of a software product can be divided into the categories corresponding to different degrees of requirements satisfaction – the set of recommended values contains: *exceeding requirements*, *target*, *minimal* and *non-acceptable*.

A quality model and assessment functions form so called quality and evaluation model. Summarizing, the model is defined by three elements (ISO/IEC 9612-1, 2001):

- a family of quality characteristics and subcharacteristics that are hierarchically ordered,
- quality measures that are assigned to the characteristics or subcharacteristics, and
- at least one assessment function.

The definition of the quality and evaluation model adheres also to the new currently elaborated series of ISO/IEC 25000 standards – Software product Quality Requirements and Evaluation (SQuaRE). SQuaRE will replace ISO/IEC 9126 – Product Quality, and ISO/IEC 14598 – Product Evaluation standards. Its goal is to deliver logically organized, unified series covering two main processes: software quality requirements specification and software quality evaluation, supported by a software measurement process (SQuaRE, 2005).

The series, however, do not cover the topics that are important in the context of the software development process, e.g. How to construct quality and evaluation models suitable for a given product and development process? Which artifacts select for evaluation as indicators for the quality of the final product? Later we illustrate some problems that are behind the questions, but they remain still open.

Software quality is the subject of numerous research, for example (Deissenboeck, Juergens, Lochmann & Wagner, 2009; Ho-Won, Seung-Gweon & Chang-Shin, 2004). An interesting review of the research results is given in (Mohagheghi, Dehlen, & Neple, 2009). The paper proposes the quality model called 6C consisting of six quality characteristics: completeness, consistency, comprehensibility, correctness, confinement, and changeability. Completeness is defined as having all the necessary information that is relevant and being detailed enough according to the purpose of modeling. Confinement is understood as an agreement with the purpose of modeling and the type of system (e.g. using relevant diagrams and being at the right abstraction level). Consistency is defined as no contradictions within the model as well as between models that represent the same aspect (e.g. data) but at different abstraction levels. Comprehensibility means understandability by the intended users (either human users or tools). Correctness is relative to the language and modeling rules or conventions. Changeability is defined as a feature supporting changes or improvements and is important for maintainability purposes.

A formalized version of quality model definition can be found in (Lamouchi, Cherif & Levy, 2008). In general the model defined there is very similar to ours, however, the notions used in (Lamouchi, Cherif & Levy, 2008) are different from those defined in ISO 9126-1 (e.g. quality goal is equivalent of characteristic, quality factor – subcharacteristic, criterion – subcharacteristic that is not further decomposed, measure – measure, rule – assessment function).

There are many different approaches to quality definition, but the ISO/IEC 9126 series of standards in our opinion propose the most matured view of quality in software development and therefore we will only reference the notions from the ISO/IEC 9126-1 from here.

BACKGROUND FOR Q-MDA

The Quality-Driven MDA (Q-MDA) is a framework for information system development, which integrates the process of software development and the process of software quality specification and evaluation. Software development process follows the MDA approach which means that the CIM, PIM, PSM models, and code are considered as intermediate artifacts. Software quality

specification and evaluation process is based on the ISO/IEC 9126 standard which entails the application of external and internal quality and evaluation models. An information system is usually embedded in an enterprise system in which there are actors constituting a direct environment of the information system. Information systems consist of parts that are hardware with operating systems, application software, and databases. Therefore, concentrating on quality-driven software development, the context where the software is placed should be taken into account. It means that quality requirements for the software are derived from the quality requirements for the information system, and the quality of the software influence on the quality of the whole information system. Later in the chapter only database systems are considered as software product.

In this Section we explain the background for the framework assuming that a database system is considered as a software product. Figure 1 presents the basic structure of the Q-MDA framework. The structure consists of MDA models and associated quality and evaluation models, further called quality models for the shortcut, represented in the form of UML packages.

There are dependency relationships between some elements in the figure. Except for standard <<trace>> dependency there are two new stereotypes of dependency relationships: <<spec>> and <<ass>>. The specification dependency <<spec>> means that a dependent element is defined on the base of an independent element. For example, Internal Quality Model – PIM is elaborated on the base of the External Quality Model for Information System and the PIM model. The assessment dependency <<ass>> links a quality model as the independent element with a MDA model or Information System and means that the model or product is assessed with respect to the specific quality model.

The root of the basic structure of the Q-MDA framework is External Quality Model for Information System. On the basis of this model, internal

Figure 1. The structure of dependencies between MDA quality models

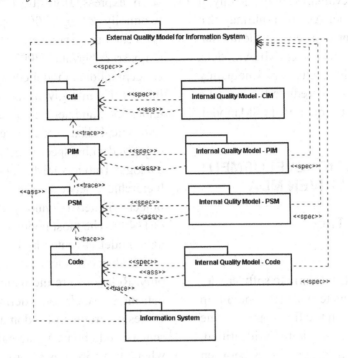

quality models for PIM, PSM and code are defined. It is worth noting that internal quality model for CIM is independent from the external quality model. The reason is that the most important quality characteristics for any CIM model are not ISO characteristics and have a logical nature: consistency and completeness. Of course, consistency relates also to the PIM and PSM models. It is implicitly assumed that all the models should be consistent, and complete, but the completeness of CIM may be evaluated by domain experts only.

The quality of the final software product – Information System – is evaluated with respect to its external quality model, and the quality of intermediate artifacts – CIM, PIM, PSM and code – with respect to their internal quality models.

Now, we explain in more detail the relationship between the quality models. The relationship between the models results from the relationship between the elements of those models, i.e. quality characteristics, measures and assessment functions.

Each quality characteristic from the external quality model should be present, if possible, in an internal quality model. The idea behind the rule is that when evaluating any intermediate artifact all characteristics concerning the final software product should be taken into account. This is not always possible because the evaluated intermediate artifacts may have not attributes suitable for a given characteristic. However, some extra characteristics may be included to the internal quality models. The inclusion may ensue, for example, from the experience that specific extra characteristics will improve the quality of the final product, or may be the result of the quality policy applied by the software manufacturer.

There is no direct relationships between the quality assessment functions in external and internal quality models. A simple rule of thumb may be recommended: the quality assessment function in the internal quality model should be defined in such a way that negative evaluation of the quality of the intermediate artifact should be a credible forecast of a negative evaluation of the quality of the final software product. A similar rule may also be applied to the relationship between the internal quality models for two subsequent MDA models. For example, the negative evaluation of the quality of PIM model should be a credible forecast of a negative evaluation of the quality of PSM model.

DATABASE SYSTEM DEVELOPMENT USING QUALITY-DRIVEN MDA

Data Models and Their Relation to MDA

Database development, similarly to software development, can be conducted using the bottom-up or top-down approach. In the first approach, the attributes for all entities are initially identified, then next the functional dependencies between the attributes are defined, and finally, on the basis of the normalization process, the schemata of the database are elaborated. This approach is effective only for small databases. If the number of attributes goes back hundreds or even thousands, it excludes the possibility of identifying all the relationships between the attributes, even for domain experts. The second approach, similarly to MDA, is based on data models that are created on different levels of abstraction. Subsequent models are derived more or less automatically from the previous ones. In general, the data models are defined at three abstraction levels: conceptual, logical and physical resulting in three different data models: conceptual data model, logical data model and physical data model.

Conceptual data model describes entities (for example, patient, service) from a considered domain, properties of these entities (e.g. first name, second name, birth date) and the relationships between entities (e.g. a patient *orders* service). The model is platform independent, that is, it abstracts from all details relating to a specific database environment. Conceptual data model can be expressed by Entity Relationship Diagrams (Connolly & Begg, 2005, pp. 342–385) or, what is recently more popular, by UML class diagrams (Elmasri & Navathe, 2007, pp. 121–123). As the conceptual data model concentrates on interesting entities in a given domain, it can be easily understood and verified by domain experts.

Logical data model describes how data are organized within specific technology. Many different logical models are distinguished, for example, hierarchical, network, relational, object-relational, object-oriented (Connolly & Begg, 2005, pp. 461–490) The most popular is still the relational data model, invented by E.F. Codd in 1970. So, our further considerations apply to that model only. Relations are the main element in logical data model. A relation is defined as a subset of the Cartesian product of n domains. It consists of a schema and a body. A schema is a set of attributes, where an attribute is an ordered pair of attribute name and attribute type. A body of n-ary relation is a set of n-ary tuples, where a tuple is an unordered set of attribute values. Tuples in relation should be identified by a so called (primary) key. A key is defined as a minimal subset of relation's attributes for which each two tuples have distinguishable values. The relationships between relations are usually expressed with the concept of foreign keys. A foreign key is an attribute in relation A that holds values of the (primary or alternative) key in relation B. A table is an accepted visual representation of a relation. The relational data model could be expressed in many ways. Usually the database supporting tools propose their own notation for that purpose, for example, Enterprise Architect. Some (e.g. Rational Rose Data Modeler) propose to use a specific profile of the UML language, dedicated for database modeling. Using a standardized version of SQL 2003 language (ISO/IEC 9075, 2003) or Common Warehouse Metamodel (CWM) Specification (CWM, 2003) could also be considered as an acceptable way of expressing the relational database model.

Physical data model describes how data are organized within a specific database management system (DBMS), for example, Oracle, MS SQL 2005 or eXist. This knowledge is needed for database programmers who are responsible for database schemata definition. Of course, the physical data model should be consistent with the logical data model (e.g. still should be a relational one). However, a specific DBMS usually offers native capabilities that can be used by database programmers (e.g. specific types, views). We assume that physical data model can also contain the realization of the part of business logic delegated to DMBS like stored procedures or transaction definitions. The physical data model is usually represented by SQL scripts accepted in the target environment. It is also possible to define these models directly in DMBS using available tools.

Sometimes, prior to conceptual data model elaboration, an additional domain data model is created. This model facilitates stakeholders to understand the considered domain. Like the conceptual data model, the domain model shows the entities that exist in a given domain and the relationships between them. However, this model is usually wider than the conceptual one as it may consist of entities that will be not present in the subsequent models – see the illustrating example in the next Section.

There is a clear correspondence between the database models and the MDA models (Dubiele-wicz, Hnatkowska, Huzar, &Tuzinkiewicz, 2006). Domain data model can be considered as a part of the CIM model, conceptual data model – because of its platform independence – as a part of PIM model, logical data model – as a part of the PSM model, while the physical data model – as a part of code.

Quality in the Context of Database Systems

Database system is an important, executable component of information system. It is usually controlled by the database management system, for example, Oracle or MS SQL. The database system is understood here as a set of data (database) with a set of database operations (insert, update, delete), and specification of access permissions.

Database system can be viewed as a software product itself, and can be evaluated against the external quality model derived from the external quality model defined for the information system. Database system is not the complete product perceived by the end-users, so it can be evaluated against the quality-in-use perspective.

We have analyzed the external quality characteristics proposed in ISO/IEC 9126-1 in respect to their applicability for the database system quality assessment. As a result, we formulated the following conclusions.

For external quality models, all the quality characteristics except the usability characteristic are applicable. The reason for excluding usability is that this characteristic deals with the end-user oriented features, like understandability, easiness to learn and attractiveness (database system does not include end-user interface).

We share the opinion of many researchers (Kifer, Brenstein & Lewis, 2006, pp. 383–455; Lightstone, Teorey & Nadeau, 2007, pp. 32–50), that among applicable quality characteristics maintainability, efficiency and security characteristics are the most important. The reason for maintainability is that software maintenance is the most expensive stage in the software life cycle (between 67% and 90% of the total life cycle costs is consumed in this stage). The efficiency of the database system has very often a crucial influence on the efficiency of the whole information system. Data stored in databases as assets owned by companies or individuals need to be secured.

We have also analyzed the internal quality characteristics proposed in ISO/IEC 9126-1 in respect to their applicability for different data models quality assessment. The conclusions of our analysis are presented in Table 1.

Table 1. Internal quality characteristics applicability to data models

MDA/ data model	Quality characteristic					
	Functionality	Reliability	Usability	Efficiency	Portability	Maintainability
CIM/domain	NA	NA	NA	NA	NA	A
PIM/conceptual	NA	PA	NA	PA	NA	A
PSM/logical	PA	PA	NA	A	PA	A
Code/physical	PA	PA	NA	A	A	A

Note. All quality characteristics come from ISO/IEC 9126-1. The meaning of the used abbreviations is as followed: A – fully applicable, NA – not applicable, PA – partially applicable.

The notion 'partially applicable' means that for a given characteristic not all its subcharacteristics are possible to be applied. For example, portability characteristic, described by four subcharacteristics (installability, adaptability, replaceability and co-existence) is partially applicable at the PSM level as only adaptability (measured with the number of data structure changes) can be estimated. The other subcharacteristics, for example, installability cannot be applied as it is inadequate for the PSM data model (PSM data model has a static nature). The characteristic *portability* is applicable at the code level, as all their subcharacteristics can be measured.

Usability characteristics is assumed to not be applicable for any data models. The reason is that usability is perceived by end-users only.

In contrast to the usability maintainability characteristic is applicable for all data models. In the opinion of (Piattini, Calero, Sahraoui & Lounis, 2001; Piattini & Genero, 2001) the most important subcharacteristics of maintainability is the analyzability measured by complexity measure. Complexity can be defined and evaluated for the data models expressed either by UML class diagrams (Piattini & Genero, 2001) or relational schema (Piattini, Calero, Sahraoui & Lounis, 2001), so it can be applied for domain, conceptual, logical, as well as physical data models.

Analyzing two efficiency subcharacteristics time behavior and resource utilization, the first one could only be estimated taking into account the specification of database system operations,

while the second one can be assessed, for example, with the measures taken from ISO/IEC 9126-3 (ISO/IEC 9126-3, 2003) at PSM and code levels.

Functionality characteristics – described by four subcharacteristics: suitability, accuracy, interoperability and security, is partially applicable because, for example, interoperability cannot be estimated based only on platform independent data models. Suitability and accuracy subcharacteristics would be evaluated only for the physical data model if system functions are implemented by DBMS (e.g. stored procedures). It is also possible to evaluate security subcharacteristic if grants are used in PSM and physical models.

Reliability characteristic similarly to functionality is only partially applicable to data models because two of its subcharacteristics are "behavior–oriented" e.g. recoverability or fault tolerance and measures proposed in ISO/IEC 9126-3 can never be measured for these models. The third subcharacteristic, maturity can be considered as applicable as it concerns to fault detections and removals in the created artifacts.

Quality-Driven Approach to Database System Development

The process of database system development within MDA is described by an activity diagram presented in Figure 2. The database development process is strongly correlated with the quality evaluation process shown in Figure 3. The quality evaluation process refines the activities

Figure 2. Database system development process (DSDP)

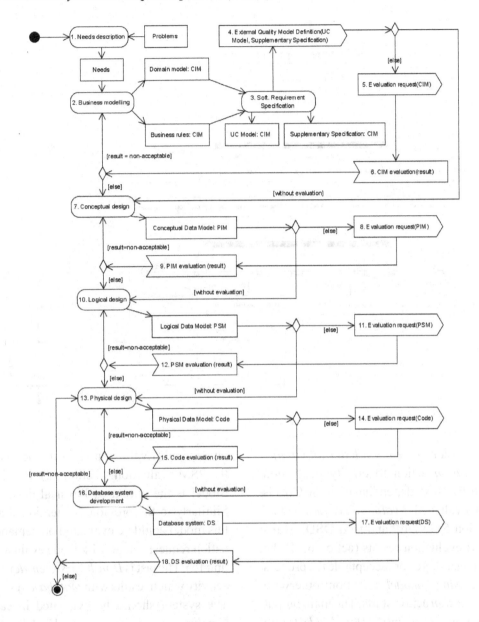

undertaken within the external quality model and internal quality model definitions. Both processes communicate with each other what is shown by the appropriate send signal actions and accept the event actions.

The database system development process (DSDP) starts with *Needs description* action. The action results with *Needs* identification which are the basis for *Business modeling* action. Business modeling produces a part of the CIM model, that is.: (a) *Domain model*, and (b) *Business rules*. They are the inputs for *Software Requirement Specification*. The aim of this action is to create the rest of the CIM model, that is: (d) *Use-case Model* (*UC Model*) gathering functional requirements, and (e) *Supplementary Specification* gathering non-functional requirements. The CIM model (especially the part with system require-

Figure 3. Quality evaluation process (QEP) of artifacts in database system development process

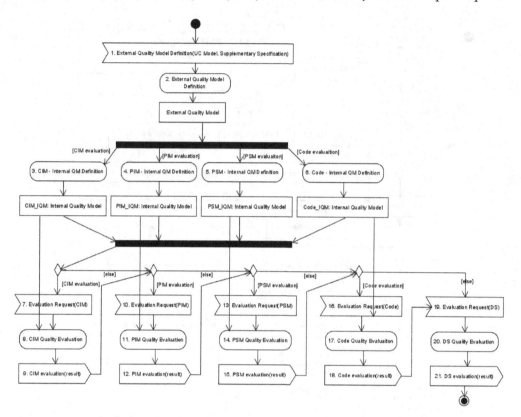

ment specification) is sent via *External Quality Model Definition* action to quality evaluation process (QEP). Next, depending on if the CIM is going to be evaluated, *Evaluation request* signal is sent (action 5) to QEP and next DSDP waits for the CIM evaluation results (action 6). If the assessment results are non-acceptable the process returns to *Business modeling* action; otherwise *Conceptual design* action starts. The main output from this action is *Conceptual Data Model* (main part of the PIM model in the context of database system). After that, depending on if the PIM is going to be evaluated, another *Evaluation request* signal is sent to QEP (action 8) and the results from the assessment are received (action 9). The next action is *Logical design*. The main output from this action is *Logical Data Model* (main part of the PSM model in the context of database system). *Logical Data Model* could be evaluated

on demand (Evaluation request – action 11, and the PSM evaluation – action 12). Physical Data Model is the output of Physical design action. Similarly to the previously mentioned artifacts, this model could be evaluated on demand (Evaluation request – action 14, Code evaluation – action 15). The last is *Database system development* activity which results with *Database system* itself. The system should be evaluated in each case (*Evaluation request* – action 17, *DS evaluation* – action 18). If the assessment results are non-acceptable the process returns to *Physical design* action when the database could be tuned.

The quality evaluation process (QEP) is started with accept event action, after which *External Quality Model Definition* is built. After that the selected, planned, internal models are created (maybe in parallel). The particular internal quality model is the input to specific evaluation action, for example *CIM_IQM* (CIM internal quality model) is the input for *CIM Quality Evaluation* action. On the one side, the evaluation actions are performed on demand, e.g. *CIM Quality Evaluation* is raised by *Evaluation Request (CIM)* (action 7); on the other side they are performed conditionally (only when planned). At the end of the accept event action chain is the evaluation request for the database system (action 19). Only this action is obligatory. Results of the assessment are sent by *DS evaluation* action.

Some activities in Figure 2 are conditional, for example, all evaluation requests for intermediate database system products (CIM, PIM, PSM, Code). The same holds in Figure 3, where appropriate internal quality models are elaborated and assessed only when it is needed. For the sake of brevity it is assumed that within the activity number 2 in Figure 3 both external models for the information system, and for the database system being a part of the information system are created, and next only the latter is taken into account.

Well defined quality models should fulfill particular demands. In (Deissenboeck, Juergens, Lochmann & Wagner, 2009) authors classify quality models – based on their purpose – into three groups: definition, assessment, and prediction models, and formulate some general requirements for each group. According to the classification, our proposal is a kind of quality modeling framework that satisfies the main requirements for the definition and assessment models, for example: (a) the metamodel shall define the structure of the definition model and an unambiguous decomposition mechanism for its contents, (b) metamodel shall allow to define the different views of quality, (c) metamodel shall cover both internal product characteristics and externally visible product characteristics, and (d) assessment of the quality criteria can be qualitative or quantitative. The requirement that is not supported by us is "the model shall describe with what techniques each quality criterion can be assessed, i.e. dynamic tests, automated static analysis, or manual review."

In (Mohagheghi & Dehlen, 2008) the authors propose a quality framework for Model Driven Engineering. The quality framework is understood that there is a 7th step procedure: (1) Identify quality goals, (2) Identify the target objects that can impact the quality goals, (3) Identify the quality-carrying properties of the target objects, (4) Specify how to evaluate the quality-carrying properties and characteristics, (5) Specify association links between the quality-carrying properties and the quality goals, and (6) Review and evaluate the framework in practice. All the aforementioned steps are carried out by our approach. What is more, some of them are defined more accurately (precise), e.g. quality goals are derived from user needs, so, in consequence, the review step could be limited (completeness is guaranteed by model construction).

EXAMPLE OF QUALITY-DRIVEN MDA APPLICATION

This section is an illustration of the proposed approach to a quality evaluation of a software product. The considered software product is a database application system handling a Heath Care Center (HCC). The system consists of two parts: a database system and a client application (thin client). This system was selected as a fairly simple, and related to commonly known matter. Furthermore, the database system is considered as a final product.

The presentation starts with the concise description of user needs and software requirements, which are the basis for external quality and evaluation model definition. Next, CIM, PIM, PSM models, and the code along with the respective internal quality and evaluation models are developed and discussed. The internal quality and evaluation models are used to estimate the elaborated artifacts. The final software product (the database system implemented in the MS SQL database management system) is assessed according to the external quality and evaluation model. All quality and evaluation models follow the ISO/IEC 9126-1 standard presented in the previous part of this chapter.

Only external and internal quality models are taken into consideration. The quality-in-use model representing a user perspective relates to the capability of the software product to enable users to achieve specified goals in a specific context of use. Definition of the quality-in-use model would require additional considerations on the grounds of a business domain which is outside of our interest.

The database system development process (DSDP) proceeds according to the activity diagram presented in Figure 2, while the quality evaluation process (QEP) proceeds according to the activity diagram presented in Figure 3. As both processes, that is DSDP and QEP are running in parallel, activities from both processes are interleaved, and therefore the description of their actions is also interleaved at inter-process communication points.

Needs Description (DSDP, Activity 1)

We consider the medical services offered by an authorized Health Care Center. The HCC offers a limited range of medical services. Each type of services has a fixed cost and an estimated average time of its accomplishment. The HCC consists of deferent medical service units, e.g. laryngology, ophthalmology, surgery. Cost of service depends on its type, and is established by the HCC. Medical services are performed by authorized personnel. Services are offered from Monday to Friday at regular hours (e.g. from 8 a.m., to 3 p.m.). The monthly volume of services performed by the HCC is limited. Patients who wish to use a medical service must register first at the reception desk, and the registration assigns the patient to a particular medical staff member. The reception desk is manned by personnel who do not carry out medical services. In the registration process the

following data are recorded: a planned date and time of the medical service, and personal data of the client. The responsibilities of the receptionists include informing patients about services, patient registering and possible changes of the registration. On the day of the service, the patient checks in at the reception desk to confirm his or her arrival, where he/she is given a token for the service. The token is passed on to medical staff who records the time when the visit starts and ends. Tokens serve also as the basis for financial reports which are prepared by the financial department of the HCC. Particularly, monthly prepared reports include:

- Workload of employees;
- Number of performed services and number of planned services partitioned by types;
- The total sum of payments for the service partitioned by types.

The HCC is characterized by the following quantities:

- 12 000 potential patients;
- 20 specialized surgeries, open for eight hours a day, with an average service time of 15 minutes per patient;
- three reception desks with a processing time of five minutes per patient.

The maximal annual capacity for services is about 20 000.

The following main problems are identified within considered domain:

- Lateness in patient's servicing what results in not optimal medical staff utilization and patients' dissatisfaction.
- Registration process is too long which results in patients' dissatisfaction and long queues for registration.
- Time consuming preparation of periodic reports.

Having to improve the quality of patient registration and delivered medical services, the following needs were established:

- From the perspective of HCC patients:
  1. Punctual carrying out of services.
  2. Quick and simple registration for services.
- From the perspective of HCC manager and financial department:
  1. Effective management of HCC's resources (employees, surgeries etc.), and assurance of high patients' satisfaction.
  2. Protection of personal data of patients.
  3. Support for reports preparation.

On the basis of the needs stated above, the CIM model is elaborated. The CIM model consists of four components. The first two – a domain model and business rules – are defined within business modeling activity, while the others – a use case model and a supplementary specification – within software requirement specification activity.

Business Modeling (DSDP, Activity 2)

The starting point for business modeling is business rules identification. We defined the following business rules belonging to different groups:

- Structural facts:
  - BR/01 – Health Care Center employs many servicemen
  - BR/02 – Serviceman is employed exactly by one Health Care Center
  - BR/03 – Serviceman can perform many service types
  - BR/04 – Service of given type can be performed by many servicemen
  - BR/05 – Health Care Center provides at least one service type. The maximal number of monthly performed services of a given type cannot exceed a given limit. The services are

offered within specified timetable at specific price.
  - BR/06 – Service type can be served by many Health Care Centers.
  - BR/07 – Patient can be registered to a given service type provided by a specific Health Care Center at specific registration date on a planned service date.
  - BR/08 – Service type provided by a specific Health Care Center can be registered to many patients.
- Invariants (must be true for all entities):
  - BR/9 – *service date* must be located in a *timetable*
  - BR/10 – the number of performed services within one month must be equal or less than the specified *monthly limit*
- Constraints:
  - BR/11 – a patient may only be registered for a service of selected type when there exists a free date and time in the *timetable* for that service and the respective *monthly Limit* is not exceeded

As a result of the business modeling, a domain model (see Figure 4) from a set of business rules was derived.

Software Requirement Specification (DSDP, activity 3)

Defining the requirements is a challenge so it is usually done gradually. The recommended approach (Leffingwell & Widrig, 2003, pp. 95–99; Kroll & Kruchten, 2003, pp. 287–310) is to start from a list of features, and to further refine them into system requirements. A feature is understood as "a service provided by the system that can be observed by a user of the system, and that fulfills a stakeholder need" (Kroll & Kruchten, 2003, pp. 294).

Figure 4. Domain model of Heath Care Center domain

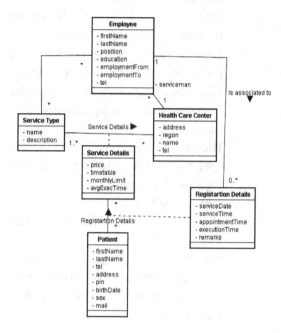

The following basic features for HCC system were identified:

- FE/01 – Patients registration
- FE/02 – Create, view, modify, and delete offered service types
- FE/03 – Service schedule management
- FE/04 – Analysis of workers activity
- FE/05 – Registration of performed services
- FE/06 – Support for medical staff
- FE/07 – Personal patient data must be protected
- FE/08 – System should response quickly
- FE/09 – System should be available at working hours

Based on the described features, a set of requirements for a system is elaborated. The description of requirements must be more detailed (than feature description) to enable system design, implementation and testing.

The system requirements are to be allocated to hardware and software components. In our case all requirements are allocated to software. HCC system consists of only two software items: database application (DA) and database system (DS). Database application is assumed to provide graphical user interface to database system, and database system is expected to realize business logic (by stored procedures) as well as to check business rules.

Software requirements (for both items) – expressed in natural language – are divided into functional and non-functional. Functional requirements are usually presented by Use Case Model (UC model), while non-functional requirements are gathered in a supplementary specification document (Kroll & Kruchten, 2003, pp. 296–299). UC Model consists of use case diagram and a set of use-case specifications (textual documents). For simplicity, the presentation of UC Model is limited to use-case diagram (see Figure 5), and short use-cases descriptions given below. The list of actors is implied from the domain problem description, domain model and described needs, while the use cases are derived from basic system features.

Use-case short description list:

- Information about medical services use-case:
    ◦ As a *Patient*

I want to obtain information about services provided by HCC in order to know what services are available. (traced from FE/02, offered to *Patient* actor)

- Performed services registration use-case:
    ◦ As a *Medical Staff Member*

I want to record details about the service I have performed in order to facilitate the preparation of reports for the HCC manager. (traced from FE/05, offered to *Medical staff* actor)

- Patient's medical treatment management use-case

Figure 5. Use-case model of Heath Care Center System

    ◦   As a *Medical Staff Member*

I want to read and update patient's medical data record in order to maintain current information about patients. (traced from FE/06, offered to *Medical staff* actor)

- Daily duties browsing use-case
    ◦   As a *Medical Staff Member*

I browse my timetable in order to know my daily duties. (traced from FE/03 and FE/06, offered to *Medical staff* actor)

- Patient list browsing use-case:
    ◦   As a *Medical Staff Member*

I browse my patient list in order to know who is planned to be serviced by me on a specific date (traced from FE/06, offered to *Medical staff* actor)

- Employee's activity planning use-case:
    ◦   As a *Manager*

I plan a timetable for medical staff members in order to manage their duties (traced from FE/03, offered to *Manager* actor)

- Employee's activity analyzing use-case:
    ◦   As a *Manager*

I prepare five kinds of reports:

R1: The burden on HCC staff,

R2: List of performed services per worker,

R3: List of offered services by HCC,

R4: List of services performed by HCC staff,

R5: List of workers who exceeded monthly limit of performed services

in order to better manage the staff members and plan their duties (traced from FE/04, offered to *Manager* actor)

- Offered services management use-case:
    ◦   As a *Manager*

I create/delete/update information regarding provided service types in order to keep information provided to patients up to date (traced from FE/02, offered to *Manager* actor)

- Patient registration use-case:
    ◦   As a *Receptionist*

I register patients for particular services and create patient's medical record for a new patient in order to better organize staff member duties (traced from FE/01, offered to *Receptionist* actor).

Next, the supplementary specification is shortly presented.

Supplementary Specification

Performance Requirements

- PR/01 – The system shall accommodate 25 users during peak usage time from 8:00 a.m. to 10:00 A.M. local time, with an estimated average session duration of 30 minutes (allocated to DS, derived from domain description)
- PR/02 – Responses to queries shall take no longer than 1 second to load data from the

database after a user submits the query (allocated to DS, derived from FE/08)

Security Requirements

- SE/01 – Users shall be required to log in to the HCS (Health Center System) system for all operations except browsing of the offered services (allocated to DA, and DS, derived from FE/07)
- SE/02 – The system shall permit medical staff to view only their own patients (allocated to DS, derived from FE/07)

Availability

- AV/01 – The HCS system shall be available to users on the corporate Intranet 99% of the time between 8:00 a.m. and 3:00 p.m. local time, and 90% of the time between 3:00 p.m. and 8:00 a.m. local time (allocated to DA, and DS, derived from FE/09)
- AV/02 – The HCS system shall be available to dial-in users 99% of the time between 8:00 a.m. and 3:00 p.m. local time, and 90% of the time between 3:00 p.m. and 8:00 a.m. local time (allocated to DA, and DS, derived from FE/09)

Operating Environment

- OE/01 – HCS system shall operate with MS Internet Explorer v. 7.0 and 8.0, Netscape v.7. web browsers (allocated to DS)
- OE/02 – HCS system shall permit employees access from the corporate Intranet only (allocated to DS)
- OE/03 – HCS system shall permit patients access from the Internet only (allocated to DS).

Synchronization Point (DSDP, Send Signal Action 4 – QEP, Accept Event Action 1)

Definition of External Quality Model Definition elaborated within the QEP is sent to the DSDP.

External Quality Model Definition (QEP, Activity 2)

This external quality model for the database application system is derived from supplementary specification for the whole system. External quality model is defined only for the database system and consists of two characteristics: *functionality* and *efficiency*. For each of them one subcharacteristic was selected, i.e. *security* for the former one, and *time behavior* for the latter. For these characteristics, the following measures were defined:

- Access Controllability (AC) – percentage of number of unauthorized executed database operations with comparing to number of all attempts of database operation executions,
- Maximal Average Response Time ($MART$) – maximal value from the set of average response time of each query type.

The definitions of the assessment functions in the context of external quality model are as followed:

$$F_{Security}(AC) = \begin{cases} \text{target} & \text{if } AC = 0\% \\ \text{non– acceptable} & \text{otherwise} \end{cases}$$

$$F_{Time-behav}(MART) = \begin{cases} \text{exceeding} & \text{if } MART \leq 0.5s \\ \text{target} & \text{if } 0.5s < MART \leq 0.8s \\ \text{minimal} & \text{if } 0.8s < MART \leq 5s \\ \text{non– functional} & \text{otherwise} \end{cases}$$

The final evaluation of the quality of database application system will be calculated using the following function:

$$F(AC, MART) = \begin{cases} non-acceptable & \text{if } F_{Security}(AC) = non-acceptable \\ F_{Time-behav}(MART) & \text{otherwise} \end{cases}$$

The functions evaluate a quality of the database application system as non-acceptable if there is no guarantee that security is fully satisfied, otherwise the quality of the database application system is the same as the quality of efficiency.

From the defined quality and evaluation model for the database system application, a new quality and evaluation model for the database system is derived. The security requirements for the database application system should be maintained by the database system which is implied by feature FE/07. The performance requirements for the database system should be stronger than those for the whole system, and are defined as followed:

$$FDS_{Time-behav}(MART) = \begin{cases} exceeding & \text{if } MART \leq 0.1s \\ target & \text{if } 0.1s < MART \leq 0.5s \\ minimal & \text{if } 0.5s < MART \leq 1s \\ non-acceptable & \text{otherwise} \end{cases}$$

$$FDS_{Security}(AC) = F_{Security}(AC)$$

Consequently, the final quality assessment function *FDS* for the database system is defined as the modification of the function *F*:

$$FDS(AC, MART) = \begin{cases} non-acceptable & \text{if } FDS_{Security}(AC) = non-acceptable \\ FDS_{Time-behav}(MART) & \text{otherwise} \end{cases}$$

CIM Internal Quality Model Definition (QEP, Activity 3)

CIM is a special model which, first of all, should be consistent with a business domain. Additionally it is expected to be internally consistent and

complete. External consistency and completeness of the model can be proved by domain experts only. The functionality and efficiency characteristics – elements of external quality model – are not adequate for the CIM internal quality model. However, it would be possible to take into account the maintainability characteristics that are not included in the external quality model. In the example, instead of the maintainability evaluation, we apply the best practices ((Leffingwell & Widrig, 2003, pp. 271–288) in specification of requirements. Therefore, the internal quality model for CIM is not defined.

PIM Internal Quality Model Definition (QEP, Activity 4)

PIM internal quality model should contain if possible all the quality characteristics from the external quality model, in our case: functionality (security) and efficiency (time-behavior). In the example, the PIM internal quality model is not considered by the following reasons. Firstly, as the security aspect is not considered in the PIM model, therefore the security characteristic is also omitted in the PIM internal quality model. Secondly, the time-behavior aspect could be considered in the PIM model but the efficiency on this level reflects the computational complexity of the considered problem rather than the efficiency of the problem solution. From a pragmatic point of view, the efficiency evaluation of the PIM model has an unessential impact on the efficiency of final software product.

PSM Internal Quality Model Definition (QEP, Activity 5)

PSM internal quality model usually ranks candidate logical models which enables the selection of the best one in context of the given non-functional demands. Internal quality model characteristics should consider all the characteristics from the external quality model. However, in some situations, it is not possible; for example, security cannot be evaluated at the PSM level, because it is not expressed here. But some new characteristics, for example, maintainability, can be added. Therefore, in our case, the proposed internal quality model consists of two quality characteristics: *efficiency* and *maintainability*.

In the example, to evaluate the quality of logical data model we will use the following basic measures:

- Number of Tables (*NT*) – number of tables defined in the logical data model,
- Number of Foreign Keys (*NFK*) – number of foreign keys defined in the logical data model,
- Number of Attributes (*NA*) – the sum of numbers of attributes in all tables of the logical data model,
- Number of Join Operations (*NJO*) – the number of joint operations in database operations serving to prepare data for reports.
- Number of database Operations (*NO*) – number of database operations defined over the database that are necessary to prepare requested reports.
- Table's Record Length (*TLR*) – the declared length of the table's record in bytes.

and the following derived measures:

- Tables Maintenance Index (*TMI*) – it is obtained by establishing the proportion of the number of attributes (*NA*) and the number of tables (*NT*) in the relational schema. The higher this measure is, the more difficult it is to maintain the tables in the schema.
- Schema Connectivity Index (*SCI*) – the proportion of the number of foreign keys (*NFK*) and the number of tables (*NT*) in the schema. The higher this measure is the more difficult it is to maintain the relational schema.

- Transaction Join Index (*TJI*) – the proportion of the total number of join operations (*NJO*) and the number of database operations (*NO*) performed over the database. The higher this measure is the less efficient is database operation performance.
- Average Length of table Record (*ALR*) – the proportion of total length of records definitions in all tables and the number of all tables. The higher this measure is the less efficient query performance is.

The measures *NT*, *NFK*, *NA*, *TMI* and *CI* come from literature (Garcia, Serrano, Cruz-Lemus, Ruiz, & Piattini, 2007), and the other are proposed by us.

The values of measures may be of different types, sometimes a set of values is not bounded. Therefore, it is convenient to transform the possible values of measures into a common, finite set of values. In this way we get normalization of measure values. In our example, we use the set of ordered values {*Low, Medium, High, Very High*} for each derived measure. In consequence, we introduced the auxiliary functions which definitions in pseudo code are given below.

For maintainability evaluation, two functions were defined: (a) *A(TMI)*, and (b) *A(SCI)*.

$$
A(TMI) = \begin{cases} VeryHigh & \text{if } TMI > 100 \\ High & \text{if } 50 < TMI \leq 100 \\ Medium & \text{if } 15 < TMI \leq 50 \\ Low & \text{if } 0 < TMI \leq 15 \end{cases}
$$

$$
A(SCI) = \begin{cases} VeryHigh & \text{if } SCI \geq 2 \\ High & \text{if } 1.5 \leq SCI < 2 \\ Medium & \text{if } 1 < SCI < 1.5 \\ Low & \text{if } 0 \leq SCI \leq 1 \end{cases}
$$

For efficiency (time-behavior) evaluation also two functions were defined: (a) *A(ALR)*, and (b) *A(TJI)*.

$$A(ALR)=\begin{cases} VeryHigh & \text{if } ALR \geq 1000 \\ High & \text{if } 500 \leq ALR < 1000 \\ Medium & \text{if } 150 < ALR \leq 500 \\ Low & \text{if } 0 \leq ALR \leq 150 \end{cases}$$

$$A(TJI)=\begin{cases} VeryHigh & \text{if } TJI > 15 \\ High & \text{if } 10 \leq TJI \leq 15 \\ Medium & \text{if } 3 \leq TJI < 10 \\ Low & \text{if } 0 \leq TJI < 3 \end{cases}$$

Having the auxiliary functions defined, we propose different assessment functions for each considered quality characteristic (*MFF* for maintainability and *EFF* for efficiency):

$$MFF(A(TMI),A(SCI)) = \begin{cases} \text{exceeding} & \text{if } A(TMI) = Low \text{ and } A(SCI) = Low \\ \text{target} & \text{if } A(TMI) \leq Medium \text{ and } A(SCI) \leq Medium \\ \text{minimal} & \text{if } A(TMI) \leq VeryHigh \text{ and } A(SCI) \leq VeryHigh \\ & \text{or } A(TMI) = VeryHigh \text{ and } A(SCI) = Low \\ & \text{or } A(TMI) = Low \text{ and } A(SCI) = VeryHigh \\ \text{non--acceptable} & \text{otherwise} \end{cases}$$

$$EFF(A(ALR), A(TJI)) = \begin{cases} \text{exceeding} & \text{if } A(ALR) = Low \text{ and } A(TJI) = Low \\ \text{target} & \text{if } A(ALR) \leq High \text{ and } A(TJI) < Medium \\ \text{minimal} & \text{if } A(TJI) \leq High \\ \text{non--acceptable} & \text{otherwise} \end{cases}$$

Final quality assessment of PSM internal quality model is defined by the following function:

$$F_{LDM}(MMF, EFF) = \begin{cases} \text{exceeding} & \text{if } MMF \geq \text{target and } EFF = \text{exceeding} \\ EFF & \text{if } EFF \leq \text{target} \\ \text{target} & \text{if } MMF \leq \text{minimal and } EFF = \text{exceeding} \end{cases}$$

Code Internal Quality Model Definition (QEP, Activity 6)

Code is a representation of the physical model presented in a target programming language. In our example, the physical model is the specification a database instance expressed in native SQL (MS SQL 2005), and it consists of three kinds of elements:

- database schema definitions (create table statements),

- database operations, e.g. stored procedures,
- database privileges specification (grant statements).

For the sake of simplicity, we decided to evaluate database schema definitions only.

The quality evaluation of the logical model gives the same result of the evaluation as the evaluation of the physical model (limited to the database schema definitions) because each element from logical model is transformed one-to-one to an element of the database schema. Therefore, there is no need to define separate internal quality model for the physical model.

Conceptual Design (DSDP, Activity 7)

Taking into account the functional requirements and the previously created domain model (CIM) a conceptual data model (PIM) was elaborated (see Figure 6). For the sake of simplicity, attribute names are hidden.

We distinguished *Person* class as a generalization of *Employee* and *Patient* classes. Additionally, analyzing attributes of *Patient* class, we found out that the feature *address* represents the independent entity of the domain (i.e. instances of *address* may exist independently of *Patient* instances). Therefore, we decided to represent the feature as a new *Address* class.

Any patient is offered services (*Orders* association class) by different HCC companies. The details relating service orders are represented by *performs* association class, while the details relating the service type (e.g. its *price*) by *provide* association class.

All entities from the domain model were transformed in the classes of the conceptual model. The transformation entails some change of entity names. Table 2 shows the tracing of the models' elements and their names.

Figure 6. Conceptual data model (PIM) for Heath Care Center System

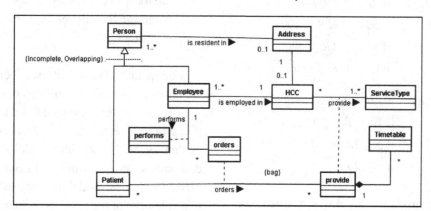

Table 2. Trace dependencies between domain and conceptual data models

Domain data model	Conceptual data model	Comments
Employee	*Employee*	A person working for HCC.
	Person	Generalization of two domain entities (*Employee*, *Patient*). It allows the disclosing of essential knowledge that the same person can be an employee and a patient.
Patient	*Patient*	A person who orders at least one service provided by HCC
	Person	Generalization of two domain entities (*Employee*, *Patient*). It allows the disclosing of essential knowledge that the same person can be an employee and a patient.
Service Type	*ServiceType*	The class *ServiceType* has the same meaning as the entity *Service* Type
Health Care Center	*HCC*	Abbreviation used in the domain problem
Service details	*provide*	Characteristics of services (timetable, price, monthly limit) provided by HCC.
Service details(timetable)	*Timetable*	An instance of the class *Timetable* represents a period of the day when a given type of service is available.
Registration details	*performs* *orders {bag}*	An ordered service performed for a patient by *Employee* on fixed date. The actual service duration is stored for the analysis purpose of service quality.
Patient(address)	*Address*	The attribute address of the entities *Patient*, *Employee* and *Health Care Center* are represented by the class *Address*. The class has own attributes needed to search detail information of places for statistic purposes.
Serviceman(address) *Health Care Center (address)*		

Logical Design (DSDP, Activity 10)

The conceptual data model PIM is the source for the transformation to the logical data model. Based on the PIM, many different PSMs can be proposed. In our case, applying different strategies of data model transformations (Garcia et al., 2007; Halpin & Morgan, 2008, pp. 681–733;

Lightstone, Teorey & Nadeau, 2007, pp. 196–220), we prepared two alternative logical data models (LDM_1, LDM_2) that are presented in Figure 7. All classes were transformed into tables, and relationships between the classes are represented either by foreign keys or by separate tables with foreign keys. The semantic of these two models is the same but their structures are different. The

Figure 7. Logical data models (PSM) for Heath Care Center System – (A) LDM₁ (B) LDM₂

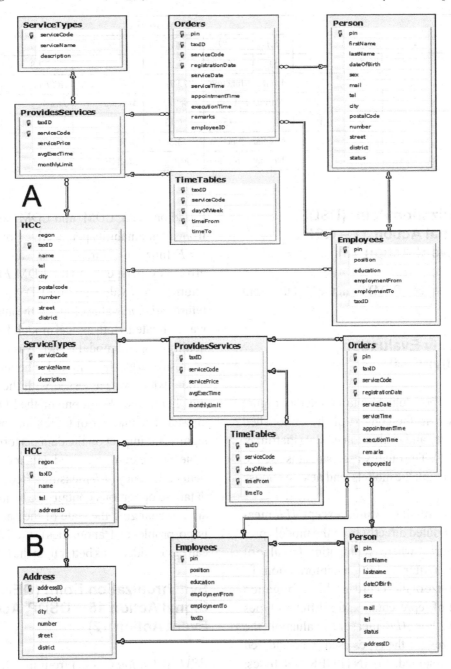

first model LDM₁ is de-normalized. Model LDM₂ is in the third normal form (3NF) which is usually considered as sufficient to ensure data integrity. Normalized data models are free of undesirable characteristics such insertion, update, and dele-

tion anomalies that may be the reason of a loss of data integrity.

All attributes from the conceptual model are present at the logical data model (no information is lost).

Table 3. Measurement values and auxiliary assessment results of logical data models LDM$_1$ and LDM$_2$

Model	Measure							
	NT	*NFK*	*NA*	*NJO*	*TMI*	*SCI*	*TJI*	*ALR*
LDM$_1$	7	8	51	14	7,28	1.14	2,8	164,57
	Auxiliary function				*A(TMI)*	*A(SCI)*	*A(TJI)*	*A(ALR)*
	Normalized value				*Low*	*Medium*	*Low*	*Medium*
LDM$_2$	8	10	49	15	6,13	1,25	3,0	131,00
	Auxiliary function				*A(TMI)*	*A(SCI)*	*A(TJI)*	*A(ALR)*
	Normalized value				*Low*	*Medium*	*Medium*	*Low*

Synchronization Point (DSDP, Send Signal Action 11 – QEP, Accept Event Action 13)

Evaluation request (PSM) from the DSDP is sent to the QEP.

PSM Quality Evaluation (QEP, Activity 14)

The quality of both logical data models (see Figure 7) is assessed in the context of the established internal quality and evaluation model (Piattini & Genero, 2001). The quality assessment is used to compare and rank the models, and next to choose the best one.

The values of all measures, except *ALR* measure, are computed directly from the models presented in Figure 7, whereas computing the value of *ALR* measure requires additional information. To estimate the size of the record in table information about a size of representation for different types is necessary. For *ALR* measure evaluation the following sizes for the types used in considered models are assumed: (a) INTEGER – 4 bytes, (b) DECIMAL – 9 bytes, (c) DATE – 8 bytes, (d) TIME – 4 bytes, and (e) CHAR(n) – n bytes. The *ALR* measure is equal to 164,57 for LDM$_1$ and 131,00 for LDM$_2$.

Table 3 gathers all the measures needed to internal quality evaluation of logical data models, as well as auxiliary assessment function results.

Based on them, LDM$_1$ and LDM$_2$ were assessed from maintainability perspective (for both models *MFF* function returns *target* value), and from efficiency perspective (for LDM$_1$*EFF* function returns *target* value, and for LDM$_2$*EFF* function returns *minimal* value). Finally, the internal quality was evaluated. Both logical models have accepted quality. Logical model LDM$_1$ was assessed with the result *target*. This model is better than LDM$_2$ model which was assessed with the result *minimal*. For further development, the LDM$_1$ model is chosen. The number of table join operations has significant impact on the data performance. Less tables in the de-normalized data model results in better efficiency (*TJI* measure). Because the set of database operations contains only queries which are not changing the state of the database (there is no problem of anomalies), the LDM$_1$ model can be considered as better than the LDM$_2$ model.

Synchronization Point (QEP, Send Signal Action 15 – DSDP, Accept Event Action 12)

PSM evaluation (result) from the QEP is sent to the DSDP.

Physical Design (DSDP, Activity 13)

In this activity, the physical data model was elaborated based on the previously prepared logical data model – LDM$_1$. We prepared SQL scripts

Box 1.

```
SELECT
        w.pin AS 'Employee', p.firstName 'First name',
        p.lastName 'Last name',          o.serviceCode 'Service',
        CAST(YEAR(o.serviceDate) AS CHAR(4))+'-'+
            CAST(MONTH(o.serviceDate) AS CHAR(4)) AS sDate,
        COUNT(*) AS "Ordered services"
FROM
        dbo.ProvidesServices ps
        JOIN dbo.Orders o ON (ps.serviceCode = o.serviceCode
                    AND ps.taxID = o.taxID)
        JOIN dbo.Employees w ON (w.pin = o.pin)
JOIN Person p ON (p.pin = w.pin)
WHERE
        o.serviceDate BETWEEN '2009-01-01' AND (SELECT GETDATE())
GROUP          BY w.pin,o.serviceCode,p.firstName,p.lastName,
YEAR(o.serviceDate), MONTH(o.serviceDate), ps.monthlyLimit
HAVING COUNT(*) > ps.monthlyLimit
ORDER BY COUNT(*) DESC, p.lastName, p.firstName;
```

executable in MS SQL environment for database schemata creation. Additionally, we defined five queries (R1, …, R5) for different reports (R1: The burden on HCC staff, R2: List of performed services per worker, R3: List of offered services by HCC, R4: List of services performed by HCC staff, R5: List of workers who exceeded the monthly limit of performed services). SQL definition of R5 query is given in Box 1.

Moreover, the grants for accessibility rights to the data for all transactions were defined.

Database System Deployment (DSDP, Activity 16)

During this activity the database is populated with data. The estimated numbers of records for particular tables in the HCC database system are as followed: 12 for *HCC*, 124 502 for *Orders*, 12 831for *Person*, 439 for *ProvidesServices*, 220 for *ServiceTypes*, and 319 for *Employees*.

Synchronization Point (DSDP, Send Signal Action 17 – QEP, Accept Event Action 19)

Evaluation request (DS) from the DSDP is sent to the QEP.

Database System Quality Evaluation (QEP, Activity 20)

During this activity, the database system is assessed against the external quality and evaluation model. The database system is assessed taking into account two characteristics: *functionality* (*security*), and *efficiency* (*time behavior*).

The database system was tested in an environment with the same parameters as the information environment in the HCC. Two kinds of tests were performed: access control tests for the whole database system, and performance tests for each transaction.

All access control tests were passed with the value of the measure $AC = 0$, which means that there was no situation of unauthorized access to data. In consequence, the assessment function $S_{ecurity}(AC)$ returns the value *target*.

Performance tests were performed during simultaneous activity of 10 users. For each user, a set of random selected 100 transactions was chosen. The following average response times were obtained for the set of defined database operations: R1 (0,87 s), R2 (0,38 s), R3 (0,12 s), R4 (0,31 s), and R5 (0,93 s).

The above results yields the value of the measure $MART = 0,93$ s. In consequence, the assessment function $E_{Time\_behav}(MART)$ returns the value *minimal*.

Taking into account the partial evaluations, eventual quality evaluation of the database system $FDS(AC, MART) = minimal$.

Synchronization Point (QEP, Send Signal Action 21 – DSDP, Accept Event Action 18)

DS evaluation (result) from the QEP is sent to the DSDP.

Received accept event action gives information on the value of database system assessment function. If the value is acceptable, the development process is finished; otherwise the database system should be improved, and we should go back to activity 13 (DSDP). There are many possibilities of database system efficiency improving, for example, by defining indexes, partitioning, and denormalization.

In our example, the value of database system assessment function is *minimal* which is considered as acceptable, and therefore both processes DSDP and QEP are completed.

FUTURE RESEARCH DIRECTIONS

MDA approach becomes widely accepted. Following the approach in software development process we assume that constructed models are consistent and complete with respect to a given domain problem, and the transformations between models are functionality preserved. For a given source model there are many possible transformations which results in multitude of target models. A natural question arises which one from the possible transformations to choose? The evident answer is: choose that transformation which gives the best model in the context of the final software product. To do it, first quality of the models should be specified and evaluated, after then the transformations should be evaluated. In the context of our considerations the following research questions are of the most importance:

- How to specify quality requirements and how to bind them to MDA models?
- How to construct quality and evaluation models suitable for a given product and development process?
- How to evaluate transformations of models?
- Which artifacts select to evaluation as indicators for the quality of the final product? How the quality of intermediate artifacts influence the quality of the final product?

In general, there are no satisfactory answers to the problems, although there some works dealing with them. For example, new UML profiles were elaborated: for Modeling and Analysis of Real-time and Embedded systems (Modeling and Analysis, 2008), and UML Profile for Modeling Quality of Service and Fault Tolerance Characteristics and Mechanisms (UML Profile for Modeling Quality, 2008).

CONCLUSION

In the chapter we presented the Q-MDA framework to software system development which combines the MDA approach with quality specification and evaluation. It enables the early examination and evaluation of developed models which results in the controlled quality of final software product. The framework is general and can be adopted for different kinds of applications, such as a database system.

The application of the framework is shown by a simple example of database system development. The example presents how to create internal quality models for intermediate artifacts as well as how to create an external quality model for the final product. The quality models cover the following quality characteristics: efficiency, maintainability and security, which seem to be crucial in the context of databases. The example also illustrates how to define assessment functions for different perspectives and how quality evaluation results can influence the development process.

REFERENCES

Common Warehouse Metamodel (CWM) Specification. *Version 1.1.* (2003). from http://www.omg.org/ technology/documents/formal/cwm_2.htm

Connolly, T., & Begg, C. (2005). *Database Systems. A practical Approach to Design, Implementation, and Management* (4th ed.). New York: Pearson Education, Inc.

Deissenboeck, F., Juergens, E., Lochmann, K., & Wagner, S. (2009). Software Quality Models: Purposes, Usage Scenarios and Requirements. In *Proc. Seventh Workshop on Software Quality* (pp. 9–14). Los Alamitos, CA: IEEE Computer Society.

Dubielewicz, I., Hnatkowska, B., Huzar, Z., & Tuzinkiewicz, L. (2006). Feasibility analysis of MDA-based database design. In W. Zamojski (Ed.), *Proceedings of International Conference on Dependability of Computer Systems. DepCoS – RELCOMEX.* (pp. 19–26). Los Alamitos: IEEE Computer Society Press.

Elmasri, R., & Navathe, S. B. (2007). *Fundamentals of database systems,* (5Th Ed.). New York: Pearson Education, Inc.

Garcia, F., Serrano, M., Cruz-Lemus, J., Ruiz, F., & Piattini, M. (2007). Managing software measurement: A metamodel–based approach. *Information Sciences, 12*(177), 2570–2586. doi:10.1016/j.ins.2007.01.018

Garvin, D. A. (1984). What does "product quality" really mean? [Los Alamitos, CA: IEEE Computer Society Press.]. *MIT Sloan Management Review, 26*(1), 25–43.

Guide to the Software Engineering Body of Knowledge (SWEBOK). (2004). Retrieved from http://www.computer.org/portal/web/swebok/about

Halpin, T., & Morgan, T. (2008). *Information Modelling and Relational Databases* (2nd ed.). Burlington, MA: Morgan Kaufman Publisher.

Ho-Won, J., Seung-Gweon, K., & Chang-Shin, Ch. (2004). Measuring Software Product Quality: A Survey of ISO/IEC 9126. *IEEE Software, 21*(5), 88–92. doi:10.1109/MS.2004.1331309

ISO/IEC 25000:(2005) (E), *Software engineering – Software Quality and Requirements Evaluation (SQuaRE) Guide to SQuaRE.*

ISO/IEC 9075:(2003) *(part 1, 2), Information technology – Database languages-SQL.*

ISO/IEC 9126-1:(2001) (E), *Software engineering – Product quality – Part 1: Quality model.*

ISO/IEC 9126-3:(2003) (E), *Software engineering – Product quality – Part 3: Internal metrics.*

Kifer, M., Brenstein, A., & Lewis, P. M. (2006). *Database Systems. An Application-Oriented Approach* (2nd ed.). New York: Addison Wesley.

Kroll, P., & Kruchten, P. (2003). *Rational Unified Process Made Easy, A Practitioner's Guide to the RUP.* Boston: Addison-Wesley Professional.

Lamouchi, O., Cherif, A. R., & Levy, N. (2008). A Framework Based Measurements for Evaluating an IS Quality. In A. Hinze, M. Kirchberg, (Ed.), *Proc. Fifth Asia-Pacific Conference on Conceptual Modelling* (pp. 39–47). Wollongong, Australia: CRPIT, 79, ACS.

Leffingwell, D., & Widrig, D. (2003). *Managing Software Requirements: A Use Case Approach.* Boston: Addison-Wesley.

Lightstone, S., Teorey, T., & Nadeau, T. (2007). *Physical Database Design. The Database Professional's Guide to Exploiting Indexes, Views, Storage, and More.* San Francisco, CA: Morgan Kaufman Publisher.

Miller, J., & Mukerji, J. (2003). *MDA Guide version 1.0.1.* Retrieved from http://www.omg.org/

Modeling and Analysis of Real-time and Embedded systems. (2008). Retrieved from http://www.omgmarte.org/ Specification.htm

Mohagheghi, P., & Dehlen, V. (2008). *Developing a Quality Framework for Model-Driven Engineering. Models in Software Engineering* (pp. 275–289). Heidelberg: Springer.

Mohagheghi, P., Dehlen, V., & Neple, T. (2009). Definitions and approaches to model quality in model-based software development – A review of literature. *Information and Software Technology, 51,* 1646–1669. doi:10.1016/j.infsof.2009.04.004

Piattini, M., Calero, C., Sahraoui, H., & Lounis, H. (2001). Object-relational database metrics. *L'Object. Edition Hermès Sciences, 17*(4), 477–498.

Piattini, M., & Genero, M. (2001). *Empirical validation of measures for class diagram structural complexity through controlled experiments.* Retrieved from http://www.iro.umontreal.ca/~sahraouh/qaoose01/genero.pdf

UML Profile for Modeling Quality of Service and Fault Tolerance Characteristics and mechanisms, v 1.1. (2008). Retrieved from http://www.omg.org/technology/documents/formal/QoS_FT.htm

Wagner, S., & Deissenboeck, F. (2007), An Integrated Approach to Quality Modelling. In *Proceedings of the 5th International Workshop on Software Quality* (pp. 1). Washington, DC: IEEE Computer Society.

ADDITIONAL READING

Ambler, S. (2006). *Refactoring Database: Evolutionary Database Design.* NY: Addison Wesley Professional.

Behkamal, B., Kahani, M., & Akbari, M. K. (2009). Customizing ISO 9126 quality model for evaluation of B2B applications. *Information and Software Technology, 51,* 599–609. doi:10.1016/j.infsof.2008.08.001

Bombardieri, M., & Fontana, F. A. (2009). Software aging assessment through a specialization of the SQuaRE quality model, In *Proc. Seventh Workshop on Software Quality* (pp. 33–38), IEEE Computer Society.

Calero, C., Sahraoui, H. A., Piattini, M., & Lounis, H. (2002). Estimating Object-Relational Database Understandability Using Structural Metrics. from www.springerlink.com/index/04jldq2uwenn5v90.pdf

Cherfi, S. S., Akoka, J., & Comyn-Wattiau, I. (2007). Perceived vs. Measured Quality of Conceptual Schemas: An Experimental Comparison. In Grundy, J., Hartmann, S., Laender, A. H. F., Maciaszek, L. and Roddick, J. F. (Ed.), *Proc. Tutorials, posters, panels and industrial contributions at the 26th International Conference on Conceptual Modeling – ER 2007* (pp. 185–190), Auckland, New Zealand, CRPIT, 83, ACS.

Cockburn, A. (2001). *Writing Effective Use Cases*. Boston: Addison Wesley.

Cortellessa, V., Di Marco, A., & Inverardi, P. (2007) Non-Functional Modeling and Validation in Model-Driven Architecture. from www.plastic.paris-rocquencourt.inria.fr/dissemination/wicsa2007_cr-2.pdf

Dubielewicz, I., Hnatkowska, B., Huzar, Z., & Tuzinkiewicz, L. (2006). An approach to evaluation of PSM. MDA database models in the context of transaction performance. *International Journal on Computer Systems and Network Security, 10*(6), 179–186.

Dubielewicz, I., Hnatkowska, B., Huzar, Z., & Tuzinkiewicz, L. (2006). An approach to software quality specification and evaluation (SPoQE). In Sacha, K. (Ed.), *Software engineering techniques: design for quality* (pp. 155–165). New York, Boston: Springer. doi:10.1007/978-0-387-39388-9_16

Dubielewicz, I., Hnatkowska, B., Huzar, Z., & Tuzinkiewicz, L. (2006). Software Quality Metamodel for Requirement, Evaluation and Assessment, In *Proceedings of Information, Simulation, Modeling* (pp. 115–122). Prerov, Czech Republic: Acta Mosis No. 105.

Dubielewicz, I., Hnatkowska, B., Huzar, Z., & Tuzinkiewicz, L. (2007). Quality-driven software development within MDA approach. *International Review on Computers and Software, 6*(2), 573–580.

ISO/IEC 14598-3:2000 (E), Information technology – Product evaluation – Part 3: Process for developers.

ISO/IEC 14598-5:1998 (E), Software engineering – Product evaluation – Part 5: Process for evaluators.

ISO/IEC 9126-2:2003 (E), Software engineering – Product quality – Part 2: External metrics.

Kleppe, A., Warmer, J., & Bast, W. (2004). *MDA Explained: The Model Driven Architecture: Practice and Promise*. Boston, MA: Pearson Education, Inc.

Lange, C. F. J., & Chaudron, M. R. V. (2005). Managing Model Quality in UML-based Software Development. In *Proceedings of the 13th IEEE International Workshop on Software Technology and Engineering Practice (STEP '05)* (pp. 7–16), Washington, DC: IEEE Compter Society.

MacDonell, S., & Martin, G. Shepperd J., & Sallis Ph. J. (1997). Metrics for Database Systems: An Empirical Study. In *Proceedings of the 4th International Symposium on Software Metrics* (pp. 99), Washington, DC: IEEE Compter Society.

Mendling, J., Reijers, H. A., & van der Aalst, W. M. P. (2010). Seven process modeling guidelines (7PMG). *Information and Software Technology, 52*, 127–136. doi:10.1016/j.infsof.2009.08.004

Mohagheghi, P., & Aagedal, J. (2007). Evaluating Quality in Model-Driven Engineering. In *International Workshop on Modeling in Software Engineering* (pp. 6), Washington, DC: IEEE Computer Society.

Naiburg, E. J., & Maksimchuk, R. A. (2002), *UML for Database Design*, Boston: Addison Wesley.

Pham, H. N., Mahmoud, Q. H., Ferworn, A., & Sadeghian, A. (2007). Applying Model-Driven Development to Pervasive System Engineering. In *Proc. of 29th International Conference on Software Engineering Workshops* (pp. 7), Washington, DC: IEEE Computer Society.

Piattini, M., & Genero, M. (2002). An Empirical Study with Metrics for Object-Relational Databases. *Lecture Notes in Computer Science*, Volume Software Quality –. *ECSQ, 2002*, 298–309.

Rawashdeh, A., & Matalkah, B. (2006). A New Software Quality Model for Evaluating COTS Components. *Jordan Journal of Computer Science, 2*(4), 373–381. doi:10.3844/jcssp.2006.373.381

Rech, J., & Bunse, C. (2008). *Model-Driven Software Development: Integrating Quality Assurance*. Information Science Reference.

Reingruber, M. C., & Gregory, W. W. (1994). *The Data Modeling Handbook: A Best-Practice Approach to Building Quality Data Models*. New York: John Wiley & Sons, Inc.

Rosenberg, D., & Scott, K. (1999). *Use Case Driven Object Modeling With UML: A Practical Approach*. Reading, MA: Addison Wesley Longman, Inc.

Ross, R. G. (1997). *The Business Rule Book* (2nd ed.). Houston, Texas: Business Rules Solutions, Inc.

Röttger, S., & Zschaler, S. (2004). Model-Driven Development for Non-functional Properties: Refinement Through Model Transformation. *The Unified Modelling Language* (pp. 275–289). [Heidelberg: Springer Berlin.]. *Lecture Notes in Computer Science, 3273*. doi:10.1007/978-3-540-30187-5_20

Shasha, D., & Bonet, P. (2003). *Database Tuning, principles, experiments and troubleshooting techniques*. San Francisco: Morgan Kaufmann Publisher.

Skene, J., & Emmerich, W. (2003) A Model-Driven Approach to Non-Functional Analysis of Software Architectures. from http://eprints.ucl.ac.uk/720/1/9.9.5ase03.pdf

Unhelkar, B. (2005). *Verification and Validation for Quality of UML 2.0 Models*. Hoboken, NY: Wiley-Interscience. doi:10.1002/0471734322

Wagner, S., Lochmann, K., Winter, S., Goeb, A., & Klaes, M. (2009). Quality Models in Practice: A Preliminary Analysis, In *Proc. 3rd International Symposium on Empirical Software Engineering and Measurement* (pp. 464–467). Lake Buena Vista, FL: IEEE Computer Society.

KEY TERMS AND DEFINITIONS

Assessment Function: A function which rates the quality of a software artifact on the basis of its measurement. The measurement brings the values of defined *measures*. The assessment function can be intended to give complete (taking into account all the quality characteristics) or partial evaluation of an artifact or set of artifacts.

Conceptual Data Model: A model of a database expressed at platform independent level; describes entities from a considered domain, properties of these entities, and the relationships between entities.

External Quality Model: A kind of *quality model* which represents the perspective of a final user which uses the software product in a specified environment and a specific context of use.

Internal Quality Model: A kind of *quality model* which represents the perspective of a software developer and relates to the intermediate artifacts that are produced during software development process.

Logical Data Model: A model of a database expressed at platform dependent level; depending on the used technology hierarchical, network, relational, object-relational, and object-oriented logical models are distinguished. Among aforementioned models, relational logical model is the most popular. The relational logical data model describes relations (that can be perceived as tables), and relationships between them.

Measure: A function defined over the values of measurable software attribute, yielding results from a well defined set (usually a numerical set).

Physical Data Model: Model of a database expressed at platform dependent level in the way accepted by a specific database management system. Beside the data it can also contain implementation of business logic in the form of stored procedures or transaction definitions.

Quality and Evaluation Model: A *quality model* with *assessment functions*.

Quality-Driven MDA Framework: A framework for model-based software development aiming at producing high quality software products; It integrates two complementary processes: MDA approach and quality specification and evaluation process, defined mainly in the ISO/IEC 9216 series of standards.

Quality Model: A set of selected quality characteristics and subcharacteristics together with the assigned *measures*. The quality model provides the basis for specifying quality requirements and evaluating quality.

Chapter 11
Exploring Business Value Models for E-Service Design

Jelena Zdravkovic
Stockholm University & Royal Institute of Technology, Sweden

Tharaka Ilayperuma
Stockholm University & Royal Institute of Technology, Sweden

ABSTRACT

Contemporary enterprises face strong pressures to increase competitiveness by engaging in alliances of several kinds. In a rapidly increasing degree, traditional organizational structures evolve towards online business using modern ICT – such as the Internet, semantic standards, process- and service-oriented architectures. For efficient applications of inter-organizational information systems, the alignment between business and ICT is a key factor. At the ICT level, Web services are used as the cornerstones for modeling the interaction points of Web applications. So far, development of Web services has focused on a technical perspective, such as the development of standards for message exchanges and service coordination. Thereby, business concepts, such as economic values exchanged among the cooperating actors, cannot be traced in Web service specifications. As a consequence, business and ICT models become difficult to keep aligned. To address this issue, the authors propose a MDA-based approach for design of software services which may be implemented using Web services and Web service coordinations. The proposal focuses on a value-explorative analysis and modeling of business services at the CIM level, and model transformations using UML 2 to the PIM level, by utilizing well-defined mappings.

INTRODUCTION

Since the emergence of the Internet, enterprises have opened their core functions to customers, suppliers, business partners and financial institutions. The intensive growth of World Wide Web has created opportunities for all kinds of enterprises to make their value offerings available to consumers as software services (i.e. e-services). An example of this is the proliferation of bookstores on the Web that let Internet users browse their catalogues, place orders, and make payments.

A problem common to actors participating in such collaborations is to identify what offerings

DOI: 10.4018/978-1-61692-874-2.ch011

they should make available as e-services for others. Business collaborations can be described using business models. A business model is made in order to make clear who the actors are in a business scenario and explain their relations, which are formulated in terms of *economic values* exchanged between the actors. Thereby, business models capture the relations between actors, and the events that result in the creation and distribution of the values among the actors.

From the technical perspective, Web services have become a common technology for modelling interactions of Web applications. So far, development of Web services has focused on structural and operational aspects. Designing applications directly to these perspectives is tedious, error prone, and business functionality remains invisible. We need to design service-oriented applications from a higher-level of abstraction to get the needed business perspective, and also make programming more productive by automating the generation of low-level technology solutions. Raising the level of abstraction to separate business specifications from implementation details is a well-established trend in system development and is one of the main goals of MDA, Model Driven Architecture (Kleppe et al., 2003).

MDA is proposed by the Object Management Group (OMG) as an approach for system development that separates business and application from the underlying platform technology. MDA guides architects and developers to define formal models at different levels of abstraction and create transformations among them. The MDA process typically involves the creation of three different types of models. Computational Independent Model (CIM) is used to describe business level information, independent of technology considerations. This model is further refined to a Platform Independent Model (PIM), which specifies a high-level design of an IT system. Finally, the PIM is transformed into a Platform Specific Model (PSM), which adds the technology details necessary for implementation on a specific

software platform. MDA follows the traditional development phases, as promoted earlier by RUP, Rational Unified Process (Kruchten, 1998), i.e. modeling of business and system requirements, system analysis, design, coding, and so forth. The two major differences from the MDA perspective, concern a shift from object composition to model transformation, and a new type of artifacts, which are based above all on formal models. Thus, when a technology changes, it is not needed to change the business specification (i.e. CIM); instead, the new technology model (PSM) can be created from the system model (PIM). In this way, each model is preserved as a product gate.

One of the major issues in the MDA discipline is the choice of model types to be used for CIMs and PIMs. In this chapter, we explain how business value models can be used at the CIM level, to provide a clear and a declarative foundation for identifying business services of an enterprise. Exploring a business model across a whole collaboration lifecycle, i.e. starting from planning to post-actualization, enable us to describe an entire enterprise-wide service portfolio within CIM. At the same level, process models are used to describe the service behavior. To enable mapping of the elicited business services further to e-services at the PIM level, we rely on the use of UML profiles that provide a standard way to set a model focus on a specific architectural style, such as in this case – service-oriented. Conceptualized in this way, the method that we propose is capable to support integration and alignment of economic value propositions of the collaborating business actors with the ICT realizations created using Web services. The method has a practical relevance for exploring the enterprise models in more depth from the business perspective, in order to identify e-services and design systems accordingly.

The chapter is structured as follows. Next section introduces business value models, and gives a brief overview of process modeling. In the section after, our MDA-based method for e-service identification and description is explained ad exemplified. The two final sections conclude the study and point out possible research directions for the business-driven system development.

BACKGROUND

Enterprise models are used to describe actors, information, resources, relations and processes of an organisation (Marshall, 2000). Business models and process models are parts of enterprise models, having distinct purposes and describing different aspects of an enterprise. Business models give a high-level view of the processes taking place in and between organizations, by identifying actors, economic values and the exchanges of values between the actors. These models provide a declarative view, i.e. they explain *"what"* of a business. Process models define the tactics of a business (i.e. *"how"*), by dealing with operational and procedural aspects of business communications. These models are typically expressed through low-level concepts such as control flow, data flow and message passing. Such concepts are not easily understood by business experts and users, who instead prefer to understand processes through business oriented notions like value exchanges.

Thereby, an approach when modelling a business that will be further realised with ICT systems, is to start with a business model to explain stable business commitments, and then complement it with process models to describe the ways those commitments are fulfilled by coordinations of business activities. In this way, it becomes possible to trace operational design decisions back to explanations and motivations expressed in business terms. A more detailed argumentation on a complementary use of business models and business process models the reader may find in studies (Gordijn et al., 2000) and (Johannesson, 2007).

Business Value Models

The purpose of a *business value model* is to describe the transfer of economic values that take place among the involved actors. These values may include goods, information, services, or money. Examples of actors are consumers, companies, and government authorities. Business models have a special characteristic in that they are formulated declaratively. There exist a number of efforts for business value modeling in the research community, such as the business ontologies (Fox, 1992), (Gordijn 2004), and (Osterwalder 2004). For our purpose we will make use of one long- and well-established business model ontology - REA (McCarthy, 1982).

The REA Framework

The Resource-Event-Agent (REA) framework was formulated originally by McCarthy (1982) and further developed in (Geerts & McCarthy, 1999). REA was first proposed as a knowledge basis for accounting information systems and focused on representing increases and decreases of value in an organization. It has been later extended to form a foundation for enterprise information systems architectures (Hruby, 2006), and it has also been applied to UN/CEFACT e-commerce frameworks (2006).

The core concepts in the REA ontology are *resource, event,* and *agent.* It is assumed that every business operation can be described as an event where two agents exchange economic values, i.e. resources. To acquire a resource, an agent (i.e. actor) has to give up some other resource. For example, in a goods purchase, the buyer has to give up money in order to receive some goods. Conceptually, two events are taking place: one where the amount of money is given away and another where an amount of goods is obtained. This combination of events is called a *duality* and is an expression of economic reciprocity - an event

Figure 1.The core elements of the REA ontology: resources (economic values), events and agents

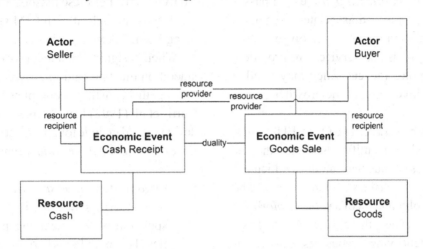

receiving some resource is always accompanied by an event provisioning another resource.

The concepts of the REA ontology are not supported with a specific graphic modeling notation. Here, we will use an entity-relationship like notation to depict the elements and relations in a REA business model, as illustrated in Figure 1. The model is created from the seller's perspective, and as such, it depicts two reciprocal economic events: Goods Sale and Cash Receipt, with accompanied resources - Goods and Money respectively.

In our proposal, we use the REA framework to describe the declarative part of the proposed CIM. We additionally extend the REA value model along a business life-cycle in order to elicit complete requirements for the exchanges of resources.

Business Life-Cycle

From the life-cycle perspective, a business typically spans a number of phases. ISO Open-EDI initiative (2006) considers a business as consisting of five phases (activities): *planning, identification, negotiation, actualization* and *post-actualization*. These phases encompass the following activities:

- In *the planning phase*, the customer and the provider are engaged in activities to identify the actions needed for selling or purchasing goods and services. As an example, a distributor sends catalogues to potential customers.
- *The identification phase* involves the activities needed to exchange information among providers and potential customers regarding selling or purchasing goods and services. For example, a provider sends a quotation to a customer.
- During *the negotiation phase*, contracts are proposed and completed. Detailed specifications of goods and services, quantity, price, terms, and conditions are determined in this phase. If required, the parties involved may make bids and put forward counter offers. For example, a customer sends offer to a provider and the provider sends the counter offer to the customer.
- *The actualization phase* includes all the activities necessary for exchanging goods and services between involved actors as agreed during negotiations. For example, the provider sends advance shipping notice when goods are prepared for shipping.

- *The post-actualization phase* encompasses all the activities and associated exchanges of information between involved actors after the goods and services are provided. For example, the customer may send a warranty invocation to the provider.

In the chapter, the described Open-EDI framework is utilized to identify resources (that is, economic values) in business models, which are to be exchanged in business collaborations. The objective is the obtainment of a *value-explorative business model*, which, thereby, can be used as a full basis for identifying the business services of the involved actors.

Process Models

Process models are used to steer day-to-day business activities of enterprises. A well-known definition describes a business process "as a specific ordering of work activities across time and place, with a beginning, an end, and clearly defined inputs and outputs; a structure for action" (Davenport, 1992). The main idea behind is that a business process is a sequence of activities that achieves a goal by transforming an input into a valuable output.

There exist many languages and notations that can be used to design business process models. Some of them are widely accepted in both industrial and academic communities, such as Business Process Modelling Notation, BPMN (White, 2006), Event-Driven Process Chains, EPC (Scheer et al. 2005) and UML 2 Activity Diagrams (Amber, 2004). MDA recommends UML as a modelling standard. UML has been widely adopted for modelling concepts and their behaviour as it enables modelling at different levels of abstraction and relationships between model elements can be established across modelling perspectives. Being based on a common meta-language, the Meta Object Facility, MOF (2005), UML facilitates the need for interoperability between different

MDA models. For these reasons, we will express the process models at both CIM and PIM levels using UML 2 Activity Diagrams.

When designing business processes, the consideration must be paid to different perspectives that together constitute a complete process model. Curtis et al. (1992) have proposed that a process design should include four perspectives: *organizational, functional, informational* and *behavioural*:

- *Organizational perspective*: This perspective describes the distribution of the responsibility for executing process activities. The main focus here is on the notion of the actor. An actor can be an organization unit, or a software system. UML 2 uses the partition notion to depict this perspective.
- *Functional perspective*: The perspective concerns how a process can be decomposed into activities that are to be executed. An activity can be either atomic, or composite. A composite activity can recursively refined to atomic activities; these notions correspond to activities and actions in UML 2 notation, respectively.
- *Informational perspective*: Here the main concern is on the resources that are manipulated by a process. A resource can be either traditional or informational. Product and services are traditional resources, while data and artifacts are informational resources. A resource is consumed or produced by a process activity. UML 2 offers the object node to depict the informational aspect.
- *Behavioural perspective*: This perspective concerns the flow of activities within a process. The control flow expresses when an activity is to be executed in relation to others. In UML 2, a number of control-flow components are available: decision and merge nodes, fork-and-join node, start and end nodes, and so forth.

With the EPC modeling technique, in addition to the outlined design perspectives, it is also possible to depict and classify the "output" perspective of a process, as a material or as a service.

In the chapter, we utilize the described framework to elicit the components of process models that the business modeler should include when modeling the service behavior in CIM and PIM, to enable a complete elicitation of the service implementation.

DESIGNING BUSINESS AND SOFTWARE SERVICES ON THE MDA BASIS

Service Modeling

In the business science community it is accepted that a *business service*, or simply *service*, is a business activity offered by a service provider to its environment. Thereby, an *e-service* is defined as the provisioning of a service over an electronic network, such as the Internet, where its functionality is commonly delivered via a Web service. A service, or an e-service, can be composite, meaning that its realization requires several other services or basic activities ordered in a process.

Design of e-services has so far mainly focused on operational aspects, such as the development of standards for message exchanges and service coordination. The terms service *orchestration* and *service choreography* have become broadly used to describe two modeling aspects of service processes (Peltz, 2003).

Orchestration is used when the objective is to obtain an executable process model, controlled from one party's perspective. The model includes business logic and a task execution order, where the tasks may be realized from both internal and external e-services. Choreography is used to model a collaborative process specification, showing an ordering of interactions of services of all the involved parties. However, a much less concern

is set on the business settings in which the services are used. At the same time, the actual use of e-services has evolved from a point-wise use towards large-scale use across enterprise boundaries (Piccinelli et al. 2001). This increase of the usage scope has resulted in a need for explicitly analyzing the business values that services deliver to rationalize their economic viability.

In the long run, e-services that do not support the business values cannot be justified. Lately, the research in both academic and industrial communities, implies that when designing service-oriented software solutions, constructive results are obtained by starting analyzing business models of enterprises (Baida et al. 2005), (Cherbakov et al. 2005), (Andersson et al. 2007). This fact, according to the referred studies, is shifting the focus of large scale e-service design to the context of economic value transfers. Thereby, two classes of services have been recognized:

- Business services which are identified on the business model level.
- E-services that realize the business services, typically implemented using Web Services.

Using this relationship between business and e-services as a guide for software service design, it becomes natural to identify and develop services in a top-down manner starting from the strategic and economic aims of an enterprise and deriving e-services aligned to those services.

Following MDA principles, a number of research studies have reported proposals for e-service design, defined in the form of a Platform Independent Model (PIM). Many of them utilize the UML profile concept to describe and scope a technology independent model, such as: a) a SOA-based model, proposed in (López-Sanz et al. 2008), b) a software service model proposed by IBM (Johnston, 2005) targeted for helping architects to map out an entire, enterprise-wide e-service portfolio, which is after detailed by developers, who provide final Web service specifications, or c) a process-oriented system model, capable of capturing e-service orchestrations (Amsden et al. 2003). Some other studies have augmented the starting abstraction level by considering the business process perspective as a basis for creating Computational Independent Model (CIM); the process activities from the CIM model are further mapped to software components or services at the PIM level (Rosen, 2003), (Vidales et al. 2008), (Kherraf et al. 2008). Being focused solely on business processes at the CIM level, that is, on an operational perspective, the aforementioned studies have not considered the business viability of e-services.

Recent research activities have proposed that when addressing business-to-IT service integration, the starting point should be the business models of enterprises (Gordijn et al., 2008), (Derzsi et al., 2008). However, even being model-oriented, these proposals do not define models and model transformations as recommended by the MDA discipline.

Our approach differs from the above referred studies in the way that we propose a MDA-based method for designing e-services that are aligned with the business services elicited in a business value model. In particular, we propose designing a service-centered CIM relying on two model types. Firstly, a REA-based value model is explored to span all the major business phases, that is, planning, identification, negotiation, actualization and post-actualization; the obtained model is used as a source for identifying business services needed to deliver the exchanged values, along a whole business cycle. Secondly, every business service is described in further details using a process orchestration. Following the argumentation given in the previous section on the need to use business and process models complementary, in this way we obtain a complete business service portfolio relevant for a multi-actor collaboration.

Transforming a given CIM to an e-service based PIM containing both declarative and be-havioral description for each elicited e-service, using a set of transformation rules. In the next section, we describe our approach for defining the outlined MDA models, and the transformations between them, and we illustrate it on the case of the on-line game provider business.

Method Description and Application

Case Study: MMOG

A Massively Multiplayer Online Games (MMOG) business involves several actors: the Game Provider, the Game Player and the Internet Service Provider. The Game Provider is the principal actor responsible for producing a game content, as well as for distributing it to the Game Players. To distribute the games, the Game Provider uses services from the Internet Service Provider (ISP) who in return receives a payment. In order to play games, the Game Player needs to pay an Internet connection from the ISP; the provider gets a payment as the compensation for the provided connection.

CIM: an Explorative Business Model with Collaboration Process Models

In MDA, the Computational Independent Model (CIM) describes the business context and requirements relevant for a system development. As such, the model plays a vital role in bridging the gap between business and technology, i.e. establishing traceability between enterprise models and system models.

In what follows, we propose a CIM that relies on the use of a REA business value model. The aim here is to describe a high-level view of the activities taking place between organizations and people, by identifying the actors involved in a business constellation, as well as the values they offer to each other. One of the major issues in business modeling concerns the need for a systematic approach for designing business value

Figure 2. ISO Open-EDI phases of a business collaboration, defined from the REA framework perspective

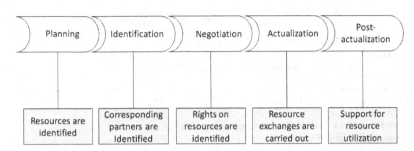

models in order to identify the offerings of the involved actors, while spanning a whole collaboration life-cycle. Thereby, as the major CIM component, we propose an explorative business model that encompasses the resource (i.e. value) assortment across a whole business life-cycle, starting from the planning up to post-actualization (see Figure 2). Such a model forms a complete basis for identification of the business services that are to be provisioned by an actor within his business portfolio. Furthermore, there is a need to describe the behavior for the identified business services, where process models are commonly utilized. Following this, we describe the basis of our method for creating CIM, in two steps:

Step 1: *Where we design a REA business value model to identify candidates for business services.*

In value modeling, it is the actualization phase, which is commonly considered when eliciting a business model (Gailly et al. 2008). In a business, the business transactions are identified upon the reciprocities of the resource transfers. In the previously given MMOG scenario, giving away a game in return for money, forms a business transaction.

Further, each identified business transaction is expanded along the planning, identification, negotiation, actualization and post actualization phases (see Section: *Business Life-Cycle*), from the perspective of the actor for which a service-oriented solution is to be developed. In REA, the

activities performed in the Open-EDI framework are the followings (see also Figure 2): in the planning and identification phases, the collaborating actors and their resources are identified respectively; in the negotiation phase the commitments to particular resource exchanges are established in the form of rights; in the actualization phase the agreed resource exchanges are carried out, and in the post-actualization phase support for resource utilization is provided.

Exploring the basic transactions along the five phases, results in the identification of new economic events and resources for supporting the planning and identification activities, negotiating and establishing of the rights on the core resources, delivering the custody of the resources, and finally, the activities for facilitating successful resource utilization.

As we have explained in section on the REA framework, in a REA business model, when offering a resource, an actor expects in return some other resource. Thereby, each pair of the events (i.e. duality) is considered as an economic symmetry and as such, gives rise to a service. When examining the five collaboration phases in details, it may be observed that in the planning, identification and negotiation phases, an event acquiring some resource is unavoidably accompanied by the other event giving away another resource in the way "all or nothing". For instance, to get a product catalog, a consumer must identify himself by providing his contact details. As another example, a negotiation cannot be completed be-

Table 1. Economic events in the Games Provisioning transaction along Open-EDI phases

Phase	Economic Events (EE), Actors (A) and Resources (R)
Plan-ning	Game Provider (A) offers Catalogue (R) to the Game Player (A). In return Game Provider (A) obtains the Attention (R) of the Game Player (A). Economic Events (EE) – Publish Games Catalogue (Game Provider), Obtain Attention (Game Player)
Identi-fication	Game Player (A) provides Accreditation (R) to the Game Provider (A). Game Provider (A) compensates with Games Info. (R) to the Game Player (A). Economic Events (EE) – Obtain Game Selection (Game Player), Offer Games Info. (Game Provider)
Nego-tiation	Game Provider (A) offers Right to Play Games (R) to the Game Player (A). Game Player (A) offers Right to Payment (R) to the Game Provider (A). Economic Events (EE) - Offer Right to Play Games (Game Provider), Obtain Right to Payment (Game Player)
Actual-ization	Game Player (A) gets the Access to Games (R) Game Provider (A) gets the custody of Money (R) Economic Events (EE) - Deliver Games (Game Provider), Obtain Payment (Game Player).
Post-actualiza-tion	Game Player (A) gets FAQ Info (R). Game Provider (A) gets Status (R). Game Player (A) provides Error Reports (R) to the Game Provider (A) Game Provider (A) offers Solutions (R) to specific problems of the Game Player (A). Economic Events (EE) - Offer FAQ, Offer Solutions (Game Provider), Obtain Error Report, Obtain Player Satisfaction (Game Player)

fore the both involved actors agree on the rights on the resources that they will provide to each other. However, following the negotiation, due to a variety of business agreements alternatives, it may be possible for the actors to give away certain resources without getting a compensation at the same time. As an example, a seller may agree with a buyer on paying certain goods after the goods are delivered. This means that in the actualization and post-actualization phases, it is possible to refine the granularity of services to correspond to single economic events, such as payment, or delivery.

Application of Step 1: *Generating a CIM/Business Model for the MMOG case*

Considering the MMOG case presented in the beginning of the section, we identify three business transactions: *Games Provisioning, Hosting Provisioning* and *Internet Access Provisioning*.

Next, the transactions identified above are expanded along planning, identification, negotiation, actualization and post actualization phases. To begin, we consider the *Games Provisioning* transaction. In Table 1, we summarize the economic events identified in this transaction along these phases.

The business model developed based on the above information is depicted in Figure 3.

Step 2: *Where we define processes to describe the behavior of the business services elicited in Step 1.*

Designing process models from the REA business model involves business modeler deciding on how to model processes to describe the behavior of services, and also determining the activities that should be defined in those processes. Below, we outline the rules for designing process models from the REA business model.

Figure 3. REA business model fragment for the Games Provisioning transaction of the MMOG case. The events are created from the MMOG perspective (i.e. provider perspective). Symbols <A>, <EE>, <R> denote actor, economic event, and resource

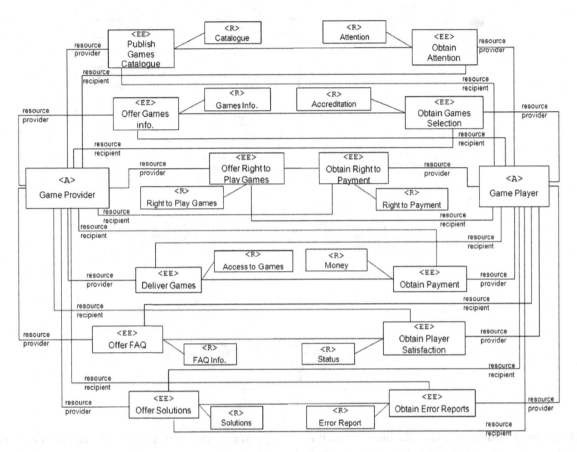

Every process should describe the behavior of a single business service elicited in the REA business model from dualities of events. A process model is created to include the service choreography, i.e. the interactions of the service with others, as well as the service orchestration (belonging to the provider of the business service, namely "the principal actor").

Every process should be modeled considering organizational, functional, informational and behavioral design aspects.

Application of Step 2: *Generating CIM/Process Models for the MMOG case*

In Figure 3, we consider, for instance, the Offer Right to Play Games and Obtain Right to Payment events forming a business service that we name *Establish Contract*. Following Step 1, a process shall be created from the perspective of the MMOG provider.

The business modeller will first consider the organizational perspective; thereby, he will create two UML partitions: *Game Player* and *Game Provider*. Starting with the functional perspective, the modeler will explore the two major tasks in this service: a) offering right to play games, which will be realized by obtaining a chosen selection of games from the player, and b) obtaining a right to payment by giving the player a contract to sign.

Figure 4. UML activity diagram exploring the details of the Establish Contract service

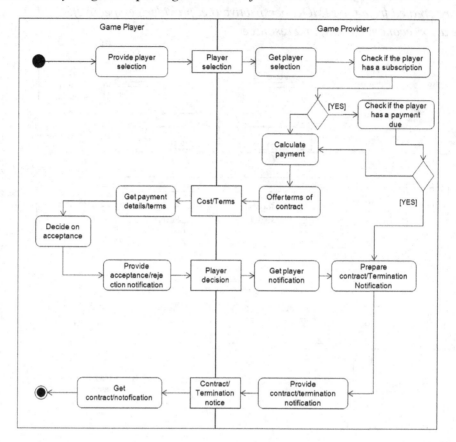

By creating a composition of the outlined activities (behavioral aspect), refining them to the level of atomic business activities and including the internal rules, the modeler will create a process model as depicted in Figure 4. When drawing the activities, he will also consider the informational aspect, i.e. the messages/documents that have to be exchanged, and model those using UML objects (see Figure 4). As a result, the obtained service process will begin when the Game Provider receives a games selection from the Game Player; then the Game Provider checks an internal database to examine if the player has a subscription with a payment due or not.. Based on this information, the provider will either offer a contract for the Game Player, or decide on a direct acceptance of the player.

Step 2 completes when the behaviors of all the services from the REA business model are well-described with the process models documented using UML 2 Activity Diagrams, and where all four process design perspectives are included. Regarding the contents of messages and documents, they may be provided using, for example, an informational model depicted with a UML class diagram, or simply, by attaching the electronic forms of documents to the depicted information objects.

To summarize, the CIM proposed in this section consists of a business value model spanning a whole collaboration life-cycle, where the business services are mapped-out, and a number of process models depicting the behavior of each of the services.

Figure 5. The conceptual e-service model (from IBM UML 2 Profile for Software Services)

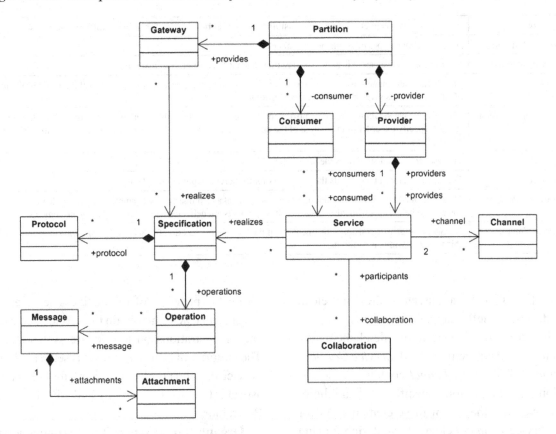

PIM: A System Model Defining E-Service Structures and Behaviors

The business and process models developed to define the proposed Computation Independent Model (CIM) are used as the input for creating a UML-based Platform Independent Model (PIM).

The process of creating a PIM from a CIM implies defining transformation rules between the two models. To create a mapping of the services elicited in the CIM, to the PIM level, we rely on the use of the UML profile concept, which in the MDA context provides a common way to focus toward a specific architectural style, to enable the model to properly capture and express specific information. A profile enables bundling of specialized semantics through the notion of stereotypes, a common UML extension mechanism. Here, we utilize the UML 2 Profile for Software Services,

as proposed by IBM (Johnston, 2005). This profile is relatively small and thereby, facilitates a reasonably straightforward modeling of e-service structures using UML Class Diagrams. To explore the e-service orchestration, i.e. service control- and data-flow, we utilize UML 2 Activity Diagrams. Thereby, the final PIM will reflect a system model including both service structure and service behavior aspects. In the next section we explain in detail the design of PIM components, as well as the rules for mapping out these components from the CIM level. In the rest of the text we will denote those two complementing PIM models as PIM/e-Service Contract, and PIM/e-Service Behavior.

Figure 5 depicts the conceptual model of IBM UML 2 Profile for Software Services. Primarily, the model consists of stereotyped extensions of the elements of UML 2 meta-model, such as Classes,

Table 2. Different elements of UML 2 Profile for Software Services

Partition	**Partition element defines responsibility or system boundaries for offering different services.**
Service Provider	A *Service Provider* provides one or more *Services*.
Service Consumer	*Service Consumer* element is used as a classifier to identify consumers of a *Service*.
Service	The *Service* element acts as a name tag of a service offered by the *Service Provider*, where the actual definition of what it offers, is given with *Service Specification*.
Service Specification	The *Service Specification* element identifies both the service interface, that is, a set of operations. The element can also specify the order of invocation of the operations associated with it, using the protocol state machine (i.e. *Protocol*).
Operation	The *Operation* element defines the atomic functionalities of the *Service* element.
Message	The *Message* element represents the containers for the service input or output data.
Message Attachment	*Message Attachment* is associated to the *Message* element as a property. For example, a *Message* element may contain product details while the images of these products are delivered as *Message Attachment* elements.
Service Gateway	The *Service Gateway* considers the openness of the *Service*, by denoting the *Service Specification* elements available to access within a partition.

Classifiers, Collaborations, etc. In the table below, we describe briefly the major elements.

In our approach, certain profile elements are not modelled explicitly in PIM. *Service Collaboration* and *Service Channel* contain the details belonging to a platform specific level and therefore, we omit the use of these elements. As for the service *Protocol* element, we define it using the UML 2 activity diagram, to define a complete orchestration for every identified e-service. In this way, the final PIM will reflect a system model including both service structure (i.e. *service contract*) and service behaviour aspects.

Defining CIM to PIM Transformations

When defining the transformation rules, the system modeler uses the CIM/Process Model and considers the functional, organizational, behavioral and informational aspects as a classification basis for transformations to PIM. The modeling focus is set on the provider of the business service, i.e. the principal actor, to obtain the service contracts and orchestrations on a software system level. The majority of transformations is set to the PIM/Service Profile (i.e. class diagram); the behavioral aspect is transformed directly to the PIM/Service Behaviour.

Organisational Aspect: The first rule concerns the distribution of responsibilities for executing services at a system level. The modelling focus is set on the provider of the business service, i.e. the principal actor, as explained earlier. The transformation rules for mapping CIM to PIM are presented in Table 3.

Design considerations: for every added Partition element type in PIM/Service Profile by following Rule 1, the elements of type Service Provider, Service, Service Specification and Service Gateway (optionally) are automatically created.

Application to MMOG Case:

Table 3.

Rule 1	a) Each non-principal actor partition in the CIM/Process Model is mapped to a Partition in the PIM to host the interaction activities of the principal actor toward that actor.
Organi-zational Aspect	b) The partition of the principal actor is refined to the partitions that will include information retrieval/storing activities, by determining the providers of these activities.

- (Rule 1,a) The partition *GamePlayer* in the CIM-level activity diagram is mapped to the *gamePlayerManagement* partition element in the PIM-level class diagram. The *gamePlayerManagement* partition will include the interactions of the Game Provider to the Game Player. For this partition, a Service Provider, Service, Service Specification and Service Gateway elements are created and named *gamePlayerManager*, *gameContract*, *gameContractInterface* and *gamePlayerManagementGateway*. The Gateway element is added to define that the service specification is accessible outside its hosting partition. (see Figure 6).

- (Rule 1,b) *subscriptionManagement* partition is added to host the information retrieval activities of the Game Provider, such as *Check if the player has a subscription* in CIM-level activity diagram in Figure 5. As in the previous example, for the created partition, Service Provider, Service and Service Specification and Gateway elements are added, as depicted in Figure 6.

Functional Aspect: the second rule concerns the transformation of the activities from CIM to PIM (Table 4).

Design considerations: following *Rule 2*, Operation elements are added in PIM/Service Profile.

Application to MMOG Case:

- (*Rule 2, a*): The activity "Provide game selection" from the CIM (see Figure 5) is mapped to the Operation "*receivePlayerSelection*" within the *gameContractInterface* (Figure 6).

- (*Rule 2, b*): the Operation element *receiveGamesCost* within *subscriptionInterface* is added (Figure 6).

- (*Rule 2, c*): the activity element *Provide contract/termination notification* in the CIM is decomposed to Operation elements "*sendContract*" and "*sendPaymentDueNotice*" within the *gameContractInterface* (Figure 6).

The *"Check if the player has a subscription"* and *"check if the player has a payment due"* in the CIM-level are the assignment-type of activities, and as such, are mapped to *"selectPlayerInformation"* and *"selectPaymentDueInformation"* in the PIM/Service Behaviour (Figure 7). In the similar way, the rest of interaction activities in CIM/Process Model are transformed, and a final operation portfolio is obtained as depicted in Figure 6.

Informational Aspect: the third rule concerns the transformation of information resources from CIM to PIM.

Design considerations: information objects in CIM are mapped to Message, and optionally, to Message Attachment elements in PIM/Service Profile, according to the described rule. The system modeller should derive information objects

Table 4.

Rule 2	a) Every activity in CIM/Process Model concerning the interactions between partitions is transformed to a send, receive, or send-receive service Operation element. b) Additional send, receive, send-receive operations are created for every new partition identified in *Rule1*, to model the interaction activities for that partitions.
Functional Aspect	c) An activity modeled in CIM is decomposed, or aggregated to conform to the functions of the existing systems (for example, "receive customer profile" in a CIM may be decomposed to "receive customer contact" and "receive customer history" in a PIM, if those information are provided by different existing system services) Activities that concern assignments (i.e. "delegations"), rules and calculations will be mapped only to the PIM/Service Behavior; as such activities do not correspond to service operations. Those activities are the part of the internal process system logic of the principal actor.

Figure 6. PIM/Service Profile (UML 2 class diagram)

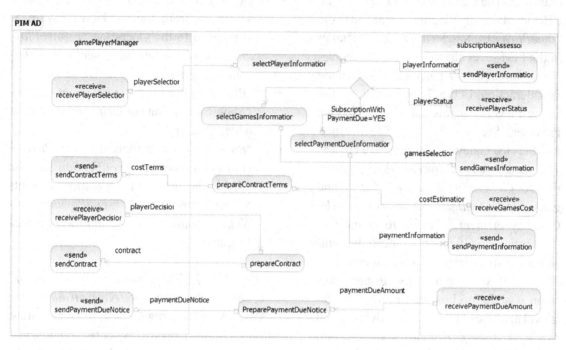

Figure 7. PIM/Service Behavior (UML 2 activity diagram)

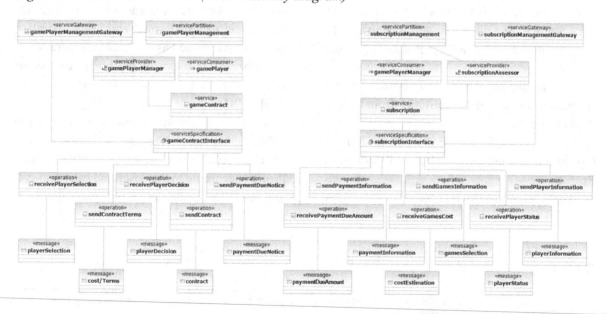

Table 5.

Rule 3	a) Every information resource is transformed to a Message element.
Informational Aspect	b) If an information resource (artifact) is supported differently due to changes in the functional aspect (*Rule 2*), then the resource granularity will be changed (decomposed, or aggregated).

Table 6.

Rule 4	The control flow as given in the CIM/Process Model is reused in PIM/Service Behavior Model; the flow is refined to support the orderings of new elements, as added with *Rule 2* (functional aspect). The internal, flow-related activities, such as rules and assignments, are mapped from CIM (rules), or created at this stage (assignments).
Behavioral Aspect	

in parallel to the functional aspect discussed previously.

Application to MMOG Case:

- (*Rule 3, a*) The information resource *"Player selection"* from the CIM (see Figure 5) is mapped to the Message element *"playerSelection"* (Figure 6).
- (*Rule 3, b*) Considering the decomposition of the activity *Provide contract/termination notification* in the functional aspects in *Rules 2(c)*, the information resource *"Contract/termination notice"* from the CIM-level activity diagram (see Figure 5) is decomposed to the Message elements *"contract"* and *"paymentDueNotice"* in PIM/Service Profile (Figure 6).

Behavioural Aspect: the fourth rule concerns the transformation of the service control-flow from CIM to PIM. Since the Service Profile model does not support modelling of control-flow, the transformation of this aspect is performed between the CIM and PIM activity diagrams. The flow in PIM-level activity diagram will generally follow the flow defined in CIM/Process Model; however, the flow will be adjusted due to the identification of new activities, and messages.

Figure 6 depicts the structure part of the PIM service model obtained when applying the five transformation rules on the CIM service *Establish Contract*.

Figure 7 depicts the behavioral part of the PIM service model obtained when applying the transformation rules on the CIM service *Establish Contract*.

To summarize, in this section we have defined a method for obtaining a PIM from a CIM using a set of ordered transformation rules. The transformations start by mapping out the business services as tagged in the CIM/Business Model to e-services in the PIM, where the PIM/Service Profile model is created to define the service contract, and a PIM/Service Behaviour model to explore the service coordination.

From the PIM to a PSM

Finally, the obtained Platform Independent Model (PIM) is transformed into a Platform Specific Model (PSM), which includes the details necessary for getting an executable software model. The primary aim of this chapter was to give an approach for transforming a business-oriented CIM to a service-oriented PIM. For that reason, in this section we will give only brief guidelines for how a PSM can be obtained from the proposed PIM.

The PIM as we have defined it in the previous sections includes both the structural and behavioral aspects of software services. As such, the model supports creating executable service-oriented solutions including service static specification and coordination. For instance, in case the Web services are the target technology platform, then the given PIM will be automatically converted to: a) WSDL documents, from the PIM/Service Profile, for specifying the Web service interfaces, operations and messages - i.e. the contracts, and b) to a workflow-like specification, such as WS-BPEL (OASIS, 2007), from the UML activity diagram, for getting the sequences of invocations of the obtained Web services and the operations.

Box 1.

```
<wsdl:message name="palyerSelection">
        <wsdl:part name="selectionInfo" type="someType"/>
</wsdl:message>
<wsdl:message name="costTerms">
        <wsdl:part name="cost" type="xsd:string"/>
</wsdl:message>
......
......
<wsdl:portType name="gameContractInterface ">
        <wsdl:operation name=" receivePlayerSelection">
        <wsdl:input message=" playerSelection"/>
        ......
        ......
        </wsdl:operation>
</wsdl:portType>
```

In our running example, the UML class diagram in the PIM is used to create WSDL specifications for two identified e-services: GameContract and Subscription (see Figure 6). For instance, the Message and Service Specification profile elements associated with these services can be mapped to WSDL Message types and PortTypes respectively. An excerpt of WSDL specification for the e-service GameContract as obtained from PIM, looks as in Box 1.

The BPEL specification for the Platform Specific Model (PSM) can be obtained by mapping the PIM models and their constituent components to different BPEL elements. For instance, the UML activity diagram is mapped to the BPEL control-flow, Operations in the class diagram to the BPEL activities, Partition elements to the BPEL partner declarations, etc. In Box 2, we exemplify a BPEL specification that will be obtained for the previously explored top e-service *Establish Contract*. In particular, the UML class diagram in Figure 6 is converted to BPEL process declaration. The control flow and the activities in the UML activity diagram from Figure 7 define the BPEL activity flow.

The automatic transformations from UML models to BPEL specifications are discussed and proposed in a number of papers; for more details the reader is referred to (White, 2005), (Amsden et al., 2003).

FUTURE RESEARCH DIRECTIONS

In MDA, models at platform independent level and platform specific level are so far mostly considered in the system development process, leaving thus the computational independent model level less explored (Vidales et al., 2008). In this chapter, we have set the base focus on defining a CIM, which elicits value-based services in a business value model along different phases of a business lifecycle. In this way obtained CIM, we have further transformed to a PIM capturing e-service structure and behaviour. From that perspective, a number of directions for future work appear as relevant:

- *Extending CIM with strategic aspects:* in regard to business-to-IT alignment, identifying consumer needs across different phases of a business collaboration and

Box 2.

```
<process name="establishContract">
        targetNameSpace=http://abc.com/simpleContractProcessing
        xmlns:lns="http://contracts.org/wsdl/contract-establishment"
        ....................
        .................... />
        <partners>
        <partner name="gamePlayerManager"
                serviceLinkType="lns:contractApproveLinkType"
                myRole="approver"/>
          <partner name="subscriptionAssessor"
        ............
        ......... />
        <partners>
        <sequence>
        <receive name="receiveSelection" partner="gamePlayerManager"
                portType="......"
        operation="receivePlayerSelection"
        ......... />
        </receive>
        <invoke name="invoke subscriptionAssessor "
        partner="subscriptionAssessor"
        portType="......"
        ...... />
        </invoke>
        ......
        ......
        </sequence>
<process>
```

mapping them to the activities required to fulfil these needs would be of a high importance. Incorporating the motivation behind the value propositions in the business model would improve the accuracy of the model specification (i.e. CIM) and thereby the identification of services. This can be achieved by, for instance, considering a goal-supported business model at the CIM level, where the values are elicited as the means for the achievement of the goals of consumers.

• *Augmenting the automation of CIM-to-PIM transformations.* A way to achieve a smoother transformation between the two models is to clearly define and structure the CIM meta-data. For instance, a UML profile including declarative business aspects (i.e. value exchanges, actors, etc.), as well as procedural (i.e. process activities and execution rules), would be helpful in getting a comprehensive meta-data model at the CIM level. To facilitate semantic matching between different models, a possibility is to use ontologies for defining meta-data;

this is already proposed in certain research studies. Having such defined CIM would also facilitate a pattern-based mapping to more specific components at the PIM level.

- *Capturing service protocols.* When defining business services, in our approach, we have considered a whole business life-cycle, i.e. planning, identification, negotiation, actualization and post-actualization phases. By identifying business and e-services on a phase-basis, as a result, at the lowest specification level, we get a number of independent service contracts and behavior specifications. This enhances the flexibility for combining services at different stages of a collaboration. To capture the information for possible orderings, for instance for the business services such as "delivery of goods" and "payment management", both the CIM and the PIM may be extended to include the information of interrelated services. However, this may be counter-productive from the service coupling perspective. Another possibility is to define the service interrelations by means of business rules and then relate those to business service definitions.

CONCLUSION

In this chapter, we have introduced an MDA-based method for designing business-oriented e-services, which may be implemented using Web services or some other related technology.

In the model driven development, a clear understanding of the usability of all the employed models is of a high importance. In our approach, business value models play a major role in the service identification, because they offer some important advantages compared to other types of enterprise models. They can illustrate a high-level description of a whole business in a single and easy-understandable view. Here, we have shown that using the REA framework, the business

modeler can elicit an explorative business service portfolio that providers make available in order to use and produce economic values along all the phases of a business collaboration (i.e. planning, identification, negotiation, actualization and post-actualization). This model forms the basis of CIM, which is further extended by modeling the behavior of every service elicited in the business model. After, using a well-defined set of mappings, CIM is transformed to a high-level system model, i.e. PIM, which in detail specifies the structure and behavior of the e-services, using UML 2. Such a formed PIM can be transformed to an executable service specification and service coordination, using for instance, Web service technology. We have illustrated the use of our method on the case of an on-line game provider.

The benefit of the proposed method is twofold. First, it enables a systematic and explorative identification of value-founded e-services, which improves the overall performance of a network of actors in business collaborations. Secondly, the method describes a straightforward approach for development of e-services and their coordinations. Using MDA as a cornerstone, the method enables traceability of low-level executable services toward economic value offerings, justifying thus the economic viability of these services.

REFERENCES

Ambler, S. (2004). *The Object Primer: Agile Model-Driven Development with UML 2.0.* Cambridge, UK: Cambridge University Press. doi:10.1017/CBO9780511584077

Amsden, J., Gardner, T., Griffin, C., & Iyengar, S. (2003). *IBM Draft UML 1.4 Profile for Automated Business Processes with a mapping to BPEL 1.0.* Retrieved March 15, 2009, from http://www.ibm.com/developerworks/rational/library/content/04April/3103/3103_UMLProfileForBusinessProcesses1.1.pdf

Anderssson, B., Johannesson, P., & Zdravkovic, J. (2007). Aligning Goals and Services through Goal and Business Modeling. *The International Journal of Information Systems and e-Business Management (ISEB), 7,* 143-169.

Baida, Z., Gordijn, J., Saele, H., Akkermans, H., & Morch, A. (2005). An Ontological Approach for Eliciting and Understanding Needs in e-Services. In: O. Pastor J.F. Cunha (Ed.), *17th Conference on Advanced Information Systems Engineering,* (LNCS Vol. 3520 pp. 400-414). Berlin: Springer-Verlag.

Cherbakov, L., Galambos, G., Harishankar, R., Kalyana, S., & Rackham, G. (2005). Impact of Service Orientation at the Business Level. *IBM Systems Journal, 44*(4), 653–668. doi:10.1147/sj.444.0653

Curtis, B., Kellner, M., & Over, J. (1992). Process Modeling. *Communications of the ACM, 35*(9), 75–90. doi:10.1145/130994.130998

Davenport, T. (1992). *Process Innovation: reengineering work through information technology.* Cambridge, MA: Harvard Business School.

Derzsi, Z., Gordijn, J., & Tan, Y. (2008) Towards model-based assessment of business-IT alignment in e-service networks from multiple perspectives. In *Proceedings of 16th European Conference on Information Systems* 2008. Retrieved March 15, 2009, from http://is2.lse.ac.uk/asp/aspecis/20080007.pdf

Fox, M. S. (1992). The TOVE Project: Towards A Common-sense Model of the Enterprise. *Enterprise Integration Laboratory Technical Report.* Retrieved May 02, 2009, from http://www.eil.utoronto.ca/enterprise-modelling/papers/fox-tove-uofttr92.pdf

Gailly, F., España, S., Poels, G., & Pastor, O. (2008). *Integrating business domain ontologies with early requirements modelling,* (LNCS vol. 5232, pp. 282-291). Berlin: Springer.

Geerts, G., & McCarthy, W. E. (1999). An Accounting Object Infrastructure for Knowledge-Based Enterprise Models . In *IEEE Intelligent Systems* (pp. 89–94). Their Applications.

Gordijn, J. (2004). E-Business Modeling Using the e3 Value Ontology . In Curry, W. (Ed.), *E-Business Model Ontologies* (pp. 98–128). London: Elsevier Butterworth-Heinemann.

Gordijn, J., Akkermans, J. M., & van Vliet, J. C. (2000). Business Modeling is not Process Modeling. In G. Goos, J. Hartmanis & van J. Leeeuwen (Ed.), *Conceptual Modeling for e-Business and the Web,* (LNCS Vol 1921, pp.40-51). Berlin: Springer-Verlag.

Gordijn, J., van Eck, P., & Wieringa, R. (2008). Requirements Engineering Techniques for e-Services . In Georgakopoulos, D., & Papazoglou, M. P. (Eds.), *Service-Oriented Computing: Cooperative Information Systems series* (pp. 331–352). Cambridge, MA: The MIT Press.

Hruby, P. (2006). *Model-Driven Design of Software Applications with Business Patterns.* Berlin: Springer Verlag.

ISO/IEC 15944-4:2006 Information technology – Business Agreement Semantic Descriptive Techniques – Part 4: Open-EDI Business Transaction Ontology. (2006). Retrieved May 04, 2009, from http://www.itu.dk/~hessellund/REA2006/papers/McCarthy.pdf

ISO/IEC 19502:2005(E). (2005). *Meta Object Facility (MOF) Specification,* Version 1.4.1. Retrieved March 08, 2009, from http://www.omg.org/cgi-bin/doc?formal/05-05-05.pdf

Johannesson, P. (2007). The Role of Business Models in Enterprise Modeling . In Krogstie, J., Opdahl, A., & Brinkkemper, S. (Eds.), *Conceptual Modeling in Information Systems Engineering* (pp. 123–140). Berlin: Springer-Verlag. doi:10.1007/978-3-540-72677-7_8

Johnston, S. (2005). *UML 2.0 Profile for Software Services*. Armonk, NY: IBM Cooperation. Retrieved March 15, 2009, from http://www.ibm.com/developerworks/rational/library/05/419_soa/

Kherraf, S., Lefebvre, E., & Suryn, W. (2008). Transformation from CIM to PIM Using Patterns and Archetypes. In *Proceedings of the 19th Australian Software Engineering Conference*, (pp. 338-346). Washington, DC: IEEE Computer Society.

Kleppe, A., Warmer, J., & Bast, W. (2003). *MDA Explained*. Reading, MA: Addison-Wesley Professional.

Kruchten, P. (1998). *The Rational Unified Process*. Reading, MA: Addison-Wesley Pub.

López-Sanz, M., Acuña, C. J., Cuesta, C. E., & Marcos, E. (2008). *UML Profile for the Platform Independent Modelling of Service-Oriented Architectures*, (LNCS Vol 4758, pp. 304-307). Berlin: Springer.

Marshall, C. (2000). *Enterprise modeling with UML: designing successful software through business analysis*. Reading, MA: Addison-Wesley Professional.

McCarthy, W. E. (1982). REA Accounting Model: A Generalized Framework for Accounting Systems in a Shared Data Environment. *Accounting Review, 57*(3), 554–578.

OASIS - Web Services Business Process Execution Language Version 2.0., WS-BPEL. (2007). Retrieved May 04, 2009, from http://docs.oasis-open.org/wsbpel/2.0/OS/wsbpel-v2.0-OS.html

Osterwalder, A. (2004). *The Business Model Ontology*. Doctoral thesis, HEC Lausanne. Retrieved May 02, 2009, from http://www.hec.unil.ch/aosterwa/

Peltz, C. (2003). Web services orchestration and choreography. *Computer, 36*(10), 46–52. doi:10.1109/MC.2003.1236471

Piccinelli, G., & Stammers, E. (2001). From E-Processes to E-Networks: an E-Service-oriented Approach. In *International Conference on Internet Computing*, (Vol. 3, pp. 549-553). CSREA Press.

Rosen, M. (2003). MDA, SOA and Technology Convergence. *MDA Journal, December 2003*. Retrieved March 15, 2009, from http://www.bptrends.com/publicationfiles/12-03%20COL%20Frankel%20-%20MDA%20SOA%20-%20Rosen.pdf.

Scheer, A., Thomas, O., & Adam, O. (2005). Process Modeling Using Event-driven Process Chains. In *Process-aware Information Systems: Bridging People and Software through Process Technology*, (pp. 119-145). Hoboken, NJ.

UN/CEFACT Modeling Methodology (UMM) User Guide. (2006). Retrieved May 04, 2009, from http://www.unece.org/cefact/umm/UMM_user-guide_220606.pdf

Vidales, M.A., Sánchez, García, A.Mª F. & Aguilar, L. J. (2008). A new MDA approach based on BPM and SOA to improve software development process. *Polytechnical Studies Review. Tékhne, 6*(9), 70–90.

White, S. (2005). Using BPMN to Model a BPEL Process. *Business Process Management Trends, March 2005*. Retrieved March 04, 2009, from http://www.businessprocess-trends.com/publicationfiles/03-05%20WP%20Mapping%20BPMN%20to%20BPEL-%20White.pdf

White, S. (2006). *Business Process Modeling Notation (BPMN). OMG / Business Management Initiative*. Retrieved May 04, 2009, from http://www.bpmi.org

ADDITIONAL READING

Anderssson, B., Johannesson, P., & Zdravkovic, J. (2007). *Aligning Goals and Services through Goal and Business Modeling. The International Journal of Information Systems and e-Business Management (ISEB), Special issue on Design and Management of Business Models and Processes in Services Science* (*Vol. 7*, pp. 143–169). Springer Berlin Heidelberg.

Gordijn, J., Akkermans, J. M., & van Vliet, J. C. (2000). Business Modeling is not Process Modeling. In: G. Goos, J. Hartmanis & van J. Leeeuwen (Ed.) Conceptual Modeling for e-Business and the Web. *Lecture Notes in Computer Science*, Vol 1921 (pp.40-51). Springer-Verlag.

Hruby, P. (2006). *Model-Driven Design of Software Applications with Business Patterns*. Springer Verlag Berlin Heidelberg.

ISO/IEC 15944-4:2006 Information technology – Business Agreement Semantic Descriptive Techniques – Part 4: Open-EDI Business Transaction Ontology (2006). Retrieved May 04, 2009, from http://www.itu.dk/~hessellund/REA2006/papers/McCarthy.pdf.

Johannesson, P. (2007). The Role of Business Models in Enterprise Modeling . In Krogstie, J., Opdahl, A., & Brinkkemper, S. (Eds.), *Conceptual Modeling in Information Systems Engineering* (pp. 123–140). Springer-Verlag. doi:10.1007/978-3-540-72677-7_8

KEY TERMS AND DEFINITIONS

Business Value Model: A business model that describe the transfer of economic values taking place among the involved actors.

REA: An ontology for defining a business value model, including three core concepts: *resource* (economic value), *event* (transfer), and *agent* (actor).

Business Process Model: An ordered set of business activities.

Open-EDI: An ISO standard for defining the phases in a business collaboration.

Business Service: A business activity offered by a service provider to its environment.

E-Service: The provisioning of a business service over an electronic network, such as the Internet.

Web Service: A technology for realising e-services.

Chapter 12
An MDA Approach for Developing Executable UML Components

Simona Motogna
Babeş- Bolyai University, Romania

Bazil Pârv
Babeş- Bolyai University, Romania

Ioan Lazăr
Babeş- Bolyai University, Romania

ABSTRACT

Model-driven Architecture frameworks provide an approach for specifying systems independently of a particular platform and for transforming such system models for a particular platform. But development processes based on MDA are not widely used today because they are in general heavy-weight processes - in most situations they cannot deliver (incrementally) partial implementations to be executed immediately. Executable UML means a execution semantics for a subset of actions sufficient for computational completeness. This chapter introduces a foundational UML (fUML) based action language (AL) and describes its concrete syntax. AL is used to describe the operations for iCOMPONENT - the proposed solution for a platform-independent component model for dynamic execution environments. Moreover, a UML profile for modeling components is defined and applied, following agile principles, to the development of service-oriented components for dynamic execution environments. The intended use of the proposed approach is enterprise systems.

INTRODUCTION

Some service-oriented component models support the dynamic availability of components at run-time and offer the possibility to build dynamically adaptable applications. However, building service-oriented components is a complex task due to the complexity of service-oriented frameworks. In this context today frameworks try to simplify the component development by allowing developers to concentrate only on implementing the business

DOI: 10.4018/978-1-61692-874-2.ch012

logic of the component and then to configure declaratively the component deployment.

In this chapter, we describe our contribution to this domain that can be expressed in:

- A fUML based action language and its concrete syntax. AL is part of the COMDEVALCO framework (Pârv, Lazăr & Motogna, 2008; Pârv, Lazăr, Motogna, Czibula & Lazăr, 2009) and we are using it to model the functionality of the components, to simulate the execution of the models and to test the models;

- A Platform-independent component model, iCOMPONENT with a corresponding UML profile for constructing components as UML models according to MDA;

- An agile MDA approach for constructing executable models for service oriented components;

- Mappings of iCOMPONENT to some existing service-oriented component frameworks.

BACKGROUND

Why

Component-based approaches lead to applications developed and deployed as a set of components. The main benefits of these approaches consist of loose coupling among the application components, third-party component selection, and increased component reuse. In traditional component-based approaches the set of components is statically configured; this means that the benefits outlined above typically extend only to the development portion of the software system life-cycle, not to the run-time portion (Escoffier & Hall, 2007).

Nowadays, there are component models and frameworks which allow components unavailable at the time of application construction to be integrated into the application later into its life-cycle, i.e. after the application has been installed

(OSGi, 2007). Such a framework should offer a dynamic execution environment, providing: (i) *dynamic availability of components* - the ability to install, update, and remove components at run-time, and to manage their provided and required interfaces; (ii) *dynamic reconfiguration* - the ability to change the configuration properties of a running component; (iii) *dynamic composition* - the ability to compose components from other existing components at runtime.

Most frameworks that support dynamic availability of components use the general principles of service-oriented component models (Cervantes & Hall, 2004), merging the concepts of service-oriented computing (Papazoglou & Georgakopoulos, 2003) into a component model.

Typically, a service-oriented component approach to build an application includes the following steps: (1) *Decompose the application into a collection of interacting services*. The semantics of these services are described independently of each other, and of any implementation. The service specifications will provide a basis for substitutability. (2) *Define a set of components implementing the application services*. A component may provide and require zero or more services. (3) *Define composite components that guide the application execution*. These composite components are described in terms of service specifications, and the concrete implementations of services will be resolved at run-time.

One of the main ideas for simplifying the construction of components is to separate the business logic of a component from the non-functional requirements related to the container in which the component execution will be managed. In such a context, developers concentrate first on implementing the business logic of the component, and then they configure declaratively the component deployment. Another important aspect of component models and frameworks refers to the development approach. Approaches in which modeling is at the core of the development activities also simplify the component construction process.

The success of using models (formal or not) is influenced in part by the availability and the degree of acceptance of modeling tools and techniques developed by the software development community. Those who build models need to perceive the usefulness of the models (Henderson & Walters, 1999), need to find a tradeoff between model complexity and its ease of use. It is convenient to build simple models, without great investments in time and intellectual effort. More important, the resulting models need to be accessible, easy to understand and analyze, and to have a reasonable degree of formality.

Executable models (Mellor & Balcer, 2002) improve even more the eficiency and reliability of an application: model excution will verify all the constraints on the model and the code will be generate only if the verification passed, and any modification of the model will be automatically reflected in the generated code.

What

As identified above, two important aspects for simplifying the construction of components consist of (1) *applying a model-driven development (MDD) approach* and (2) *separating the business logic of a component from the nonfunctional requirements*.

Model-driven development approaches. The Model-driven Architecture (MDA) frameworks provide an approach for specifying systems independently of a particular platform and for transforming the system specification into one for a particular platform. MDA is considered the OMG approach to Model Driven Engineering (MDE) (Balasubramanian, Gokhale, Karsai, Sztipanovits & Neema, 2006; Batory 2006). MDE approaches can be based either on MDA, or on Domain Specific Modeling. MDE appeared as a solution to applications that have to deal with increased platform complexity and domain concepts, aiming to raise the level of abstraction in

program specification and to increase automation in program development. The system can be developed based on models at different levels of abstraction, and then model transformations partially automate some steps of program development. But development processes based on MDA are not widely used today because most of them are viewed as heavy-weight processes - they cannot deliver (incrementally) partial implementations to be executed as soon as possible.

In this context, executing UML models became a necessity for development processes based on extensive modeling. For such processes, models must act just like code, and UML 2 and its Action Semantics (OMG, 2007) provide a foundation to construct executable models. In order to make a model executable, it must contain a complete and precise behavior description. Unfortunately, creating such a model is a tedious task or an impossible one because of many UML semantic variation points.

Executable UML (Mellor & Balcer, 2002) means execution semantics for a subset of actions sufficient for computational completeness. Two basic elements are required for such subsets: an action language and an operational semantics. The action language specifies the elements that can be used while the operational semantics establishes how the elements can be placed in a model, and how the model can be interpreted. Again, creating reasonable-sized executable UML models is difficult, because the UML primitives from the UML Action Semantics package are too low level.

The fUML standard (OMG, 2008) provides a simplified subset of UML Action Semantics package and it also simplifies the context to which the actions need to be applied. However, an easy-to-use concrete textual syntax is still needed in order to speed up the process of creating executable models.

An agile MDA process (Mellor, 2005) applies the main Agile Alliance principles (e.g. testing first, immediate execution) into a classical MDA process. In other words, "models are linked together, rather than transformed, and they are then all mapped to a single combined model that is then translated into code according to a single system architecture" (Mellor, 2005). The verification gap between a model and the corresponding code can be reduced by generating small parts of code as soon as possible, parts that are generated from the model, and that can be executed imediately.

Separation of the business logic and non-functional requirements targets two important aspects in software development. First at all, the developer will concentrate on the functionality without concern for data access or presentation aspects. Secondly, such an approach will support reuse on a larger scale. Early comercial component models such as Component Object Model (COM) (Microsoft, 1995), Enterprise Java-Beans 2.1 (Sun, 2003), and CORBA Component Model (OMG, 2002) propose specific application programming interfaces, so they do not offer a clear separation between functional and non-functional requirements. These approaches increase the development costs and decrease the potential reuse of the components.

There are many other component models developed by the academic community which provide solutions for the separation problem but do not provide dynamic execution environment features (Lau & Wang, 2005). Some of these frameworks - such as iPOJO (Escoffier & Hall, 2007), OSGi framework (OSGi, 2007), SCA (OASIS, 2007) - which have similar features to the approach presented in this chapter, are discussed in more detail in the Related work section.

How: ComDeValCo Framework

MDA and Agile principles represent the driven principle of our proposal, a framework for Software Component Definition, Validation, and Composition, ComDeValCo (Pârv, Lazăr & Motogna, 2008; Pârv, Lazăr, Motogna, Czibula & Lazăr, 2009).

The framework is intended to cover component development and component-based system development. Component development starts with its definition, using an object-oriented modeling language, and graphical tools. Modeling language provides the necessary precision and consistency, and use of graphical tools simplifies developer's work. Once defined, component models are passed to a verification and validation (V&V) process, which is intended to check their correctness and to evaluate their performances. When a component passes V&V step, it is stored in a component repository, for later (re)use.

Component-based system development takes the components already stored in repository and uses graphical tools, intended to: select components fulfilling a specific requirement, perform consistency checks regarding component assembly and include a component in the already existing architecture of the target system. When the assembly process is completed, and the target system is built, other tools will perform V&V, as well as performance evaluation operations on it.

ComDeValCo consists of:

- A modeling language used to describe components models (presented in the following sections).

- A component repository, which stores and retrieves software components and systems, and represents the persistent part of the framework, containing the models of all fully validated components. After passing the verification and validation step, component models are store into the repository, from where they can be reuse in system development.

- A toolset aimed to help developers to define, check, and validate software components and systems, and to provide maintenance operations for the component repository. The toolset is intended to automate many tasks and to assist developers in performing component definition and V &

V, maintenance of component repository, and component assembly.

The framework offers a solution to the current issues stated in the previous section. Its basic features can be summarizes in:

- **Supports separation of business logic and non-functional requirements**: Using a platform-independent component model developers concentrate only on defining the business logic, all dynamic execution environment features being managed by the proposed infrastructure.
- **Support MDA** using executable models. The benefits of such an approach are: a higher level of abstraction (developers concentrate on the application level of abstraction), a clearer separtion of concerns, and a more direct translation from PIM to PSM. Actions are specified in an action language, and consequently the implementations code can be generated from such an UML model.
- **Supports agile MDA**: services, structure and deployment models are linked together and test-driven development is applied to simple components in order to obtain incrementally, small pieces of code that can be executed immediately.

EXECUTABLE UML ACTIVITIES

In order to offer a good support for agile MDA processes, a modeling language should provide a metamodel, together with graphical and textual notations for easy manipulation of language elements. All language constructs should be simple and easy to handle for both the developers and users of the model. Consequently, the syntax definition uses a procedural style.

Three requirements were imposed on the Action Language (AL): completeness, in the sense that all the required elements of the model can be described with the language constructs, minimality, i.e. AL omits all unnecessary details, and extensibility. It was defined in the initial phase, implementing the procedural paradigm, and then enhanced with modular issues. AL has the following features:

- all elements are objects, instances of classes defined at logical level, with no relationship to a concrete programming language; this means that component models are platform-independent, (PIM);
- top-level language constructs cover both complete software systems - Program (the only executable) and concrete software components (not executable by themselves, but ready to be assembled into a software system) - Procedure, Function, Module, Class, Interface, Connector, Component;
- there is a 1:1 relationship between the internal representation of the component model - an aggregated object - and its external representation;
- the dimensions of extensibility are: the statement set, the component definition, the data type definition, and the set of components;
- it allows automatic code generation for component PIMs towards concrete programming languages, according to MDA specifications. One can define mappings from the modeling elements to specific constructs in a concrete programming language in a declarative way. Another extensibility dimension is the concrete programming language.

Also, AL needs to create the abstract representation for the statements and control structures as provided by programming languages, and it must support complex expressions and easy access to parameters and variables.

fUML (OMG, 2008) is a computationally complete and compact subset of UML (OMG, 2007), designed to simplify the creation of executable UML models. fUML standard chooses a data flow abstract representation of the behavior. Though a difficult task, the action language needs to hide all the data flow aspects of the abstract representation. This aspect is more obvious in the case of parameters and variables that are represented in the behavior with rather complex systems of output pins (that provide the values), fork nodes (that duplicate the values), input pins (that use the values) and object flow.

Such an action language might not suit all needs, and might not be usable in certain domains, but a compromise has to be made in order to create an action language that allows the users to quickly create executable models and that can be adopted easily by the majority of users. If the resulted action language has a well structured abstract representation, it will be possible to apply model transformations and generate code to structured programming languages with little effort. Thus, the executable models for which the behavior is created with such an action language can be converted to several platforms.

Concrete Syntax Definition for Activities

The proposed action language uses for its abstract syntax only elements allowed by the fUML standard. The concrete syntax of the action language resembles the syntax of existing structured programming languages, with some elements inspired by OCL. Throughout this chapter, EBNF notation (Wirth, 1977) will be used to express specific syntactical rules. Part of the ComDeValCo framework, AL is used to model the functionality of the components, to simulate the execution of the models and to test the models.

An excerpt from the syntactical rules is given in Example 1. Some of them are explained in

greater detail later (grammar elements are *italic*, while fUML constructs are given in Courier New).

The basic constructs activities, statements are explained in detail below. Expressions and other syntactical constructs have also been defined, and a complete description can be found in (Lazăr, Lazăr, Pârv, Motogna & Czibula, 2009).

Activities

The action language allows the user to construct UML Activities, using only the elements included in the fUML standard. The Activities may be declared either in Packages or Classifiers, and they may be set as the methods of Operations.

As described in rules **(1)-(6)**, an Activity may have Parameters, and for each Parameter there is one input / output ActivityParameterNode or both, depending on the direction of the corresponding Parameter (in [default value], inout, out, return). The value of the Parameter gets in or out of the Activity through the ActivityParameterNodes and is exposed to the actions in the activity using ForkNodes (similar to variables). The Activity is structured in statements, using StructuredActivityNodes and ControlFlow edges to enforce the sequential flow between the statements (blocks of statements).

The textual syntax requires only the signature (activity name and the list of parameters). The *act_name* and *par_name* nonterminals should be proper identifier names for the activity and parameter, respectively, while *type* can be any classifier. The default direction of a parameter is *in*. The direction of the return parameter is *return*.

Statements

The activity is made up of blocks of statements, some of which may be composed of another blocks of statements (e.g. *if, foreach* statements). Each statement - see rule **(7)** - is represented using a StructuredActivityNode, containing all its actions and edges that provide its functionality. The state-

Example 1.

```
(1)       activity::= act_ name "(" {params} ")"":" ret_ param block
(2)       params::= param { "," param } ;
(3)       param::= [direction] par_name ":" type
(4)       direction::= "in" | "inout" | "out"
(5)       ret_ param::= type
(6)       block::= "{" {stmt} "}"
(7)       stmt::= block | assign_prop_stmt | call_oper_stmt | call_act_stmt |
            def_var_stmt |
                  assign_var_stmt | if_stmt | while_stmt | foreach_stmt |
                  return_stmt
(8)       assign_prop_stmt::= [obj "."] property ":=" expr ";"
(9)       call_oper_stmt::= oper_expr ";"
(10)      call_act_stmt::= act_expr ";"
(11)      def_var_stmt::= "def" var ":" type [mult_up] [":=" expr] ";"
(12)      mult_up::= "[" (size | "*") "]"
(13)      assign_var_stmt::= var ":=" expr ";"
(14)      if_stmt::= "if"  "(" cond ")" block ["else" block]
(15)      while_stmt::= "while" "(" cond ")" block
(16)      foreach_stmt::= "foreach" "(" var [":" type] "in" list ")" block
(17)      return_stmt::= "return" [expr] ";"
```

ments are executed as a sequence, the control being enforced with ControlFlows. The only exception to this structure is the presence of ForkNodes that are used to simulate the variables and parameters, which are placed after the statements that declare them or set values to them.

This structure (blocks of statements) favors both model transformation and code generation from PIMs created with the action language towards PSMs (Platform-Specific Models), expressed using structured programming languages (e.g. Java, C++). This is true based on recursive composition, namely the functionality of each statement is nested inside a node.

If statement is represented with a ConditionalNode, having one Clause object (or two, if *else* branch is present, see rule **(14)**), properly ordered by using their successor/predecessor properties. The ConditionalNode contains all test and body executable nodes, and the clauses will properly reference them as test or body nodes. The decider pin for a *cond* clause will always be the output pin of its test node. The *cond* nonterminal denotes any expression returning a boolean value. The *else* clause will always have a true clause test, meaning that the test node will consist of one ValueSpecificationAction for the true LiteralBoolean. The body node for each clause is a block of statements and is represented using a single StructuredActivityNode, which will contain the actions for the statements. When the *else* clause is missing, the ConditionalNode is not assured, meaning that it is possible that no test will succeed; otherwise, the ConditionalNode is determinate, i.e. at most one test will succeed.

While statement (rule **(15)**) is represented with a tested first LoopNode. The LoopNode has a built-in system of loop input/variable/output pins, which is used to pass in and out the outer variables that are used and updated inside. The

LoopNode contains no action for the setupPart. It contains all the actions for the test and bodyPart properties, which will simply reference the used actions (contained as nodes). The test actions will have to output a boolean value, and the decider pin for the test will always be the output pin of its test actions (the condition expression). The bodyPart contains the actual body actions (inside one block node) and, if needed, the extra actions and control nodes needed to update the loop input/variable/output pins.

ForEach statement is similar to the *While* statement (see rule **(16)**), with the only difference that its action iterates over lists of elements: body actions are executed in sequence for each element in the list. It is represented with a StructuredActivityNode containing the actions (body of statements) and the argument *iterative* ExpansionRegion. The list is passed to the input ExpansionNode of the ExpansionRegion, and the region executes the body actions for each element. The current list element is made available inside the statement using a ForkNode (similar to a variable).

Every activity that has a return parameter must have a *return* statement at the end of every possible navigation path through the code. If there is no return parameter, there is no need to have an explicit *return* statement. The type of the return expression must conform to the type of the return parameter.

The expression actions inside a *return* statement send the result value to a MergeNode found directly in the Activity, which forwards it to the return ActivityParameterNode. Also, the *return* statement gives the control to the MergeNode placed before the ActivityFinalNode, which forwards it to the final node, forcing the execution of the activity to end. There is a need to use the MergeNodes before the return parameter node and final node, because there could be multiple return statements in the activity, which means there will be multiple edges going to these nodes. And these nodes will not execute unless all the edges pass a token, which is an impossible situation.

The MergeNodes will pass each token on outgoing edge immediately as it arrives, which means that the tokens are able to get to their intended destination.

Other Syntactical Constructions: Variables

The textual syntax allows to declare a simple variable or a list (array) variable and to set an initial value, or to default to null or an empty list (rules **(11)** – **(13)**). The lower bound of the output pins providing values for the single value variables or the input pins receiving values from the single value variables might be 0. This is because the value of a variable can be null, which means that there is no token. When declaring a list variable, the OutputPin has the multiplicity of the variable, as declared in text. The textual syntax uses the standard UML way of declaring multiplicities, mentioning only the upper bound (the lower bound is set to 0 by default).

If no default value is provided, a ValueSpecificationAction, having as value the LiteralNull null is used implicitly (the action has a result OutputPin with the same multiplicity as the declared variable). The *var* nonterminal is the variable name and the *type* can be any classifier. The *expr* result type must match the *type*. The *mult up* (multiplicity upper bound) can be any positive integer value (*size*), or "***", which means the variable list is unbounded.

To access the value of a variable, it is simply referenced by name; in the abstract syntax, this is done using an ObjectFlow from the last accessible ForkNode that provides a value for the variable (it has the same name as the variable).

EXAMPLE

The example model consists of a POS (Point of Sale) class, which contains a list of Products and is the entry point of the system, as shown in Figure

1.a). The user can make a new Sale (stored in POS as the currentSale) by invoking the makeNewSale operation and by adding SaleItems to the current sale in the form of product code and quantity. The POS object finds the Product associated with the given product code by using a private findProduct activity, and, if present, passes the product and quantity to the currentSale. The Sale creates a new SaleItem instance and adds it to its list of sale items.

The findProduct activity is a private activity of the POS class. Figure 1.b) shows the concrete syntax of this activity, while Figure 1.c) shows the fUML abstract syntax of the findProduct activity. The activity has one in-parameter, for which there exists an input ActivityParameterNode; its value is exposed to the actions using a ForkNode. The activity has also a return parameter for which

there exists an output ActivityParameterNode, named return. A MergeNode is placed before this parameter node, as argued in the previous section.

The activity will be structured in statements, using StructuredActivityNodes and ControlFlow edges to enforce the sequential flow between the statements (blocks of statements). The actions for each statement will be grouped inside one StructuredActivityNode. The only exception is represented by the ForkNodes that expose the variable/parameter values, and which are placed on the same level as the statement nodes, though no ControlFlow edges connect to them, only ObjectFlow edges.

The concrete syntax as presented in Figure 1.b) is quite simple, and easy to be followed. Line 2 shows how a multivalue property may

Figure 1. AL example and corresponding fUML representation

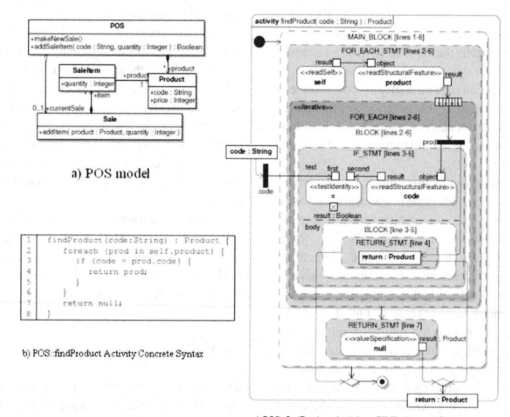

a) POS model

```
1   findProduct(code:String) : Product {
2       foreach (prod in self.product) {
3           if (code = prod.code) {
4               return prod;
5           }
6       }
7       return null;
8   }
```

b) POS::findProduct Activity Concrete Syntax

c) POS::findProduct Activity - fUML Abstract Syntax

be accessed (self.product) and line 3 shows how a simple property can be accessed (prod.code).

ICOMPONENT PROFILE

iCOMPONENT (injected component) (Lazăr, Pârv, Motogna, Czibula & Lazăr, 2008) has been designed as a platform-independent component model that can be used to develop service-oriented components for dynamic execution environments. This section describes the iCOMPONENT metamodel and its corresponding UML profile, and the next section presents how it can be used in an agile MDA approach.

The set of stereotypes used to model injected components are: Module, Component, Domain, Node, DynamicExecutionEnvironment, provides, requires, validate, invalidate, controller, and config, as shown in Figure 2.

Modules. The Module stereotype extends the UML 2 DeployedArtifact metaclass and represents the unit of deployment. A Module may contain classes, interfaces, components, component instances, and other resources. The set of model elements that are manifested in the module (used in the construction of the module) is indicated by the manifestation property of the DeployedArtifact.

Component types. The Component stereotype extends the Class metaclass (from UML StructuredClasses) and represents a component type. A Component may define properties and methods since it is a structured class. The configuration properties of a component must be marked with the config stereotype, which contains an attribute for indicating a setter operation to be called when the component container injects the value for a given configuration property.

The provides stereotype is used for publishing services and their properties. This stereotype extends both UML InterfaceRealization and Port metaclasses in order to allow modeling of published services as simple classes that implement interfaces, as well as components that have attached ports. The property attribute can be used to export the service properties, expressed as a set of (key, value) pairs.

The requires stereotype can be used for requiring services. This stereotype extends both UML Association and Port metaclasses such that the required services may be modeled as simple classes that have unidirectional associations with interfaces, as well as components that have attached

Figure 2. UML profile for iCOMPONENT

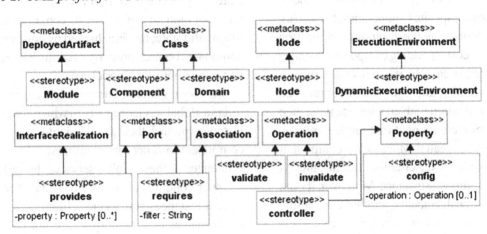

ports. The filter attribute can be used to filter the required services, based on their properties.

The UML provided/required interfaces do not contain such attributes, which explains why the provides and requires stereotypes were introduced. The two attributes are essential in the service-oriented component model because they contain information needed for component matching. For example, consider two components *EnglishDictionary* and *FrenchDictionary* implementing the same interface *Dictionary* and an *EnglishSpellChecker* component that requires a *Dictionary*. If the two concrete dictionary components are adnotated with a property representing the language (*language=English*, respectively *language=French*), then the spell checker component can choose which interface implementation to use: *filter=(language=English)*.

Composite components. UML 2.0 offers two ways of modeling subcomponents: subcomponents as parts and subcomponents as nested elements. The composites in iCOMPONENT use UML composite structures in order to indicate their internal structure. In this context, subcomponents modeled as parts are shared components which may be referenced by many composite components.

Component instances. The execution environment creates (target) component instances in two ways: (a) by creating the instances specified by Modules, and (b) by creating the instances specified as parts of composite Components. In case (a), the module containing the component definition indicates that a corresponding component instance must be created. In case (b), if a composite structure diagram attached to the component contains an instance specification with an interface type, then an instance of a component that implements the interface will be created when such a component type is available. After creation, the instance is bound to the composite instance. Moreover, if such a bound instance disappears, another compatible one can be instantiated to replace the missing service required by the composite. This mechanism

is called dynamic substitution of services. In both cases, the component instances are specified as InstanceSpecification objects of type Component. The values of the InstanceSpecification's slots are used to configure the component instance's properties (using member field injection). The component's required references (services) will be injected by the execution environment.

Component binding. The execution environment creates for each component instance a container, wrapping the instance, which automatically manages the activities of providing and requiring interfaces. When a component is added to the dynamic execution environment, it enters the *invalid* state. The component enters the *valid* state and its provided interfaces are published into a service registry when the container resolves its dependencies, i.e. the required interfaces.

Lifecycle controllers. iCOMPONENT proposes a simple notification mechanism between a component and its container: (a) After a module is installed it enters the *installed* state. When all the model elements required by a module (its module dependencies) are available, the module enters the *resolved* state. A resolved module can be started and the module enters the *active* state. (b) The component instances configured by the module will be created in the *active* state and destroyed when the module leaves this state. When a module becomes *active*, its components enter the *invalid* state; they become *valid* only after validation. A valid component can require its container to enter the invalid state; this is achieved by configuring a component boolean property as controller property using the controller stereotype.

Service registries. The execution environment offers a global service registry in which component instances publish their provided interfaces. Other component instances may automatically acquire references to these global services through their wrapper containers. In order to isolate the component instances and services of an application, the instances of a composite are not published globally by default. Each composite component has its own service registry which is used by all component instances of the same composite for providing and requiring services. Because a composite may contain other composites, a mechanism for importing and exporting services is needed; this way, a composite can export a service to its parent or can import a service from its parent.

Nodes and dynamic execution environments. Node stereotype extends UML Node metaclass. A node may deploy several modules and therefore possible several components instantiated by these modules. The DynamicExecutionEnvironment stereotype extends Node, in which you can use: (a) the properties associated to a service that is published by a component, and (b) dynamic binding using filters for selecting the services required by a component, in a similar way to the iPOJO approach (Escofier & Hall, 2007).

Domain. A Domain represents the architecture - a complete configuration for system deployment, and consists of nodes and connectors between nodes. It may have several nodes, each containing several components. Here a node is seen as a process on a computer. The binding of the components in a specific domain does not depend of the nodes in which the components are deployed.

AGILE MDA APPROACH FOR SERVICE-ORIENTED COMPONENTS

The models can be constructed using any UML case tool, and their execution can be performed with any fUML-compliant tool (such as fUML plugin from MagicDraw (Model Driven Community, 2009)). As discussed above, COMDEVALCO workbench is such a tool, being designed according to these requirements (Motogna, Lazăr, Pârv & Czibula, 2009; Lazăr, Pârv, Motogna, Czibula & Lazăr, 2007; 2009). The iCOMPONENT profile may be easily applied to develop service-oriented components for dynamic execution environments.

The proposed agile MDA approach consists of applying the following steps in the specified order: (1) the model is described on different layers: services, structure and deployment, then (2) for simple components proceed with test-first component development. The approach is applied for the following example: a case study that prints the product prices of a given store. The store has a product catalog containing product information (code, description, and price without taxes and discounts). The printing procedure must consider the discount strategies the store may have for each product and the application of VAT.

Services Model

The services model, typically defined by the system analyst, describes the services that will be provided by the system. The modules that refer to services model may include any data type, such as classes, interfaces, or components. The interfaces contain the operations provided by the services.

At this step, the model should be defined with the separation of responsibilities in mind. The modules will contain required operation or will simply delegate execution to corresponding operation from another module within the model.

Figure 3.a shows the services model, illustrating the separation of responsibilities. The StoreService interface contains the required operations for printing the product prices with taxes and discounts. StoreService's operations can simply delegate execution to their corresponding operations from ProductCatalog and PriceCalculator. The Pricing-Strategy interface is designed to represent both discount and VAT price adjustments. The services module includes all these interfaces as well as the Product business entity.

Structural Model: Composite Components

The structural model, typically defined by the system architect, indicates component instances that implement the services. At this stage, the system is decomposed into a set of components, simple

Figure 3. (a) Services model and (b) structural model

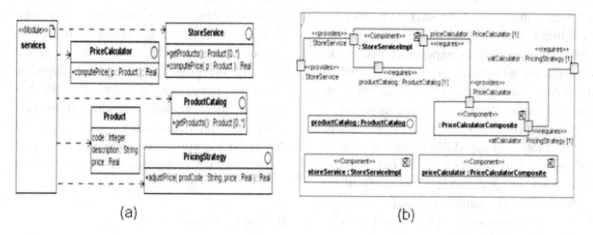

(a)   (b)

or composite. **Composite components** help the architect to decompose the system functionality in a hierarchical way. Each composite component has attached a composite structure diagram, describing its internal structure, using component parts (simple or composite) and connectors between ports, and specifying which components will be instantiated. The rules for the construction of the diagram are:

- the internal structure of a component uses instances of other components, connected through ports;
- the provided and required ports, as well as their multiplicity, should be specified;
- to select a certain service implementation satisfying some criteria, use the property attribute corresponding to provides and filter attribute corresponding to requires;
- the InstanceSpecification objects indicate which components should be created and their corresponding property values.

Instances will be created according to the rules specified by iCOMPONENT profile. The hierarchical composition works such that components acquire services from their parent, and provide services to their parent.

Figure 3.b shows the composite structure diagram of the Store composite component. Store uses three shared subcomponents; one of them, PriceCalculatorComposite, is a composite too. The provided and required interfaces are represented as ports and the components are linked using connectors.

Deployment Model

The deployment model is specified using UML Node and DynamicExecutionEnvironment constructs, as shown above. The dependencies in this model represent the required runtime dependencies between modules (see Figure 4(a)). All monolithic implementations reference only interfaces, but composite components may use other components as parts.

At this moment, the domain has to be specified, with its included nodes, and the deployment of modules within nodes – as shown in Figure 4(b). There are two nodes, corresponding to CatalogApp and TaxServices. Next, the module must indicate which components will be instantiated during execution and which nodes are involved in each instantiation process.

Coresponding to the domain specification above, Figure 5 shows the component instances created at runtime in their corresponding nodes.

Figure 4. Deployment model

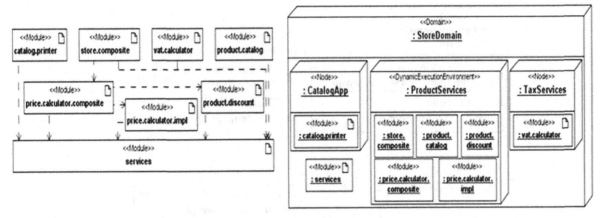

(a) Module dependencies   (b) Domain and nodes

StoreComposite acquires vatCalculatorImpl service and publishes it for its part components, then creates instances for its parts.

Test-First Component Development

When the decomposition is complete, the next step is to define simple or monolithic components solving the initial problem. For each new feature of the system being developed, the proposed agile MDA process includes the sequence of following test-first design steps (Beck, 2002):

- **Add a test**. Developers write the tests using either graphical or textual notations. Both

are compiled into the same UML repository model. The tests are conformant with UML testing specifications (OMG, 2005). During the activity construction process, the framework allows the use of inline expressions, represented and evaluated according to the pull model for actions.

Figure 6a) shows how tests for ProductDiscount module are created, including initialization of the component properties productCode and discountPercentage. Using AL, the implementation:

assert 90 = pricingStrategy.adjustPrice ("3",100);

Figure 5. Component instances

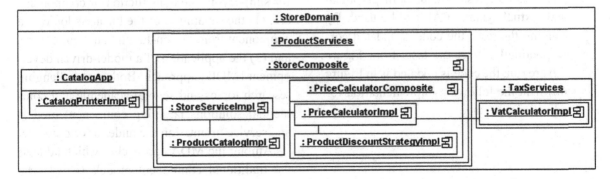

Figure 6. a)Product discount tests; b) Product discount

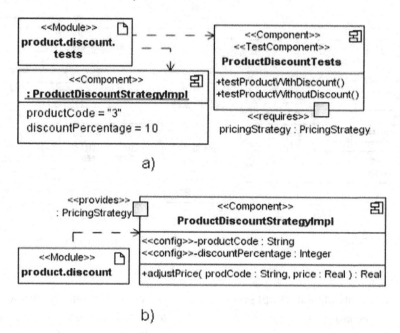

is introduced in testProductWithDiscount method, and

assert 100 = pricingStrategy.adjustPrice(''1'',100);

is introduced in testProductWithoutDiscount method in ProductDiscountTest.

- **Run the tests**. The methods of the components have an empty body, only the conditions are specified
- **Add production code**. The third step is to update the functional code to make it pass the new test. Again, both graphical and textual syntax of AL can be used. By running the tests, the code is updated correspondingly. After the tests from Figure 6a) are run, the code is updated is in Figure 6b) with the following implementation for adjustPrice method:

```
if (productCode = self.productCode)
        return (1-discountPercent-
age/100)* price;
else
        return price;
```

- **Run the tests**. This last step means running the tests again. Once the tests pass the next step is to start over implementing a new system feature.

RELATED WORK

As shown in the first section, two important issues for simplifying the construction of components are: (1) the separation of the business logic of a component from its non-functional requirements and (2) the application of a model-driven development (MDD) approach. Both are challenging research topics and several academic and commercial solutions targeting component models and service orientation are under development.

Among the MDA approaches which address the traditional component models (e.g. Corba

Component Model), the standard specification for deployment and configuration of component-based distributed applications (OMG, 2006) should be mentioned.

Other MDA approaches referring to embedded systems (Cano, Martinez, Seepold, & Aguilar 2007) or pervasive systems (Bottaro, Bourcier, Escofier, & Lalanda, 2007; Bourcier, Chazalet, Desertot, Escofier & Marin, 2006; Munoz, Pelechano, & Fons, 2004) address the dynamic execution environment features and the separation problem.

Academic solutions, such as Fractal (Bruneton, Coupaye, Leclercq, Quema & Stefani, 2004) and SOFA 2.0 (Bures, Hnetynka & Plasil, 2006) are open component models that provide all dynamic features but do not offer a clear separation of the functional and non-functional requirements.

iPOJO (injected Plain Old Java Objects) (Escofier & Hall, 2007) is a service-oriented component framework supporting the service-oriented component model concepts and dynamic availability of components, following the POJO (Plain Old Java Object) approach. All service-oriented aspects, such as service publication, the required service discovery and selection are managed by an associated component container. The operations in iPOJO are similar to iCOMPONENT operations, but our approach is platform-independent, while iPOJO is restricted to Java.

Also, the current version of iPOJO does not provide a clear separation of the business logic and non-functional requirements for all operations discussed above. More precisely, only dynamic availability of components and composition of components are supported, while the dynamic reconfiguration of components can be performed only using the OSGi Configuration Admin service.

Another framework which supports dynamic availability and reconfiguration of components is the OSGi framework (OSGi, 2007), which offers a service-oriented component model. OSGi components are bound using a service-oriented interaction pattern, and their structure is described declaratively. However, OSGi does not offer a clear separation between business logic and the non-functional requirements.

Service Component Architecture (SCA) Assembly Model specification (OASIS, 2007) proposes a definition of composite components similar to iPOJO; in addition, the components may be distributed in several locations/nodes within the same domain. Another remarkable feature of SCA is that it allows specification of component implementations which are not necessary classes; they can be business processes also. However, there are also some drawbacks of SCA: it doesn't indicate any solution for controlling the lifecycle of components and does not allow the user to attach properties to a published service and to filter services specifying some conditions.

Table 1 enumerates the main elements used to develop service-oriented components for dynamic execution environments and gives the mapping between these elements from iCOMPONENT, iPOJO and SCA frameworks. These two frameworks were taken into consideration as specific target platforms for models created using our proposed UML profile.

Table 1. iCOMPONENT, iPOJO, and SCA mappings

iCOMPONENT	iPOJO	SCA
Domain	-	Domain
Node	-	Node
DynamicExecutionEnvironment	OSGi implementation	-
Module	Bundle	Contribution
Component	Component	Component
Composite component	Composite	Composite
provides	provides	Service
Requires	Requires	Reference
validate and invalidate	validate and invalidate	-
controller	controller	-
Config	Property	Property

As the table suggests, the main difference between iCOMPONENT and SCA on one hand, and iPOJO, on the other hand, is that iPOJO does not support distributed service architecture. iCOMPONENT supports it, by distributing the modules in the nodes of the dynamic execution environment. Comparing iCOMPONENT with SCA, one may observe that SCA does not have lifecycle controllers, i.e. a notification mechanism between a component and its container such that the component can participate to its lifecycle events.

In conclusion, COMDEVALCO framework allows service-oriented applications to be modeled independently of any platform, then these models can be executed, and in the end, complete code is generated targeting such a platform (SCA, iPOJO), providing that the differences highlighted in the table were taken into consideration.

FUTURE RESEARCH DIRECTIONS

Future developments of COMDEVALCO framework include: improving model V&V capabilities, model transformation and SOAML compliance. More precisely, model V&V will cover the investigation of multi-modal test execution techniques in the context of fUML by using UML composite structures and test data concepts.

The COMDEVALCO toolset will also include model transformation capabilities, referring to the generation of full executable code from executable models.

CONCLUSION

This chapter describes COMDEVALCO framework, made up of: a concrete syntax for fUML, iCOMPONENT - a platform-independent component model for dynamic execution environments, and an agile MDA approach for building executable models. To the best of our knowledge, no other existing works combines executable models, agile MDA, and platform-independent service-oriented component models for dynamic execution environments.

Our proposal is compared to other specific platforms, like iPOJO and SCA. By using iCOMPONENT profile, COMDEVALCO models can be constructed with any UML tool and can be executed in any executable UML tool.

The intended use of COMDEVALCO framework is twofold. The first target is component-based development, since COMDEVALCO conforms to UML and MDA standards, providing a complete framework for executable service-oriented component models.

The second target is of an academic nature. COMDEVALCO can be used in many Software Engineering courses as an example of applying model-driven principles in the software development process. At a beginner level, students get used earlier with model-based development, while at an advanced level the framework may be used for model-driven V&V tasks.

ACKNOWLEDGMENT

The research is supported by the grant ID 546, sponsored by NURC - Romanian National University Research Council (CNCSIS).

REFERENCES

Balasubramanian, K., Gokhale, A., Karsai, G., Sztipanovits, J., & Neema, S. (2006). Developing Applications Using Model-Driven Design Environments. *Computer, 39*(2), 33–40. doi:10.1109/MC.2006.54

Batory, D. (2006). Multilevel models in model-driven engineering, product lines, and metaprogramming. *IBM Systems Journal, 45*(3), 527–539. doi:10.1147/sj.453.0527

Beck, K. (2002). *Test-Driven Development By Example*. Boston: Addison Wesley.

Bottaro, A., Bourcier, J., Escofier, C., & Lalanda, P. (2007). Autonomic Context-Aware Service Composition in a Home Control Gateway. In *Proceedings of IEEE International Conference on Pervasive Services* (pp. 223-231), Istanbul, Turkey.

Bourcier, J., Chazalet, A., Desertot, M., Escofier, C., & Marin, C. (2006). A Dynamic-SOA Home Control Gateway. In *Proceedings of IEEE International Conference on Services Computing* (pp. 463–470), Chicago.

Bruneton, E., Coupaye, T., Leclercq, M., Quema, V., & Stefani, J.-B. (2004). An Open Component Model and Its Support in Java. In Crnkovic, I., Stafford, J.A., Schmidt, H.W., & Wallnau, K. (Eds.), *Component-Based Software Engineering,* (LNCS Vol. 3054, pp. 7-22). Berlin: Springer.

Bures, T., Hnetynka, P., & Plasil, F. (2006). SOFA 2.0: Balancing Advanced Features in a Hierarchical Component Model. In *Proceedings SERA* (pp. 40-48). Seattle: IEEE Computer Society.

Cano, J., Martinez, N., Seepold, R., & Aguilar, F.L. (2007). Model-driven development of embedded system on heterogeneous platforms. In *Procedings of Forum on Specification and Design Languages* (pp. 243–248). Barcelona, Spain: ECSI.

Cervantes, H., & Hall, R. S. (2004). A Framework for Constructing Adaptive Component-Based Applications: Concepts and Experiences. In Crnkovic, I., Stafford, J.A., Schmidt, H.W., Wallnau, K. (Eds.), *7th Symposium on Component-Based Software Engineering:* (LNCS Vol 3054, pp. 130-137). Berlin: Springer.

Escofier, C., & Hall, R. S. (2007). Dynamically Adaptable Applications with iPOJO Service Components. In Lumpe, M. & Vanderperre, W. (Eds.), *Proc. 6th Conference on Software Composition,* (LNCS Vol 4829, pp. 113-128). Berlin: Springer.

Henderson, P., & Walters, R. J. (1999). System Design Validation Using Formal Models. In *10th IEEE International Workshop in Rapid System Prototyping 146*(3), 10-14.

Lau, K.-K., & Wang, Z. (2005). A Taxonomy of Software Component Models. In *Proceeding of 31st EUROMICRO Conference of Software Engineering and Advanced Applications* (pp. 88-95). Washington, DC: IEEE Computer Society.

Lazăr, C.-L., Lazăr, I., Pârv, B., Motogna, S., & Czibula, I.-G. (2009). Using an fUML Action Language to Construct UML Models, In *11th International Symposium on Symbolic and Numeric Algorithms for Scientific Computing*, Timisoara, Romania.

Lazăr, I., Pârv, B., Motogna, S., Czibula, I.-G., & Lazăr, C.-L. (2007). An Agile MDA Approach for Executable UML Structured Activities. *Studia Univ. Babeş-Bolyai. Informatica, LII*(2), 101–114.

Lazăr, I., Pârv, B., Motogna, S., Czibula, I.-G., & Lazăr, C.-L. (2008). iCOMPONENT: A Platform-independent Component Model for Dynamic Execution Environments, In *10th International Symposium on Symbolic and Numeric Algorithms for Scientific Computing* (pp. 257-264), Timisoara, Romania. Washington, DC: IEEE Computer Society.

Mellor, S. J. (2005). *Agile MDA*, Technical report, OMG. Retrieved May 20, 2009, from http://www.omg.org/mda/mda_files/Agile_MDA.pdf

Mellor, S. J., & Balcer, M. J. (2002). *Executable UML: A Foundation for Model-Driven Architecture*. Boston: Addison Wesley.

Microsoft. (1995). *Component Object Model*. Redmond, WA: Microsoft, Inc. Retrieved May 20, 2009, from: http://www.microsoft.com/com/

Microsystems, S. (2003). *Enterprise JavaBeans Specification*. Retrieved October 2007, from: http://java.sun.com/products/ejb/docs.html

Model Driven Community. (2009). *fUML Magic-Draw plugin*. Retrieved Oct, 2009, from: http://portal.modeldriven.org/content/fuml-reference-implementation-download

Motogna, S., Lazăr, I., Pârv, B., & Czibula, I. (2009). An Agile MDA Approach for Service-Oriented Components. In J. Happe, B. Zimmerova (Eds.) *6th International Workshop on Formal Engineering approaches to Software Components and Architectures (FESCA), PreProceedings* (pp. 2-17). York, Electronic Notes in Theoretical Computer Science.

Munoz, J., Pelechano, V., & Fons, J. (2004). Model Driven Development of Pervasive Systems. *ERCIM News, 58*, 50–51.

OASIS. (2007). *SCA Service Component Architecture. Assembly Model Specification*, Version 1.1. Retrieved October 2007, from: http://www.oasis-opencsa.org/sca

OMG. (2002). *CORBA Components Specification*, Version 3.0. Retrieved October 2007, from: http://www.omg.org/technology/documents/formal/components.htm

OMG. (2005). *UML 2.0 Testing Profile Specification*. Retrived October 2007, from: http://www.omg.org/cgi-bin/apps/doc?formal/05-07-07.pdf

OMG. (2006). *Deployment and Configuration of Component-based Distributed Applications Specification*, Version 4 Retrieved October 2007, from: http://www.omg.org/technology/documents/formal/deployment.htm

OMG. (2007). *UML Superstructure Specification*, Rev. 2.1.2, Retrieved October 2007, from: http://www.omg.org/docs/formal/07-11-02.pdf

OMG. (2008). *Semantics of a Foundational Subset for Executable UML Models* (*FUML*), Retrieved April 2009, from: http://www.omg.org/spec/FUML/

OSGi Alliance. (2007). *OSGi Service Platform Core Specification*, Release 4, Version 4.1., Retrieved October 2007, from: http://www.osgi.org/

Papazoglou, M., & Georgakopoulos, D. (2003). Service-Oriented Computing. *Communications of the ACM, 46*(10), 25–28.

Pârv, B., Lazăr, I., & Motogna, S. (2008). ComDeValCo Framework - the Modeling Language for Procedural Paradigm. *International Journal of Computers, Communications & Control, 3*(2), 183–195.

Pârv, B., Lazăr, I., Motogna, S., Czibula, I.-G., & Lazăr, C.-L. (2009) ComDeValCo Framework - Procedural and Modular Issues. In *2nd International Conference Knowledge Engineering: Principles and Techniques* (pp. 189-193), Cluj-Napoca, Romania, Studia Universitatis Babeş-Bolyai.

Wirth, N. (1977). What can we do about the unnecessary diversity of notation for syntactic definitions? *Communications of the ACM, 20*(11), 822–823. doi:10.1145/359863.359883

KEY TERMS AND DEFINITIONS

Component-Based Development: Software systems are developed and deployed as a set of components, providing loose coupling among the application components, third-party component selection, and increased component reuse (Escofier & Hall, 2007).

Test-Driven Development: is a software development technique that relies on repeatedly apply small unit testing in order to detect system behavior and write the corresponding code (Beck, 2002)

Service-Oriented Component Model: adopts the service oriented approach of late binding among components via services. Thus, the application is consists of component composition, and at run time it adapts based on availibility of the services (Cervantes & Hall, 2004).

Agile MDA: applies the main agile principles into a classical MDA process;"models are linked together, rather than transformed, and they are then all mapped to a single combined model that is then translated into code according to a single system architecture" (Mellor, 2005)

Executable UML: represents an execution semantic for a subset of actions sufficient for computational completeness. Two basic elements are required for such subsets: an action language and an operational semantics (Mellor & Balcer, 2002).

Action Language: part of excutable UML, uses only elements allowed by fUML standard and should create abstract representantions for all the elements the model requires (Mellor & Balcer, 2002).

Execution Environment: manages application compositions based on service availability and provides deployment and intergration (Cervantes & Hall, 2004).

Section 3
Modeling of Product Lines and Patterns

Chapter 13
Model–Driven Impact Analysis of Software Product Lines

Hyun Cho
University of Alabama, USA

Jeff Gray
University of Alabama, USA

Yuanfang Cai
Drexel University, USA

Sonny Wong
Drexel University, USA

Tao Xie
North Carolina State University, USA

ABSTRACT

Software assets, which are developed and maintained at various stages, have different abstraction levels. The structural mismatch of the abstraction levels makes it difficult for developers to understand the consequences of changes. Furthermore, assessing change impact is even more challenging in software product lines because core assets are interrelated to support domain and application engineering. Model-driven engineering helps software engineers in many ways by lifting the abstraction level of software development. The higher level of abstraction provided by models can serve as a backbone to analyze and design core assets and architectures for software product lines. This chapter introduces model-driven impact analysis that is based on the synergy of three separate techniques: (1) domain-specific modeling, (2) constraint-based analysis, and (3) software testing. The techniques are used to establish traceability relations between software artifacts, assess the tradeoff of design alternatives quantitatively, and conduct change impact analysis.

DOI: 10.4018/978-1-61692-874-2.ch013

INTRODUCTION

Changes are inevitable in software development and maintenance. Software adaptation and evolution represent changes that occur throughout the software lifecycle from conception to termination, such that change management influences both cost and quality (Lehman & Belady, 1985). Thus, impact analysis, which identifies the ripple effects of proposed software changes, is beneficial before developers make actual modification to a software asset. However, it is challenging for developers to analyze multiple candidate options for changes and make decisions that may have significant consequences (Arnold & Bohner, 1993; Bohner, 2002). Furthermore, it is difficult for developers to understand the consequences of changes across various software assets due to the structural mismatch of abstraction levels at different stages of the software lifecycle (De Lucia et al., 2008).

The challenges of software change are even more problematic for a software product line, which supports the derivation of a wide range of software products (members of a product family) through composing or modifying the core assets of its architecture. Developers can make changes to the problem domain and/or application domain of a software product line either to enhance the core architecture, impacting all the derived products, or to add more products as new members in the product family. Making changes to a software product requires the consideration of multiple constraints from different stakeholders and users of the product line family. It is possible that one stakeholder proposes a change to the requirements to maximize the value of his/her own product derived from the product family, but the change may positively or negatively influence other products or other properties of the product family.

Impact analysis (Arnold & Bohner, 1993; Bohner, 2002) accepts as input a root asset to which an initial proposed change is made, and then performs three main steps: (1) The analysis

traces the relationships between the root asset and other assets to identify related assets; (2) The analysis examines each related asset to determine if it will be affected by the proposed change, and if so, what changes must be made by developers to accommodate the initial proposed change; (3) The analysis adds the effort to make additional changes on related assets to the total needed effort, producing an estimated scope and cost of the proposed change as the results of the analysis. Analyzing the impact of changes before performing actual modification to an asset has been recognized as an important task in the software development lifecycle (Arnold & Bohner, 1993; Bohner, 2002; Jönsson, 2007; Anquetil et al., 2008). The analysis results can serve as a preliminary input to planning project costs and predicting software system quality (Ajila, 1995). Despite its importance, the majority of support offered in current requirements and design tools provides only limited functionality. For example, given multiple alternatives to accommodate a change, quantitative and automated techniques are needed to assess the tradeoffs of each alternative, to balance the constraints from different perspectives, and to minimize the impact on existing products. Furthermore, it is difficult to assess change impact on heterogeneous software artifacts generated at different stages of the software development process. Manually creating traceability relations (the basis of impact analysis) is time-consuming, error-prone, and tedious. Although predicting change impact facilitates project planning and quality prediction, it is often omitted because of these preceding obstacles.

The Unified Modeling Language (UML) has been widely used for system analysis and design and a large number of UML diagrams have been developed to assist with lifecycle concerns. Some researchers have proposed impact analysis based on UML models to accomplish changes in the system while minimizing potential consequences, such as cost overrun and intermingled evolutions (Briand et el., 2006; Briand et el., 2002). However, the UML is a general-purpose modeling language that tries to do many things for a broad range of uses. This nature of the UML can often limit the specificity of the abstraction and representation in which a system is modeled. An alternative to the UML has been realized in the adoption of domain-specific modeling languages (Gray et al., 2007), which allow the expression of a model in a form that is more natural (in terms of the abstractions and visualization of the model) manner to model an application and product line. This chapter presents our approach for using domain-specific modeling, in conjunction with impact analysis, to understand the effect of changes on a product line.

This contribution describes our approach for impact analysis based on model-driven engineering that targets software product lines, addressing the challenges listed in this introduction. The approach uses domain-specific modeling techniques to automate establishment of traceability relations, adopts constraint-based analysis techniques to quantitatively assess the tradeoffs of design alternatives, and employs a systematic testing framework to conduct change impact analysis.

BACKGROUND

This section presents the necessary background information needed to understand our approach, including the design and construction of domain-specific models, analyzing the impact of changes, and evaluating the alternatives of accommodating changes. Model-Driven Engineering (MDE) serves as a backbone of analysis and design activities in software product line development, which is a two-stage process including the stages of domain engineering (Bayer et al., 1999; Kang et al., 1990; Tracz, 1995; Czarnecki, 2006) and application engineering. Configuration management records and manages every change activity and configuration item. Impact analysis is performed in the process of change management, which controls the entire process of change (e.g., identification of changes, authorization and validation).

SOFTWARE PRODUCT LINES

According to the Software Engineering Institute, "A software product line is a group of software products sharing a common set of features that satisfy a well-defined set of market needs and that are developed from a set of common core assets for a specific application domain" (SEI-CMU, 2010). The notion of software product lines has received substantial attention since the 1990s and has proven itself in a large number of organizations (SEI-CMU, 2010; Weiss & Lai, 1999). Unlike single product development, a Software Product Line (SPL) is characterized by three essential phases: core asset development, product development, and management of technology and organization. In the phase of core asset development, core assets such as platform characteristics and components are developed or mined through domain analysis and then a series of products are produced on the basis of these core assets under the prescribed attached processes in the phase of product development. The management phase manages and supports both development activities and organization structure to maximize their performance.

Many organizations have realized the benefits of software product lines, such as reducing time to market and product-development costs, improving process predictability, enhancing product quality, achieving large-scale productivity gains, and increasing customer satisfaction (Clements & Northrop, 2001). For example, Hewlett Packard (Toft et al., 2000) reported that they shortened time-to-market three-fold, reduced typical defect density by a factor of 25, and reused code up to 70% across participating printer product lines. However, it is quite difficult to achieve similar levels of benefits as in the HP case. The main reasons are that few organizations could use the same domain model as HP even though they may be in the same business. Furthermore, each organization has different levels of software development capabilities. Most of all, the way that product development is performed with software product lines is quite different from development of a single product. Thus, success in adoption and institutionalization of a software product line requires an organization to evolve its development process and methods, as well as the structure of the organization itself.

Unlike single-product development, the development of a product as an instance of a software product line follows a two-stage process: domain engineering and application engineering. The domain engineering stage focuses on developing core assets that contain variability and are reusable throughout a complete product line. Domain analysis is a key phase in domain engineering. During the domain analysis phase, engineers model the common and variable features as a feature model and specify the constraints among features to transform them into reusable core assets (Clements & Northrop, 2001). These assets are the design elements of a product line architecture and the basis of a product instantiation, with a proper variability management mechanism. After the engineers identify commonality and variability of the domain during domain analysis, the engineers design a product line architecture and its domain components in the domain design phase. The engineers should design a product line architecture to be platform-independent and to accommodate necessary variation management mechanisms (e.g., dynamic reconfiguration of features at runtime) (Gomaa & Hussein, 2004).

Application engineering instantiates a concrete product that is specific to customer requirements. The goal of application engineering is to produce the derivation of products as product line members through the selection, customization, integration, or transformation of the product specification and the appropriate assets developed in domain engineering. Application engineering begins with application analysis, whose goals are to determine the application-specific requirements and to analyze the impacts of selection from various platform-specific architectural design decisions (e.g., hardware resources, programming languages, binding time, and middleware). In the application design phase, engineers create platform-specific architecture and assets by selecting and customizing core assets developed in the domain engineering phase.

MODEL-DRIVEN ENGINEERING (MDE)

Model-Driven Engineering (MDE) has emerged as a promising paradigm in software engineering by emphasizing the use of models not just for documentation and communication purposes, but as first-class artifacts to be transformed into other work products (e.g., other models, source code, and test scripts) (Schmidt, 2006). Models may range from general-purpose modeling languages such as the Unified Modeling Language (UML) to domain-specific modeling languages (DSMLs), which assist domain experts in working within their own problem space without being concerned about technical details of the solution space (e.g., programming languages and middleware). DSMLs also provide an accessible way to communicate with stakeholders who are not familiar with the fast changing technologies.

The general approach to developing DSMLs consists of three different modeling layers: the model, metamodel, and meta-metamodel (Kurtev, Bézivin, Jouault, & Valduriez, 2006). Each model layer defines a representation structure and a global typing system that is used by the layer beneath it (i.e., each model conforms to its defining meta-layer). For example, a meta-metamodel is a model that defines a metamodel (i.e., the metamodel conforms to the meta-metamodel definition). The top-level meta-metamodel has a special definition – it can be used to define itself such that no higher

Figure 1. Metamodel for feature diagram language

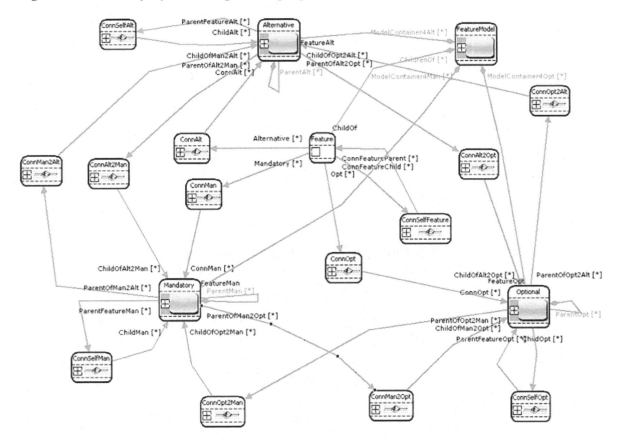

layer is needed. The MOF (MetaObject Facility) (OMG MOF, 2006) is an example of a common meta-metamodel. For example, the metamodel of UML describes the constituents of all well-formed models such as Use case, Class, relationships, and properties. The UML metamodel definition is specified in MOF. A model represents an instance of a metamodel, and specifies an actual software system. A model must conform to its defining metamodel.

According to the report of practitioners who have adopted MDE for software product lines (SPLs) (Weiss & Lai, 1999; Pohjonen & Tolvanen, 2002), MDE can provide the role of the technological backbone for supporting product line development. DSMLs and specialized tools such as model transformation engines and code generators have been adopted and used based on the concepts

available in specific domains. For example, domain analysis normally models commonality and variability with a feature model. MDE provides tools necessary to model and manage commonality and variability in a software product line. Figure 1 and Figure 2 describe a metamodel for a feature modeling language (Figure 1), along with a sample feature model that is defined in this language (Figure 2). The idea of a feature model was proposed by Kang et al. (1990) to represent all possible commonality and variability of an SPL in a single model using features and their relationships. Mandatory features are the common features across the product lines. Alternative and optional features are features that represent variations of the products to accommodate specific product requirements. Optional features are used if more than one feature is selectable for the

Figure 2. Feature diagrams for mobilemedia application

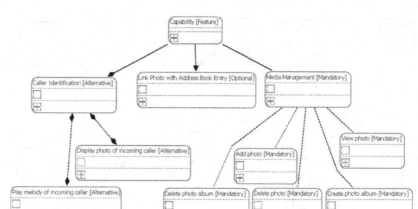

a) Feature model representing application capabilities

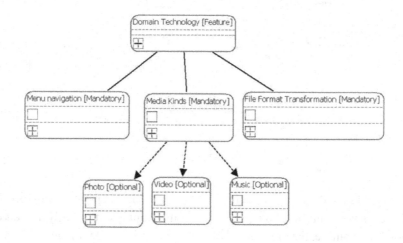

b) Feature model representing domain technologies

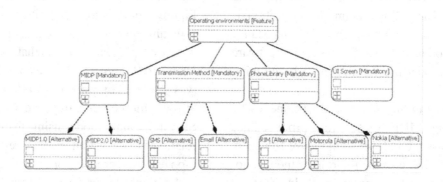

c) Feature model representing operating environments

products but alternative features allow selecting no more than one feature.

To model a system as a feature model, the metamodel should define three key concepts of feature modeling as mentioned earlier: Mandatory, Alternative, and Optional features. The feature metamodel also defines the relationships among these concepts, such as mandatory-to-alternative, which means that a parent feature is mandatory, but has alternative sub-features. Figure 2 shows a feature model for the MobileMedia application, which we use in a case study for applying our approach (described later in this chapter). Each rectangle represents features that are Mandatory, Alternative, or Optional. Each line shows the relationship between features through different line styles and arrow heads. For example, the relationship emanating into or out of a Mandatory feature does not have an arrow head. A line emanating from an Alternative feature uses a diamond arrow head and a line emanating from an Optional feature uses a normal arrow head. A solid line represents the relationship within a feature space, which is categorized into capability, domain, operation, implementation, and feature types (e.g., Mandatory, Alternative, and Optional). A dotted line represents the relationship among domain features. A mandatory-to-alternative relation is represented as a dotted line with no arrow head and an alternative-to-optional relation is represented as a dotted line with a diamond arrow head.

CONFIGURATION MANAGEMENT & CHANGE MANAGEMENT

Configuration and change management play the roles of the artifact management backbone to develop high quality software. Configuration management tracks changes of all the development artifacts such that the artifacts are not limited to source code. Change management tracks the status of development activities such as tasks, defect removals, and feature enhancement requests. IEEE standard 1042-1987 (IEEE 1042, 1987) describes four main activities in configuration management: configuration identification, configuration control, status accounting, and audit and review. The main tasks of configuration identification are identifying configuration items that comprise the structure of the artifacts and their properties, and making them unique and accessible. After configuration items are identified, configuration control manages the lifecycle of each item by creating baselines. Status accounting assumes the role of recording and reporting the status of configuration items. A configuration item's completeness and consistency are validated through audit and review (IEEE 1042, 1987).

From the early conceptual phase through phases of completion to retirement, a software product is constantly changing. The success of these changes is determined by whether the modified software meets its requirements and the changes finish on time and within budget. Thus, if the changes are not managed properly, software development and maintenance suffer from poor software quality, unnecessary rework, and failed changes. The second layer describes key information of the change management process, which begins by submitting change requests. Before proceeding to actual artifact changes, a change manager analyzes the impact of configuration items from the changes. After impact analysis, the change control manager determines whether to approve or deny the change requests. For an authorized change, the actual change is implemented and validated.

THE ORIGIN OF SOFTWARE CHANGE

According to Pineherio et el (1996), software changes come from either the social and business context of the system or from the improved understanding of the constraints as the maturity level of software development is increased. Thus, it is very difficult to list all of the causes of changes. Researchers have characterized and categorized various types of changes with the expectation that such categorization can assist engineers in producing software with a lower defect density by preventing the occurrence of common undesirable types of change. In addition, the classification of changes may help to understand the nature of a change to minimize the crosscutting impacts. Lientz & Swanson (1984) distinguished the types of software maintenance as perfective, adaptive, and corrective. Buckley et al. (2005) developed a taxonomy for changes from a mechanisms perspective. Their approach focuses on the "how, what, when, and where" of an evolutionary change (i.e., any change request, such as requirement changes, bug fixes, and regulation changes that can occur throughout the software lifecycle). Chaplin et al. (2001) proposed 12 distinct categories on the purpose of maintenance. Based on related literature, the origin of a change can be classified according to the location of the change:

- **Internal change**: An internal change is a change whose origin comes from the software development lifecycle. As software development proceeds, engineers better understand the requirements, system, and development infrastructures (e.g., database, middleware and programming language). This enhanced understanding causes changes; for example, engineers restructure a design to use several design patterns to minimize dependency on concrete implementations (Gamma et al., 1994), or adopt an N-tier architecture to enforce reusability of the system. In addition, a defect is an important source of an internal change, which fixes the defect.

- **External change**: Unlike internal changes, the origin of an external change comes from outside a development organization (e.g., marketing and customer demand,

Table 1. Examples of changes in SPL (based on McGregor, 2005)

	Internal	**External**
Anticipated Evolution	Restructuring Introduction of new technology Optimization / Performance	Changes of regulation Changes of business environment Feature enhancement
Unanticipated Evolution	Defects	Software Faults

new or revised regulations, and feature enhancement).

Change management in a SPL can be different from that of a single product. Changes in a software product line are more predictive and manageable because most changes are based on technically anticipated and proactively researched requirements that are related to advances in the technologies and business. As described by McGregor (2005), the core assets of a software product line are designed and implemented with numerous variation management mechanisms based on technology and business forecasting. Thus, the variation mechanisms that accommodate evolution of a software product line can be anticipated. Table 1 classifies examples of change according to the origin of the change and the types of evolution.

IMPACT ANALYSIS

As software systems continue to become more complex, estimating expected changes is more difficult and often leads to inaccurate predictions. Lindvail & SanDahl (1998) empirically showed that developers predict the impact of change optimistically, which results in the underprediction of actual changes by a factor of 1.5 to 2.2. This result suggests that even experienced developers can predict the scope of changes with at most 50%

accuracy. This underprediction of actual changes results in serious problems in software development and management. Thus, systematic impact analysis is necessary to improve the accuracy of the estimation of changes when change requests are introduced to the software development and maintenance phases.

Impact analysis identifies potential consequences of a change request and can predict what artifacts need to be added, deleted, or modified to accommodate a change request. Impact analysis normally follows two steps: Identification and Estimation. The identification step identifies potential consequences from the change. Traceability relations between artifacts play a pivotal role in identifying the potential consequences because the links connect between different software artifacts such as requirements, design documentation, source code, and test cases. Traceability relations help with the task of impact analysis in three main ways. First, a traceability relation assists in verifying that a system meets its requirements by tracing from requirements to tests, and vice versa. Thus, a traceability relation helps to determine whether a specification is completely implemented and covered by tests. Second, a traceability relation helps to comprehend the system under analysis. When a system is developed top-down, a traceability relation helps a maintainer or tester in finding relevant documents such as design and requirements documents, and assists in understanding the core concept for estimating the scope and cost of system changes. Finally, a traceability relation helps to analyze the impact of changes by locating needed information to be updated and recorded when there are change requests. After the identification step, the estimation step assesses the impacts of possible changes and computes an estimate for the necessary modification, schedule, and cost based on the potential consequences.

Although performing impact analysis before doing an actual modification offers several benefits to software development and management, it is often done only when absolutely necessary.

Such uncommon practice is because the current practice of impact analysis typically is performed manually, such that the increasing volume of heterogeneous artifacts and their interrelationships is very burdensome to manage. In some tool chains, such as IBM Rational tools (IBM Rational DOORS, 2009), impact analysis can be automated through integration, but it is very rare that an organization focus its complete tool chain on just one vendor. Furthermore, there is no sufficient method to describe the semantics of software change relationships and the traceability of those relationships.

MODEL-DRIVEN IMPACT ANALYSIS FOR SPLS

This section presents our approach for performing impact analysis based on model-driven engineering (MDE), addressing the problems discussed in the previous two sections. The process of impact analysis is initiated from the submission of change requests. There could be multiple alternatives to accommodate the proposed changes. Assessing these alternatives before implementation is challenging because of the lack of models to express and evaluate both existing products and envisioned changes. It is also difficult to establish traceability relations between assets, which are represented through different abstractions depending on a specific development stage. For example, requirements are normally expressed with natural language and subsequent design may be expressed with visual models. Across the lifecycle stages, there is often a difference in the granularity of the software representation and a lack of automation to support analysis and evaluation of design candidates. Our approach consists of three integrated parts: building domain-specific models to represent both existing products and proposed changes, assessing tradeoffs of each alternative (to accommodate the proposed changes) using a constraint-based design testing framework, and

Figure 3. Procedure for model-driven impact analysis

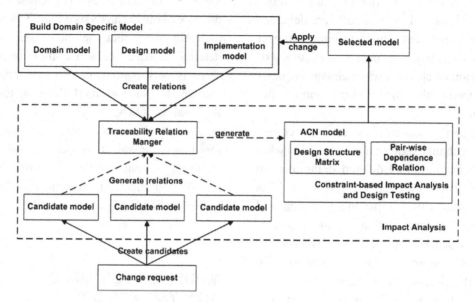

applying the selected alternative to accommodate the changes. Figure 3 shows the procedure for using our approach.

Our approach starts with building domain-specific models for requirements, designs, implementations, and tests. Each model is linked to each other through a traceability relation to verify that the descendent model satisfies requirements or constraints of its precedent, as well as to analyze the impacts of changes. When a change request is introduced to one of the models, an engineer may query the traceability relations to obtain information about which model elements should be modified to create candidate models. Based on this information, several different change candidates are constructed and these candidates are passed on to the constraint-based impact analysis part to select a model that maintains a high independence in the level of design and design volatility. The procedures for impact analysis can be done automatically given that the candidate change models are provided and traceability relations are established across all the artifacts. After traceability relations are linked to every artifact, adding or modifying traceability relations can be done semi-automatically by in-teracting with engineers. Each of the key parts in Figure 3 is described in the subsequent subsections.

BUILDING DOMAIN-SPECIFIC MODELS

The ability to define new modeling languages for specific domains of interest is a key advantage of MDE over general-purpose modeling languages that are fixed on a specific notation (e.g., UML). Domain-specific models for MDE are built from three main steps:

1. **Analyze the domain**. To better understand the requirements and needs for a specific modeling language, engineers should conduct domain analysis to recognize the usage scenarios and concepts that need to be expressed in a new modeling language. In this step, engineers define the exact scope of the domain model and clarify the intended use of the modeling tool, often through experts who would be users of the modeling language.

Figure 4. A sample Design Structure Matrix (DSM)

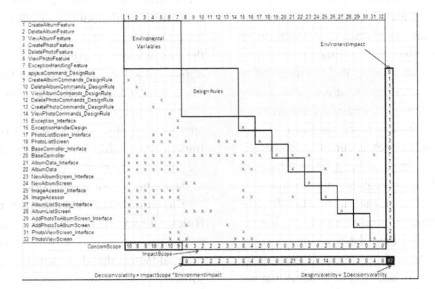

2. **Define a metamodel for the domain**. After understanding the domain and the needs of a modeling language for that domain, engineers then define a metamodel formally. The metamodel itself is specified using the language of a meta-metamodel, such as MOF (OMG MOF, 2006).

3. **Build a domain-specific modeling tool**. Many meta-configurable modeling tools can generate a new modeling environment from a metamodel, such as GME (GME, 2010) and MetaEdit+ (MetaEdit+, 2010). However, engineers must consider the integration of domain-specific modeling tools with the existing development environment before adopting a new modeling language.

As shown in Figure 4, at least six models (i.e., feature model, design model, implementation model, test model, impact analysis model, and trace model) are required to analyze the impacts of potential changes. However, the number of models that need to be considered during impact analysis may vary depending on the objective of the impact analysis. For example, if the primary interest is on the impact of test cases from potential changes, the only analysis that is needed involves the actual change request and the candidate test cases that are affected by the request.

The first step of our approach is to model all the variations of a software product line by using a DSML. Each modeling language has a corresponding metamodel that captures the essence of the domain. It may be possible to use several different general-purpose modeling tools and DSMLs. However, they should provide sufficient APIs to integrate with each other. Particularly, to support a software product line, the available tools may have capabilities to capture the common and variable properties that are required to analyze the impact of changes across the lifecycle (e.g., from the very beginning of the development to the deployment of the project) or versioning its model evolution.

The second step is to construct an infrastructure for the impact analysis (e.g., traceability relation) between each model. Although the traceability relation allows traversing bi-directionally, the traceability relation is actually intended to point artifacts from the subsequent development phase to its precedent. For instance, traceability relations between requirements and domain model elements are created so that each domain model element can point to its relevant requirements. Engineers must generate the initial traceability relation by indicating the source and destination of a relation manually from a tool called the traceability relation manager. After the initial traceability relations are established, engineers can manage the traceability links in a semi-automated way based on the metamodel designed for a specific software product line. If a change is introduced in one of the models, a traceability relation manager queries and gathers relevant information for this change to construct an infrastructure for the impact analysis (e.g., traceability relation). This procedure may be guided through the impacted artifacts by highlighting unmatched model elements that are missing traceability relations or have suspiciously matched model elements (i.e., the impact changes of model elements must be examined for those that have an indirect traceability relation).

The third step is to analyze impact and design tests based on constraints. This step is described in the next section and can be performed automatically by referring to traceability relations.

CONSTRAINT-BASED IMPACT ANALYSIS & DESIGN TESTING

After establishing traceability relations within a domain-specific model, our approach further transforms the model into an augmented constraint network(ACN) that represents the assumptions and constraints from different perspectives embedded in heterogeneous software artifacts. A design testing framework (Cai et al., 2007) is similar to program testing, but considers the envisioned changes as test inputs. This testing framework uses ACN as a computational core and the test output is a set of quantitative modularity metric values, such as the volatility (Sethi et al., 2009) of the resulting design under given changes. To assess how each alternative impacts the modular structure of the product family, designers can test

these alternatives under the same changes and compare these alternatives based on the computed metric values. In this section, we first introduce the concept of *environmental parameters* and *design rules* that form the basis of our approach. Then we introduce the ACN that formalizes these concepts and forms the computational core of the approach. Finally, we describe the design testing framework, as shown in Figure 5. In particular, we introduce the modularity metrics that are used as the output of our framework.

Environmental Parameters and Design Rules. Sullivan et al. (2001) introduced Environmental Parameters into software models to capture external factors that drive software changes. In a software product line, features are one kind of environmental factor because features drive changes to the product line and are usually not controlled by the designers. According to Baldwin & Clark (2000), a design rule is a stable decision that decouples otherwise coupled decisions and thus creates independent modules. A module is independent if it depends only on design rules, but not on other independent modules. For example, MobileMedia adopts the model-view-controller (MVC) architecture, in which the view (user interface) components and controller components use the Java Command API as the communication framework so that the UI components are decoupled from the controllers. Accordingly, the Java Command API is a design rule. Design rules are the most important architectural decisions that frame the modular structure of the design and influence its stability.

Given a software design, our design testing framework tests its modularity variation under a changing environment. To compare two design alternatives, we test them against the same set of environmental parameters to see which alternative generates the least impact on the original design, and which one produces the best modularized and most stable structure, determined by their design rules. Uniformly modeling environmental and design variables is the first step toward automated

Figure 5. A design testing framework

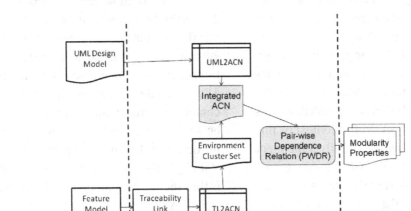

design testing. Next, we introduce such a modeling technique.

Augmented Constraint Network. Cai (2006) developed the ACN as a logic-based design modeling technique, which consists of a set of variables that can model any dimension of software, including environmental conditions and design rules. A variable with a given value models a concrete decision or condition in a dimension. Their relations are modeled as logical constraints. An ACN also includes a dominance relation (DR) that formalizes the notion of a design rule - the asymmetric dependencies among design decisions, and a cluster set (CS) in which each cluster models one way a design can be aggregated. In the rest of the chapter, we refer to an external condition as a concern variable or environmental variable, and interchangeably refer to a design decision as a decision, design variable, or variable.

ACN entails a paradigm-agnostic means to compute modularity properties of a design, and precisely defines a pair-wise dependence relation (PWDR) among design decisions: if a decision y depends on x, that is, $(x, y) \in$ PWDR, then there must exist a consistent state of the ACN. Changing the value of x violates some constraints and makes the constraint network inconsistent, and the value of y needs to be changed in a way that restores consistency.

From an ACN, a Design Structure Matrix (DSM) (Baldwin & Clark, 2000) can be automatically generated to visualize the modular structure of an application. A DSM is a square matrix in which the columns and rows are labeled with design variables, and a marked cell is used to model that the decision on the row depends on the decision on the column. Figure 4 depicts a DSM that models one release of MobileMedia. The blocks along the diagonal represent the modules in the system. All the DSMs shown in this chapter are automatically derived from ACNs. The first block includes seven variables and denotes the features in this release as environmental conditions. The second block contains the design rules of the architecture. The rest of the blocks represent the components. We uniformly represent environmental conditions, design rules, and other design decisions as an ACN, which we then solve to generate pair-wise dependency relations that capture the modular structure of the design. Next, we assess change impact with a design testing framework.

A Design Testing Framework. Figure 5 illustrates our design testing framework. The test input consists of two parts: a software design, which can be represented using prevailing design models (such as a UML class diagram, domain-specific model, or a component diagram) and the environment that this design is embedded, such as requirements and features. In the context of this chapter, a software design is a UML component diagram representing a software product line, and its environment is represented as a feature model. The output of the testing framework is a modularity property measured against a set of software modularity and stability metrics. Within the framework, we translate the design model into an ACN (UML2ACN) (Wong & Cai, 2009, Sethi et al., 2009) that contains only design decisions. Given the feature model, we establish a traceability relation, which we also translate into an ACN that represents the environmental parameters of the design (TL2ACN). We use a variable to represent each feature and use a constraint to model the assumption between a feature and the components that implement it. We integrate these two ACNs into one ACN (Integrated ACN), from which we generate a PWDR and calculate the modularity and stability metric values. In this section, we mainly introduce the stability and modularity metrics (Sethi et al., 2009) whose values are the output of our framework.

Design Stability Metrics. Software stability is usually measured based on how software components depend on each other syntactically, such as the number of classes outside a package that depend on classes within the package. However, it is possible that some part of the system is highly coupled, but is not subject to any environmental changes. As a result, the design could have a low stability value, but in reality, is highly stable. We thus use a DecisionVolatiltiy metric to measure the stability of a design decision, x, and a DesignVolatility metric to measure the stability of the whole design.

As introduced in our prior work (Sethi et al., 2009), the DecisionVolatiltiy metric assesses the stability of a decision in terms of the number of environmental conditions that influence it (EnvrImpact) and its own impact scope (ImpactScope). The rationale is that the more environmental conditions influencing x, the more likely x will be subject to change; the more decisions x can influence, and the more impact x will have on the stability of the whole design. The DesignVolatility is thus the summation of all individual DecisionVolatiltiy values. We chose these metrics because in model-driven systems, features and domain requirements are usually explicit and integrated with the underlying design and implementation models, and these stability metrics directly measure the impact of these environmental conditions, unlike other prevailing coupling and cohesion based metrics.

Figure 4 shows the MobileMedia DSM in which variables are clustered into environment, design rule, and component blocks (shown as blocks consisting of two variables). This DSM visually shows how the volatility metrics can be calculated from the PWDR relation; the numbers in the column to the right of the DSM are the total number of environmental variables that influence the variable on the corresponding row. The numbers in the row next to the last row of the DSM are the impact scope of the variable on the column. The numbers further below are the DecisionVolatility value of each variable, which sums to the DesignVolatility value shown in the cell with dark background and white text. From the DecisionVolatility values, we identify the most unstable variable.

In this case, AlbumData_Interface seems to be the most volatile decision (DecisionVolatility=21). Although it influences only three other variables, it turned out to be heavily influenced by multiple environmental conditions. This observation is confirmed by MobileMedia designers: whenever a feature is added, deleted or changed, the data set that needed to be accessed has to be changed, hence a change in the AlbumData_Interface. It is important to note that, for the sake of simplicity, the Volatility metrics count only the number of environment variables that impact design decisions. They do not model how likely these environmental conditions will change. It is possible that a design variable suffers impact from many environmental conditions, but none of them will change. As a result, the variable may have a very high volatility value measured by the analysis but be highly stable in reality. The volatility metrics can be extended with the probability of change for each environmental condition. We can then use the extended metrics to conduct sensitivity analysis to assess design stability under uncertainty.

Independence Level (IL) metric. The key property of a modular structure is to allow tasks to be accomplished in parallel and independently. According to Baldwin & Clark (2000), a module generates value in the form of options: "a module creates an option to invest in a search for a superior replacement and to replace the currently selected module with the best alternative discovered, or to keep the current one if it is still the best choice." Intuitively, the more independent modules there are in an architecture, the higher the option values that can be generated. Prevailing models, however, use classes, aspects, or components as modules, which are usually not independent. To explicitly measure how a system supports independent task assignments and option generation, we chose an Independence Level (IL) metric introduced in our recent work (Sethi et al. 2009, Wong et al. 2009) to measure design modularity.

The IL metric quantifies the extent to which a design can support module-wise independent searching and replacement; that is, its ability to generate option values. Baldwin and Clark's net option valuation (NOV) statistically accounts for the options value embedded in a software structure, requiring the user to estimate a number of economic parameters based on software modular structure, such as the technical potential and cost of each module. We identify independent modules

from an architecture as the first step towards more sophisticated option value reasoning.

To identify independent modules, we first cluster the variables in the PWDR generated from the ACN into a design rule hierarchy (DRH) using our previous algorithm (Wong et al., 2009). Figure 6 shows a DSM clustered into a DRH from the DSM shown in Figure 4. The DSM shows a hierarchy with three layers. The lower-right block (white background) contains independent modules that depend on the layers preceding them. The variables in cluster "Level1" contain decisions that only make assumptions about the decisions in cluster "Level0" and influence the decisions in the lower-right block. Moreover, once the decisions in Level0 are made, the clusters of decisions in Level1 can be made independently and concurrently. The only truly independent modules are the clusters in the lower-right block. All other variables are environmental parameters or design rules that make these modules independent from each other.

Clustering a DSM into a design rule hierarchy reveals several modularity properties. In Figure 6, the cells show that a number of dependencies are clustered. For example, there are 33 decisions in Level1 that depend on decisions in Level0. The DSM thus shows the impact scope of each variable and each level. In addition, because only the modules in the last level are independent, the more variables in the last level, the larger part of the

Figure 6. A DSM that is clustered into a Design Rule Hierarchy

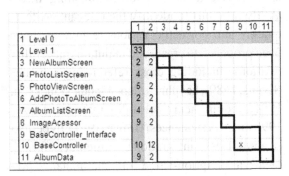

system can be freely swapped or evolved under stable design rules, and the better the design is modularized. We thus define a simplified option-oriented Independence Level metric as the percentage of the variables falling into the last level of the design rule hierarchy. For example, the Independence Level of the MobileMedia design is 0.28, meaning that about 28% of the Mobile-Media design is independent and can effectively generate option value.

Another stability metric that we consider is change impact. Similar to a conventional change impact metric that quantifies changes in code, this metric quantifies modified elements in an ACN model to analyze, for instance, the satisfaction of pivotal design principles, such as the open-closed principle (i.e., software is open to extension, but closed to modification) (Meyer, 2000). By comparing the number of variables that are added, removed, or changed in two ACNs that model consecutive design releases, we can easily calculate the number of variables that are added, removed, and changed.

ESTABLISHING TRACEABILITY RELATIONS

Impacts are analyzed based on traceability relations, which link heterogeneous artifacts that are developed in different lifecycle stages. The variety of artifacts makes it difficult to create the traceability relations correctly and consistently. Thus, one of the key parts of the impact analysis is to devise a method for establishing traceability relations to identify the relevant artifacts quickly and correctly. Various techniques have been proposed to create and maintain traceability relations, including cross referencing schemes (Evans, 1989), keyphrase dependencies (Jackson, 1991), requirement traceability matrices (Davis, 1990), matrix sequences (Brown, 1991), hypertext (Kaindl, 1991), integration documents (Lefering, 1993), assumption-based truth maintenance net-

works (Smithers et al., 1991), constraint networks (Bowen et al., 1990).

Some practitioners (Alves-Foss et al., 2002; Maletic et al., 2005) have adopted XML to represent traceability relations. As XML is platform-independent and vendor-independent, it is frequently used to exchange messages between heterogeneous systems; store, retrieve, and process documentation; manage information, and configure system environments. For example, most commercial and open source software design tools (e.g., IBM Rational Rose, IBM Rational Rhapsody, ArgoUML, SysML, and MagicDraw UML) adopted XML as the representation medium for storing design models and configuring tool options. In addition to XML, the World Wide Web Consortium proposed three language derivatives from XML: XLink (XLink, 2001), XPath (XPath, 1999), and XPointer (XPointer, 2002). These languages allow traceability relations to be embedded into models and other specifications (e.g., source code and test cases).

XLink is the XML link language that was designed to be used in many domains that need to link software applications. XLink defines a link through universal resource identifiers and it allows XML documents to assert linking relationships among more than two resources, associate metadata with a link, and express links that reside in a location separated from the linked resources. XPath is the XML Path language, which is a query language that uses navigation path expressions to select nodes or node-sets in an XML document. XPointer is the XML Pointer language, which is used as a basis for fragment identifiers for any resource whose type is encoded according to the XML standard. Because most models used in our approach adopt XML to represent the information needed for impact analysis across software artifacts, we use XLink and other XML language derivatives to specify the features needed for traceability relations. Listing 1 shows the part of an XML document type definition (DTD) that defines the traceability relations between a

Listing 1. Example of a Traceability Relation Between a Feature Model and Class Diagram

```
<?xml version="1.0" encoding="UTF-8" standalone="no"?>
<link-from-class-to-feature>
<!--Comment-->
<Files SourceFile="MobileMedia.dia"
      TargetFile="MobileMedia.fm"/>
<link desc="Link from AlbumListScrren to Create photo album"
      source_name="AlbumListScrren"
      source_path="/dia:diagram/dia:layer/dia:object[@type='UML - Class'][1]"
      target_name="Create photo album"
      target_path="//RealRoot/ModelContainer4Man"
      relation = "Refined"/>
<link desc="Link from AddPhotoToAlbum to Add photo"
      source_name="addPhotoToAlbum"
      source_path="/dia:diagram/dia:layer/dia:object[@type='UML - Class'][3]"
      target_name="Add photo"
      target_path="//RealRoot/ModelContainer4Man"
      relation = "Refined"/>
<link desc="Link from PhotoViewScreen to Delete photo album"
      source_name="PhotoViewScreen"
      source_path="/dia:diagram/dia:layer/dia:object[@type='UML - Class'][6]"
      target_name="View photo"
      target_path="//RealRoot/ModelContainer4Man"
      relation = "Refined"/>
</link-from-class-to-feature>
```

feature model and class diagram. Each relation is generated automatically by using the traceability relation manager. The types of links are described as XML tags in the form "link-from-<source>-to-<target>". For example, Listing 1 describes link information from a class diagram to a feature model, such that the link type is specified as "<link-from-class-to-feature>" in the second line.

CASE STUDY: MODEL-DRIVEN IMPACT ANALYSIS OF A MOBILE MEDIAL SPL

This section introduces a case study that demonstrates the application of model-driven impact analysis to an example software product line in the domain of Mobile Media (Young, 2005), which represents multimedia software that supports several different mobile phones (e.g., Android, iPhone, and Blackberry). The products used in the case study demonstrate various combinational features according to a customer's requirements and the device's hardware constraints. In particular, the case study explores the use of these devices in a collaborative environment where new requirements and features become necessary. The product is thus subject to a number of heterogeneous changes, including enhancing the core architecture, or adding a new application to the product family. A key part of the case study is the demonstration of how various models are

Table 2. Capabilities of the MobileMedia Product Line. Adapted from (Young, 2005;Figuerideo et al., 2008; Huynh et al., 2008)

Type	Feature	Brief description	Constraints	R1	R3	R4	R5	R6	R7	R8
Mandatory	Create media folder	Create new media folder to categorize media to be added		P					M	V
	Add media	Add photo, video, or music to the file system		P					M	V
	Delete media	Delete photo, video, or music from the file system permanently		P					M	V
	Label media	Label photo, video, or music with text for search purposes			P				M	V
	View/Play media	Display a selected photo on the device screen; or, play video or music	Photo: View Video/Music: Play	P					M	V
Optional	Send media	Send media to others by transmission method	Predefined the transmission method					I	M	
	Specify favorite photos	Associate contact list with a photo in the device file system				I				
	Sort media	Sort media by preference			P				M	
	Keep multiple copies of photos						I			
Alternative	Caller Identification	*Display photo for incoming call*: Display caller's photo if caller's photo is linked with address book entry	Link between photo and address book							
		Play melody for incoming call: Play customized ring tone per caller	Link between music and address book							

used to analyze the impact of changes, and how to use the design testing framework to select and assess the optimal candidates.

MobileMedia is an evolved version of MobilePhoto that was developed at the University of British Columbia (Figuerido et al., 2008). It is designed to support different software product lines for various phone vendors (e.g., Apple, RIM, Motorola, and Nokia) and exploits both object-oriented and aspect-oriented techniques. MobileMedia can handle photo, video, and music data on mobile devices, such as cellular phones. Throughout its evolution, MobileMedia was released through eight different versions of design and implementation. Each version added some new functionality or restructured the previous version

to achieve an improved modularized structure. In some versions, feature types were changed from mandatory to alternative.

Release 1 of MobileMedia was the core design that only included photo-related functions, such as adding or deleting photos and photo albums. Release 2 added exception handling as a mandatory feature. Release 3 added photo labeling as a mandatory feature and photo sorting as an optional feature. Releases 4, 5, and 6 each added an optional feature, such as specifying favorite photos. Release 7 involved changing the mandatory characteristic of photo manipulations to become an alternative feature, and adding another alternative feature, music manipulation. The final release added another alternative feature that provided

Table 3. Domain Technologies of MobileMedia

Type	Feature	Brief description	Constraints
Optional	Media types	Specify media type to be used in the system, such as Photo, Video, and Music	At least one media type should be selected

Table 4. Operational Environments of MobileMedia

Type	Feature	Brief description
Alternative	MIDP	MobileMedia supports version 1 or 2 of the Mobile Information Device Profile (MIDP)
Alternative	Phone Library	Each cellular phone manufacturer provides their own phone library. MobileMedia can be operated on devices from RIM (Blackberry), Motorola, and Nokia.
Alternative	Transmission Method	Transmission method describes the way to send media (e.g., photo, video, or music) to other users. The media can be sent by either SMS or Email.

Table 5. Implementation Technologies of MobileMedia

Type	Feature	Brief description
Alternative	Design Pattern	Some common design patterns (e.g., Chain of Responsibility) are used to handle feature-specific actions by each feature.
Alternative	Thread Management	A controller uses threads to provide the services in the background to avoid resource contention issues from incoming phone calls or external events
Alternative	File Management	File management is implemented based on J2ME's Record Management System (RMS) and manages all activities of storing and retrieving media content
Mandatory	Exception Handling	Manages exceptions such as invalid file path, image format, and name of album; Implemented at Release 2

the capability to manipulate video. The evolution of MobileMedia features is summarized in Table 2. P, M, and V represent the media type of each release: photo, music, and video, respectively. Because the primary change request of Release 2 was focused on exception handling features, R2 is not shown in the above table.

In addition to Table 2, which shows the capability features of MobileMedia and the changes at each release, Table 3 through Table 5 capture additional domain information. Table 3 describes the media types and the related technologies that are key domain technologies for the MobileMedia system. Table 4 lists the operational environment of MobileMedia. Because MobileMedia executes on a mobile phone, it is largely affected by the mobile manufacture's development environments,

such as a mobile phone library or the Mobile Information Device toolkit (Topley, 2002). Table 5 describes technologies that were used to implement MobileMedia. As MobileMedia was developed using Java and should support multitasking, the implementation of design patterns and thread management are important factors for implementation. However, Young (2005) classified features without a proper range of development decisions (i.e., the features were described only operationally in the sense of system capabilities). We found that this incomplete classification leads to missing traceability relations between feature models and class diagrams. For example, MobileMedia was designed and implemented to use a threading mechanism to avoid resource contention issues between device display and incoming phone calls.

However, the designed thread mechanism cannot be linked to its feature model because the original work considered only capability features. Thus, we employed a layered approach proposed by Young (2005) and recovered missing features through the traceability relations that we added.

BUILDING DOMAIN-SPECIFIC MODELS FOR MOBILE MEDIA SPL

To construct the foundation for model-driven impact analysis, we defined three different metamodels that represent languages for specifying feature models, traceability relations, and ACN. The metamodel for the feature model and an example instance model were shown in Figure 1 and Figure 2 in the previous Model-Driven Engineering section. For this case study, we used the Generic Eclipse Modeling System (GEMS) to define the various modeling languages and their instances (White & Schmidt, 2005).

Five entities and connections are defined for the metamodel for a traceability relation language. LinkModel is an entity that serves as a functioning container; this entity is not shown explicitly in a traceability relation instance. Both DesignModelSrc and DesignModelDst represent source and destination design elements for relations, respectively. The two models are linked by the relationship Refined. Unlike the refinement relationship in UML, the refinement relationship for a traceability relation is bi-directional. Thus, UML models can serve as the sources for a traceability relation with a feature model as the destination. In addition, other entities such as implementation, test cases, and test reports are defined to represent the key development artifacts within the impact analysis process. The relationships between entities are modeled through one of the named relations: Realized, Verified, Validated, and Tested. An instance of a traceability relation is shown in Listing 1. As discussed earlier, this figure illustrates the traceability relations between a feature model and a UML class diagram. Each traceability relation has a Refined relationship.

An additional metamodel is defined to represent a language for specifying ACN models. Such models can serve as an input model for impact analysis. The ACN metamodel can assist in guiding the transformation of a traceability relation into an instance representing an ACN. The ACN metamodel introduces inheritance to analyze the impact from the variations among features, design, or implementation. In an ACN, all model elements are generalized as a component with a body and an interface. Components are related to each other by a dominant relationship according to the vulnerability of the design or implementation changes. For example, interfaces dominate implementations. Normally, the decisions informing an interface change the way a component is implemented, but changes in an implementation may not force modifications to an interface.

Listing 2 shows part of an ACN instance that is based on the metamodel of ACN. This textual representation of the ACN instance corresponds to the input that is used by the ACN tool, and is generated from a model. The first three sections of the ACN representation are derived from an existing feature model or UML model. In an ACN, feature models are specified as variables and UML components are specified as two separate implementation and interface variables. The suffixes _impl and _interface represent an implementation body and an interface of a component, respectively. Each implementation or interface as a design dimension where decisions will be made, we abstractly model each dimension as having at least two possible decisions, one that is currently known and the other that is unknown, representing future changes. Accordingly, we model each variable as having two values, *orig* and *other.* In order to assess change impact, we care only that a decision will change, but do not care about *what* the decision is describing.

The fourth section models the constraint network for an ACN component. The constraints

Listing 2. An Example ACN Model (excerpt from MobileMedia ACN Model)

```
DesignSpace MobileMedia
{
//Section 1:
//ACN Component models which are derived from a UML Class diagram
    AddPhotoToAlbum_impl: {other,orig};
    AddPhotoToAlbum_interface: {other,orig};
    AlbumData_impl: {other,orig};
    AlbumData_interface: {other,orig};
//Section 2:
//ACN Component models which are derived from a feature model
    AlbumListScreen: {other,orig};
    AddPhotoToAlbum: {other,orig};
    PhotoListScreen: {other,orig};
    PhotoViewScreen: {other,orig};
//Section 3:
//ACN Component models for design rule
    ViewAlbumCommands_DesignRule: {other,orig};
    CreatePhotoCommands_DesignRule: {other,orig};
    DeletePhotoCommands_DesignRule: {other,orig};
    DeleteAlbumCommands_DesignRule: {other,orig};
    CreateAlbumCommands_DesignRule: {other,orig};
//Section 4:
//Constraint Network model derived from Class relationships
    AddPhotoToAlbum_impl = orig => AddPhotoToAlbum_interface = orig;
    AlbumData_impl = orig => ImageAccessor_interface = orig;
    ImageData_interface = orig => ViewAlbumFeature = orig;
    AlbumData_interface = orig => ViewAlbumFeature = orig;
//Section 5:
//Dominant relationship between classes
    [AddPhotoToAlbum _impl, AddPhotoToAlbum _interface];
    [AlbumData_impl, AlbumData_interface];
    [PhotoViewScreen_impl, Constants_interface];
//Section 6:
//Dominant relationship between feature and design rule
    [AlbumListScreen, ViewAlbumCommands_DesignRule];
    [AddPhotoToAlbum, CreatePhotoCommands_DesignRule];
    [PhotoListScreen, CreatePhotoCommands_DesignRule];
};
```

model the assumption relation between decisions. Instead of modeling the concrete states of each component and their relations, we abstractly model the fact that in any design, decisions are made for each component and other components make assumptions about these known decisions. For example, the first constraint in Section 4 models that the implementation decision on AddPhotoToAlbum is based on the assumption that AddPhotoToAlbum's interface is as originally agreed. Finally, the last two sections specify the dominant relationship between ACN model elements, showing that the decisions on interfaces dominate implementation decisions and that the design rule decisions dominate other non-design rule decisions.

The metamodels representing traceability and ACN were not created to build modeling tools, but to assist in the transformation between the representations used to capture traceability and analysis information. For example, when a traceability relation and other models (e.g., a feature model or class diagram) are transformed, their representations are parsed by referring to their metamodels. The transformation assists in generating the ACN model, which conforms to its own metamodel.

CONSTRAINT-BASED IMPACT ANALYSIS FOR MOBILE MEDIA EVOLUTION

To illustrate how to perform impact analysis using the various modeling languages described in this section, assume that there have been two previous releases of the MobileMedia product line and a set of change requests have emerged for the next release (e.g., counting the number of times a photo has been viewed, sorting photos by viewing frequency, or editing the photo's label). To analyze the impact of these change requests, a temporary feature model and a set of design models can be used to define a traceability relation between the anticipated changes. Two possible candidate designs are illustrated in Figure 7, which are refined from a temporary feature model. Both candidate designs have two common design decisions: (1) modifying the PhotoListScreen class to provide a sorted view that is based on the number of times a photo has been viewed and (2) introducing the NewLabelScreen class for editing the photo label. Each candidate design represents different approaches for managing the photo count and editing the photo label.

In design (a) of Figure 7, PhotoViewScreen has extended its functionalities as a controller to address new counting and editing of photo information. PhotoViewScreen manages the new changes by controlling the collaborations of two new classes, CountPhotoView and NewLabelScreen. In addition, PhotoListScreen references the view count information in CountPhotoView to display photos by its view preference. In design (b), the ImageUtil class was modified to manage the number of photo views by extending an attribute of each photo. Also, PhotoViewScreen was modified to count the number of photo views and pass the count information to the ImageUtil class. For editing the photo label, two new classes (PhotoController and NewLabelScreen) were designed.

When candidate designs are stable, the impact analysis of the new designs can commence by generating an ACN model using two tools (called UML2ACN and TL2ACN), which generate an ACN model from either a UML class diagram or a traceability relation model, respectively. The usage of such tools can be observed in the impact analysis process shown in Figure 5. The generated ACN model is then transformed into a DSM.

The DSM for this case study, as shown in Figure 8, provides information about the stability and modularity of the design, as well as illustrating the graphical design dependency. The Overall Design Volatility and the Decision Volatility measure the stability of the design, and the Independence Level for Design measures the modularity.

Figure 7. Candidate Designs for Release 3

a) Candidate design based on collaboration controller

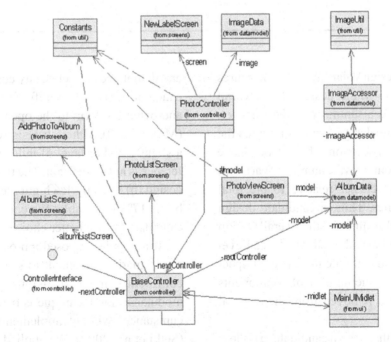

b) Candidate design based on attribute extension

Figure 8. Result of Impact Analysis for Candidate Design (a)

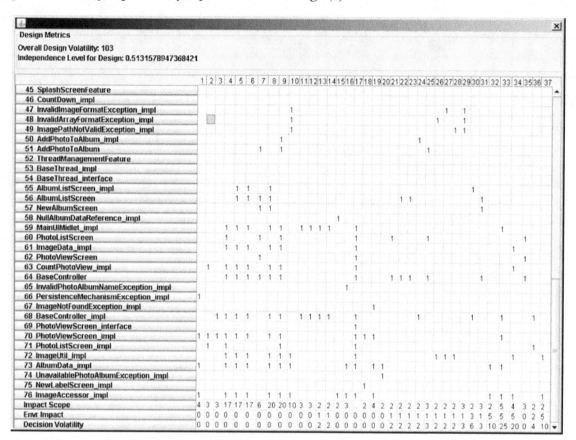

The Overall Design Volatility metric measures the stability of the whole design. The Overall Design Volatility is a summary of the Decision Volatility across the design, which measures the stability of a design decision. The Independence Level for Design computes the number of variables in an independent cluster relative to the total number of variables. Thus, a candidate design should be designed to minimize the Overall Design Volatility and maximize the Independence Level for Design. We also compute the change impact analysis in terms of the number of components added, deleted, and removed from the original design.

Table 6 shows that design candidate (a) is less volatile to change requests than design (b). In addition, although these two alternatives require adding the same number of new components and do not need to delete any component, design candidate (a) will modify fewer components, and better conform to the open-closed principle (Meyer, 2000). Although design candidate (b) has a slightly higher level of independence, the difference is not significant. The tradeoff shows that design (b) has only 1% higher level of flexibility but is 17% less stable. We conclude that design candidate (a) is a better choice.

To assess the proposed approach, we performed a systematic assessment to see if designers can confidently make decisions, such as which modularization technique is better in which circumstances without implementing the systems (Sethi et al., 2009). We applied the metrics to a series of releases of a software product line for MobileMedia. Both aspect-oriented (AO) and object-oriented (OO) editions of MobileMedia

Table 6. Summary of Impact Analysis for Candidate Designs

	Design (a)	Design (b)
Overall Design Volatility	103	121
Independence Level for Design	0.51	0.52
Components added	2	2
Components modified	3	6
Components deleted	0	0

were used and compared. Modularity and stability were key requirements in both editions, which underwent changes through 8 releases. UML component diagrams were available for all the AO and OO releases. Key external factors, the features driving new releases, were documented and considered. Their stability and modularity properties were computed based on the automatically generated ACN models and the proposed metrics.

Finally, we compared the findings obtained from our assessment with the conclusions obtained from in-depth analyses previously made from the source code (Figuerido et al., 2008). Our purpose was to compare the conclusions leading to decisions. The results showed that our approach reached highly consistent conclusions against that of implementation-level analysis. Moreover, the small numbers of discrepancies reveal issues in previously conducted implementation-level analysis. For example, our approach automatically detected several indirect dependencies between external concerns and internal components that were not picked up by source code analysis. These new metrics also led to new insights, e.g., showing how the superior option-generation ability observed in AO decomposition is paired with its lower stability. These positive results imply the possibility of faithfully assessing software stability and modularity at the level of higher-level models without the cost of implementation.

FUTURE RESEARCH DIRECTIONS

There are several remaining challenges and limitations that suggest areas for future work. The metrics that we presented in this chapter are focused on design issues. It would be a useful goal to increase the connection between design metrics and source code metrics as an effort to improve the transition between lifecycle phases as related to analysis of predictive change. Combining the results from a suite of metrics across the lifecycle may improve the ability to predict the overall cost of change and its effect on the project schedule. Many new areas of research can be investigated in this area of combining lifecycle metrics. An additional area for future work that we will soon explore is the extension of the functionality of the traceability relation to provide more query-specific opportunities (e.g., to enable the designer to issue queries based on suspicions that their own intuition suggests about a particular design and a set of change requests). Such query-specific traceability relations could assist in finding the depth of a link or a related attribute that appears in a trace.

CONCLUSION

This chapter introduced our approach for analyzing the impact of changes to software product lines (SPLs) through model-driven engineering. Software changes are a natural and inevitable part of a product line's lifecycle, similar to single product development. However, impact analysis for SPLs is more complex and difficult than that of a single product development because software changes for SPLs can occur at any level of the system domain (e.g., either problem domain or application domain), and the impacts of these changes are propagated to the other domain. Thus, the support of automated tools and systematic assessment of candidate changes is highly necessary to produce impact analysis results that can be used to inform important decisions about software evolution. Our approach offers several benefits for domain analysis by exploiting domain-specific modeling languages and a systematic design testing framework for impact analysis. The domain-specific modeling languages help to identify and specify a domain's characteristics, which consist of a number of different constraint sets, with graphical notations and make it possible to lift the abstraction and representation of a software change such that it can be analyzed and separated from specific platform and environment details that would exist at the implementation level. Traceability relations make it possible to detect and query multiple options for changes and multiple constraints from different stakeholders and users of the product line. By utilizing XML, a traceability relation can have a foundation to resolve the structural abstraction mismatch at different stages of the software development lifecycle. Thus, traceability relations can provide a streamlined foundation for domain analysis and it can reduce the effort to find relevant information across the domains for changes. In addition, a traceability relation provides information to generate constraint information, environmental parameters, and design rules, automatically for impact analysis. The results of constraint-based impact analysis provide guidance on which change option has significant consequences by analyzing multiple candidate options.

ACKNOWLEDGMENT

This work is supported in part by NSF CAREER award CCF-1052616 and CCF-1052616, and NSF grants CCF-0916891 and DUE-0837665.

REFERENCES

Ajila, S. (1995). Software Maintenance: An approach to impact analysis of object changes. *Software, Practice & Experience*, 25(10), 1155–1181. doi:10.1002/spe.4380251006

Alves-Foss, F., de Leon, D., & Oman, P. (2002). Experiments in the use of XML to enhance traceability between object-oriented design specifications and source code. *Hawaiian International Conference on System Sciences*, Big Island, HI, (pp. 3959-3966).

Anquetil, N., Grammel, B., & da Silva, I. Noppen, J.A.R. Khan, S., Arboleda, H., Rashid, A., & Garcia, A. (2008). Traceability for model-driven, software product line engineering. *ECMDA Traceability Workshop*, Berlin, Germany, (pp. 77-86).

Arnold, R. S., & Bohner, S. A. (1993). Impact Analysis: Towards a framework for comparison. *International Conference on Software Maintenance*, Montreal, Canada, (pp. 292-301).

Baldwin, C. Y., & Clark, K. B. (2000). Design Rules: *Vol. 1. The Power of Modularity*. Cambridge, MA: MIT Press.

Bayer, J., Flege, O., Knauber, P., Laqua, R., Muthig, D., Schmid, K., et al. (1999). PuLSE: A methodology to develop software product lines. *Symposium on Software Reusability*, Los Angeles, CA, (pp. 122-131).

Bohner, S. A. (2002). Software Change Impacts: An evolving perspective. *International Conference on Software Maintenance*, Montreal, Canada, (pp. 263-271).

Bowen, J., O'Grady, P., & Smith, L. (1990). A constraint programming language for lifecycle engineering. *Artificial Intelligence in Engineering*, 5(4), 206–220. doi:10.1016/0954-1810(90)90022-V

Briand, L. C., Labiche, Y., O'Sullivan, L., & Sówka, M. M. (2006). Automated impact analysis of UML models. *Journal of Systems and Software*, 79(3), 339–352. doi:10.1016/j.jss.2005.05.001

Briand, L. C., Labiche, Y., & Soccar, G. (2002). Automating impact analysis and regression test selection based on UML designs. *International Conference on Software Maintenance*, Montreal, Canada, (pp. 252-261).

Brown, P.G. (1991). QFD: Echoing the voice of the customer. *AT&T Technical Journal*, March/April, 21-31.

Buckley, J., Mens, T., Zenger, M., Rashid, A., & Kniesel, G. (2005). Towards a taxonomy of software change. *Journal of Software Maintenance and Evolution: Research and Practice*, *17*(5), 309–332. doi:10.1002/smr.319

Cai, Y. (2006). *Modularity in Design: Formal Modeling and Automated Analysis*. Ph.D. thesis, University of Virginia.

Cai, Y., Huynh, S., & Xie, T. (2007). A framework and tool supports for testing modularity of software design. *International Conference on Automated Software Engineering*, Atlanta, GA, (pp. 441-444).

Cai, Y., & Sullivan, K. (2006). Modularity analysis of logical design models. *International Conference on Automated Software Engineering*, Tokyo, Japan, (pp. 91-102).

Chaplin, N., Hale, J., Khan, K., Ramil, J., & Tan, W. (2001). Types of software evolution and software maintenance. *Journal of Software Maintenance and Evolution: Research and Practice*, *13*(1), 3–30. doi:10.1002/smr.220

Clements, P., & Northrop, L. (2001). *Software Product Lines: Practices and Patterns*. Reading, MA: Addison-Wesley.

Czarnecki, K., & Helsen, S. (2006). Feature-based survey of model transformation approaches. *IBM Systems Journal*, *45*(3), 621–645. doi:10.1147/sj.453.0621

Davis, A. M. (1990). *Software Requirements: Analysis and Specification*. New York: Prentice-Hall, Inc.

De Lucia, A., Fasano, F., & Oliveto, R. (2008). *Traceability management for impact analysis* (pp. 21–30). Beijing, China: Frontiers of Software Maintenance.

Evans, M. W. (1989). *The Software Factory*. Chichester, UK: John Wiley and Sons.

Figueiredo, E., Cacho, N., Sant'Anna, C., Monteiro, M., Kulesza, U., Garcia, A., et al. (2008). Evolving software product lines with aspects: An empirical study on design stability. *International Conference on Software Engineering*, Leipzig, Germany, (pp. 261-270).

Gamma, E., Helm, R., Johnson, R., & Vlissides, J. (1994). *Design Patterns: Elements of Reusable Object-Oriented Software*. Reading, MA: Addison-Wesley.

GME – Generic Modeling Environment. (2010). (Version 10) [Software]. Available from http://www.isis.vanderbilt.edu/Projects/gme/

Gomaa, H., & Hussein, M. (2003). Dynamic software reconfiguration in software product families. *International Workshop on Software Product Family Engineering*, Siena, Itlay, (pp. 435–444).

Gray, J., Tolvanen, J., Kelly, S., Gokhale, A., Neema, S., & Sprinkle, J. (2007). Domain-specific modeling. In *Handbook of Dynamic System Modeling* (pp. 7-1–7-20). Boca Raton, FL: CRC Press. doi:10.1201/9781420010855.pt2

Huynh, S., Cai, Y., Song, Y., & Sullivan, K. (2008). Automatic modularity conformance checking. *International Conference on Software Engineering*, Leipzig, Germany, (pp. 411-420).

IBM Rational DOORS. (2010). [Software]. Available from http://www-01.ibm.com/software/awdtools/doors/

IEEE. 1042. (1987). *IEEE Guide to Software Configuration Management*. IEEE/ANSI Standard 1042-1987.

Jackson, J. (1991). A keyphrase based traceability scheme. *IEE Colloquium on Tools and Techniques for Maintaining Traceability During Design*, London, UK, (pp. 2/1-2/4).

Jönsson, P. (2007). *Exploring Process Aspects of Change Impact Analysis*. Blekinge Institute of Technology Doctoral Dissertation Series. No 2007:13.

Kaindl, H. (1993). The missing link in requirements engineering. *ACM SIGSOFT Software Engineering Notes*, *18*(2), 30–39. doi:10.1145/159420.155836

Kang, K., Cohen, S., Hess, J., Novak, W., & Peterson, A. (1990). *Feature-oriented domain analysis (FODA) feasibility study*. Technical Report CMU/SEI-90-TR-21, Software Engineering Institute, Carnegie Mellon University, Pittsburgh, PA.

Kurtev, I., Bézivin, J., Jouault, F., & Valduriez, P. (2006). *Model-based DSL frameworks*. *Object-Oriented Programming, Systems, Languages, and Applications* (pp. 602–616). Portland, OR: Companion Proceedings.

Lefering, M. (1993). An incremental integration tool between requirements engineering and programming in the large. *International Symposium on Requirements Engineering*, San Diego, CA, (pp. 82-89).

Lehman, M. M., & Belady, L. (1985). *Program evolution: processes of software change*. New York: Academic Press Professional.

Lientz, B. P., & Swanson, E. B. (1980). *Software Maintenance Management: A Study of the Maintenance of Computer Application Software in 487 Data Processing Organizations*. Reading, MA: Addison-Wesley.

Lindvall, M., & Sandahl, K. (1998). How well do experienced software developers predict software change? *Journal of Systems and Software*, *43*(1), 19–27. doi:10.1016/S0164-1212(98)10019-5

Maletic, J. I., Collard, M. L., & Simoes, B. (2005). An XML based approach to support the evolution of model-to-model traceability links. *International Workshop on Traceability in Emerging Forms of Software Engineering*, Long Beach, CA, (pp. 67-72).

McGregor, J. (2005). *The evolution of product-line assets*. Technical Report CMU/SEI-2003-TR-005, Software Engineering Institute, Carnegie Mellon University, Pittsburgh, PA. *MetaEdit+* (2010). [Software]. Available from http://www.metacase.com/

Meyer, B. (2000). *Object-Oriented Software Construction*. New York: Prentice Hall, Inc.

Mitschke, R., & Eichberg, M. (2008). Supporting the evolution of software product lines. *Traceability Workshop*, Berlin, Germany, (pp. 87-96).

MOF 2.0 (2006). *Meta Object Facility*. Retrieved from http://www.omg.org/spec/MOF/2.0/

Pinheiro, F. A., & Goguen, J. A. (1996). An Object-Oriented Tool for Tracing Requirements. *IEEE Software*, *13*(2), 52–64. doi:10.1109/52.506462

Pohjonen, R., & Tolvanen, J.-P. (2002). Automated production of family members: Lessons learned. *OOPSLA Workshop on Product Line Engineering The Early Steps: Planning, Modeling, and Managing*, Seattle, WA.

Schmidt, D. (2006). Model-driven engineering. *Computer*, *39*(2), 25–32. doi:10.1109/MC.2006.58

SEI-CMU. (2010). *Software Product Lines*. Retrieved from http://www.sei.cmu.edu/productlines/

Sethi, K., Cai, Y., Wong, S., Garcia, A., & Sant'Anna, C. (2009). From retrospect to prospect: Assessing modularity and stability from software architecture. *Conference on Software Architecture and European Conference on Software Architecture*, Cambridge, UK, (pp. 269-272).

Smithers, T., Tang, M. X., & Tomes, N. (1991). *The Maintenance of Design History in AI-Based Design*, DAI Research Paper 571, Department of Artificial Intelligence, University of Edinburgh, Scotland.

Toft, P., Coleman, D., & Ohta, J. (2000). HP product generation consulting: A cooperative model for cross-divisional product development for a software product line. *First Conference on Software Product Lines*, Denver, CO, (pp. 111-132).

Tracz, W. (1995). DSSA (Domain-Specific Software Architecture): Pedagogical example. *ACM SIGSOFT Software Engineering Notes*, *20*(3), 49–62. doi:10.1145/219308.219318

Weiss, D., & Lai, C. (1999). *Software Product Line Engineering: A family-based Software Development Process*. Reading, MA: Addison-Wesley.

White, J., & Schmidt, D. (2005). Simplifying the development of product line customization tools via the Generic Eclipse Modeling System. *OOPSLA Eclipse Technology eXchange Workshop*, San Diego, CA.

Wong, S., & Cai, Y. (2009). Predicting change impact from logical models. *International Conference on Software Maintenance*, Edmonton, Canada, (pp. 464-470).

Wong, S., Cai, Y., Valetto, G., Simeonov, G., & Sethi, K. (2009). Design rule hierarchy and task parallelism. *International Conference on Automated Software Engineering*, (pp. 197—208).

XLink. (2001). *XML Linking Language*. Retrieved from http://www.w3.org/TR/xlink/

XPath. (1999). *XML XPath Language*. Retrieved from http://www.w3.org/TR/xpath/

XPointer. (2002). *XML Pointer Language*. Retrieved from http://www.w3.org/TR/xptr/

Young, T. (2005). *Using AspectJ to Build a Software Product Line for Mobile Devices*. Master's thesis, University of British Columbia, Vancouver, Canada.

KEY TERMS AND DEFINITIONS

Model-Driven Engineering: Model-Driven Engineering (MDE) emphasizes the use of models not just for documentation and communication purposes, but as first-class artifacts to be transformed into other work products (e.g., other models, source code, and test scripts).

Impact Analysis: Impact analysis analyzes the range of impact from changes to a software system. The result of impact analysis is used to estimate the cost of such changes.

Traceability Relation: Traceability relation is the basis of impact analysis and informs how development artifacts are related to each other.

Software Product Lines: Software product lines represent a paradigm to develop a series of family products by maximizing the reuse of the commonalities among the software products and customizing variants for specific customers.

Augmented Constraint Network (ACN): Augmented Constraint Network (ACN) is a way to measure modularity of the design, especially measure design volatility under given changes. The metric is formed from the Environmental Parameter and Design Rule.

Environment Parameter: An environment parameter represents factors that drive software changes. For example, changes in interfaces must drive changes in internal design and implementation.

Design Rule: A design rule is another factor that is used to make a software change. Unlike environment parameters, design rules are used to measure the dependency in internal design.

Chapter 14
Systematic Use of Software Development Patterns through a Multilevel and Multistage Classification

Sofia Azevedo
Universidade do Minho, Portugal

Ricardo J. Machado
Universidade do Minho, Portugal

Alexandre Bragança
Instituto Superior de Engenharia do Porto, Portugal

Hugo Ribeiro
Primavera Business Software Solutions, Portugal

ABSTRACT

Software patterns are reusable solutions to problems that occur often throughout the software development process. This chapter formally states which sort of software patterns shall be used in which particular moment of the software development process and in the context of which Software Engineering professionals, technologies and methodologies. The way to do that is to classify those patterns according to the proposed multilevel and multistage pattern classification based on the software development process. The classification is based on the OMG modeling infrastructure or Four-Layer Architecture and also on the RUP (Rational Unified Process). It considers that patterns can be represented at different levels of the OMG modeling infrastructure and that representing patterns as metamodels is a way of turning the decisions on their application more objective. Classifying patterns according to the proposed pattern classification allows for the preservation of the original advantages of those patterns and avoids that the patterns from a specific category are handled by the inadequate professionals, technologies and methodologies. The chapter illustrates the proposed approach with the classification of some patterns.

DOI: 10.4018/978-1-61692-874-2.ch014

INTRODUCTION

In the context of software development, patterns are provided as reusable solutions to recurrent problems. In other words, software patterns are reusable solutions to problems that occur often throughout the software development process. Pattern classifications emerged as a way to organize the many patterns that have been synthesized. *Pattern classification* is the activity of organizing patterns into groups of patterns that share a common set of characteristics. The simple fact of organizing patterns into classifications is a way of building a stronger knowledge on patterns, which allows understanding their purpose, the relations between them and the best moments for their adoption (Gamma, Helm, Johnson, & Vlissides, 1995).

Despite their use within the software development process, the use of patterns may not be systematic. In the context of this chapter, the systematic use of software development patterns means that decisions on the application of patterns are less subjective and more objective. Besides that, a lot of pattern classifications were conceived until the present day, yet none of them formally stated which sort of patterns shall be used in which particular moment of the software development process. This chapter will provide for specific directives on how to systematically adopt patterns within a multilevel and multistage software development process. A multilevel and multistage classification of patterns will be the foundation of such systematic use of patterns.

A multistage software development process can be defined as a software development process composed of some stages organized in a consecutive temporal order. Each stage is separated from the contiguous ones by well defined borders. Moreover each particular stage is composed of a flow of well defined activities. Each stage's activities are conducted by specific professionals, using specific technologies (frameworks, languages, tools), under the directives of specific methodologies (processes, notations and methods) to achieve specific goals. Borders are well defined if the shift in the professionals, technologies, methodologies and goals that takes place when moving from one stage to another is identified in terms of the development process. A multilevel software development process can be defined as a software development process concerned with the levels of abstraction in which the different artifacts involved in the development of software are handled. In the context of this chapter, those levels are the levels of the OMG (OMG, 2009a) modeling infrastructure or Four-Layer Architecture (Atkinson & Kühne, 2003), depicted in Figure 1. The OMG modeling infrastructure comprises a hierarchy of model levels just in compliance with the foundations of MDD (Model-Driven Development) (Atkinson & Kühne, 2003). Each model in the Four-Layer Architecture (except for the one at the highest level) is an instance of the one at the higher level. The first level (*user data*) refers to the data manipulated by software. Models of user data are called *user concepts models* and are one level above the user data level. Models of user concepts models are *language concepts models*. These are models of models and so are called metamodels. A metamodel is a model of a modeling language. It is also a model whose

Figure 1. The OMG modeling infrastructure or Four-Layer Architecture

M3: Meta-Object Facility
M2: UML concepts
M1: User concepts
M0: User data

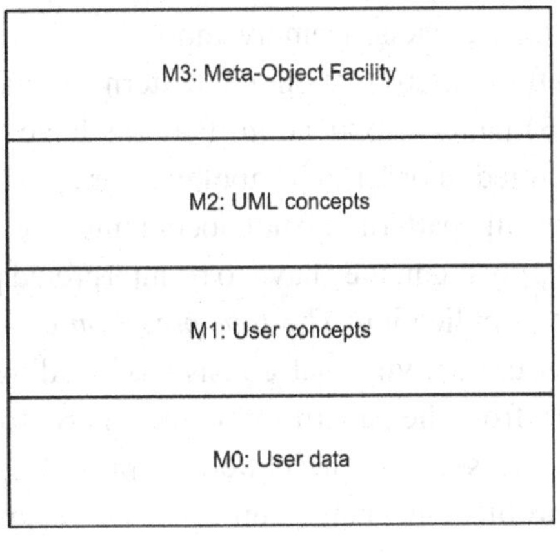

elements are types in another model. An example of a metamodel is the UML (Unified Modeling Language) metamodel (OMG, 2009b). It describes the structure of the different models that are part of it, the elements that are part of those models and their respective properties. The *language concepts metamodels* are at the highest level of the modeling infrastructure. The objects at the user concepts level are the model elements that represent objects residing at the user data level. At the user data level, data objects may be the representation of real-world items.

Patterns are provided by pattern catalogues such as (Adams, Koushik, Vasudeva, & Galambos, 2001; Beck, 2008; Buschmann, Meunier, Rohnert, Sornmerlad, & Stal, 1996; Eriksson & Penker, 2000; Fowler, 1997, 2003b; Gamma, Helm, Johnson, & Vlissides, 1995; Larman, 2001; Pree, 1995). Pattern languages are more than pattern catalogues (collections of patterns). A pattern language is composed of patterns for a particular (small and well-known) domain. Those patterns must cover the development of software systems down to their implementation. A pattern language must also determine the relationships between the patterns the language is composed of. The language's patterns are its vocabulary, and the rules for their implementation and combination are its grammar (Buschmann, Meunier, Rohnert, Sornmerlad, & Stal, 1996).

The *adoption* of a pattern (pattern adoption) is composed by the set of activities that consist of using the pattern somehow when producing software artifacts. Namely those activities are: (1) pattern interpretation; (2) pattern adaptation; and (3) pattern application. Patterns have to be interpreted in order to be applied. For the reason that usually patterns are not documented by those who apply them, they have to be interpreted prior to their application. The *interpretation* of a pattern is the activity that consists of reading the pattern from the pattern catalogue and reasoning about the solution the pattern is proposing for that problem in that given context. Following

the interpretation activity, the adoption process may require the patterns to be adapted somehow (Beck, 2008; Fowler, 2003a). The *adaptation* of a pattern is the activity of modifying the pattern from the catalogue without corrupting it (corrupting the pattern includes corrupting the pattern's semantics and the pattern's abstract syntax). Finally the *application* of a pattern is its actual use in the development of software, whether to develop software products or families of software products, or to inspire the conception of design artifacts since some patterns are not identifiable in the source code as they are not meant to give origin to code directly (Soukup, 1995).

Habitually pattern catalogues represent patterns at the M1-level of the OMG modeling infrastructure or Four-Layer Architecture. We consider that leveraging patterns to the M2-level is a way of turning the decisions on their application more objective as well as of reducing the misinterpretation of patterns from catalogues and the corruption of patterns during the pattern adaptation process. Misinterpretation and corruption of patterns can lead to the irremediable loss of the advantages of adopting those patterns. Considering the OMG modeling infrastructure as a multilevel architecture, *multilevel instantiation* (or the instantiation of M2-level patterns at the M1-level) shall occur during the adoption of patterns.

This chapter is an original contribution to the improvement of the software products' quality given that it provides for some directives on how to adopt software patterns in such a way that the original advantages of the adopted pattern are preserved. The originality of the contribution is due to the novelty character of the pattern classification, which relies on the fact that it is based on the software development process. The classification we propose represents a benefit in terms of the process of developing software as it allows knowing (by classifying the patterns according to it) in which moment of the software development process to use the patterns and in the context of which Software Engineering professionals, technologies and methodologies. This chapter contributes for MDD since it addresses the OMG modeling infrastructure through the multilevel character of the proposed classification. The classification considers that patterns can be represented at different levels of the OMG modeling infrastructure, which influences their interpretation. The usefulness of a multilevel and multistage pattern classification resides in avoiding that the patterns from a specific category are handled by the inadequate professionals, technologies and methodologies. By classifying the patterns (in this case the software development patterns) we assure that the professionals with the right skills (who use the technologies and methodologies adequate to their profile) use the right pattern categories. For instance it would be inadequate for a product manager to use a pattern from the Gang of Four (GoF) book (Gamma, Helm, Johnson, & Vlissides, 1995). That would not produce the desired effects of using such kind of pattern.

This chapter is structured as follows: Section 2 affords a state-of-the-art that suits the purpose of substantiating the strength of our approach; Section 3 aims at clarifying the relation of patterns, pattern classifications and the proposed pattern classification with the theme of the book; Section 4 is devoted to exhibiting the proposed pattern classification in abstract terms before formalizing categories and positioning patterns at those categories; Section 5 is targeted at demonstrating the feasibility of the solution we are going to propose to the systematic use of software development patterns by using some concrete examples of patterns positioned at distinct categories of our classification to illustrate the different types of patterns we have formalized; finally Section 6 exposes some concluding remarks.

BACKGROUND

Typically patterns are adopted at later phases of the software development process. The analysis and design phases of software development are disregarded. Most of the times analysis and design decisions are not documented and that originates missing knowledge on how the transition from previous stages to the implementation stage was performed. Knowing design decisions without design documentation as a helper of this activity is only possible if those decisions can be transmitted by the people who know them. When talking about patterns, design decisions have to be perfectly known so that an activity of pattern discovery can be applied to a software solution with the purpose of discovering the original pattern (the pattern in the catalogue) from the implementation. If the original pattern is successfully reengineered from the implementation, then it means that most likely the advantages of the original pattern are present in that software solution. It is pertinent to understand how patterns from catalogues, after being interpreted, adapted and applied, can be constrained in such a way that the advantages enclosed in the solution each of those patterns proposes cannot be observed. Buschmann, *et al.* (Buschmann, Henney, & Schmidt, 2007b) referred that patterns may be implemented in many different ways; still patterns are not vague in the solution structure they propose. The diversity in the instantiations of a pattern is due to the specificity of the concrete problems being addressed. What must be assured is the "spirit of the pattern's message" as Buschmann, *et al.* called it. In the development of software it must be assured that not only the advantages of the original pattern are visible (directly or indirectly) in the software solution but also that patterns are adopted throughout all the process phases since patterns address all of them as we will be seeing in the next section of this chapter. Besides these two considerations it must be noted that the development of software is not performed exclusively based on patterns but it is a microprocess or nanoprocess when compared to the whole software development process as Buschmann, *et al.* stated.

Pattern classifications are useful for understanding pattern catalogues better and providing input for the discovery of new patterns that fit into the already existing pattern categories (Gamma, Helm, Johnson, & Vlissides, 1995). Patterns are classified into categories according to different classification criteria and are organized in pattern catalogues according to classification schemas that support the different classification criteria each particular schema contemplates. Classification schemas can be unidimensional or multidimensional depending on whether they obey to a single or more than one criterion. Throughout this chapter (due to simplification purposes) we are going to use the term pattern classification instead of the complete term pattern classification schema.

The pattern classifications of (Beck, 2008; Eriksson & Penker, 2000; Gamma, Helm, Johnson, & Vlissides, 1995; Pree, 1995; Tichy, 1997; Zimmer, 1995) have not been explicitly defined within a procedural referential, thus we are not able to know beforehand which software pattern shall be used at what moment during the process of developing software in general as well as in the context of which Software Engineering professionals, technologies and methodologies. These procedural concerns include also the adoption of a modeling infrastructure to prevent subjective pattern application decisions, and situations of misinterpretation and corruption of patterns from catalogues while interpreting and adapting the patterns respectively. At last the classifications we are going to present next have not elaborated on the nature of the domain to which patterns are most adequately applicable. Considering that nowadays families of software products are commonly developed with domain-specific artifacts, taking the adequacy of patterns to particular domain natures into account is relevant in order to choose between the patterns that are most applicable to a domain-specific software product or family of products.

The first pattern classification we mention is from the GoF (Gamma, Helm, Johnson, & Vlissides, 1995). They classified design patterns according to two criteria: purpose and scope. The purpose of a pattern states that pattern's function. According to the purpose, patterns can be *creational, structural* or *behavioral.* Creational patterns are concerned with the creation of objects. Structural patterns are targeted at the composition of classes or objects. Behavioral patterns have to do with the interaction between classes or objects and their responsibility's distribution. The scope of a pattern is its applicability either to classes or to objects. *Class patterns* are related to the relationships between classes. *Object patterns* are related to the relationships between objects. Despite the GoF's classification considering more than one criterion, it is not multidimensional as the criteria have not been combined to determine pattern categories. The GoF's classification is concerned with the function of the pattern (what the pattern does) and its applicability to low level implementation elements (how the pattern will be handled in the software construction moment). The classification does not refer to explicit procedural questions on the development of software with the use of patterns (when patterns shall be used, by whom, with what technologies and methodologies, and at which levels of abstraction) or to questions with the applicability of patterns to specific domain natures. The same is true for the classification we are going to mention next.

A classification of patterns according to their relationships was proposed by Zimmer (Zimmer, 1995). Zimmer classified the relationships into three categories: *X uses Y in its solution* (the solution of X contains the solution of Y), *X is similar to Y* (both patterns address a similar type of problem) and *X can be combined with Y* (both patterns can be combined, in spite of the solution of X not containing the solution of Y). This classification may give hints on the selection and composition of patterns, nevertheless it does not provide for directives on the nature of the domain the patterns are more adequate to, on the right moment to adopt the patterns, within which Software Engineering discipline's context and on how to respect a modeling infrastructure when adopting the patterns.

A classification of general-purpose design patterns (patterns traversal to all application domains) was proposed by Tichy in (Tichy, 1997). Tichy proposed nine categories to organize design patterns. The categories were determined based on the problems solved by the patterns. The proposed categories were *decoupling* (which has to do with the division of a software system into independent parts), *variant management* (which is associated with the management of commonalities among objects), *state handling* (which is the handling of objects' states) and others. Again, neither procedural concerns, nor concerns with the applicability of patterns to particular domain nature types were evidenced by this classification that relies on the types of problems patterns propose to solve.

The Pree's and the Beck's classifications we are going to expose next do not also evidence hints on which moments of the software development process to adopt patterns, in the context of which Software Engineering discipline, respecting a modeling infrastructure and the applicability of patterns to domain natures in particular.

Wolfgang Pree (Pree, 1995) categorized design patterns by distinguishing between the purpose of the design pattern approach and its notation. Notation can be informal textual notation (plain text description in a natural language), formal textual notation (like a programming language) or graphical notation (like class diagrams). Purpose expresses the goal a design pattern is pursuing. The *Components* category indicates that design patterns are concerned with the design of components rather than frameworks. The *Frameworks I* category indicates that design patterns are concerned with describing how to use a framework. The *Frameworks II* category indicates that design patterns represent reusable framework designs. Pree's classification scratches very superficially the question of modeling as it distinguishes between patterns represented with code (formal

textual notation in the Pree's classification) and those represented with models (graphical notation in the Pree's classification) but it does not elaborate on how to work respecting different levels of abstraction throughout the process of developing software.

Kent Beck's (Beck, 2008) implementation patterns translate good Java programming practices whose adoption produces readable code. He claims these are patterns because they represent repeated decisions under repeated decision's constraints. Kent Beck's implementation patterns are divided into five categories: (1) class, with patterns describing how to create classes and how classes encode logic; (2) state, with patterns for storing and retrieving state; (3) behavior, with patterns for representing logic; (4) method, with patterns for writing methods (like method decomposition, method naming); and (5) collections, with patterns for using collections. Kent Beck claims his implementation patterns describe a style of programming. These implementation patterns address common problems of programming. For instance Kent Beck advises to use the pattern *Value Object* if the intention is to have an object that acts like a mathematical value, or the pattern *Initialization* for the proper initialization of variables, or the pattern *Exception* to express non-local exceptional flows appropriately, or the pattern *Method Visibility* to determine the visibility of methods while programming, or the pattern *Array* as the simplest and less flexible form of collection. Kent Beck uses Java in order to exemplify the pattern (as a different presentation of it) instead of a model or a structured text. Despite the programming practices having to be considered by the software development process, this classification does not care about the process of adopting patterns within the whole software development process.

Not only design patterns and implementation patterns are used when developing software. The classification of Eriksson and Penker (Eriksson & Penker, 2000) addresses business-level patterns like those we are going to mention just now. The *Core-Representation* pattern dictates how to model the core objects of a business (the *business objects* e.g. customer, product, order) and their representations (e.g. the representation of a business object within the information system may be a window or another graphical user interface element as the representation of a debt is an invoice and the representation of a country may be the country code). The *Document* pattern shows how to model documents (e.g. how to handle different versions and copies of a document). The *Geographic Location* pattern illustrates how to model addresses (which is of interest to mail-order companies, post offices, shipping companies). The *Organization and Party* pattern demonstrates how to model organizational charts. The *Product Data Management* pattern indicates the way to model the structure of the relationship between documents and products (the structure varies from one business to another). The *Thing Information* pattern (used in e-business systems) models the thing (resource in the business model) and the information about the thing (the information in the information system about that resource). The *Title-Item* pattern (used by stores and retail outlets) is to model items (e.g. a loan item) and their titles (e.g. a book title). The *Type-Object-Value* pattern (used by geographical systems) depicts how to model the relationship between a type (e.g. country), an object (e.g. Portugal) and a value (e.g. +351). Eriksson and Penker classified business-level patterns into three categories: *resource and rule patterns*, *goal patterns* and *process patterns*. The *resource and rule patterns* provide for guidelines on how to model the rules (used to define the structure of the resources and the relationships between them) and resources (people, material/information and products) from a business domain. The *goal patterns* are intimately related to goal modeling. The main idea is that the design and implementation of a system depends on the goals of the system (how it is used once built). At last the *process patterns* are related to process-oriented

models (such as workflow models). Process patterns prescribe ways to achieve specific goals for a set of resources, obeying to specific rules that express possible resource states.

The classification we are going to mention next is elaborated on the software development phases. Siemens' (Buschmann, Meunier, Rohnert, Sornmerlad, & Stal, 1996) two-dimensional pattern classification (from the book "Pattern-Oriented Software Architecture" (POSA), volume 1, or just POSA 1) was defined with two classification criteria (*pattern categories* and *problem categories*). Every pattern is classified according to both criteria. The *pattern categories* determined were *architectural patterns*, *design patterns* and *idioms*. They are related to phases and activities in the software development process. Architectural patterns are used at early stages of software design, particularly in the structure definition of software solutions. Design patterns are applicable to former stages of software design, particularly to the refinement or detailing of what Buschmann, *et al.* call the *fundamental architecture of a software system*. Idioms are adequate to implementation stages, where software programs are written in specific languages. The *problem categories* determined were *from mud to structure, distributed systems, interactive systems, adaptable systems, structural decomposition, organization of work, access control, management, communication* and *resource handling*. As an example *Structural Decomposition patterns* support the decomposition of subsystems into cooperating parts and *Organization of Work patterns* support the definition of collaborations for the purpose of providing complex services. These categories express typical problems that arise in the development of software. Placing some patterns in a specific category is a useful activity since it allows eliciting related problems in software development. However this pattern classification does not address the analysis phases (business modeling and requirements) of the software development process as the multilevel and multistage pattern classification does.

The POSA 1 (Buschmann, Meunier, Rohnert, Sornmerlad, & Stal, 1996) and the POSA5 (Buschmann, Henney, & Schmidt, 2007b) are the most general POSA references. The POSA 2 (Schmidt, Stal, Rohnert, & Buschmann, 2000) contains a pattern language for concurrent and networked software systems. The POSA 3 (Kircher & Jain, 2004) contains a pattern language for resource management. The POSA 4 (Buschmann, Henney, & Schmidt, 2007a) contains a pattern language for distributed computing. As referred in the POSA 5 by its authors the classifications in the POSAs 2, 3 and 4 are intention-based, which is why they haven't been included in this chapter's literature review. This chapter is targeted at software development patterns in general, not intention-based software development patterns.

In the POSA 5 Buschmann, *et al.* reflect on the terminology used in the pattern classification in the POSA 1 and conclude that the pattern classification from the POSA 1 has terminology problems. The terms used to distinguish disjoint categories (*architectural patterns*, *design patterns* and *idioms*) actually do not refer to pretty disjoint categories. These authors refer that architectural activities and the application of *idioms* can also be considered design activities. They also refer that since the POSA 1 they have concluded that the term *design pattern* is to designate software development patterns in general and to distinguish them from patterns that have nothing to do with software. It does not mean that they have to do with design activities. For this reason they conclude that the term *design pattern* used in the pattern classification in the POSA 1 should have been replaced with some other name to refer to the GoF patterns. Concerning the *architectural patterns* Buschmann, *et al.* conclude that all patterns are architectural in nature, so there cannot be a category called *architectural patterns*. To Buschmann, *et al.* design is the activity of making decisions on the structure or behavior of a software system and architecture is about the most significant design decisions for a system (and not all

design decisions). Therefore although all patterns are intrinsically architectural, not all of them are applicable to architectural activities. Concerning the *idioms*, Buschmann, *et al.* conclude that the term *idiom* has some ambiguity since sometimes it refers to a solution for a problem specific to a given programming language and some other times it refers to conventions for the use of a programming language. An *idiom* can even refer to both situations. Buschmann, *et al.* also conclude that *idioms* can refer to patterns used within the context of a specific domain, architectural partition or technology, thus they conclude that the term *idiom* should have been *programming language idiom* as a programming language is a specific solution domain. For instance the pattern *Iterator* is an *idiom* specific to C++ and Java, although it differs between these two specific languages.

Since all architecture is design (Clements et al., 2002) the consideration of Buschmann, *et al.* that there cannot be a pattern category for architectural patterns makes sense (they are patterns of design). However not all design is architecture (Clements et al., 2002), which means that a distinction between patterns that address architecture and patterns that address design has to be made. Architectures do not define implementations, they rather constrain downstream activities of design and implementation. The architecture defines the system structure. The software architect shall leave the implementation details veiled. Design patterns shall address details of implementation (like the GoF patterns do).

The matter with *idioms* that Buschmann, *et al.* mention in the POSA 5 has been solved by Kent Beck in (Beck, 2008). Kent Beck's implementation patterns express good programming practices (or the conventions for the use of programming languages). Kent Beck uses Java in order to exemplify his implementation patterns, which shall be applicable to other programming languages. Kent Beck's implementation patterns are not Java or other language-specific patterns that are just a different representation of design patterns (Grand, 2002; Stelting, 2002).

PATTERNS AND MODEL-DRIVEN SOFTWARE DEVELOPMENT

Atkinson and Kühne discuss the foundations of MDD in (Atkinson & Kühne, 2003). The goal of MDD is to raise the abstraction level at which software programs are written by reducing the software development effort needed to produce a software product or set of software products. That effort is reduced by allowing modeling artifacts to actually deliver more to the software product or set of software products under development than they do when used just for documentation purposes. Automated code generation from visual models is one of the main characteristics of MDD and the ultimate goal of the model transformation cycle. The other main characteristic of MDD is the reduction of models' sensitivity to change by (1) making them accessible and useful (therefore understandable in the first place) by all stakeholders; (2) changing models while the systems that rely on them are running; (3) storing the models in formats that other tools can use; and (4) automating the process of translating platform-independent models to platform-specific models and the former to code. Point 1 is achieved through notation, point 2 through dynamic language extension (through the runtime extension of the set of types available for modeling, which are the *language concepts* previously mentioned in this chapter), point 3 through interoperability and point 4 through user-definable mappings. An MDD infrastructure must provide for visual modeling and the means for defining visual modeling languages, which are abstract syntax, concrete syntax, well-formedness rules (constraints on the abstract syntax) and semantics. Such infrastructure must also provide for the use of OO (Object-Oriented) languages that allow extending the set of types available by those languages' APIs (Application Programming

Interfaces) despite in a static way (not at runtime as MDD actually requires). Describing the previously mentioned concepts from the *language concepts metamodel* level, the concepts from the *language concepts* level and the also previously mentioned *user concepts* in a metalevel way (e.g. with the OMG modeling infrastructure) allows adding new *language concepts* dynamically at runtime. Finally an MDD infrastructure must provide for the means to define model transformations by the user in order to translate models ultimately into code of a specific implementation platform. A means to define model transformations is to use the model transformation languages QVT (Query/View/Transformation) (OMG, 2008) or ATL (ATLAS Transformation Language) (The Eclipse Foundation, 2010).

MDD relies on models that can be used as input to automated transformations (Swithinbank et al., 2005). In (Ruben & Vjeran, 2009) it is stated that the transformation of models into code can be facilitated by using software development patterns. The means to obtain that is to pack patterns as reusable assets with encapsulated implementation. We consider that a packed pattern can contain either the (pattern's) model and the code or just the model since not all patterns are to be directly converted into programming code. Depending on the type of pattern, it can be translated into code that can be directly included in the software solution under development in the programming environment for further manipulation or it can be imported in the modeling environment to be used in the modeling of the software solution by customizing the pattern's model elements and relating them with the remaining model elements. If the packed pattern contains the model and the code, then both the inclusion of the code in the software solution in the programming environment and the import of the model in the modeling environment can be performed. These ways patterns can be involved in the visual modeling of software systems and/or the automated code generation from visual models used in the development of those software systems just like MDD requires. According to (Greenfield & Short, 2004) a code template can be attached to the pattern to generate code from the model to which the pattern has been applied. Finally we consider that there is no point in using implementation patterns as packed patterns that can be imported in the programming environment as most of the times they depend on modeled elements parameters to be instantiated. In fact some of those patterns are already available in the programming environment through context menus of source code elements generated from models.

The models used to develop a software product or family of products evolve along the software development lifecycle and according to MDD end up in code. Pattern classifications help the actors involved in MDD software development processes to choose the most convenient patterns (in the form of models) to be incorporated into the models that are later transformed into code. By dividing patterns into categories all pattern classifications contribute to the use of patterns to develop software according to the MDD directives as the effort to select patterns without them would be higher, which would not contribute to the goal of MDD (raising the abstraction level at which software programs are written by reducing the software development effort). Patterns in the form of models also help raising the abstraction level at which software programs are written. Those that are not represented as models because they are to be only in code contribute to MDD by being considered in the process of automating code generation from visual models, during which the structure of code is thoroughly defined for the code that is generated from the visual models. For instance if the model from which we are to generate code incorporates the *Getter/Setter* pattern, we have to consider the implementation patterns like those in (Beck, 2008) applicable to the target platform in order to generate source code for the getters/setters (operations) (Swithinbank et al., 2005).

Especially the pattern classifications that reveal some kind of software development procedural notion contribute to MDD given that it is more likely that the most adequate patterns are selected. That is because those classifications avoid the wrong patterns to be handled by the wrong professionals, technologies and methodologies that make more sense in the context of a specific process' phase(s). Specific professionals, technologies and methodologies are more skilled to handle specific kinds of models that address specific kinds of problems in specific moments of MDD software development processes. This means that specific professionals, technologies and methodologies are more skilled to handle specific kinds of patterns (in the form of models) to be applied to the specific kinds of models they handle as input to the automatic generation of code. Those patterns address specific kinds of problems, which can be better understood by those professionals due to their skills and profile. The pattern classification we propose in this chapter is particularly based on a software development process, which is the RUP (Rational Unified Process) (Kruchten, 2000). The proposed pattern classification is also related to the OMG modeling infrastructure in the sense that it demands for the patterns to be classified according to the abstraction level at which they are represented (the OMG modeling infrastructure's levels M2, M1 or M0) for the reasons we will expose further on in this chapter.

THE MULTILEVEL AND MULTISTAGE CLASSIFICATION

Our multilevel and multistage pattern classification has three dimensions: the level (from the OMG modeling infrastructure), the Software Engineering discipline (based on the RUP) and the stage of the software development process (also based on the RUP). The classification adopts also an attribute, besides the three dimensions: the nature of the domain.

The Classification Explained

Domains can be of horizontal nature or of vertical nature. The vertical domains represent particular business domains and correspond to activity sectors (e.g. banking, insurance, trading, industry). The horizontal domains are traversal to the vertical domains, which means that they represent areas of knowledge common to every business domain (e.g. accounting, human resources, stock, project management). This does not mean that business applications (banking applications for example) shall contemplate all horizontal domains but it means that horizontal applications (for instance accounting applications) shall be usable by all the businesses possible, although there is a part of each horizontal domain that is only applicable to each business domain (e.g. there are accounting rules specific to the banking sector).

The multilevel character of our classification lies on the different levels of the OMG modeling infrastructure, which provides for a multilevel, four-layer modeling architecture. The classification's RUP-based Software Engineering discipline dimension provides for clear hints on the professionals who shall handle specific types of patterns, with particular technologies and methodologies. At last the classification's multistage character is given by the dimension associated with the RUP-based phases of the software development process. Our hypothesis is that the development of software can take more advantage of patterns and their proposed solutions if their adoption occurs at the right moment of the process of developing a software solution and within the context of the right Software Engineering professionals, technologies and methodologies, respecting the levels patterns shall follow throughout the adoption process, which involves dealing with models at different levels of abstraction as well. We consider that the positioning of patterns at the wrong category of any process-based classification leads to a misinterpretation of those same patterns, resulting in an unsuccessful adoption. By unsuc-

cessful adoption we mean a constriction of the original patterns' advantages. Although our effort is towards minimizing the effects of pattern misinterpretation, pattern adaptation can still and will most likely occur over the pattern models we are going to expose in this chapter. Our classification (especially due to its multilevel character) reduces the chances of pattern misinterpretation since it reaches the metamodeling level (M2-level from the OMG modeling infrastructure). Unsuccessful pattern adoptions can lead to software solutions where the adopted patterns are unrecognizable.

Patterns vary in their abstraction level. Actually the same pattern may be positioned at different abstraction levels according to its representation. Normally the interpretation of a pattern is performed directly from the catalogue to the particular context of the product or the family of products. This way both the representation of the pattern in the catalogue and the interpretation of that same pattern are situated at the M1-level, which may not be adequate if the goal is to systematically use patterns and reduce the unsuccessful pattern adoptions during software production. Thinking about software families the matter with software product lines and software patterns may lie on the instantiation of M2 artifacts at the M1 layer, which again indicates the relevance of the abstraction level concerning the adoption of software patterns.

We are adopting the geometrical terminology to represent the pattern classification. Patterns can be positioned at the *pattern positioning geometrical space* placed in the first octant of the orthonormal referential like Figure 2 (on the left) shows. Actually that space may be partitioned into cubes. As patterns can be classified with three possible values according to two of the three axes of the referential and with four possible values according to the other axis, the pattern positioning geometrical space can be divided into $3 \times 3 \times 4$ cubes as can also be seen from Figure 2 (on the left). The fourth criterion is the domain nature and in the case of the pattern positioned at the pattern positioning geometrical space in the figure it takes

Figure 2. Orthonormal referential with the dimensions of the multilevel and multistage classification on the axes plus the pattern categorization three-dimensional space (on the left). The projections of a pattern's positioning in a two-dimensional area (on the right)

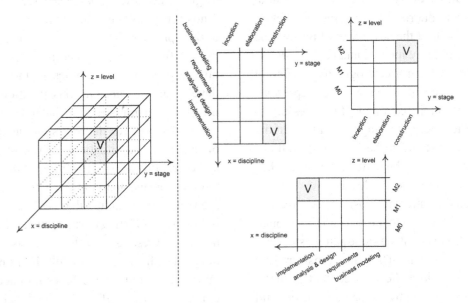

the value vertical (V). That is why the grey cube representing the pattern is tagged with a *V* (the domain nature is not a dimension, it is an attribute so it does not correspond to an axis). Figure 2 (on the right) presents the projections of the pattern's positioning represented in a three-dimensional space on the left of the figure, this time in a two-dimensional area. The possible values of each dimension are attached to the axes. They will be detailed further on in this section of the chapter.

As we have already argued, leveraging patterns to the M2-level is a way of turning the decisions on the application of patterns more objective as well as of reducing the misinterpretation of patterns at the M1-level with all the disadvantages that subjective decisions and misinterpretation bring into the software development process and the quality of the software product itself. Multilevel instantiation shall occur during the adoption of patterns in order to systematize their use. Patterns are positioned at the pattern positioning geometrical space (according to the axes representing the Software Engineering disciplines and the OMG modeling infrastructure levels) with

regards to their representations: the M2 model (pattern M2), the M1 model (pattern M1) and the M1 code. As we will see later on in this chapter, the pattern in the M1 representation is an instance of the pattern in the M2 representation, whereas the code is a transformation of the pattern's M1 model into a specific programming language code. The abstraction level decreases when moving from models at the M2-level to the code. Pattern catalogues represent patterns with M1 models and M1 code (source code). They do not propose patterns using their M2 representation (or metamodels). That is not our approach as it will be detailed in the next section of this chapter. The course of the artifacts inside the pattern positioning geometrical space as well as the course's projection on the discipline×level plan indicates that a small process within the whole software development process must occur when systematically dealing with patterns, which includes multilevel instantiation and transformation of models into code.

The reason for representing patterns in catalogues in their M1 representation is due to the willing of not compromising the applicability of patterns to a broader domain coverage. This is the risk of rising the abstraction level from M1 to M2. Naturally every risk has some potential for success and the risk of rising the abstraction level carries with it the advantage of turning the pattern adoptable by more domains. In order to adapt a pattern from a catalogue to a different domain than the one considered for representing the pattern in the catalogue it is necessary to know in which areas to change it and for that the pattern's structure has to be known as well. To know the structure of the pattern, the pattern has to be represented at the M2-level.

Although the pattern may assume several representations according to the level it is positioned at, we are talking about the same pattern since the diverse representations of the pattern answer to the same problem, within the same context, with the same solution, driven by the same recurrent and predictable forces (Beck, 2008; Gamma, Helm, Johnson, & Vlissides, 1995; Meszaros & Doble, 1997). Having various representations for the same pattern implies that the M2 representation of a pattern covers more functionality, therefore reaching higher levels of functional completeness than the M1 representation.

The Classification's Dimensions and Attribute

Next each criterion (the dimensions and the attribute) of the multilevel and multistage classification are described. As we have already stated the multilevel and multistage classification considers the moment of the software development process during which specific kinds of patterns, what we call pattern types (see section 3.3 for more information on the multilevel and multistage pattern types), shall be used. The *Discipline* dimension represents these different moments in the process of developing software. The multilevel and multistage classification considers as well the context in which patterns shall be used in terms of Software Engineering professionals, technologies

and methodologies. Stages of software development are defined by different profiles of Software Engineering professionals who work with different kinds of technologies and methodologies tailored to their profiles. The *Stage* dimension represents these different stage-related professionals, technologies and methodologies in the process of developing software. Our classification takes also in a modeling infrastructure that has been adopted to avoid subjective decisions on the application of patterns, and situations of misinterpretation and corruption of patterns from catalogues while interpreting and adapting them respectively. The modeling infrastructure that has been considered is the OMG modeling infrastructure. The *Level* dimension represents the different levels of the OMG modeling infrastructure. Finally the multilevel and multistage classification takes into account that domain-specific artifacts for the development of families of software products are common these days, which means that the applicability of patterns to particular domain natures allows to choose between the patterns that are most adequate to a domain of a software product or family of products. The *Domain Nature* attribute represents the different (both) domain natures to which patterns are most applicable (or the applicability of patterns to both domain natures).

As the subtitles indicate, the *Discipline* dimension can take the values {*business modeling, requirements, analysis & design, implementation*} and the *Stage* dimension can take the values {*inception, elaboration, construction*}. The *Level* dimension corresponds to the levels of the OMG modeling infrastructure {M1, M2}. For now M3 is not being considered. We are not representing M3 in the figures because M3 can be represented with (UML) models and we haven't yet worked our classification at that level. Despite that, M0 is represented in the figures to remember the reader that after M1 code (compile-time code) we have M0 code (runtime code) but runtime code is not relevant to our classification. The *Domain Nature* attribute which has already been explained earlier in this section of the chapter can take the values {*vertical, horizontal, agnostic*}.

In order to use this classification do the following: (1) analyze the pattern you want to classify according to the dimensions *Discipline* and *Stage*, and give a value to each of those dimensions for that pattern you are classifying; (2) conclude on the pattern type (see section 3.3 for more information on the multilevel and multistage pattern types and how the dimensions *Discipline* and *Stage* determine the pattern type); (3) determine the pattern's level, which corresponds to giving a value to the *Level* dimension; (4) if the pattern is not represented in its M2 representation, draw an M2 model of the pattern; (5) by looking at the M2 representation of the pattern describe its semantics in textual form; and finally (6) by looking at the pattern's M2-level textual description and at the pattern's description in the catalogue classify the pattern in what its domain nature is concerned, which is equivalent to tagging the pattern with one of the three possible values for the *Domain Nature* attribute.

The assignment of patterns to particular chunks of the classification is dependent on the pattern type, therefore on the RUP's textual descriptions of its disciplines and phases (to conduct step 1). In order to determine the pattern's level the classifier (the subject who classifies) must be familiarized with the Four-Layer Architecture since he has to understand if the concepts the pattern presents are situated at the M2 or at the M1 levels. The classifier has to know the notion of multilevel instantiation. The classification process is dependent on the subject who conducts the process. Determining the pattern type is subjective as it implies looking at the textual descriptions of the RUP's disciplines and phases. Analyzing textual descriptions is subjective (at least in this approach). Determining the pattern's level is also subjective (at least in this approach) because it depends on the classifier's knowledge.

The Discipline Dimension

The RUP's Business Modeling Software Engineering Discipline

The RUP's *Business Modeling* discipline shall comprise activities of derivation of the software requirements the system to be developed must support in order to be adequate to the target organization and of analyzing how that system fits into the organization. The goal of the *Business Modeling* discipline is to model an organizational context for the system.

The RUP's Requirements Software Engineering Discipline

The RUP's *Requirements* discipline shall comprise activities of stakeholder request elicitation and of transformation of those requests into requirements on the system to be developed. Those requirements shall span the complete scope of the system. The requirements on what the system shall do have to be agreed with the stakeholders (customer and others). The goal of the *Requirements* discipline is to provide developers with a better understanding of the requirements the system must fulfill based on the customer's (or other stakeholder's) requests. It is also the goal of this discipline to delimit the boundaries of the system to be developed.

The RUP's Analysis & Design Software Engineering Discipline

The RUP's *Analysis & Design* discipline shall comprise activities of transformation of the requirements elicited with the stakeholders into a design of the system to be deployed. The design of the system shall contemplate an architecture for the system. The goal of this discipline is to specify the design of the system to be developed.

The RUP's Implementation Software Engineering Discipline

The RUP's *Implementation* discipline shall comprise activities of development, unit testing of the developed components and integration of the software components that will allow the system requested by the stakeholders to be deployed based on the design specifications elaborated in the context of the *Analysis & Design* discipline. When developing the system, the organization of the code shall be defined according to the layers of the subsystems to implement. Developing the system through components implies that all the components produced by different teams are integrated into an executable system. The goal of this discipline is to translate the design elements that came up in the context of the *Analysis & Design* discipline into implementation elements (source files, binaries, executable programs and others).

The Stage Dimension

The RUP's Inception Software Development Stage

The RUP's *Inception* stage shall comprise activities of discrimination of the critical use cases of the system and the primary operation scenarios vital to the design tradeoffs that will have to be made further on during the process. At least one candidate architecture shall be exhibited (and maybe demonstrated) and shall support the primary scenarios (or at least some of them) in order for the stakeholders to agree upon the fulfillment of the requests they exposed to the Software Engineers responsible for the requirements elicitation. The goal of this stage is to ensure that the software development project is both worth doing and possible to execute.

The RUP's Elaboration Software Development Stage

The RUP's *Elaboration* stage shall comprise activities of architecture handling like conceiving a baseline architecture of the system, thus providing a stable basis for the further design and implementation work which will take place during the *Construction* stage. This architecture shall contemplate and reflect the most significant requirements for the architecture of the system.

Architectural prototypes shall be used to evaluate the stability of the architecture. The goal of this stage is to elaborate an architectural foundation for the upcoming detailed design and implementation efforts.

The RUP's Construction Software Development Stage

The RUP's *Construction* stage shall comprise activities of development of deployable software products from the baseline architecture of the system elaborated during the prior stage. The design, development and testing of all the requested functionality for the system shall be completed during this stage. The construction of the software system shall be conducted in an iterative and incremental way. It is during the construction of that software system that remaining use cases and other requirements are described, others are further detailed, the design built during the previous stage is enlivened and the implemented software is tested. The goal of this stage is to develop a complete software product ready to transition to the users.

The Level Dimension

The *Level* dimension of the classification corresponds to the levels of abstraction of the Four-Layer Architecture. Each model in the Four-Layer Architecture except for the one at the highest level is an instance of the one at the higher level. The M0-level refers to the data manipulated by software. The M1-level refers to models of user concepts. The M2-level refers to UML concepts models. These are models of models and so are called metamodels. A metamodel is a model whose elements are types in another model (an example of a metamodel is the UML metamodel). It describes the structure of the models, the elements that are part of those models and their respective properties. The meta-metamodels are at the highest level of the modeling infrastructure, the MOF (Meta-Object Facility) (OMG, 2006) or M3-level.

The Domain Nature Attribute

The *Domain Nature* attribute indicates whether the pattern is more adequate to vertical domains (industry, commerce, services and others) or to horizontal domains (accounting, stock, project management and others). Some patterns as it will be evidenced later in this chapter are domain nature agnostic, which means that they are applicable both to vertical and to horizontal domains.

THE PATTERN TYPES

Following are the pattern types from the multilevel and multistage classification. A pattern type represents a kind of pattern that has been classified with the same *Discipline* dimension's value and the same *Stage* dimension's value. A description is provided for each of the pattern types as well as the classification according to the *Discipline* and *Stage* dimensions. The classification of pattern types according to the *Level* dimension does not make sense as it depends on the representation of the pattern and has no influence on the definition of the pattern types themselves. The pattern types are: business patterns, analysis patterns, enterprise patterns, architectural patterns, design patterns and implementation patterns. These names have been chosen because they are the most common pattern names in the literature and make the most sense in our definitions of the pattern types.

This section will expose some examples of patterns that were classified with different pattern types. The patterns in this section suit the purpose of demonstrating how we have applied the multilevel and multistage classification of patterns. We provide for a representation of the patterns as M2-level (meta)models and as M1-level models (when applicable).

Be aware that some of the patterns we are going to analyze in this section have not been classified with the same pattern type name we have classified them with using our classification. For instance the *Posting* pattern has been classified as a business pattern by Pavel Hruby in (Hruby, 2006) but we classify it as an analysis pattern.

The Business Patterns

The term *business pattern* was inspired on IBM's definition of business pattern (Adams, Koushik, Vasudeva, & Galambos, 2001).

Business patterns are more pertinent in the context of vertical domains. They make the most sense to be handled during the *Inception* stage by professionals, technologies and methodologies from the *Business Modeling* and *Requirements* disciplines.

Business patterns are used to describe a solution to accomplishing a business objective. They shall address the users of the solution, the organization's software systems the users interact with (or the organization itself) and the organization's information (available through those systems or the organization itself). Business patterns may refer to e-business solutions that convey an organizational framing, validity and conformance of the solution to the business problem the solution is trying to solve. Software solutions shall be sustained by the business and this is achieved with the adoption of business patterns.

We can see examples of business patterns in (Adams, Koushik, Vasudeva, & Galambos, 2001) and also in (Eriksson & Penker, 2000).

Figure 3 (on the left) illustrates the positioning of business patterns according to the *Stage* and the *Discipline* dimensions.

The Domain Model Pattern

The *Domain Model* pattern's goal is to produce an object model of the domain or business area. A domain model must distinguish between the data the business involves and the business rules (or the rules used by the business). The behavior expressed by these business rules shall be placed in the business object that really needs it. Figure 3

Figure 3. The business patterns' positioning according to the Stage and the Discipline dimensions (on the left). The Domain Model pattern modeled at both the M2 and the M1 levels of the OMG modeling infrastructure (on the right)

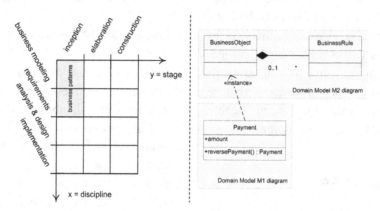

(on the right) shows a model with an example of the *Domain Model* pattern in the M1 representation as well as the M2 representation of the pattern. The *Domain Model* pattern is composed of two types of concepts: business objects (or domain objects) and business rules. This is evidenced by the *Domain Model* M2 model in Figure 3 (on the right).

The *Domain Model* pattern suits the modeling of every business domain possible as every business domain has business objects and business rules on those objects. Even though the pattern is applicable to all business domains it is not appropriate to the modeling of a horizontal domain or to the modeling of structural business domain commonalities, which makes of it applicable to domains of vertical nature.

The *Domain Model* pattern does not show how to model objects or rules for a specific business domain but the types of concepts the pattern handles are business-related and shall be instantiated in order to model business domains. Besides and more important than that, the *Domain Model* pattern allows to model objects and rules that shall be handled by the solution to the business problem the solution is trying to solve. The *Domain Model* pattern is a very atomic pattern as it does not address the users of the solution or the

organization's software systems the users interact with (or the organization itself); nonetheless it is adequate to reach the business domain model from the candidate architecture that shall be exhibited to the stakeholders. For all of these reasons we consider that the *Domain Model* pattern shall be classified as a business pattern.

By looking at the RUP's textual descriptions of its disciplines and phases, we concluded that the *Domain Model* pattern shall be used during the *Inception* software development stage and in the context of the *Business Modeling* and *Requirements* Software Engineering disciplines as seen in the previous section of this chapter. During the *Inception* stage a domain model must be built from a candidate architecture that translates the critical use cases and the primary operation scenarios. That domain model may be achieved with the application of the *Domain Model* pattern. The pattern shall help translating the requirements elicited with the stakeholders. Those requirements have to be adequate to the target organization, which is a concern of the *Requirements* discipline.

The Analysis Patterns

The term *analysis pattern* was inspired on Fowler's definition of analysis pattern (Fowler, 1997).

Figure 4. The analysis patterns' positioning according to the Stage and the Discipline dimensions (on the left). The Posting pattern modeled at both the M2 and the M1 levels of the OMG modeling infrastructure (on the right)

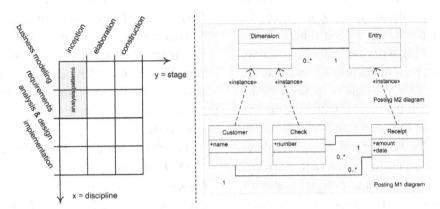

Analysis patterns are more applicable to horizontal domains. They shall be used during the *Inception* stage by professionals, technologies and methodologies from the *Business Modeling* and *Requirements* disciplines. In spite of being called analysis patterns it does not make sense to use them in the context of the *Analysis & Design* discipline. They have been called so because *analysis pattern* is a terminology spread out through the literature and also because Fowler's definition of analysis pattern inspired ours. In an older informal terminology the development of software was composed of three phases: analysis, design and implementation. With RUP formalizing the dimension of business modeling in the process of software development, analysis was divided into business modeling and requirements. The former design discipline corresponds to RUP's *Analysis & Design*.

Analysis patterns are solutions to recurrent problems in many (business) domains. They are composed of concepts that represent structural commonalities when modeling many different business domains.

We can see examples of analysis patterns in (Fowler, 1997).

Figure 4 (on the left) shows the positioning of analysis patterns according to the *Stage* and the *Discipline* dimensions.

Business patterns and analysis patterns are *dual patterns* since they coexist in the context of the *Inception* stage and of both the *Business Modeling* and the *Requirements* disciplines. Business patterns are not necessarily about software but they have to give input on how the software requirements of a business domain are adequate to an organization. Analysis patterns have to consider its adequacy to the target organization. They both have to be used during the earliest period of the software solution's development, when requirements are elicited and agreed with the stakeholders.

The Posting Pattern

Previously in (Hruby, 2006) the *Posting* pattern has been classified as a business pattern by Pavel Hruby. According to the multilevel and multistage classification the *Posting* pattern is classified as an analysis pattern. It is applicable to horizontal domains.

The point of the *Posting* pattern is to keep the history of economic events (commitments, contracts or claims) or in other words the history of interactions between economic agents for the exchange of economic resources like the purchase of products, the sale of services, invoices and corresponding payments, among others. Some examples of posting types are inventory posting, finance posting, man-hours posting and distance posting. Figure 4 (on the right) exposes a model with an example of the *Posting* pattern in the M1 representation as well as the M2 representation of the pattern. The *Posting* pattern contemplates two types of concepts: dimensions and entries. A posting dimension is either an economic agent or an economic resource. The purpose of the dimension is to provide additional information about the economic event or in other words provide descriptive information about the posting entries. A posting entry is an entry of a commitment, a contract or a claim. The purpose of the entry is to keep track of the history of economic events. In Figure 4 (on the right) we can see that Customer and Check are two posting dimensions of the posting entry Receipt. Most probably the Customer class represents the economic agent involved in the economic event represented by the entry class Receipt whereas the Check class represents the economic resource.

The *Posting* pattern is constituted by concepts belonging to a horizontal domain (the accounting domain). Nevertheless the *Posting* pattern has only the concept of posting entry in common with the *Accounting* pattern (in the *Accounting* pattern the concept of posting entry corresponds to the concept of agreement).

The arguments for classifying the *Posting* pattern as an analysis pattern as well as for its adequacy to the *Inception* software development stage and the *Business Modeling* and *Requirements* Software Engineering disciplines are the same we described beforehand for the *Accounting* pattern.

The Enterprise Patterns

The term *enterprise pattern* was inspired on Fowler's considerations about enterprise patterns and enterprise software in (Fowler, 2009).

Enterprise patterns are most adequate to vertical domains. They are more relevant in the context of the *Elaboration* stage by professionals, technologies and methodologies from the *Analysis & Design* discipline.

Enterprise patterns are used in the development of software systems on which various businesses rely on and run (the so called enterprise software systems). Normally the architecture of such systems is a layered architecture. Conception decisions on layered architectures are design decisions that have to be taken inside a logical layer or between different logical layers. Often single enterprise applications need to interact so enterprise patterns have also to propose solutions to the integration of enterprise applications problem. Validations, calculations and business rules on the data an information system manipulates vary according to the domain and change as the business conditions change. Enterprise applications must respond to ever changing business requirements.

Enterprise patterns address architectural concerns as well as the architecture patterns we will be talking next but whereas enterprise patterns are mainly concerned with topological architecture, architectural patterns are mainly concerned with logical architecture.

This chapter does not consider the notion of *enterprise* as the RUP does not consider it. The RUP is a Software Engineering process framework. IBM has delivered a RUP plug-in called RUP SE (RUP for Systems Engineering) (Cantor, 2003). The RUP SE has enlarged the RUP with the consideration that the development of large-scale systems must be concerned with software, hardware, workers and information. The RUP SE considers different perspectives on

Figure 5. The enterprise patterns' positioning according to the Stage and the Discipline dimensions (on the left). The Service Layer pattern modeled at both the M2 and the M1 levels of the OMG modeling infrastructure (on the right)

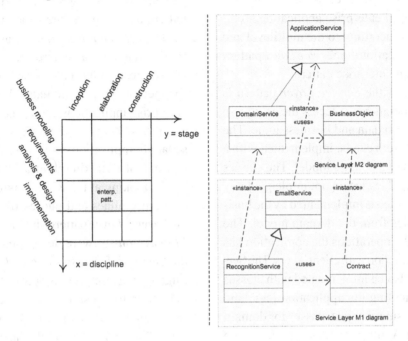

the system (logical, physical, informational, and others). The RUP SE is shortly a framework for addressing the overall system's issues. The RUP SE addresses behavioral requirements (the way the system shall behave in order to fulfill its role in the enterprise). The RUP does not express such concern with the enterprise in which the system will play its role. In fact this kind of concern is more from the field of Systems Engineering than from the field of Software Engineering. When we talk about system requirements in the context of Software Engineering we are specifically talking about software system requirements. The system requirements are derived from an understanding of the enterprise, its services and the role that the system (software-based or not) plays in the enterprise. For instance the RUP SE suggests that the enterprise shall be partitioned into the system and its actors in order to derive the system requirements. In the RUP SE an enterprise is faced as

a set of collaborating systems that collaborate to realize enterprise services, mission and others. The system attributes are obtained from an analysis of the enterprise needs. As this chapter talks about software system development patterns in the context of RUP (not RUP SE), this chapter is related to Software Engineering, not to Systems Engineering, which means that this chapter's *enterprise patterns* have nothing to do with the concept of *enterprise* from the Systems Engineering field. The term *enterprise pattern* comes from the term *enterprise application architectural pattern* from Folwer's book "Patterns of Enterprise Application Architecture" (Fowler, 2003b).

We can see examples of enterprise patterns in (Fowler, 2003b).

Figure 5 (on the left) depicts the positioning of enterprise patterns according to the *Stage* and the *Discipline* dimensions.

The Service Layer Pattern

In (Fowler, 2003b) Fowler classified the *Service Layer* pattern as an enterprise application architectural pattern. According to the multilevel and multistage classification the *Service Layer* pattern is classified as an enterprise pattern.

The purpose of the *Service Layer* pattern is to provide for operations to access the enterprise application's stored data and business logic. The *Service Layer* pattern can be implemented with a set of facades over a domain model. The classes implementing the facades do not implement any business logic, which is implemented by the business object's rules from the domain model. The facades gather the operations the application has available for interaction with client layers. The Service Layer can also be implemented with classes directly implementing the application logic and delegating on business object classes for domain logic processing. Application logic is grouped into classes of related application logic. These classes are application service classes. Figure 5 (on the right) depicts an example of this second strategy for implementing the *Service Layer* pattern at the modeling level. The figure shows a model with an example of the *Service Layer* pattern in the M1 representation as well as the M2 representation of the pattern. As we may conclude from the figure the *Service Layer* pattern is composed of two types of concepts: application services and domain services. Business objects are also represented in the models as the domain services rely on them for business logic. The domain services act as intermediates between the application services and the business objects since they provide for calls to application logic in application services and for calls to business logic residing on business objects. These last calls are made inside the service operations the domain services provide for, which correspond to the use cases the actors want to perform with the application.

As the main focus of the *Service Layer* is the domain service acting as a bridge between the application logic and the business logic, and not implementing any business domain logic (just accessing it) we have tagged this particular enterprise pattern as domain nature agnostic.

The *Service Layer* pattern has been classified in this chapter as an enterprise pattern because it is used to develop enterprise software systems for specific business domains. When developing enterprise applications, logical layers are essential and the concern of the *Service Layer* pattern (to separate application logic from business logic) proves that we talking about an enterprise pattern.

By looking at the RUP's textual descriptions of its disciplines and phases we concluded that the *Service Layer* pattern shall be used during the *Elaboration* software development stage and in the context of the *Analysis & Design* Software Engineering discipline. Since splitting application logic from business logic is an architectural decision with impacts at the level of the baseline software system architecture it makes sense to adopt the *Service Layer* pattern during the *Elaboration* stage and by the professionals, technologies and methodologies responsible for the software design.

The Architectural Patterns

The term *architectural pattern* was inspired on Buschmann, *et al.* and Zdun (Buschmann, Meunier, Rohnert, Sornmerlad, & Stal, 1996; Zdun & Avgeriou, 2005).

Architectural patterns are more appropriate to horizontal domains. They shall be picked up from catalogues for usage during the *Elaboration* stage by professionals, technologies and methodologies from the *Analysis & Design* discipline.

Architectural patterns are used in the definition of the structure of software solutions. The architecture of a system is the design artifact that represents the functionality-based structure of that system and shall address quality or non-functional attributes wished-for the system. Architectural patterns shall help improving both the functional and the quality attributes of software systems.

Figure 6. The architectural patterns' positioning according to the Stage and the Discipline dimensions (on the left). The MVC pattern modeled at both the M2 and the M1 levels of the OMG modeling infra-structure (on the right)

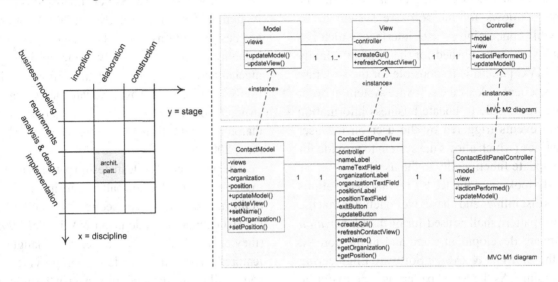

We can see examples of architectural patterns in (Buschmann, Meunier, Rohnert, Sornmerlad, & Stal, 1996).

Figure 6 (on the left) shows the positioning of architectural patterns according to the *Stage* and the *Discipline* dimensions.

Enterprise patterns and architectural patterns are *dual patterns* since they coexist in the context of the *Elaboration* stage and of the *Analysis & Design* discipline.

The Model-View-Controller Pattern

Originally in (Buschmann, Meunier, Rohnert, Sornmerlad, & Stal, 1996) the MVC (*Model-View-Controller*) pattern has been classified by Buschmann, *et al.* as an architectural pattern. According to the multilevel and multistage classification the MVC pattern is classified as an architectural pattern. It is adequate to both horizontal and vertical domains, so it is agnostic relatively to the domain nature.

The purpose of the MVC pattern is to ensure the consistency between the user interface and the business information of a software system. The

separation of the user interface from the business information of a software system provides for user interface flexibility. Figure 6 (on the right) depicts an example of a model of the MVC pattern in the M1-level and also the MVC pattern represented in the M2-level. The MVC pattern is composed of three types of classes: a model, a view and a controller. The model contains the business information that is to be presented to the user. The view obtains the information from the model and displays it to the user. The controller is responsible for requesting the business information updating on the model upon user action (event) on the graphical interface (view). It takes the business information from the view and requests for the model's updating with that information.

Although the model component contains business information the MVC pattern is adequate to both horizontal and vertical domains, which makes of it agnostic in what its domain nature is concerned. The pattern can either be adopted if the business information is relative to horizontal business objects or to vertical business objects.

The MVC pattern is classified as an architectural pattern according to the multilevel and multistage classification since it is used to define the structure of the software system, namely the structure of the client-side of the system. The pattern allows for the software system to be flexible concerning its user interface, which is a quality attribute wished-for that system. Mainly the MVC pattern is responsible for the structure of the client-side of the software system in order for it to be able to update business information upon events triggered by the user on the user interface (which allows the system to provide for the update functionality to the user).

By looking at the RUP's textual descriptions of its disciplines and phases we concluded that the MVC pattern shall be used during the *Elaboration* software development stage and in the context of the *Analysis & Design* Software Engineering discipline. As the MVC pattern is used to define the structure of the client-side of the system, addressing both the update functionality and the user interface flexibility (non-functional requirement), it shall be part of the system's architecture, which shall be part of the system's design specification. The system's baseline architecture shall contemplate the most significant architectural requirements, and the MVC pattern addresses the consistency between the user interface and the business information of the software system (which is a requirement vital to interactive software systems).

The Design Patterns

The term *design pattern* was inspired on the GoF's patterns (Gamma, Helm, Johnson, & Vlissides, 1995).

Design patterns are domain nature agnostic, which means that they are both applicable to vertical and to horizontal domains. They shall be manipulated during the *Construction* stage by professionals, technologies and methodologies from the *Analysis & Design* discipline.

Although the GoF described design patterns as OO software patterns we consider design patterns

are those that are applicable to the refinement or detailing of the software system architecture. For instance Larman's GRAS (General Responsibility Assignment Software) (Larman, 2001) patterns are design patterns since they have to do with behavioral aspects that only come up during a mechanistic design phase of the software solution's development (by mechanistic we mean structural or behavioral mechanisms more refined than components from logical architectures) (Larman, 2001).

The presence of code in design patterns is only to give examples. Design patterns are independent of the languag, as we can see from the GoF catalogue (Gamma, Helm, Johnson, & Vlissides, 1995) (they only talk about OO concepts, not language features). The sample code section provides for code to illustrate the example given in the motivation section, where the reader is given a scenario to illustrate a design problem in order for him to better understand the more abstract description of the pattern that follows the motivation section. Again the code is an illustration of the pattern's applicability.

Figure 7 (on the top left) depicts the positioning of design patterns according to the *Stage* and the *Discipline* dimensions.

Figure 7 (on the bottom left) illustrates the difference between our definition of design pattern and GoF's. The lighter grey area corresponds to the pattern positioning space of the GoF catalogue. The darker grey area corresponds to the pattern categorization area of our classification where we position *our* design patterns. These areas have been drawn taking only the *Discipline* and the *Stage* dimensions into consideration as the *Level* dimension does not allow demonstrating the difference between both definitions. We consider that design patterns shall only be used during the *Construction* stage of the software development process as the Software Engineering professionals, technologies and methodologies of the *Analysis & Design* are the most adequate to handle these patterns due to their professional

Figure 7. The design patterns' positioning according to the Stage and the Discipline dimensions (on the top left). The difference between our design patterns and the GoF's according to the Stage and the Discipline dimensions (on the bottom left). The Adapter pattern modeled at both the M2 and the M1 levels of the OMG modeling infrastructure (on the right)

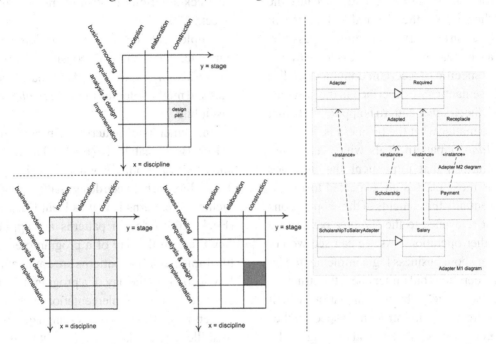

profile and adequacy to the *Construction* stage's activities and goals. We also consider that if design patterns are handled throughout the whole software development stages and by the people and tools (technologies and methodologies) of every Software Engineering discipline, the advantages predicted in pattern catalogues of the adopted design patterns are not going to be preserved and that the design patterns in the catalogues are not going to be used in their full potential by the people most skilled to handle them.

The Adapter Pattern

In the past in (Gamma, Helm, Johnson, & Vlissides, 1995) the *Adapter* pattern has been classified as a design pattern by the GoF but in the sense of OO software pattern. According to the multilevel and multistage classification the *Adapter* pattern is classified as a design pattern. It is applicable to

both horizontal and vertical domains, which makes of it a domain nature agnostic pattern.

The *Adapter* pattern (also known as *Wrapper*) has to do with a class converting the interface of one class to be what another class expects. Figure 7 (on the right) shows a model exemplifying the *Adapter* pattern in its M1 representation as well as the M2 representation of the pattern. This is what the *Adapter*'s implementation described at the M2-level should look like: "The Adapter must have an input parameter of the Adapted's type in its constructor and extend the Required and call the Adapted's appropriate operation inside the operation required by the Receptacle". The *Adapter*'s description at the M2-level in terms of semantics is the following: "The Receptacle requires the Adapted to be adapted to the Required through the Adapter (the process is called *adaptation*). The goal is for the Receptacle to be able to call the Required's operation from an instance of the Adapted".

The *Adapter* pattern is independent from any domain (or domain nature agnostic) because the adapter, the adapted, the required and the receptacle objects can belong to every domain possible. As long as the semantics or business logic (at the M1-level) specific of a certain domain complies to the M2 semantics we described in the previous paragraph the *Adapter* pattern is applicable to that domain no matter what the business is.

The *Adapter* pattern deals with classes and their operations that implement the interface operations those classes are expected to implement. Essentially the contents of those operations that are of relevance to the *Adapter* pattern are calls to other operations. As we can see we are not arguing about business logic implemented by the class' operations but rather about the structure of the classes targeted by the adaptation, which means we are discussing structural aspects rather than behavioral. Nevertheless and once again the *Adapter* pattern shall be applied during the mechanistic design phase of the system's development when classes shall be derived from architectural components. The *Adapter* pattern in its semantics shall be used to detail the baseline software system architecture and be part of a design specification containing the interface design of the classes involved in the *adaptation* process. For all of these reasons we have classified the *Adapter* pattern as a design pattern.

By looking at the RUP's textual descriptions of its disciplines and phases we concluded that the *Adapter* pattern shall be used during the *Construction* software development stage and in the context of the *Analysis & Design* Software Engineering discipline as already argued in this chapter. The adequacy of such stage and discipline to the *Adapter* pattern is intimately related to the reasons we have just exposed for classifying the *Adapter* pattern as a design pattern.

The Implementation Patterns

The term *implementation pattern* was inspired on Beck's definition of implementation pattern (Beck, 2008).

Implementation patterns are domain nature agnostic. They shall be considered during the *Construction* stage by professionals, technologies and methodologies from the *Implementation* discipline.

Implementation patterns are in fact the patterns in Kent Beck's catalogue (Beck, 2008) for instance and not Java or other language-specific patterns. The difference between design patterns and implementation patterns is that as Kent Beck claimed (Beck, 2008) design patterns are applicable a few times in the day of a programmer whereas his implementation patterns are applicable every few seconds in the day of a programmer. He also claimed that his implementation patterns teach readers how to use certain OO language constructs regardless of the language (despite him using a trivial subset of Java to exemplify the patterns). Java patterns or other language-specific patterns are just a different representation of design patterns (Grand, 2002; Stelting, 2002) (e.g. in (Stelting, 2002) Java is *applied* to the GoF patterns and other patterns). A different representation changes the pattern's level in the classification (e.g. in the case of the patterns from (Stelting, 2002) they had to be situated at the M1 (code) level in order for them to be called *Java* patterns). Kent Beck refers his patterns are applicable when all domain-specific questions are solved and developers are left with solely technical issues.

Figure 8 illustrates the positioning of implementation patterns according to the stage and the discipline dimensions.

The Value Object Pattern

In (Beck, 2008) the *Value Object* pattern has been classified as a class pattern. In the context of the multilevel and multistage classification the *Value*

Figure 8. The implementation patterns' positioning according to the stage and the discipline dimensions

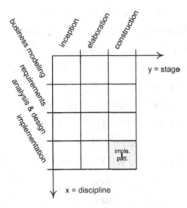

Object pattern is classified as an implementation pattern. It is adequate to both horizontal and vertical domains, which means that it is domain nature agnostic.

The purpose of the *Value Object* pattern is to create objects that once created cannot have the values of the variables they handle changed. The solution is to set the value of those variables when the object is created through its constructor. No other assignments shall be made to those variables elsewhere in the object's class. Operations on the object shall always return new objects that shall be stored by the requester of the operation. Shortly value objects are objects representing mathematical values, which are values that do not change over time (have no state). For instance a transaction (value object) shall not change over time, rather an account changes over time (a transaction implies a change of state in the account). It does not make sense to model implementation patterns as they are only to exist in code, not in models, which implies that they are always represented at the M1-level (compile-time code).

The *Value Object* pattern shall be involved in the coding of both horizontal and vertical domain software systems since it is about the construction of objects that shall not change over time, the as-

signment of values to those objects' variables and the operations on those (value) objects.

The *Value Object* pattern has been classified as an implementation pattern because it is about the technical details of using classes (an OO language construct), in this case to create objects that shall have no state (whose variables' values shall not change over time).

By looking at the RUP's textual descriptions of its disciplines and phases we concluded that the *Value Object* pattern shall be used during the *Implementation* software development stage and in the context of the *Construction* Software Engineering discipline as previously mentioned in this chapter. The *Value Object* is related to the development of software systems, particularly to the development of implementation elements (source code).

FUTURE RESEARCH DIRECTIONS

Future work concerning the software patterns in the context of the software development process involves studying how patterns evolve over the time of that process. This evolution demands for the comprehension of the relationships between software patterns (especially those positioned at consecutive stages). It also demands for the analysis of how time implies that software patterns are associated with each other in a chain. The gap between patterns used at different stages shall be bridged in order to have a complete multistage software development process that contemplates different artifacts (software patterns and other artifacts like use case models, component models and others). In fact software patterns used at different stages solve the same problem at different levels of abstraction.

Software patterns may be used to detail logical software system architectures (expressed through component models). As software patterns are normally presented in class models, the detailing of those architectures requires knowing how to apply the concept of class to the concept of (logical) component.

The consideration of software patterns within the context of the software development process claims for the specialization of the actors who intervene in that process with specific roles during the adoption of those patterns. It is relevant to study the impacts of other software development processes (besides the RUP) in the proposed pattern classification.

Developing software product lines with software patterns (and other artifacts) may have some particular implications. Some variability mechanisms may have to be taken into account in software patterns. The use of those mechanisms may be constrained to a specific level of the OMG modeling infrastructure (the M2-level) and to specific pattern types. It may be necessary to define all the possible M2-level concepts (e.g. classes, attributes, operations) and/or the values of those concepts (e.g. class names, class attributes, class operations) as well as the application of all of them to all or some of the product line's members. The whole matter with software product lines and software patterns may mainly lie on the instantiation of M2-level artifacts at the M1-level.

Finally it is important to determine which software patterns may and shall be made available in modeling infrastructures (either through libraries of software pattern metamodels or models, or through domain-specific languages).

CONCLUSION

Some lessons have been learned on the application of the multilevel and multistage pattern classification to some patterns from the literature. After looking at the RUP's textual descriptions of its disciplines and phases some patterns were not classified with the pattern type we expected they would be classified with. This means that a procedural referential such as the RUP is important to classify patterns, mainly because it gives the

classification a notion of software development process. It also means that the awareness of the adequacy of a pattern in a catalogue to a specific discipline and stage changed after the multilevel and multistage pattern classification has been elaborated. Initially before an in depth analysis of the RUP's textual descriptions and the definitions of the various pattern types we expected that (1) analysis patterns did not make sense in the context of the RUP's *Business Modeling* discipline; (2) design patterns made sense in the context of both the RUP's disciplines of *Analysis & Design* and *Implementation*, and of both the RUP's *Elaboration* and *Construction* stages; and (3) patterns that could be contextualized in the RUP's *Implementation* discipline and in the RUP's *Construction* phase were language-specific patterns. After analyzing RUP's textual descriptions and the pattern type definitions we concluded that (1) analysis patterns do make sense in the context of the RUP's *Business Modeling* discipline; (2) design patterns make only sense in the context of the RUP's *Analysis & Design* discipline and the RUP's *Construction* stage; and (3) language-specific patterns are a translation of design patterns into some language, not implementation patterns.

One of the reasons that was in the genesis of the creation of the multilevel and multistage classification was to provide for some guidance on the adoption of software development patterns in order to avoid loosing the original advantages of the pattern throughout the adoption process. For this reason we have considered that the pattern classification had to rely on the software development process. The benefits of such an approach to pattern classification are: (1) the knowledge of the moment from the software development process in which to use specific kinds of patterns; and (2) the knowledge of who the Software Engineering professionals most skilled to handle those specific kinds of patterns in each stage of the software development process are, considering their instruments (technologies and methodologies).

The systematic character of the multilevel and multistage classification is based on the objectiveness of the decisions on the application of software development patterns, which may be assured with the adoption of a modeling infrastructure. A systematic use of software development patterns is likely to also prevent the misinterpretation and corruption of patterns from catalogues when interpreting and adapting them respectively.

Besides being concerned with the stages and the Software Engineering professional's skills and the instruments they handle to conduct Software Engineering activities, and besides translating concerns with the systematic use of software development patterns the multilevel and multistage classification is also concerned with the nature of the domain, which is one of the criteria that compose the classification. Therefore the multilevel and multistage classification is focused on domain-based software development. The classification also focuses on model-driven software development since it incorporates through its multilevel character the OMG modeling infrastructure by considering that patterns can be represented at different levels of that infrastructure, which influences their interpretation.

The multilevel and multistage pattern classification is innovative in some ways relatively to the existing literature. Most pattern classifications do not classify patterns based on the software development process. The only classification that does, disregarded the analysis phases (business modeling and requirements) of the software development process. The multilevel and multistage classification though addresses business modeling and requirements.

REFERENCES

Adams, J., Koushik, S., Vasudeva, G., & Galambos, G. (2001). *Patterns for e-Business: A Strategy for Reuse*. Indianapolis, Indiana: IBM Press.

Atkinson, C., & Kühne, T. (2003). Model-Driven Development: A Metamodeling Foundation. *IEEE Software*, *20*(5), 36–41. doi:10.1109/MS.2003.1231149

Beck, K. (2008). *Implementation Patterns*. Upper Saddle River, NJ: Addison-Wesley.

Buschmann, F., Henney, K., & Schmidt, D. C. (2007a). *Pattern-Oriented Software Architecture: A Pattern Language for Distributed Computing*. Hoboken, NJ: Wiley.

Buschmann, F., Henney, K., & Schmidt, D. C. (2007b). *Pattern-Oriented Software Architecture: On Patterns and Pattern Languages*. Hoboken, NJ: Wiley.

Buschmann, F., Meunier, R., Rohnert, H., Sornmerlad, P., & Stal, M. (1996). *Pattern-Oriented Software Architecture: A System of Patterns*. Hoboken, NJ: Wiley.

Cantor, M. (2003). Rational Unified Process for Systems Engineering - Part III: Requirements Analysis and Design. *The Rational Edge*, from http://www.ibm.com/developerworks/rational/rationaledge

Clements, P., Bachmann, F., Bass, L., Garlan, D., Ivers, J., & Little, R. (2002). *Documenting Software Architectures: Views and Beyond*. Upper Saddle River, NJ: Addison-Wesley.

Eriksson, H.-E., & Penker, M. (2000). *Business Modeling With UML: Business Patterns at Work*. Hoboken, NJ: Wiley.

Fowler, M. (1997). *Analysis Patterns: Reusable Object Models*. Upper Saddle River, NJ: Addison-Wesley.

Fowler, M. (2003a). Patterns. *IEEE Software*, *20*(2), 56–57. doi:10.1109/MS.2003.1184168

Fowler, M. (2003b). *Patterns of Enterprise Application Architecture*. Upper Saddle River, NJ: Addison-Wesley.

Fowler, M. (2009). *Patterns in Enterprise Software* from http://martinfowler.com/articles/enterprisePatterns.html

Gamma, E., Helm, R., Johnson, R., & Vlissides, J. (1995). *Design Patterns: Elements of Reusable Object-Oriented Software*. Upper Saddle River, NJ: Addison-Wesley.

Grand, M. (2002). *Patterns in Java: A Catalog of Reusable Design Patterns Illustrated with UML*. Hoboken, NJ: Wiley.

Greenfield, J., & Short, K. (2004). *Software Factories: Assembling Applications with Patterns, Models, Frameworks, and Tools*. Hoboken, NJ: Wiley.

Hruby, P. (2006). *Model-Driven Design Using Business Patterns*. Berlin: Springer-Verlag.

Kircher, M., & Jain, P. (2004). *Pattern-Oriented Software Architecture: Patterns for Resource Management*. Hoboken, NJ: Wiley.

Kruchten, P. (2000). *The Rational Unified Process: An Introduction*. Upper Saddle River, NJ: Addison-Wesley.

Larman, C. (2001). *Applying UML and Patterns: An Introduction to Object-Oriented Analysis and Design and the Unified Process*. Upper Saddle River, NJ: Prentice Hall.

Meszaros, G., & Doble, J. (1997). A Pattern Language for Pattern Writing. In Martin, R. C., Riehle, D., & Buschmann, F. (Eds.), *Pattern Languages of Program Design 3* (pp. 529–574). Upper Saddle River, NJ: Addison-Wesley.

OMG. (2006). *Meta-Object Facility: Core Specification - version 2.0* from http://www.omg.org

OMG. (2008). *Meta Object Facility 2.0 Query/View/Transformation: Specification - version 1.0* from http://www.omg.org

OMG. (2009a). *Object Management Group* from http://www.omg.org

OMG. (2009b). *Unified Modeling Language: Superstructure - version 2.2* from http://www.omg.org

Pree, W. (1995). *Design Patterns for Object-Oriented Software Development*. Upper Saddle River, NJ: Addison-Wesley.

Ruben, P., & Vjeran, S. (2009). Framework for Using Patterns in Model-Driven Development. In Papadopoulos, G. A., Wojtkowski, G., Wojtkowski, W., Wrycza, S., & Zupančič, J. (Eds.), *Information Systems Development: Towards a Service Provision Society* (pp. 309–317). Berlin, Heidelberg: Springer-Verlag.

Schmidt, D., Stal, M., Rohnert, H., & Buschmann, F. (2000). *Pattern-Oriented Software Architecture: Patterns for Concurrent and Networked Objects*. Hoboken, NJ: Wiley.

Soukup, J. (1995). Implementing Patterns. In Coplien, J. O., & Schmidt, D. C. (Eds.), *Pattern Languages of Program Design* (pp. 395–412). Upper Saddle River, NJ: Addison-Wesley.

Stelting, S. (2002). *Applied Java Patterns*. Upper Saddle River, NJ: Prentice Hall.

Swithinbank, P., Chessell, M., Gardner, T., Griffin, C., Man, J., & Wylie, H. (2005). *Patterns: Model-Driven Development Using IBM Rational Software Architect*. Indianapolis, Indiana: IBM Press.

The Eclipse Foundation. (2010). ATL Project from http://www.eclipse.org/m2m/atl

Tichy, W. F. (1997). *A Catalogue of General-Purpose Software Design Patterns*. Paper presented at the 23rd Technology of Object-Oriented Languages and Systems (TOOLS-23), Santa Barbara, California, USA.

Zdun, U., & Avgeriou, P. (2005). *Modeling Architectural Patterns Using Architectural Primitives*. Paper presented at the 20th Annual ACM SIGPLAN International Conference on Object-Oriented Programming, Systems, Languages, and Applications (OOPSLA 2005), San Diego, California, USA.

Zimmer, W. (1995). Relationships between Design Patterns. In Coplien, J. O., & Schmidt, D. C. (Eds.), *Pattern Languages of Program Design* (pp. 345–364). Upper Saddle River, NJ: Addison-Wesley.

KEY TERMS AND DEFINITIONS

Software pattern: reusable solution to a problem that occurs often throughout the software development process.

Pattern Classification: Activity of organizing patterns into groups of patterns that share a common set of characteristics.

Multilevel Software Development Process: Software development process concerned with the levels of abstraction in which the different artifacts involved in the development of software are handled.

Multistage Software Development Process: Software development process composed of some stages organized in a consecutive temporal order.

Pattern Adoption: Set of activities that consist of using the pattern somehow when producing software artifacts.

Pattern Interpretation: Activity that consists of reading the pattern from the pattern catalogue and reasoning about the solution the pattern is proposing for that problem in that given context.

Pattern Adaptation: Activity of modifying the pattern from the catalogue without corrupting it (corrupting the pattern includes corrupting the pattern's semantics and the pattern's abstract syntax).

Pattern Application: Actual use of a pattern in the development of software, whether to develop software applications or families of software applications, or to inspire the conception of design artifacts.

Multilevel Instantiation: Instantiation of M2-level patterns at the M1-level during the adoption of patterns.

Multilevel and Multistage Pattern Classification: Pattern classification concerned with the levels of abstraction in which the different software patterns are handled and composed of some stages organized in a consecutive temporal order.

Chapter 15
Reducing Enterprise Product Line Architecture Deployment and Testing Costs via Model Driven Deployment, Configuration, and Testing

Jules White
Virginia Tech, USA

Brian Dougherty
Vanderbilt University, USA

ABSTRACT

Product-line architectures (PLAs) are a paradigm for developing software families by customizing and composing reusable artifacts, rather than handcrafting software from scratch. Extensive testing is required to develop reliable PLAs, which may have scores of valid variants that can be constructed from the architecture's components. It is crucial that each variant be tested thoroughly to assure the quality of these applications on multiple platforms and hardware configurations. It is tedious and error-prone, however, to setup numerous distributed test environments manually and ensure they are deployed and configured correctly. To simplify and automate this process, the authors present a model-driven architecture (MDA) technique that can be used to (1) model a PLA's configuration space, (2) automatically derive configurations to test, and (3) automate the packaging, deployment, and testing of con-figurations. To validate this MDA process, the authors use a distributed constraint optimization system case study to quantify the cost savings of using an MDA approach for the deployment and testing of PLAs.

INTRODUCTION

Emerging trends and challenges. *Product-line architectures (PLAs)* enable the development of a group of software packages that can be retargeted for different requirement sets by leveraging common capabilities, patterns, and architectural styles (Cements 2001). The design of a PLA is typically guided by *scope, commonality, and variability*

DOI: 10.4018/978-1-61692-874-2.ch015

(SCV) analysis (Coplien 1998). SCV captures key characteristics of software product-lines, including their (1) *scope*, which defines the domains and context of the PLA, (2) *commonalities*, which describe the attributes that recur across all members of the family of products, and (3) *variabilities*, which describe the attributes unique to the different members of the family of products.

Although PLAs simplify the development of new applications by reusing existing software components, they require significant testing to ensure that valid variants function properly. Not all variants that obey the compositional rules of PLA function properly, which motivates the need for powerful testing methods and tools. For example, connecting two components with compatible interfaces can produce a non-functional variant due to assumptions made by one component, such as boundary conditions, that do not hold for the component to which it is connected (Weyuker 1998).

The numerous points of variability in PLAs also yield variant configuration spaces with hundreds, thousands, or more possible variants. It is therefore crucial that PLAs undergo intelligent testing of the variant configuration space to reduce the number of configurations that must be tested. A key challenge in performing intelligent testing of the solution space is determining which variants will yield the most valuable testing results, such as performance data.

Solution approach → Model-driven testing and domain analysis of product-line architectures. Model-driven Architectures (MDA) (Karsai 2008, Brown 2008, Paige 2009) are a development paradigm that employs models of critical system functionality, model analysis, and code generation to reduce the cost of implementing complex systems. MDA models capture design information, such as software component response-time, that are not present in third-generation programming languages, such as Java and C++. Capturing these critical design properties in a structured model allows developers to perform analyses, such as

queuing analyses of a product-line architecture, to catch design flaws early in the development cycle when they are less costly to correct.

A further benefit of MDA is that code generators and model interpreters can be used to traverse the model and automatically generate portions of the implementation or automate repetitive tasks (Trujillo 2007). For example, Unified Modeling Language (UML) models of a system can be transformed via code generation into class skeletons or marshalling code to persist objects as XML. Model interpreters can be used to automatically execute tests of code using frameworks (Chen 2007), such as Another Neat Tool (ANT) and JUnit.

MDA offers a potential solution to the challenges faced in testing large-scale PLAs. MDA can be used to model the complex configuration rules of a PLA, analyze the models to determine effective test strategies, and then automate test orchestration. Effectively leveraging MDA to improve test planning and execution, however, requires determining precisely what PLA design properties to model, how to analyze the models, and how best to leverage the results of these analyses.

This chapter focuses on techniques and tools for modeling, analyzing, and testing PLAs. First, we introduce the reader to *feature modeling* (Kang 1990, Asikainen 2004, Kang 2002), which is a widely used modeling methodology for capturing PLA variability information. Second, we describe approaches for annotating feature models with probabilistic data obtained from application testing that help predict potentially flawed configurations. Next, we present numerical domain analysis techniques that can be used to help guide the production of PLA test plans. Finally, we present the structure and functionality of a FireAnt, which is an open-source Eclipse plug-in for modeling PLAs, performing PLA domain analysis to derive test plans, and automating and orchestrating PLA testing for Java applications

BACKGROUND

To explore the characteristics of testing PLAs, we have developed an Enterprise Java Beans (EJB)-based *Constraints Optimization System (CONST)* that schedules pickup requests to vehicles. As shown in Figure 1, CONST manages a list of items that must be scheduled for pickup, a list of times that the items must arrive by, and a list of vehicles and drivers that are available to perform the pickup. CONST uses a constraint-optimization engine to find a cost effective assignment of drivers and trucks to pickups.

CONST's optimization engine can be used to schedule a wide variety of shipment types. In one configuration, for example, the system could schedule limousines to customers requiring a ride, whereas in another configuration the system could dispatch trucks to highway freight shipments. CONST's optimization engine must therefore be customizable at design-time to handle these various domains effectively.

CONST must also be customizable at run-time to adapt to changing operating conditions. During peak traffic times, for instance, its optimization engine may need to use traffic-aware routing algorithms, whereas during off-peak times, it may switch to faster traffic-unaware algorithms. Depending on the target domain, CONST also needs to handle failures differently. For example, when scheduling limousines to pickups a degradation of the time required to schedule a reservation below a threshold may require CONST's constraint engine to adapt to improve performance. When scheduling highway freight shipments, however, the threshold may be higher since pickup and drop-off windows are more flexible.

To support the degree of customization described above, we developed CONST as a PLA using SCV analysis, as follows:

- The **scope** is the constraint optimization system architecture and the associated components that address the domain

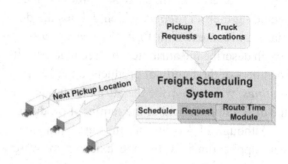

Figure 1. Highway freight shipment scheduling architecture

of scheduling shipments to vehicles, e.g., computing route times between vehicles and shipments, maintaining a list of waiting shipments, and calculating the cost of assigning a vehicle to a shipment.

- The **commonality** is the set of components and their interactions that are present in all configurations of CONST, which include the scheduler updating the schedule, the route time module answering requests from the schedule, and the dispatcher sending routing orders to vehicles.

- The **variability** includes how the list of waiting shipments is prioritized, how the system calculates the cost of assigning each vehicle/driver combination to pickups, how late pickups and dropoffs are handled, and how the system handles response time degradation.

By applying the SCV analysis to CONST we designed a PLA that enables the customization of its optimization engine for various domains.

CONST variants are composed of two main assemblies of components: the *PickupList* and the *Optimizer*. The *PickupList* may be implemented as either (1) a *prioritized list* for domains, such as freight shipments, where some cargos have higher priorities, or (2) a *FIFO* list for other domains, such as taxi scheduling. The *Optimizer* is composed of a *ConstraintsOptimizationModule*, *RouteTimeModule*, *GeoDatabaseModule*, and

DispatchingModule, each of which has different valid configurations. The *DispatchModule* has two valid implementations for different system to driver communication models. The *Route-TimeModule* has three different implementations. The *ConstraintsOptimizationModule* can be configured with three different algorithms. Finally, the *GeoDatabase* can use two different vendor implementations. These composition options support a total of 72 valid variants to construct from the PLA.

Although PLAs can increase software reuse and amortize development costs, PLA configuration spaces are hard to analyze and test manually. Deploying, configuring, and testing a PLA in numerous configurations without intelligent modeling, domain analysis, and automation is expensive and/or infeasible. Large-scale product variants may consist of thousands of component types and instances (Sharp 1999) that must be tested. This large solution space presents the following key challenges to developing a PLA:

- **Challenge 1: Manually managing a PLA's configurations and constraints**. Traditional processes of identifying valid PLA variants involve software developers determining manually the software components that must be in a variant, the components that must be configured, and how the components must be composed. Such manual approaches are tedious and error-prone and are a significant source of system downtime (Oppenheimer 2003). Manual approaches also do not scale well and become impractical with the large configuration spaces typical of PLAs. In CONST, for example, there may be thousands of variations on freight types, licensing requirements, freight handling procedures, and local laws applying to transportation that require the PLA to have a substantial amount of variability.

- **Challenge 2: Determining what PLA configurations to test through domain analysis**. With hundreds or thousands of potential configurations, testing each possible configuration may not be feasible or cost effective. Developers must determine which PLA configurations will yield the most valuable information about the capabilities of different regions of the PLA configuration space. Determining how to perform this domain analysis is hard. For example, it may not be clear which freight routing algorithms in CONST yield poor performance when used together in a configuration.

- **Challenge 3: Managing the complexity of configuring, launching, and testing hundreds of valid configuration and deployment**. *Ad hoc* techniques often employ build and configuration tools, such as Make and Another Neat Tool (ANT), but application developers still must manage the large number of scripts required to perform the component installations, launch tests, and report results. Developing these scripts can involve significant effort and require in-depth understanding of components. Understanding these intricacies and properly configuring applications is crucial to their providing proper functionality and quality of service (QoS) requirements (Krishna 2005). Incorrect system configuration due to operator error has also been shown to be a significant contributor to down-time and recovery (Oppenheimer 2003). Developing custom deployment and configuration scripts for each variant leads to a significant amount of reinvention and rediscovery of common deployment and configuration processes. As the number of valid variants increases, there is a corresponding rise in the complexity of developing and maintaining each variant's deployment, configuration, and testing infrastructure. Automated techniques can be used to manage this complexity (Sloane 2000, Edwards 2004, Memon 2004).

- **Challenge 4: Evolving deployment, configuration, and testing processes as a PLA evolves**. A viable PLA must evolve as the domain changes, which presents significant challenges to the maintenance of configuration, deployment, and testing processes. Small modifications to composition rules can ripple through the PLA, causing widespread changes in the deployment, configuration, and testing scripts. Maintaining and validating the large configuration and deployment infrastructure is hard. Moreover, as PLA components evolve, it is essential that intelligent regression testing be performed on PLA variants to identify those that may become non-functional due to unforeseen side effects. For example, a change in a CONST component for assigning costs to shipments may have wide ranging affects on numerous configurations of the optimization engine. With a large variant solution space, it becomes-even more difficult to rapidly evolve and validate the PLA.

The next section describes how we resolve these challenges via model-driven PLA testing and domain analysis techniques.

MODEL-DRIVEN TESTING AND DOMAIN ANALYSIS TECHNIQUES FOR PRODUCT-LINE ARCHITECTURES

This section introduces modeling techniques for capturing PLA configuration rules and then describes how these models can be annotated with results from testing. It also presents constraint-based optimization techniques that can be used to analyze the model to derive configurations to test.

Figure 2. MDA solution architecture

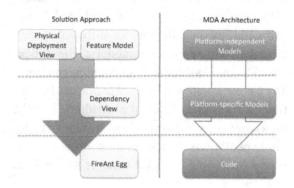

An overview of the solution techniques and how they correspond to standard MDA models is shown in Figure 2. The platform-independent *Feature Model* and *Physical Deployment View* models are first created by developers to capture the variability in the software and the constraints on its deployment to hardware. The *Dependency View* models is a platform-specific model for mapping features to actual implementation. Finally, the *Egg* is a code archive produced by the process for the automated testing infrastructure.

Feature Modeling

To address *Challenge 1*, a modeling methodology is needed to capture the SCV of the application and reason about correct and incorrect configurations of the PLA. A widely used technique for formally representing the variability in a PLA is *feature modeling* (Kang 1990, Asikainen 2004, Kang 2002). Feature modeling describes the SCV of a PLA using a tree-like structure where each node in the tree represents a software *feature*. The SCV defines the points of variability in the application and the feature model can serve as the model that captures this variability information.

Features are an abstraction for an increment of functionality or a point of variability in the software architecture. For example, Figure 2 shows a partial feature model of CONST. The feature *Prioritized* represents whether or not the

Figure 3. Segment of CONST feature model

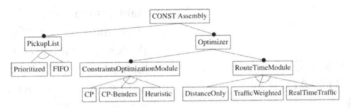

configuration of CONST is designed to handle prioritized shipments.

Each unique configuration of a PLA is represented as a selection of features from the feature model. A unique feature selection is called a *variant*. The goal of PLA configuration with feature models is to find a variant that adheres to all of the configuration rules of the PLA and simultaneously meets the functional and non-functional requirements of the project.

As shown in Figure 2, the configuration rules of a PLA are encoded into the parent-child relationships in the feature model tree. The most basic feature modeling rule is that a feature can be selected if and only if its parent is also selected. The root feature must always be selected. In Figure 2, the *Prioritized* feature can only be selected if the parent *PickupList* feature is also selected.

Points of variability in the PLA and their constraints on configuration are specified as special types of parent-child relationships. The children of a feature can be combined into an XOR group where exactly one of the child features can be selected at a time. The children can also form a cardinality group, where the selection of the child features must conform to a cardinality expression. For example, a feature can specify that between 1...3 of its children can be selected.

MAPPING TEST RESULT DATA TO FEATURE MODEL QUALITY ATTRIBUTES

Addressing *Challenge 2* requires developing an understanding of how test results map to points

of variability in the PLA. For example, if all tests that include the features HazMat and TankerMonitoring fail, developers should be able to map this information to the feature model in order to further investigate the failure or add additional constraints to mark the feature set as invalid. To tackle this challenge, a combination of statistical analysis and feature modeling techniques can be used.

Quality Attributes (Kang 2002) are an extension of feature modeling whereby attribute information is stored along with each feature. Cost information, for example, can be stored as an attribute on each feature to provide guidance on the overall configuration cost of a PLA variant. In terms of testing, a powerful approach to mapping test information to feature models is to use probabilistic data for quality attributes.

Probabilistic quality attributes are used to understand the probability that a set of feature selections will reach a desired goal. For example, given the current selection of features, what further set of features are most commonly selected to complete the feature selection. In terms of testing, probabilistic data can be used to understand the probability that the feature selection will fail one or more tests if a given set of additional features is added. If TankerMonitoring is selected, adding the HazMat feature will guarantee failure and thus its quality attribute will be set to 100%.

Values for the quality attributes are derived by evaluating the historical results of past tests. If two features have been tested together in three different variants and failed in one of them, the probability of failure for selecting both features would be 33%. Initially, no historical test data may be available, in which case, all values are set to 0%.

FEATURE MODELS AND CONSTRAINT SATISFACTION PROGRAMMING

To help address Challenge 2, a method is needed to aid developers in deriving configurations to tests. Given a set of probabilistic quality attribute values, it may not be straightforward to understand which combination of features will yield the largest information gain for testing. The problem is that selecting a set of features to maximize a function of the features is an NP-Hard problem. To address this issue, automated methods can be used to automatically derive the set of features that will yield the best information gain.

Constraint Satisfaction Problems (CSPs) (Benavides 2005) are mathematical models that specify a set of variables and a set of constraints governing the values that those variables may be assigned. There are numerous automated tools, called constraint solvers, for automatically deriving solutions to CSPs that adhere to the CSP constraints and maximize or minimize a function of the variables. Feature models can be translated into CSPs where the solution to the CSP yields a valid selection of features. Moreover, the CSP can be solved using a constraint solver for a selection of features that maximizes or minimizes a function of the feature model features, which can help developers automatically derive configurations to test and address Challenge 2.

MAPPING FEATURE MODELS TO CSPS

A CSP is a problem defined by a set of variables for which values must be derived that meet a set of constraints. For example, $Y > 0$, $X + Y < 10$, $X \neq Y$, is a simple CSP over the integer variables

X and Y. A valid solution, called a labeling of the variables, to the CSP is $X = 2$, $Y = 1$.

Constraint solvers offer the ability to automatically derive solutions to a CSP that maximize or minimize a given function. For example, a CSP could be asked to derive a solution to the CSP that maximizes the value of $X - Y$. The optimal solution in this case would be $X = 8$, $Y = 1$.

A feature model can be transformed into a CSP such that deriving a valid solution to the CSP produces a valid selection of features in the feature model. The transformation is achieved by:

1. A preorder traversal of the feature model is performed starting from the root feature
2. As the ith feature is traversed, a variable f_i is added to the CSP
   a. The variable f_i has the domain [0,1]
   b. After solving the CSP, a value of 1 for f_i indicates that the feature is selected
3. As the ith feature is traversed, for each quality attribute, k, of the feature, a variable a_{ik} is added to the CSP. The value of a_{ik} is set to the numerical value of that quality attribute for the ith feature.
4. The constraint, $f_0 = 1$, is added to ensure that the root feature is selected in any derived configuration
5. A second preorder traversal of the feature model is performed and at each feature, constraints encoding the parent/child relationships in the feature model are encoded as follows

if f_k is a mandatory child of f_i, the constraint $f_k = 1 \Leftrightarrow f_i = 1$

if f_i has children f_k and f_p in an XOR relationship, the constraint $f_i = 1 \Leftrightarrow (f_k = 1 \text{ xor } f_p = 1)$

if f_i has an optional child f_k, $f_k = 1 \Rightarrow f_i = 1$

Using this transformation process, a CSP is produced for which a correct labeling of the variables, $f_i \in F$, yields a feature selection that adheres to the feature model roles. For each feature, f_i, if $f_i = 1$, then the corresponding feature in the feature model is selected in the configuration. Similarly, if $f_i = 0$, the corresponding feature is not selected in the configuration.

Once the feature model is translated into a CSP, a constraint solver can be used to derive configurations that maximize or minimize functions of the features and quality attributes. For example, assume that the kth quality attribute of each feature is the cost of selecting it. The solver can be asked to derive a minimal cost configuration by asking the solver to derive a solution that minimizes the function: $Cost(F) = \Sigma f_i a_{ik}$

For each feature, f_i, if the feature is selected, its value is set to 1. In the function provided to the solver, this will cause the sum for $Cost(F)$ to incur the cost of the ith feature a_{ik}. If f_i, is not selected, is set to 0, which causes its cost to be zeroed out and not included in the sum.

DERIVING TEST PLANS THAT MAXIMIZE INFORMATION GAIN

As discussed earlier, statistical information from test results can be encoded into a feature model's quality attributes. Automatic configuration using a CSP can be used to both help plan test processes to maximize the intake rate of statistical test data. Furthermore, a CSP-based configuration derivation process can find configurations that have the greatest or least probability of functioning correctly based on current statistical data gleaned from test results.

For example, assume that based on previous tests and statistical analysis, a failure quality attribute, a_i, has been constructed. Each quality attribute, a_i, specifies the probability that the configuration will fail one or more tests if it the feature f_i is selected. Using this failure probability attribute, configurations of the feature model can be derived that have the greatest probability of failure based on the provided feature model and failure statistics.

In the CSP, we can encode the probability of a configuration failing as $Fail(F) = Max(f_0 a_0, f_1 a_1, \dots f_n a_n)$, where n is the number of features. Determining a configuration that maximizes the probability of failure simply requires asking the constraint solver to derive a configuration that maximizes $Fail(F)$. Moreover, configurations with low probabilities of failures can be generated by requesting that the solver minimize the value of $Fail(F)$.

As *Challenge 4* pointed out, the test plans must be evolved as the PLA evolves and new test results are obtained. Using a CSP-based configuration derivation process, new configurations to test can automatically be derived as the PLA changes. Moreover, the test plans can also be updated as each test results sheds more light on the PLA configuration space.

TEST AUTOMATION FROM FEATURE MODELS.

To address Challenge 3, which is the complexity of deploying, configuring, and testing a PLA, we have developed *FireAnt*. FireAnt is an MDA tool that allows application developers to describe the components that form the common building blocks of their PLA and to construct feature models specifying how the blocks can be composed to form valid variants. FireAnt significantly reduces the cost of testing a PLA in the following key ways:

Test, Deployment, and Configuration Infrastructure Generation. FireAnt allows developers to describe the target hardware where variants will be deployed. Using a target hardware definition and the artifact mapping, FireAnt can automatically package all the archive files required to deploy each variant, as well as generate the required configuration scripts. These scripts may be in implemented in a variety of languages. Currently, FireAnt provides bindings for generating Another Neat Tool (ANT) build files.

Test Automation. FireAnt can use CSP configuration derivation techniques to generate a global configuration script that remotely deploys, configures, and tests variants automatically on each possible hardware target.

FireAnt was developed using the *Generic Eclipse Modeling System* (GEMS) (White 2005), which is an open-source MDA environment built as an Eclipse plug-in. A GEMS-based metamodel describing the domain of PLA deployment, configuration, and testing was constructed and interpreted to create the FireAnt domain-specific modeling language (DSML) for PLAs. FireAnt's modeling environment uses GEM's support for multiple views to capture the feature model, deployment, configuration, and testing requirements of a PLA. The remainder of this section discusses how each of these views can be used to manage the complexity of testing a PLA and how the view addresses each of the challenges.

FIREANT FEATURE MODELING

To facilitate the analysis of the variant solution space and address Challenge 1 requires a formal grammar to describe the structure of the PLA and its valid configurations. This customization grammar can then be used to automatically generate and explore the variant solution space using the CSP techniques. In FireAnt, the *Logical Composition View* is a feature model for capturing the SCV of a PLA. This view allows developers to formalize what features are available in the PLA, the hierarchical relationships between features, and the rules for selecting groups of features.

To capture a formal definition of the PLA, the components on which it is based must be modeled. The *Feature* element is the basic building block in the Logical Composition View. A Feature represents an indivisible unit of functionality, such as an EJB or CORBA component. In the CONST application, the various algorithm implementations for the constraints optimization engine are represented as Features. A configuration is a valid composition of Features that produces a complete set of application functionality. Each configuration may require different source artifacts depending on the features that it contains.

The feature model rules are specified through composition predicates. FireAnt supports that standard feature modeling constraints for AND, Exclusive OR and optional features. The children of each feature are connected through a composition predicate to their parent to specify the rules governing their selection. In CONST, for example, the *ConstraintsOptimizationModule* is connected to the Exclusive OR predicate, which can be connected to each algorithm packaged with the optimizer to create a variant. This composition indicates that the *ConstraintOptimizationModule* is composed from one of the three algorithms.

To specify the compositional variability in the PLA, developers build Component, Assembly, and Predicate trees, which we call *Logical Composition* Trees. At the root of the tree is an Assembly representing the entire PLA. The root Assembly, Predicate, and children specify the modules that must be present to complete the PLA. Each level down the tree specifies the composition of smaller pieces of functionality.

In the CONST system, the root of the feature model is the CONST Assembly. The CONST Assembly is connected to an AND predicate and the predicate is in turn connected to the PickupList and Optimizer Assemblies, which specifies that both a PickupList and Optimizer must be present in CONST variants. The CONST Logical Composition tree is shown in Figure 4.

Figure 4. Feature model notation

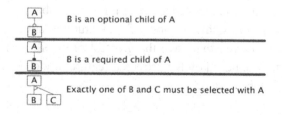

Figure 5. CONST logical composition tree

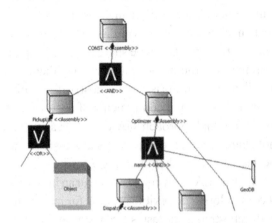

Figure 6. Logical deployment tree for the Geo-Database assembly

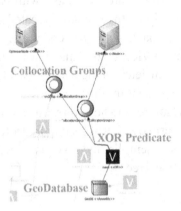

By capturing PLA compositional variability in a feature model through the Logical Composition tree, developers can formally specify how valid variants are composed. With a formal specification of the variant construction rules, FireAnt can automatically explore the variant solution space to discover all valid compositional variants of the PLA.

DEPENDENCY AND DEPLOYMENT VIEWS

Simply capturing the configuration rules for the PLA is not sufficient to automate deployment and testing. FireAnt must have a specification of how the features in the feature model map down to individual source artifacts. For example, if the *ConstraintsOptimizationModule* is selected, what Java jar files need to be packaged into the final variant that is tested.

To automate the packaging and configuration of variants and address Challenge 3, a dependency model must be developed to associate each feature with physical artifacts, such as JAR files, it relies on. This mapping from physical artifacts to PLA components can be used to automatically manage and package the artifacts and configuration scripts required for each variant. The depen-

dency model is a platform-specific model in the MDA paradigm.

The Dependency View manages the complexity of organizing and maintaining all the various physical artifacts required to deploy and configure a variant. A variant may contain hundreds of components, each with multiple physical artifacts required for their deployment. As the number of variants grows, it becomes hard to package all physical artifacts required to deploy a variant. Our CONST application, for example, has 72 unique valid package combinations that can be created for the variants. Each possible package requires a unique artifact set.

In distributed applications, developers may need to test the deployment of the application across different numbers and configurations of hardware. FireAnt's *Physical Deployment View* allows developers to specify rules on how features and their associated artifacts can be mapped to a series of remote hosts. Because the physical deployment view is not tied to any specific hardware or software implementation, it is a platform-independent model. FireAnt then takes each of these possible deployment variants and determines the unique packaging combinations of artifacts that are required for all possible valid deployments. Each unique package is called an *Egg*.

The *Physical Composition View* shows which physical artifacts are associated with each egg. Individual zip archives can be created for each deployment package by traversing the Physical Composition View trees. This view manages the complexity of determining what physical artifacts should be present in for the deployment of each variant's features to a host. FireAnt can automatically collect and zip all of the required artifacts for a variant's Assemblies by traversing the Physical Composition Tree.

EMPIRICALLY EVALUATING FIREANT GENERATIVE AND ANALYTIC CAPABILITIES

A method for estimating the point at which developing a PLA becomes more cost effective than a traditional development approach is described in (Coplien 1998). This paper defines the average economic or time cost of developing a variant manually without a PLA to be C_0 and the cost of the same development with automation to be C_1. To develop N variants using a manual approach, therefore, has a total cost of $N*C_0$. A is defined to be the initial overhead of performing SCV analysis and creating reusable components. C_1 is assumed to be smaller than C_0. The cost of developing the same N variants with a PLA is $A + N * C_1$.

For small numbers of variants, the initial cost A does not make a PLA cost effective. As the number of variants, N, grows, however, a PLA becomes more cost effective since $C_1 < C_0$. This section expands on this formula to estimate the cost of testing N variants developed manually and N variants developed with a PLA. We then show how FireAnt can decrease the initial cost A of developing a testing infrastructure for a PLA.

In the context of testing, we let T_0 be the cost of manually developing the infrastructure to test a variant and T_1 be the cost of developing the same infrastructure for a PLA variant. T_1 should be significantly smaller than T_0, since tests for determining the correctness of individual components can be reused for each variant. Moreover, any tests that check the correctness of a common element among the variants can be shared. To develop the testing infrastructure for a new variant, therefore, T_1 will only be comprised of the cost of developing tests for the unique components of each variant. With a manual approach, however, the variants do not share common components and tests cannot be shared among them making $T_0 > T_1$.

With a PLA, conversely, we incur an initial cost A of developing a flexible process for integrating and orchestrating the tests shared between variants. Even with the use of automation tools, such as those available for running JUnit tests, a developer must manually specify which tests to run for each variant. The total cost of testing N variants is $N*T_0$ for the manual approach and $A+N*T_1$ for the PLA. The goal of developing a testing infrastructure of a PLA is therefore to minimize A and ensure that the overhead of creating reusable tests does not make $T_1 > T_0$.

The remainder of this section reports the results from a series of experiments on our CONST case study described in *Section 2*. The goal of these experiments was to evaluate the extent to which FireAnt minimizes the initial cost A and does not require excess testing overhead that would increase T_1. Each experiment was repeated using several variations of the PLA to investigate how the performance of FireAnt scaled as the solution space grew. For testing, we used FireAnt 2.0 with a 2.2 Mhz AMD Athlon 3200 with 1 gigabyte of RAM running Windows XP and Eclipse 3.1.0. Our test cases were written using JUnit.

SOLUTION SPACE EXPLORATION TIME

In our CONST case study, we evaluated the time required by FireAnt to discover and visualize all valid variants. Our initial implementation of CONST contained 17 EJBs, each packaged in

Figure 7. Solution space exploration time

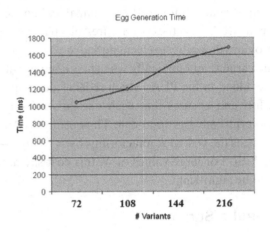

individual Enterprise Application Resource (EAR) files with separate XML deployment descriptors to facilitate packaging. To analyze the impact of refactoring, which is the modification of the systems code and models, and its affect on FireAnt and the solution space, we created a new type of PickupList that was a hybrid priority/FIFO list. A waiting request's priority was determined by the time multiplied by the priority. Adding this PickupList implementation increased the number of valid variants to 108.

In our second refactoring, we provided two new graph representations for the optimization algorithm. One implementation used an in-memory graph representation. The second implementation used a disk-based graph representation scheme to reduce memory footprint. This refactoring increased the number of valid variants to 144. In the final refactoring, we combined both the PickupList and algorithm refactoring, which produced 216 valid variants. For each PLA, we calculated the time for FireAnt to generate all of the valid configurations (Eggs). The results of the tests are shown in Figure 7.

Figure 7 shows that the time required, D_v, to explore the solution space scaled at a rate of approximately $N * D_I + K$, where D_I is the time required by FireAnt to discover a single variant and K a constant overhead. The maximum time required was less than 2 seconds. It can be seen that $D_I = (D_V (72) - D_V (216)) / 144 < 700 / 144 = 4.8$ms. We posit that to discover the same set of variants manually, the time required would be $V(N) * N * D_0 + K$, where $D_0 > D_I$ $V(N)$ is a function of N, and $V(N) > V(N-1) \geq 1$ for all N.

These results show that the discovery of a single variant is slower with a manual process and the time to discover all variants becomes increasingly worse as the number of variants grows, which stems from the inability of manual methods to scale as the complexity increases. Even without a $V(N)$ manual scaling factor and optimistically assuming $D_0 = 1000$ms, the FireAnt aided method is roughly 200 times faster. If a PLA architecture is used with a manual approach for assigning tests to variants, A varies in proportion to $V(N)$. By using FireAnt, $V(N)$ is removed and D_I is far smaller than D_0, and thus, the cost, A, is significantly reduced for large numbers of variants.

Packaging Time

FireAnt also has the ability to collect all the resources needed to deploy a variant and package them in separate zip files for deployment across a group of nodes. FireAnt uses the Eggs and Dependency Tree to calculate the minimum physical artifacts required for each node's package. Along with the package generator, we created a translator that generates ANT build scripts for the deployment of the variant's packages. FireAnt can support generation of other scripting languages. We chose ANT, however, since it is platform-independent and well supported.

For each variant/deployment configuration, FireAnt generates local ANT scripts that are executed on each node to perform the Assembly installations. The generated ANT scripts invoke the appropriate PreDeployment, Deployment, and PostDeployment scripts required to install each component. After installing each component or assembly, the generated ANT scripts invoke any tests associated with the element in the Depen-

Figure 8. FireAnt packaging time

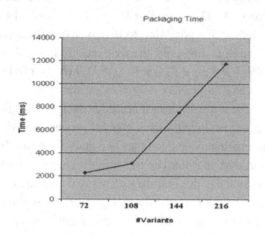

dency view, which enables automated testing of each variant. FireAnt also generates a global deployment script to execute the deployment, configuration, and testing of each variant consecutively. Developers simply provide the scripts to configure and deploy the individual assemblies and / or components.

We used our AMD Athlon 3200 test platform to measure, O_v, which is how long it took FireAnt to package all of the resources and generate the ANT build scripts for each of the variants. We then measured the time required for FireAnt to collect and zip the files for each package. The results are shown in Figure 8.

The results in this figure show that using Fire-Ant, $O_v = N * P_1 + K$, where P_1 is the time taken to package and generate the configuration script for a single variant using FireAnt and K is a constant overhead. Again, a manual approach to accomplishing the same task would require that $O_v = V(N) * N * P_0 + K$, where P_0 is the time to manually package a variant, $P_0 > P_1$, $V(N)$ is a function of N, and $V(N) > V(N-1) \geq 1$ for all N. As can be seen from the results, $P_1 < (12000 - 2000) / 144 = 69.4$ms.

Assuming that a manual process could package all the artifacts required for a variant in 1000ms (which is extremely optimistic), the FireAnt aided

method is still ~14 times faster. The FireAnt method again removes a $V(N)$ manual scaling factor, as well, from the cost A. FireAnt's packaging provides the ability to calculate and re-package all the variants automatically when new components are added to the PLA, which reduces developer effort and ensures that each variant's package footprint is always up-to-date. Thus, using FireAnt reduces the cost of R refactorings by $R * (V(N) - 1) * 14$. For large values of N, this cost savings will be significant.

Results Summary

FireAnt automates (1) the generation of deployment scripts for variants, (2) the packaging of artifacts for variants, and (3) the testing of variants. These capabilities reduce the upfront cost, A, and enable rigorous testing of PLAs. They also address each of the four key challenges outlined earlier.

Due to the large number of variants it becomes costly for PLA developers to manually find and manage all possible variants without MDA tool support. This complexity increases the initial cost, A, of developing a PLA testing infrastructure since a developer must find all valid variants and determine which tests are required to ensure the proper functioning of each. In other words, $A \geq Dv + Ov$, where D_v is the time required to find each valid variant and O_v is the time required to generate an orchestration script for each variant that will execute the proper tests.

FireAnt reduces the initial cost A by automatically exploring the solution space and producing visualizations of valid variants for the developer. These capabilities significantly aid developer understanding of PLA variability and enables for the automated testing and packaging of each variant. Without automating the identification of variants of the PLA to test, it is hard to ensure that the PLA is tested properly, which is important in mission-critical domains.

FUTURE RESEARCH DIRECTIONS

In future work, we are pursuing the use of FireAnt to create self-tuning installations. Many high-performance parallel computing applications, such as the Automatically Tuned Linear Algebra Software (ATLAS) (Whaley 2000), run performance tests in multiple configurations as part of the installation process. These applications can then interpret the performance results to optimize themselves for the given hardware.

We also plan to expand on the ATLAS approach by allowing FireAnt users to define a fitness function based on the performance metrics collected from the individual component tests. The FireAnt test automation framework will then be used to iteratively deploy variants in various configurations in an attempt to maximize this fitness function.

Developers will only need to create the tests to collect the appropriate data, such as service rate, and then provide the logic to perform analyses on the results, such as throughput analysis using queuing networks, to score the configurations. FireAnt will use this cost function to automatically deploy, configure, test, and score each candidate variant in each valid component to hardware configuration. After all testing completes, FireAnt will collect the results and install the variant/component to hardware configuration with the highest score.

CONCLUSION

Product-line architectures (PLAs) can significantly improve the reuse of software components and decrease the cost of developing applications. The large number of valid variations in a PLA must be tested to ensure that only working configurations are used. Due to the large solution spaces it is infeasible or overly costly to use traditional *ad hoc* methods to test a PLA's variants.

By using MDA tools to capture the compositional and deployment variability in PLAs, we showed that much of the deployment, configuration, and testing of PLAs can be automated. This automation frees developers to focus on implementing reusable components and deployment and configuration scripts for known working units of functionality. Our experiments have shown that FireAnt can significantly reduce both the initial cost, A, of developing a PLA and the testing cost T_1 of each variant. FireAnt accomplishes this cost reduction by automating tedious and error-prone manual tasks, such as solution space exploration.

The following are our lessons learned from developing FireAnt and applying it to the EJB-based *Constraints Optimization System (CONST)* that schedules pickup requests to vehicles:

- **There is a larger up-front cost to adopt an automated test platform.** Initially, the cost of developing models for the MDA testing process increases development cost. Over time, however, this startup cost is amortized across variants of the SPL saving time and money.
- **Choosing the right statistical analysis technique for test results is an important concern.** This chapter introduces a few statistical analyses that can be used to populate quality attribute values from test results. There are a wide array of other types of analyses that can be used as well.
- **There may be unanticipated problems caused by the composition of two or more features** that may not be scriptable by FireAnt. For example, complex changes in source code may be needed. More work is needed to identify how to automate the generation of the deployment and configuration glue of PLA variants.
- **Deployment variations greatly expand the solution space** since each variant must be tested with each deployment variation. It is thus important to only model realistic deployment scenarios to restrict this space.

REFERENCES

Asikainen, T., Männistö, T., & Soininen, T. (2004). Representing Feature Models of Software Product Families Using a Configuration Ontology. In *Proceedings of the ECAI 2004, Workshop on Configuration*, Valencia, Spain.

Batory, D., Sarvela, J., & Rauschmayer, A. (2004). Scaling step-wise refinement. *IEEE Transactions on Software Engineering, 30*(6), 355–371.

Benavides, D., Trinidad, P., & Ruiz-Cortes, A. (2005). Automated Reasoning on Feature Models. In *Proceedings of the 17th Conference on Advanced Information Systems Engineering*, LNCS, (pp. 491-503).

Bosch, J., Florijn, G., Greefhorst, D., Kuusela, J., Obbink, J., & Pohl, K. (2002). Variability issues in software product lines. *Lecture Notes in Computer Science*, 13–21.

Brown, A. (2008). MDA Redux: Practical Realization of Model Driven Architecture. In *Proceedings of the Seventh International Conference on Composition-Based Software Systems (ICCBSS 2008)*, (pp. 174–183).

Chen, M., Qiu, X., Xu, W., Wang, L., Zhao, J., & Li, X. (2007). UML Activity Diagram-Based Automatic Test Case Generation For Java Programs. *The Computer Journal*.

Clements, P. C., & Northrop, L. (2001). *Software Product Lines – Practices, and Patterns*. Reading, MA: Addison-Wesley.

Coplien, J., Hoffman, D., & Weiss, D. (1998). Commonality and Variability in Software Engineering. *IEEE Software, 15*(6), 37–45. doi:10.1109/52.730836

Dai, Z. R. (2004). Model-driven Testing with UML 2.0, In *Proceedings of the Second European Workshop on Model Driven Architecture (MDA)*, Canterbury, UK.

Ding, H., Kihwal, L., & Sha, L. (2005). Dependency Algebra: A Theoretical Framework for Dependency Management in Real-Time Control Systems. In *Proceedings of the 12th IEEE International Conference on the Engineering of Computer-Based Systems*, Greenbelt, MD.

Edwards, G., Deng, G., Schmidt, D., Gokhale, A., & Natarajan, B. (2004). Model-driven Configuration and Deployment of Component Middleware Publisher/Subscriber Services. In *Proceedings of the 3rd ACM Conference on Generative Programming and Component Engineering*, Vancouver, CA.

France, R., & Rumpe, B. (2007). Model-driven development of complex software: A research roadmap. In *International Conference on Software Engineering*, (pp. 37–54). IEEE Computer Society Washington, DC, USA.

Gokhale, A., Schmidt, D., Natarajan, B., Gray, J., & Wang, N. (2003). *Model-Driven Middleware*. Middleware for Communications.

Gomaa, H., & Webber, D. (2004). Modeling adaptive and evolvable software product lines using the variation point model. In *Proceedings of the Proceedings of the 37th Annual Hawaii International Conference on System Sciences (HICSS'04)-Track*, vol. 9, (pp. 05–08).

Guo, J., Liao, Y., Gray, J., & Bryant, B. (2005). Using connectors to integrate software components. In *Proceedings of the International Conference on the Engineering of Computer-Based Systems (ECBS)*, Greenbelt, MD.

Hallsteinsen, S., Hinchey, M., Park, S., & Schmid, K. (2008). Dynamic Software Product Lines. *Computer, 41*(4), 93–95. doi:10.1109/MC.2008.123

Harrold, M., Liang, D., & Sinha, S. (1999). An Approach to Analyzing and Testing Component-Based Systems. In *Proceedings of the ICSE'99 Workshop on Testing Distributed Component-Based Systems*, Los Angeles, CA.

Hatcliff, J., Deng, W., Dwyer, W., Jung, G., & Prasad, V. (2003) Cadena: An Integrated Development, Analysis, and Verification Environment for Component-based Systems. In *Proceedings of the 25th International Conference on Software Engineering*, Portland, OR.

Kang, K., Cohen, S. G., Hess, J. A., Novak, W. E., & Peterson, S. A. (1990). *Feature Oriented Domain Analysis (FODA) - Feasibility Study, Technical report CMU/SEI-90-TR-21*, Carnegie-Mellon University, Pittsburg, PA.

Kang, K., Lee, J., & Donohoe, P. (2002). Feature-oriented product line engineering. *IEEE Software*, *19*(4), 58–65. doi:10.1109/MS.2002.1020288

Kang, K. C., Lee, J., & Donohoe, P. (2002). Feature-oriented Product Line Engineering. *IEEE Software*, *19*(4), 58–65. doi:10.1109/MS.2002.1020288

Karsai, G., Neema, S., & Sharp, D. (2008). Model-driven architecture for embedded software: A synopsis and an example. *Science of Computer Programming*, *73*(1), 26–38. doi:10.1016/j.scico.2008.05.006

Krishna, A., Turkay, E., Gokhale, A., & Schmidt, D. (2005). Model-Driven Techniques for Evaluating the QoS of Middleware Configurations for DRE Systems. In *Proceedings of the 11th IEEE Real-Time and Embedded Technology and Applications Symposium*, San Francisco, CA.

Kumar, V. (1992). Algorithms for Constraint-Satisfaction Problems: A Survey. *AI Magazine*, *13*(1), 32–44.

Laguna, M., & Gonzaonza, M. G, B., & Marque, J. (2007). Seamless development of software product lines. In *Proceedings of the 6th international conference on Generative programming and component engineering*, (pp. 94).

Ledeczi, A., Bakay, A., Maroti, M., Volgysei, P., Nordstrom, G., Sprinkle, J., & Karsai, G. (2001). *Composing Domain-Specific Design Environments*. IEEE Computer.

Mannisto, T., Soininen, R., & Sulonen, R. (2001). Product Configuration View to Software Product Families. In *Proceedings of the 10th Int. Workshop on Software Configuration Management (SCM-10) of ICSE*, Ontario, Canada.

Matena, V., & Hapner, M. (1999). *Enterprise Java Beans Specification, Version 1.1*. Sun Microsystems.

Memon, A., Porter, A., Yilmaz, C., Nagarajan, A., & Schmidt, D. Natarajan. B. (2004). Skoll: Distributed Continuous Quality Assurance. In *Proceedings of the 26th International Conference on Software Engineering*, Edinburgh, Scotland, (pp. 459-468).

Metzger, A., Heymans, P., Pohl, K., Schobbens, P., & Saval, G. (2007). Disambiguating the documentation of variability in software product lines: A separation of concerns, formalization and automated analysis. In *Proceedings of the Requirements Engineering Conference*, (pp. 243–253).

Oppenheimer, D., Ganapathi, A., & Patterson, D. (2003). Why do Internet Services Fail, and What can be Done about It? In *Proceedings of the USENIX Symposium on Internet Technologies and Systems*, Seattle, WA.

Paige, R., Hartman, A., Rensink, A. (2009). *Model Driven Architecture Foundtions and Applications*.

Popovic, M., & Velikic, I. (2005). A Generic Model-Based Test Case Generator. In *Proceedings of the 12th IEEE International Conference on the Engineering of Computer-Based Systems (ECBS)*, Greenbelt, MD.

Sharp, D. (1999). Avionics Product Line Software Architecture Flow Policies, In *Proceedings of the 18th IEEE/AIAA Digital Avionics Systems Conference (DASC)*, St. Louis, MO.

Sloane, A. (2000). Modeling Deployment and Configuration of CORBA Systems with UML. In *Proceedings of the 22nd International Conference on Software Engineering*, Limerick, Ireland.

Trujillo, S., Batory, D., & Diaz, O. (2007). Feature oriented model driven development: A case study for portlets. In *Proceedings of the 29th international conference on Software Engineering*, (pp. 44–53).

Voelter, M., & Groher, I. (2007). Product line implementation using aspect-oriented and model-driven software development. In *Proceedings of the International Conference on Software Product Lines*, (pp. 233–242).

Wang, N., Gill, C., Schmidt, C., & Subramonian, V. (2004). Configuring Real-time Aspects in Component Middleware. In *Proceedings of the Conference on Distributed Objects and Applications*, Cyprus, Greece.

Weyuker, E. J. (1998). *Testing Component-based Software: A Cautionary Tale. IEEE Software*. September/October.

Whaley, R. C., Petitet, A., & Dongarra, J. J. (2000). *Automated empirical optimizations of software and the atlas project. Technical report*. Knoxville: Dept. of Computer Sciences, Univ. of TN.

White, J., Benavides, D., Dougherty, B., & Schmidt, D. (2009). Automated Reasoning for Multi-step Configuration Problems. In *Proceedings of the Software Product Lines Conference (SPLC)*. San Francisco, USA.

White, J., & Schmidt, D. (2005). Simplifying the Development of Product-Line Customization Tools via MDA. In *Proceedings of the Workshop on MDA for Software Product Lines, ACM/IEEE 8th International Conference on Model Driven Engineering Languages and Systems*, Montego Bay, Jamaica.

White, J., Schmidt, D. C., Benavides, D., Trinidad, P., & Ruiz-Cortez, A. (2008). Automated Diagnosis of Product-line Configuration Errors in Feature Models. In *Proceedings of the Software Product Lines Conference (SPLC)*, (pp. 225–234). Limerick, Ireland.

KEY TERMS AND DEFINITIONS

Product-Line Architecture: A software architecture that is designed with specific points of variability to allow it to be adapted for different requirement sets.

FireAnt: A product-line deployment and testing automation tool.

Model Interpreters: Executable code that can read a model and generate output, such as source code artifacts or analyses.

Feature Modeling: A modeling technique that uses commonality and variability analysis to map the configuration space of a software product-line.

Constraint Satisfaction Problems: Mathematical formulations that specify a set of variables and constraints governing the allowed values of the variables.

Quality Attributes: Annotations added to a feature model to specify numeric properties of a feature.

Constraint Solver: An executable program that automates the derivation of correct solutions to a constraint satisfaction problem.

Chapter 16

Applying UML Extensions in Modeling Software Product Line Architecture of a Distribution Services Platform

Liliana Dobrica
University Politehnica of Bucharest, Romania

Eila Ovaska
VTT Technical Research Centre of Finland, Finland

ABSTRACT

UML provides the means to use specific variation mechanisms to describe hierarchical systems. However, it does not support a description of variation, as it is required for service architecture. UML built-in extension mechanisms refine its specification. This chapter presents the extensions of the UML for representing variations in the software product line architecture of middleware services. The product line is defined as a middleware services framework that includes several products. The products realize different functionality by using various modern software technologies of spontaneous networks. Architecture design produces descriptions at two abstraction levels from multiple viewpoints. The modeling of service architectures benefits from a more familiar and widely used notation that improves stakeholders' understanding of the architectural artifacts. A standard based notation also enables more extensive tool support for manipulating architecture models.

INTRODUCTION

For several years the focus of our research has been product line architecture design and analysis. An important goal is to define a method for modeling software product line architecture of a distribution services platform. An essential issue is to explic-itly represent variation and indicate locations for which changes are allowed in design. In this way, the diagrammatic description of the product line architecture defined by using the method helps in instantiating it for a particular product or in its evolution for future use. From the product line architecture documented diagrammatically, it is easy to detect what kind of modifications, omis-

DOI: 10.4018/978-1-61692-874-2.ch016

sions and extensions are permitted, expected or required. Initially, the method can be described by defining and using a framework that consisted of, among other ingredients, an underlying model, referring to the kinds of constructs are represented, manipulated and analyzed by the model and, a language, which is a concrete means of describing the constructs, considering possible diagrammatic notations. In order to achieve an optimal method, these ingredients can be defined or selected more properly. Some of them may already be available, from the literature, tool vendors or as open source distribution, whereas others may have to be specially developed.

Nowadays a considerable interest exists in applying UML to modeling the reference architecture of a software product line. The work in this chapter presents UML extensions for the management of variability in the space of software product line architectures. The extensions are described based on several predefined architectural views and exemplified on a case study. The aim is to introduce and utilize new constructs that indicate variability and represent a profile of the extended UML concepts intended primarily for use in modeling product line architectures. The new constructs are used together with other UML concepts of superstructure to provide a complete modeling tool set.

The case study that is exemplified to validate the UML notation extensions for architectural designs is represented by a set of four software products. The goal is to model the architecture of a software framework for distributed middleware services that includes common and variable features. Moreover, the result, the model, takes account of not only the known styles and design patterns, but also separation of concerns, variability sources, and locality criteria. By separating different concerns in distinct views and identifying different variability sources we manage complexity and reduce the risk of non-anticipation variation. Locality criteria facilitate determining

what information goes into architecture model and what implementation specific is.

Our case study defines and applies concepts and principles about product line architecture modeling as a state of art research needed for theory development to establish the basis for understanding the research domain. The definition of middleware as "a variety of distributed computing services and application development supporting environments that operate between the application logic and underlying system" (Charles, 1999) is similar to software product line definition that is "a set of products sharing a common, managed set of features that satisfy the specific needs of a particular mission" (Clements & Northrop, 2000, 2002). Thus, building the architecture of a framework for distributed middleware services is equivalent to modeling product line architecture. Distributed computing services represent the shared common, managed set of features that satisfy the specific distribution needs.

This chapter is organized as follows. As a background, in the beginning we discuss concepts related to architecture modeling and variability. Our focus is on different types of variability that are visible in an architecture description. Next section introduces our perspective on modeling variability by UML extensions for service architecture description. Then we introduce the case study to illustrate our approach in modeling variability for product line architecture of distributed middleware services. Finally, in the last section, we provide some future research directions and concluding remarks.

BACKGROUND

Architecture Description

Components and services. The architecture of any software system is defined in terms of components and interactions among those components. Product line architecture is defined in the same terms and is the main tangible element shared by all the product line members. Product line architecture components cover common functionality and support variability. In the literature differences could be identified in what a component is. The UML User's Guide (OMG, 2005) defines a component as a physical entity rather than a logical entity as needed for architecture description. (Shaw & Garlan, 1996) consider that computational components, such as layers in a hierarchical system, define architecture. Later on, a new definition (Bachman et al., 2000) focuses on design rules that impose a standard coordination model on all components. These rules take the form of a component model, or a set of standards and conventions to which components must conform. From a product line architecture perspective, (Webber, 2001) defines a component as *"a group of coherent classes conforming to a reference architecture which may contain variation points. It is a large grain deployable unit."*

Modern distributed systems are software-intensive systems that embody service architecture and provide a variety of services for their users. A service is the capability of an entity (the server) to perform, upon request of another entity (the client), an act that can be perceived and exploited by the client. Services are constructed by a set of software components, which are *"units of composition with contractually specified interfaces and explicit context dependencies"* (Szyperski, 1997).

Architecture development. There are several architectural development approaches that can be adopted to service based software systems development. The Model-Driven Architecture described in (OMG, 2003) is an approach that guides the specification of information systems. The idea is to separate descriptions of functionality from the implementation specifications and thus provide the interoperability and portability of a system. Implementation independent descriptions of functionality last longer than implementation specifications that change as soon as a better technology is available. Here a model means a formal

specification of part of the function, structure and/or behavior of a system. A formal specification expects either textual or graphical language with strictly defined syntax and semantics.

Architecture development concentrates on multiple views. An architectural view as a representation of a whole system from a perspective of a related set of concerns is recommended by IEEE Std 1417-2000 (IEEE, 2000). View-oriented design approaches start with 4+1 approach of (Krutchen, 1995), that uses the logical, process, physical and development views. After this approach other new ones have been introduced (Jaaksi, Alto& Vatto, 1999; Hofmeister, Nord & Soni, 2000). Among these approaches there is no agreement on a common set of views or on the way to describe software architecture. The need for different architectural views depends mainly on three issues: the complexity of the system, the domain and the number of different stakeholders (Purhonen, Niemelä, & Matinlassi, 2004).

Methods. Architectural views have formed the basis of a number of design methods during the last few years. A considerable interest exists in applying UML to modeling software product lines (Gomaa, 2005; Dobrica & Niemela, 2007). Various views of UML (i.e. use cases, design view) may be used for modeling product line architectures. During the last decade many methods have been developed to create such models using UML notation (Atkinson, Bayer & Muthig, 2000; Coriat, Jourdan & Boisbourdin, 2000; El Kaim, Cherki, Josset, Paris & Ollagnon, 2000; Gomaa & Gianturco, 2002). Their focus was to provide a common understanding of the product line domain and to determine the commonalities and variabilities in the product line. The first generation of methods Feature-Oriented Domain Analysis (Kang, Cohen, Hess, Novak & Peterson, 1990) and Scope, Commonality and Variability (Coplien, Hoffman & Weiss, 1998) scoped the common core and uncovered the commonalities and variabilities. They defined a common set of all members in the family not a subset of the members. The next generation of methods based on variation point model (Webber, 2001) represented, by using or extending UML notation, the points of variation and hence explicitly described where in the PLA software evolution can occur. A model of a variation point adds detail into the modeling process, communicating in this way to reusers where and how to realize a product line member unique variant.

Variability

Mechanisms. An important aspect of product line architectures is variation among products, defined as variation in space (Bosch, 2000). In the past variability in software systems has been handled in an implicit manner. Due to increasing complexity, present-day software systems require a more explicit approach. It becomes important to understand how to express variability, what are the options possible (Jaring & Bosch, 2002). In software design a variability mechanism is a wide range of generalization and specialization techniques. (Jacobson, Griss & Jonsson, 1997) defined inheritance, uses, extensions, parameterization, configuration and generation. *Inheritance* creates subtypes or subclasses that specialize abstract types or classes at their variation point. Use case inheritance mechanism is for *uses*. *Extensions* are particular type-like attachments that can be used to express variant in use case and object components. *Parametrization* is for types and classes using templates, frames and macros. *Configuration* variation points are used to declaratively or procedurally connect optional or alternative components and variants into complete configurations. *Generation* provides derived components and various relationships from languages and templates. Product line architecture developers exploit these mechanisms in defining changes for each product member (Bass, Clements & Kazman 2003) or variation points (Webber & Gomaa, 2002). A variation point does not only identify locations at which the variation will occur, but it also identifies the mechanism for a reuser to extend it. (Svahnberg, van Gurp & Bosch, 2002) establish the factors that need to be considered for selecting an appropriate mechanism for implementing variability based on consequences and identify two major mechanisms, configuration management and design patterns. Many of the most commonly used design patterns are discussed in detail in (Buschmann, Meunier, Rohnert, Sommerlad & Stahl, 1996; Gamma, Helm, Johnson & Vlissides, 1995). Nevertheless, variation is difficult to model in architectural descriptions. An approach that models variation in product families using patterns is provided in (Keepence & Mannion, 1999). The authors use the family requirements specification to build an architecture that is independent of all requirements that differentiate one member from another. A requirement that make this difference is called discriminant. There are three basic types of discriminants: single discriminants, multiple discriminants and option discriminants. These types are similar to mandatory, alternative and optional features identified by (Kang et al., 1990), where features describe the functional as well as the quality characteristics of a system. Feature modeling is the key concept in software product lines, being an important phase during domain engineering with the purpose to analyze commonalities and differences among products into a features model, which is used to develop domain models, such as architecture models. Various relationships exist among features such as generalization, aggregation, utilization or mutual dependency (Dobrica & Ovaska, 2009; Szasz & Vilanova, 2008).

Sources of variation. A set of different alternatives for dealing with variation among products may be captured in various views of product line architecture. This facilitates the designer constructing a product to have the potential solutions to choose from. Identifying and separating sources of variation could be a systematization of concerns regarding anticipated variation. Several sources of variation have been introduced in (Bachmann &

Bass, 2001). These are: v*ariation in data*, where a particular data structure may vary from one product to another; *variation in function,* where a particular function may exist in some products and not in others; *variation in control flow,* where a particular pattern of interaction may vary from one product to another; *variation in technology,* where the platform (operating system, hardware, dependence on middleware, run-time system for programming language) may vary in exactly the same mode as the function; *variation in quality goals,* where the particular quality goals are important for a product; *variation in environment,* where the style in which a product interacts with its environment may vary.

Since the focus of this chapter is on how to describe variability on the architecture level, we will try to deal with variability that is visible in the architecture views. In practice, analysis of these sources is useful when the variability is architecturally relevant.

Product line architecture model. Currently there are several methods for modeling product line architectures based on UML. Several researchers have tried to use and extend UML notation for variability specification. They have introduced new symbols tagged to UML elements (McComas et al., 2000; Morisio, Travassos & Stark, 2000). The projection of variability on the software architecture through UML elements is realized in (Cherki, El Kaim, Josset & Paris, 2000) by using a package to represent a hot spot with the stereotype <<hot spot>> and tagged any collaboration with a variant with "variation point". Variability is also visible in the UML models with the variation points technique defined in (Coriat et al, 2000) providing information for a reuser to choose a variant. The mechanism of attaching attributes to each variation point, by using a class to represent it, defines the transformation to apply when doing a product derivation. Using systematically this technique requires development of specific scripts and programs to manage it, since it is not integrated in UML modeling tools. (Webber &

Gomaa, 2002) goes a step further and shows to a reuser how to build a variant. Her approach provides an excess of information to be managed by the designer in a low-level pattern.

Explicit modeling of the similarities and variations among members of the product lines by using the UML notation is also allowed separating various views. (Atkinson et al., 2000) in KobrA establish a suite of UML diagrams to represent structural, behavioral and functional models for specification and a decision model that contains information about how these models change for the different applications and thus describes the different variants of a Komponent, where this term is a shorthand for a KobrA component. A view integration approach described by (Gomma & Shin, 2003) extends the use case view and the static view for modeling product lines and a domain of product lines. It integrates the feature model with the UML package notation to define the use case view, where new stereotypes are introduced. Class diagrams with new UML stereotypes that differentiate classes are used for static modeling of the product line domain. Variability in multiple-views has been defined by a functional view with use cases, a static view with class diagrams and a dynamic view through a collaboration model and a state-chart model.

All these methods have some similarities with our approach by allowing explicit modeling of the commonalities and variations in a product line. However none of them defines UML standard extensions to be used particularly for services architecture design to describe variations that could be specified in product line architectures. Our goal is to extend UML for product lines architectures modeling using standard UML extensions mechanisms of stereotypes, constraints and tagged values (OMG, 2005). In our approach the model is prepared for change by analyzing various sources of variability that are visible in architecture description. Concrete components are defined for the prime reason of encapsulating variabilities, while abstract components are provided with the optimal balance generic/specific based on the different sources of variation analyzed for each product line member.

MODELING VARIABILITY BY UML EXTENSIONS

UML as a standard provides the means to use specific variation mechanisms to describe hierarchical systems (ways to decompose systems into smaller subsystems). However, the standard does not support a description of variation, as is required for service architecture description. UML 2.0 supports the refinement of its specification through three built-in extension mechanisms: constraints, tagged values and stereotypes. Figure 1 presents tabular forms for specifying the new refinements that have been considered. For instance, a definition of a stereotype in a table identifies the following: stereotype name, the base class of the stereotype that matches a class or subclass in the UML metamodel, the direct parent of the stereotype being defined, an informal description with possible explanatory comments and constraints associated with the stereotype. Also, the stereotype notation is specified.

We present in the following the main ideas of concerning variability that can be realized in the architecture views of our method by using UML extensions.

The method for service architectures design has two abstraction levels: conceptual and concrete (Matinlassi, Niemelä, & Dobrica, 2002). Conceptual level means abstract, i.e. delayed design decisions concerning, e.g. technologies to be selected or details in functionality, whereas the concrete level illustrates realization of conceptual architecture. Architecture design produces descriptions at both abstraction levels from four viewpoints: structural, behavior, deployment and development. The structural view is concerned with the composition of software components, whereas the behavior view takes the dynamics

Figure 1. Examples of stereotypes, constraints and tag definitions

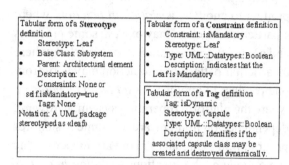

into consideration. The deployment view refers to the allocation of software components to various computing environments. The development view represents the categorization and management of domains, technologies and work allocation. Our focus is on structural, behavior and deployment views presented first on conceptual level, then on concrete level of service architecture description. The development view is not in the scope of this chapter, however detailed information is provided in (Niemela, Matinlassi & Lago, 2003).

Conceptual Level

Conceptual structural view. Variation in this view is divided into structural variation (between Leaf/ Subsystem components) and internal variation (within Leaf components). We separate components and configurations from each other to enable variation. Flexible and adaptable structures are needed to instantiate components and bind them into configurations during product derivation.

Structural variation has to offer the possibility of preventing automatic selection of all Leaf or Subsystem components included in a System during product derivation. Variability is included in this view by using specific stereotypes for the architectural elements as shown in Figure 2. Thus we consider a Leaf or a Subsystem is further stereotyped in:

Figure 2. Variable points and internal variation of a mandatoryLeaf component included in conceptual structural view

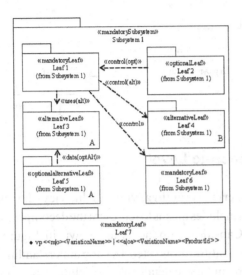

- «mandatoryLeaf» or «mandatorySubsystem»
- «alternativeLeaf» or «alternativeSubsystem»
- «optionalAlternativeLeaf» or «optionalAlternativeSubsystem»
- «optionalLeaf» or «optionalSubsystem».

If it's required, in case of «alternative» or «optionalAlternative» variability of a Leaf or Subsystem, the inclusion in the package symbol of a reference to the anticipated product that requires specific architectural element may be permitted.

Some of the constraints that govern variability modeling cannot be expressed by the UML metamodel. They concern the following:

- If a «mandatorySubsystem» only consists of «optionalLeaf» components, at least one of them must be selected during the derivation process; otherwise, a «Subsystem» that only consists of «optionalLeaf» components must be an «optionalSubsystem».
- Two «alternativeLeaf» or «alternativeSubsystem» components of different products

are exclusive, meaning that only one can be selected for a product. The product is specified at the bottom of the symbol.

- There should be no relationships between *alternative* or *optionalAlternative* components; they belong to different products. All relations to an *optional* component must also be optional.

The relationships are stereotyped: «control», «data», «uses», «control (opt)», «data (opt)», «uses (opt)», «control (optAlt)», «data (optAlt)», «uses (optAlt)».

We define *internal variation* only for Leaf components. A Leaf component is on the lowest hierarchical level and may perform functional requirements variable for different products. The internal variation of Leaf components is designated by a ● symbol as shown in Figure 2 for *Leaf7*. Although the symbol is not included in the UML standard, (Jacobson et al., 1997) and later (Webber, 2001) introduced this symbol for variation points. The UML tag syntax

●*vp <<m|o><VariationName>> | <<a|oa><VariationName><ProductId>>*

shows the parts of an internal variation so that the developer can build a product. Mandatory (m) or optional (o) functionality (*VariationName*) of a Leaf component is specified in the tag syntax. In the case of alternative (*a*) or optionalAlternative (*oa*) the product identifier (*ProductId*) is also specified.

Conceptual behavior view. This view may be mapped directly onto a hierarchy of UML collaboration diagrams. The elements are roles/instances of the Subsystem stereotypes defined in the conceptual structural view (Figure 3).

Variable parts of a collaboration or interaction diagram are represented with dashed lines or alternative branches. Optional messages between ServiceComponents use dashed lines with solid arrowheads. Collaboration diagrams describe each

Figure 3. Variability notation in conceptual behavior view

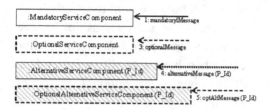

Figure 4. DeploymentNode, DeploymentUnits and Leaf elements

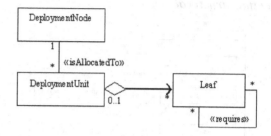

operation that is part of the specification requirements. Similar to the structural view, *alternative* and *optionalAlternative* ServiceComponents may be represented in this view. An identifier of the specific product that requires a particular interaction should be introduced and represented in the diagram.

Conceptual deployment view. In UML a deployment diagram shows the structure of the nodes on which the components are deployed. The concepts related to a deployment diagram are Node and Component. DeploymentNode is a UML Node that represents a processing platform for various services. The notation used for DeploymentNode is a Node stereotyped as «DeploymentNode». UML notation for Node (a 3-dimensional view of a cube) is appropriate for this architectural element.

A DeploymentUnit is composed of one or more conceptual leaf components as shown in Figure 4. Clustering is done according to a mutual requirement relationship between leafs. It cannot be split or deployed on more than one node. The stereotype, «deploymentUnit» is a specialization of the ArchitecturalElement stereotype and applies only to Subsystem, which is a subclass of Classifier in the UML metamodel. The other stereotypes «mandatory», «mandatoryActive», «mandatoryPassive», «optional» and «alternative» are specializations of the DeploymentUnit stereotype and also apply to Subsystem. *Exclude* is a new stereotype of UML association introduced in this diagram.

Concrete Level

Concrete structural view. In this view the notation includes means to represent the decomposition of Capsule components as shown in Figure 5. This feature allows step-by-step understanding of more and more details of the architecture model. Decomposition also shows possible variations. A Capsule cannot only be decomposed into component Capsules, but can also be decomposed so that new functionality is revealed.

Between abstract components there are decomposition relationships. Concrete components of particular products are obtained by specialization. The notation of Capsules specifies particular product (A) or subset of products (B, C) at the bottom of the symbol. Looking top-down, the AbstractComponents encapsulated in the «TopCapsule» are decomposed into «subsystemCapsule» abstract components: CapsuleS$_1$,…, Cap-

Figure 5. Structural variation in concrete view

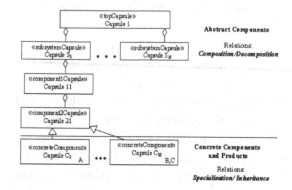

suleS$_N$. Decomposition continues on «component1Capsule», «component2Capsule» and so on, if necessary. In each component, abstract functions of the corresponding sub-domains are collected, which are subsets of the parent abstract functions. For each product, an abstract component is specialized in a «concreteComponent». This view may include indication regarding products or product sets, thus providing information about the reusability of each component.

Concrete behavior view. This view describes how the system reacts in response to external stimuli and is mostly modeled using two main important diagrams: a state diagram and a message sequence diagram. State machines are used with the concrete structural view's entities: capsules, ports and protocols. Standard UML state charts are applied for modeling the state machines of capsules, which in combination with inheritance, facilitates reuse.

Variability is included in notation and state decomposition. As for notation, parts that are not needed in all products are represented with dashed lines (optional states) or a different fill pattern and Product_Id (alternative states). State decomposition is the other source of variants. The decomposition of a state may be shown by a small symbol in the top left corner of a state symbol. Figure 6 presents variable point notations in state diagrams.

Figure 6. Variable points notation in state diagrams

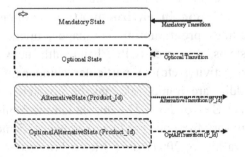

Concrete deployment view. This view is mapped directly on the deployment diagram of UML. UML deployment diagrams are much less well explained in the standard than other elements of UML. However, nodes - the UML elements which represent processing elements – are Classifiers in UML, which means that they can have instances, play roles in collaborations, realize interfaces, etc. They can also contain instances of components.

CASE STUDY

Description and Analysis

The starting point of our exercise represents descriptions of core classes implemented in four products that focus on distribution of middleware services. The products represent the following software systems: a dynamic distributed platform, a Bluetooth connectivity component for Java, a Jini service framework, and a video camera demonstration for Jini service framework. In this section we introduce the products by describing their main functional features validated through implementation.

The first product, the dynamic distributed platform, is a framework for distributed applications. Its can be synthesized in "to perform all that is required for the task of distribution". The goal is to connect pieces of distributed applications that may reach each other over various means of communications. The second product that contributed to the development of our framework is the Bluetooth connectivity component, which is an example of a component that can establish connectivity through new media, protocols and connectivity methods. This was designed to be used in applications that employ spontaneous wireless communications. Considering the features of our framework, the second product represents a specific component added to the communication services. The functionality of the third product, the

Jini service framework, is described completely by three properties. a) It creates a set of extendible classes that would automatically perform the most important functions required from a Jini service or service user. b) It transfers legacy client-server applications into Jini services with minimal changes, and c) It creates a new Jini service that has distinct types for a service user and a service session. The fourth product, the video camera demonstration system, represents a distributed application that has been implemented as a proof-of-concept to demonstrate the functionality of the third product. The provided service is a live video stream from a camera. The service user needs all necessary code from the service for viewing the video stream. The differences between these products express variation in our product line architecture model. In the following we will analyze each source of variation that brings variants, considering the four products of the case study.

Variation in function: Directory Service is a component important for a middleware framework. A 'proactive mode" of Directory Service (Bustamante, Widener & Schwan, 2002) is a variant through which clients can subscribe to be notified about changes in their objects of interest. Clients use filters to remotely tune the detail and granularity of notifications. Three products have the same requirements in functionality, i.e. distribution of applications and the Bluetooth connectivity component has a variant of communication service based on a different communication protocol.

Variation in data: We distinguish video camera demonstration that functions with multimedia streams. Architecturally, of concern is fidelity, which is the property that defines the degree to which data presented at a client matches the reference copy at a server (Noble, Narayannan, Tilton, Flinn & Walker, 1997). Fidelity includes consistency and the type of data. Data consistency means high availability of shared data in intermittent network systems (Hongisto, 2002) and this is essential in Bluetooth connectivity

component. The types of data are based on time, state and frequency. Frame rate is a key issue in video streaming. Application developers make tradeoffs among these dimensions.

Variation in control flow: Generally, event-driven communication is used for coordination and a broker for mediation between middleware and applications. However, services with a proactive directory service use data-flow architectural style for being aware of changes in the environment that could affect the components' functionality and quality. An adapter customizes the interfaces and data exchanged. We identified proxy pattern, asynchronous operations and lookup service.

Variation in technology: A particular component of the framework may be required in one product and not in another. The operating system or the hardware may vary from a product to another. Jini technology, remote method invocation, a specific connectivity card or a specific format for video streams are variabilities.

Variation in quality goals: Interoperability, scalability, portability and adaptability, survivability, agility and fidelity are few of the quality characteristics of middleware domain that could vary for a distributed services framework. Reusability, maintainability, modifiability and extensibility may vary when evolution is of concern. For example the synchronization of states between cooperating service components may be achieved via a publisher-subscriber mechanism or via a direct calling connection. The choice of one or another of these two options embodies a choice of the importance of performance and (modifiability, reusability) and this choice may be different in different products.

Variation in environment: Environment includes programming languages, operating systems, resources (CPU, bandwidth, network connectivity, etc). A particular component of middleware framework may be invoked from either C++ or Java. The invocation mechanism may vary from one product to another (Niemelä & Vaskivuo, 2004). Java Media Framework is specifically required by video camera demonstration product.

Modeling Architectural Views

In the process of designing the architecture of the framework from the four products related through common features we selected one of them as a reference product because it contains the core functional features. Then we tried to add, modify and change its components so that to include new functions, data, technology, environment adaptations of the other three products. We considered only variations that are architecturally visible. Discussion of our experience is in the following.

Conceptual level. The conceptual structural view of the framework is presented in Figure 7 and it represents an abstraction of the layers, *«subsystem»* components that have assigned modules, *«leaf»* components, identified in the various products. Our exercise demonstrates that in case of several complex products, members of the same product line, we cannot represent all the variabilities from high-level to lower-level/ detailed specifications. The diagram would become very complex for understanding by other stakeholders, users of this view. Consequently, *«Leaf»* components can be decomposed further in more detail in case that other variabilities must be revealed, by using the same UML extensions defined for this view. We consider that in a diagram

Figure 7. Conceptual structural view

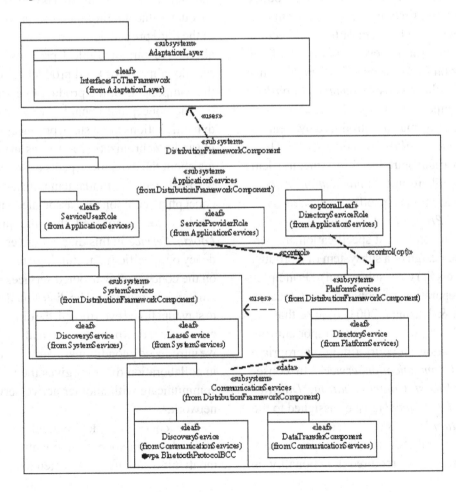

Figure 8. Conceptual deployment view

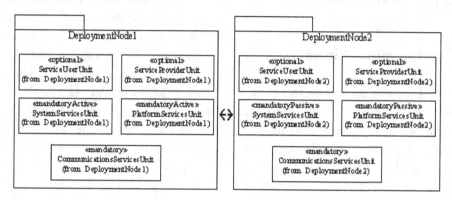

the level of description of conceptual components is appropriate when it reveals an understanding of the coarse-grain common and variable features included in each product member. As a software product line, our framework has various particularities. One of these is that features of a product can be included entirely in a leaf component of a structural view. A subsystem of the architecture conceptual structural view responsible of all communication is *CommunicationServices*. This subsystem may have several *CommunicationProtocol* (leaf components) assigned to it. New means of communication may be introduced by creating new *CommunicationProtocol* components. Thus, we have a variant introduced in structural leaf components, where in *CommunicationProtocol* component variation is specified as •*vpa alternative BluetoothProtocolBCC* (Figure 8).

Changes in component specification are performed in the design of a subsystem of a product (i.e. DiscoveryService subsystem). Principles related to separation of concerns and locality thesis (Eden & Kazman, 2003) require that the architectural components with an important role in communication move to a more appropriate subsystem, *CommunicationServices*. In consequence, *Multicast Communication, DataResolver* and *UDPProtocol* must be assigned to the *CommunicationServices* subsystem.

Another variant of the distribution framework layer with the same required functionality is

exhibited in the architecture of the third product. The conceptual components of this subsystem are connected in a different way from the one described in the architecture of the first product, thus the flow of control is different. Since we choose the functional features of the first product as reference for our product line architecture, the functionality of the third product is added to the structure as an alternative variant. Table 1 presents mapping of functionality of the third product components to the components of the product line architecture.

The conceptual behavior view specifies the dynamic actions the system, produces their ordering and synchronization and gives an understanding about the dynamic aspects of services. When we analyzed the fundamental behavior of the conceptual components associated in the third product we discovered that the presence of *Lookup Service* in this diagram gives the dependency on specific Jini technology that cannot suit on the concept of distributed services for a spontaneous environment. The distributed system has to stay functional even though the directory service may be shut down. In order to realize this variant we introduced a conditional clause. Thus, a branch in collaboration diagram gives the possibility to communicate with another active service in the network.

The conceptual deployment view consists of DeploymentNode components and DeploymentUnit components allocated to nodes. In this

Table 1. Mapping services between JSF and DisMis

JSF	DisMis
ApplicationServiceProvider & ApplicationService User/Consumer	ApplicationServiceProvider & ApplicationService User/Consumer
LookupService	DirectoryService, DataStorageService
Proxy	Proxy
Discovery Protocol	NetworkMonitorService
Join Protocol	Service Registration
ServiceRegistrar	-

Table 2. Components of the concrete structural view

Capsule level	Capsule Name
topCapsule	DisMis Framework
subsystemCapsule	AdaptationLayer, AbstractDistributionFramework, DistributionFramework
component-1Capsule	ApplicationServices, DistributionAndCommunicationServices
component-2Capsule	CommunicationServices, SystemServices, PlatformServices
component-3Capsule	CommunicationProtocol
concreteComponent	JiniAdaptationLayer, VCDAdaptationLayer, VCDDistributionFramework DDPApplicationServices, JiniApplicationServices, DDPDistAndCommServices, JiniServices, CommProtocols, BluetoothProtocolCapsule

view it is necessary the specification with UML stereotypes of different types of deployment units. It is significant to remark the presence of variants in nodes of «mandatory», «mandatoryActive» and «mandatory Passive» deployment units (Figure 8).

Concrete level. The views that have been developed for modeling architecture on the concrete level are structural, behavior and deployment. Variability from various sources is represented in the concrete structural view by using architectural elements and relationships extended from UML.

Thus, components are subsystem capsules or component capsules at level 1..n, and relationships are concrete interfaces with ports, connectors and protocols. Table 2 specifies the capsule level and the names of capsules in this view.

Decomposition relationships describe the hierarchical structure of abstract components. The vertical range of abstract components consists of several levels, from the *topCapsule* component (*DisMis Framework*) to *component3Capsule* level component (*CommunicationProtocol*). Inheritance mechanism and specialization are used to obtain various concrete components.

Our case study shows that a technology dependent product, like Java Services Framework, whose components bring variability in the flow of control due to Jini technology cannot be easily added to the product line architecture model. Jini and JSF are conceptually on the same level of

abstraction with the concept of DDP, because they share mostly the same services and structures. JSF is then, a wrapper to Jini, comprising mostly all of the same features and sharing the similar structures. However because the concepts of Jini and DPP meet only at a very high abstract level, all of the conceptual and concrete substructures of them are mostly different and at least not interchangeable. The difficulty to be dealt with occurs when the other components of the *DistributionandCommunicationServices* component1 Capsule have to be able to deal with specific Jini technology and Java language. The costs of changes would be too high. Variations should be kept as local as possible, thus we decided to specialize its concrete components, *JiniServices*, on an upper hierarchical level than other concrete components. *Communication Services*, *SystemServices* and *PlatformServices* are contained in *DDPDistrAndCommServices* capsule. Futhermore, mandatory communication protocols are encapsulated in *CommunicationProtocols* capsule. Optional *BluetoothProtocol* that varies on a different technology and environment to provide data consistency is localized in one capsule. Thus we avoided changing of a mandatory component into a variant due to optional relations with an optional variant. Similar approach has been applied to *JiniAdaptationLayer* and *JiniApplicationServices*, which vary depending on Jini services technology. *VCDAdaptationLayer* and *VCD DistributionFramework* are variants which make it possible to create interface with video camera service for controlling the camera and transferring data as multimedia stream in motion JPG format.

FUTURE RESEARCH DIRECTIONS

This chapter extensively introduced a comprehensive description regarding applying UML extensions in modeling software product line architecture of a distribution services platform. A major challenge for future research is to refine the models by increasing the semantics, which is an essential foundation for offering tool support and for handling the huge complexity of the variability more effectively. For example we need to refine the two levels of abstraction and mechanisms for mapping the concepts and the variability defined at one level to another level in a consistent manner. The introduction of model-driven development approach for software product line engineering is still a key research challenge.

Currently, our approach supports representation of variation in functionality, data, control, technology and environment. Variation in quality goals is partly supported, and that is why another major challenge for future research is on representing execution qualities, such as reliability and availability, in architectural models. Execution qualities are important especially in service architectures that our method is intended for. Several steps have been performed towards this and the work in progress has been described in (Raatikainen, Niemelä, Myllärniemi & Männistö, 2008).

CONCLUSION

This chapter has described how UML standard concepts can be extended to address the challenges of variability in space of software product line architectures for middleware services. Particularly, a new UML profile has been defined to be integrated in a systematic approach, a quality-driven architecture design and quality analysis method. UML standard extensibility mechanisms can be used to express diagrammatic notations of each view of the architecture. Integrated use of a standard profile and a design method as described here would allow extensive and systematic use and maintenance of software product line architectures.

Software product line engineering is the best candidate for applying model-driven development.

REFERENCES

Atkinson, C., Bayer, J., & Muthig, D. (2000). Component-based Product Line Development: The KobrA Approach. In Donohoe, P. (Ed.), *Software Product Lines. Experience and Research Directions* (pp. 289–310). Boston: Kluwer Academic Publishers.

Bachman, F., Bass, L., Buhman, C., Comella-Dorda, S., Long, F., & Robert, J. (2000). *Technical Concepts of Component-Based Software Engineering*. Pittsburgh, PA: Software Engineering Institute, Carnegie Mellon University.

Bachmann, F., & Bass, L. (2001). Managing Variability in Software Architectures. *ACM SIGSOFT Software Engineering Notes*, *26*(3), 126–132. doi:10.1145/379377.375274

Bass, L., Clements, P., & Kazman, R. (2003). *Software Architecture in Practice* (second edition), *The SEI Series in Software Engineering*. Westford, MA: Addison-Wesley.

Bosch, J. (2000). *Design and Use of Software Architecture – Adopting and Evolving a Product Line Approach.* Reading, MA: Addison- Wesley Professional, ACM Press.

Buschmann, F., Meunier, R., Rohnert, H., Sommerlad, P., & Stahl, M. (1996). *Pattern-Oriented Software Architecture – A System of Patterns.* West Sussex, UK: Willey.

Bustamante, F. E., Widener, P., & Schwan, K. (2002). Scalable Directory Services Using Proactivity. In *Proceedings of the 2002 ACM/IEEE conference on Supercomputing* (pp.1-12). Los Alamitos, CA: IEEE Computer Society Press.

Charles, J. (1999). Middleware moves to the forefront. *Computer, 32*(5), 17–19. doi:10.1109/MC.1999.762786

Cherki, S., El Kaim, W., Josset, P., & Paris, F. (2000). Domain Analysis and Product-Line Scoping: a Thomson-SCF Product-Line Case Study. In P. Knauber & G. Succi (Eds), *Software Product Lines: Economics, Architectures, and Implications, Proceedings of Workshop #15 at 22th International Conference on Software Engineering (ICSE 2000), Limerick, Ireland* (pp. 65-73), Fraunhofer IESE Report No. 070.00/E, 2000.

Clements, P., & Northrop, L. (2000). *A Framework for Software Product Line Practice, Version 3.0.* Pittsburgh, PA: Software Engineering Institute, Carnegie Mellon University.

Clements, P., & Northrop, L. (2002). *Software Product Lines: Practices and Pattern, The SEI Series in Software Engineering.* Reading, MA: Addison-Wesley Professional.

Coplien, J., Hoffman, D., & Weiss, D. (1998). Commonality and Variability in Software Engineering. *IEEE Software, 15*(6), 37–45. doi:10.1109/52.730836

Coriat, M., Jourdan, J., & Boisbourdin, F. (2000). The SPLIT Method. In Donohoe, P. (Ed.), *Software Product Lines. Experience and Research Directions* (pp. 147–166). Boston: Kluwer Academic Publishers.

Dobrica, L., & Niemela, E. (2007). Modeling Variability in the Product Line Architecture of Distributed Middleware Services. In H. Arabnia & H. Reza (Eds) *Proceedings of the 2007 International Conference on Software Engineering Research and Practice, June 25-28, Las Vegas, NV,* (vol. 1, p.269-275). CSREA Press.

Dobrica, L., & Ovaska, E. (2009). A service based approach for a cross domain reference architecture development. In S. Jablonski & L. Maciaszek (Eds) *ENASE 2009 - 4th International Conference on Evaluation of Novel Approaches to Software Engineering* (pp. 33-44). Lisbon, Portugal: INSTICC Press.

Eden, A. H., & Kazman, R. (2003). Architecture, Design, Implementation. In *The 25th International Conference on Software Engineering (ICSE 2003), May 3-10, Portland, Oregon, USA,* (pp.149-159). Washington, DC: IEEE Computer Society.

El Kaim, W., Cherki, S., Josset, P., Paris, F., & Ollagnon, J.-C. (2000). Applied Technology for Designing a PL Architecture of a Pilot Training System. In P. Knauber & G. Succi (Eds.) *Software Product Lines: Economics, Architectures, and Implications, Proceedings of Workshop #15 at 22th International Conference on Software Engineering (ICSE 2000), Limerick, Ireland* (pp. 55-65). Fraunhofer IESE Report No. 070.00/E, 2000.

Gamma, E., Helm, R., Johnson, R., & Vlissides, J. (1995). *Design Patterns: Elements of Reusable Object-oriented Software.* Reading, MA: Addison-Wesley Publishing.

Gomaa, H. (2005). *Designing Software Product Lines with UML: From Use Cases to Pattern-Based Software Architecture*. Redwood City, CA: Addison Wesley Longman Publishing Co., Inc.

Gomaa, H., & Gianturco, M. (2002). Domain modeling for World Wide Web based on Software Product Lines with UML. In C. Gacek (Ed) *Software Reuse: Methods, Techniques, and Tools, 7th International Conference on Software Reuse, ICSR-7, Austin, TX, USA, April 15-19, 2002, Proceedings*, (LNCS 2319, pp. 78-99). Berlin: Springer-Verlag.

Gomaa, H., & Shin, M. E. (2003). Variability in Multiple-View Models of Software Product Lines. *Procs. Intl Workshop on Software Variability Management, ICSE'03, Portland, Oregon, May 3-11* (pp. 63-68). Washington, DC: IEEE Computer Society.

Hofmeister, C., Nord, R., & Soni, D. (2000). *Applied Software Architecture*. Boston, MA: Addison-Wesley Longman Publishing Co., Inc.

Hongisto, M. (2002). Shadow: Smart and highly adaptive data sharing over weak connections. *1st International Conference on Mobile and Ubiquitous Multimedia, Oulu, Finland, December 11-13*. Oulu, FI: Oulu University Press.

IEEE. (2000). *IEEE Std1417:2000 - Recommended Practice for Architectural descriptions of Software Intensive Systems*. Los Alamitos, CA: IEEE.

Jaaksi, A., Alto, J.-M., & Vatto, K. (1999). *Tried & True Object Development: Industry-Proven Approaches with UML*. New York: Cambridge University Press.

Jacobson, I. Griss, & M., Jonsson, P. (1997). *Software Reuse-Architecture, Process and Organization for Business Success*. New York: ACM Press.

Jaring, M., & Bosch, J. (2002). Representing Variability in Software Product Lines: A Case Study. In *Proceedings of the Second International Conference on Software Product Lines* (LNCS 2379, pp. 15-36). London: Springer-Verlag.

Kang, K., Cohen, S., Hess, J., Novak, W., & Peterson, S. (1990). *Feature-Oriented Domain Analysis, Technical Report No. CMU/SEI-90-TR-21, Software Engineering Institute*. Pittsburgh, PA: Carnegie Mellon University.

Keepence, B., & Mannion, M. (1999). Using patterns to Model Variability in Software Architectures. *IEEE Software, 16*(4), 102–108. doi:10.1109/52.776957

Kruchten, P. (1995). The 4+1 view model of architecture. *IEEE Software, 12*(6), 42–50. doi:10.1109/52.469759

Matinlassi, M., Niemelä, E., & Dobrica, L. (2002). *Quality-driven architecture design and quality analysis method – A revolutionary initiation approach to product line architecture, VTT Publications 456*. Espoo, Finland: VTT Technical Research Centre of Finland.

McComas, D., Leake, S., Stark, M., & Morisio, M. Travassos, & G., White, M. (2000). Addressing Variability in a Guidance, Navigation, and Control Flight Software Product Line. In *Proceedings of Product Line Architecture Workshop, The First Software Product Line Conference (SPLC1), Denver Co, USA, Fraunhofer IESE-Report No. 053.00/E, August 2000* (pp. 85-96).

Morisio, M., Travassos, G., & Stark, M. (2000). Extending UML to Support Domain Analysis. In *Proceedings of the 15th IEEE International Conference on Automated software engineering* (pp.321). Washington, DC: IEEE Computer Society.

Niemelä, E., Matinlassi, M., & Lago, P. (2003). Architecture-centric approach to wireless service engineering. *IEC Annual Review of Communications, 56*, 875–889.

Niemelä, E., & Vaskivuo, T. (2004). Agile Middleware of Pervasive Computing Environments. In *Proceedings of the Second IEEE Anual Conference on Pervasive Computing and Communications Workshops* (p.192). Washington DC: IEEE Computer Society.

Noble, B. D., Narayannan, D., Tilton, J. E., Flinn, J., & Walker, K. R. (1997). Agile Application-Aware Adaptation for Mobility. *ACM SIGOPS Operating Systems Review, 31*(5), 276–287. doi:10.1145/269005.266708

OMG. (2003). *MDA Guide Version 1.0.1.* (J. Miller, & J. Mukerji, Eds). Document No. omg/2003-06-01, date: 12th June 2003. Retrieved from http://www.omg.org/docs/omg/03-06-01.pdf (Access: 15 July 2005).

OMG. (2005). *OMG Unified Modeling Language*: *Superstructure*, Version 2.0. Retrieved from http://www.omg.org/spec/UML/2.0/Superstructure

Purhonen, A., Niemelä, E., & Matinlassi, M. (2004). Viewpoints of DSP software and service architectures. *Journal of Systems and Software, 69*(1-2), 57–73. doi:10.1016/S0164-1212(03)00050-5

Raatikainen, M., Niemelä, E., Myllärniemi, V., & Männistö, T. (2008). Svamp – An Integrated Approach for Modeling Functional and Quality Variability. In *Proceedings of Second International Workshop on Variability Modeling of Software Intensive Systems VaMoS08*, ICB-Research Report No.22, January 2008, (pp.89-96). Essen, Germany: ICB, University of Duisburg-Essen.

Shaw, M., & Garlan, D. (1996). *Software Architecture*. Upper Saddle River, NJ: Prentice Hall.

Svahnberg, M., van Gurp, J., & Bosch, J. (2002). *A taxonomy of Variability Realization Techniques*, Technical Paper ISSN: 1103-1581. Sweden: Blekinge Institute of Technology.

Szasz, N., & Vilanova, P. (2008). Statecharts and variabilities. *Proceedings of Second International Workshop on Variability Modeling of Software Intensive Systems VaMoS08*, ICB-Research Report No.22, January 2008, p. 131-140. Essen, Germany: ICB, University of Duisburg-Essen.

Szyperski, C. (1997). *Component Software –Beyond Object –Oriented Programming*. Harlow, UK: Pearson Education Limited.

Webber, D. (2001). *The variation point model for software product lines.* Ph.D Dissertation, George Mason University.

Webber, D., & Gomaa, H. (2002), *Modeling variability with the variation point model.* In C. Gacek (Ed.), *Software Reuse: Methods, Techniques, and Tools, 7th International Conference on Software Reuse, ICSR-7, Austin, TX, USA, April 15-19, 2002, Proceedings*, (LNCS 2319, pp. 109-122). Berlin: Springer-Verlag.

KEY TERMS AND DEFINITIONS

Model: A model means a formal specification of part of the function, structure and/or behavior of a system. A formal specification expects a language with strictly defined syntax and semantics.

Software Architecture: Software architecture of a software system is the structure or structures of the system, which comprise software elements, the externally visible properties of those elements and the relationships among them. Structures of interest could be static and dynamic, while external properties manifest functionality and quality properties.

Architectural View: An architectural view is a representation of the whole system that illustrates how the architecture addresses one or more concerns held by one or more of its stakeholders. The need for different architectural views depends on the complexity of the system, the domain and the number of stakeholders. It is not possible to capture the functional and quality properties of a complex system in a single comprehensible model that is understandable by all stakeholders.

Software Product Line: A software product line is defined as a set of products sharing a common, managed set of features that satisfy the specific needs of a particular mission.

Variability: Product line architecture components cover common functionality and support variability. Variability among products at architectural level could be specified explicitly using variation points or implicitly using a wide range of generalization and specialization techniques.

Feature: A feature describes funct`ional or quality characteristics of a system. Feature modeling is a key concept in software product lines.

Service: A service is a capability of an entity (the server) to perform, upon request of another entity (the client) an act that can be perceived and exploited by the client.

Middleware services: Middleware services represent a variety of distributed computing services and application development supporting environments those operate between the application logic and underlying system.

Chapter 17
Model–Driven Requirements Specification for Software Product Lines

Mauricio Alférez
Universidade Nova de Lisboa, Portugal

Ana Moreira
Universidade Nova de Lisboa, Portugal

Vasco Amaral
Universidade Nova de Lisboa, Portugal

João Araújo
Universidade Nova de Lisboa, Portugal

ABSTRACT

Model-driven methods for requirements specification in Software Product Lines (SPLs) support the construction of different models to provide a better understanding of each SPL feature and intended use scenarios. However, the different models must be composed to show the requirements of the target applications and, therefore, help to understand how features will be integrated in a new product of a software product line. Although well-established standards for creating metamodels and model transformations exist, there is currently no established foundation that allows practitioners to distinguish between the different modeling and composition approaches for requirements models. This chapter provides an overview of different approaches for specifying requirements models and composing models for specific products of an SPL. In particular, it emphasizes one of the most recurring specification techniques: model-driven and use case scenario-based specification. This technique, in combination with feature models and the Variability Modeling Language for Requirements (VML4RE), integrates our approach for model-driven requirements specification for SPLs.

DOI: 10.4018/978-1-61692-874-2.ch017

INTRODUCTION

Software Product Lines are increasingly being adopted by major and medium-sized industrial players to quickly address change requests and improving time to market. SPLs enable modular, coarse-grained reuse through a set of core and varying software elements addressing a particular application domain (Clements & Northrop, 2002). Software Product Line (SPL) engineering is a promising approach to increase software quality and productivity. It encompasses the creation and management of families of products for a particular domain, where each product in the family is derived from a shared set of core assets, following a set of prescribed rules (Clements & Northrop, 2002).

An SPL product shares, with other systems, properties or functionalities that are relevant to some stakeholders. These are usually called "features" and express not only commonalities, but also variabilities that allow us to distinguish among products. The term "commonalities" refers to features that are mandatory to every product in an SPL. It is used to reference the parts of the requirements that are related to SPL common features. The term "variabilities" refers to the variable (optional, variation points and variants) features of an SPL. *Optional* features are not mandatory and might not be included in some of the products of an SPL. A *variation point* identifies a particular concept within the SPL requirements specification as being variable and it offers a number of *variants*. A *variant* describes a particular variability decision, such as a specific choice among *alternative variants*. Typically, we can model the available features and their dependencies (e.g., if feature X is selected, feature Y also must be selected) using a feature model (Czarnecki & Eisenecker, 2000; Kang, Cohen, Hess, Novak, & Peterson, 1990), that helps to capture the commonalities and variabilities of a family of products.

To understand each SPL feature and intended use scenarios of target products, Model-driven methods for requirements specification support the construction of different models that design the product behavior. However, to show the requirements of the target products, different models must be composed to help to understand and communicate to users, managers, testers and programmers the intended behavior of the new product to be produced from the SPL. Although well-established standards for creating metamodels and model transformations such as Meta-Object Facility (OMG, 2009a) exist, there is currently no established foundation for specifying requirements models for SPLs and compositing these models for specific products. This chapter introduces a classification of several existing approaches for model-driven requirements specification for Software Product Lines and focuses on exploiting use scenario-based techniques. We make explicit the different ways of specification taking into account the concrete syntax of the requirements models and the separation of three core components needed to specify and compose requirements models:

- the base models that specify requirements. For example, specifications of use scenarios using use cases models complemented with activity diagrams;
- variability information that makes explicit which are the SPL features that are common to all the products and which are the features that are particular to some products of the SPL; and
- configuration knowledge, which establishes the mapping between features and base models that specify requirements, for example, associating feature expressions, in the form of logical propositions, to specific model fragments. Also, in Model-Driven Development (MDD), configuration knowledge may include the specification of the transformations of SPL requirements models to compose models for specific products.

This chapter is structured as follows. Section "Requirements Modeling for SPLs" provides an overview of both textual and graphical notations for modeling SPL requirements and different ways to compose requirements. That section motivates this work, showing some shortcomings in previous approaches. Section "A Model-Driven Requirements Specification Approach for SPLs" constitutes the major contribution of this work. It presents our approach for model-driven requirements specification for SPLs. This approach employs use case models and activity diagrams to represent one of the most recurring techniques for requirements modeling such as use case scenario specifications. We employ feature models to model variability information in combination with specially tailored composition rules for requirements models provided by the Variability Modeling Language for Requirements (VML4RE). The final sections of this chapter synthesize our contributions to the field of model-driven requirements specifications for SPLs, address future research directions, and conclude this chapter.

REQUIREMENTS MODELING FOR SPLS

The success of a SPL depends on abstraction and decomposition mechanisms supporting modular treatment of its commonalities and variabilities (Alves, et al., 2006; Figueiredo, et al., 2008). SPLs can most easily accommodate changes and be instantiated to specific products if all varying and core software elements are defined in a modular fashion, from requirements to architecture and implementation. Mainstream techniques to support modular realization of software variabilities are focused on code. Typical examples of these techniques are object-oriented mechanisms, design patterns, and conditional compilation (Alves, et al., 2006; Figueiredo, et al., 2008). However, less attention has been given to the use of models as a key asset during requirements engineering.

One of the most recurring techniques used to specify requirements both in single and SPL systems is use case scenario modeling (Alexander & Maiden, 2004; Cockburn, 2001; Jacobson, 1992). Each use case describes how actors (i.e., persons, organizations or other (sub)systems) will interact with the system to be developed to achieve a specific goal. One or more scenarios may be generated from a use case, corresponding to the detail of each possible way to achieve that goal. Scenarios can help to (Alexander & Maiden, 2004; Cockburn, 2001):

- validate requirements;
- generate acceptance criteria for requirements;
- verify the level of abstraction of each requirement;
- help to create initial system architectures.

A number of different approaches for use case scenario variability modeling have been proposed for SPLs, such as (Alférez, Santos, et al., 2009; Bonifacio & Borba, 2009; Czarnecki & Antkiewicz, 2005; Eriksson, Börstler, & Borg, 2005; Gomaa, 2004). These approaches differ in their notation which is based on graph models such as use case and activity models (OMG, 2009b), or text, such as the black-box notation to represent use case scenarios (Alexander & Maiden, 2004). Each of the approaches has its own advantages and drawbacks. A free-format textual representation of requirements usually requires a short-time of elaboration at the expense of some ambiguity due to interpretation of the natural language. On the other hand, using a graph-based representation allows using a standard language to express the requirements, such as, conditionals, control flows and parallelism, therefore, contributing to avoid ambiguity.

In addition to choosing between textual or graphical notations for the requirements specifications, developers have to decide whether or not to mix requirements specifications and variability data in their SPL models. Adding variability data to textual or graph-based requirements models is used to make explicit the relationships between their fragments and SPL features. Next, we will briefly introduce both approaches using both text- and graph-based requirements models. In these approaches we start with free format textual-based requirements descriptions. This approach was the base for more structured approaches such as use scenario-based approaches that can be supported by Model Driven Development (MDD) techniques. Our objective with this is to establish a foundation that allows to distinguish between the different modeling approaches for requirements models and also to motivate the use of model-driven techniques.

Mixing Variability into the Requirements Specification

The first approaches for describing variability that we look at are based on text. Textual descriptions can be in general very expressive because they are based on natural language. Also, despite the fact that the use of domain specific models to specify requirements has been growing, the textual descriptions are still very popular. One of the reasons is that all stakeholders are able to read the specification, and to write does not require modeling skills. However, as it will be shown in this section, requirements expressed using free-from textual descriptions lacks of rigor and may fail to communicate unambiguously variability information.

Unformatted Textual Specifications

Natural language can be used to express optional and alternative parts in the specifications using phrases related to SPL features. For example, the sentence: "*the Security System should support either PIN entry via Keypad, Fingerprint Scanning or Retina Scanning*", does not make clear the number of alternatives that different clients

may require for their products. For example, some may select the cheaper alternative for his product; others may prefer a more sophisticated one integrated in their solution, while others may want any possible combination of the three for extra security. After successive changes in the specification, the number of possible choices and their impact in other features may become complex to control, and the use of natural language will result inefficient and insufficient to express correctly and unambiguously the variable parts in the SPL. Therefore, even when the requirements are carefully written to avoid ambiguities, it is virtually impossible in a large project to assure their quality after successive modifications.

Structured Textual Specifications

Given what was discussed in the last section, a way to document variability in a more concise and unambiguous manner is necessary. Table 1 (a) exemplifies a more understandable way to express the requirements based on formats similar to those provided by (Gomaa, 2004; Pohl, 2006). This structured textual format also shows which and how many alternatives of a variation point can be selected for a specific product.

Therefore, structuring the requirements specifications by expressing the kind of variability with key phrases such as "only one", "two from all", etc., reduces the ambiguity of a simply unformatted textual requirements approach. This intuitive approach can be complemented with a textual language to describe variability and features. Using a structured language usually allows reducing the size of the specification and helps to restrict the way in which the developer elaborates the requirements specification. Consequently, in the case of textual requirements descriptions, each model written using a structured language will have to follow some construction rules. These rules are defined by the language grammar that performs the role of a *metamodel*, as it is known in the MDD domain.

Table 1. (a) Expressing variability textually; (b) Expressing variability textually using a description language

(a)
SPL-Requirement # X. The security system shall support only one of the following alternative devices for user authentication:
V1 (Variation point #1): Authentication Device
<u>Only one</u> of the following variants can be selected for **V1**:
V1.1 PIN using Keypad
V1.2 Fingerprint Scanner
V1.3 Retina Scanner

(b)
SmartHome: **all** (electronicWindows, security?)
Security: **all** (AuthenticationDevice, AlarmType)
AuthenticationDevice: **one-of** (keypad, fingerprintScanner, retinaScanner)
AlarmType: **more-of** (siren, light)

Table 1 (b) shows a short example, inspired in the Feature Description Language (FDL) proposed by Deursen and Klint (Deursen & Klint, 2001). The base of FDL consists of a number of feature definitions which is the feature name followed by ":" and the feature expression. In this example the variation points start with upper case while the variants (e.g., keypad, fingerprints, retinaScanner) and optional features (e.g., security) start with lower case in the feature expression side. Also, supposing that security is an optional feature, its name is followed by the "?" sign. However, while this approach works well for small problems, it can be difficult to keep an overview of variabilities and dependencies as the number of features and options increases. Furthermore, many times it is necessary to express by means of additional models, usually based on graphs, what is the expected behavior of the features. Also, it is necessary to specify how the presence or absence of specific sets of features affects the behavior of the target system.

Graph-Based Specifications

The discussion above highlights the need for a more efficient solution. For this reason, graph-based models are sometimes preferred to design and communicate the requirements of the system. A number of authors such as Gomaa (Gomaa, 2004), and Bragança and Machado (Bragança & Machado, 2007) add variability information into the requirements models. Currently, there is no standard that restricts the way in which the variability information should be added and represented in the concrete syntax of the requirements models. However, the use of stereotypes and model annotations is a common practice for both UML-based models and a number of Domain Specific Languages (DSL) (DSM forum website). Stereotypes and annotations help to make explicit what parts of the models are common to all the products of the product line (also called *kernel*, *mandatory* parts, or *commonalities*) and which parts are variable (i.e., not common) among all the products (also called *variabilities*).

Figure 1 is based on the notation proposed by Gomaa (Gomaa, 2004) and uses stereotypes such as "Kernel" and "Alternative" to mark what is common and what the alternatives are. Similarly, supposing that not all the products will include the security feature, the security package is labeled with an "Optional" stereotype.

This kind of diagrams could be complemented with cardinality using, for example, UML notes as shown by (Bragança & Machado, 2007). For example, a note showing a cardinality of "1..3" attached to the "Authenticate User" would express that a minimum of 1 and a maximum of 3 alternatives could be chosen to be included in a single product. This kind of specifications has some drawbacks. First, the models could be polluted with stereotypes, some of them to indicate SPL variability and others to express standard UML

Figure 1. Expressing variability graphically using stereotypes

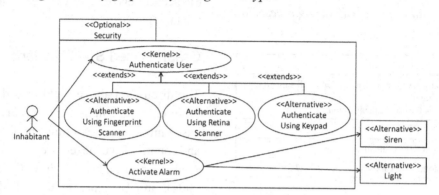

semantics, such as "extends" and "includes". Hence, it would not be clear which "extension" use cases are created to offer possible alternative use case scenarios for a single product, and which use cases are created to show SPL alternatives, for example. This situation may become complex if the modeller is using a UML profile to model in a specific domain that requires the use of additional stereotypes. Therefore, to augment the models' understandability, it would be better to follow a separation of concerns approach (Filman, Elrad, Clarke, & Aksit, 2004; Moreira, Rashid, & Araújo, 2005) and separate variability information from the concern requirements specification.

Separating Variability Information and Requirements Specification

There are some patterns that have been followed when variability information and requirements specifications are separated. The first one is about linking parts of the requirements specification (also called model fragments) to a feature model. Feature models (Czarnecki & Eisenecker, 2000; Kang, et al., 1990) are a well accepted means for expressing requirements in a domain on an abstract level. They are applied to describe variable and common features of products in a product line, and to derive and validate configurations of software systems. The second pattern is about the use of mechanisms of composition based on adding or

removing optional model fragments according to features' selections in a feature model.

Linking Requirements Models to Features Models

One of the patterns used as prerequisite to compose models for specific products is to link fragments of the requirements models to features in a feature model. These links enable the adaptation of base requirements models based on features' selection. A feature model groups hierarchically from general to more specific common and variable features using a refinement relationship. This may also include cardinality as in (Czarnecki, Helsen, & Eisenecker, 2004) to express properties such as the number of alternative features that can be chosen for specific variation points, that is for example, "the number of authentication devices that can be included to guarantee a secure system". On the other side, requirements models, such as use cases and activity diagrams, express the intended behavior of a system focusing on the clear representation of use scenarios to the SPL and products' stakeholders.

The base mechanism to link requirements model fragments to features is to use a correspondence table (also called: mapping table), as presented by (Gomaa, 2004), (Pohl, Böckle, & van der Linden, 2005) and (Alférez, et al., 2008). Also, with the advent of MDD technologies, the use of tools such as FeatureMapper (Heidenreich, 2010), FMP (Antkiewicz & Czarnecki, 2004; Czarnecki & Antkiewicz, 2005), and VML4RE (Alférez, Santos, et al., 2009) ease the linking between features and other models. The mechanisms used for ease the linking between requirements models and features range from more usable visual editors with facilities such as drag-and-drop and multiple selection of model fragments, to mechanisms to create links programmatically, for example, using quantification and queries on the models' properties to determine correspondence between features and model fragments. The goal of all these mechanisms is to ease the arduous task of creating and maintaining links manually between many features and model fragments as happens with the use of simple mapping tables.

Composition of Requirements Models

After linking fragments of the requirements models to features in a feature model, the model fragments can be composed to show the requirements of the target applications and, therefore, help to understand how features will be integrated in a new product of a software product line. The way of composing the target model of a product is based on removing (i.e., *Negative Variability*) or adding (i.e., *Positive Variability*) model fragments to a base requirements model. Next we explain these mechanisms.

Negative Variability Composition Mechanism
Negative variability selectively takes away parts of a model based on the presence or absence of features in configuration models, such as feature model configurations (Volter & Stahl, 2006). When using negative variability, developers have to model the overall SPL requirements. Then, after linking model fragments to certain features in a feature model, some model fragments are taken away from the base model according to a certain features' selection for a particular product. Typically, requirements composition approaches have

followed negative variability mechanisms. Some examples of approaches using mostly negative variability mechanisms are proposed by Eriksson (Eriksson, et al., 2005) and Czarnecki and Antkiewicz (Czarnecki & Antkiewicz, 2005).

Positive Variability Composition Mechanism
To reduce requirements models composition to a simple removal of some fragments (e.g., a use case, a scenario step, etc.) according to a specific feature model selection (also called feature model configuration) is straightforward. However, it may difficult to specify the overall SPL requirements at the beginning of the development process. The composition mechanism where the target model is composed adding model fragments to a base model is called "positive variability". This starts with a minimal base model and selectively adds additional parts (Volter & Stahl, 2006). The base model generally represents the model fragments that are common to all products within the product line. Model fragments related to varying features are attached to the requirements models based on the presence or absence of features in the configuration models, such as feature model configurations. Some authors that propose approaches that employ positive variability mechanisms are Eriksson (Eriksson, 2006) that instantiate parametric features with specific values in use case scenario descriptions, and Alférez et. al. (Alférez, Santos, et al., 2009) that add and modify specific model fragments in use cases models and activity diagrams.

However, to compose requirements models for a specific product may require to insert and remove model fragments. One situation when it may happen is when we need to insert model fragments related to a feature that is incompatible with other feature that was already added into the base model. Therefore, composition requires to remove and to insert model fragments. This demands the need of richer composition mechanisms that allow both negative and positive variability to derive target requirements models as we show later in this chapter.

Other Mechanisms to Support Variability Composition

Apart from the use of positive and negative variability mechanisms, there are situations in which the adaptation of the fragments in a model depends on the simultaneous presence and absence of a specific combination of features. Czarnecki and Antkiewicz (Czarnecki & Antkiewicz, 2005) recognize this fact. They expressed use case scenarios using UML activity diagrams and annotate them with *presence conditions*. These presence conditions are expressions that can be evaluated to false or true according to the set of features selected for a specific product. Although this approach uses a separate feature model to express variability information, this, as well as Eriksson's approach (Eriksson, 2006), fails to fully separate "configuration knowledge" from the requirements specifications. The result is that the requirements models turn out full of textual annotations expressing presence conditions for each fragment of the models, including fine-grained elements like "actions" and control flows.

A MODEL-DRIVEN REQUIREMENTS SPECIFICATION APPROACH FOR SPLS

Until now we have mentioned three elements in the definition of Model-Driven Requirements Specification for Software Product Lines:

- *Requirements specification* that defines use scenarios describing the expected behavior of the SPL's members. These scenarios might be optional, have parameters, and modify the behavior of other use scenarios.
- *Feature models* that make explicit what features are common or variable and model the dependencies between features. Feature

models also contribute to the composition process, since they are used for checking if a product configuration represents a valid member of the product line.

- *Configuration knowledge* defined as a set of instructions that relates feature expressions to transformations (Czarnecki & Eisenecker, 2000) can be used for automatically generate product models. However, configuration knowledge is sometimes tangled with the base requirements specification raising understandability and maintainability problems.

Next, we describe our approach for keeping separated requirements elements, feature models and configuration knowledge to contribute to the understandability and maintainability of the three types of models. This approach uses models and specially-tailored composition rules to customize use case scenarios based on activity diagrams and use case models. Graph-based models such as use case and activity diagrams help to avoid ambiguity and add more rigor to the specifications (Pohl, et al., 2005).

Separation of Concerns in the Definition of Model-Driven Requirements Specification

The idea of linking features and requirements models' fragments, separating configuration knowledge, and supporting positive and negative variability mechanisms, is used in the Variability Modeling Language for Requirements (VML4RE) (Alférez, Santos, et al., 2009). Figure 2 sketches the idea behind the separation of concerns marked with the labels 1- 4:

1. *SPL requirements specifications* are expressed using different models such as use case models and activity diagrams that express use scenarios. These models conform to the UML metamodel (OMG, 2009b).

Figure 2. Linking features to requirements model fragments separating configuration knowledge

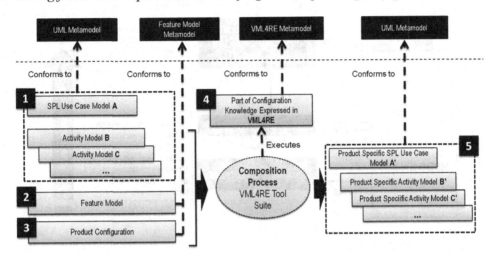

2. *Feature model* that makes explicit common and variable features as well as the dependencies between them. Each feature can be associated to fragments in the SPL requirements specification, and particular fragments in the SPL requirements specifications such as use cases, actors, activities, etc, can be associated to several features in the feature model.

3. *Product configuration* contains the selection of features that will be included in the specific product and that will be derived from the SPL.

4. *Configuration knowledge* establishes the mapping between features and base models that specify requirements, and expresses how to compose the base models according to some transformation rules to produce requirements models for target products. This information, together with the dependencies between features described in the feature model (e.g., feature "retina Scanner" excludes feature "fingerprint Scanner"), helps to derive target products correctly from a set of reusable SPL requirements models. Other information that is part of configuration knowledge, and that is usually attached directly to the feature model are the potential

bad feature interactions and default values for features selections.

In our approach the metamodel of the source models such as A, B and C in Figure 2 will be the same for the target models A', B', C', respectively. This means, for example, that if the model B (Figure 2-1) is an activity diagram representing an SPL use case scenario, the resultant product specific requirements model B' (Figure 2-5), where B' means a composed model created based on B, will be an activity diagram as well. Product specific models like A', B' or C' are generated for a specific product described by a product configuration (Figure 2-3). Each product configuration contains a selection of features in the feature model (Figure 2-2). The composition process is guided by the configuration knowledge. The VML4RE represent part of the configuration knowledge for requirements models that is related with the transformation of the models. This specifies how to link model fragments with features in the feature model programmatically using quantification, and also allows describing a composition workflow. In particular VML4RE uses composition actions specially tailored for graph-based use case scenarios like use case models and activity diagrams.

Figure 3. Raising the abstraction level to ease the use MDD transformations in requirements models

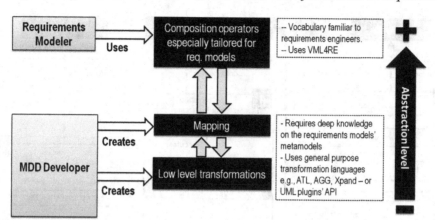

Raising the Abstraction Level to Specify Requirements Models Transformations

Figure 3 sketches the idea of using a domain specific language such as VML4RE to raise the level of abstraction to express the composition of the requirements models. In comparison with the technical background required by developers, requirements modelers simply have to employ the familiar vocabulary provided by VML4RE. Naturally, composition actions used by the requirements modeler in VML4RE are mapped to low level transformations of the requirements models. Therefore, to create more composition actions it is necessary the intervention of either a model-driven developer that knows the details of the UML use case and activity diagrams and masters general purpose model transformation languages such as ATL (Jouault & Kurtev, 2005), AGG (Taentzer, 2003), Xpand (openArchitectureWare.org), or that understands how to modify programmatically the base specifications using the Application Programming Interface (API) provided by the respective tool used to model the requirements, e.g., UML tools plug-in for the Eclipse Framework (Eclipse Foundation).

Table 2 shows examples of a subset of composition actions in VML4RE that are available for the requirements modeler. The names of specific elements in the models are in *italics* while the keywords of the language are in **bold**. It is important to note that the composition actions is address positive and negative variability as it was described in the Section "Composition of Requirements Models".

Semantics of VML4RE Composition Actions

The semantics of each VML4RE composition action can be defined in terms of a model-to-

Table 2. Some composition rules in VML4RE

Insert : package, use case, actor, use case links, activity, activities and relationships between activities.
Examples:
insert (packagepackageX**into ucModel**useCaseModelY**);**
insert (UClinks_of_type: associatedWith { fromactor_ X**touseCaseA**, *useCaseB, UseCaseC* });**
insert (InsertActivityLinksactivityA**to**activityB**with guard-** guard**);**
insert (InsertActivityLinksactivityA**to**activityC**);**
insert (actor Cameras **into ucModel** uc**);**
Remove: the same elements than can be inserted using the **insert** types.
Replace: activities by activities and activity models, actors by actors, use case by use case, etc

Figure 4. Graph rule to insert an association between actorD and useCaseC in packageB

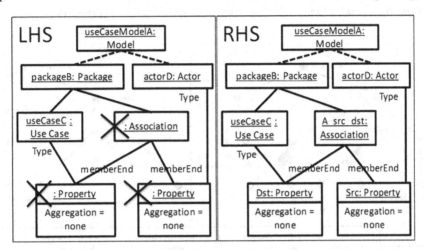

model transformation where the metamodel of source and target models is UML. Transformations can be presented by the left hand side (LHS) and right hand side (RHS) graphs. In general, a graph transformation is a graph rule *r: L —› R* for LHS graph *L* to a RHS graph *R*. The process of applying *r* to a graph *G* involves finding a graph monomorphism, *h*, from *L* to *G* and replacing *h(L)* in *G* with *h(R)* (Grzegorz, 1997).

Let's take as an example from (Alférez, Santos, et al., 2009). It shows the "Insert Use Case Links" action using the use case link type "*associatedWith*", which connects an actor and a use case using an association link

(insert_(UCLinks_of_type:_associatedWith_{_from_**actorD_**to_**useCaseModelA. PackageB.useCaseC**});). The intended transformation of the use case model can be presented by the left hand side (LHS) and right hand side (RHS) graphs in Figure 4, where the inputs are a use case model, a use case, a use case's package, and an actor. If there is already an association between the actor and the use case in the same package, the transformation is not applied to avoid duplicates. This is expressed with the cross in some elements in the LHS graph that act as negative application conditions (NAC). It means that any match against the LHS graph cannot have a

packageB with any existing association between *actorD* and the *useCaseC*.

The notation used to define this graph transformation is similar to the one used by (Markovic & Baar, 2005) where the LHS and RHS patterns are denoted by a generalized form of object diagrams. However, for visual simplicity we added dashed lines between elements to represent any number of containments (in this case, package's containments). We defer to (Markovic & Baar, 2005) for the readers interested in details of this notation.

It is important to note that VML4RE requirements modelers do not need to build graph-based transformations, know the details of the metamodels, or to master general purpose transformation language or technologies. VML4RE provides requirements-specific composition actions that facilitate the specification of the composition of the base models.

Home Automation Case Study

To clarify the idea and the use of these composition rules, we have modeled a subset of the Smart Home. This is a home automation software product line being developed by Siemens AG (Morganho, et al., 2008). We already used part of this case study

Figure 5. (1) Smart home feature model; (2) feature model configuration for the economic home; (3) use case model for the Smart Home SPL; (4) use case model for the economical edition of the Smart Home SPL

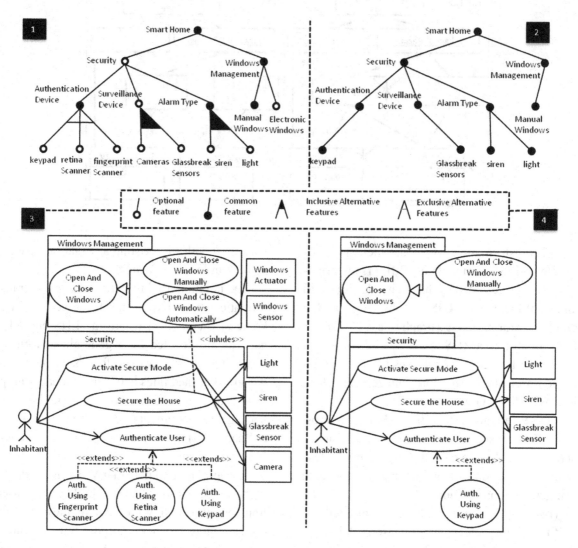

to exemplify the different textual approaches in the Section "Requirements modeling for SPLs" using several authentication devices, keypad, retina scanner, fingerprint scanner. Figure 5-1 provides a feature model that includes these features as well as others related with security and windows management, while the Figure 5-2 presents one of its possible configurations, the "Economical Smart Home". Some optional features that are expensive and add more cost to the system are not included in such Economical product. Therefore,

retina and fingerprint scanners, as well as cameras, are not part of the final product.

As far as the Security feature is concerned, inhabitants can initiate the secure mode by activating the glass break sensors or/and camera surveillance devices (Glass Break Sensors and Cameras features). If an alarm signal is sent by any of these devices, and according to the security configuration of the house, the Smart Home decides to (i) Secure the house by activating the alarms (Siren and Lights features), and/or (ii) closing windows

Figure 6. Simplified Smart Home ActivateSecureMode use case scenario before and after a replace activity action

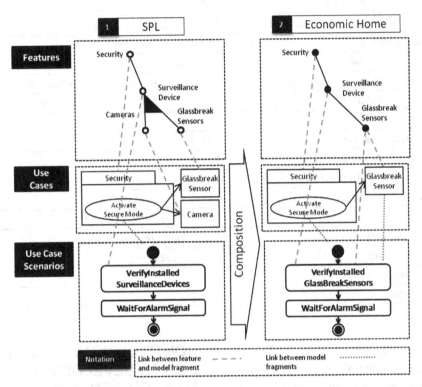

and doors (Electronic Windows feature) (see use case model in Figure 5-3). Smart Home can also choose to open or close windows automatically to regulate the temperature inside the house as an option to save energy (Electronic Windows feature). Alternatively to the electronic windows, the inhabitants could always be able to open and close the windows manually (Manual Windows feature). In Figure 5-4 we show the intended target use case model for the Economic home.

We chose use cases whose detailed behavior is modeled using activity models. This alternative provides models that conform to a metamodel (i.e., the metamodel of UML activity diagrams), thereby reducing the ambiguity in the specifications (Pohl, et al., 2005). The detailed specification of use cases as activity models also enables customizations of use cases realizing specific SPL configurations.

Figure 6-1 shows a simplified SPL scenario for the "activate secure mode" use case and how it

was customized for the Economic home that only have glassbreak sensors as available surveillance device (Figure 6-2). This figure also shows the links between features in the feature model and specific model fragments, and links between model fragments in different levels of abstraction of the requirements specification that helps to understand the relationships between the different models. The composition of the elements is expressed using a VML4RE model as the one shown in Table 3.

The VML4RE specification in Table 3 expresses how to configure the models for a specific product. Therefore, it contributes to express configuration knowledge as it was sketched in Figure 2-4. The VML4RE specification references the requirements models and specifies composition rules. In the specification it is possible to use expressions such as "and (glassbreak, not (cameras))" (see Table 3 - line 8), which means that the composition rules inside brackets will be

Table 3. Part of the VML4RE Model for the Smart Home

01	import features <"/featureModel.fmp">;	17	}
02	import core <"/UseCaseAndActivityModels.uml'>;	18	variant for (GlassbreakSensor) {
03	concern SmartHomeSPL { //...//	19	insert (actor GlassbreakSensor);
04	variant for ElectronicWindows {	20	insert (UCLinks_of_type: associatedWith {
05	remove (useCase OpenWindowsAutomatically);	21	from actor GlassbreakSensor to
06	remove (actor WindowsActuator);	22	useCase ActivateSecureMode})
07	}	23	}
08	variant for and (glassbreak, not (cameras)){	24	}
09	replace (activity activateSecureMode::	25	variant for (cameras){
10	VerifyInstalledSurveillanceDevices by	26	insert (actor camera);
11	activity verifyInstalledGlassBreakSensors);	27	}
12	}	28	variant for not (cameras){
13	variant for not (security){	29	remove (actor camera);
14	remove (package security);	30	}//...//
15	remove (actor glassbreakSensor);	31	}
16	remove (actor camera);	32	

executed if the expression evaluates to TRUE. This is, when the "glassbreak" sensors feature is included but not the "cameras" feature in the feature model configuration. The VML4RE tool (AMPLE, 2009) receives as input the SPL use cases and activity models, the feature model configuration and the VML4RE specification. As outputs, the VML4RE tool generates: (i) use cases of a product; and (ii) activity models that describe product's use scenarios.

There are composition rules that add elements to the SPL model and there are others that remove or replace elements. The specification in Table 3 shows familiar vocabulary such as useCase, activity, actor, etc.. The modeler does not require to know metamodel complexities such as the link between the UML metaclasses "Use case", "Association" and "Property" to express "simply" things such as for example the insertion of an association relationship between an actor and a use case. Also, the way of expressing what happens when a variant feature is selected or not is very intuitive as it can be appreciated for the case of the variant "cameras" (Table 3, lines 25-30).

CONTRIBUTIONS OF MODEL-DRIVEN DEVELOPMENT TO REQUIREMENTS ENGINEERING IN SPLS

The use of models, metamodels and models transformations in MDD provide the possibility of using models as key assets in the development process. Some of the contributions of using approaches for model-driven development requirements engineering in SPLs such as the one presented in Section "A Model-Driven Requirements Specification Approach for SPLs" are:

- *Rigor of the specifications through the verification of the conformity of the models with their metamodels:* The models that express the requirements specifications conform to metamodels that can be verified. The verification of the models is important as it is required to produce models written in a known metamodel. If the metamodel of the model is known, it is possible to create transformation rules that are described based on the metaclasses of the source and target models' metamodels. Therefore, a chain of transformation rules and additional increments of information in the requirements specification models could be applied to refine them to more detailed models such as design models, or initial architectural models.

- *Employ a correct abstraction level to express the requirements*: the use of domain specific languages such as feature models and VML4RE helps to express efficiently composition, variability and configuration knowledge of requirements models in the vocabulary and in the way that the users understand. This is a big contribution to the solution of the problem of abstraction mismatch (Sánchez, Loughran, Fuentes, & Garcia, 2008) that difficult the use MDD techniques use by non technical-oriented people.

- *Testing and understanding the behavior of specific products in the SPL*: The automatic derivation of requirements models for a specific product is useful to both (i) understanding which requirements and features are involved in the development of an SPL product, and (ii) to support the testing and documentation activities. In particular, activity models are an example of requirements artifacts that are well suited for business process modeling and for modeling the logic captured by a single use case or scenario.

FUTURE RESEARCH DIRECTIONS

There are several issues to address that are common for model-driven specification approaches not only in requirements analysis, but also for architectural and detailed design, for example: co-evolution management of multiple interrelated models, verification and validation of the produced

models, and usability of composition language. However, there are two main research directions in requirements specification. The first is related to the representation of non-functional requirements, business rules, and the use of specific requirements models for systems engineering; and the second is related to the detection of potential unwanted feature interactions analyzing the semantic of the composed models.

To specify interactions between functional and non-functional requirements during requirements modeling, other models, such as goal models (Chung, Nixon, Yu, & Mylopoulos, 1999; Yu) can be used. Such models also allow studying the actors and their dependencies, thus encouraging a deeper understanding of the business process. Therefore, we plan to use these kinds of models to specify also non-functional properties of SPLs systems. Besides, it is important to investigate the relationship of the models used in our approach and OMG (Object Management Group (OMG)) standards for business modeling such as: Business Motivation Model (BMM) (Object Management Group (OMG), 2008a), Semantics of Business Vocabulary and Rules (SBVR) (Object Management Group (OMG), 2008b), and also for systems engineering, such as the requirements package of the Systems Modeling Language (SysML) (Object Management Group (OMG), 2010).

Another future research trend is the detection of feature interactions after the composition of their respective models. A feature interaction occurs when the behavior of a feature inhibits or subverts the behavior of another one in an unwanted or unexpected way. Therefore, feature interaction detection contributes to produce products whose features interact as expected and without conflicts (Alférez, Moreira, et al., 2009).

CONCLUSION

This chapter provided an overview of both textual and graphical notations for modeling SPL requirements and different ways to compose requirements. Also, it shows our approach for model-driven requirements specification for SPLs. It separates requirements specifications, variability information and configuration knowledge to reach a better understandability of the models. This approach employs use cases whose detailed scenarios are modeled using activity models. The further elaboration of use cases with activity models; in contrast to free-format textual descriptions, facilitates to have models suitable to be processed by MDD tools and to produce useful information such as the customized models for specific products in a SPL.

ACKNOWLEDGMENT

This work was partially supported by the European Project AMPLE, contract IST-33710, and the grant SFRH/BD/46194/2008 of Fundação para a Ciência e a Tecnologia, Portugal.

REFERENCES

Alexander, I., & Maiden, N. (2004). *Scenarios, Stories, Use Cases*. Chichester, UK: Wiley.

Alférez, M., Kulesza, U., Sousa, A., Santos, J., Moreira, A., Araújo, J., et al. (2008). *A Model-Driven Approach for Software Product Lines Requirements Engineering*. Paper presented at the 20th International Conference on Software Engineering & Knowledge Engineering, Redwood City, CA.

Alférez, M., Moreira, A., Kulesza, U., Araújo, J., Mateus, R., & Amaral, V. (2009). *Detecting Feature Interactions in SPL Requirements Analysis Models*. Paper presented at the 1st International Workshop on Feature-Oriented Software Development Denver, Colorado.

Alférez, M., Santos, J., Moreira, A., Garcia, A., Kulesza, U., Araújo, J., et al. (2009). *Multi-View Composition Language for Software Product Line Requirements*. Paper presented at the 2nd Int. Conference on Software Language Engineering, Denver, USA.

Alves, V., Gheyi, R., Massoni, T., Kulesza, U., Borba, P., & Lucena, C. (2006, 2006). *Refactoring Product Lines*. Paper presented at the Proceedings of the 5th International Conference on Generative Programming and Component Engineering, Portland, Oregon, USA.

AMPLE. (2009). *Ample Project*. from http://www.ample-project.net/

Antkiewicz, M., & Czarnecki, K. (2004). *FeaturePlugin: Feature Modeling Plug-in for Eclipse*. Paper presented at the 2004 OOPSLA workshop on eclipse technology eXchange.

Bonifacio, R., & Borba, P. (2009). *Modeling Scenario Variability as Crosscutting Mechanisms*. Paper presented at the Aspect Oriented Software Development.

Bragança, A., & Machado, R. J. (2007). *Automating Mappings between Use Case Diagrams and Feature Models for Software Product Lines*. Paper presented at the 11th International Software Product Line Conference.

Chung, L., Nixon, B., Yu, E., & Mylopoulos, J. (1999). *Non-Functional Requirements in Software Engineering* (1 ed.). Amsterdam: Kluwer Academic Publishers.

Clements, P., & Northrop, L. M. (2002). *Software Product Lines: Practices and Patterns*. Boston: Addison-Wesley.

Cockburn, A. (2001). *Writing Effective Use Cases*. Boston: Addison-Wesley.

Czarnecki, K., & Antkiewicz, M. (2005). *Mapping Features to Models: A Template Approach Based on Superimposed Variants*. Paper presented at the 4th International Conference on Generative Programming and Component Engineering.

Czarnecki, K., & Eisenecker, U. W. (2000). *Generative Programming: Methods, Tools, and Applications*. New York: ACM Press/Addison-Wesley Publishing Co.

Czarnecki, K., Helsen, S., & Eisenecker, U. (2004). *Staged Configuration Using Feature Models*. Paper presented at the Third International Conference in Software Product Lines, Boston, Massachusetts, USA.

Deursen, A. v., & Klint, P. (2001). Domain-Specific Language Design Requires Feature Descriptions. *Journal of Computing and Information Technology, 10*. DSM forum website. (n.d.). DSM Forum: Domain-Specific Modeling. from http://www.dsmforum.org/

Eclipse Foundation. (n.d.). MDT-UML2Tools. from http://www.eclipse.org/uml2/

Eriksson, M. (2006). *An Approach to Software Product Line Use Case Modeling. Unpublished Doctoral Degree, UMEÅ University*. Sweden: UMEÅ.

Eriksson, M., Börstler, J., & Borg, K. (2005). *The PLUSS Approach - Domain Modeling with Features, Use Cases and Use Case Realizations*. Paper presented at the 9th International Conference on Software Product Lines.

Figueiredo, E., Cacho, N., Sant'Anna, C., Monteiro, M., Kulesza, U., Garcia, A., et al. (2008). *Evolving software product lines with aspects: an empirical study on design stability*. Paper presented at the 30th International Conference on Software Engineering (ICSE 2008).

Filman, R. E., Elrad, T., Clarke, S., & Aksit, M. (2004). *Aspect-Oriented Software Development*. Addison-Wesley.

Gomaa, H. (2004). *Designing Software Product Lines with UML: From Use Cases to Pattern-Based Software Architectures*. Reading, MA: Addison-Wesley.

(1997). InGrzegorz, R. (Ed.). Handbook of Graph Grammars and Computing by Graph Transformation: *Vol. I. Foundations*. River Edge, NJ: World Scientific Publishing Co., Inc.

Heidenreich, F. (2010). *FeatureMapper: Mapping Features to Models*. from http://featuremapper.org/

Jacobson, I. (1992). *Object-oriented Software Engineering: A Use CASE Approach*. Reading, MA: Addison Wesley.

Jouault, F., & Kurtev, I. (2005). *Transforming Models with ATL*. Paper presented at the Model Transformations in Practice Workshop at MoDELS 2005.

Kang, K., Cohen, S., Hess, J., Novak, W., & Peterson, A. (1990). *Feature-Oriented Domain Analysis (FODA) Feasibility Study (Technical report, CMU/SEI-90-TR-021)*. Software Engineering Institute, Carnegie Mellon University.

Markovic, S., & Baar, T. (2005). *Refactoring OCL Annotated UML Class Diagram*. Paper presented at the International Conference On Model Driven Engineering Languages And Systems

Moreira, A., Rashid, A., & Araújo, J. (2005, 2005). *Multi-Dimensional Separation of Concerns in Requirements Engineering*. Paper presented at the Proceedings of the 13th IEEE International Conference on Requirements Engineering, France.

Morganho, H., Gomes, C., Pimentão, J. P., Ribeiro, R., Grammel, B., Pohl, C., et al. (2008). *Requirement Specifications for Industrial Case Studies* (AMPLE Project, Deliverable D5.2). Object Management Group (OMG). *Object Management Group*. from http://www.omg.org/

Object Management Group (OMG). (2008a). *Business Motivation Model*. from http://www.omg.org/spec/BMM/1.0

Object Management Group (OMG). (2008b). *Semantics of Business Vocabulary and Business Rules (SBVR)*. from http://www.omg.org/spec/SBVR/1.0/PDF

Object Management Group (OMG). (2010). *Systems Modeling Language (SysML)*. from http://www.omg.org/spec/SBVR/1.0/PDF

OMG. (2009a). *OMG's MetaObject Facility (MOF)*. from http://www.omg.org/mof/

OMG. (2009b). *Unified Modeling Language*. from http://www.uml.org/

openArchitectureWare.org. (n.d.). *openArchitectureWare*. from http://www.openarchitectureware.org/

Pohl, K. (2006). Panel on Product Line Research: Lessons Learned from the last 10 years and Directions for the next 10 years. In *10th International Software Product Line Conference (SPLC 2006)*. Retrieved from http://www.sei.cmu.edu/splc2006/SPLC06-ResearchPanel-KP.pdf

Pohl, K., Böckle, G., & van der Linden, F. (2005). *Software Product Line Engineering: Foundations, Principles and Techniques*. Berlin, Germany: Springer.

Sánchez, P., Loughran, N., Fuentes, L., & Garcia, A. (2008). *Engineering Languages for Specifying Product-derivation Processes in Software Product Lines*. Paper presented at the 1st International Conference on Software Language Engineering (SLE).

Taentzer, G. (2003). *AGG: A Graph Transformation Environment for Modeling and Validation of Software*. Paper presented at the 2nd International Workshop on Applications of Graph Transformations with Industrial Relevance (AGTIVE), Virginia, USA.

Volter, M., & Stahl, T. (2006). *Model-Driven Software Development*. Glasgow, UK: Wiley.

Yu, E. (n.d.). *i* an Agent-oriented Modelling Framework*. from http://www.cs.toronto.edu/km/istar/

KEY TERMS AND DEFINITIONS

Software Product Line (SPL) Engineering: Is a development approach to increase software quality and productivity. It addresses the creation and management of a family of software products for a particular domain instead of developing each product separately.

Feature: Is a property or functionality that is relevant to some stakeholders and that allows to distinguish between products in a SPL. In a family of software products most of the features are *common* while some features *vary* between the family members.

Common Feature: Is a kind of *feature* that expresses a property that is common to all the products in a SPL.

Variable Feature: Is a kind of *feature* that expresses a property that is not common to all the products in a SPL.

Feature Model: Is a model for expressing requirements in a domain on an abstract level. They are applied to describe variable and common features of products in a product line, and to derive and validate configurations of software systems.

Optional Feature: Is a kind of feature that may not be included in some of the products of the SPL.

Variation Point: Identifies a particular concept within the SPL requirements specification as being variable and it offers a number of variants.

Variant: Describes a particular variability decision, such as a specific choice among alternative variants.

Model Composition: In its basic sense means to combine two or more models to modify one or more models, or to create a new one. Composition in SPL helps to create models for specific SPL products using composition actions and model transformations.

Section 4
Surveys

Chapter 18
Domain Modeling Approaches in IS Engineering

Marite Kirikova
Riga Technical University, Latvia

ABSTRACT

In information systems engineering there is a long history of development and application of different domain modeling approaches, methods and techniques. The chapter surveys and analyzes enterprise models, systems development artifacts, enterprise architectures, enterprise modeling tools, and information systems change management issues from the point of view of information systems engineering. The purpose of this work is to share experience from information systems engineering with model driven architecture community and to reveal strong and weak sides of domain modeling approaches and tools used in information systems engineering which, in turn, would help to see where further research and development efforts are needed in order to achieve maximum value from systems development efforts in the area of information systems engineering and model driven architecture. The chapter focuses on methods used in information systems engineering and, according to its purpose, does not consider in detail domain modeling approaches that are well known to model driven development/engineering/architecture community.

INTRODUCTION

The purpose of this chapter is to provide an overview of domain modeling approaches and techniques used in information systems (IS) engineering. IS engineering is an area where different types of domain models were used as

DOI: 10.4018/978-1-61692-874-2.ch018

a basis for software development long before the name of model driven approach and model driven architecture was coined (MDA, 2009; Miller & Mukerji, 2003). IS engineering views not only software, but also requirements and domain models, as systemic artifacts that can be traced, analyzed, and reused in different systems development tasks. Examination of historical evolvement, level of completeness, complexity, and usability of these models, methods, and tools may provide a better understanding of tendencies, problems, and constraints in model driven domain analysis and software development. The paper mainly focuses on the requirements phase of IS engineering, where domain modeling to some extent is similar to development of CIM (Computation Independent Model) in MDA (Model Driven Architecture) (Miller & Mukerji, 2003; Lankhorst, M., 2005; Gherbi et al., 2009; Kheraff et al., 2008).

Background section concerns different approaches of domain modeling used for requirements identification. In requirements engineering (as a part of IS engineering) at least some means for systemic elicitation and amalgamation of requirements are usually applied. One can see that emphasis on particular issues in domain analysis has been changed by putting IS users or business systems in the main focus at different levels of abstraction and using different representation frameworks. The section will show the spectrum of approaches and the way how requirements knowledge is integrated in some of the representative methods. It consists of two subsections. The first one discusses domain modeling in IS engineering; the second one briefly considers domain modeling in model driven software development.

Models developed during requirements engineering phase are essential IS engineering artifacts. The scope and use of these artifacts depend on the approach of IS development. For instance, agile and enterprise modeling driven methods differ considerably in their creation and use of systems development artifacts (Kirikova, 2004; Stirna & Kirikova, 2008). Dependence of domain modeling approaches on systems development methods is analyzed in section "Domain modeling artifacts in different IS development approaches".

While in Background section the main emphasis is on diversity of requirements engineering approaches in terms of domain analysis methods applied for requirements identification, in section "Role of enterprise architectures in domain model-

ing and analysis" the domain analysis frameworks are analyzed taking Enterprise Architectures into the main focus. This section also includes analysis of multilevel systems representations in general. Section "Role of tool support in use of domain modeling approaches" briefly discusses issues of tool support for domain analysis. Here the gap between knowledge utilized in enterprise modeling tools and tools supporting UML (UML, 2009) is analyzed. The discussion is continued in section "Domain models and change management" where systems change management issues are considered. The paper ends by brief description of future work and conclusions.

BACKGROUND

This section discusses domain modeling from the viewpoint of two related but still bit alienated communities, namely IS engineering and software engineering. The main difference is in points of emphasis of approaches. According to the purpose of the chapter the section focuses on basic approaches in the IS engineering (subsection "Domain modeling in IS engineering"). Nevertheless, several approaches known in software engineering and, in particular in domain model driven approaches, are discussed as a related work in subsection "Domain modeling in model driven software engineering".

Domain Modeling in IS Engineering

In IS engineering the main purpose of domain modeling is identification of system of requirements for the IS to be built. In fact, IS engineering implies that requirements are engineered not just transferred from the heads of end-users via programmers to software. There are numerous approaches of requirements engineering that have been reported in different scientific conferences and on consulting company web pages (see, e.g.,

Sawyer et al., 2007). We can classify all approaches in the following two main groups:

- Group 1: Approaches with the main focus on software user requirements
- Group 2: Approaches with the main focus on the enterprise model

Group 1 approaches relay upon the viewpoint of software user with respect to the intended use of software and then try to establish the system of software requirements that could satisfy the user needs. The first contemporary, tool supported, approaches of this type were reported in late eighties of the previous century. For instance, Martin (1988) states that "functional and data base requirements should be developed together, followed by compilation of performance requirements. Parallel top-down development of the functional and data base requirements differs from the classical systems analysis approach of defining functional capabilities first and then determining the supporting data requirements. It also differs from the approach ..."define and implement data base and necessary reports will take care of themselves...""". Soon Coad and Yourdon (1990) say that it is practically impossible to develop functional and data requirements for the whole system in parallel (consistency problem); therefore object-oriented approach is necessary to do it in parallel, but in smaller pieces. This eventually leads to Jacobsen's et al. (1995) use cases which nowadays are a well known means for requirements elicitation. Switching to piece-like user requirements introduces the problem of information integration that is still not solved despite of availability of advanced requirements management tools such as Requisite Pro and DOORS (IBM, 2009). Another problem in software user requirements oriented approaches is dealing with many diverse views (Sommerwille & Sawyer, 1997), which also require sophisticated methods for integrating information acquired from different viewpoints. Thus the focus on

user requirements, in essence, does not give an opportunity to validate the relationship between business domain and requirements domain and software development domain. This is because of non-formal means of requirements integration, decision back-tracing difficulties and complexity, and the fact that integrated view on the domain where the software system is to operate has never been established.

Group 2 approaches aim at building the domain model and then deriving the requirements from the domain model. It is necessary to emphasize that the notion "domain model" here is used not in terms of a particular UML class model but in terms of an integrated system of models that reflect the enterprise where software is to be applied (Bubenko Jr. et al., 1992; Lamsweerde, 2008). In this section two representative approaches of Group 2 are considered, namely, the Enterprise Modeling (Bubenko Jr.et al., 1992) and i* (Yu & Mylopoulos, 1994). Both approaches are in use more than 10 years. Enterprise Modeling is based on the enterprise model (EM) which can be represented at three conceptual levels: meta-meta level that consists of six models; meta-level that describes semantic contents of each of six models defined at meta-meta-level; and instance level where the actual enterprise model is developed. Instance level models can be further decomposed according to modeling needs. The meta-meta level EM is reflected in Figure 1. It consists of six interrelated models: Goals, Resources and Actors, Concepts, Business processes, Business Rules, and IS Requirements and Components models. The Business Rules model was added to EM later when the methodology evolved into enterprise knowledge development methodology (EKD) (Bubenko Jr. et al., 2001). The way the EM is presented in Figure 1 differs from the original representation. The difference here is introduced to simplify further discussion in this chapter where EKD will be compared to other methodologies. Dotted arrow-headed lines show that all requirements are derived from mutually related enterprise models,

Figure 1. Meta-meta level of EM

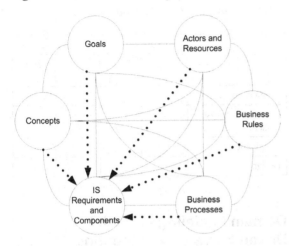

Figure 2. Correspondence between EM and i* models

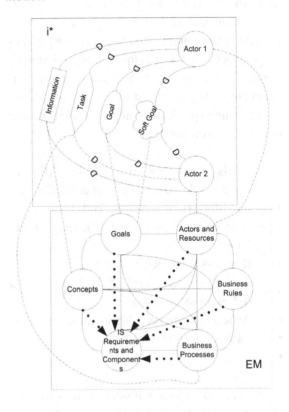

each of which represents a particular view on the enterprise or "world" (Bubenko jr. & Kirikova, 1995). A basic essential feature of the enterprise modeling approach involves development of models on the plastic sheets by stakeholders. It means that their knowledge is shared during the process of domain model development.

Modeling of strategic relationships, initially called i*, uses domain representation that focuses on actors and relationships between them. Activities of the actors depicted at the upper level of the model can be represented in the so-called strategic rationale models, where different types of decompositions can be reflected. i* utilizes four types of relationships between actors, namely, soft goal relationship, goal relationship, task relationship, and information relationship. The relationship shows the dependence of one actor on others, e.g., owner of the goal depends on the one who fulfills the goal. Correspondence between EM and i* model is reflected in Figure 2. Actors of i* can be mapped to the EM Resources and Actors model, goal and soft goal dependencies may be reflected in Goals model (taking into consideration inter-model links), task dependency could be reflected in Business Process model (taking into consideration inter-model links), and information dependency could be

shown using Concepts model of EM and inter-model links.

Comparison of both methodologies shows that they can reflect a similar scope of the domain model, however, the primary emphasis of the modeling differs. The enterprise model focuses on whole domain in each of its meta-meta-level models while i* reflects the domain as a network of interdependent actors. It seems that using model transformation algorithms it could be possible to some extent to derive EM from i* model and vice versa. It is interesting that both domain modeling approaches (EM based and i*) or their modifications have been recognized as goal-oriented/driven approaches (Kavakli & Loucopoulos, 2004). Modifications of i* can be classified also as agent-oriented (Panserini et al., 2006; Lapouchnian & Lesperance, 2006) and aspect-oriented (Rashid & Chitchyan, 2008) approaches.

This shows that (1) in requirements engineering there are particular issues that almost always are to be taken into consideration – such as those reflected in EM and i*; and (2) usually a particular perspective is taken as the leading or dominating one. Some of leading perspectives in IS engineering in general and in requirements engineering in particular that are used in different Group 2 approaches follow:

- Goals or objectives (Kavakli & Loucopoulos, 2004; Quartel et al., 2009)
- Intentions (Rolland et al., 2007)
- Business processes (e.g., Ouyang et al., 2009)
- Business rules (Ross, 2003)
- Agents (Panserini et al., 2006; Lapouchnian & Lesperance, 2006)
- Aspects (Rashid & Chitchyan, 2008)
- Values (Gordijn, 2002)
- Etc.

Success of domain modeling depends on the expressiveness of model framework in use (Kirikova, 2000a). Another important issue is the way in which knowledge about the domain is integrated. Table 1 reflects model based knowledge integration points for two groups of requirements engineering approaches discussed in this section.

Table 1 shows that different approaches have various capacities for model based knowledge integration. From the point of view of software developer it might be of small importance where exactly the point of integration resides. However, from the point of view of IS development, it is essential that human knowledge would be consistent with models that are used for enterprise and software design (Alter, 2008). On the other hand, higher up on the grey ladder reflected in Table 1 there is the point of knowledge integration – it's easier to validate the requirements and manage their change.

Table 1. Knowledge integration points in requirements engineering approaches

	Group 1		Group 2	
	Use Cases	View-points	i*	EM
Human knowledge				X
Domain/Enterprise model			X	
Requirements		X		
Design	X			

Domain Modeling in Model Driven Software Engineering

Model driven engineering concerns forward and reverse engineering of systems focusing on models of system developed for different purposes (Bezivin et al., 2007). In model driven development/ engineering/architecture domain modeling usually occurs at the level of CIM (Schmidt, 2006; Bezivin, 2006; Sparx Systems, 2007). The following models and model combinations have been used by different researchers and practitioners for domain description at the upper level of MDA:

- Environment of the system and requirements for the system (Miller & Mukerji, 2003)
- Business model, Domain Model, Business requirements (Lankhorst et al, 2005)
- Task model and Use Case model (Valverde et al., 2007)
- Requirements models (Gherbi et al., 2009)
- Knowledge about functionality and structure of the problem domain (Osis et al., 2007, Osis & Asnina, 2008)
- Semantics of business vocabulary and business rules (Diouf et al., 2008)
- Communication contracts, Global policies, Failover, Infrastructure capabilities (Biffl et al., 2007)

Table 2. Systems artifact dependence on systems development methods

	Domain/Enterprise Model	*IS Model*	*Requirements Model*	*Software Design Model*
Agile	n/a or tacit, fragmentary	Tacit, fragmentary	From Tacit fragmentary to semi-formal fragmentary	From tacit to semi-formal
Plan-driven	From tacit to semi-formal	From tacit to semi-formal	From tacit to formal	From tacit to formal

- Product line requirement model (Kabanda et al., 2006)
- Business systems (Slack, 2005)
- Business process model; System requirements model (Visual Use Cases) (Kheraff et al., 2008)
- Enterprise integration Model: Organization model, Process model; Data model, System model (Shuangxi & Yushun, 2007)
- Business Motivation Model (OMG, 2008)
- Domain specific languages (e.g. Kelly & Tolvanen, 2008)
- Etc.

While the domain model representation approaches used in model driven software engineering form a wide spectrum of models and techniques, none of them present any break-through method. The main tendency, especially in domain specific languages, is to arrive at a class model that comprises nouns and verbs describing a domain model. This is about the same knowledge represented in Concepts model of EM. This can be regarded as a domain model in a narrow sense. Majority of the approaches listed in this subsection do not provide means for domain model completeness and consistency analysis. They are focused more on the language of domain description (Lin et al., 2007) than on information flows that are the main object of interest in IS engineering approaches. This leads to the thought that the role of IS is not yet well understood in the context of MDA (Kirikova et al., 2010). Therefore in the rest of the paper the focus of the discussion will be on IS engineering oriented methods and tools.

DOMAIN MODELING ARTIFACTS IN DIFFERENT IS DEVELOPMENT APPROACHES

All IS development approaches can be put on the axis with "agile" on one end and "plan-driven" on the other end. While each of these approaches has its specific application area, recently there has emerged a tendency towards integration of best practices of both above-mentioned groups of approaches. This section focuses on commonalities and a difference of artifacts (mainly domain models) used in agile and plan-driven systems development approaches; and ponders about integration possibilities of these artifacts.

Domain modeling is human activity that leads to the creation of different types of domain representations. These representations may be tacit (in human minds) and explicit/externalized (on paper or in software tool). The nature and scope of the domain models depend on the way in which IS is being developed. Both the domain modeling method and systems development method matter. In Table 1 knowledge integration points were presented for different requirements engineering methods. Table 2 shows how artifacts depend on systems development methods (Kirikova, 2004; Stirna & Kirikova, 2008).

Agile IS development approach has proved to be a widely used means for systems development (Ambler, 2002). This approach is based on intensive communication between software developers and so-called 'customer on site'. Modeling techniques are used, however models themselves in most cases have a very short life span as they are documented on whiteboards and are usually not

Table 3. Share-ability of domain models

Agile approach		Plan driven approach				
Knowledge	Group 1 Use Cases	Knowledge	Group 1		Group 2	
Tacit knowledge about the domain (mental models)	Shared between customer on site and developers		Use Cases	Viewpoints	i*	EM
Domain model	Undeveloped	Tacit knowledge about the domain (mental models)	Not shared	Not shared	Usually not shared	Shared by business users and (optionally) developers
		Domain model	Undeveloped	Undeveloped	Exists	Exists

intended for further use. Their main aim is to aid mental model development. Nevertheless, the scope of documented artifacts changes with the complexity of the domain and the IS to be built. The more complex the systems, the more complex and elaborated are hard models developed during agile systems development. The following artifacts are most common in agile modeling (Ambler, 2007): Business rule definition; Component diagram (UML); Constraint definition; Data model; Deployment diagram (UML); Essential use case; External interface; Features; Glossary; Network Diagram; Organization chart; Package diagram; Specification language; Technical Requirement; Use case diagram; User interface flow diagram; Workflow diagram. One can see that these artifacts do not include a holistic domain model, e.g., the one that could be represented by EM or i* models. On the other hand, plan-driven approach may utilize different types of models including a holistic domain model. Looking from the point of view of availability of externalized knowledge about the domain, the plan-driven methods seem to be more reliable because of the utilization of semi-formal or even formal models. However, tacit knowledge should not to be neglected in systems development (Kirikova, 2004). While hard models in agile approaches may be less developed, mental models, due to extensive communication between users and developers of the

software, can be much more shared than in plan-driven approaches.

Nested Table 3 illustrates how share-ability of domain knowledge differs in agile approach and various development options that are available in plan-driven approaches. In agile development Use Cases is practically the only often used in practice requirements acquisition method among the methods that were described in previous section. This is due to the relative simplicity of development of Use Cases comparing to enterprise models such as EM or i* (Kirikova, 2001).

Table 3 shows that domain model is undeveloped in agile approach and in Group 1 options of plan-driven approach. The fact that mental models are shared in agile approach suggests better applicability of the approach in terms of software system acceptance. It also suggests that plan-driven methods without the domain model development and without knowledge sharing among system stakeholders and developers would hardly promote successful software development projects. With plan-driven methods only in the case of EM both hard domain model and shared domain knowledge are present. In case of classical enterprise modeling method or EKD methodology (Bubenko jr. et al., 2001) knowledge is shared among business domain stakeholders. Usually this is not the case in agile development. However, in EKD methodology knowledge between business stakeholders and developers might be less intensively shared than in agile systems development methods. Thus we can conclude that domain modeling artifacts be their holistic models as EM or just fragmentary domain model elements like business rule definition, aid in knowledge sharing and mental model development of business stakeholders and IS developers. On the other hand, holistic domain models, if properly designed, managed and shared could aid the development of systems, which due to their size or complexity need semi-formal or formal aids for ensuring their completeness and consistency (Kirikova, 1998; Kirikova, 2000b). During the last decade the interest in holistic domain models has grown. These models are usually associated to particular enterprise architectures that define particular cognitive framework for related domain modeling artifacts (Schekkerman, 2006).

ROLE OF ENTERPRISE ARCHITECTURES IN DOMAIN MODELING AND ANALYSIS

The notion of enterprise architecture has evolved from information technology and has become a well known term in business development. Several books have been published presenting different enterprise architectures (Schekkerman, 2006; Saha, 2007). This chapter does not attempt to analyze all enterprise architectures. It tries to look at their inherent structure and comment on their applicability in the context of MDA. MDA is regarded as multilevel architecture that comprises three levels PSM (Platform Specific Model), PIM (Platform Independent Model) and CIM. This hierarchy of models is regarded as abstraction hierarchy where PIM abstracts from the particular technology, and CIM abstracts from the way software fulfills the expectations of its users. Thus MDA is one-dimensional abstraction architecture. The question is how expressive and how reliable

such architecture can be and how does it relate to well-known enterprise architectures.

Cognitive engineering (Rasmussen et al., 1994) suggests reflecting complex system in two-dimensional framework, namely, means-ends hierarchy taken orthogonally to part-of hierarchy. The following means-ends hierarchy is suggested by Rasmussen et al. (1994):

- *Purposes and constraints*: properties necessary and sufficient to establish relations between the performance of the system and the reasons for its design, that is, the purposes and constraints of its coupling to the environment. Categories are in terms referring to properties of environment.
- *Abstract functions and priority measures*: properties necessary and sufficient to establish priorities according to the intention behind the design and operation: Topology of flow and accumulation of mass, energy and information, people, monetary value. Categories in abstract terms, referring rather to system, not environment.
- *General functions*: Properties necessary and sufficient to identify the 'functions' which are to be coordinated irrespective of their underlying physical processes. Categories according to recurrent, familiar input/output relationships.
- *Physical Processes and Activities*: properties necessary and sufficient for control of physical work activities and use of equipment: To adjust operations in order to match specifications or limits: to predict response to control actions; to maintain and repair equipment. Categories according to underlying physical processes and equipment.
- *Physical Form and Configuration*: properties necessary and sufficient for classification, identification, and recognition of particular material objects and their configurations, for navigation in the system.

Categories in terms of objects, their appearance and location.

Depending on the nature and features of the systems for the part-of relationship different variations of number of levels and their names are presented in Rasmussen et al. (1994). From the point of view of MDA an interesting fact in means-ends hierarchy is that categories in terms of objects are used only at the bottom level of the hierarchy. Another issue to be considered is that human thought via hierarchies, as illustrated in the book, does not go just top-down or bottom-up, but freely moves in four directions in two-dimensional space with a tendency to start at the purpose of total system and end at the physical processes or materials of components.

Since eighties of previous century the best known enterprise architecture is Zachman two-dimensional framework that tries to take into consideration all issues relevant in domain/enterprise modeling (Finkelstein, 2006; Zachman, 1987). One of the dimensions of Zachman architecture presents the following modeling perspectives:

- Planner (objectives, scope), contextual
- Owner (conceptual), enterprise model
- Designer (logical), system model
- Builder (Physical), technology model
- Subcontractor (out of context), detailed representation
- Functioning enterprise

It suggests the following abstractions to be considered orthogonally to each above-mentioned perspective:

- What (data)
- How (function)
- Where (network)
- Who (people)
- What (time)
- Why (motivation)

It is necessary to point out here that there is a difference between the multi-hierarchical abstractions such as in MDA where higher level of abstraction abstracts from all issues that where abstracted from in lower levels of abstraction. In Zachman's framework aspect-oriented abstractions are used. In nested Table 4 all three above discussed frameworks (MDA, cognitive engineering, and Zachman) are reflected.

The underlying issue in IS development is that in terms of MDA the hierarchy CIM-PIM-PSM does not take into consideration existence of part-of relationship between CIM and PIM. Additionally, this hierarchy does not take into consideration the role of information in this context. IS is one of the subsystems of the enterprise, and software is a part of this and only this subsystem, unless it is embedded in the mechanical device that can perform physical functions. There are some enterprise architectures that take into consideration the role of information, like Extended Enterprise Architecture Framework (Schekkerman, 2006), where columns are structured similar to Zachman architecture and rows have meanings: Business, Information, IS, Technology, but overall meaning of the cells differs considerably from Zachman architecture. Extended Enterprise Architecture Framework architecture is interoperability oriented. Its rows keep together essential issues of the enterprise while columns are organized so that they reflect means-ends hierarchy to some extent (Rasmussen et al., 1994).

The spectrum of enterprise architectures shows that none of them is organized in a clean means-ends part-of orthogonal matrix as suggests cognitive engineering. Nevertheless, it is possible to allocate different systems mentioned above (enterprise, IS, etc.) in such orthogonal hierarchy (Table 5). This type of representation is valid only in situations when the enterprise already has software resources that will be reused in the new system. If the system is built for the enterprise which has not yet used any software,

Table 4. Different architectures

MDA	Cognitive engineering					
Levels of abstraction:		Total System	Sub-system	Function unit	Sub-assembly	Component
CIM	Purposes and Constraints	Why				
	Abstract functions and Priority measures	Why	What			
PIM	General functions	Why	What	How		
	Physical processes and Activities		What	How		
PSM	Physical Form and Configuration			How		

Zachman Architecture						
	What	How	Where	Who	When	Why
Contextual	e.g., List of things	e.g., List of Processes	e.g., List of Locations	e.g., Organizational Structure	e.g., List of Events	e.g., List of Objectives
Enterprise Model	e.g., Enterprise Model	e.g., Business Process Model	e.g., Business Logistics	e.g., Work Flow	e.g., Master Schedule	e.g., Business plan
System Model	e.g., Logical Data model	e.g., Application Architecture	e.g., Distributed Architecture	e.g., Human Interface	e.g., Processing Structure	e.g., Business Rules
Technology Model	e.g., Physical Data Model	e.g., System Model	e.g., Technology Architecture	e.g., Presentation Interface	e.g., Control Structure	e.g., Rule Design
Detailed representation	e.g., Data definition	e.g., Program	e.g., Network Architecture	e.g., Security Architecture	e.g., Timing Definition	e.g., Rule Specification
Functioning enterprise	e.g., Data	e.g., Function	e.g., Network	e.g., Organization	e.g., Schedule	e.g., Strategy

PSM would be in the same column as Software Systems Model.

Table 5 shows that (1) enterprise model is an important issue in MDA; (2) IS model is to be constructed before the software systems model; (3) the PIM to be built is just a part of other platform specific models of the enterprise. The framework in the Table 5 helps to not neglect that the enterprise, in essence, always is computation dependent if we understand by computation any means for information processing, not just software. This is a matter of investigation how this framework maps to Zachman architecture, which still does not have a meta-model, which could explain all its features (Chen & Pooley, 2009).

Enterprise architectures offer a wider variety of issues to be considered comparing to domain models discussed in previous section. Actually the domain model could be organized according to any architecture in use. The question is about usability of each issue in a particular systems development context and possibility of enterprise model development, documentation and maintenance, where availability of appropriate tools is an essential issue.

Table 5. MDA in cognitive engineering framework

	Total System	Sub-system	Function unit	Sub-assembly	Component
Purpses and Constraints	Enterprise Model				
Abstract functions and Priority measures		IS Model			
General functions			Software Systems Model (PIM)		
Physical processes and Activities				PSM for the software to be developed	
Physical Form and Configuration					Software components/objects to be developed

ROLE OF TOOL SUPPORT IN USE OF DOMAIN MODELING APPROACHES

In the beginning of the 21st century there was a gap between different tools needed in IS development. There were tools for requirements management (RM, 2009; INCOSE, 2009), tools for enterprise modeling capable to support model construction according to different enterprise architectures fully or partly, such as ARIS, Casewise (Casewise, 2009), Popkin Systems Architect, etc. (it should be noted here that there are tools that claim to be enterprise modeling tools, yet do not provide the functionality for enterprise model development). There were around 200 business process modeling tools on the market that did support the business process modeling, but did not give an opportunity to model other aspects of the enterprise (domain) (Kirikova & Makna, 2005), and there were software development tools such as IBM Rational Rose and others that sometimes were claimed to be enterprise modeling tools while offering purely class diagram for the enterprise (domain) model. Tool market has recently seen quite considerable changes, where the best enterprise modeling tools have merged with software development tools, e.g., IBM acquired Telelogic with its requirements management and enterprise modeling capabilities and Software AG became the dominating share

holder of IDS Scheer which possesses ARIS, relied upon by about 7500 companies in the world (ARIS, 2009). This means that software vendors have understood real value of domain modeling and tools that support this activity.

In Background section the domain modeling was considered from the point of view of IS engineering and the term 'enterprise modeling' was used. However, during the last decade enterprise modeling has become popular not only in IS development context, but also in the context of business process management. P. Harmon (2007) writes: "Unfortunately, any discussion of Enterprise Modeling is complicated because there is considerable confusion about just what constitutes Enterprise Modeling. The largest source of confusion is the Zachman Framework. Zachman created a framework designed to classify the types of information one might want to store about the enterprise. There's nothing wrong with the Zachman Framework, but it has led many people to assume that Enterprise Modeling is really just another name for letting IT (Information Technology) set up a database and then classify all the IT resources the company has". He suggests that real enterprise modeling needs the following tools:

- *Tools for Strategy work* - tools that can be used to define and document strategy statements, mission statements, goals, and

Table 6. Toolset capabilities

Toolset	ESOM	EAM	RE	CM	SD	Source
IBM Rational (Including IBM Rational Systems Architect and Websphere Business Modeller)	+	+	+	+	+	http://www-01.ibm.com/software/rational/
ARIS + Software AG tools	+	+	+	+	+	http://www.ids-scheer.com/international/en
Casewise	+	+	+	+	-	http://www.casewise.com/
ADONIS	+	+	+	+	BPEL only	http://www.boc-group.com/
QPR	+	+	+	+	Workflow only	http://www.qpr.com/products-overview.html
Sparx Systems Toolset	-	+	+	+	+	http://www.sparxsystems.eu/

policies; tools that can define organization or business models and track stakeholders and their concerns.

- Tools *for Defining Value Chains* and high level business processes, e.g., Value Chain Group's VRM and Supply Chain Council's SCOR framework (VRM, 2007; SCOR, 2009).
- *Tools for performance monitoring and for evaluating managerial performance* that can capture process performance metrics and show how they are aligned through the process hierarchy.
- *Tools for identifying and prioritizing process efforts*, i.e., tools that can help to track performance of company processes and identify, which processes would benefit from redesign or improvement efforts. These tools can also simulate changes and cost change efforts to help determine where the company will get the greatest return on a process change project.

This suggests that enterprise modeling implies more than domain modeling discussed in Background section and section "Role of enterprise architectures in domain modeling and analysis". Therefore for enterprise development, including the development of enterprise IS on one hand, and for software development for the enterprise on

another hand, the following basic functionalities of software toolkit would be relevant:

- Enterprise strategic and operational management (includes functionality of all 4 above-mentioned groups of tools suggested by P. Harmon (2007) (ESOM)
- Enterprise architecture modeling (EAM)
- Requirements engineering (RE)
- Change management (CM)
- Software development (SD)

This shows that domain modeling might be considered as a scope of the first four functionalities. Table 6 shows some popular tool sets and tries to reflect their current functionalities according to the above-mentioned list. We should remember, however, that current tool development is so dynamic that information presented in Table 6 may soon be out of date.

Toolsets amalgamated in Table 6 are just some examples of tools that can be used for domain modeling. The purpose of the table is to show that there is a clear tendency to merge all five functionalities of the tools presented in the table. Another issue is the use of those sophisticated tools in enterprises. Forrester's survey of 196 enterprise architects about their use of enterprise architecture modeling tools showed that 64% of corporations with more than 5000 employees use enterprise architecture tools. However, only 26%

of small enterprises use enterprise architecture tools partly due to a lower level of IT complexity, but mainly because of cost and ease-of-use barriers (Peyret, 2006). This suggests that the more advanced versions that are more user-friendly are expected in the tool market.

Tendencies in tool development make us think that in terms of MDA, CIM probably will evolve in sophisticated model families that currently represent functionalities ESOM, EAM, RE, and CM.

DOMAIN MODELS AND CHANGE MANAGEMENT

One of the important issues in contemporary IS development is frequent changes in the system dictated by turbulent external environment. This section examines the role of domain models in change management. Methods, approaches, and tools discussed in previous sections show that contemporary IS engineering utilizes sophisticated domain models where literarily almost each issue of the enterprise has its own model where it is brought into focus and related to other issues. This means that theoretically the majority of relevant changes in the enterprise can be reflected in domain models and their impact on different subsystems of the enterprise may be traced at different levels of abstraction.

The claim of MDA is independent development of business and technologies (MDA, 2009) in terms of PIM and PSM, i.e., the behavior of application is separated from the specific code. It is partly achieved by separating human tasks from software tasks in business process model and then generating the application in terms of business process execution language (Matjaz & Kapil, 2008). Therefore a business process model becomes the central element in enterprise and IS change management. Information processing is reflected in a business process model. Thus a business process model is the one that shows which information processing tasks (of the modeled

ones) are assigned to human actors and which - to software. This is the main issue in IS engineering as it enables to define requirements for software to be built and to analyze information flows among human actors, inside the software, and between human actors and software (Kirikova et al., 2010).

Analysis of IS theories and enterprise architectures has revealed the following main change objects in IS change management (Makna, 2009):

- Data (any recorded information electronically in databases or in paper files, or on other means of information transfer)
- Knowledge
- IS users
- IS activities
- Business process activities (other than IS activities)
- Territory (where the business process is performed)
- Resources
- Products

To achieve proper change managements from an IS engineering viewpoint it is necessary that domain model would reflect or in some way would be related to all above mentioned change elements. Referring to Table 6, at least one tool reflects each of the change objects except of knowledge. This shows that the relationship between tacit human knowledge and externalized knowledge reflected in domain models is not addressed properly in most of domain modeling tools and methods. Some efforts to solve this problem have been reported in terms of active knowledge modeling of enterprises (Lillehagen & Kroghstie, 2008) and agile enterprise modeling (Stirna & Kirikova, 2008). Active enterprise modeling generates and maintains specific role oriented models on the basis of the domain model. Agile enterprise modeling prescribes to relate enterprise architecture to more manual enterprise modeling means than enterprise modeling or EKD discussed in Background section.

FUTURE RESEARCH DIRECTIONS

It is necessary to take into consideration that domain modeling does not exclude people from IS and software development. Therefore three knowledge domains are relevant in IS change management, namely, business knowledge, IS knowledge, and software systems knowledge. This shows that identification of software requirements is not possible without clear detection of IS as a subsystem of software application domain (enterprise in the context of this paper). Following this line of thought it might be worth considering also IS for business and IS for software and hardware development and maintenance as separate IS subsystems in enterprise models and tools.

CONCLUSION

This chapter discussed and analyzed domain modeling from the point of view of IS engineering. It was done by comparing several requirements engineering approaches that are used for software requirements identification, by analysis of domain modeling artifacts in agile and plan-driven methods, by discussion on enterprise architecture frameworks, and by brief analysis of change management issues in IS development. The main conclusions based on the above presented material are as follows:

1. Domain modeling is a part of requirements engineering activities.
2. The higher up on the ladder: Design, Requirements, Enterprise Model, Human knowledge; is the knowledge integration point – the easier is the validation of requirements, i.e., knowledge integration on higher level facilitates systemic enterprise, IS and software development.
3. The fact that mental model is shared in agile approach suggest better applicability of this approach in terms of software system ac-

ceptance. It also suggests that plan- driven methods without the domain model development and without knowledge sharing among system stakeholders and developers would hardly promote successful software development projects.

4. Domain modeling artifacts be their holistic models as EM or just fragmentary domain model elements, aid in knowledge sharing and mental model development of business stakeholders and developers.
5. Holistic domain models, if properly designed, managed, and shared could aid the development of systems by semi-formal or formal aids of ensuring their completeness and consistency.
6. Use of cognitive engineering framework would help to understand and model the domain, IS, and software.
7. Currently domain modeling already is well supported by appropriate software tools. These tools are helpful for IS change management, however the relationship between domain models and human knowledge is not yet properly addressed.

All above-mentioned issues in the paper were analyzed and discussed in a brief manner. However, the list of related works given in references enables the readers to obtain more details on issues of their interest.

REFERENCES

Alter, S. (2008). Defining IS as work systems: implications for the IS field. *European Journal of IS, 17*, 448–469.

Ambler, S. (2002). *Agile modeling: Effective practices for extreme programming and the unified process* (1st ed.). New York: John Wiley & Sons Inc.

Ambler, S. (2007, November 27). *Overcoming Requirements Modeling Challenges*. Retrieved October, 2009, from http://www.agilemodeling. com/essays/requirementsChallenges.htm.

ARIS. (2009). Retrieved October, 2009, from http:// www.ids-scheer.com/international/en.

Bezivin, J. (2006). Model driven engineering: an emerging technical space. In R. Lammel, J. Saraiva, & J. Visser (Eds.), *GTTSE 2005* (LNCS 4143, pp. 36-64). Berlin: Springer-Verlag.

Bezivin, J., Barbero, M., & Jouault, F. (2007). On the Applicability Scope of Model Driven Engineering. In *Proceedings of Fourth International Workshop on Model-Based Methodologies for Pervasive and Embedded Software*, 2007. MOMPES '07. IEEE, v 0-7695-2769-8/07.

Biffl, St., Mordinyi, R., & Scatten, A. (2007) A Model-driven approach using explicit stakeholder quality requirement model for building dependable information systems. In *Proceedings of the Fifth International Workshop on Software Quality (WoSQ'07)*. Washington, DC: IEEE.

Bubenko, J., Jr., & Kirikova, M. (1995). "Worlds" in requirements acquisition and modelling. In H. Kangassalo et al. (Ed.), *Information Modelling and Knowledge Bases VI*, (pp. 159-174.). Amsterdam: IOS Press.

Bubenko, J. A. Jr. et al. (1992). *Computer support for Enterprise Modelling in Requirements Acquisition From Fuzzy to Formal*, ESPRIT III Project 6612: Deliverable 3-1-3-R1 Part B.

Bubenko, J. A., Jr., Persson, A., & Stirna, J. (2001). *User guide of the knowledge management approach using enterprise knowledge patterns, deliverable D3, IST Programme project "Hypermedia and Pattern Based Knowledge Management for Smart Organisations"*. Retrieved October, 2009, from Department of Computer and Systems Sciences, Royal Institute of Technology (Stockholm, Sweden) website http://www.dsv. su.se/~js/ekd_user_guide.html.

Casewise. (2009). Retrieved October, 2009, from http://www.casewise.com

Chen, Zh., & Pooley, R. (2009). Rediscovering Zachman Framework using Ontology from Requirement Engineering Perspective. In *Proceedings of Annual IEEE International Computer Software and Application Conference*, (pp. 3-8). Washington, DC: IEEE.

Coad, P., & Yourdon, E. (1990). *Object-Oriented Analysis* (2nd ed.). New York: Prentice hall.

Diouf, M., Musumbu, K., & Maabout, S. (2008). Methodological aspects of semantics enrichment in Model Driven Architecture. In *Proceedings of the Third International Conference on Internet and Web Applications and Services* (pp. 205–210). Washington, DC: IEEE.

Finkelstein, C. (2006). *Enterprise Architecture for Integration: Rapid Delivery Methods and Technologies*. Boston: Artech House.

Gherbi, T., Borne, I., & Meslati, D. (2009). MDE and mobile agents: another reflection on agent migration. In *Proceedings of 11th International Conference on Computer Modelling and Simulation, UKSim 2009,* (pp. 468-473).

Gordijn, J. (2002). *Value Bassed Requirements Engineering*. Doctor of Philosophie Thesis, Vrije University, Amsterdam, the Netherlands.

Harmon, P. (2007). *Enterprise Modeling*. Retrieved October, 2009, from http://www.bptrends. com/publicationfiles/advisor20071023.pdf

IBM Systems and software development tools. (2009). Retrieved October, 2009, from http:// www-01.ibm.com/software/rational/offerings/ architecture

INCOSE. (2009). *Requirements Management Tools Survey*. Retrieved October, 2009, from http://www.incose.org/ProductsPubs/Products/ rmsurvey.aspx

Jacobsen, I., Erikson, N., & Jacobsen, A. (1995). *The Object Advantage: Business Process Reengineering with Object Technology*. Wokingham, UK: Addison-Wesley.

Kabanda, S., & Adigun, M. (2006). Extending Model Driven Architecture benefits to requirements engineering. In *Proceedings of SAICSIT*, University of Zululand (pp. 22-30).

Kavakli, E., & Loucopoulos, P. (2004). Goal Driven Requirements Engineering: Analysis and Critique of Current Methods. In Krogstie, J., Halpin, T., & Siau, K. (Eds.), *Information Modeling Methods and Methodologies (Adv. topics of Database Research)* (pp. 102–124). Hershey, PA: IDEA Group.

Kelly, S., & Tolvanen, J.-P. (2008). *Domain-Specific Modeling: Enabling Full Code Generation*. Chichester, UK: John Wiley & Sons, Ltd.

Kheraff, S., Lefebvre, E., & Suryn, W. (2008). Transformation from CIM to PIM using patterns and archetypes. In *Proceedings of 19th Australian Conference on Software Engineering*, 2008 (pp. 338-346). Washington, DC: IEEE.

Kirikova, M. (1998). Consistency of Information in Requirements Engineering. In Charrel, J. P., Jaakkola, H., Kangassalo, H., & Kawaguchi, E. (Eds.), *Information Modelling and Knowledge bases IX* (pp. 192–205). Amsterdam: IOS Press.

Kirikova, M. (2000a, May). Explanatory capability of enterprise models. *Data & Knowledge Engineering, 33*(2), 119–136. doi:10.1016/S0169-023X(99)00048-8

Kirikova, M. (2000b). Potential role of enterprise models in organisational knowledge processing. In Kawaguchi, E., Kangassalo, H., Jaakkola, H., & Hamid, I. A. (Eds.), *Information modelling and knowledge bases XI* (pp. 114–127). Amsterdam: IOS Press.

Kirikova, M. (2001). Business modelling and use cases in requirements engineering. In Jaakkola, H., Kangassalo, H., & Kawaguchi, E. (Eds.), *Information modelling and knowledge bases XII* (pp. 410–420). Amsterdam: IOS Press.

Kirikova, M. (2004). Interplay of tacit and explicit knowledge in Requirements Engineering. In H. Fujitaand, & V. Gruhn (Eds.), *New Trends in Software Methodologies, Tools and Techniques: Proceedings of the third SoMet_W04* (pp. 77-86.). Amsterdam: IOS Press.

Kirikova, M., Finke, A., & Grundspenkis, J. (2010). What is CIM: an information system perspective. In J. Grunspenkis, M. Kirikova, Y. Manopoulos, & L. Novickis (Eds.), *Advances in Databases and Information Systems associated Workshops and Doctoral Consortium of the 13th East European Conference (ADBIS 2009)* (LNCS 5968, pp. 169-176). Berlin: Springer.

Kirikova, M., & Makna, J. (2005). Renaissance of Business Process Modelling. In Vasilecas, O., Caplinskas, A., Wojtkowski, G., Wojtkowski, W., & Zupancic, J. (Eds.), *IS Development Advances in Theory, Practice, and Education* (pp. 403–414). Berlin: Springer.

Lankhorst, M. (2005). *Enterprise architecture at work, modelling, communication, and analysis*. Berlin: Springer.

Lapouchnian, A., & Lesperance, Y. (2006). Modeling mental states in agent-oriented requirements engineering. In E. Dubois, & K. Pohl (Eds.), *Advanced IS engineering. Proceedings of the 18th International conference (CAISE 2006), Luxembourg, Luxembourg, June 5-9, 2006* (LNCS 4001, pp. 480-494). Berlin: Springer.

Lillehagen, F., & Kroghstie, J. (2008). *Active Knowledge Modeling of Enterprises*. Berlin: Springer. doi:10.1007/978-3-540-79416-5

Lin, Y., Gray, J., & Jouault, F. (2007). DSMDiff: a differentiation tool for domain-specific models. *European Journal of Information Systems, 16*(4), 349–361. doi:10.1057/palgrave.ejis.3000685

Makna, J. (2009). Business process aware IS change management in SMEs. In *Advances in Databases and IS, Proceedings of the 13th East European Conference (ADBIS 2009),* (pp. 28-42). Berlin: Springer.

Martin, C. F. (1988). *User-centered requirements analysis.* Englewood Cliffs, NJ: Prentice Hall.

Matjaz, B. J., & Kapil, P. (2008). *Business Process Driven SOA using BPMN and BPEL.* Birmingham, UK: Packt Publishing.

MDA. (2009). *OMG Model Driven Architecture.* Retrieved October, 2009, from http://www.omg.org/mda

Miller, J., & Mukerji, J. (Eds.). (2003). *MDA Guide, Version 1.0.1.*

OMG. (2008). *Business Motivation Model Version 1.* Retrieved April, 2010, from http://www.omg.org/spec/BMM/1.0/PDF

Osis, J., & Asnina, E. (2008). Enterprise Modeling for Information System Development within MDA. In *41st Hawaii International Conference on Systems Science (HICSS-41 2008)* (pp. 490-490). Waikoloa, Big Island, HI: IEEE Computer Society.

Osis, J., Asnina, E., & Grave, A. (2007). Formal Computation Independent Model of the Problem Domain within the MDA. In *10th International Conference on Information System Implementation and Modeling* (pp. 47-54). Hradec nad Moravici, Czech Republic: Jan Štefan MARQ.

Ouyang, C., Dumas, M., Van Der Aalst, W. M. P., Ter Hofstede, A. H. M., & Mendling, J. (2009). From business process models to process-oriented software. In *ACM transactions on Software. Engineering and methodology (TOSEM), 19*(1), 2:1-2:37.

Panserini, L., Perini, A., Susi, A., & Mylopoulos, J. (2006). From stakeholder intensions to software agent implementations. In E. Dubois & K. Pohl (Eds.), *Advanced IS engineering. Proceedings of the 18th International conference (CAISE 2006), Luxembourg, Luxembourg, June 5-9, 2006* (LNCS 4001, pp. 465-479). Berlin: Springer.

Peyret, H. (2006). *Enterprise Architecture Modeling Tools Not Yet Ready For Prime Time.* Retrieved October, 2009, from http://www.forrester.com/Research/Document/Excerpt/0,7211,39437,00.html.

Quartel, D., Engelsman, W., Jonkers, H., & van Sinderen, M. (2009). A goal-oriented requirements modelling language for enterprise architecture. In *Proceedings of the 13th IEEE International Enterprise Distributed Object Computing Conference (EDOC 2009), Auckland, New Zealand, September 1-2, 2009* (pp. 3-13). Los Alamitos, CA: IEEE Computer Society Press.

Rashid, A., & Chitchyan, R. (2008). Aspect-oriented requirements engineering: a roadmap. In *Proceedings of the 2008 ACM Conference on Computer Supported Cooperative Work, San Diego, California, USA, November 8-12, 2008* (pp. 35-41). New York: Association for Computing Machinery, Inc.

Rasmussen, J., Pejtersen, A. M., & Goodstein, L. P. (1994). *Cognitive systems engineering.* New York: John Wiley & Sons, Inc.

RM. (2009). *Requirements Management Software.* Retrieved October, 2009, from http://www.jiludwig.com/Requirements_Management_Tools.html.

Rolland, C., Kaabi, R. S., & Kraiem, N. On Intentional Services Oriented Architecture (ISOA). In J. Krogstie, A.L. Opdahl & G. Sindre (Eds.), *Advanced IS engineering. Proceedings of the 19th International conference (CAISE 2007), Trondheim, Norway, June 11-15, 2007,* (LNCS 4495, pp. 574-588). Berlin: Springer.

Ross, R. G. (2003). *Principles of the Business Rule Approach*. Reading, MA: Addison Wesley.

Saha, P. (2007). *Handbook of Enterprise Systems Architecture in Practice*. Hershey, PA: IGI Global.

Sawyer, P., Paech, B., & Heymans, P. (Eds.). Requirements Engineering: Foundation for Software Quality. (2007). In *Proceedings of the 13th International Working Conference (REFSQ 2007), Trondheim, Norway, June 11-12, 2007* (LNCS 4542). Berlin: Springer.

Schekkerman, J. (2006). *How to Survive in the Jungle of Enterprise Architecture Frameworks: Creating or Choosing an Enterprise Architecture Framework*. Bloomington, IN: Trafford Publishing.

Schmidt, D. C. (2006). *Model-driven engineering*. IEEE 0018-9162/06, (pp.25-30).

SCOR. (2009). *SCOR Frameworks*. Retrieved October, 2009, from https://www.supply-chain.org/resources/scor

Shuangxi, H., & Yushun, F. (2007). Model Driven and Service Oriented Enterprise Integration-The method, framework and platform. In *the Proceedings of the Sixth International Conference on Advanced Language Processing and Web Information Technology*, (pp. 504-509). Washington, DC: IEEE.

Slack, S. E. (2009). *The business analyst in model-driven architecture*. Retrieved May, 2009, from http://www.ibm.com/developerworks/library/ar-bamda/index.html

Sommerville, I., & Sawyer, P. (1997). *Requirements Engineering: A good practice Guide*. Chichester, UK: John Wiley & Sons.

Sparx Systems. (2007). *MDA Overview, Sparx Systems*. Retrieved April, 2010, from http://www.sparxsystems.com

Stirna, J., & Kirikova, M. (2008). How to support agile development projects with enterprise modelling. In Johannesson, P., & Soderstrom, E. (Eds.), *IS Engineering: From Data Analysis to Process Networks* (pp. 159–185). Hershey, PA: IGI Publishing.

UML. *Unified Modeling Language*. (2009). Retrieved October, 2009, from http://www.uml.org

Valverde, F., Panach, I., & Pastor, O. (2007). An abstraction interaction model for MDA software production method. In A.H.F. Laender, L. Maciaszek, and J.F. Roddik (Eds.), *The 26th International Conference on Conceptual Modeling – ER 2007 – Tutorials, Posters, Panels and Industrial Contributions*, 83. Auckland, New Zealand: Conferences in Research and Practice in Information Technology

van Lamsweerde, A. (2008). Requirements engineering: from craft to discipline. In *Proceedings of the 13th international Workshop on Early Aspects, Leipzig, Germany, May 12 - 12, 2008* (pp. 238-249). New York: Association for Computing Machinery, Inc.

VRM. (2007). *The Value Reference Model*. Retrieved October 2009, from http://www.value-chain.org/en/cms/?1960

Yu, E. S. K., & Mylopoulos, J. (1994). From E-R to "A-R" – Modelling Strategic Actor Relationships for Business Process Reengineering. In *Proceedings of the 13th International Conference on the Entity-Relationship Approach*, Manchester, UK.

Zachman, J. (1987). A Framework for IS Architecture. *IBM Systems Journal, 26*(3). doi:10.1147/sj.263.0276

KEY TERMS AND DEFINITIONS

Information System: Information system is a system of natural and artificial data processing units where at least some of them can transfer or generate meaning from the data available in the system.

Information Systems Engineering: Methodological, at least partly transparent, traceable, and manageable design and development of useful information systems.

Domain: System that has (or will have) as its part an information system which is a subject of particular design and/or development efforts.

Model: A simplified representation of the system.

Knowledge: Systemic representation of a system(s) by natural or/and artificial knowledge holder.

Natural Knowledge: Dynamic representation of the world and ideas in human brains.

Tacit Knowledge: Knowledge that can be externalized only partly.

Explicit Knowledge: Externalized knowledge.

Information: Interpretation of data by particular knowledge holder.

Chapter 19
Model–Driven Performance Evaluation of Web Application Portals

Nilabja Roy
Vanderbilt University, USA

Douglas C. Schmidt
Vanderbilt University, USA

ABSTRACT

Web application portals cater to various types of concurrent users and requests. The number of requests varies by time of day and day of week. Despite the variation in workload, it is important to provide the expected performance (response time) to users of these applications. To assure an appropriate level of performance, web application portals should be analyzed and evaluated throughout their software development lifecycles. Model Driven Architecture (MDA) provides a structured process for developing and analyzing web application portals from the requirement analysis to the ultimate deployment. This chapter examines recent advances in performance analysis methods for web application portals and shows how they can be integrated with MDA methods to analyze performance analysis throughout their software development lifecycles.

INTRODUCTION

Emerging trends and challenges. The advent of web-based applications, such as shopping, social networking, photos, videos, music, gaming, and chat, are increasing the popularity and accessibility of the Internet. There is also growing focus on application integration platforms, such as Sun's Java Composite Application Platform Suite, Facebook's Application Platform, and Oracle's

DOI: 10.4018/978-1-61692-874-2.ch019

Application Development Framework, where a single portal can provide many services. These integrated web sites are referred in this paper as *web application portals*, which are Internet sites that provide multiple services to users. For example, users of social networking sites, such as Facebook (www.facebook.com) and MySpace (www.myspace.com), upload recent photos and videos, exchange messages and chat with each other, and play online games with friends.

Figure 1 shows the architecture of a typical web application portal, such as www.priceline.

Figure 1. A travel site that provides interface to hotels, flights, rental cars, and cruises

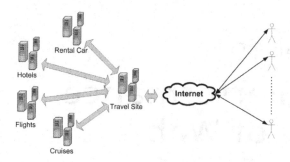

com or www.hotwire.com, that help users build vacation packages with choices for flights, hotels, rental cars, and cruises. Users submit requests to the portal, which in turn contacts various service providers for each service and forwards responses to users. Web application portals should be scalable to support a variety of services and the large number of customers accessing the services simultaneously. The scalability requirements for these sites typically grow as the number of service providers increases.

Competition between providers of web application portals is also growing. Providers have different marketing differentiators and focus on different features and services. For example, IMDb (www.imdb.com) focuses on detailed movie information, whereas yahoo-movies (www.movies.yahoo.com) focus on movie ratings and theater showings. Although both features are useful, they serve different sets of users with somewhat different interests. With multiple services, differentiated focus, and large customer bases, such web portals are a complex composition of different sources of non-determinism, which complicates the evaluation of web application portal performance.

Regardless of the features and services offered by web application portals, successful providers must ensure key quality of service (QoS) properties, such as end-to-end request response time, system availability, and scalability. For example, online travel sites, such as Expedia(www.expedia.

com) or Orbitz(www.orbitz.com), aim to provide the best travel deals to customers within a reasonable time frame, which may vary from person-to-person and from application-to-application. In particular, user submitting travel queries may be willing to wait longer for the best deals than users searching for a phone number. Given the proliferation of web-based application portals in the Internet, users who are not satisfied with one provider can often switch to alternative providers, which incentivizes providers to enhance the QoS of their web application portals.

To remain viable in today's competitive environment, therefore, developers and administrators of web application portals must address a number of issues, such as (1) what software/hardware architecture will provide the necessary performance at scale, (2) how should the software be modularized, (3) how can applications and systems be configured to ensure high performance, (4) how particular application design performs under certain usage patterns, and (5) how many (and what type) of machines are required to achieve the required performance. Addressing these issues can help developers of web application portals design systems that can provide the required QoS for current and planned usage models.

In many cases, however, web portal application performance is evaluated late in the system lifecycle, i.e., after the software is developed and deployed on the target hardware. At this point, it is hard to correct mistakes in the system design that yield poor performance. What is needed, therefore, are techniques that analyze and predict the performance of web-based applications earlier in the lifecycle and can help guide developers choices of alternative portal designs. These techniques need not provide exact predictions, but they do need to accurately capture general trends and provide quantifiable numbers that enable developers to select the most appropriate alternative designs.

Developers and administrators must address various challenges to ensure that web portal applications meet their QoS requirements. For example, application performance depends on multiple factors, such as the underlying middleware, operating system, third party-tools, and hardware, each of which must be properly understood and quantified. Performance also depends on the hardware used to deploy applications. Developers who deploy applications therefore need techniques and tools that can provide quantifiable numbers to help choose the right configurations. Likewise, administrators need techniques and tools that can provide quantifiable numbers that help choose the right configuration and deployment options.

A common technique for predicting the performance of applications in large-scale systems involves the creation and evaluation of analytical and/or simulation models (Menasce et al., 2004). Analytical modeling creates a mathematical representation of the system that can predict application performance under various conditions. Simulation modeling creates a representation of the actual system, implementing the model using a simulation package (such as C++Sim), executing the model, and analyzing execution output. Developers of web application portals face the following two challenges, however, when trying to create and evaluate analytical and/or simulation models in their domain:

The performance of large-scale, multi-tiered web application portals are not accurately predicted using conventional analytic and simulation modeling techniques, such as processor usage measurement, simple queuing modeling, or exponential arrival rates.

A large gap has historically existed between the performance problems of interest to domain experts and the expression of these problems in conventional performance modeling technologies. For example, admission control policies in web servers and multi-threaded software contention are hard to analyze accurately using conventional queuing theory techniques, such as closed and open models (Menasce et al., 2004).

Solution approach → Model-driven techniques and tools that can predict web application

portal performance accurately and help close the gap between domain-oriented performance problems and conventional performance modeling technologies. Model-driven tools based on the OMG's *Model-Driven Architecture* (MDA) technologies (Miller, 2003) provide a structured process for software development and evaluation based on specifying and transforming *platform-independent models* (PIMs) into *platform-specific models* (PSMs) that capture key performance attributes, such as execution time and processor utilization (Cortellessa et al., 2006a). The use of model-driven tools enables the refinement of performance models throughout the software development lifecycle to predict performance with greater accuracy (Skene and Emmerich, 2003). Simulation modeling based on several techniques such as queuing networks and colored Petri nets, can also be used to estimate application performance. Emulation-based approaches, such as the CUTS (Slaby et al., 2006) system execution modeling environment, are another way of estimating large-scale application performance.

This book chapter explores current research in the area of analytic and simulation modeling and describes how new techniques (such as regression based modeling and innovative workload prediction) can be used to accurately evaluate and predict web application portal performance. It also discusses how these techniques can be combined with model-driven tools and applied to web application portals. These model-driven techniques and tools provide developers and administrators with the flexibility to tune key model parameters to enable detailed sensitivity analysis. For example, the scalability of an admission control policy in a web server can be evaluated by increasing the number of concurrent client requests until the response time reaches a certain upper bound, which accurately estimates application behavior as the number of clients increase.

The chapter covers the general steps to follow when conducting a model-driven performance

Figure 2. Model-driven steps to improve web application portal performance

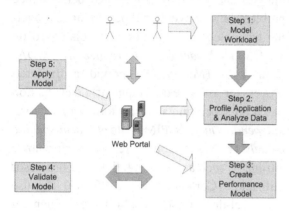

evaluation, which are shown in Figure 2 and summarized below.

Step 1: Workload modeling, which models the incoming workload to the system. Workload is affected by various factors, such as time of day, days of a month, and holiday season (Menasce and Almeida, 2002). Web portal applications have a variety of workload patterns, such as holiday crowd, evening crowd, and lunch time requests, which are hard to characterize. Modeling techniques, such as customer behavior modeling, fitting request data to distributions, correlations, and auto-correlations, can be used to accurately model the modern day workload pattern of a web portal. The initial workload modeling parameters, such as customer behavior modeling can be input as a part of PIM of the MDA process. These parameters can be subsequently transformed into actual values (such as the number of customers) in the PSM.

Step 2: Profile application and analyze data, which profiles the individual application components during unit testing. In early stages of an application's lifecycle (e.g., at the PIM level), usage data can be approximated using data for similar components from previous projects, operational experience, or representative workload models. The objective at this point is to build an approximate model of the application's performance, not

an exact one. Actual profiled values can later be inserted at the PSM level to provide more accurate model-driven performance evaluation.

Step 3: Create a performance model, which can be a simulation model or an analytical model, each of which has their pros and cons. If a system can be modeled using analytic techniques, the result is accurate. In many web portals, however, exact analytic models cannot be built since they involve so many dimensions, such as workload variance, operating system and middleware complexities, database transactions, and network bottleneck. In these cases, approximate models must be built to estimate performance by simplifying many of the concepts outlined above (Menasce et al., 2004). Another approach is to create a simulation, which may give better results than analytical models, depending upon the number of iterations performed to generate a set of data that represents the distribution functions used to model various random variables. Both simulation and analytical models can be generated from PIM or the PSM level. The models at the PIM level will be approximate, whereas those at the PSM level will be more accurate.

Step 4: Validate model, which evaluates both simulation and analytical models against actual application execution traces after the model is built. If there is a large discrepancy, the workload model must be revisited at both the PIM and the PSM level and the earlier steps repeated, as shown in Figure 2. This process is important since a performance model of a web portal must be accurate so that estimations made by it can be used with a high degree of confidence. In particular, system management decisions and planning done using such performance models may not work if the performance model is not accurate.

Step 5: Apply model, which can use validated models to help guide application configuration decisions by developers and administrators. For example, various alternative configurations can be evaluated to determine which architectures to choose. This step can be automated as part of a *model interpreter*, which parses the model at the PIM and the PSM level and analyzes it. Administrators can use an interpreter to answer key provisioning and management questions, such as the number of machines to use, the proper way to distribute the components over the machines, and the amount of replication required. System developers want to find out the system bottlenecks for a particular architecture used, as well as compare various architectures to determine which design alternatives best rectify the bottlenecks.

The remainder of this chapter summarizes prior work on applying MDA to evaluate system performance; discusses workload modeling in web portals; It then goes on to discuss application profiling and data analysis, performance modeling techniques, such as queuing network or Petri net models that estimate performance of web application portals; It next presents model validation and demonstrates the application of performance modeling to deploy and configure web application portals.

BACKGROUND

The OMG has standardized the *Model-Driven Architecture* (MDA) approach to include a three-phase process composed of *Computation Independent Models* (CIMs), *Platform-Independent Models* (PIMs), and *Platform-Specific Models* (PSMs). CIMs model the requirements and the overall functionalities of the application. PIMs model the behavior (e.g., via UML Activity diagrams and Sequence diagrams) and the structure (e.g., UML Component diagrams) of applications that satisfy the requirements modeled in CIM. PIMs can be converted automatically into PSMs that map the behavior and structure of the PIMs onto specific software platforms, such as J2EE or.NET. At the PSM level, the deployment mapping of the various components onto different hardware can also be modeled. If the PSM is modeled in great detail, significant amounts

of code can be generated to help automate and simplify the development process.

The OMG MDA has historically focused on enhancing the software development process and making it more structured and standard. As discussed in "Introductions" Section, however, the success of a web portal depends heavily on its ability to meet user performance requirements. Web portal non-functional properties, such as response time, maximum capacity, and bottleneck analysis, must therefore be evaluated in early life-cycle phases (such as software architecture and design) so that major performance defects are not manifest in later phases (e.g., system integration and testing).

Although performance analyses will necessarily be approximate during early phases, they can be refined as applications mature. These analyses can therefore be merged along with the stepwise MDA process with performance models built at each level of CIM, PIM, and PSM. With progress in each step of MDA, new information about the software is added to the models. This iterative process also helps to refine the performance models and ensure their accuracy.

APPLYING MDA TO PERFORMANCE EVALUATION

Prior work has attempted to convert high-level software architecture models to a corresponding performance models, such as queuing networks or a petri-net models. These models can later be analyzed or simulated to extract performance characteristics. The resulting performance values can then be fed back to architecture models and presented to the users, who can use these values to deploy and configure the application in a better way. The next section discusses recent research in the area of extending MDA for analysis of non-functional aspects such as performance and reliability of a web application portal. The discussion begins by presenting the overall architecture

Figure 3. Non functional MDA framework

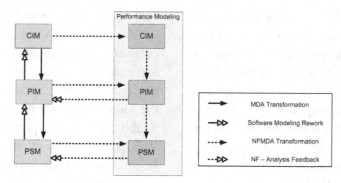

of Non-Functional MDA followed by details of Software Performance MDA.

Non-Functional Model Driven Architecture

Cortellessa et al (Cortellessa et al., 2007) propose a framework that extends the MDA by incorporating performance evaluation at each step of the development process of software applications, such as a web application portal. They introduced Software Performance Model Driven Architecture (SPMDA) in (Cortellessa et al. 2006a) that embeds new models and transformations to facilitate performance validations. SPMDA was later extended to Non-Functional Model Driven Architecture (Cortellessa et al., 2007) to include other non-functional application characteristics, such as reliability or security. This work shows that platform-independent/specific aspects also occur in non-functional dimensions. Using these models thus enables the analysis of performance or reliability aspects of web application portals within an MDA framework.

Figure 3 shows the structure of the Non-Functional MDA framework for the specific case of performance, which extends MDA by adding a set of models and transformations that consider non-functional application characteristics. In MDA, a model transformation refines a model so it is more detailed. In contrast, Non-Functional

MDA defines a horizontal transformation that can convert one model into another model at the same level of detail, but with a different aspect/perspective, such as the following:

A **Computation-Independent Non-Functional Model**, which represents the requirements and constraints related to non-functional aspects, such as performance, reliability, and availability. In MDA, UML Use Case diagrams are often used to present software functional requirements. These diagrams can be annotated with non-functional requirements, such as "response time of a user authentication should be less than 1 sec" or "The availability of the auction site should be 99%".

A **Platform-Independent Non-Functional Model**, which represents the application logic of the system and includes an estimate of the amount of resources that a system requires. The PIM consists of the structural and behavioral aspects of the application. For example, it can contain a UML Component diagram that lists all the classes/components (structure) in the web application portal or the UML Sequence diagram containing the sequence of operations (behavior) to satisfy each use case involving the classes/components.

A **Platform-Specific Non-Functional Model**, which merges the structural and behavioral aspects of the model with the actual platform used to deploy the application. In MDA, a platform is typically middleware, such as J2EE or .NET, used to deploy the application. In the non-functional context, however, the underlying hardware characteristics may also be used to measure actual resource usage values, such as CPU usage for each transaction.

The following are examples of transformations defined by the Non Functional MDA framework shown in Figure 3:

MDA Transformations are the default transformations prescribed by MDA consisting of transformations from CIM to PIM and then to PSM.

NF-MDA Transformations are horizontal transformations that transform the MDA models so the non-functional performance aspects can be analyzed. This transformation occurs in a two-step process: (1) the model is annotated with additional data, such as workload details, and (2) the annotated model is then transformed into a form suitable for analyzing non-functional characteristics, such as response times of each service. In this transformation, input is also taken from the upper level model in the non-functional models. For example, the Platform Independent Non-Functional Model is generated largely from PIM, but also uses input from Computation-Independent Non-Functional Model.

NF-Analysis Feedback is the result of non-functional analysis passed back to the original MDA models. These results depend upon the phase at which the analysis is conducted. Analysis at the PIM level can only provide upper or lower bounds of non-functional parameters or overloaded components, whereas analysis at the PSM level can provide more accurate analysis results.

Software Modeling Rework is the transformation that occurs as a result of the analysis. For example, the analysis could point out flaws in the original system design. To address these flaws, it may be necessary to change the application design, e.g., redesign component interaction to avoid bottlenecks. There may also be cases where the PIM and CIPM are affected due to some analysis results given by Platform Specific Non-Functional Model.

Figure 4 shows the instances of the Non Functional MDA framework in the various non-

Figure 4. Different instances of the non functional MDA framework

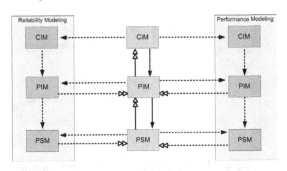

functional areas, such as performance, reliability, and safety. In Figure 4 the models on the left are the performance models generated out of the MDA models CIM, PIM and PSM. On the right are the models which estimate reliability of the system.

Performance Modeling in Model Driven Architecture

As shown above, the Non Functional MDA framework can be used to model and evaluate non-functional parameters of software, including application performance. Below, we describe the performance aspects of Non Functional MDA that are composed of the Computation Independent Performance Modeling, Platform Independent Performance Modeling and the Platform Specific Performance Modeling.

Computation Independent Performance Modeling (CIPM)

The CIPM expresses application performance requirements, which could be produced from a *service level agreement* (SLA) between clients and application developers. For example, an SLA of a web application portal, such as eBay, could state that the response time for creating an auction should not be more that 1 sec with a workload of a maximum of 1,000 users. These types of requirements should be annotated onto

Figure 5. Use case diagram annotated with workload and performance requirement (a) Performance requirement of different Services;(b) Characterizing incoming load

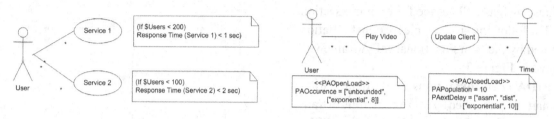

software application models so the performance models can check to see if developed applications satisfy their requirements. Most research (Cortellessa et al., 2006a;Balsamo and Simeoni, 2001; Balsamo and Marzolla, 2005; Cortellessa et al., 2007) proposes adding these requirements onto UML Use Case diagram. Workload details, such as incoming data rate, type of user behavior (e.g., streaming requests or interactive requests) can also be added at this stage. Some examples of workload characterization are shown in Figure 5.

Figure 5(a) shows an annotation on the Use Case diagram of a web portal that provides two services. Service 1 has a response time upper bound of 1 sec with a customer population of 200, where Service 2 has a response time upper bound of 2 secs with a customer population of 100. Figure 5(b) presents additional details about the incoming workload data. The following types of workloads—*open workload* and *closed workload*—are represented by two users based on the UML profile for schedulability, performance, and time specification (OMG, 2002):

The <<PAOpenLoad>> stereotype signifies an *open workload* that has a stream of requests arriving at a given rate in some predetermined pattern, such as Poisson arrivals. In the open workload for the use case "Play Video," the tag PAOccurence (Balsamo and Marzolla, 2005) expresses that the request rate is unbounded, i.e., there is a continuous stream of requests, the arrival pattern follows an exponential distribution and the mean inter-arrival time is 8 time units.

The <<PAClosedLoad>> stereotype describes a *closed workload* that has a fixed number of active users or jobs that cycle between submitting requests and spending an external delay period (also known as "think time") outside the system between the end of one response and the next request. In the closed workload for the use case "Update Client," a fixed number of users each send requests; when the response comes each client spends some time "thinking" before sending the next request. Here the tag *PAPopulation* gives the number of fixed users and *PAextDelay* gives the external delay, which is exponentially distributed with a mean of 10 time units.

Platform Independent Performance Modeling (PIPM)

The PIPM is derived from the PIM that consists of the application structural and behavioral models. The PIPM contains the classes and objects that are the building blocks of the application and the interaction between them to satisfy the use cases given in the CIM. At this point, an estimation of the service demand for each function of a component is made. For example, a search for a particular item in an auction site could involve N high-level statements, which in turn could involve K database calls and M remote calls.

From previous historical data, average resource demands for database read and write calls and remote calls can be used to estimate the service demand for the function. The accuracy of this estimate depends upon the hardware used in historical data. Since the current environment might use completely different hardware set, these performance measures cannot be used to compare against actual system performance, but they can (1) approximate the upper and lower bounds of system performance, (2) identify likely system bottlenecks, and (3) compare performance tradeoffs between different application design alternatives, such as using thread pools versus thread-per-client.

The process of transforming a PIM to a PIPM consists of two steps. First, the PIM models are annotated to include performance characteristics, such as service demands. Second, the annotated models are converted into a form that can be analyzed to identify initial performance results. Below we show how PIM models are annotated with performance parameters.

Annotation of the PIM with Performance Data. In (Cortellessa et al., 2006b; Cortellessa et al., 2007) a PIM is represented by UML Component diagrams and Sequence diagrams. Both the diagrams are annotated with performance data as shown below:

Component Diagrams

Component diagrams are mainly annotated with two types of information, (i) functions provided by a component are annotated with its estimated Service Demand and (ii) scheduling policy on pending service requests for each component.

Figure 6a shows how a component diagram is annotated with service demand and scheduling policy using the UML profile for Schedulability, Performance, and Time (Balsamo and Marzolla, 2005). In the Component diagram each component is annotated by means of the <<PAhost>> stereotype, which indicates the scheduling policy of the software components (note that in the figure all components have FIFO scheduling policy). Each provided service is annotated with <<PAstep>> stereotype to indicate the service demand (i.e., PAdemand tag value) that the service requires. The service demand is expressed in number of

high-level operations that represent a measure of the complexity of the steps the component must execute to provide the required service. For example, op1 service provided by Comp2 has an associated service demand equal to four high-level operations, which means that Comp2 executes four high-level operations to provide op1.

Sequence Diagram

The sequence diagrams are annotated with two types of information: (1) probabilities over the branching points, and (2) average number of loop iterations.

The same <<PAstep>> stereotype is also used in the Sequence diagram to annotate branching probabilities to various paths in the system behaviors (i.e., PAprob tag value) under the constraint that the sum of the probabilities of all alternatives must equal to 1. In the Sequence diagram of Figure 6b there are two alternatives annotated with parametric probabilities (i.e., $P1 and 1-$P1, respectively) whose sum is always 1. Finally, the Sequence diagram shown in Figure 6b is also annotated with the <<PAclosedLoad>> stereotype that describes the arrival process of the requests.

Conversion of annotated PIM to Execution Graph. The PIPM is represented by an Execution Graph (60,2), which is a flow graph that models the software dynamics. The building blocks in an Execution Graph are (1) basic nodes that model sequential operations, (2) fork and join nodes that model concurrency, (3) loop nodes that model iterative constructs, (4) branching nodes that model alternative paths, and (5) composite nodes that model separately specified macro-steps. In addition to the software dynamics, an Execution Graph attaches a demand vector to each basic node to model the resources needed to execute the corresponding operation.[1] Each element of the demand vector represents a high-level metric, such as screen operation or message sending (Smith and Williams, 2002).

An estimated amount of each metric can be attached to any basic block in the Execution Graph.

Figure 6. Annotated sequence and component diagrams

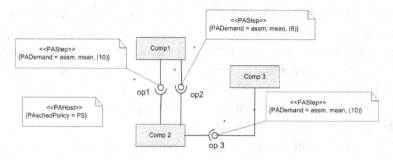

Figure 6a. Component diagram Annotated with Service Demands and Scheduling Policy

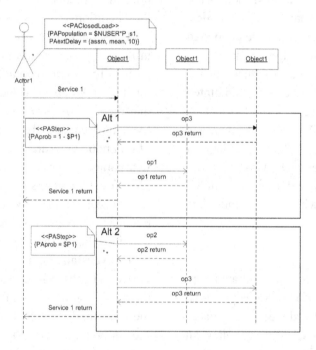

Figure 6b. Sequence Diagram Annotated with Branching Probabilities and Loop Iterations

An Execution Graph is therefore a platform-independent performance model which is not bound to any platform. The results of an Execution Graph provide an intuitive estimate of application performance. The annotated PIM (i.e., the Use Case and Sequence diagrams) is transformed into an Execution Graph via the following steps:

Probabilities on a Use Case diagram are combined to compute the probability of each use case

to occur. This also represents the probability that the corresponding Sequence diagram is executed.

An Execution Graph is built for each Sequence diagram by visiting the diagram and piecewise translating each fragment encountered in an Execution Graph specific pattern.

Execution Graph patterns are then combined following the structure of the Sequence diagram. During the visit, the performance annotations are used to build demand vectors attached to Execution Graph basic blocks.

Finally, all Execution Graphs are combined into a single graph that starts with a branching node, where each Execution Graph represents an alternative path. The probabilities over the outgoing paths correspond to the ones present in the Use Case diagram.

The tool supporting the modeling of Execution Graphs (i.e., SPEED (Smith et al., 1997)) allows standalone and worst-case analysis of an Execution Graph. SPEED is software performance engineering tool that automatically transforms high level architecture diagrams, such as UML activity diagrams, into detailed performance models based on queuing networks. These models can be solved and performance estimates can be produced. Typical performance estimates include end-to-end response times and device utilization. Obviously, the validity of the analysis depends on the estimates of model parameters.

Platform Specific Performance Model (PSPM)

As described above, in the PIM the structural and behavioral models are mapped onto a platform, such as J2EE or.NET. This PIM must be enriched with hardware-specific details, such as CPU speed and network latency, to enable the computation of performance characteristics, such as response time, throughput, and resource utilizations. UML Deployment diagrams can be used to include the hardware details for a particular installation, including the computers and the network. These diagrams can be annotated with hardware details that can later be converted into performance models (Balsamo and Marzolla, 2005).

Figure 7a shows a deployment diagram with three resources (Client, Video Server, and the Network) and annotated with hardware performance details. The nodes are annotated with the <<PAHost>> stereotype defined in the OMG's Schedulability, Performance, and Time specifica-

tion. The scheduling policy can be specified with the PAschedPolicy tag: the tag values for "FIFO", "SJF"(Shortest Job First) and "PS" (Processor Sharing) scheduling policies are considered. The PArate tag specifies the relative speed of the processor. The deployment diagram in Figure 7a can be combined with the PSM and used to generate a performance model, such as a Queuing Network or a Petri Net shown in Figure 7b. This figure shows a queuing network that models the client terminals, network, and the video server. This performance model then can be used to evaluate the performance of the web portal application using either an analytical or a simulation method.

In (Balsamo and Marzolla, 2005) a queuing network model is created with multiple service centers and different classes. Each service center represents the resources in the deployment diagram. If there are different workloads, each

Figure 7. Deployment diagram and the corresponding queuing network model

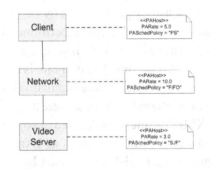

Figure 7a. Deployment Diagram of an Online Video Server

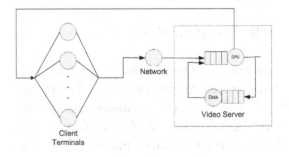

Figure 7b. Queuing Network Model of a Video Server generated from Deployment Diagram and PSM

workload is represented by a job class. Performance measures, such as resource utilizations, response time and queue lengths on each service center can be computed using the queuing network model and be interpreted within the PSM. The utilization and queue length of a service center is actually the utilization and the mean number of waiting requests for a resource in the PSM. The response time of each job class in the queuing network is the response time of the corresponding workload in the PSM.

At this point, a performance model based on simulation can also be built from the PSM, as described in (Balsamo and Marzolla, 2003; Balsamo and Marzolla, 2004) where the tool UML-PSI is used to develop a discreet event simulation model from the annotated UML diagrams. UML-PSI uses the annotated UML models as described above to develop a C++ program that simulates the software system. The UML diagrams are converted into a XMI format that is then used to develop the simulation model.

The workload details in UML-PSI are extracted from Use Case diagrams. Activity or Sequence diagrams provide the actions performed by the software. The hardware details are extracted from Deployment diagrams. The program is run using user-supplied inputs, such as simulation time and confidence intervals. The results are then inserted into a XMI document that is used to populate the UML diagrams with tags, such as PArespTime. This annotated model can be used by software architects and developers to ensure performance goals are met.

Model Transformations

As mentioned in Section titled "Non-Functional Model Driven Architecture" the MDA models must be transformed into performance models that can be used to estimate application performance. We now describe various transformations that can be used.

ATLAS Transformation Language-based Model Transformation. The ATLAS Transformation Language (ATL) is a model transformation language developed by University of Nantes and INRIA (Cortellessa et al., 2008). ATLAS defines both a metamodel and a textual concrete syntax. An ATL transformation program is composed of rules that define how the elements of a source model are matched and navigated to create and initialize the elements of the target model. ATL can be used to automate the model transformations required at each stage of the MDA process when an MDA model is transformed into the corresponding performance model. The source and the target models in such cases will be UML metamodels (OMG, 2001).

At the stage where a PSM is converted to a PSPM, a Queuing Network or Petri Net metamodel (such as PMIF-extended metamodel (Cortellessa et al., 2008) can be used. A method of using ATL is shown in (Cortellessa et al., 2008) to perform the model transformations at each stage in the software lifecycle. The Sap-One tool (Cortellessa et al., 2006a) is used to showcase the ATL capabilities. First, the UML diagrams (e.g., annotated UML Use Case, Component and Sequence diagrams) are pruned of any elements not used for the transformation. The diagrams are then annotated with the MDA stereotypes and tags. These diagrams are then converted into the queuing network model that is composed of Nodes, Arcs, Workload, and ServiceRequest elements. A Node is a server and contains a queue that consists of the jobs waiting to use the server. The Arcs connect the Nodes. A Workload represents a collection of jobs with similar characteristics, such as resource requirement and incoming rate.

WORKLOAD MODELING (STEP 1 FROM FIGURE 2)

This section describes the various factors affecting the workload of a web application portal, including

Table 1. Transition probabilities between different services

	home	browse	browse_cat	browse_reg	br_cat_reg	Srch_it_cat	Srch_it_reg	view_items	Probabilities
home	0	0.01	0.0025	0.0025	0.0025	0.0025	0.0025	0.0025	0.0026
browse	1	0	0.0075	0.0075	0.0075	0.0075	0.0075	0.0075	0.01
browse_cat	0	0.7	0	0	0	0	0	0	0.007
browse_reg	0	0.29	0	0	0	0	0	0	0.0029
br_cat_reg	0	0	0	0.99	0	0	0	0	0.0029
Srch_it_cat	0	0	0.99	0	0	0.44	0	0.74	0.3343
Srch_it_reg	0	0	0	0	0.99	0	0.44	0	0.1371
view_items	0	0	0	0	0	0.55	0	0	0.2436
vu_usr_info	0	0	0	0	0	0	0	0.15	0.0747
vu_bid_hst	0	0	0	0	0	0	0	0.1	0.0386
view_items_reg	0	0	0	0	0	0	0.55	0	0.0999

demand for various services, sequence of service invocations, and roles played by customers. It also describes the methods and strategies that have been proposed in recent research to characterize those factors and produce workload models. These workload models can then be used the evaluate web application portal performance.

The workload modeling process starts from live traces of the system that contains logs of incoming user requests to the system. The traces represent actual workload and may potentially contain a substantial amount of data. Since processing such a large amount of data for performance evaluation is often unrealistic it may be necessary to find some inherent patterns in the data. This pattern can then be represented through the use of probabilistic models and statistical distributions.

The models should be generic enough so they can be used for a wide set of performance evaluations. For example a web application portal, such as an auction site like ebay, can have a number of different types of users, such as casual browsers, sellers, buyers, bidders, and reviewers. Users will likely invoke different services on the portal in different sequences, depending upon their objectives. By studying the observed log of

user behaviors, it is possible to characterize the sequence of activities of a particular type of user.

Table 1 shows a possible set of transitions of a user doing simple browsing. It also contains the probability of a browsing user invoking a particular service after another. The row and the column headings consist of the various available services. Element $x_{i,j}$ is the entry in the ith row and the jth column and represents the probability of invoking the ith row service after invoking the jth column service. For example, consider the entry $X_{5,7}$ which is equal to 0.99, which conveys that a typical user invokes "Search_it_reg", 99% of the times after invoking ""Browse_Cat_Reg". Such a set of transition can be estimated from the observed logs. In this manner, the behavioral patterns of different categories of users can be understood.

A technique called *Customer Behavior Modeling Graph* (CBMG) is presented in (Menasce and Almeida, 2002). This technique represents user behavior patterns in the form of probabilistic models. Figure 8a shows such a diagram of a typical user moving from one web page to the other. The figure consists of a set of states and transitions. The states are connected through transitions. Each state represents a web page or

Figure 8. Service access probabilities and customerbehavior modeling graph

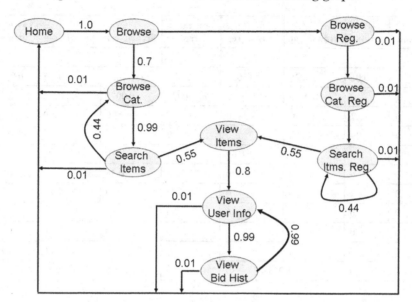

Figure 8a. Customer Behavior Modeling Graph of a Typical User

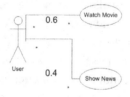

Figure 8b. A typical user with probabilities for accessing each service

service provided by the application. The transition from each state to another has a probability associated with it.

As shown in Figure 8a, a user viewing the "Browse" web page can navigate to the "Browse Regions" page with a probability of 0.3 and to the "Browse Category" page with a probability of 0.7. Similarly a user in "Search Items" can "View Item" with 0.55 chance or go back to the "Browse Category" page. These probabilistic models can be solved using standard techniques (Zhang et al., 2007). Recent work (Zhang et al., 2007, Roy et al., 2009) on web application portal performance modeling and designing has applied these techniques to model the behavior of typical

users. Moreover, the use of formal techniques to solving such models appears in (Zhang et al., 2007). After solving the models, the percentage of user calls for a particular service can be estimated and used with either simulation or analytical models to evaluate the performance of web portal applications.

The user behavior patterns described above can be represented in a standard way by extending the MDA Use Case diagrams.

Figure 8b shows the annotation of the Use Case diagram with a typical user and probabilities for each use case. Here the user plays a typical role such as bidder or seller in an auction site. Each type of user will have a different probability of accessing the web application portal. For example, a bidder could enter 35% of the time, a seller 20% of the time, and a casual browser entering 45% of the time. After users enter, they have different probabilities of accessing each service. For example, in Figure A, the user has a 75% probability of invoking Service 1 and 25% probability of invoking Service 2. This probability value can be used to assign the chance to invoke a particular use case and its corresponding Activity diagram or Sequence diagram. These steps are defined formally in (Cortellessa and Mirandola, 2000) with a system with m types of users and n use cases. Let p_i ($I = 1, \ldots, m$) be the probability of the ith user accessing the system with $\sum_{i=1}^{m} p_i = 1$. $P_{i,j}$ is the probability that the ith user makes use of the jth use case with $j = 1, \ldots, n$ and $\sum_{j=1}^{n} P_{ij} = 1$. The probability of a sequence diagram x being invoked is thus $P(x) = \sum_{i=1}^{m} p_i * P_{ix}$. The probability values of $P(x)$ are used to estimate the workload for each type of Sequence diagram.

PROFILE APPLICATION AND ANALYZE DATA (STEP 2 FROM FIGURE 2)

Application profiling is used to determine the resource requirements of each component in the web portal application, including the CPU time required for each user bid on an item or disk time required for each user login authentication. This profiling can be done while unit testing the component. It is important that measurements are performed accurately and the data are interpreted properly to minimize errors. A key challenge in profiling is not introducing unnecessary/excessive overhead while measuring performance since this could skew the results. This section describes various methods of application profiling, along with statistical techniques to accurately interpret the profiled data.

Profile Application

In previous work (Daniel G. Waddington and Roy, 2007) we conducted an extensive survey of common profiling techniques to capture multithreaded behavior in applications. Many of these techniques can also be used to extract more general information, such as resource usage like processor cycles and size of various queues, such as the tcp accept queue. The various categories we used to classify profiling techniques include:

Compiler-based instrumentation. This type of instrumentation can be done at various places, such as:

Source code instrumentation, which could be done by manually inserting tracing code into the source code or using aspect-oriented techniques, such as AspectC++ (Spinczyk et al., 2002). The advantage with source code instrumentation is the ease of tracing application-specific events, such as start and end of a transaction.

Static binary Code instrumentation, which is done by many profiling tools, such as GNU gprof. Other tools, such as DynaInst (Buck and Hollingsworth, 2000, Wa et al., 1999), insert tracing code to binaries. The advantage of static binary code instrumentation is that the original source is not needed or affected.

Dynamic binary code instrumentation, which is done while the application is running (Buck and Hollingsworth, 2000; Keung Luk et al., 2005). The advantage with dynamic binary code instrumentation is the ability to enable/disable tracing when required. Moreover, the source code is not affected and applications need not be stopped/restarted.

Operating system and middleware profiling. Applications rely on operating systems and middleware for various services, such as thread management, file system usage, and remote calls. Profiling probes can therefore be inserted in to the operating system to capture traces and distributed message passing can be traced using middleware, as follows:

Inserting probes into operating system services. Operating system and middleware libraries can be instrumented to intercept application calls to system services (Cantrill and Doeppner Jr., 1997). One problem with this approach is that it can be hard to relate the calls to application-specific events, such as the start/end of a session or transaction.

Operating system performance counters. Operating systems and middleware often store data related to running applications, including processor utilization, memory usage, cache misses, and network utilization (Microsoft, 2003). This data could be correlated with running applications.

Distributed system monitoring, which captures message traces between distributed components to help developers understand the behavior of the complete application (Object Computing Inc., 2010). These traces can be recorded by instrumenting stubs and skeletons generated for each component and used to generate distributed call graphs.

Virtual machine profiling. Applications are increasingly run in virtual machine environments, such as the *Java Virtual Machine* (JVM) or the Microsoft.NET *Common Language Runtime* (CLR). Having tracing enabled within a JVM or CLR instances help record application behavior, as follows:

Virtual machine sampling inspects the program counter and call stack of the VM at periodic intervals to detect which application methods are executing (Binder, 2005). This sampling can also be performed after a certain number of bytecodes execute.

Profiling via VM hooks, where virtual machines like JVM and CLR provide hooks to insert application profiling (Hilyard, J. 2010). These hooks can detect the entry/exit of methods and record trace information.

Bytecode instrumentation, which involves rewriting bytecode to insert profiling code within the application logic (Dmitriev, 2002). This approach generally has less overhead than profiling via VM hooks or direct source code instrumentation and can be done at compile-time, load-time, or at run-time.

Aspect-oriented techniques, which can be used to instrument bytecode of applications (Boner, 2004). Aspect-oriented tools accept advice written in high-level languages and insert the corresponding bytecode at the desired point in an application.

Hardware-based profiling. Hardware profiling is often used in safety-critical systems since it is faster, and more accurate. It has minimum overhead and is thus useful for certain types of system behavior, such as recording memory cache hits/misses, though detecting events at the application level is often infeasible. Examples of hardware-based profilers include the following:

On-chip performance counters, which are specialized circuits added to most microprocessors to collect events and measure execution timing (Intel Corporation, 2006). Higher-level APIs are used to access these performance counters.

On-chip debugging interfaces. Additional debugging information (such as the active process id, program tracing, and breakpointing on specified instructions) at the hardware level is provided by *In Circuit Emulators* (ICE) (IEEE, 2007). Many modern microprocessors provide explicit support of ICE.

Analyze Data

The previous section gave a range of methods that can be used to profile applications. The best method(s) to select often depend on application-specific details (such as sources of non-determinism and amount of variability and the profiling intent (such as for run-time control or static time benchmarks. Whatever the method of profiling, however, the data gathered from the profiling must be analyzed properly to accurately evaluate application performance.

Non-Determinism in Application Performance

Two instances of the same operation may not produce similar timing characteristics due to sources of non-determinism (Kalibera et al., 2005), such as

Memory allocation, which is due to the selection of the virtual addresses for the code and data of the process and the assignment of the physical pages to back the allocated virtual addresses. This assignment is often different for each instance of the process, which can cause different distributions of cache hits and misses. A different number of cache hits/miss will also result in changes in operation execution times (Kalibera et al., 2005).

Code compilation, which is due to compilers using random name-mangling for symbols that can cause linkers to place the symbols in different orders and different memory addresses in object files. It also causes the execution time of operations to change.

System events, which can cause changes in the performance of software programs. For example, hardware or software interrupts can occur randomly during the execution of software applications.

Thread scheduling, which applications can use to handle multiple workloads concurrently. Different systems may run different thread schedules, thereby causing their execution time to vary.

Applications running in managed environments, such as JVMs or the CLR, also have sources of non-determinism (Georges et al., 2007), including:

JIT compilation. Some virtual machines use timer-based compilation and optimizations that may cause different runs of the same program to have different execution times.

Garbage collection. Managed environments collect unused memory (garbage) periodically during application run-time. The instant at which garbage collection runs can affect application determinism.

Statistical Methods to Interpret Measured Data

Due to the sources of non-determinism present in the experimental setup, the performance measurement of applications often has errors. To minimize/remedy the impact of these errors, rigorous statistical methods are needed (Georges et al., 2007; Kalibera et al., 2005) to extract the correct data from the measured data. The general steps to follow are:

Measure the variable multiple times. Prevalent methods (Georges et al., 2007; Kalibera et al., 2005) advice that variables of interest should be measured a number of times within a run and also across multiple runs of the process to prune away the effects of non-determinism within the application. Multiple measurements can be used in off-line benchmarks, but is impractical for runtime monitoring since corrective decisions might be needed after observing a single sample and there might not be the time to wait for multiple measurements. During initial benchmarking (e.g., during pre-deloyment), multiple measurements can be performed across multiple runs to identify the distribution of the variable. During on-line monitoring, however, there cannot be multiple runs since that would entail the stopping and restarting of the whole application.

Use sample mean and variance to characterize the variable. According to the Central Limit Theory (Feller, 1945), the average and variance of the total sample population are often good estimates of the actual mean and variance of the distribution. Central Limit Theory states that for large number of samples (typically > 30), the sample average is approximately normally distributed with mean equal to the population mean and standard deviation equal to $\sigma/\sqrt{n}$, where n is the number of samples and σ is the standard deviation of the population.

Use confidence intervals with given confidence level. Since the sample mean just estimates the actual mean of the random variable, there should be an interval around the mean value that has a given probability of containing the actual mean. In general, the higher the probability, the shorter is the interval. A confidence interval of 99% will thus be shorter than a confidence interval of 90%. The confidence interval is equally spread around the mean and has a value $c=2z_{1-\alpha/2}*s/\sqrt{n}$, where s is the sample variance and $z_{1-\alpha/2}$ is typically located from a pre-computed table.

Eliminate the influence of outliers by using median. A process for removing the influence of outliers on the final estimated mean is given by (Kalibera et al., 2005). Here the data for each run is sampled to create n sub-selections. The average for each of these is calculated, M_j. The median of these n averages are then used to represent the entire run. This process is performed for each run and the result of the benchmark is $M=1/m\backslash\sum_{j=1}M_j$. The variance for each run is also calculated similarly by generating subsets and calculating the median of the variances of all the subsets in the runs.

Use of confidence intervals for comparison. While evaluating application performance, it is important to compare the estimated variables against each other. Due to the inherent non-determinism present in the calculation of the variables, however, it is erroneous to simply compare the estimated values of the variables. It is therefore important to compare the confidence intervals of the two values. If the confidence intervals do not overlap then it can be concluded with a given probability (equal to the used confidence level) that the two values differ from each other. Otherwise, it cannot be concluded that there is a change in performance. The ratio of the difference between the two estimations can be used to estimate the quantity of performance change (Kalibera et al., 2005).

Reconfiguring the system to adapt to changes must be careful to avoid thrashing, which can occur if the system adapts to a new configuration due to an erroneous reading while subsequent readings cause it to revert back to the previous configuration. One solution is to define a range

of values and enable the system to adapt only if the measured value exceeds the range. This approach reduces thrashing but the breadth of the range must be defined properly, which depends upon the application. The range values can be identified using prior profiling and simulation/analytic methods.

Applying Profiled Data to MDA Models

The Section titled "Platform Independent Performance Modeling" discussed how the PIM must be annotated with performance data, such service demands of functions of a component or loop iterations. These data can be gathered from historical data since the actual hardware may not be determined at the PIM phase. After the hardware is selected for the web application portal and profiled data is available, the PIM/PSM can be annotated with the data that is extracted from the measurement and subsequent analysis. Parameters such as service demands can include the CPU or disk time taken by each component function. Similarly, probabilities over branching points or average loop iterations can also be monitored by measurements and used to annotate the MDA models. These MDA models can be used to generate performance models that can be used for various analyses, such as capacity planning or application placement of web application portals.

CREATE A PERFORMANCE MODEL (STEP 3 FROM FIGURE 2)

This section describes common performance modeling techniques for web application portals, examines the pros and cons of each technique, and summarizes the research needed to make the techniques more feasible in practice. We include a discussion on both simulation models and analytical models in the context of modeling web application portal performance.

Simulation Modeling

Simulation modeling creates a representation/model of the system being studied. The model can be implemented using a simulation package, such as C++Sim (Lee et al., 2001). Although simulation models can be made as detailed as required, they take much longer to execute (Marzolla and Balsamo, 2004). Using such simulation packages, it is possible to simulate web application portals. Once a simulation model is built, it can be run under a wide range of workload and hardware/software environment. From these runs, various performance estimates such as response time, throughput can be made. Common methods of generating simulation models of web application portals are summarized below.

Models Based on Queuing Network

SMART2 (Anciano et al.) is a performance evaluation tool targeted to relational transactional applications, which can be used for web application portals. It is a Java application that interacts with the Oracle RDBMS and the Queuing Network Analysis Package (QNAP2) (Veran and Potier, 1984) (which is a software product including a queuing network description language and a discrete-event simulator). SMART2 simulations can compute common performance metrics of web application portals, such as response time and throughput. It also produces an event trace that can be used for debugging. Users of SMART2 specify the hardware and software environment, the details of the web application portal, and the workload that can be modeled as discussed in section titled "Workload Modeling". SMART2 uses this input to generate a model of the web application portal and then uses QNAP2 to simulate the model and present the results to users.

SPEED (Smith et al., 1997) is a queuing network modeling tool that is similar to SMART2. Users input a software processing sequence and

the environment details, which SPEED then uses to create a queuing network model of the specifications. This model can then be used for either an analytic or simulation solution of the web application portal, according to user preferences. Other tools, such as SimML (Arief and Speirs, 2000) build simulation models from UML diagrams that specify application activity.

Models Based on Application Flow

Fahringer et al. (Fahringer et al., 2003) suggest a method of simulating scientific applications that have little non-determinism and few alternate executions paths. They use a tool called MetaPL (Mazzocca et al., 2000) to model the application. Applications are described using MetaPL constructs, such as control-flow constructs (e.g., loops and switch statements), task management constructs (e.g. spawn, exit, and wait), message passing constructs (e.g., send and receive), and blocks of code that can be annotated with timing information. A cost function can also be used to relate processing time with input size. MetaPL generates a trace of the application that is then used by another tool called HeSSE (Mazzocca et al., 2000) to simulate the application. HeSSE is a simulation tool targeted towards distributed systems. These tools can also be used for modeling of web application portal since the basic constructs used by MetaPL are also applicable to web application portals.

Analytical Modeling

Analytical modeling creates a mathematical representation of the system being studied. This representation can then be used to estimate various performance estimates of the system. A web application portal can also be modeled using analytical methods by creating a math representation of the portal. Once built, the model can be used to predict performance of the web portal under various conditions. The complexity of developing analytical models is different from simulation models since they require fewer resources in terms of programming manpower, hardware and software but on the other hand require strong analytical skills. They can also be solved in lesser time (Menasce et al., 2004), though certain behaviors (such as blocking resources or simultaneous resource possession) are hard to model using analytic techniques. Below we discuss the various analytical methods that can be used to model web application portals.

Models Based on System Workload

Caporuscio et al. (Caporuscio et al., 2005) proposes an online framework for managing performance of the Siena publish/subscribe middleware. This performance management process uses monitored data to identify reconfiguration points. A reconfiguration point is reached when the processor utilization of a host increases beyond a designated threshold. An analytical model of the application is created using monitored data, which conveys the arrival rates of requests and notifications to each server. When there is the need for re-configuration, several alternative configurations are tested by creating different models for each. The models are solved and the results are compared. The configuration that produces the model with the best results is chosen to become the new configuration.

The model used in (Caporuscio et al., 2005) is based on monitored data that captures the number of arrival publisher/subscriber, forwarding, and notification requests to a server within a time period. The arrival rates, average service and throughout are calculated from this information. As before, this information is used to determine the utilization and waiting queue size of each server. All the inputs to the above model are very generic and are applicable to web application portals also. Thus such a model can easily be used to do performance evaluation of web application portals.

Models Based on Petri Nets

Porcarelli et al. (Porcarelli et al., 2004) use a stochastic dependability model of the system to reconfigure a system to recover from faults. This model is based on stochastic Petri nets (Balbo, 2002), which add non-deterministic timing to the transitions in the Petri net. A Petri net model is created for each system component, such as links, hosts, and application software components. They use a dependability modeling and evaluation tool called *DEpendability Evaluation of Multiple-phased systems* (DEEM) for solving the model and providing performance estimates.

Kounev (Kounev, 2006) used Queuing Petri Nets(Bause, 1993)which combines queuing networks and Petri nets to model the performance of distributed component-based systems. (Kounev, 2006) conducts a case study of the performance evaluation of a J2EE application server and then presents a performance evaluating method for modeling thread contention in a load balancer used with the application server. The focus in (Kounev, 2006) is on modeling the number of threads in a thread pool for the load balancer.

Models Based on Software Architecture

Garlan et al. (Garlan et al., 2001) use an architectural model to represent a system in terms of its principal run-time parts (such as its runnable components) and the pathways of communication (such as connectors). Architectural models are useful for run-time monitoring and system adaptation since they provide a high level abstraction of low-level components (such as abstracting a network route using a connector). For example, low-level network routes can be represented as a network connector with values such as throughput, congestion, and latency. Moreover architectural models are often close to implementation structures, thereby helping to map architectural reconfiguration decisions to the proper implementation component(s).

Combining Simulation and Analytical Techniques

Simulation techniques generally produce more accurate solutions compared to analytical solutions, whereas analytical solutions generally produce much faster results. Combining these two techniques can often be used to produce more accurate performance results. For example, simulations could be used before deployment to obtain accurate application configurations, while analytical models could be used at run-time to reconfigure the application to address uncertain events.

The following is a methodology for combining simulation and analytical techniques:

1. Prepare a simulation model before deployment
2. Validate and tune it to make it as accurate as possible
3. Use model to configure application
4. Derive an analytical model from it.
5. Use the analytical model at run-time to reconfigure application

This methodology leverages the strengths of each modeling technique and can thus be used to ensure application QoS.

VALIDATE MODEL (STEP 4 FROM FIGURE 2)

This section discusses the step of validating a performance model with actual runtime results, which is important since if a model is inaccurate management decisions based on it can have errors and expected benefits may not occur. Model validation consists of running the modeled system under certain conditions of workload and measuring the performance. The model is also run under similar environment and the estimated performance parameters are recorded. The two results are then compared to check how closely the model predicted the actual results.

There is typically some imprecision in the model prediction, but as long as it is within permissible bounds the model may be accepted as being representative. If there is a large degree of imprecision the model creation stage should be revisited and changes to the model made until its estimates are close to the real measured result. In case of a web application portal this process is the same, i.e., the portal should be profiled and performance measures (such as response time, device utilizations, and throughput) recorded for a particular workload. After that, the model can be used to make predictions under similar workload and the estimated results can be compared with the actual results.

Urgaonkar et al. (Urgaonkar et al., 2005) present an extensive validation of an analytical model of a multi-tiered web application portal model. Their work builds two versions of the model and validates them against real data to determine which model provides more accurate results. They use two popular benchmarks Rubis and Rubbos to validate the models. Rubis implements the core functionality of an auction site application, whereas Rubbos is a bulletin board application modeled after an online news forum, such as Slashdot. Urgaonkar et al. modified the benchmark to adjust the workload so that their model could be verified. The authors then chose various architecture patterns, such as EJB-based implementation vs. servlet-based implementation, and measured key performance metrics, such as response time, utilizations, and throughput, using different workload values. The models were then used to predict the performance under those workload. After comparing the actual results with the predictions made by both models they found that one model give more accurate results. This model was then used for system management decisions, such as capacity planning and resource provisioning.

Stewart et al (Stewart and Shen, 2005) present a model of a component-based web application portal. Their focus is on modeling network usage overhead and its affect on performance. They also conduct extensive validation of the model against the RUBiS benchmark using three versions of the model: (1) not considering any network influence, (2) considering remote method invocation but no network delays, and (3) considering both. The models were then validated against various workloads and the results were validated. They found that the third model (which considers both network delay and remote method invocation) had the most accurate result. The models were then validated against various factors that could influence results, such as cluster size (models of larger systems should not introduce errors), request mixes (the model should work for all request mix), heterogeneous machines (mix of different kind machines should not the modeling accuracy), placement and replication strategy (performance with different placement and replication strategy should be accurately predicted by the model).

APPLY MODEL (STEP 5 FROM FIGURE 2)

This section describes techniques for applying analytical and simulation models to aid the management of web application portals by evaluating system performance. System performance evaluation can then be used to solve several configuration and deployment related problems. For example, an analytical model can help conduct capacity planning for a web application portal by estimating the amount of hardware resource required to serve a certain quantity of concurrent users with acceptable QoS. These techniques can be coded in the form of model interpreters that conduct analysis on the performance model generated from a corresponding MDA model based on user input. For example, users may want to perform capacity planning or application placement for a web portal

application and automate this analysis by running the model interpreter on the performance model.

The rest of this section discusses the various applications of performance modeling.

Capacity Planning

Capacity planning is a useful application of a performance model since it helps administrators and deployers estimate the hardware resources required to serve the incoming workload with the constraint of satisfying user QoS requirements and SLAs. Without accurate estimates, administrators may fail to adequately meet application performance and resource requirements, e.g., leading to unacceptable workload surges due to special events, such as new product advertisement campaigns or breaking political/cultural news.

The first step in capacity planning is to estimate the new workload levels, which can often be found by studying historical data from similar events in the past and from trends in the current data. After determining the anticipated workload, the resource requirements of applications can be estimated using a performance model. The performance models will be computed against the new workload to extract the resource requirements.

These additional resources can then be provisioned to ensure the designated QoS. Stewart et. al. (Stewart and Shen, 2005) performs capacity planning on heterogeneous machines and predicts future requirements as workload increases. They use a component placement algorithm based on simulated annealing (Granville et al., 1994), which is a random sampling based optimization algorithm that gradually reduces the sampling space following an "annealing schedule". This approach uses a regression-based performance model to devise a component placement and a replication strategy for multi-component web applications.

It is also important to accurately forecast future workload based upon past trends. Accurate forecasting enables administrators to provision resources properly so that QoS is maintained.

Urgaonkar et al (Urgaonkar et al., 005a) present a workload predictor that uses trends in incoming workload to a web application portal to predict future workload. Such workload normally has long-term variations and is affected by time-of-day or seasonal effects. Their workload predictor estimates the peak arrival rate in the next interval by maintaining a record of the peak arrival rate for the similar interval (say between noon and 1pm) in the past several days. It creates a histogram of the peak rates and computes a probability distribution of the arrival rate for that interval. The peak workload is then estimated by choosing a high percentile of the arrival rate distribution for that interval, thereby predicting a peak workload that is close to the worst case loading of the application.

These capacity planning methods can be included in a model interpreter and automatically applied on the performance model that is generated from the corresponding MDA models. Users simply need to invoke the model with certain parameters, such as target workload, and the analysis can be conducted and presented to users by the interpreter.

Application Placement

Application placement addresses the problem of mapping various components of a web application portal onto available computing nodes. The challenge is to use the hardware resources in such a way that each component receives sufficient resources to provide acceptable QoS while minimizing resource waste. Various versions of this problem exist. For example, one problem involves placing the components of multiple applications onto the hardware resources in a shared hosting platform, such as a data center (Urgaonkar et al., 005a). Here the challenge is supporting a maximum number of user requests while keeping the average response time within a certain threshold.

In general, the application placement problem is NP-Hard, though there are various approximate algorithms that provide efficient solutions for many practical scenarios. For example, Stewart et. al. (Stewart and Shen, 2005) searches through the space of all possible placement using the component placement algorithm based on simulated annealing method as discussed in the previous section. This algorithm checks the application performance for each placement using a performance model, so an accurate model of the web application portal is needed. For such application placement algorithms, analytical models are required. The models must be simple enough so that the run-time complexity of the algorithm is low enough to solve application placement for large systems within realistic times. The analytical model used in (Stewart and Shen, 2005) is based on linear fitting, which records profiles of resource usage by each component for different levels of workload. These samples are then used to fit linear equations that model the resource requirements of each component against workload.

Urgaonkar et. al (Urgaonkar et al., 2009) identify resource needs of application components by profiling them and uses the results to create a model of the application resource requirements. This model consists of the minimum CPU requirements over a time period, the usage distribution, and the overbooking tolerance (which specifies the probability with which a component's requirements may be violated). They also define an algorithm for mapping the application components onto the available computing nodes. The algorithm uses the resource requirements of each component given by the performance model while assigning the components onto the available hardware resources.

Admission Control

Admission control is another area that can benefit from using system performance models. For example, large-scale web application portals can experience "flash crowds" (Welsh and Culler, 2003) that cause an unexpected surge in workload. In such situations, admission control helps to limit the total number of clients on a server so that the QoS of each admitted customer is maintained. The clients that cannot be admitted can be redirected to other replicated servers. A key challenge when conducting admission control is determining the capacity of each application, i.e., how many parallel users can a server support. This information can be determined using a detailed performance evaluation of the system which can be done using the capacity planning techniques discussed in the above section. A performance model can be built by doing such an evaluation, which can also be used later online to determine which clients to admit.

Session policing techniques are described in, (Urgaonkar et al., 2005a; Urgaonkar et al., 2005) using an analytical model based on queuing theory. Such admission control mechanisms maximize some metric, such as revenue, of a web application portal. By ensuring the admitted clients receive their allotted QoS, therefore, the revenue of the web application portal is ensured. Otherwise, if all clients are allowed admission, none would get their allotted QoS, thereby reducing the number of clients that can access the portal, which in turn reduces revenue.

The work in, (Urgaonkar et al., 2005a; Urgaonkar et al., 2005) use a multi-class queuing model to predict application performance. In this model, there are multiple classes of users, each generating different revenue. The objective is to allow more users with the higher revenue. A heuristic is used to iteratively assign the set of users to each class. At every step, the heuristic uses the queuing model to estimate the response time of each class and ensure that response time SLAs are not violated.

Cost Analysis

Cost analysis can also be done using performance models from the perspective of revenue generation and profit calculation. Capacity planning using performance modeling can help architects and administrators understand the hardware resource requirement for a particular installation supporting a certain set of clients. This planning helps calculate the cost of the installation. Total revenue generation can be computed from clients that can be supported and from workload forecasting. Using these two parameters, therefore, cost analysis of web application portals can be computed. Performance models can also be used for system optimization, e.g., to minimize the cost of machines or maximizing user admission. Here the goal is to accommodate the maximum number of users who provide the most value.

Stewart et al. (Stewart and Shen, 2005) present a cost effective analysis. The problem they address is how to buy machines for future increase in workload. There are three types of machines, each with different costs. The power of the machines also varies, e.g., more powerful machines are costlier. Their model uses linear fitting to estimate performance parameters of the system. Their analysis determined that buying the least powerful machines gives the best benefit in terms of cost. Although more powerful machines perform better, they cost more and raise the cost. In contrast, less powerful machines are sufficient to meet the required response time SLAs.

FUTURE RESEARCH DIRECTIONS

This section discusses the future research directions in the area of model driven performance evaluation of web application portals. As mentioned in Section titled "Applying MDA to Performance Evaluation", the overall framework of MDA with CIM, PIM and PSM can be used for performance evaluation at different stages of the web application portal software development lifecycle. The CIM stage can be used for more sophisticated performance specification, such as load characteristics and performance requirements. Incoming load in a web portal depends on many factors, such as time of the day, day of the week or seasonal variations. It is not always possible to predict the exact load on a particular day but analyzing historical data it is possible to get an idea for the increase in load and thus deploy resources accordingly. The CIM can therefore provide specification of load distribution and variation, which can help allocate resources proactively in advance so that performance in not hampered.

Model transformation is an important area where much future research is needed. Model transformation converts high-level structural models of an application onto performance models. In the process, it also considers the hardware usage, such as the number of machines and the machine specification required for performance prediction. Improved model transformation will convert structural models into performance models with the least amount of manual help and can then be easily used for analyzing application performance. Changes in load or component performance when updated at the CIM or PIM level can be easily incorporated into the performance model, which then provides updated performance measures. This information helps analysts better analyze a particular scenario, as well as create other improved scenarios.

Improved system management algorithms and techniques can be integrated with the MDA driven performance modeling in the form of interpreters. Other techniques, such as capacity planning, application placement, admission control and optimized cost analysis, can be improved when integrated with MDA tools. These interpreters can use the structural model parameters and the performance models to give answers to queries setup by analysts. Example queries include "the number of machines required when load increases to a higher value" or "placement of components of an application to the different machines".

The research directions described above will enhance the area of model driven performance evaluation so it will be more widely applicable. In turn, greater applicability will enable the use of analytical techniques in every phase of the software development process, which today often are ignored until the final product is implemented.

CONCLUSION

This chapter surveys the broad area of model-driven performance evaluation and system management issues in the domain of web application portals. It also explained the general steps of performance evaluation in the web application portals domain and showed these steps fit into the overall MDA framework. Web application portals are typically used by large-scale, multi-tiered enterprises, such as eBay or Amazon, to provide many web services. Clients using such applications perform various different roles with different sequence of invocations on the services. Ideally, applications should adhere to service level agreement (SLAs) that give an upper bound on the response times that users experience. Likewise, web application portal administrators want to serve as many concurrent clients to maximize revenue. It is therefore essential to conduct accurate performance analyses of web application portals so the proper SLAs and concurrent users can be set and the appropriate amount of hardware can be provisioned.

Traditional methods of performance evaluation techniques, such as queuing theory, are not directly applicable to web application portals. Specialists must therefore expend a significant amount of effort to analyze portal performance. Model Driven Architecture (MDA) provides a promising strategy for simplify the analysis of web application performance. Recent research has investigated the ways to use MDA-based methods analyze application performance. Performance-related information can be added to the general MDA framework at each phase of the process. For example, response time bounds can be specified at the requirements phase (CIM), architecture/design performance in the second phase (PIM), and detailed platform-specific performance in the third phase (PSM). MDA models and the PSM phase then can be converted into performance models, such as queuing network models or Petri net models, which can then be analyzed mathematically and/or simulated and the results presented to system administrators or architects.

Our survey of recent research on model-driven performance evaluation yields the following observations:

The performance of a web application portal depends heavily upon the incoming workload. The workload must therefore be modeled properly. Workload modeling can benefit by combining it with the MDA CIM phase, which makes the requirements analysis more formal and allow integrating it into the software development process.

The performance bounds specified by SLAs are essential for providing clients with a satisfactory user experience to survive in the competitive market that web application portals typically face. The SLA bounds should therefore also be included as part of the CIM and checked after a performance model is available.

The performance of a web application portal depends upon the core architecture or design, which can be selected during the PIM phase. Performance analysis at this stage can help system administrators or select the appropriate design strategies.

At the PSM phase, a platform is selected for the web application portal. Code generated and developed for application may also be available. Profiling of the components done during unit testing will provide service demands that can give actual performance measures on a real platform and can be checked with initial SLA bounds that are present in the CIM model.

Before deployment, different model interpreters that perform various system management decisions, such as capacity planning, application placement, cost analysis, can be run against the performance model. These model interpreters can help guide the deployment and configuration of web application portals and enable administra-tors to comply with the SLA bound and provide maximum QoS.

REFERENCES

Anciano, L., Savino, N., Corbacho, J., & Puig-janer, R. (1998) Extending SMART2 to predict the behaviour of PL/SQL-based applications. In *Proc. of 10th Int. Conf. on Modelling Techniques and Tools for Computer Performance Evaluation (Tools' 98)*, (pp. 292–305).

Arief, L. B., & Speirs, N. A. (2000). A uml tool for an automatic generation of simulation programs. In *WOSP '00: Proceedings of the 2nd international workshop on Software and performance*, (pp. 71–76), New York: ACM.

Balbo, G. (2002). *Introduction to stochastic petri nets* (pp. 84–155). Lectures on Formal Methods and Performance Analysis.

Balsamo, S., & Marzolla, M. (2003). Simulation modeling of UML software architectures. In *Proc. of ESM'03, the 17th European Simulation Multiconference*, (pp. 562–567).

Balsamo, S., & Marzolla, M. (2005). Performance evaluation of UML software architectures with multiclass Queueing Network models. In Proceedings of the *5th international workshop on Software and performance*, (pp. 42). New York: ACM.

Balsamo, S., & Simeoni, M. (2001). On trans-forming UML models into performance models. In *ETAPS01: Workshop on Transformations in UML*. Citeseer.

Bause, F. (1993). Queueing petri nets - a formal-ism for the combined qualitative and quantita-tive analysis of systems. In *Proceedings of the 5th International Workshop on Petri nets and Performance Models*, (pp. 14–23). Washington, DC: IEEE Computer Society.

Binder, W. (2005). A Portable and Customizable Profiling Framework for Java Based on Bytecode Instruction Counting. In *Programming languages and systems: third Asian symposium, APLAS 2005, Tsukuba, Japan, November 2-5, 2005*, (pp. 178). Berlin: Springer Verlag.

Bolch, G., Greiner, S., de Meer, H., & Trivedi, K. (1998). *Queueing networks and Markov chains: modeling and performance evaluation with computer science applications*. New York: Wiley-Interscience.

Boner, J. (2004). AspectWerkz - Dynamic AOP for Java. In *Proceeding of the 3rd International Conference on Aspect-Oriented Development (AOSD 2004)*, March 2004, Lancaster, UK.

Buck, B., & Hollingsworth, J. K. (2000). An API for Runtime Code Patching. *International Journal of High Performance Computing Applications*, 317–329. doi:10.1177/109434200001400404

Cantrill, B., & Doeppner, T. W. (1997) Threadmon: A Tool for Monitoring Multithreaded Program Performance. In *Proceedings of the 30th Hawaii International Conference on Systems Sciences*, (pp. 253-265, January 1997).

Caporuscio, M., Marco, A. D., & Inverardi, P. (2005). Run-time performance management of the siena publish/subscribe middleware. In *WOSP '05: Proceedings of the 5th international workshop on Software and performance*, (pp. 65–74). New York: ACM.

Cortellessa, V., Di Gregorio, S., & Di Marco, A. (2008). Using atl for transformations in software performance engineering: a step ahead of java-based transformations? In *WOSP '08: Proceedings of the 7th international workshop on Software and performance*, (pp. 127–132). New York: ACM.

Cortellessa, V., Di Marco, A., & Inverardi, P. (2006a). Software performance model-driven architecture. In *SAC '06: Proceedings of the 2006 ACM symposium on Applied computing*, (pp. 1218–1223). New York: ACM.

Cortellessa, V., Di Marco, A., & Inverardi, P. (2006b). Software performance model-driven architecture. In *SAC '06: Proceedings of the 2006 ACM symposium on Applied computing*, (pp. 1218–1223). New York: ACM.

Cortellessa, V., Di Marco, A., & Inverardi, P. (2007). Integrating Performance and Reliability Analysis in a Non-Functional MDA Framework. In *Fundamental approaches to software engineering: 10th international conference, FASE 2007, held as part of the Joint Conferences on Theory and Practice of Software, ETAPS 2007*, Braga, Portugal, March 24-April 1, 2007: (pp. 57). Berlin: Springer-Verlag Inc.

Cortellessa, V., & Mirandola, R. (2000). Deriving a queueing network based performance model from uml diagrams. In *WOSP '00: Proceedings of the 2nd international workshop on Software and performance*, (pp. 58–70). New York: ACM.

Daniel, G., Waddington, R. N., & Schmidt, D. C. (2007). Dynamic analysis and profiling of multi-threaded systems. In Tiako, P. (Ed.), *Designing Software-Intensive Systems: Methods and Principles*. Hershey, PA: Idea Group Inc.

Dmitriev, M. (2002). Application of the HotSwap Technology to Advanced Profiling. In *Proceedings of the First Workshop on Unanticipated Software Evolution, held at ECOOP 2002 International Conference*, Malaga, Spain.

Fahringer, T., Mazzocca, N., Rak, M., Pllana, S., Villano, U., Madsen, G., et al. (2003). Performance modeling of scientific applications: Scalability analysis of lapw0. In *Proceedings Eleventh Euromicro Conference on Parallel, Distributed and Network-Based Processing*, (pp. 5-12), Genoa, Italy 2003.

Feller, W. (1945). The fundamental limit theorems in probability. *Bulletin of the American Mathematical Society*, *51*, 800–832. doi:10.1090/S0002-9904-1945-08448-1

Garlan, D., Schmerl, B., & Chang, J. (2001). Using gauges for architecture-based monitoring and adaptation. In *Working Conference on Complex and Dynamic Systems Architecture*, Brisbane, Australia.

Georges, A., Buytaert, D., & Eeckhout, L. (2007). Statistically rigorous java performance evaluation. In *Proceedings of the 2007 OOPSLA conference* (pp. 57–76).

Granville, V., Krivanek, M., & Rasson, J. (1994). Simulated annealing: a proof of convergence. *IEEE Transactions on Pattern Analysis and Machine Intelligence, 16*, 652–656. doi:10.1109/34.295910

Hilyard, J. (2010) No Code Can Hide from the Profiling API in the .NET Framework 2.0. *MSDN Magazine January 2005*. Retrieved 28th May 2010 from http://msdn.microsoft.com/en-us/magazine/cc300553.aspx

IEEE. (2001). IEEE Standard Test Access Port and Boundary-scan Architecture. *IEEE Std*. 1149.1-2001.

Intel Corporation. (2006) *Intel 64 and IA-32 Architectures Software Developer's Manual,* (Vol. 3B, System Programming Guide, Part 2). Retrieved 4 January 2007 from http://www.intel.com/products/processor/manuals/

Jensen, K. (1996). *Coloured Petri nets: basic concepts, analysis methods, and practical use*. Berlin: Springer Verlag.

Kalibera, T., Bulej, L., & Tuma, P. (2005). Benchmark precision and random initial state. In *Proceedings of the 2005 International Symposium on Performance Evaluation of Computer and Telecommunications Systems, SPECTS 2005*, (pp. 853–862). Citeseer.

Keung Luk, C., Cohn, R., Muth, R., Patil, H., Klauser, A., & Lowney, G. (2005). Pin: Building customized program analysis tools with dynamic instrumentation. In *Programming Language Design and Implementation* (pp. 190–200). New York: ACM Press.

Kounev, S. (2006). Performance modeling and evaluation of distributed component-based systems using queueing petri nets. *IEEE Transactions on Software Engineering, 32*(7), 486–502. doi:10.1109/TSE.2006.69

Lee, C., Kim, J., Stach, J., & Park, E. K. (2001). Simulating agent based processing in an ads using c++ sim. In *ISADS '01: Proceedings of the Fifth International Symposium on Autonomous Decentralized Systems*, (pp. 231). Washington, DC: IEEE Computer Society.

Marzolla, M., & Balsamo, S. (2004). Uml-psi: The uml performance simulator. In *Quantitative Evaluation of Systems, 2004* (pp. 340–341). QEST. doi:10.1109/QEST.2004.1348057

Mazzocca, N., Rak, M., & Villano, U. (2000). The transition from a pvm program simulator to a heterogeneous system simulator: The hesse project. In *Proceedings of the 7th European PVM/MPI Users' Group Meeting on Recent Advances in Parallel Virtual Machine and Message Passing Interface*, (pp. 266–273). London: Springer-Verlag.

Menasce, D., & Almeida, V. (2002). *Capacity Planning for Web Services: metrics, models, and methods*. Upper Saddle River, NJ: Prentice Hall.

Menasce, D., Dowdy, L., & Almeida, V. (2004). *Performance by design: computer capacity planning by example*. Upper Saddle River, NJ: Prentice Hall PTR.

Microsoft. (2003). Windows Server 2003 Performance Counters Reference. *TechNet*. (Electronic media) Retrieved May 28, 2010, from http://technet.microsoft.com/en-us/library/cc776490%28WS.10%29.aspx

Miller, J. (2003). *Model-Driven Architecture Guide*. Object Management Group.

Object Computing Incorporated. (2006). *A Window into your Systems*. [Electronic media] Retrieved 28th May 2010 from http://www.ociweb.com/products/OVATION

OMG (2001). *Unified Modeling Language (UML) v1.4.* Object Management Group, OMG Document formal/2001-09-67 edition.

OMG (2002). UML Profile for Schedulability, Performance, and Time Specification. *Object Management Group, Final Adopted Specification* ptc/02-03-02 edition.

Porcarelli, S., Castaldi, M., Gi, F. D., & Inverardi, P. (2004). A framework for reconfiguration-based fault-tolerance in distributed systems. In *Architecting dependable systems II* (pp. 343–358). Berlin: Springer Verlag.

Roy, N., Xue, Y., Gokhale, A., Dowdy, L., & Schmidt, D. C. (2009). A component assignment framework for improved capacity and assured performance in web portals. In *OTM '09: Proceedings of the Confederated International Conferences, CoopIS, DOA, IS, and ODBASE 2009 on On the Move to Meaningful Internet Systems*, (pp. 671–689). Berlin: Springer-Verlag.

Sendall, S., & Kozaczynski, W. (2003). Model transformation: The heart and soul of model-driven software development. *IEEE Software, 20*(5), 42–45. doi:10.1109/MS.2003.1231150

Skene, J., & Emmerich, W. (2003). Model Driven Performance Analysis of Enterprise Information Systems. *Electronic Notes in Theoretical Computer Science, 82*(6). doi:10.1016/S1571-0661(04)81033-8

Slaby, J. M., Baker, S., Hill, J., & Schmidt, D. C. (2006). Applying system execution modeling tools to evaluate enterprise distributed real-time and embedded system qos. In *RTCSA '06: Proceedings of the 12th IEEE International Conference on Embedded and Real-Time Computing Systems and Applications*, (pp. 350–362). Washington, DC: IEEE Computer Society.

Smith, C., & Williams, L. (2002). *Performance Solutions: a practical guide to creating responsive, scalable software.* Boston: Addison-Wesley.

Smith, C. U., Smith, C. U., Williams, L. G., & Williams, L. G. (1997). *Performance engineering evaluation of object-oriented systems with speed. Computer Performance Evaluation Modelling Techniques and Tools* (pp. 135–154). Berlin: Springer.

Spinczyk, O., Gal, A., & Schröder-Preikschat, W. (2002). Aspectc++: an aspect-oriented extension to the c++ programming language. In *CRPIT '02: Proceedings of the Fortieth International Conference on Tools Pacific*, (pp. 53–60). Darlinghurst, Australia: Australian Computer Society, Inc.

Stewart, C., & Shen, K. (2005). Performance modeling and system management for multi-component online services. In *Proceedings of the 2nd conference on Symposium on Networked Systems Design & Implementation*, (Vol. 2, pp. 71–84). Berkeley, CA: USENIX Association.

Urgaonkar, B., Pacifici, G., Shenoy, P., Spreitzer, M., & Tantawi, A. (2005). An Analytical Model for Multi-tier Internet Services and its Applications. *SIGMETRICS Perform. Eval. Rev., 33*(1), 291–302. doi:10.1145/1071690.1064252

Urgaonkar, B., Shenoy, P., Chandra, A., & Goyal, P. (2005a). Dynamic provisioning of multi-tier internet applications. In *ICAC '05: Proceedings of the Second International Conference on Automatic Computing*, (pp. 217–228).

Urgaonkar, B., Shenoy, P., & Roscoe, T. (2009). Resource overbooking and application profiling in a shared Internet hosting platform. [TOIT]. *ACM Transactions on Internet Technology, 9*(1), 1–45. doi:10.1145/1462159.1462160

Veran, M., & Potier, D. (1984). QNAP-2: A Portable Environment for Queueing Systems Modelling. In Potier, D. (Ed.), *Modelling Techniques and Tools for Performance Analysis* (p. 25). Amsterdam: North-Holland.

Wa, R., Hunt, G., Hunt, G., Brubacher, D., & Brubacher, D. (1999). Detours: Binary Interception of Win32 Functions. In *Proceedings of the 3rd USENIX Windows NT Symposium*, (pp. 135–143). Citeseer.

Welsh, M., & Culler, D. (2003). Adaptive overload control for busy internet servers. In *USITS'03: Proceedings of the 4th conference on USENIX Symposium on Internet Technologies and Systems*, (pp 4–4). Berkeley, CA: USENIX Association.

Winston, W., & Goldberg, J. (1994). *Operations research: applications and algorithms*. Belmont, CA: Duxbury press.

Zhang, Q., Cherkasova, L., Mathews, G., Greene, W., & Smirni, E. (2007). R-capriccio: a capacity planning and anomaly detection tool for enterprise services with live workloads. In *Middleware '07: Proceedings of the ACM/IFIP/USENIX 2007 International Conference on Middleware*, (pp. 244–265). New York: Springer-Verlag, Inc.

ADDITIONAL READING

In addition to the references made in this chapter, we recommend the following materials on this subject:

"Queueing networks and Markov chains: modeling and performance evaluation with computer science applications" (Bolch et al., 1998) covers detailed techniques of queuing network analysis in the area of computing systems. It contains methods to model non-exponential service and arrival times which helps in modeling real world systems.

"Operations research: applications and algorithms" (Winston and Goldberg, 1994) discusses various methods to forecast workload patterns. It contains algorithms for optimizing cost and efficient resource usage which can be used along with performance modeling techniques to come up with efficient system management.

"Coloured Petri nets: basic concepts, analysis methods, and practical use" (Jensen, 1996) discusses the theory behind Colored Petri Nets and ways in which it can be used to model analyze and model systems. This will help in coming up with models of systems which can predict performance.

"Model transformation: The heart and soul of model-driven software development" (Sendall and Kozaczynski, 2003) discusses model transformation basics and how it is important in the context of Model Driven Architecture. It is very important to automatically transform structural models into performance models for ease of use.

KEY TERMS AND DEFINITIONS

Queuing Theory: It is the mathematical study of waiting lines or queues. Queues occur in many places in our daily life from cars waiting in line on a toll booth to queues for paying for lunch in cafeteria to logging into to an online mail service. In this chapter, queuing theory is referred to its use in analyzing computer systems.

Petri Nets: It is a mathematical modeling language for distributed systems. It consists of places and transitions with arcs connecting them and tokens moving amongst them. The tokens remain in places. One particular distribution of tokens in the different places represents a state of the system. The transitions can fire to move tokens from one place to another and signifies change in state.

Computation Independent Model (CIM): It is a higher level model of the system and presents what the system is required to do. It hides the details related to information technology and does not contain any implementation detail.

Platform Independent Model (PIM): It specifies the details of the application components and their behavior but hides the details of the underlying infrastructure or platform. It abstracts out the functionalities of the platform in the form of generic services which are used by the application components.

Platform Specific Model (PSM): It combines the PIM model and combines it with the details of a particular platform on which it will be implemented. This is required for the final implementation of the system.

Model Transformation: It defines the conversion of a model belonging to one metamodel type to another of a different metamodel type. There could also be endogenous transformation when the source and target models are of the same metamodel.

Web Application Portals: Integrated websites which provide the user with a variety of services.

ENDNOTE

[1] At this level in the hierarchy the amount of resources needed cannot be specified by classical measures (such as CPU time and disk accesses) since no real platform has been associated with the application at the PIM phase.

Compilation of References

Abrahao, S., & Poels, G. (2007). Experimental Evaluation of an Object-oriented Function Point Measurement Procedure. *Information and Software Technology*, *49*(4), 366–380. doi:10.1016/j.infsof.2006.06.001

Abrahao, S., & Poels, G. (2009). A Family of Experiments to Evaluate a Functional Size Measurement Procedure for Web Applications. *Journal of Systems and Software*, *82*(2), 253–269. doi:10.1016/j.jss.2008.06.031

Adams, J., Koushik, S., Vasudeva, G., & Galambos, G. (2001). *Patterns for e-Business: A Strategy for Reuse*. Indianapolis, Indiana: IBM Press.

Ahmad, R., Yuqing, F., Cheng, Z., & Jihua, Z. (2006). Closing Information Loops with Extended PLM. In *CSECS'06: Proceedings of the 5th WSEAS International Conference on Circuits, Systems, Electronics, Control & Signal Processing* (pp. 344–349). Stevens Point, WI: World Scientific and Engineering Academy and Society (WSEAS).

Ajila, S. (1995). Software Maintenance: An approach to impact analysis of object changes. *Software, Practice & Experience*, *25*(10), 1155–1181. doi:10.1002/spe.4380251006

Akbar, M., Manning, E., Shoja, G., & Khan, S. (2001). Heuristic Solutions for the Multiple Choice Multi-dimension Knapsack Problem. *Lecture Notes in Computer Science*, 659–668. doi:10.1007/3-540-45718-6_71

Alexander, I., & Maiden, N. (2004). *Scenarios, Stories, Use Cases*. Chichester, UK: Wiley.

Alférez, M., Kulesza, U., Sousa, A., Santos, J., Moreira, A., Araújo, J., et al. (2008). *A Model-Driven Approach for Software Product Lines Requirements Engineering*. Paper presented at the 20th International Conference on Software Engineering & Knowledge Engineering, Redwood City, CA.

Alférez, M., Moreira, A., Kulesza, U., Araújo, J., Mateus, R., & Amaral, V. (2009). *Detecting Feature Interactions in SPL Requirements Analysis Models*. Paper presented at the 1st International Workshop on Feature-Oriented Software Development Denver, Colorado.

Alférez, M., Santos, J., Moreira, A., Garcia, A., Kulesza, U., Araújo, J., et al. (2009). *Multi-View Composition Language for Software Product Line Requirements*. Paper presented at the 2nd Int. Conference on Software Language Engineering, Denver, USA.

Alter, S. (2008). Defining IS as work systems: implications for the IS field. *European Journal of IS*, *17*, 448–469.

Alves, C., & Castro, J. (2001). CRE: A systematic method for COTS components selection. In *Brazilian Symposium on Software Engineering*, (pp. 193–207).

Alves, V., Gheyi, R., Massoni, T., Kulesza, U., Borba, P., & Lucena, C. (2006, 2006). *Refactoring Product Lines*. Paper presented at the Proceedings of the 5th International Conference on Generative Programming and Component Engineering, Portland, Oregon, USA.

Alves-Foss, F., de Leon, D., & Oman, P. (2002). Experiments in the use of XML to enhance traceability between object-oriented design specifications and source code. *Hawaiian International Conference on System Sciences*, Big Island, HI, (pp. 3959-3966).

Amazon Elastic Compute Cloud (Amazon EC2). (n.d.) Retrieved March 2010 from http://aws.amazon.com/ec2/

Ambler, S. (2004). *The Object Primer: Agile Model-Driven Development with UML 2.0*. Cambridge, UK: Cambridge University Press. doi:10.1017/CBO9780511584077

Ambler, S. (2002). *Agile modeling: Effective practices for extreme programming and the unified process* (1st ed.). New York: John Wiley & Sons Inc.

Ambler, S. (2007, November 27). *Overcoming Requirements Modeling Challenges*. Retrieved October, 2009, from http://www.agilemodeling.com/essays/requirementsChallenges.htm.

Amelunxen, C., Königs, A., Rötschke, T., & Schürr, A. (2006). MOFLON: A Standard-Compliant Metamodeling Framework with Graph Transformations. In A. Rensink & J. Warmer (Eds.), *Lecture Notes in Computer Science (LNCS), Model Driven Architecture - Foundations and Applications: 2nd European Conference* (pp. 361–375). Berlin: Springer Verlag.

AMPLE. (2009). *Ample Project*. from http://www.ample-project.net/

Amsden, J., Gardner, T., Griffin, C., & Iyengar, S. (2003). *IBM Draft UML 1.4 Profile for Automated Business Processes with a mapping to BPEL 1.0*. Retrieved March 15, 2009, from http://www.ibm.com/developerworks/rational/library/content/04April/3103/3103_UMLProfileForBusinessProcesses1.1.pdf

Anciano, L., Savino, N., Corbacho, J., & Puigjaner, R. (1998) Extending SMART2 to predict the behaviour of PL/SQL-based applications. In *Proc. of 10th Int. Conf. on Modelling Techniques and Tools for Computer Performance Evaluation (Tools '98)*, (pp. 292–305).

Anderssson, B., Johannesson, P., & Zdravkovic, J. (2007). Aligning Goals and Services through Goal and Business Modeling. *The International Journal of Information Systems and e-Business Management (ISEB), 7,* 143-169.

Anquetil, N., Grammel, B., & da Silva, I. Noppen, J.A.R. Khan, S., Arboleda, H., Rashid, A., & Garcia, A. (2008). Traceability for model-driven, software product line engineering. *ECMDA Traceability Workshop,* Berlin, Germany, (pp. 77-86).

Antkiewicz, M., & Czarnecki, K. (2004). *FeaturePlugin: Feature Modeling Plug-in for Eclipse*. Paper presented at the 2004 OOPSLA workshop on eclipse technology eXchange.

Antón, A. I. (1996). Goal-Based Requirements Analysis. *Second IEEE International Conference on Requirements Engineering (ICRE '96)* (pp. 136-144). Colorado Springs, CO: IEEE.

Archimate. (n.d.). *ArchiMate resource tree*. Retrieved April 8, 2010, from http://www.archimate.org/ART/

Arief, L. B., & Speirs, N. A. (2000). A uml tool for an automatic generation of simulation programs. In *WOSP '00: Proceedings of the 2nd international workshop on Software and performance,* (pp. 71–76), New York: ACM.

ARIS. (2009). Retrieved October, 2009, from http://www.ids-scheer.com/international/en.

Arlow, J., & Neustadt, I. (2005). *UML2 and the Unified Process: Practical Object-Oriented Analysis and Design*. Reading, MA: Addison-Wesley, Pearson Education.

Armbrust, M., Fox, A., Griffith, R., Joseph, A., Katz, R., Konwinski, A., et al. (2009). *Above the Clouds: A Berkeley View of Cloud Computing*. Technical Report 2009-28, UC Berkeley.

Arnold, R. S., & Bohner, S. A. (1993). Impact Analysis: Towards a framework for comparison. *International Conference on Software Maintenance*, Montreal, Canada, (pp. 292-301).

Asikainen, T., Männistö, T., & Soininen, T. (2004). Representing Feature Models of Software Product Families Using a Configuration Ontology. In *Proceedings of the ECAI 2004, Workshop on Configuration*, Valencia, Spain.

Asnina, E. (2006). The Formal Approach to Problem Domain Modelling Within Model Driven Architecture. In *Proceedings of the 9th International Conference "Information Systems Implementation and Modelling" (ISIM'06), April 25-26, 2006, Přerov, Czech Republic, 1st edn.* (pp. 97-104). Ostrava, Czech Republic: Jan Štefan MARQ.

Asnina, E. (2006a). Formalization aspects of problem domain modeling within Model Driven Architecture. In *Databases and Information Systems. Seventh International Baltic Conference on Databases and Information Systems. Communications, Materials of Doctoral Consortium, July 3-6, 2006, Vilnius, Lithuania* (pp. 93-104). Vilnius, Lithuania: Technika.

Asnina, E. (2009). A formal holistic outline for domain modeling. *Local Proceedings of Advances in Databases and Information Systems, 13th East-European Conference, ADBIS 2009, Associated Workshops and Doctoral Consortium, Riga, Latvia, September 7-10, 2009* (pp. 400-407). Riga Technical University.

Asnina, E., & Osis, J. (2010). Computation independent models: bridging problem and solution domains. In J. Osis, & O. Nikiforova (Ed.), *Proceedings of the 2nd International Workshop on Model-Driven Architecture and Modeling Theory-Driven Development MDA & MTDD 2010, In conjunction with ENASE 2010, Athens, Greece, July 2010* (pp. 23-32). Portugal: SciTePress.

Atkinson, C., & Kühne, T. (2003). Model-Driven Development: A Metamodeling Foundation. *IEEE Software, 20*(5), 36–41. doi:10.1109/MS.2003.1231149

Atkinson, C., Bayer, J., & Muthig, D. (2000). Component-based Product Line Development: The KobrA Approach. In Donohoe, P. (Ed.), *Software Product Lines. Experience and Research Directions* (pp. 289–310). Boston: Kluwer Academic Publishers.

Bachman, F., Bass, L., Buhman, C., Comella-Dorda, S., Long, F., & Robert, J. (2000). *Technical Concepts of Component-Based Software Engineering*. Pittsburgh, PA: Software Engineering Institute, Carnegie Mellon University.

Bachmann, F., & Bass, L. (2001). Managing Variability in Software Architectures. *ACM SIGSOFT Software Engineering Notes, 26*(3), 126–132. doi:10.1145/379377.375274

Baida, Z., Gordijn, J., Saele, H., Akkermans, H., & Morch, A. (2005). An Ontological Approach for Eliciting and Understanding Needs in e-Services. In: O. Pastor J.F. Cunha (Ed.), *17th Conference on Advanced Information Systems Engineering*, (LNCS Vol. 3520 pp. 400-414). Berlin: Springer-Verlag.

Balasubramanian, K., Gokhale, A., Karsai, G., Sztipanovits, J., & Neema, S. (2006). Developing Applications Using Model-Driven Design Environments. *IEEE Computer, 39*(2), 33–40. doi:10.1109/MC.2006.54

Balasubramanian, K., Schmidt, D., Molnar, Z., & Ledeczi, A. (2007). Component-based system integration via (meta)model composition. In *14th Annual IEEE International Conference and Workshops on the Engineering of Computer-Based Systems* (pp. 93–102). Washington, D.C.: IEEE Computer Society.

Balbo, G. (2002). *Introducation to stochastic petri nets* (pp. 84–155). Lectures on Formal Methods and Performance Analysis.

Baldwin, C. Y., & Clark, K. B. (2000). Design Rules: *Vol. 1. The Power of Modularity*. Cambridge, MA: MIT Press.

Balogh, Z., & Varró, D. (2009). *Model Transformation by Example using Inductive Logic Programming. Software and Systems Modeling*. Berlin: Springer.

Balsamo, S., & Marzolla, M. (2003). Simulation modeling of UML software architectures. In *Proc. of ESM'03, the 17th European Simulation Multiconference*, (pp. 562–567).

Balsamo, S., & Marzolla, M. (2005). Performance evaluation of UML software architectures with multiclass Queueing Network models. In Proceedings of the *5th international workshop on Software and performance*, (pp. 42). New York: ACM.

Balsamo, S., & Simeoni, M. (2001). On transforming UML models into performance models. In *ETAPS01: Workshop on Transformations in UML*. Citeseer.

Bass, L., Clements, P., & Kazman, R. (2003). *Software Architecture in Practice* (second edition), *The SEI Series in Software Engineering*. Westford, MA: Addison-Wesley.

Batory, D. (2006). Multilevel models in model-driven engineering, product lines, and metaprogramming. *IBM Systems Journal, 45*(3), 527–539. doi:10.1147/sj.453.0527

Bause, F. (1993). Queueing petri nets - a formalism for the combined qualitative and quantitative analysis of systems. In *Proceedings of the 5th International Workshop on Petri nets and Performance Models*, (pp. 14–23). Washington, DC: IEEE Computer Society.

Bayer, J., Flege, O., Knauber, P., Laqua, R., Muthig, D., Schmid, K., et al. (1999). PuLSE: A methodology to develop software product lines. *Symposium on Software Reusability*, Los Angeles, CA, (pp. 122-131).

Beck, K. (2002). *Test-Driven Development By Example*. Boston: Addison Wesley.

Beck, K. (2008). *Implementation Patterns*. Upper Saddle River, NJ: Addison-Wesley.

Benavides, D., Trinidad, P., & Ruiz-Cortes, A. (2005). Automated Reasoning on Feature Models. *17th Conference on Advanced Information Systems Engineering (CAiSE05, Proceedings)*, (LNCS, 3520, pp. 491–503).

Berard, E. V. (1998). *Be Careful With "Use Cases"*. The Object Agency, Inc.

Bettin, J. (2002, Novermber). *Measuring the potential of domain-specific modeling techniques*. Paper presented at the 17th Annual ACM Conference on Object-Oriented Programming, Systems, Languages, and Applications. Seattle, WA.

Bezivin, J. (2006). Model driven engineering: an emerging technical space. In R. Lammel, J. Saraiva, & J. Visser (Eds.), *GTTSE 2005* (LNCS 4143, pp. 36-64). Berlin: Springer-Verlag.

Bezivin, J., Barbero, M., & Jouault, F. (2007). On the Applicability Scope of Model Driven Engineering. In *Proceedings of Fourth International Workshop on Model-Based Methodologies for Pervasive and Embedded Software*, 2007. MOMPES '07. IEEE, v 0-7695-2769-8/07.

Bézivin, J., Jouault, F., & Valduriez, P. (2004). On the Need for Megamodels. In *Proceedings of Workshop on Best Practices for Model-Driven Software Development at the 19th Annual ACM Conference on Object-Oriented Programming, Systems, Languages, and Applications*, Vancouver, British Columbia, Canada.

Biddle, R., Noble, J., & Tempero, E. (2002). *Supporting reusable use cases. LNCS 2319* (pp. 210–226). Berlin: Springer.

Biffl, St., Mordinyi, R., & Scatten, A. (2007) A Model-driven approach using explicit stakeholder quality requirement model for building dependable information systems. In *Proceedings of the Fifth International Workshop on Software Quality (WoSQ '07)*. Washington, DC: IEEE.

Binder, W. (2005). A Portable and Customizable Profiling Framework for Java Based on Bytecode Instruction Counting. In *Programming languages and systems: third Asian symposium, APLAS 2005,* Tsukuba, Japan, November 2-5, 2005, (pp. 178). Berlin: Springer Verlag.

Blair, G., Bencomo, N., & France, R. (2009). Models@run.time. *IEEE Computer, 42*(10), 22–27.

Boehm, B. (1987). Improving Software Productivity. *Computer, 20*(9), 43–57. doi:10.1109/MC.1987.1663694

Bohner, S. A. (2002). Software Change Impacts: An evolving perspective. *International Conference on Software Maintenance*, Montreal, Canada, (pp. 263-271).

Bolch, G., Greiner, S., de Meer, H., & Trivedi, K. (1998). *Queueing networks and Markov chains: modeling and performance evaluation with computer science applications*. New York: Wiley-Interscience.

Boner, J. (2004). AspectWerkz - Dynamic AOP for Java. In *Proceeding of the 3rd International Conference on Aspect-Oriented Development (AOSD 2004)*, March 2004, Lancaster, UK.

Bonifacio, R., & Borba, P. (2009). *Modeling Scenario Variability as Crosscutting Mechanisms*. Paper presented at the Aspect Oriented Software Development.

Bosch, J., Florijn, G., Greefhorst, D., Kuusela, J., Obbink, J., & Pohl, K. (2002). Variability issues in software product lines. *Lecture Notes in Computer Science*, 13–21.

Bosch, J. (2000). *Design and Use of Software Architecture – Adopting and Evolving a Product Line Approach*. Reading, MA: Addison-Wesley Professional, ACM Press.

Bottaro, A., Bourcier, J., Escofier, C., & Lalanda, P. (2007). Autonomic Context-Aware Service Composition in a Home Control Gateway. In *Proceedings of IEEE International Conference on Pervasive Services* (pp. 223-231), Istanbul, Turkey.

Bourcier, J., Chazalet, A., Desertot, M., Escofier, C., & Marin, C. (2006). A Dynamic-SOA Home Control Gateway. In *Proceedings of IEEE International Conference on Services Computing* (pp. 463–470), Chicago.

Bowen, J., O'Grady, P., & Smith, L. (1990). A constraint programming language for life-cycle engineering. *Artificial Intelligence in Engineering*, *5*(4), 206–220. doi:10.1016/0954-1810(90)90022-V

Bragança, A., & Machado, R. J. (2007). Adopting computational independent models for derivation of architectural requirements of software product lines. In *Fourth International Workshop on Model-Based Methodologies for Pervasive and Embedded Software (MOMPES'07)* (pp. 91-101). Washington, DC: IEEE.

Bragança, A., & Machado, R. J. (2007). *Automating Mappings between Use Case Diagrams and Feature Models for Software Product Lines*. Paper presented at the 11th International Software Product Line Conference.

Briand, L. C., Labiche, Y., O'Sullivan, L., & Sówka, M. M. (2006). Automated impact analysis of UML models. *Journal of Systems and Software*, *79*(3), 339–352. doi:10.1016/j.jss.2005.05.001

Briand, L. C., Labiche, Y., & Soccar, G. (2002). Automating impact analysis and regression test selection based on UML designs. *International Conference on Software Maintenance*, Montreal, Canada, (pp. 252-261).

Brown, A. W., Carney, D. J., Morris, E. J., Smith, D. B., & Zarrella, P. F. (1994). *Principles of CASE tool integration*. New York: Oxford University Press, Inc.

Brown, A. (2008). MDA Redux: Practical Realization of Model Driven Architecture. In *Proceedings of the Seventh International Conference on Composition-Based Software Systems (ICCBSS 2008)*, (pp. 174–183).

Brown, P.G. (1991). QFD: Echoing the voice of the customer. *AT&T Technical Journal*, March/April, 21-31.

Bruneton, E., Coupaye, T., Leclercq, M., Quema, V., & Stefani, J.-B. (2004). An Open Component Model and Its Support in Java. In Crnkovic, I., Stafford, J.A., Schmidt, H.W., & Wallnau, K. (Eds.), *Component-Based Software Engineering*, (LNCS Vol. 3054, pp. 7-22). Berlin: Springer.

Bryant, B. B., Lee, B. S., Cao, F., Zhao, W., Burt, C. C., & Gray, J. (2003). From Natural Language Requirements to Executable Models of Software Components. In *Proceedings of the Monterey Workshop on Software Engineering for Embedded Systems, 2003*, 51–58.

Bubenko, J. A. Jr. et al. (1992). *Computer support for Enterprise Modelling in Requirements Acquisition From Fuzzy to Formal*, ESPRIT III Project 6612: Deliverable 3-1-3-R1 Part B.

Bubenko, J. A., Jr., Persson, A., & Stirna, J. (2001). *User guide of the knowledge management approach using enterprise knowledge patterns, deliverable D3, IST Programme project "Hypermedia and Pattern Based Knowledge Management for Smart Organisations"*. Retrived October, 2009, from Department of Computer and Systems Sciences, Royal Institute of Technology (Stockholm, Sweden) website http://www.dsv.su.se/~js/ekd_user_guide.html.

Bubenko, J., Jr., & Kirikova, M. (1995). "Worlds" in requirements acquisition and modelling. In H. Kangassalo et al. (Ed.), *Information Modelling and Knowledge Bases VI*, (pp. 159-174.). Amsterdam: IOS Press.

Buck, B., & Hollingsworth, J. K. (2000). An API for Runtime Code Patching. *International Journal of High Performance Computing Applications*, 317–329. doi:10.1177/109434200001400404

Buckley, J., Mens, T., Zenger, M., Rashid, A., & Kniesel, G. (2005). Towards a taxonomy of software change. *Journal of Software Maintenance and Evolution: Research and Practice*, *17*(5), 309–332. doi:10.1002/smr.319

Bures, T., Hnetynka, P., & Plasil, F. (2006). SOFA 2.0: Balancing Advanced Features in a Hierarchical Component Model. In *Proceedings SERA* (pp. 40-48). Seattle: IEEE Computer Society.

Buschmann, F., Henney, K., & Schmidt, D. C. (2007a). *Pattern-Oriented Software Architecture: A Pattern Language for Distributed Computing*. Hoboken, NJ: Wiley.

Buschmann, F., Henney, K., & Schmidt, D. C. (2007b). *Pattern-Oriented Software Architecture: On Patterns and Pattern Languages*. Hoboken, NJ: Wiley.

Buschmann, F., Meunier, R., Rohnert, H., Sommerlad, P., & Stahl, M. (1996). *Pattern-Oriented Software Architecture – A System of Patterns*. West Sussex, UK: Willey.

Bustamante, F. E., Widener, P., & Schwan, K. (2002). Scalable Directory Services Using Proactivity. In *Proceedings of the 2002 ACM/IEEE conference on Supercomputing* (pp.1-12). Los Alamitos, CA: IEEE Computer Society Press.

Buyya, R., Yeo, C., Venugopal, S., Broberg, J., & Brandic, I. (2009). Cloud Computing and Emerging IT Platforms: Vision, Hype, and Reality for Delivering Computing as the 5ᵗʰ Utility. *Future Generation Computer Systems*, *25*(6), 599–616. doi:10.1016/j.future.2008.12.001

Cai, Y. (2006). *Modularity in Design: Formal Modeling and Automated Analysis*. Ph.D. thesis, University of Virginia.

Cai, Y., & Sullivan, K. (2006). Modularity analysis of logical design models. *International Conference on Automated Software Engineering*, Tokyo, Japan, (pp. 91-102).

Cai, Y., Huynh, S., & Xie, T. (2007). A framework and tool supports for testing modularity of software design. *International Conference on Automated Software Engineering*, Atlanta, GA, (pp. 441-444).

Cano, J., Martinez, N., Seepold, R., & Aguilar, F. L. (2007). Model-driven development of embedded system on heterogeneous platforms. In *Procedings of Forum on Specification and Design Languages* (pp. 243–248). Barcelona, Spain: ECSI.

Cantor, M. (2003). Rational Unified Process for Systems Engineering - Part III: Requirements Analysis and Design. *The Rational Edge*, from http://www.ibm.com/developerworks/rational/rationaledge

Cantrill, B., & Doeppner, T. W. (1997) Threadmon: A Tool for Monitoring Multithreaded Program Performance. In *Proceedings of the 30th Hawaii International Conference on Systems Sciences,* (pp. 253-265, January 1997).

Cao, X.-x., Miao, H.-k., & Chen, Y.-h. (2008). Transformation from computation independent model to platform independent model with pattern. [English Edition]. *Journal of Shanghai University*, *12*(6), 515–523. doi:10.1007/s11741-008-0610-2

Caporuscio, M., Marco, A. D., & Inverardi, P. (2005). Run-time performance management of the siena publish/subscribe middleware. In *WOSP '05: Proceedings of the 5th international workshop on Software and performance*, (pp. 65–74). New York: ACM.

Carle, G., & Biersack, E. (1997). Survey of Error Recovery Techniques for IP-based Audio-visual Multicast Applications. *IEEE Network Magazine*, *11*(6), 24–36. doi:10.1109/65.642357

Carzaniga, A., Rutherford, M., & Wolf, A. (2004). A routing scheme for content-based networking. *INFOCOM*, *2*, 918–928.

Casewise. (2009). Retrieved October, 2009, from http://www.casewise.com

Cervantes, H., & Hall, R. S. (2004). A Framework for Constructing Adaptive Component-Based Applications: Concepts and Experiences. In Crnkovic, I., Stafford, J.A., Schmidt, H.W., Wallnau, K. (Eds.), *7th Symposium on Component-Based Software Engineering:* (LNCS Vol 3054, pp. 130-137). Berlin: Springer.

Chambers, J. M., Cleveland, W. S., & Tukey, P. A. (1983). *Graphical methods for data analysis. The Wadsworth statistics/probability series*. Belmont, CA: Wadsworth.

Chaplin, N., Hale, J., Khan, K., Ramil, J., & Tan, W. (2001). Types of software evolution and software maintenance. *Journal of Software Maintenance and Evolution: Research and Practice, 13*(1), 3–30. doi:10.1002/smr.220

Chappel, O. (2005, October). *Term-fact modeling, the key to successful rule-based systems*. Retrieved November 10, 2009, from Business Rules Journal / BRCommunity: http://www.BRCommunity.com/a2005/b250.html

Charles, J. (1999). Middleware moves to the forefront. *Computer, 32*(5), 17–19. doi:10.1109/MC.1999.762786

Che, Y., Wang, G., Wen, X., & Ren, B. (2009). Research on Computational Independent Model in the Enterprise Information System Development Mode Based on Model Driven and Software Component. *International Conference on Interoperability for Enterprise Software and Applications China, 2009. IESA '09*. (pp. 85 - 89). Washington, DC: IEEE.

Chen, M., Qiu, X., Xu, W., Wang, L., Zhao, J., & Li, X. (2007). UML Activity Diagram-Based Automatic Test Case Generation For Java Programs. *The Computer Journal*.

Chen, Zh., & Pooley, R. (2009). Rediscovering Zachman Framework using Ontology from Requirement Engineering Perspective. In *Proceedings of Annual IEEE International Computer Software and Application Conference*, (pp. 3-8). Washington, DC: IEEE.

Cherbakov, L., Galambos, G., Harishankar, R., Kalyana, S., & Rackham, G. (2005). Impact of Service Orientation at the Business Level. *IBM Systems Journal, 44*(4), 653–668. doi:10.1147/sj.444.0653

Cherki, S., El Kaim, W., Josset, P., & Paris, F. (2000). Domain Analysis and Product-Line Scoping: a Thomson-SCF Product-Line Case Study. In P. Knauber & G. Succi (Eds), *Software Product Lines: Economics, Architectures, and Implications, Proceedings of Workshop #15 at 22th International Conference on Software Engineering (ICSE 2000), Limerick, Ireland* (pp. 65-73), Fraunhofer IESE Report No. 070.00/E, 2000.

Chitchyan, R., & Oldevik, J. (2006). A Runtime Model for Multi-dimensional Separation of Concerns. *Models@run.time, held at MODELS 2006*, Genova, Italy, October 2006.

Chung, L., Cooper, K., & Courtney, S. (2004). COTS-aware requirements engineering and software architecting. In *Proceedings of the SERP*. Citeseer.

Chung, L., Nixon, B., Yu, E., & Mylopoulos, J. (1999). *Non-Functional Requirements in Software Engineering* (1 ed.). Amsterdam: Kluwer Academic Publishers.

Cleary, D. (2000). Web-*based development and functional size measurement*. Paper presented at IFPUG Annual Conference, San Diego, USA

Clements, P., & Northrop, L. (2001). *Software Product Lines: Practices and Patterns*. Reading, MA: Addison-Wesley.

Clements, P., Bachmann, F., Bass, L., Garlan, D., Ivers, J., & Little, R. (2002). *Documenting Software Architectures: Views and Beyond*. Upper Saddle River, NJ: Addison-Wesley.

Clements, P., & Northrop, L. (2000). *A Framework for Software Product Line Practice, Version 3.0*. Pittsburgh, PA: Software Engineering Institute, Carnegie Mellon University.

Coad, P., & Yourdon, E. (1990). *Object-Oriented Analysis* (2nd ed.). New York: Prentice hall.

Cockburn, A. (2000). *Writing Effective Use Cases*. Reading, MA: Addison-Wesley Professional.

Common Warehouse Metamodel (CWM) Specification. *Version 1.1*. (2003). from http://www.omg.org/ technology/documents/formal/cwm_2.htm

Comos Industry Solutions Gmb, H. (2009). *Comos ET.* Retrieved June 21, 2009, from Comos Industry Solutions GmbH: http://www.comos.com/elektrotechnik.html?&L=1

Connolly, T., & Begg, C. (2005). *Database Systems. A practical Approach to Design, Implementation, and Management* (4th ed.). New York: Pearson Education, Inc.

Conway, C., & Edwards, S. (2004). Ndl: a domain-specific language for device drivers. In *Proceedings of the 2004 ACM SIGPLAN/SIGBED conference on languages, compilers, and tools for embedded systems* (pp. 30–36). New York: ACM

Coplien, J., Hoffman, D., & Weiss, D. (1998). Commonality and Variability in Software Engineering. *IEEE Software, 15*(6), 37–45. doi:10.1109/52.730836

Coplien, J., Hoffman, D., & Weiss, D. (1998). Commonality and Variability in Software Engineering. *IEEE Software, 15*(6), 37–45. doi:10.1109/52.730836

Coriat, M., Jourdan, J., & Boisbourdin, F. (2000). The SPLIT Method. In Donohoe, P. (Ed.), *Software Product Lines. Experience and Research Directions* (pp. 147–166). Boston: Kluwer Academic Publishers.

Cortellessa, V., & Mirandola, R. (2000). Deriving a queueing network based performance model from uml diagrams. In *WOSP '00: Proceedings of the 2nd international workshop on Software and performance*, (pp. 58–70). New York: ACM.

Cortellessa, V., Di Gregorio, S., & Di Marco, A. (2008). Using atl for transformations in software performance engineering: a step ahead of java-based transformations? In *WOSP '08: Proceedings of the 7th international workshop on Software and performance*, (pp. 127–132). New York: ACM.

Cortellessa, V., Di Marco, A., & Inverardi, P. (2006b). Software performance model-driven architecture. In *SAC '06: Proceedings of the 2006 ACM symposium on Applied computing*, (pp. 1218–1223). New York: ACM.

Cortellessa, V., Di Marco, A., & Inverardi, P. (2007). Integrating Performance and Reliability Analysis in a Non-Functional MDA Framework. In *Fundamental approaches to software engineering: 10th international conference, FASE 2007, held as part of the Joint Conferences on Theory and Practice of Software, ETAPS 2007,* Braga, Portugal, March 24-April 1, 2007: (pp. 57). Berlin: Springer-Verlag Inc.

Curtis, B., Kellner, M., & Over, J. (1992). Process Modeling. *Communications of the ACM, 35*(9), 75–90. doi:10.1145/130994.130998

Cybulski, J. L., Neal, R. D. B., Kram, A., & Allen, J. C. (1998). Reuse of early life-cycle artifacts: workproducts, methods and tools. *Annals of Software Engineering, 5,* 227–251. doi:10.1023/A:1018983220136

Czarnecki, K., Helsen, S., & Eisenecker, U. (2005). Staged configuration through specialization and multi-level configuration of feature models. *Software Process Improvement and Practice, 10*(2), 143–169. doi:10.1002/spip.225

Czarnecki, K., & Helsen, S. (2006). Feature-based survey of model transformation approaches. *IBM Systems Journal, 45*(3), 621–645. doi:10.1147/sj.453.0621

Czarnecki, K., & Eisenecker, U. W. (2000). *Generative Programming: Methods, Tools, and Applications.* New York: ACM Press/Addison-Wesley Publishing Co.

Czarnecki, K., & Antkiewicz, M. (2005). *Mapping Features to Models: A Template Approach Based on Superimposed Variants.* Paper presented at the 4th International Conference on Generative Programming and Component Engineering.

Czarnecki, K., Foster, J. N., Hu, Z., Lämmel, R., Schürr, A., & Terwilliger, J. F. (2009). Bidirectional Transformations: A Cross-Discipline Perspective. GRACE Meeting notes, state of the art, and outlook. In *International Conference on Model Transformations (ICMT)*, Zurich, Switzerland, (pp. 260–283).

Czarnecki, K., Helsen, S., & Eisenecker, U. (2004). *Staged Configuration Using Feature Models.* Paper presented at the Third International Conference in Software Product Lines, Boston, Massachusetts, USA.

Dai, Z. R. (2004). Model-driven Testing with UML 2.0, In *Proceedings of the Second European Workshop on Model Driven Architecture (MDA)*, Canterbury, UK.

Daniel, G., Waddington, R. N., & Schmidt, D. C. (2007). Dynamic analysis and profiling of multi-threaded systems. In Tiako, P. (Ed.), *Designing Software-Intensive Systems: Methods and Principles*. Hershey, PA: Idea Group Inc.

Dardenne, A., van Lamsweerde, A., & Fickas, S. (1993). Goal-directed requirements acquisition. [). Amsterdam, The Netherlands: Elsevier North-Holland, Inc.]. *Science of Computer Programming, 20*, 3–50. doi:10.1016/0167-6423(93)90021-G

Davenport, T. (1992). *Process Innovation: reengineering work through information technology*. Cambridge, MA: Harvard Business School.

Davis, A. M. (1990). *Software Requirements: Analysis and Specification*. New York: Prentice-Hall, Inc.

De Lucia, A., Fasano, F., & Oliveto, R. (2008). *Traceability management for impact analysis* (pp. 21–30). Beijing, China: Frontiers of Software Maintenance.

Debnath, N., Leonardi, M. C., Mauco, M. V., Montejano, G., & Riesco, D. (2008). Improving model driven architecture with requirements models. In *Proceedings of the Fifth International Conference on Information Technology: New Generations* (pp. 21-26). Washington, DC: IEEE.

Deissenboeck, F., Juergens, E., Lochmann, K., & Wagner, S. (2009). Software Quality Models: Purposes, Usage Scenarios and Requirements. In *Proc. Seventh Workshop on Software Quality* (pp. 9–14). Los Alamitos, CA: IEEE Computer Society.

Denton, T., Jones, E., Srinivasan, S., Owens, K., & Buskens, R. W. (2008). NAOMI – An Experimental Platform for Multi–modeling. In K. Czarnecki, I. Ober, J.-M. Bruel, A. Uhl, & M. Völter (Eds.), *Lecture Notes in Computer Science (LNCS), Model driven engineering languages and systems, 11th international conference, MoDELS 2008, Toulouse, France, September 28 - October 3, 2008; proceedings* (pp. 143–157). Berlin: Springer.

Denton, T., Jones, E., Srinivasan, S., Owens, K., & Buskens, R. (2008). NAOMI-An Experimental Platform for Multi-modeling. In *Proceedings of the 11th international conference on Model Driven Engineering Languages and Systems*, (pp. 143–157). Berlin: Springer.

Derzsi, Z., Gordijn, J., & Tan, Y. (2008) Towards model-based assessment of business-IT alignment in e-service networks from multiple perspectives. In *Proceedings of 16th European Conference on Information Systems 2008*. Retrieved March 15, 2009, from http://is2.lse.ac.uk/asp/aspecis/20080007.pdf

Desfray, P. (2004). *Making a success of preliminary analysis using UML*. Retrieved November 10, 2009, from Softeam: http://www.objecteering.com/ressources_white-papers.php

Deursen, A. v., & Klint, P. (2001). Domain-Specific Language Design Requires Feature Descriptions. *Journal of Computing and Information Technology, 10*. DSM forum website. (n.d.). DSM Forum: Domain-Specific Modeling. from http://www.dsmforum.org/

Ding, H., Kihwal, L., & Sha, L. (2005). Dependency Algebra: A Theoretical Framework for Dependency Management in Real-Time Control Systems. In *Proceedings of the 12th IEEE International Conference on the Engineering of Computer-Based Systems*, Greenbelt, MD.

Diouf, M., Musumbu, K., & Maabout, S. (2008). Methodological aspects of semantics enrichment in Model Driven Architecture. In *Proceedings of the Third International Conference on Internet and Web Applications and Services* (pp. 205–210). Washington, DC: IEEE.

Diskin, Z., Kadish, B., Piessens, F., & Johnson, M. (2000). Universal arrow foundations for visual modeling. In *Proc. Diagramms'2000: 1st Int. Conference on the theory and application of diagrams,* (LNAI No. 1889, pp. 345-360). Berlin: Springer.

Dmitriev, M. (2002). Application of the HotSwap Technology to Advanced Profiling. In *Proceedings of the First Workshop on Unanticipated Software Evolution, held at ECOOP 2002 International Conference*, Malaga, Spain.

Dobrica, L., & Niemela, E. (2007). Modeling Variability in the Product Line Architecture of Distributed Middleware Services. In H. Arabnia & H. Reza (Eds) *Proceedings of the 2007 International Conference on Software Engineering Research and Practice, June 25-28, Las Vegas, NV,* (vol. 1, p.269-275). CSREA Press.

Dobrica, L., & Ovaska, E. (2009). A service based approach for a cross domain reference architecture development. In S. Jablonski & L. Maciaszek (Eds) *ENASE 2009 - 4th International Conference on Evaluation of Novel Approaches to Software Engineering* (pp. 33-44). Lisbon, Portugal: INSTICC Press.

Donald, B. (1989). *Error Detection and Recovery in Robotics,* (LNCS 33). Berlin: Springer-Verlag.

Dörr, H., & Schürr, A. (2004). Special section on tool integration applications and frameworks. *International Journal on Software Tools for Technology Transfer, 6*(3), 183–185.

Dromey, R. G. (2006). Formalizing the Transition from Requirements to Design. In He, J., & Liu, Z. (Eds.), *Mathematical Frameworks for Component Software - Models for Analysis and Synthesis* (pp. 156–187). World Scientific Series on Component-Based Development.

Dubielewicz, I., & Hnatkovska, B. (2005). Structural specification of business processes. In *Proceedings of 8th Conference "Information Systems Implementation and Modeling", April 19-20, 2005, Hradec nad Moravici, Czech Republic* (pp. 111-118). Ostrava, Czech Republic: Jan Štefan MARQ.

Dubielewicz, I., Hnatkowska, B., Huzar, Z., & Tuzinkiewicz, L. (2006). Feasibility analysis of MDA-based database design. In W. Zamojski (Ed.), *Proceedings of International Conference on Dependability of Computer Systems. DepCoS–RELCOMEX.* (pp. 19–26). Los Alamitos: IEEE Computer Society Press.

Ebert, J., Riediger, V., & Winter, A. (2008). Graph Technology In Reverse Engineering, The TGraph Approach. In R. Gimnich, U. Kaiser, J. Quante, & A. Winter, (Eds.), *10th Workshop Software Reengineering (WSR 2008),* (vol. 126 of *GI Lecture Notes in Informatics*, pp. 67-81), Bonn, Germany.

Eclipse Foundation. (n.d.). MDT-UML2Tools. from http://www.eclipse.org/uml2/

Eclipse Modeling Format (EMF). (n.d.). Retrieved March 2010, from http://www.eclipse.org/modeling/emf/

Eden, A. H., & Kazman, R. (2003). Architecture, Design, Implementation. In *The 25th International Conference on Software Engineering (ICSE 2003), May 3-10, Portland, Oregon, USA,* (pp.149-159). Washington, DC: IEEE Computer Society.

Edwards, G., Deng, G., Schmidt, D., Gokhale, A., & Natarajan, B. (2004). Model-driven Configuration and Deployment of Component Middleware Publisher/Subscriber Services. In *Proceedings of the 3rd ACM Conference on Generative Programming and Component Engineering*, Vancouver, CA.

Eker, J., Janneck, J., Lee, E., Liu, J., Liu, X., & Ludvig, J. (2003). Taming heterogeneity - the ptolemy approach. *Proceedings of the IEEE, 91*(1), 127–144. doi:10.1109/JPROC.2002.805829

El Kaim, W., Cherki, S., Josset, P., Paris, F., & Ollagnon, J.-C. (2000). Applied Technology for Designing a PL Architecture of a Pilot Training System. In P. Knauber & G. Succi (Eds.) *Software Product Lines: Economics, Architectures, and Implications, Proceedings of Workshop #15 at 22th International Conference on Software Engineering (ICSE 2000), Limerick, Ireland* (pp. 55-65). Fraunhofer IESE Report No. 070.00/E, 2000.

Elmasri, R., & Navathe, S. B. (2007). *Fundamentals of database systems,* (5Th Ed.). New York: Pearson Education, Inc.

Eriksson, H.-E., & Penker, M. (2000). *Business Modeling with UML: Business Patterns at Work.* Toronto: John Wiley & Sons, Inc.

Eriksson, M. (2006). *An Approach to Software Product Line Use Case Modeling. Unpublished Doctoral Degree, UMEÅ University.* Sweden: UMEÅ.

Eriksson, M., Börstler, J., & Borg, K. (2005). *The PLUSS Approach - Domain Modeling with Features, Use Cases and Use Case Realizations.* Paper presented at the 9th International Conference on Software Product Lines.

Escofier, C., & Hall, R. S. (2007). Dynamically Adaptable Applications with iPOJO Service Components. In Lumpe, M. & Vanderperre, W. (Eds.), *Proc. 6th Conference on Software Composition,* (LNCS Vol 4829, pp. 113-128). Berlin: Springer.

Evans, M. W. (1989). *The Software Factory.* Chichester, UK: John Wiley and Sons.

Fahringer, T., Mazzocca, N., Rak, M., Pllana, S., Villano, U., Madsen, G., et al. (2003). Performance modeling of scientific applications: Scalability analysis of lapw0. In *Proceedings Eleventh Euromicro Conference on Parallel, Distributed and Network-Based Processing,* (pp. 5-12), Genoa, Italy 2003.

Farlex Inc. (2009). *Causality.* Retrieved November 4, 2009, from The Free Dictionary Com: http://encyclopedia. thefreedictionary.com/causality

Fellbaum, C. (Ed.). (1998). *WordNet: An Electronic Lexical Database.* MIT Press.

Feller, W. (1945). The fundamental limit theorems in probability. *Bulletin of the American Mathematical Society, 51,* 800–832. doi:10.1090/S0002-9904-1945-08448-1

Ferg, S. (2003, February 15). *What's Wrong with Use Cases?* Retrieved January 30, 2010, from Jackson Methods home page: http://www.jacksonworkbench.co.uk/steve-fergspages/papers/ferg--whats_wrong_with_use_cases. html

Figueiredo, E., Cacho, N., Sant'Anna, C., Monteiro, M., Kulesza, U., Garcia, A., et al. (2008). *Evolving software product lines with aspects: an empirical study on design stability.* Paper presented at the 30th International Conference on Software Engineering (ICSE 2008).

Filman, R. E., Elrad, T., Clarke, S., & Aksit, M. (2004). *Aspect-Oriented Software Development.* Addison-Wesley.

Finkelstein, C. (2006). *Enterprise Architecture for Integration: Rapid Delivery Methods and Technologies.* Boston: Artech House.

Firesmith, D. G. (2002). *Use Cases: the Pros and Cons.* Retrieved November 30, 2009, from Knowledge Systems Corporation: http://www.ksc.com/article7.htm

Fowler, M. (1997). *Analysis Patterns: Reusable Object Models.* Upper Saddle River, NJ: Addison-Wesley.

Fowler, M. (2003a). Patterns. *IEEE Software, 20*(2), 56–57. doi:10.1109/MS.2003.1184168

Fowler, M. (2003b). *Patterns of Enterprise Application Architecture.* Upper Saddle River, NJ: Addison-Wesley.

Fowler, M. (2009). *Patterns in Enterprise Software* from http://martinfowler.com/articles/enterprisePatterns.html

Fox, M. S. (1992). The TOVE Project: Towards A Common-sense Model of the Enterprise. *Enterprise Integration Laboratory Technical Report.* Retrieved May 02, 2009, from http://www.eil.utoronto.ca/enterprise-modelling/papers/fox-tove-uofttr92.pdf

France, R., & Rumpe, B. (2007). Model-driven development of complex software: A research roadmap. In *International Conference on Software Engineering,* (pp. 37–54). IEEE Computer Society Washington, DC, USA.

Fronckowiak, J. (2008). Auto-scaling Web sites using Amazon EC2 and Scalr. In *Amazon EC2.* Articles and Tutorials.

Gailly, F., España, S., Poels, G., & Pastor, O. (2008). *Integrating business domain ontologies with early requirements modelling,* (LNCS vol. 5232, pp. 282-291). Berlin: Springer.

Gamma, E., Helm, R., Johnson, R., & Vlissides, J. (1995). *Design Patterns: Elements of Reusable Object-oriented Software*. Reading, MA: Addison-Wesley Publishing.

Garcia, F., Serrano, M., Cruz-Lemus, J., Ruiz, F., & Piattini, M. (2007). Managing software measurement: A metamodel–based approach. *Information Sciences*, *12*(177), 2570–2586. doi:10.1016/j.ins.2007.01.018

Garlan, D., Schmerl, B., & Chang, J. (2001). Using gauges for architecture-based monitoring and adaptation. In *Working Conference on Complex and Dynamic Systems Architecture*, Brisbane, Australia.

Garrido, J. L., Noguera, M., González, M., Hurtado, M. V., & Rodríguez, M. L. (2006). Definition and use of computation independent models in an MDA-based groupware development process. *Science of Computer Programming*, *66*(1), 25–43. doi:10.1016/j.scico.2006.10.008

Garvin, D. A. (1984). What does "product quality" really mean? [Los Alamitos, CA: IEEE Computer Society Press.]. *MIT Sloan Management Review*, *26*(1), 25–43.

Geensys. (2009). *GEENSYS Homepage*. Retrieved July 27, 2009, from Geensys http://www.geensys.com/.

Geerts, G., & McCarthy, W. E. (1999). An Accounting Object Infrastructure for Knowledge-Based Enterprise Models. In *IEEE Intelligent Systems* (pp. 89–94). Their Applications.

Generic Eclipse Modeling System (GEMS). (n.d.). Retrieved March 2010 from http://www.eclipse.org/gmt/gems/

Genero, M., Piattini, M., Abrahao, S., Insfran, E., Carsi, J., & Ramos, I. (2007). A controlled experiment for selecting transformations based on quality attributes in the context of MDA. In *First International Symposium on Empirical Software Engineering and Measurement* (pp.498-498). Washington, DC: IEEE Computer Society

Georges, A., Buytaert, D., & Eeckhout, L. (2007). Statistically rigorous java performance evaluation. In *Proceedings of the 2007 OOPSLA conference* (pp. 57–76).

Gherbi, T., Borne, I., & Meslati, D. (2009). MDE and mobile agents: another reflection on agent migration. In *Proceedings of 11th International Conference on Computer Modelling and Simulation, UKSim 2009*, (pp. 468-473).

Giese, H., & Wagner, R. (2009). From model transformation to incremental bidirectional model synchronization. *Software and Systems Modeling*, *8*(1), 21–43. doi:10.1007/s10270-008-0089-9

GME – Generic Modeling Environment. (2010). (Version 10) [Software]. Available from http://www.isis.vanderbilt.edu/Projects/gme/

Gokhale, A., Schmidt, D., Natarajan, B., & Wang, N. (2002). Applying model-integrated computing to component middleware and enterprise applications. *Communications of the ACM*, *45*(10), 65–70. doi:10.1145/570907.570933

Gokhale, A., Schmidt, D., Natarajan, B., Gray, J., & Wang, N. (2003). *Model-Driven Middleware*. Middleware for Communications.

Gomaa, H. (2004). *Designing Software Product Lines with UML: From Use Cases to Pattern-Based Software Architectures*. Reading, MA: Addison Wesley.

Gomaa, H., & Gianturco, M. (2002). Domain modeling for World Wide Web based on Software Product Lines with UML. In C. Gacek (Ed) *Software Reuse: Methods, Techniques, and Tools, 7th International Conference on Software Reuse, ICSR-7, Austin, TX, USA, April 15-19, 2002, Proceedings*, (LNCS 2319, pp. 78-99). Berlin: Springer-Verlag.

Gomaa, H., & Hussein, M. (2003). Dynamic software reconfiguration in software product families. *International Workshop on Software Product Family Engineering*, Siena, Itlay, (pp. 435–444).

Gomaa, H., & Shin, M. E. (2003). Variability in Multiple-View Models of Software Product Lines. *Procs. Intl Workshop on Software Variability Management, ICSE'03, Portland, Oregon, May 3-11* (pp. 63-68). Washington, DC: IEEE Computer Society.

Gomaa, H., & Webber, D. (2004). Modeling adaptive and evolvable software product lines using the variation point model. In *Proceedings of the Proceedings of the 37th Annual Hawaii International Conference on System Sciences (HICSS'04)-Track*, vol. 9, (pp. 05–08).

Gordijn, J. (2004). E-Business Modeling Using the e3 Value Ontology. In Curry, W. (Ed.), *E-Business Model Ontologies* (pp. 98–128). London: Elsevier Butterworth-Heinemann.

Gordijn, J., van Eck, P., & Wieringa, R. (2008). Requirements Engineering Techniques for e-Services. In Georgakopoulos, D., & Papazoglou, M. P. (Eds.), *Service-Oriented Computing: Cooperative Information Systems series* (pp. 331–352). Cambridge, MA: The MIT Press.

Gordijn, J. (2002). *Value Bassed Requirements Engineering.* Doctor of Philosophie Thesis, Vrije University, Amsterdam, the Netherlands.

Gordijn, J., Akkermans, J. M., & van Vliet, J. C. (2000). Business Modeling is not Process Modeling. In G. Goos, J. Hartmanis & van J. Leeeuwen (Ed.), *Conceptual Modeling for e-Business and the Web,* (LNCS Vol 1921, pp.40-51). Berlin: Springer-Verlag.

Graham, S., & Rhodes, S. (1973). Practical Syntactic Error Recovery in Compilers. In *Symposium on Principles of Programming Languages*, (pp. 52-58), Boston.

Grand, M. (2002). *Patterns in Java: A Catalog of Reusable Design Patterns Illustrated with UML.* Hoboken, NJ: Wiley.

Grangel, R., Chalmeta, R., & Campos, C. (2007). Using UML Profiles for Enterprise Knowledge Modelling. In *Proceedings of the 26th International Conference on Conceptual Modeling (ER 2007), the 3rd International Workshop on Foundations and Practices of UML (FP-UML 2007), LNCS, Computer Science, Theory & Methods* (pp. 125-132). Berlin: Springer Verlag.

Granville, V., Krivanek, M., & Rasson, J. (1994). Simulated annealing: a proof of convergence. *IEEE Transactions on Pattern Analysis and Machine Intelligence, 16,* 652–656. doi:10.1109/34.295910

Gray, J., Lin, Y., & Zhang, J. (2006). Automating Change Evolution in Model-Driven Engineering. *IEEE Computer. Special Issue on Model-Driven Engineering, 39*(2), 51–58.

Gray, J., Tolvanen, J., Kelly, S., Gokhale, A., Neema, S., & Sprinkle, J. (2007). Domain-specific Modeling. In Fishwick, P. (Ed.), *Handbook of Dynamic System Modeling* (pp. 7-1–7-20). Boca Raton, FL: CRC Press.

Greenfield, J., & Short, K. (2004). *Software Factories: Assembling Applications with Patterns, Models, Frameworks, and Tools.* Hoboken, NJ: Wiley.

Grundspenkis, J. (1997). Causal model driven knowledge acquisition for expert diagnostic system development. In Wang, K., & Pranavicius, H. (Eds.), *Application of AI to Production Engineering. Lecture Notes of the Nordic-Baltic Summer School'97* (pp. 251–268). Kaunas, Lithuania: Kaunas University Press.

Grundspenkis, J. (1974). Fault localisation based on topological feature analysis of complex system model. In *Diagnostics and Identification*, (pp. 38-48).

Grundspenkis, J. (1996). Automation of knowledge base development using model supported knowledge acquisition. In *Databases and Information Systems: Proceedings of the 2nd International Baltic Workshop, Tallinn, June 12-14, 1996, 1,* (pp. 224-233). Tallinn, Estonia: Institute of Cybernetics.

Grundspenkis, J. (2004). Automated transformation of the functional model into the diagnosis knowledge base. In *Proceedings of 5th Int. Conf. on Quality, Reliability and Maintenance, QRM2004, Oxford, April 1-2 (Ed. McNulty)* (pp. 295-298). London: Professional Engineering Publishing.

Grundspenkis, J., & Blumbergs, A. (1981). Investigation of complex system topological model structure for analysis of failures. In *Issues of Technical Diagnosis*, (pp. 41-48).

(1997). InGrzegorz, R. (Ed.). Handbook of Graph Grammars and Computing by Graph Transformation: *Vol. I. Foundations*. River Edge, NJ: World Scientific Publishing Co., Inc.

Guide to the Software Engineering Body of Knowledge (SWEBOK). (2004). Retrieved from http://www.computer.org/portal/web/swebok/about

Guo, J., Liao, Y., Gray, J., & Bryant, B. (2005). Using connectors to integrate software components. In *Proceedings of the International Conference on the Engineering of Computer-Based Systems* (ECBS), Greenbelt, MD.

Guttman, M., & Parodi, J. (2007). *Real-life MDA: solving business problems with model driven architecture*. New York: Morgan Kaufmann Publishers.

Hailpern, B., & Tarr, P. (2006). Model-driven development: the good, the bad, and the ugly. *IBM Systems Journal, 45*(3), 451–461. doi:10.1147/sj.453.0451

Hallsteinsen, S., Hinchey, M., Park, S., & Schmid, K. (2008). Dynamic Software Product Lines. *Computer, 41*(4), 93–95. doi:10.1109/MC.2008.123

Halpin, T., & Morgan, T. (2008). *Information Modelling and Relational Databases* (2nd ed.). Burlington, MA: Morgan Kaufman Publisher.

Harmon, P. (2007). *Enterprise Modeling.* Retrieved October, 2009, from http://www.bptrends.com/publicationfiles/advisor20071023.pdf

Harrold, M., Liang, D., & Sinha, S. (1999). An Approach to Analyzing and Testing Component-Based Systems. In *Proceedings of the ICSE'99 Workshop on Testing Distributed Component-Based Systems*, Los Angeles, CA.

Hatcliff, J., Deng, W., Dwyer, W., Jung, G., & Prasad, V. (2003) Cadena: An Integrated Development, Analysis, and Verification Environment for Component-based Systems. In *Proceedings of the 25th International Conference on Software Engineering*, Portland, OR.

Hayes, B. (2008). Cloud Computing. *Communications of the ACM, 51*(7), 9–11. doi:10.1145/1364782.1364786

Heidenreich, F. (2010). *FeatureMapper: Mapping Features to Models.* from http://featuremapper.org/

Henderson, P., & Walters, R. J. (1999). System Design Validation Using Formal Models. In *10th IEEE International Workshop in Rapid System Prototyping 146*(3), 10-14.

Hendryx, S. (2003a, January). *A Home for Business Models in the OMG.* Retrieved November 30, 2009, from Business Rules Journal: http://www.BRCommunity.com/b127.php

Hendryx, S. (2003b). *Integrating Computation Independent Business Modeling Languages into the MDA with UML 2.* Retrieved November 30, 2009, from Object Management Group: http://www.omg.org/docs/ad/03-01-32.doc

Hendryx, S. (2003b, November 14). *Architecture of business modeling.* Retrieved April 8, 2010, from http://www.semanticcore.org/white_papers.htm

Hendryx, S. (2003c). *Integrating computation independent business modeling languages into the MDA with UML 2.* Retrieved November 10, 2009, from Object Management Group: http://www.omg.org/docs/ad/03-01-32.doc

Hendryx, S. (2005, September). Are system requirements business rules? *Business Rules Journal, 6* (9). Retrieved November 10, 2009, from http://www.BRCommunity.com/a2005/ b249.html

Hilyard, J. (2010) No Code Can Hide from the Profiling API in the. NET Framework 2.0. *MSDN Magazine January 2005.* Retrieved 28th May 2010 from http://msdn.microsoft.com/en-us/magazine/cc300553.aspx

Hoffert, J., Schmidt, D., & Gokhale, A. (2007). A QoS policy configuration modeling language for publish/subscribe middleware platforms. In *Proceedings of the International Conference on Distributed Event-Based Systems* (pp. 140–145). New York: ACM.

Hofmeister, C., Nord, R., & Soni, D. (2000). *Applied Software Architecture*. Boston, MA: Addison-Wesley Longman Publishing Co., Inc.

Hongisto, M. (2002). Shadow: Smart and highly adaptive data sharing over weak connections. *1st International Conference on Mobile and Ubiquitous Multimedia, Oulu, Finland, December 11-13.* Oulu, FI: Oulu University Press.

Ho-Won, J., Seung-Gweon, K., & Chang-Shin, Ch. (2004). Measuring Software Product Quality: A Survey of ISO/IEC 9126. *IEEE Software, 21*(5), 88–92. doi:10.1109/MS.2004.1331309

Hruby, P. (2006). *Model-Driven Design of Software Applications with Business Patterns.* Berlin: Springer Verlag.

Hruby, P. (2006). *Model-Driven Design Using Business Patterns.* Berlin: Springer-Verlag.

Huang, S., & Fan, Y. (2007). Model driven and service oriented enterprise integration - the method, framework and platform. In *Proceedings of the Sixth International Conference on Advanced Language Processing and Web Information Technology (ALPIT 2007)* (pp. 504-509). Washington, DC: IEEE Computer Society.

Huynh, S., Cai, Y., Song, Y., & Sullivan, K. (2008). Automatic modularity conformance checking. *International Conference on Software Engineering,* Leipzig, Germany, (pp. 411-420).

IBM Rational DOORS. (2010). [Software]. Available from http://www-01.ibm.com/software/awdtools/doors/

IBM Systems and software development tools. (2009). Retrieved October, 2009, from http://www-01.ibm.com/software/rational/offerings/architecture

IEEE. (2000). *IEEE recommended practice for architectural description of software-intesive systems.* Washington, DC: IEEE Architecture Working Group.

IEEE. (2000). *IEEE Std 1417:2000 - Recommended Practice for Architectural descriptions of Software Intensive Systems.* Los Alamitos, CA: IEEE.

IEEE. (2001). IEEE Standard Test Access Port and Boundary-scan Architecture. *IEEE Std.* 1149.1-2001.

IEEE. 1042. (1987). *IEEE Guide to Software Configuration Management.* IEEE/ANSI Standard 1042-1987.

INCOSE. (2009). *Requirements Management Tools Survey.* Retrieved October, 2009, from http://www.incose.org/ProductsPubs/Products/rmsurvey.aspx

Institut National de Recherche en Informatique et en Automatique (INRIA). (2009). *Model transformation at Inria.* Retrieved December 07, 2009, from Institut National de Recherche en Informatique et en Automatique (INRIA) http://modelware.inria.fr/

Intel Corporation. (2006) *Intel 64 and IA-32 Architectures Software Developer's Manual,* (Vol. 3B, System Programming Guide, Part 2). Retrieved 4 January 2007 from http://www.intel.com/products/processor/manuals/

International Standard, ISO/IEC 19502 (2005, November 01).

International Standard, ISO/IEC 19503 (2005, November 01).

International Standard, IEC 61346-1 (1996-2003).

ISO/IEC 15944-4:2006 Information technology – Business Agreement Semantic Descriptive Techniques – Part 4: Open-EDI Business Transaction Ontology. (2006). Retrieved May 04, 2009, from http://www.itu.dk/~hessellund/REA2006/papers/McCarthy.pdf

ISO/IEC 19502:2005(E). (2005). *Meta Object Facility (MOF) Specification,* Version 1.4.1. Retrieved March 08, 2009, from http://www.omg.org/cgi-bin/doc?formal/05-05-05.pdf

ISO/IEC 25000:(2005) (E), *Software engineering – Software Quality and Requirements Evaluation (SQuaRE) Guide to SQuaRE.*

ISO/IEC 9075:(2003) *(part 1, 2), Information technology – Database languages-SQL.*

ISO/IEC 9126-1:(2001) (E), *Software engineering – Product quality – Part 1: Quality model.*

ISO/IEC 9126-3:(2003) (E), *Software engineering – Product quality – Part 3: Internal metrics.*

Jaaksi, A., Alto, J.-M., & Vatto, K. (1999). *Tried & True Object Development: Industry-Proven Approaches with UML.* New York: Cambridge University Press.

Jackson, J. (1991). A keyphrase based traceability scheme. *IEE Colloquium on Tools and Techniques for Maintaining Traceability During Design,* London, UK, (pp. 2/1-2/4).

Jackson, M. (1999). *The Real World.* Retrieved November 20, 2009, from Problem Analysis and the Problem Frames Approach. Jackson Methods Home Page: http://www.jacksonworkbench.co.uk/stevefergspages/pfa/index.html

Jackson, M. (2005). *Problem Frames and Software Engineering*. Retrieved November 30, 2009, from Problem Analysis and the Problem Frames Approach. Jackson Methods Home Page: http://www.jacksonworkbench.co.uk/stevefergspages/pfa/index.html

Jacobsen, I., Erikson, N., & Jacobsen, A. (1995). *The Object Advantage: Business Process Reengineering with Object Technology*. Wokingham, UK: Addison-Wesley.

Jacobson, I., Christerson, M., Jonsson, P., & Overgaard, G. (1992). *Object-Oriented Software Engineering: A Use Case Driven Approach*. Reading, MA: Addison-Wesley.

Jacobson, I., Griss, M., & Jonsson, P. (1997). *Software reuse: architecture process and organization for business success*. New York: ACM Press.

Jaring, M., & Bosch, J. (2002). Representing Variability in Software Product Lines: A Case Study. In *Proceedings of the Second International Conference on Software Product Lines* (LNCS 2379, pp. 15-36). London: Springer-Verlag.

Java Jetty Server. (n.d.). Retrieved March 2010 from http://www.mortbay.org/jetty/

JavaScript Object Notation (JSON). (n.d.). Retrieved March 2010 from http://www.json.org/

Jeary, S., Fouad, A., & Phalp, K. (2008). Extending the model driven architecture with a pre-CIM level. In *Proceedings of the 1st International Workshop on Business Support for MDA co-located with TOOLS EUROPE 2008*. Retrieved October 30, 2009, from http://ftp.informatik.rwth-aachen.de/Publications/CEUR-WS/Vol-376/

Jensen, K. (1997). Coloured Petri nets. Basic concepts, analysis methods and practical use. Monographs in theoretical computer science. 2nd corrected printing: *Vol. 1. Basic Concepts*. Berlin: Springer-Verlag.

Jensen, K. (1996). *Coloured Petri nets: basic concepts, analysis methods, and practical use*. Berlin: Springer Verlag.

Johannesson, P. (2007). The Role of Business Models in Enterprise Modeling. In Krogstie, J., Opdahl, A., & Brinkkemper, S. (Eds.), *Conceptual Modeling in Information Systems Engineering* (pp. 123–140). Berlin: Springer-Verlag. doi:10.1007/978-3-540-72677-7_8

Johnston, S. (2005). *UML 2.0 Profile for Software Services*. Armonk, NY: IBM Cooperation. Retrieved March 15, 2009, from http://www.ibm.com/developerworks/rational/library/05/419_soa/

Jones, C. (2009). Positive and negative innovations in software engineering. *International Journal of Software Science and Computational Intelligence, 1*(2), 20–30.

Jönsson, P. (2007). *Exploring Process Aspects of Change Impact Analysis*. Blekinge Institute of Technology Doctoral Dissertation Series. No 2007:13.

Jouault, F., Allilaire, F., Bézivin, J., & Kurtev, I. (2008). ATL: A Model Transformation Tool. *Science of Computer Programming, 72*(1&2), 31–39. doi:10.1016/j.scico.2007.08.002

Jouault, F., & Kurtev, I. (2005). *Transforming Models with ATL*. Paper presented at the Model Transformations in Practice Workshop at MoDELS 2005.

Jouault, F., Bezivin, J., Chevrel, R., & Gray, J. (2006). Experiments in Runtime Model Extraction. *Models@run.time, held at MODELS 2006*, Genova, Italy, October 2006.

Jurack, S., Lambers, L., Mehner, K., & Taentzer, G. (2008). Sufficient Criteria for Consistent Behavior Modeling with Refined Activity Diagrams. In K. Czarnecki, I. Ober, J.-M. Bruel, A. Uhl, & M. Völter (Eds.), *Lecture Notes in Computer Science (LNCS), Model driven engineering languages and systems. 11th international conference, MoDELS 2008, Toulouse, France, September 28 - October 3, 2008; proceedings* (pp. 341–355). Berlin: Springer.

Kabanda, S., & Adigun, M. (2006). Extending Model Driven Architecture benefits to requirements engineering. In *Proceedings of SAICSIT*, University of Zululand (pp. 22-30).

Kaindl, H. (1993). The missing link in requirements engineering. *ACM SIGSOFT Software Engineering Notes, 18*(2), 30–39. doi:10.1145/159420.155836

Kaindl, H., Smialek, M., Svetinovic, D., Ambroziewicz, A., Bojarski, J., Nowakowski, W., et al. (2007). *Requirements specification language definition.* Project Deliverable D2.4.1, ReDSeeDS Project, Retrieved June 17, 2009 from www.redseeds.eu

Kalibera, T., Bulej, L., & Tuma, P. (2005). Benchmark precision and random initial state. In *Proceedings of the 2005 International Symposium on Performance Evaluation of Computer and Telecommunications Systems, SPECTS 2005,* (pp. 853–862). Citeseer.

Kalnins, A., Barzdins, J., & Celms, E. (2005). Model Transformation Language MOLA. In *Proceedings of MDAFA 2004,* (LNCS 3599, pp. 62-76). Berlin: Springer.

Kang, K. C., Lee, J., & Donohoe, P. (2002). Feature-oriented Product Line Engineering. *IEEE Software, 19*(4), 58–65. doi:10.1109/MS.2002.1020288

Kang, K., Cohen, S., Hess, J., Novak, W., & Peterson, A. (1990). *Feature-oriented domain analysis (FODA) feasibility study.* Technical Report CMU/SEI-90-TR-21, Software Engineering Institute, Carnegie Mellon University, Pittsburgh, PA.

Kanyaru, J. M., Coles, M., Jeary, S., & Phalp, K. (2008). Using visualisation to elicit domain information as part of the model driven architecture (MDA) approach. In *Proceedings of the 1st International Workshop on Business Support for MDA co-located with TOOLS EUROPE 2008.* Retrieved October 30, 2009, from http://ftp.informatik.rwth-aachen.de/Publications/CEUR-WS/Vol-376/

Kappel, G., Kapsammer, E., Kargl, H., Kramler, G., Reiter, T., Retschitzegger, W., et al. (2006). Lifting Metamodels to Ontologies - A Step to the Semantic Integration of Modeling Languages. In *Proceedings of International Conference on Model Driven Engineering Languages and Systems (MoDELS),* (LNCS 4199, pp. 528–542), Genova, Italy. Berlin: Springer-Verlag.

Karsai, G., Neema, S., & Sharp, D. (2008). Model-driven architecture for embedded software: A synopsis and an example. *Science of Computer Programming, 73*(1), 26–38. doi:10.1016/j.scico.2008.05.006

Kavakli, E., & Loucopoulos, P. (2004). Goal Driven Requirements Engineering: Analysis and Critique of Current Methods. In Krogstie, J., Halpin, T., & Siau, K. (Eds.), *Information Modeling Methods and Methodologies (Adv. topics of Database Research)* (pp. 102–124). Hershey, PA: IDEA Group.

Kavimandan, A., & Gokhale, A. (2008). Automated middleware QoS configuration techniques using model transformations. In *Proceedings of the 14th IEEE Real-Time and Embedded Technology and Applications Symposium* (pp. 93–102). Washington, D.C.: IEEE Computer Society

Keepence, B., & Mannion, M. (1999). Using patterns to Model Variability in Software Architectures. *IEEE Software, 16*(4), 102–108. doi:10.1109/52.776957

Kelly, S., & Tolvanen, J.-P. (2008). *Domain-Specific Modeling: Enabling Full Code Generation.* Chichester, UK: John Wiley & Sons, Ltd.

Kent, S. (2002). Model Driven Engineering. In *Proceedings of the Third International Conference on Integrated Formal Methods,* (pp. 286–298). London: Springer-Verlag.

Keung Luk, C., Cohn, R., Muth, R., Patil, H., Klauser, A., & Lowney, G. (2005). Pin: Building customized program analysis tools with dynamic instrumentation. In *Programming Language Design and Implementation* (pp. 190–200). New York: ACM Press.

Kherraf, S., Lefebvre, E., & Suryn, W. (2008). Transformation from CIM to PIM Using Patterns and Archetypes. In *Proceedings of the 19th Australian Software Engineering Conference,* (pp. 338-346). Washington, DC: IEEE Computer Society.

Kifer, M., Brenstein, A., & Lewis, P. M. (2006). *Database Systems. An Application-Oriented Approach* (2nd ed.). New York: Addison Wesley.

Kindler, E., & Wagner, R. (2007). *Triple Graph Grammars: Concepts, Extensions, Implementations, and Application Scenarios: Technical Report*. University of Paderborn, Germany. Retrieved November 27, 2008, from http://wwwcs.uni-paderborn.de/cs/ag-schaefer/Veroeffentlichungen/Quellen/Papers/2007/tr-ri-07-284.pdf.

Kircher, M., & Jain, P. (2004). *Pattern-Oriented Software Architecture: Patterns for Resource Management*. Hoboken, NJ: Wiley.

Kirikova, M. (2000a, May). Explanatory capability of enterprise models. *Data & Knowledge Engineering*, *33*(2), 119–136. doi:10.1016/S0169-023X(99)00048-8

Kirikova, M. (1998). Consistency of Information in Requirements Engineering. In Charrel, J. P., Jaakkola, H., Kangassalo, H., & Kawaguchi, E. (Eds.), *Information Modelling and Knowledge bases IX* (pp. 192–205). Amsterdam: IOS Press.

Kirikova, M. (2001). Business modelling and use cases in requirements engineering. In Jaakkola, H., Kangassalo, H., & Kawaguchi, E. (Eds.), *Information modelling and knowledge bases XII* (pp. 410–420). Amsterdam: IOS Press.

Kirikova, M. (2000b). Potential role of enterprise models in organisational knowledge processing. In Kawaguchi, E., Kangassalo, H., Jaakkola, H., & Hamid, I. A. (Eds.), *Information modelling and knowledge bases XI* (pp. 114–127). Amsterdam: IOS Press.

Kirikova, M., & Makna, J. (2005). Renaissance of Business Process Modelling. In Vasilecas, O., Caplinskas, A., Wojtkowski, G., Wojtkowski, W., & Zupancic, J. (Eds.), *IS Development Advances in Theory, Practice, and Education* (pp. 403–414). Berlin: Springer.

Kirikova, M. (2004). Interplay of tacit and explicit knowledge in Requirements Engineering. In H.Fujitaand, & V.Gruhn (Eds.), *New Trends in Software Methodologies, Tools and Techniques: Proceedings of the third SoMet_W04* (pp. 77-86.). Amsterdam: IOS Press.

Kirikova, M., Finke, A., & Grundspenkis, J. (2010). What is CIM: an information system perspective. In J.Grunspenkis, M.Kirikova, Y.Manopoulos, & L.Novickis (Eds.), *Advances in Databases and Information Systems associated Workshops and Doctoral Consortium of the 13th East European Conference (ADBIS 2009)* (LNCS 5968, pp.169-176). Berlin: Springer.

Klar, F., Königs, A., & Schürr, A. (2007). Model transformation in the large. In *ESEC-FSE '07: Proceedings of the the 6th joint meeting of the European software engineering conference and the ACM SIGSOFT symposium on the foundations of software engineering* (pp. 285–294). New York: ACM.

Klar, F., Rose, S., & Schürr, A. (2008). A Meta-Model-Driven Tool Integration Development Process. In R. Kaschek, G. Fliedl, C. Kop, & C. Steinberger (Eds.), *Information Systems and e-Business Technologies, 2nd International United Information Systems Conference, UNISCON 2008, Klagenfurt, Austria, April 22-25, 2008. Proceedings* (LNBI Vol. 5. pp. 201–212). Berlin: Springer-Verlag.

Klar, F., Rose, S., & Schürr, A. (2009). TiE - A Tool Integration Environment. In J. Oldevik, G. K. Olsen, T. Neple, & D. S. Kolovos (Eds.), *CTIT Workshop Proceedings, Proceedings of the 5th ECMDA Traceability Workshop* (pp. 39–48).

Kleppe, A., Warmer, J., & Bast, W. (2003). *MDA Explained*. Reading, MA: Addison-Wesley Professional.

Kolmogorov, A. N. (1999). *Elements of the theory of functions and functional analysis*. New York: Dover Publications.

Kolmogorov, A. N., & Fomin, S. V. (1975). *Introductory real analysis* (Silverman, R. A., Ed.). Mineola, NY: Courier Dover Publications.

Körtgen, A.-T., & Heukamp, S. (2008). Correspondence Analysis for Supporting Document Re-Use in Development Processes. In *Proceedings of the 11th World Conference on Integrated Design & Process Technology (IDPT 2008). Asia University Taichung, Taiwan, June 1-6, 2008* (pp. 194–205).

Körtgen, A.-T., & Mosler, C. (2008). Recovering Structural Consistency between Design and Implementation using Correspondence Relations. In D. A. Karras, D. Wei, & J. Zendulka (Eds.), *International Conference on Software Engineering Theory and Practice (SETP-08). Orlando, Florida, USA, July 7-10 2008* (pp. 53–60).

Kounev, S. (2006). Performance modeling and evaluation of distributed component-based systems using queueing petri nets. *IEEE Transactions on Software Engineering, 32*(7), 486–502. doi:10.1109/TSE.2006.69

Krishna, A., Turkay, E., Gokhale, A., & Schmidt, D. (2005). Model-Driven Techniques for Evaluating the QoS of Middleware Configurations for DRE Systems. In *Proceedings of the 11th IEEE Real-Time and Embedded Technology and Applications Symposium*, San Francisco, CA.

Kristensen, L., Christensen, S., & Jensen, K. (1998). The practitioner's guide to coloured Petri nets. *International Journal on Software Tools for Technology Transfer, 2*, 98–132. doi:10.1007/s100090050021

Kristensen, L., Jurgensen, J., & Jensen, K. (2004). Application of coloured Petri nets in system development. In J. Desel, W. Reisig, & G. Rozenberg (Eds.), *Lectures on Concurrency and Petri Nets. Advanced in Petri Nets. Proc. of 4th Advanced Course on Petri Nets* (LNCS 3098, pp. 626-685). Berlin: Springer-Verlag.

Kroll, P., & Kruchten, P. (2003). *Rational Unified Process Made Easy, A Practitioner's Guide to the RUP*. Boston: Addison-Wesley Professional.

Kruchten, P. (1995, November). The 4+1 view model of architecture. *IEEE Software*, 42–50. doi:10.1109/52.469759

Kruchten, P. (1998). *The Rational Unified Process*. Reading, MA: Addison-Wesley Pub.

Kruchten, P. (2000). *The Rational Unified Process: An Introduction*. Upper Saddle River, NJ: Addison-Wesley.

Kruchten, P. (1995). The 4+1 view model of architecture. *IEEE Software, 12*(6), 42–50. doi:10.1109/52.469759

Kühne, T. (2006). Matters of (Meta-) Modeling. *Software and Systems Modeling*, (4), 369–385.

Kumar, V. (1992). Algorithms for Constraint-Satisfaction Problems: A Survey. *AI Magazine, 13*(1), 32–44.

Kurtev, I., Bézivin, J., Jouault, F., & Valduriez, P. (2006). Model-based DSL frameworks. In *OOPSLA '06: Companion to the 21st ACM SIGPLAN symposium on object-oriented programming systems, languages, and applications* (pp. 602–616). New York: ACM.

Laguna, M. A., López, O., & Crespo, Y. (2004). Reuse, Standardization, and Transformation of Requirements, (LNCS 3107, pp. 329-338). Berlin: Springer

Laguna, M., & Gonzaonza, M. G, B., & Marque, J. (2007). Seamless development of software product lines. In *Proceedings of the 6th international conference on Generative programming and component engineering*, (pp. 94).

Lamouchi, O., Cherif, A. R., & Levy, N. (2008). A Framework Based Measurements for Evaluating an IS Quality. In A. Hinze, M. Kirchberg, (Ed.), *Proc. Fifth Asia-Pacific Conference on Conceptual Modelling* (pp. 39–47). Wollongong, Australia: CRPIT, 79, ACS.

Lankhorst, M. (2005). *Enterprise architecture at work, modelling, communication, and analysis*. Berlin: Springer.

Lapouchnian, A., & Lesperance, Y. (2006). Modeling mental states in agent-oriented requirements engineering. In E. Dubois, & K. Pohl (Eds.), *Advanced IS engineering. Proceedings of the 18th International conference (CAISE 2006), Luxembourg, Luxembourg, June 5-9, 2006* (LNCS 4001, pp. 480-494). Berlin: Springer.

Lara, J., & de, , Jaramillo, Ermel, C., Taentzer, G., & Ehrig, K. (2004). Parallel Graph Transformation for Model Simulation applied to Timed Transition Petri Nets. *Electronic Notes in Theoretical Computer Science, 109*, 17–29. doi:10.1016/j.entcs.2004.02.053

Larman, C. (2001). *Applying UML and Patterns: An Introduction to Object-Oriented Analysis and Design and the Unified Process*. Upper Saddle River, NJ: Prentice Hall.

Lau, K.-K., & Wang, Z. (2005). A Taxonomy of Software Component Models. In *Proceeding of 31st EUROMICRO Conference of Software Engineering and Advanced Applications* (pp. 88-95). Washington, DC: IEEE Computer Society.

Lazăr, I., Pârv, B., Motogna, S., Czibula, I.-G., & Lazăr, C.-L. (2007). An Agile MDA Approach for Executable UML Structured Activities. *Studia Univ. Babeş-Bolyai. Informatica, LII*(2), 101–114.

Lazăr, C.-L., Lazăr, I., Pârv, B., Motogna, S., & Czibula, I.-G. (2009). Using an fUML Action Language to Construct UML Models, In *11th International Symposium on Symbolic and Numeric Algorithms for Scientific Computing*, Timisoara, Romania.

Lazăr, I., Pârv, B., Motogna, S., Czibula, I.-G., & Lazăr, C.-L. (2008). iCOMPONENT: A Platform-independent Component Model for Dynamic Execution Environments, In *10th International Symposium on Symbolic and Numeric Algorithms for Scientific Computing* (pp. 257-264), Timisoara, Romania. Washington, DC: IEEE Computer Society.

Leal, L., Pires, P., & Campos, M. (2006). Natural MDA: Controlled Natural Language for Action Specifications on Model Driven Development. In *Proceedings of OTM 2006*, (LNCS 4275, pp. 551–568).

Ledeczi, A., Bakay, A., Maroti, M., Volgyesi, P., Nordstrom, G., Sprinkle, J., & Karsai, G. (2001). Composing Domain-specific Design Environments. *IEEE Computer, 34*(11), 44–51.

Ledeczi, A., Maroti, M., Bakay, A., Karsai, G., Garrett, J., Thomason, C., et al. (2001b). The generic modeling environment. In *Workshop on Intelligent Signal Processing, Budapest, Hungary*, vol. 17.

Ledeczi, A., Nordstrom, G., Karsai, G., Volgyesi, P., & Maroti, M. (2001a). On metamodel composition. In *IEEE CCA*.

Lee, C., Kim, J., Stach, J., & Park, E. K. (2001). Simulating agent based processing in an ads using c++ sim. In *ISADS '01: Proceedings of the Fifth International Symposium on Autonomous Decentralized Systems*, (pp. 231). Washington, DC: IEEE Computer Society.

Lefering, M. (1993). An incremental integration tool between requirements engineering and programming in the large. *International Symposium on Requirements Engineering*, San Diego, CA, (pp. 82-89).

Leffingwell, D., & Widrig, D. (2003). *Managing Software Requirements: a use case approach* (2nd ed.). Reading, MA: Addison-Wesley.

Lehman, M. M., & Belady, L. (1985). *Program evolution: processes of software change*. New York: Academic Press Professional.

Leonardi, M. C., & Mauco, M. V. (2004). Integrating natural language oriented requirements models into MDA. In [WER]. *Proceedings of Workshop on Requirements Engineering, 2004*, 65–76.

Li, G., & Jacobsen, H. (2005). Composite subscriptions in content-based publish/subscribe systems. In *Proceedings of the 6th International Middleware Conference* (pp. 249-269). New York: Springer-Verlag New York, Inc.

Lieberherr, K. J., & Xiao, C. (1993, April). Object-oriented software evolution. *IEEE Transactions on Software Engineering, 19*(4), 313–343. doi:10.1109/32.223802

Lientz, B. P., & Swanson, E. B. (1980). *Software Maintenance Management: A Study of the Maintenance of Computer Application Software in 487 Data Processing Organizations*. Reading, MA: Addison-Wesley.

Lightstone, S., Teorey, T., & Nadeau, T. (2007). *Physical Database Design. The Database Professional's Guide to Exploiting Indexes, Views, Storage, and More*. San Francisco, CA: Morgan Kaufman Publisher.

Lillehagen, F., & Kroghstie, J. (2008). *Active Knowledge Modeling of Enterprises*. Berlin: Springer. doi:10.1007/978-3-540-79416-5

Lin, Y., Gray, J., & Jouault, F. (2007). DSMDiff: a differentiation tool for domain-specific models. *European Journal of Information Systems, 16*(4), 349–361. doi:10.1057/palgrave.ejis.3000685

Lindvall, M., & Sandahl, K. (1998). How well do experienced software developers predict software change? *Journal of Systems and Software, 43*(1), 19–27. doi:10.1016/S0164-1212(98)10019-5

López-Sanz, M., Acuña, C. J., Cuesta, C. E., & Marcos, E. (2008). *UML Profile for the Platform Independent Modelling of Service-Oriented Architectures,* (LNCS Vol 4758, pp. 304-307). Berlin: Springer.

Loyall, J., Ye, J., Shapiro, R., Neema, S., Mahadevan, N., Abdelwahed, S., et al. (2004). A Case Study in Applying QoS Adaptation and Model-Based Design to the Design-Time Optimization of Signal Analyzer Applications. *Military Communications Conference (MILCOM),* Monterey, California.

Makna, J. (2009). Business process aware IS change management in SMEs. In *Advances in Databases and IS, Proceedings of the 13th East European Conference (ADBIS 2009),* (pp. 28-42). Berlin: Springer.

Maletic, J. I., Collard, M. L., & Simoes, B. (2005). An XML based approach to support the evolution of model-to-model traceability links. *International Workshop on Traceability in Emerging Forms of Software Engineering,* Long Beach, CA, (pp. 67-72).

Mannisto, T., Soininen, R., & Sulonen, R. (2001). Product Configuration View to Software Product Families. In *Proceedings of the 10th Int. Workshop on Software Configuration Management (SCM-10) of ICSE,* Ontario, Canada.

Markovic, S., & Baar, T. (2005). *Refactoring OCL Annotated UML Class Diagram.* Paper presented at the International Conference On Model Driven Engineering Languages And Systems

Markovitch, Z., & Rekners, Y. (1998). Synthesis of systems model on basis of topological minimodels. *Automatic Control and Computer Sciences, 32*(3), 59–66.

Markovitch, Z., & Markovitcha, I. (2000). Modelling as a tool for therapy selection. In *Proc. Of the 14th European Simulation Multiconference "Simulation and Modelling,"* (pp. 621-623), Ghent, Belgium.

Markovitch, Z., & Stalidzans, E. (2000). Expert based model building using incidence matrix and topological models. In *Proc. Of the 12th European Simulation Symposium "Simulation in Industry 2000",* (pp. 328-332), Hamburg, Germany.

Markovitcha, I., & Markovitch, Z. (1970). Mathematical model of pathogenesis of hard differentiable diseases. *Cybernetics and Diagnostics, 4,* 21–28.

Marshall, C. (2000). *Enterprise modeling with UML: designing successful software through business analysis.* Reading, MA: Addison-Wesley Professional.

Martin, C. F. (1988). *User-centered requirements analysis.* Englewood Cliffs, NJ: Prentice Hall.

Marzolla, M., & Balsamo, S. (2004). Uml-psi: The uml performance simulator. In *Quantitative Evaluation of Systems, 2004* (pp. 340–341). QEST. doi:10.1109/QEST.2004.1348057

Matena, V., & Hapner, M. (1999). *Enterprise Java Beans Specification, Version 1.1.* Sun Microsystems.

Matinlassi, M., Niemelä, E., & Dobrica, L. (2002). *Quality-driven architecture design and quality analysis method – A revolutionary initiation approach to product line architecture, VTT Publications 456.* Espoo, Finland: VTT Technical Research Centre of Finland.

Matjaz, B. J., & Kapil, P. (2008). *Business Process Driven SOA using BPMN and BPEL.* Birmingham, UK: Packt Publishing.

Mazzocca, N., Rak, M., & Villano, U. (2000). The transition from a pvm program simulator to a heterogeneous system simulator: The hesse project. In *Proceedings of the 7th European PVM/MPI Users 'Group Meeting on Recent Advances in Parallel Virtual Machine and Message Passing Interface,* (pp. 266–273). London: Springer-Verlag.

McCarthy, W. E. (1982). REA Accounting Model: A Generalized Framework for Accounting Systems in a Shared Data Environment. *Accounting Review, 57*(3), 554–578.

McComas, D., Leake, S., Stark, M., & Morisio, M. Travassos, & G., White, M. (2000). Addressing Variability in a Guidance, Navigation, and Control Flight Software Product Line. In *Proceedings of Product Line Architecture Workshop, The First Software Product Line Conference (SPLC1), Denver Co, USA, Fraunhofer IESE-Report No. 053.00/E, August 2000* (pp. 85-96).

McGregor, J. (2005). *The evolution of product-line assets.* Technical Report CMU/SEI-2003-TR-005, Software Engineering Institute, Carnegie Mellon University, Pittsburgh, PA. *MetaEdit+* (2010). [Software]. Available from http://www.metacase.com/

MDA. (2009). *OMG Model Driven Architecture.* Retrieved October, 2009, from http://www.omg.org/mda

Mellor, S., Scott, K., Uhl, A., & Weise, D. (2004). *MDA distilled: principles of model-driven architecture.* Reading, MA: Addison-Wesley Professional.

Mellor, S. J., & Balcer, M. J. (2002). *Executable UML: A Foundation for Model-Driven Architecture.* Boston: Addison Wesley.

Mellor, S. J. (2005). *Agile MDA,* Technical report, OMG. Retrieved May 20, 2009, from http://www.omg.org/mda/mda_files/Agile_MDA.pdf

Memon, A., Porter, A., Yilmaz, C., Nagarajan, A., & Schmidt, D. Natarajan. B. (2004). Skoll: Distributed Continuous Quality Assurance. In *Proceedings of the 26th International Conference on Software Engineering,* Edinburgh, Scotland, (pp. 459-468).

Menasce, D., & Almeida, V. (2002). *Capacity Planning for Web Services: metrics, models, and methods.* Upper Saddle River, NJ: Prentice Hall.

Menasce, D., Dowdy, L., & Almeida, V. (2004). *Performance by design: computer capacity planning by example.* Upper Saddle River, NJ: Prentice Hall PTR.

Mens, T., Czarnecki, K., & Van Gorp, P. (2005). A Taxonomy of Model Transformations. In Bézivin, J., & Heckel, R. (Eds.), *Language Engineering for Model-Driven Software Development.*

Meszaros, G., & Doble, J. (1997). A Pattern Language for Pattern Writing. In Martin, R. C., Riehle, D., & Buschmann, F. (Eds.), *Pattern Languages of Program Design 3* (pp. 529–574). Upper Saddle River, NJ: Addison-Wesley.

Metzger, A., Heymans, P., Pohl, K., Schobbens, P., & Saval, G. (2007). Disambiguating the documentation of variability in software product lines: A separation of concerns, formalization and automated analysis. In *Proceedings of the Requirements Engineering Conference,* (pp. 243–253).

Meyer, B. (2000). *Object-Oriented Software Construction.* New York: Prentice Hall, Inc.

Microsoft. (1995). *Component Object Model.* Redmond, WA: Microsoft, Inc. Retrieved May 20, 2009, from: http://www.microsoft.com/com/

Microsoft. (2003). Windows Server 2003 Performance Counters Reference. *TechNet.* (Electronic media) Retrieved May 28, 2010, from http://technet.microsoft.com/en-us/library/cc776490%28WS.10%29.aspx

Microsystems, S. (2003). *Enterprise JavaBeans Specification.* Retrieved October 2007, from: http://java.sun.com/products/ejb/docs.html

Miller, G. (1956). The magical number seven, plus or minus two: some limits on our capacity for processing information. *Psychological Review, 63*(2), 81–97. doi:10.1037/h0043158

Miller, J., & Mukerji, J. (2003). *MDA Guide version 1.0.1.* Retrieved from http://www.omg.org/

Mitschke, R., & Eichberg, M. (2008). Supporting the evolution of software product lines. *Traceability Workshop,* Berlin, Germany, (pp. 87-96).

Model Driven Community. (2009). *fUML MagicDraw plugin.* Retrieved Oct, 2009, from: http://portal.modeldriven.org/content/fuml-reference-implementation-download

Modeling and Analysis of Real-time and Embedded systems. (2008). Retrieved from http://www.omgmarte. org/ Specification.htm

MOF 2.0 (2006). *Meta Object Facility*. Retrieved from http://www.omg.org/spec/MOF/2.0/

Mohagheghi, P., & Dehlen, V. (2008). *Developing a Quality Framework for Model-Driven Engineering. Models in Software Engineering* (pp. 275–289). Heidelberg: Springer.

Mohagheghi, P., Dehlen, V., & Neple, T. (2009). Definitions and approaches to model quality in model-based software development – A review of literature. *Information and Software Technology, 51*, 1646–1669. doi:10.1016/j. infsof.2009.04.004

Moon, M., Yeom, K., & Chae, H. S. (2005). An approach to developing domain requirements as a core asset based on commonality and variability analysis in a product line. *IEEE Transactions on Software Engineering, 31*(7), 551–569. doi:10.1109/TSE.2005.76

Moreira, A., Rashid, A., & Araújo, J. (2005, 2005). *Multi-Dimensional Separation of Concerns in Requirements Engineering*. Paper presented at the Proceedings of the 13th IEEE International Conference on Requirements Engineering, France.

Moreno-Vozmediano, R., Montero, R., & Llorente, I. (2009). Elastic Management of Cluster-based Services in the Cloud. In *Proceedings of the 1st Workshop on Automated Control for Datacenters and Clouds,* Barcelona, Spain, (pp. 19– 24).

Morganho, H., Gomes, C., Pimentão, J. P., Ribeiro, R., Grammel, B., Pohl, C., et al. (2008). *Requirement Specifications for Industrial Case Studies* (AMPLE Project, Deliverable D5.2). Object Management Group (OMG). *Object Management Group*. from http://www.omg.org/

Morisio, M., Seaman, C., Basili, V., Parra, A., Kraft, S., & Condon, S. (2002). COTS-based software development: Processes and open issues. *Journal of Systems and Software, 61*(3), 189–199. doi:10.1016/S0164-1212(01)00147-9

Morisio, M., Travassos, G., & Stark, M. (2000). Extending UML to Support Domain Analysis. In *Proceedings of the 15ᵗʰ IEEE International Conference on Automated software engineering* (pp.321). Washington, DC: IEEE Computer Society.

Motogna, S., Lazăr, I., Pârv, B., & Czibula, I. (2009). An Agile MDA Approach for Service-Oriented Components. In J. Happe, B. Zimmerova (Eds.) *6th International Workshop on Formal Engineering approaches to Software Components and Architectures (FESCA), PreProceedings* (pp. 2-17). York, Electronic Notes in Theoretical Computer Science.

Mukherjee, P., Kovacevic, A., Benz, M., & Schürr, A. (2007). Towards a Peer-to-Peer Based Global Software Development Environment. In K. Herrmann & B. Bruegge (Eds.), *Vol. 121. Lecture Notes in Informatics, Software Engineering 2008. Fachtagung des GI-Fachbereichs Softwaretechnik, 18. - 22.02.2008 in München,* (pp. 204–216). Bonn, Germany: Gesellschaft für Informatik.

Munoz, J., Pelechano, V., & Fons, J. (2004). Model Driven Development of Pervasive Systems. *ERCIM News, 58*, 50–51.

Nagl, M. (1996). *Building Tightly Integrated Software Development Environments: The IPSEN Approach.* (LNCS Vol. 1170). Berlin: Springer.

Nechypurenko, A., Wuchner, E., White, J., & Schmidt, D. (2007). Application of Aspect-based Modeling and Weaving for Complexity Reduction in the Development of Automotive Distributed Realtime Embedded Systems. In *Proceedings of the 6th International Conference on Aspect-Oriented Software Development,* Vancouver, British Columbia, (pp. 10).

Niemelä, E., Matinlassi, M., & Lago, P. (2003). Architecture-centric approach to wireless service engineering. *IEC Annual Review of Communications, 56*, 875–889.

Niemelä, E., & Vaskivuo, T. (2004). Agile Middleware of Pervasive Computing Environments. In *Proceedings of the Second IEEE Anual Conference on Pervasive Computing and Communications Workshops* (p.192). Washington DC: IEEE Computer Society.

Noble, B. D., Narayannan, D., Tilton, J. E., Flinn, J., & Walker, K. R. (1997). Agile Application-Aware Adaptation for Mobility. *ACM SIGOPS Operating Systems Review, 31*(5), 276–287. doi:10.1145/269005.266708

OASIS - Web Services Business Process Execution Language Version 2.0., WS-BPEL. (2007). Retrieved May 04, 2009, from http://docs.oasis-open.org/wsbpel/2.0/OS/wsbpel-v2.0-OS.html

OASIS. (2006). *Web services brokered notification 1.3.* Retrieved December 11, 2009 from http://docs.oasis-open.org/wsn/wsn-ws_brokered_notification-1.3-spec-os.pdf.

OASIS. (2007). *SCA Service Component Architecture. Assembly Model Specification*, Version 1.1. Retrieved October 2007, from: http://www.oasis-opencsa.org/sca

Object Computing Incorporated. (2006). *A Window into your Systems.* [Electronic media] Retrieved 28th May 2010 from http://www.ociweb.com/products/OVATION

Object Management Group. (2006, January). *Meta Object Facility (MOF) core specification.* Retrieved December 2009, from http://www.omg.org/spec/MOF/2.0/PDF/

Object Management Group. (2006a). *Meta Object Facility (MOF) 2.0 Core Specification.* OMG Available Specification. Retrieved June 25, 2009, from Object Management Group: http://www.omg.org/cgi-bin/doc?formal/06-01-01.pdf.

Object Management Group. (2006b). *Object Constraint Language (OCL), Version 2.0.* OMG Available Specification. Retrieved June 25, 2009, from Object Management Group http://www.omg.org/cgi-bin/doc?formal/06-05-01.pdf.

Object Management Group. (2008). *Meta Object Facility (MOF) 2.0 Query/View/Transformation Specification.* OMG Available Specification. Retrieved July 27, 2009, from Object Management Group http://www.omg.org/spec/QVT/1.0/PDF/.

Object Management Group. (2009). *OMG Model Driven Architecture.* Retrieved July 21, 2009, from Object Management Group http://www.omg.org/mda/.

Object Management Group. (2007). *Data distribution service for real-time systems, version 1.2.* Retrieved June 8, 2009, from http://www.omg.org/spec/DDS/1.2.

Object Management Group. (2004-1). *Event service specification version 1.2.* Retrieved December 11, 2009, from http://www.omg.org/cgi-bin/doc?formal/2004-10-02.

Object Management Group. (2004-2). *Notification service specification version 1.1.* Retrieved December 11, 2009, from http://www.omg.org/cgi-bin/doc?formal/2004-10-11.

Object Management Group. (2003). *MDA Guide Version 1.0.1,* omg/03-06-01.

Object Management Group. (2006). *Meta Object Facility Core Specification*, version 2.0, formal/2006-01-01.

Object Management Group. (2009). *Unified Modeling Language: Superstructure*, version 2.2, formal/09-02-02.

Object Management Group (OMG). (2008a). *Business Motivation Model.* from http://www.omg.org/spec/BMM/1.0

Object Management Group (OMG). (2008b). *Semantics of Business Vocabulary and Business Rules (SBVR).* from http://www.omg.org/spec/SBVR/1.0/PDF

Object Management Group (OMG). (2010). *Systems Modeling Language (SysML).* from http://www.omg.org/spec/SBVR/1.0/PDF

OMG (2001). *Unified Modeling Language (UML) v1.4.* Object Management Group, OMG Document formal/2001-09-67 edition.

OMG (2002). UML Profile for Schedulability, Performance, and Time Specification. *Object Management Group, Final Adopted Specification* ptc/02-03-02 edition.

OMG. (2002). *CORBA Components Specification*, Version 3.0. Retrieved October 2007, from: http://www.omg.org/technology/documents/formal/components.htm

OMG. (2003). *MDA Guide Version 1.0.1.* (J. Miller, & J. Mukerji, Eds). Document No. omg/2003-06-01, date: 12th June 2003. Retrieved from http://www.omg.org/docs/omg/03-06-01.pdf (Access: 15 July 2005).

OMG. (2005). *OMG Unified Modeling Language: Superstructure*, Version 2.0. Retrieved from http://www.omg.org/spec/UML/2.0/Superstructure

OMG. (2005). *UML 2.0 Testing Profile Specification.* Retrived October 2007, from: http://www.omg.org/cgi-bin/apps/doc?formal/05-07-07.pdf

OMG. (2006). *Deployment and Configuration of Component-based Distributed Applications Specification*, Version 4 Retrieved October 2007, from: http://www.omg.org/technology/documents/formal/deployment.htm

OMG. (2006). *Meta-Object Facility: Core Specification - version 2.0* from http://www.omg.org

OMG. (2007). *UML Superstructure Specification*, Rev. 2.1.2, Retrieved October 2007, from: http://www.omg.org/docs/formal/07-11-02.pdf

OMG. (2008). *Business Motivation Model Version 1.* Retrieved April, 2010, from http://www.omg.org/spec/BMM/1.0/PDF

OMG. (2008). *Meta Object Facility 2.0 Query/View/Transformation: Specification - version 1.0* from http://www.omg.org

OMG. (2008). *Semantics of a Foundational Subset for Executable UML Models* (*FUML*), Retrieved April 2009, from: http://www.omg.org/spec/FUML/

OMG. (2009, February). *UML 2.2 Superstructure.* Retrieved January 30, 2010 from http://www.omg.org/spec/UML/2.2/

OMG. (2009a). *Object Management Group* from http://www.omg.org

OMG. (2009a). *OMG's MetaObject Facility (MOF).* from http://www.omg.org/mof/

OMG. (2009b). *Unified Modeling Language: Superstructure - version 2.2* from http://www.omg.org

OMG. (2009b). *Unified Modeling Language.* from http://www.uml.org/

OMG. (2010a). *Object management group/Business process management initiative.* Retrieved January 10, 2010, from http://www.bpmn.org/

OMG. (2010b). *UML® resource page.* Retrieved January 10, 2010, from Unified Modeling Language http://www.uml.org/

openArchitectureWare.org. (n.d.). *openArchitectureWare.* from http://www.openarchitectureware.org/

Oppenheimer, D., Ganapathi, A., & Patterson, D. (2003). Why do Internet Services Fail, and What can be Done about It? In *Proceedings of the USENIX Symposium on Internet Technologies and Systems*, Seattle, WA.

OSGi Alliance. (2007). *OSGi Service Platform Core Specification*, Release 4, Version 4.1., Retrieved October 2007, from: http://www.osgi.org/

Osis, J., Asnina, E., & Grave, A. (2008). Formal problem domain modeling within MDA. [CCIS]. *Communications in Computer and Information Science*, 22(3), 387–398.

Osis, J., Gefandbein, J., Markovitch, Z., & Novozhilova, N. (1991). *Diagnosis based on graph models: by the examples of aircraft and automobile mechanisms.* Moscow: Transport. (in Russian)

Osis, J. (1970). Mathematical description of complex system functioning. [Kibernetika i Diagnostika]. *Cybernetic and Diagnosis*, 4, 7–14.

Osis, J., Asnina, E., & Grave, A. (2008). Computation independent representation of the problem domain in MDA. *e-Informatica. Software Engineering Journal*, 2(1), 29–26. Retrieved from http://www.e-informatyka.pl/wiki/e-Informatica_-_Volume_2.

Osis, J. (1969). Topological Model of System Functioning (in Russian). *Automatics and Computer Science. J. of Acad. of Sc.*, 6, 44–50.

Osis, J., Asnina, E., & Grave, A. (2007). Computation Independent Modeling within the MDA. In *Proceedings of, ICSSTE07*, 22–34.

Osis, J. (1972). *Diagnostics of complex systems (Dissertation of Dr. Habil. Sc. Eng.).* Riga, Latvia: Latvian Academy of Sciences.

Osis, J. (1973). Some questions of microprogramming optimization using topological model properties. In *Cybernetic methods in the diagnosis,* (pp. 30-34).

Osis, J. (1997). Development of Object-Oriented Methods for Hybrid System Analysis and Design. In *Proc. of the 23rd Conference of the Association of Simula Users (ASU),* (pp. 162-170). Stara Lesna, Slovakia.

Osis, J. (2003). Extension of software development process for mechatronic and embedded systems. In *Proceeding of the 32nd International Conference on Computer and Industrial Engineering* (pp. 305-310). Limerick, Ireland: University of Limerick.

Osis, J. (2004). Software development with topological model in the framework of MDA. In *Proceedings of the 9th CaiSE/IFIP8.1/EUNO International Workshop on Evaluation of Modeling Methods in Systems Analysis and Design (EMMSAD'2004) in connection with the CaiSE'2004, 1,* (pp. 211 – 220). Riga, Lativa: RTU.

Osis, J. (2006). Formal computation independent model within the MDA life cycle. *International transactions on system science and applications, 1* (2), 159-166.

Osis, J., & Asnina, E. (2008a). A Business model to make software development less intuitive. In *Proceedings of 2008 International Conference on Innovation in Sofware Engineering (ISE 2008)* (pp. 1240-1245). Vienna, Austria: IEEE Computer Society Publishing.

Osis, J., & Asnina, E. (2008b). Enterprise modeling for information system development within MDA. In *Proceedings of the 41st Hawaii International Conference on Systems Science (HICSS-41 2008), 7-10 January 2008, Waikoloa, Big Island, HI, USA* (p. 490). Washington, DC: IEEE Computer Society.

Osis, J., & Beghi, L. (1997). Topological modelling of biological systems. In D. Linkens, & E. Carson (Ed.), *Proceedings of the 3rd IFAC Symposium on Modelling and Control in Biomedical Systems, University of Warwick, 23-26 March 1997* (pp. 337-342). Oxford, UK: Elsevier Science Publishing.

Osis, J., Asnina, E., & Grave, A. (2007a). Computation independent modeling within the MDA. In *Proceedings of IEEE International Conference on Software, Science, Technology & Engineering (SwSTE07), 30-31 October 2007, Herzlia, Israel* (pp. 22-34). Washington, DC: IEEE Computer Society, Conference Publishing Services (CPS).

Osis, J., Asnina, E., & Grave, A. (2007b). MDA oriented computation independent modeling of the problem domain. In *Proceedings of the 2nd International Conference on Evaluation of Novel Approaches to Software Engineering (ENASE 2007), Barcelona, Spain,* (pp. 66 -71).

Osis, J., Asnina, E., & Grave, A. (2007). Formal Computation Independent Model of the Problem Domain within the MDA. In *10th International Conference on Information System Implementation and Modeling* (pp. 47-54). Hradec nad Moravici, Czech Republic: Jan Štefan MARQ.

Osis, J., Sukovskis, U., & Teilans, A. (1997). Business process modeling and simulation based on topological approach. In *Proceedings of the 9th European Simulation Symposium and Exhibition,* (pp. 496-501), Passau, Germany.

Osis, J., Sukovskis, U., & Teilans, A. (1997). Business process modeling and simulation based on topological approach. In *Proceedings of the 9th European Simulation Symposium and Exhibition,* (pp. 496-501), Passau, Germany.

Osterwalder, A. (2004). *The Business Model Ontology.* Doctoral thesis, HEC Lausanne. Retrieved May 02, 2009, from http://www.hec.unil.ch/aosterwa/

Ouyang, C., Dumas, M., Van Der Aalst, W. M. P., Ter Hofstede, A. H. M., & Mendling, J. (2009). From business process models to process-oriented software. In *ACM transactions on Software. Engineering and methodology (TOSEM), 19*(1), 2:1-2:37.

Paige, R., Hartman, A., Rensink, A. (2009). *Model Driven Architecture Foundtions and Applications.*

Panserini, L., Perini, A., Susi, A., & Mylopoulos, J. (2006). From stakeholder intensions to software agent implementations. In E. Dubois & K. Pohl (Eds.), *Advanced IS engineering. Proceedings of the 18th International conference (CAISE 2006), Luxembourg, Luxembourg, June 5-9, 2006* (LNCS 4001, pp. 465-479). Berlin: Springer.

Papazoglou, M., & Georgakopoulos, D. (2003). Service-Oriented Computing. *Communications of the ACM, 46*(10), 25–28.

Pârv, B., Lazăr, I., & Motogna, S. (2008). ComDeValCo Framework - the Modeling Language for Procedural Paradigm. *International Journal of Computers, Communications & Control, 3*(2), 183–195.

Pârv, B., Lazăr, I., Motogna, S., Czibula, I.-G., & Lazăr, C.-L. (2009) ComDeValCo Framework - Procedural and Modular Issues. In *2nd International Conference Knowledge Engineering: Principles and Techniques* (pp. 189-193), Cluj-Napoca, Romania, Studia Universitatis Babeş-Bolyai.

Peltz, C. (2003). Web services orchestration and choreography. *Computer, 36*(10), 46–52. doi:10.1109/MC.2003.1236471

Peyret, H. (2006). *Enterprise Architecture Modeling Tools Not Yet Ready For Prime Time.* Retrieved October, 2009, from http://www.forrester.com/Research/Document/Excerpt/0,7211,39437,00.html.

Piattini, M., Calero, C., Sahraoui, H., & Lounis, H. (2001). Object-relational database metrics. *L'Object. Edition Hermès Sciences, 17*(4), 477–498.

Piattini, M., & Genero, M. (2001). *Empirical validation of measures for class diagram structural complexity through controlled experiments.* Retrieved from http://www.iro.umontreal.ca/~sahraouh/qaoose01/genero.pdf

Piccinelli, G., & Stammers, E. (2001). From E-Processes to E-Networks: an E-Service-oriented Approach. In *International Conference on Internet Computing,* (Vol. 3, pp. 549-553). CSREA Press.

Piccinini, G., & Scarantino, A. (2008). *Computation vs. information processing: How they are different and why it matters.* Retrieved November 30, 2008, from Conference on Computation and Cognitive Science 2008 http://people.pwf.cam.ac.uk/mds26/cogsci/program.html

Pilgrim, J. (2007). Measuring the level of abstraction and detail of models in the context of mdd. In *Second International Workshop on Model Size Metrics* (pp. 105–114). Heidelberg: Springer-Verlag

Pinheiro, F. A., & Goguen, J. A. (1996). An Object-Oriented Tool for Tracing Requirements. *IEEE Software, 13*(2), 52–64. doi:10.1109/52.506462

Podeswa, H. (2005). *UML for the IT Business Analyst: A Practical Guide to Object-Oriented Requirements Gathering.* Boston: Thomson Course Technology PTR.

Pohjonen, R., & Tolvanen, J.-P. (2002). Automated production of family members: Lessons learned. *OOPSLA Workshop on Product Line Engineering The Early Steps: Planning, Modeling, and Managing,* Seattle, WA.

Pohl, K., Böckle, G., & van der Linden, F. (2005). *Software Product Line Engineering: Foundations, Principles and Techniques.* Berlin, Germany: Springer.

Pohl, K. (2006). Panel on Product Line Research: Lessons Learned from the last 10 years and Directions for the next 10 years. In *10th International Software Product Line Conference (SPLC 2006).* Retrieved from http://www.sei.cmu.edu/splc2006/SPLC06-ResearchPanel-KP.pdf

Poole, J. (2001). Model-driven architecture: Vision, standards and emerging technologies. In *Workshop on Metamodeling and Adaptive Object Models, ECOOP.*

Popovic, M., & Velikic, I. (2005). A Generic Model-Based Test Case Generator. In *Proceedings of the 12th IEEE International Conference on the Engineering of Computer-Based Systems* (ECBS), Greenbelt, MD.

Porcarelli, S., Castaldi, M., Gi, F. D., & Inverardi, P. (2004). A framework for reconfiguration-based fault-tolerance in distributed systems. In *Architecting dependable systems II* (pp. 343–358). Berlin: SpringerVerlag.

Pratt, T. W. (1971). Pair Grammars, Graph Languages and String-to-Graph Translations. *Journal of Computer and System Sciences, 5*, 560–595.

Pree, W. (1995). *Design Patterns for Object-Oriented Software Development.* Upper Saddle River, NJ: Addison-Wesley.

Premraj, R., Shepperd, M., Kitchenham, B., & Forselius, P. (2005). An empirical analysis of software productivity over time. In *11th IEEE International Symposium on Software Metrics* (37). Washington, DC: IEEE Computer Society.

Purhonen, A., Niemelä, E., & Matinlassi, M. (2004). Viewpoints of DSP software and service architectures. *Journal of Systems and Software, 69*(1-2), 57–73. doi:10.1016/S0164-1212(03)00050-5

Quartel, D., Engelsman, W., Jonkers, H., & van Sinderen, M. (2009). A goal-oriented requirements modelling language for enterprise architecture. In *Proceedings of the 13th IEEE International Enterprise Distributed Object Computing Conference (EDOC 2009), Auckland, New Zealand, September 1-2, 2009* (pp. 3-13). Los Alamitos, CA: IEEE Computer Society Press.

Raatikainen, M., Niemelä, E., Myllärniemi, V., & Männistö, T. (2008). Svamp – An Integrated Approach for Modeling Functional and Quality Variability. In *Proceedings of Second International Workshop on Variability Modeling of Software Intensive Systems VaMoS08*, ICB-Research Report No.22, January 2008, (pp.89-96). Essen, Germany: ICB, University of Duisburg-Essen.

Ralston, A., & Reilly, E. I. (Eds.). (1993). *Encyclopedia of computer science* (3 ed.). New York: Van Nostrand Reinhold Company.

Rappa, M. (2004). The Utility Business Model and the Future of Computing Services. *IBM Systems Journal, 43*(1), 32–42. doi:10.1147/sj.431.0032

Rashid, A., & Chitchyan, R. (2008). Aspect-oriented requirements engineering: a roadmap. In *Proceedings of the 2008 ACM Conference on Computer Supported Cooperative Work, San Diego, California, USA, November 8-12, 2008* (pp. 35-41). New York: Association for Computing Machinery, Inc.

Rasmussen, J., Pejtersen, A. M., & Goodstein, L. P. (1994). *Cognitive systems engineering.* New York: John Wiley & Sons, Inc.

ReDSeeDS. (n.d.) *Requirements Driven Software Development System (ReDSeeDS) project. EU 6th framework IST project (IST-33596).* Retrieved June 17, 2009 from http://www.redseeds.eu

Reifer, D. (2000). Web development: estimating quick-to-market software. *IEEE Software, 17*(6), 57–64. doi:10.1109/52.895169

Rein, M., Ambroziewicz, A., Bojarski, J., Nowakowski, W., Straszak, T., Kalnins, A., et al. (2008). *Initial ReDSeeDS Prototype. Project Deliverable D5.4.1, ReDSeeDS Project.* Retrieved June 17, 2009, from www.redseeds.eu

Richters, M., & Gogolla, M. (1998). On formalizing the UML object constraint language OCL. *Lecture Notes in Computer Science*, 449–464.

RM. (2009). *Requirements Management Software.* Retrieved October, 2009, from http://www.jiludwig.com/Requirements_Management_Tools.html.

Robbes, R., & Lanza, M. (2008). Example-based Program Transformation. In *Proceedings of International Conference on Model Driven Engineering Languages and Systems (MoDELS),* (LNCS 5301, pp. 174–188), Toulouse, France. Berlin: Springer-Verlag.

Rodriguez, A., Fernández-Medina, E., & Piattini, M. (2007). Towards CIM to PIM transformation: From secure business processes defined in BPMN to usecases. In *Proceedings of the International Conference on Business Process Management, Brisbane, Australia,* (pp.408–415).

Rolland, C., Kaabi, R. S., & Kraiem, N. On Intentional Services Oriented Architecture (ISOA). In J. Krogstie, A.L. Opdahl & G. Sindre (Eds.), *Advanced IS engineering. Proceedings of the 19th International conference (CAISE 2007), Trondheim, Norway, June 11-15, 2007,* (LNCS 4495, pp. 574-588). Berlin: Springer.

Rosen, M. (2003). MDA, SOA and Technology Convergence. *MDA Journal, December 2003.* Retrieved March 15, 2009, from http://www.bptrends.com/publication-files/12-03%20COL%20Frankel%20-%20MDA%20SOA%20-%20Rosen.pdf.

Ross, R. G. (2003). *Principles of the Business Rule Approach.* Reading, MA: Addison Wesley.

Roy, N., Xue, Y., Gokhale, A., Dowdy, L., & Schmidt, D. C. (2009). A component assignment framework for improved capacity and assured performance in web portals. In *OTM '09: Proceedings of the Confederated International Conferences, CoopIS, DOA, IS, and ODBASE 2009 on On the Move to Meaningful Internet Systems,* (pp. 671–689). Berlin: Springer-Verlag.

Ruben, P., & Vjeran, S. (2009). Framework for Using Patterns in Model-Driven Development. In Papadopoulos, G. A., Wojtkowski, G., Wojtkowski, W., Wrycza, S., & Zupančič, J. (Eds.), *Information Systems Development: Towards a Service Provision Society* (pp. 309–317). Berlin, Heidelberg: Springer-Verlag.

Rumbaugh, J., Blaha, M., Premerlani, W., Eddy, F., & Lorensen, W. (1990). *Object-oriented modeling and design.* Upper Saddle River, NJ: Prentice Hall.

Saaksvuori, A., & Immonen, A. (2008). *Product Lifecycle Management. Springer-11643 /Dig. Serial].* Berlin: Springer-Verlag.

Sabin, D., & Freuder, E. (1996). Configuration as composite constraint satisfaction. In *Proceedings of the Artificial Intelligence and Manufacturing Research Planning Workshop,* (pp. 153–161). Chesapeake, VA: AAAI Press.

Saha, P. (2007). *Handbook of Enterprise Systems Architecture in Practice.* Hershey, PA: IGI Global.

Sánchez, P., Loughran, N., Fuentes, L., & Garcia, A. (2008). *Engineering Languages for Specifying Product-derivation Processes in Software Product Lines.* Paper presented at the 1st International Conference on Software Language Engineering (SLE).

Sawyer, P., Paech, B., & Heymans, P. (Eds.). Requirements Engineering: Foundation for Software Quality. (2007). In *Proceedings of the 13th International Working Conference (REFSQ 2007), Trondheim, Norway, June 11-12, 2007* (LNCS 4542). Berlin: Springer.

Schach, S. R. (1999). *Classical and Object-Oriented Software Engineering with UML and Java* (International edition). New York: WCB/McGraw-Hill.

Scheer, A., Thomas, O., & Adam, O. (2005). Process Modeling Using Event-driven Process Chains. In *Process-aware Information Systems: Bridging People and Software through Process Technology,* (pp. 119-145). Hoboken, NJ.

Schekkerman, J. (2006). *How to Survive in the Jungle of Enterprise Architecture Frameworks: Creating or Choosing an Enterprise Architecture Framework.* Bloomington, IN: Trafford Publishing.

Schmidt, D. (2002). Middleware for real-time and embedded systems. *Communications of the ACM, 45*(6), 43–48. doi:10.1145/508448.508472

Schmidt, D. (2006). Model-Driven Engineering. *IEEE Computer, 39*(2), 25–32.

Schmidt, D., Stal, M., Rohnert, H., & Buschmann, F. (2000). *Pattern-Oriented Software Architecture: Patterns for Concurrent and Networked Objects.* Hoboken, NJ: Wiley.

Schneider, G., & Winters, J. (2001). *Applying Use Cases. A Practical Guide* (2nd ed.). Reading, MA: The Addison-Wesley.

Schneider, D., & Becker, M. (2008). Runtime Models for Self-adaptation in the Ambient Assisted Living Domain. *Models@run.time, held at MODELS 2008,* Toulouse, France, October 2008.

Schürr, A., & Dörr, H. (2005). Special Section on Model-based Tool Integration. *Software and Systems Modeling, 4*(2), 109–170.

Schürr, A., Schäfer, W., Stürmer, I., & Legros, E. (2009). MATE - A Model Analysis and Transformation Environment for MATLAB Simulink. In *Lecture Notes in Computer Science (LNCS)*. Heidelberg: Springer Verlag.

Schürr, A. (1995). Specification of Graph Translators with Triple Graph Grammars. In E. W. Mayr, G. Schmidt, & G. Tinhofer (Eds.), *Graph-Theoretic Concepts in Computer Science, 20th International Workshop, WG '94 Herrsching, Germany, June 1618, 1994 Proceedings,* (LNCS Vol. 903, pp. 151–163). Berlin: Springer.

Schürr, A., & Klar, F. (2008). 15 Years of Triple Graph Grammars - Research Challenges, New Contributions, Open Problems. In *Lecture Notes in Computer Science (LNCS), 4th International Conference on Graph Transformation* (pp. 411–425). Heidelberg: Springer Verlag.

SCOR. (2009). *SCOR Frameworks.* Retrieved October, 2009, from https://www.supply-chain.org/resources/scor

SEI-CMU. (2010). *Software Product Lines.* Retrieved from http://www.sei.cmu.edu/productlines/

Selic, B. (2003, September/October). The pragmatics of model-driven development. *IEEE Software*, 19–25. doi:10.1109/MS.2003.1231146

SEMAT. (n.d.). Retrieved January 20, 2010, from www.semat.org

Sendall, S., & Kozaczynski, W. (2003). Model transformation: The heart and soul of model-driven software development. *IEEE Software, 20*(5), 42–45. doi:10.1109/MS.2003.1231150

Sethi, K., Cai, Y., Wong, S., Garcia, A., & Sant'Anna, C. (2009). From retrospect to prospect: Assessing modularity and stability from software architecture. *Conference on Software Architecture and European Conference on Software Architecture*, Cambridge, UK, (pp. 269-272).

Sharp, D. (1999). Avionics Product Line Software Architecture Flow Policies, In *Proceedings of the 18th IEEE/AIAA Digital Avionics Systems Conference (DASC)*, St. Louis, MO.

Shaw, M., & Garlan, D. (1996). *Software Architecture.* Upper Saddle River, NJ: Prentice Hall.

Shuangxi, H., & Yushun, F. (2007). Model Driven and Service Oriented Enterprise Integration-The method, framework and platform. In *the Proceedings of the Sixth International Conference on Advanced Language Processing and Web Information Technology*, (pp. 504-509). Washington, DC: IEEE.

Siemens, A. G. (2006). *Configuring Hardware and Communication Connections with STEP 7: Manual.* Order number: 6ES7810-4CA08-8BW0. Retrieved June 07, 2009, from http://support.automation.siemens.com/WW/llisapi.dll/csfetch/18652631/S7hwV54_e.pdf?func=cslib.csFetch&nodeid=18653484&forcedownload=true

Siemens, A. G. (2009). *SIMATIC STEP 7 Programming Software.* Retrieved October 09, 2008, from http://www.automation.siemens.com/simatic/industriesoftware/html_76/products/step7.htm

Skene, J., & Emmerich, W. (2003). Model Driven Performance Analysis of Enterprise Information Systems. *Electronic Notes in Theoretical Computer Science, 82*(6). doi:10.1016/S1571-0661(04)81033-8

Slaby, J. M., Baker, S., Hill, J., & Schmidt, D. C. (2006). Applying system execution modeling tools to evaluate enterprise distributed real-time and embedded system qos. In *RTCSA '06: Proceedings of the 12th IEEE International Conference on Embedded and Real-Time Computing Systems and Applications*, (pp. 350–362). Washington, DC: IEEE Computer Society.

Slack, S. E. (2009). *The business analyst in model-driven architecture.* Retrieved May, 2009, from http://www.ibm.com/developerworks/library/ar-bamda/index.html

Sloane, A. (2000). Modeling Deployment and Configuration of CORBA Systems with UML. In *Proceedings of the 22nd International Conference on Software Engineering*, Limerick, Ireland.

Smiałek, M., Bojarski, J., Nowakowski, W., Ambroziewicz, A., & Straszak, T. (2007). Complementary use case scenario representations based on domain vocabularies. *Model Driven Engineering Languages and Systems, (. LNCS, 4735*, 544–558.

Smith, C., & Williams, L. (2002). *Performance Solutions: a practical guide to creating responsive, scalable software*. Boston: Addison-Wesley.

Smith, C. U., & Williams, L. G. (1997). *Performance engineering evaluation of object-oriented systems with speed. Computer Performance Evaluation Modelling Techniques and Tools* (pp. 135–154). Berlin: Springer.

Smithers, T., Tang, M. X., & Tomes, N. (1991). *The Maintenance of Design History in AI-Based Design*, DAI Research Paper 571, Department of Artificial Intelligence, University of Edinburgh, Scotland.

Sommerville, I., & Sawyer, P. (1997). *Requirements Engineering: A good practice Guide*. Chichester, UK: John Wiley & Sons.

Soukup, J. (1995). Implementing Patterns. In Coplien, J. O., & Schmidt, D. C. (Eds.), *Pattern Languages of Program Design* (pp. 395–412). Upper Saddle River, NJ: Addison-Wesley.

SourceForge.net ReDSeeDS pages. (n.d.) Retrieved December 11, 2009, http://sourceforge.net/apps/mediawiki/redseeds/

Sowa, J., & Zahman, J. (1992). Extending and formalizing the framework for information systems architecture. *IBM Systems Journal, 31*(3), 590–616. doi:10.1147/sj.313.0590

Sparx Systems. (2007). *MDA Overview, Sparx Systems*. Retrieved April, 2010, from http://www.sparxsystems.com

Sparx Systems. (n.d.). *Enterprise Architect tool.* Retrieved June 17, 2009, from http://www.sparxsystems.com.au/

Spinczyk, O., Gal, A., & Schröder-Preikschat, W. (2002). Aspectc++: an aspect-oriented extension to the c++ programming language. In *CRPIT '02: Proceedings of the Fortieth International Conference on Tools Pacific*, (pp. 53–60). Darlinghurst, Australia: Australian Computer Society, Inc.

Stelting, S. (2002). *Applied Java Patterns*. Upper Saddle River, NJ: Prentice Hall.

Stewart, C., & Shen, K. (2005). Performance modeling and system management for multi-component online services. In *Proceedings of the 2nd conference on Symposium on Networked Systems Design & Implementation*, (Vol. 2, pp. 71–84). Berkeley, CA: USENIX Association.

Stirna, J., & Kirikova, M. (2008). How to support agile development projects with enterprise modelling. In Johannesson, P., & Soderstrom, E. (Eds.), *IS Engineering: From Data Analysis to Process Networks* (pp. 159–185). Hershey, PA: IGI Publishing.

Strommer, M., & Wimmer, M. (2008). A framework for model transformation by-example: Concepts and tool support. In *Proceedings of the 46th International Conference on Technology of Object-Oriented Languages and Systems*, Zurich, Switzerland, (pp. 372–391).

Strommer, M., Murzek, M., & Wimmer, M. (2007). Applying Model Transformation by-example on Business Process Modeling Languages. In *Proceedings of the 3rd International Workshop on Foundations and Practices of UML*, Auckland, New Zealand, (pp. 116–125).

Sun Microsystems. (07-June-2002). *Java Metadata Interface (JMI) Specification*. JSR 040 Java Community Process. Retrieved October 28, 2009, from http://jcp.org/en/jsr/detail?id=40.

Sun Microsystems. (2007). *mdr: netbeans.org: Metadata Repository home*. Retrieved July 27, 2009, from Sun Microsystems: http://mdr.netbeans.org/

Sun Microsystems. (2002). *Java Message Service version 1.1*. Retrieved December 11, 2009 from http://java.sun.com/products/jms/docs.html.

Sun, Y., White, J., & Gray, J. (2009). Model Transformation by Demonstration. In *Proceedings of International Conference on Model Driven Engineering Languages and Systems (MoDELS)*, (LNCS 5795, pp. 712-726), Denver, CO. Berlin: Springer-Verlag.

Svahnberg, M., van Gurp, J., & Bosch, J. (2002). *A taxonomy of Variability Realization Techniques*, Technical Paper ISSN: 1103-1581. Sweden: Blekinge Institute of Technology.

Swithinbank, P., Chessell, M., Gardner, T., Griffin, C., Man, J., & Wylie, H. (2005). *Patterns: Model-Driven Development Using IBM Rational Software Architect*. Indianapolis, Indiana: IBM Press.

Szasz, N., & Vilanova, P. (2008). Statecharts and variabilities. *Proceedings of Second International Workshop on Variability Modeling of Software Intensive Systems VaMoS08*, ICB-Research Report No.22, January 2008, p. 131-140. Essen, Germany: ICB, University of Duisburg-Essen.

Szyperski, C. (1997). *Component Software –Beyond Object –Oriented Programming*. Harlow, UK: Pearson Education Limited.

Taentzer, G. (2003). *AGG: A Graph Transformation Environment for Modeling and Validation of Software*. Paper presented at the 2nd International Workshop on Applications of Graph Transformations with Industrial Relevance (AGTIVE), Virginia, USA.

Tekinerdogan, B., Aksit, M., & Henninger, F. (2007). Impact of evolution of concerns in the model-driven architecture design approach. *Electronic Notes in Theoretical Computer Science*, *163*, 45–64. doi:10.1016/j.entcs.2006.10.015

Tichy, W. F. (1997). *A Catalogue of General-Purpose Software Design Patterns*. Paper presented at the 23rd Technology of Object-Oriented Languages and Systems (TOOLS-23), Santa Barbara, California, USA.

Toft, P., Coleman, D., & Ohta, J. (2000). HP product generation consulting: A cooperative model for cross-divisional product development for a software product line. *First Conference on Software Product Lines*, Denver, CO, (pp. 111-132).

Tracz, W. (1995). DSSA (Domain-Specific Software Architecture): Pedagogical example. *ACM SIGSOFT Software Engineering Notes*, *20*(3), 49–62. doi:10.1145/219308.219318

Trujillo, J., Soler, E., Fernández-Medina, E., & Piattini, M. (2009). A UML 2.0 profile to define security requirements for data warehouses. *Computer Standards & Interfaces*, *31*, 969–983. doi:10.1016/j.csi.2008.09.040

Trujillo, S., Batory, D., & Diaz, O. (2007). Feature oriented model driven development: A case study for portlets. In *Proceedings of the 29th international conference on Software Engineering*, (pp. 44–53).

UL IMCS. *MOLA pages*. (n.d.). Retrieved June 17, 2009, from http://mola.mii.lu.lv/

UML Profile for Modeling Quality of Service and Fault Tolerance Characteristics and mechanisms, v1.1. (2008). Retrieved from http://www.omg.org/technology/documents/formal/QoS_FT.htm

UML. *Unified Modeling Language*. (2009). Retrieved October, 2009, from http://www.uml.org

UN/CEFACT Modeling Methodology (UMM) User Guide. (2006). Retrieved May 04, 2009, from http://www.unece.org/cefact/umm/UMM_userguide_220606.pdf

University of Paderborn Software Engineering Group. (2007). *Fujaba-Homepage*. Retrieved July 27, 2009, from University of Paderborn Software Engineering Group: http://wwwcs.uni-paderborn.de/cs/fujaba/.

Urgaonkar, B., Pacifici, G., Shenoy, P., Spreitzer, M., & Tantawi, A. (2005). An Analytical Model for Multi-tier Internet Services and its Applications. *SIGMETRICS Perform. Eval. Rev.*, *33*(1), 291–302. doi:10.1145/1071690.1064252

Urgaonkar, B., Shenoy, P., & Roscoe, T. (2009). Resource overbooking and application profiling in a shared Internet hosting platform. [TOIT]. *ACM Transactions on Internet Technology, 9*(1), 1–45. doi:10.1145/1462159.1462160

Urgaonkar, B., Shenoy, P., Chandra, A., & Goyal, P. (2005a). Dynamic provisioning of multi-tier internet applications. In *ICAC '05: Proceedings of the Second International Conference on Automatic Computing*, (pp. 217–228).

Valverde, F., Panach, I., & Pastor, O. (2007). An abstraction interaction model for MDA software production method. In A.H.F. Laender, L. Maciaszek, and J.F. Roddik (Eds.), *The 26th International Conference on Conceptual Modeling – ER 2007 – Tutorials, Posters, Panels and Industrial Contributions,* 83. Auckland, New Zealand: Conferences in Research and Practice in Information Technology

van Lamsweerde, A. (2008). Requirements engineering: from craft to discipline. In *Proceedings of the 13th international Workshop on Early Aspects, Leipzig, Germany, May 12 - 12, 2008* (pp. 238-249). New York: Association for Computing Machinery, Inc.

Varro, D. (2006). Model Transformation by Example. In *Proceedings of International Conference on Model Driven Engineering Languages and Systems,* (LNCS 4199, pp. 410–424), Genova, Italy. Berlin: Springer-Verlag.

Varró, D., & Balogh, Z. (2007). Automating Model Transformation by Example using Inductive Logic Programming. In *Proceedings of the 2007 ACM Symposium on Applied Computing,* Seoul, Korea, (pp. 978–984).

VDI-Richtlinie, VDI 2219 (2002, November).

VDI-Richtlinie, VDI 2206 (2004, June 01).

Veran, M., & Potier, D. (1984). QNAP-2: A Portable Environment for Queueing Systems Modelling. In Potier, D. (Ed.), *Modelling Techniques and Tools for Performance Analysis* (p. 25). Amsterdam: North-Holland.

Vidales, M.A., Sánchez, García, A.Mª F. & Aguilar, L. J. (2008). A new MDA approach based on BPM and SOA to improve software development process. *Polytechnical Studies Review. Tékhne, 6*(9), 70–90.

Voas, J. (1998). Certifying off-the-shelf software components. *Computer, 31*(6), 53–59. doi:10.1109/2.683008

Voelter, M., & Groher, I. (2007). Product line implementation using aspect-oriented and model-driven software development. In *Proceedings of the International Conference on Software Product Lines,* (pp. 233–242).

Volter, M., & Stahl, T. (2006). *Model-Driven Software Development.* Glasgow, UK: Wiley.

VRM. (2007). *The Value Reference Model.* Retrieved October 2009, from http://www.value-chain.org/en/cms/?1960

Wa, R., Hunt, G., Hunt, G., Brubacher, D., & Brubacher, D. (1999). Detours: Binary Interception of Win32 Functions. In *Proceedings of the 3rd USENIX Windows NT Symposium,* (pp. 135–143). Citeseer.

Wagner, S., & Deissenboeck, F. (2007), An Integrated Approach to Quality Modelling. In *Proceedings of the 5th International Workshop on Software Quality* (pp. 1). Washington, DC: IEEE Computer Society.

Wang, N., Schmidt, D., Gokhale, A., Gill, C., Natarajan, B., & Rodrigues, C. (2003). Total quality of service provisioning in middleware and applications. *Microprocessors and Microsystems, 27*(2), 45–54. doi:10.1016/S0141-9331(02)00096-0

Wang, C., Wang, Q., Ren, K., & Lou, W. (2009). Ensuring Data Storage Security in Cloud Computing. In *Proceedings of 17th IEEE International Workshop on Quality of Service,* Charleston, SC, (pp. 1-9).

Wang, N., Gill, C., Schmidt, C., & Subramonian, V. (2004). Configuring Real-time Aspects in Component Middleware. In *Proceedings of the Conference on Distributed Objects and Applications,* Cyprus, Greece.

Warmer, J., & Kleppe, A. (2003). *The object constraint language: getting your models ready for MDA.* Boston: Addison-Wesley Longman Publishing Co., Inc.

Webber, D. (2001). *The variation point model for software product lines.* Ph.D Dissertation, George Mason University.

Webber, D., & Gomaa, H. (2002), *Modeling variability with the variation point model*. In C. Gacek (Ed.), *Software Reuse: Methods, Techniques, and Tools, 7th International Conference on Software Reuse, ICSR-7, Austin, TX, USA, April 15-19, 2002, Proceedings*, (LNCS 2319, pp. 109-122). Berlin: Springer-Verlag.

Weiser, M. (1984). Program Slicing. *IEEE Transactions on Software Engineering*, 10, 352–357. doi:10.1109/TSE.1984.5010248

Weiss, D., & Lai, C. (1999). *Software Product Line Engineering: A family-based Software Development Process*. Reading, MA: Addison-Wesley.

Welsh, M., & Culler, D. (2003). Adaptive overload control for busy internet servers. In *USITS'03: Proceedings of the 4th conference on USENIX Symposium on Internet Technologies and Systems*, (pp 4–4). Berkeley, CA: USENIX Association.

Weske, M. (2007). *Business process management. Concepts, languages, architectures*. Berlin: Springer-Verlag.

Weyuker, E. J. (1998). *Testing Component-based Software: A Cautionary Tale. IEEE Software*. September/October.

Whaley, R. C., Petitet, A., & Dongarra, J. J. (2000). *Automated empirical optimizations of software and the atlas project. Technical report*. Knoxville: Dept. of Computer Sciences, Univ. of TN.

White, J., Dougherty, B., & Schmidt, D. C. (2008b). *Selecting Highly Optimal Architecture Feature Sets with Filtered Cartesian Flattening*. Journal of Software and Systems - Special Issue on Design Decisions and Design Rationale in Software Architecture.

White, J., & Schmidt, D. (2005). Simplifying the Development of Product-Line Customization Tools via MDA. In *Proceedings of the Workshop on MDA for Software Product Lines, ACM/IEEE 8th International Conference on Model Driven Engineering Languages and Systems*, Montego Bay, Jamaica. Additional Reading SECTION Batory, D., Sarvela, J., & Rauschmayer, A. (2004). Scaling step-wise refinement. *IEEE Transactions on Software Engineering*, 30(6), 355–371.

White, J., & Schmidt, D. (2005). Simplifying the development of product line customization tools via the Generic Eclipse Modeling System. *OOPSLA Eclipse Technology eXchange Workshop*, San Diego, CA.

White, J., Benavides, D., Dougherty, B., & Schmidt, D. (2009). Automated Reasoning for Multi-step Configuration Problems. In *Proceedings of the Software Product Lines Conference (SPLC)*. San Francisco, USA.

White, J., Dougherty, B., & Schmidt, D. C. (2008a). *Ascent: An algorithmic technique for designing hardware and software in tandem*. Tech. Rep. ISIS-08-907, ISIS-Vanderbilt University.

White, J., Schmidt, D. C., Benavides, D., Trinidad, P., & Ruiz-Cortez, A. (2008). Automated Diagnosis of Product-line Configuration Errors in Feature Models. In *Proceedings of the Software Product Lines Conference (SPLC)*, (pp. 225–234). Limerick, Ireland.

White, S. (2005). Using BPMN to Model a BPEL Process. *Business Process Management Trends, March 2005*. Retrieved March 04, 2009, from http://www.business-process-trends.com/publicationfiles/03-05%20WP%20Mapping%20BPMN%20to%20BPEL-%20White.pdf

White, S. (2006). *Business Process Modeling Notation (BPMN). OMG / Business Management Initiative*. Retrieved May 04, 2009, from http://www.bpmi.org

Wimmer, M., Strommer, M., Kargl, H., & Kramler, G. (2007). Towards Model Transformation Generation By-Example. In *Proceedings of the 40th Hawaii International Conference on Systems Science*, Big Island, HI, (pp. 285).

Winston, W., & Goldberg, J. (1994). *Operations research: applications and algorithms*. Belmont, CA: Duxbury press.

Wirth, N. (1977). What can we do about the unnecessary diversity of notation for syntactic definitions? *Communications of the ACM*, 20(11), 822–823. doi:10.1145/359863.359883

Wong, S., & Cai, Y. (2009). Predicting change impact from logical models. *International Conference on Software Maintenance*, Edmonton, Canada, (pp. 464-470).

Wong, S., Cai, Y., Valetto, G., Simeonov, G., & Sethi, K. (2009). Design rule hierarchy and task parallelism. *International Conference on Automated Software Engineering,* (pp. 197—208).

Woo, H. G., & Robinson, W. N. (2002). Reuse of scenario specifications using an automated relational learner: a lightweight approach. In *Proceedings of IEEE Joint International Conference on Requirements Engineering,* (pp. 173-180).

World Wide Web Consortium. (2008). *W3C XML Schema.* Retrieved July 27, 2009, from World Wide Web Consortium: http://www.w3.org/XML/Schema.

Xiong, M., Parsons, J., Edmondson, J., Nguyen, H., & Schmidt, D. (2007, April). *Evaluating technologies for tactical information management in net- centric systems.* Paper presented at the Defense Transformation and Net-Centric Systems conference, Orlando, Florida.

XLink. (2001). *XML Linking Language.* Retrieved from http://www.w3.org/TR/xlink/

XPath. (1999). *XML XPath Language.* Retrieved from http://www.w3.org/TR/xpath/

XPointer. (2002). *XML Pointer Language.* Retrieved from http://www.w3.org/TR/xptr/

Young, T. (2005). *Using AspectJ to Build a Software Product Line for Mobile Devices.* Master's thesis, University of British Columbia, Vancouver, Canada.

Yu, E. (1997). Towards modelling and reasoning support for early-phase requirements engineering. In *Proceedings of the 3rd IEEE Int. Symp. on Requirements Engineering (RE'97)* (pp. 226-235). Washington, DC: IEEE.

Yu, E. (n.d.). *i* an Agent-oriented Modelling Framework.* from http://www.cs.toronto.edu/km/istar/

Yu, E. S. K., & Mylopoulos, J. (1994). From E-R to "A-R" – Modelling Strategic Actor Relationships for Business Process Reengineering. In *Proceedings of the 13th International Conference on the Entity-Relationship Approach,* Manchester, UK.

Zachman, J. (1987). A Framework for IS Architecture. *IBM Systems Journal, 26*(3). doi:10.1147/sj.263.0276

Zdun, U., & Avgeriou, P. (2005). *Modeling Architectural Patterns Using Architectural Primitives.* Paper presented at the 20th Annual ACM SIGPLAN International Conference on Object-Oriented Programming, Systems, Languages, and Applications (OOPSLA 2005), San Diego, California, USA.

Zhang, Q., Cherkasova, L., Mathews, G., Greene, W., & Smirni, E. (2007). R-capriccio: a capacity planning and anomaly detection tool for enterprise services with live workloads. In *Middleware '07: Proceedings of the ACM/IFIP/USENIX 2007 International Conference on Middleware,* (pp. 244–265). New York: Springer-Verlag, Inc.

Zimmer, W. (1995). Relationships between Design Patterns. In Coplien, J. O., & Schmidt, D. C. (Eds.), *Pattern Languages of Program Design* (pp. 345–364). Upper Saddle River, NJ: Addison-Wesley.

Zündorf, A., Schürr, A., & Winter, A. J. (1998). Story Driven Modeling. *ACM Transactions on Software Engineering and Methodology*

About the Contributors

Janis Osis graduated Latvian University cum lauda and received diploma of Electrical engineering in electrical systems (1953), Dr.sc.ing. in automatics from Kaunas Technological University, Lithuania (1961), Dr.habil.sc.ing. in system analysis from Latvian Academy of Sciences (1972). Since 1965 his research interests are topological modeling of complex systems with applications in technical and medical diagnostics. Recent fields of interest are object-oriented system analysis, modeling and design, formal methods of software engineering, software development within the framework of MDA by means of topological functioning model. His work experience includes teacher and researcher positions - at University of Latvia: an assistant, Faculty of Mechanics; Riga Technical University: a lecturer, Faculty of Energetic; a docent and a dean, Faculty of Automatics and Computer Engineering; a professor, Faculty of Computer Science and Information Technology since 2001. The list of publications contains more than 250 titles including 15 books. He is an honorary member of Latvian Academy of Sciences and a member of the International Editorial Board of the journal Automatic Control and Computer Sciences, Allerton Press, Inc.

Erika Asnina is a Docent (the position similar to Assistant Professor) in the Department of Applied Computer Science, Institute of Applied Computer Systems at Riga Technical University, Latvia. She also worked 5 years as a software developer. Her research interests include software quality assurance, business modeling, model-driven software development, model transformation languages and software engineering. Erika received MS in computer systems with specialization in applied computer science in 2003 and engineering science doctor's degree (Dr.sc.ing. or Ph.D.) in information technology with specialization in system analysis, modeling and design in 2006 from Riga Technical University. She has published 18 conference papers.

* * *

Mauricio Alférez is a PhD candidate in Computer Science/Informatics at Faculdade de Ciências e Tecnologia, Universidade Nova de Lisboa, Portugal. His main research topics are requirements engineering, model-driven development, variability management and aspect-oriented software engineering. He worked in research as well as in the industry: EAFIT University, Colombia; West Indies Union, Jamaica; and Termopaipa Power Plant - STEAG A.G, Colombia. Since 2007 he is being working for the project of the European Union for the improvement of development techniques for Software Product Lines – AMPLE. He is member of the Research Center for Informatics and Information Technologies (CITI) and the Software Engineering group at Universidade Nova de Lisboa since 2007. He publishes and participates as a reviewer of international events. More information can be found at http://citi.di.fct. unl.pt/member/member.php?id=80.

Vasco Amaral is presently Assistant Professor at UNL (Portugal) and full member of the CITI (Research Center for Informatics and Information Technologies) Portuguese Research Institution. Holds a PhD. by the University of Mannheim in Germany, worked in the past as software engineer on High Energy Physics Computing and Very Large Databases at CERN (Switzerland), DESY (Germany), and LIP (Portugal). Has been working in the last years on the general topic of Software Languages Engineering, centered on the use of Model-Driven Development (MDD) approaches, at both the Foundations and Application level. Vasco is presently focusing his research on the topics of Verification, Model Composition and Transformations, Multi-Paradigm Modeling, DSL Engineering approaches, DSL Experimental Evaluation, and MDD education. Is organizer of several events like MPM@MODELS, PPPJ, INFORUM and served in the past as part of the scientific Committee of events and journals like ICEIS, DEXA, BIRD, ANT, ISDTA, Journal of Visual Languages Computing and MODEVVA@MODELS.

João Araújo is an Assistant Professor of the Department of Informatics at the Universidade Nova de Lisboa, Portugal and full member of the CITI (Research Center for Informatics and Information Technologies) Portuguese Research Institution. He holds a PhD in Computer Science from Lancaster University, UK, in the area of Requirements Engineering. His principal research interests are in Requirements Engineering in general and Early Aspects in particular, where, he has published several papers on this topic in international conferences and workshops. He was co-founder and has been a co-organizer of the Early Aspects workshop at AOSD, OOPSLA, SPLC and ICSE conferences since 2002. Additionally, he served on the organization committees of MoDELS, CIbSE, RE and ICSE in the past few years. He is currently the Workshop co-chair of RE'10. He served as a guest editor of the Special issue on Early Aspects at Transactions on AOSD journal in 2007.

Sofia Azevedo is at present a researcher both at the Universidade do Minho (Portugal) and at the biggest Portuguese software house in the area of enterprise resource planning (Primavera Business Software Solutions). Her research work is being developed in the area of Information Systems and Technologies, particularly in the area of Software Engineering. Sofia has previously worked also in the area of Software Engineering at Philips Research Europe (The Netherlands) and at Nokia Siemens Networks (Portugal). In 2006 she graduated from the Universidade de Aveiro (Portugal) in Information Systems and Technologies and obtained her M.Sc. diploma in 2008 from the Universidade do Minho in Information Systems under the subject of UML metamodeling and domain-specific languages. Currently she is developing work on software product lines and multistage software development processes.

Alexandre Bragança is a Faculty member of the Department of Informatics Engineering from the School of Engineering (ISEP) of the Polytechnic Institute of Porto (IPP) in Portugal. He is also a researcher from the Centro Algoritmi of the Universidade do Minho (Portugal). His research focuses on Software Engineering, particularly model-driven development and its applications in software product lines. He holds a Ph.D. in Informatics from the Universidade do Minho, a M.Sc. in Electronics and Computer Engineering from the Universidade do Porto (Portugal), and a D.Eng. degree in Informatics from the School of Engineering of the Polytechnic Institute of Porto (Portugal). Alexandre Bragança has also more the 15 years of professional experience in leading several Software Engineering projects developed at major Portuguese companies.

Yuanfang Cai is an Assistant Professor in the Computer Science Department at Drexel University. She received her M.S. and Ph.D. degrees from the University of Virginia. Her primary research interests include formal design modeling and automated, quantitative analysis techniques to reason about design structure and related outcomes early in the development process. She is a member of the ACM and the IEEE.

Edgars Celms holds a PhD in computer science. He is currently a leading researcher at the Institute of Mathematics and Computer Science (IMCS UL) and a lecturer at the University of Latvia. His area of interest is transformation languages, model driven development (MDD) and advanced programming technologies. He has also experience in topics related to UML (Unified Modelling Language), modelling and meta-modelling. He has participated in various tool development projects e.g., Generic Modelling Tool, METAclipse. Most recently he has been involved in the ReDSeeDS project financed from the 6th Framework Program for Scientific Research of the European Union. In private he spends time with his family and takes part in different types of orienteering activities.

Hyun Cho is a Ph.D. student in the Department of Computer Science at the University of Alabama. His research interests include domain-specific modeling, model transformation techniques, software product line engineering, and aspect-oriented software development. He received his BS and MS in Electronics Engineering from Daegu University, South Korea. Before entering graduate study, he was a Senior Engineer at Samsung working as a lead with the digital printer product line. He is a student member of the ACM.

Liliana Dobrica holds a full professorship at the University Politehnica of Bucharest, Romania, where she is a member of the Department of Control and Industrial Informatics of Faculty of Automatic Control and Computers. She received the MSc degree in 1991 in automatic control and the PhD degree in 1998 in control systems from University Politehnica of Bucharest. She worked as a post-doctoral researcher at VTT Technical Research Centre of Finland, Oulu in 2000. Her research interests include software architecture, software product lines and model driven development of software and systems engineering. Her current research projects focuses on quality analysis and service based architecture modeling for embedded systems. She has published several books, journal and conference papers and she is a member of ACM.

Brian Dougherty is a Ph.D student in Computer Science at Vanderbilt University. Brian's research focuses on hardware/software co-design, heuristic constraint-based deployment algorithms, and design space exploration. He is the co-leader of the ASCENT project, a tool for analyzing hardware/software co-design solution spaces. Brian is also a developer for the Generic Eclipse Modeling System (GEMS). He received his B.S. in Computer Science from Centre College, Danville, KY in 2007 and his MS from Vanderbilt University in 2009.

Iwona Dubielewicz received MSc degree and PhD degree in Computer Science in 1972 and 1977 respectively, both from the Wroclaw University of Technology, Poland. Her PhD dissertation was associated with the use of formal languages in software engineering. Since 1977 she has been working as a professor assistant at the Institute of Informatics, Wroclaw University of Technology. Her main scientific interests include, but are not limited to software development methodologies, modeling languages, and quality of the software systems and processes. She is a member of Polish Committee for Standardization. Since 1994 she has been involved in the development of several international standards for Polish Comittee. Iwona Dubielewicz has over 40 publications in the international journals and conference proceedings from different areas of software engineering.

Aniruddha S. Gokhale is an Assistant Professor of Computer Science and Engineering in the Dept. of Electrical Engineering and Computer Science at Vanderbilt University, Nashville, TN, USA. He received his BE (Computer Eng) from Pune University in 1989; MS (Computer Science) from Arizona State University, Tempe, AZ in 1992; and D.Sc (Computer Science) from Washington University, St. Louis, MO in 1998. Prior to joining Vanderbilt, he was a Member of Technical Staff at Bell Labs, Lucent Technologies in New Jersey. Dr.Gokhale is a member of IEEE and ACM. Dr. Gokhale's research combines model-driven engineering and middleware for distributed, real-time and embedded systems. He is the research lead on the CoSMIC MDE tool suite.

Jeff Gray is an Associate Professor in the Department of Computer Science at the University of Alabama. His research interests include model-driven engineering, aspect orientation, code clones, and generative programming. Jeff received a Ph.D. in Computer Science from Vanderbilt University and both the BS and MS in Computer Science from West Virginia University. He is a member of the ACM and a Senior Member of the IEEE.

Bogumila Hnatkowska received MSc degree and PhD degree in Computer Science in 1992 and 1997 respectively, both from the Wroclaw University of Technology, Poland. Her PhD dissertation was associated with the use of formal methods in software engineering. Since 1998 she has been working as a professor assistant at the Institute of Informatics, Wroclaw University of Technology. Her main scientific interests include, but are not limited to software development processes, modeling languages, model driven development, model transformations, and quality of the software products. She is a member of programme committees of several international conferences. Bogumila Hnatkowska has over 60 publications in international journals and conference proceedings from different areas of software engineering.

Joe Hoffert is a Ph.D. student in the Department of Electrical Engineering and Computer Science at Vanderbilt University. His research focuses on QoS support at design and run-time for pub/sub systems. He is currently working on autonomic adaptation of transport protocols using machine learning within QoS-enabled pub/sub middleware to attain timeliness and reliability for distributed event-based systems, in particular systems using the OMG's Data Distribution Service (DDS). He previously worked for Boeing in the area of model-based integration of embedded systems and distributed constructive simulations. He received his B.A. in Math/C.S. from Mount Vernon Nazarene College (OH) and his M.S. in C.S. from the University of Cincinnati (OH).

Zbigniew Huzar received the M.Sc., Ph.D. and habilitation degrees in Computer Science from Wrocław University of Technology, Poland, in 1969, 1974 and 1990, respectively. During 1978-1984 he was deputy director of Computer Center, during 1984-2003 he served as a head of Informatics Center, during 2004- 2008 as director of the Institute of Applied Informatics, and since 2008 as director of the Institute of Informatics, Wrocław University of Technology, Poland. The scope of his scientific interests concerns software engineering, in particular, covers methods of formal specification and design of real-time systems, and model-based software development. He is author and co-author of 10 books. He is a member of the Polish Information Processing Society and editor-in-chief of the e-Informatica Software Engineering Journal.

Tharaka Ilayperuma has a Licentiate in Philosophy (PhL) degree from Stockholm University in the field of value-oriented enterprise modeling. He is currently finalizing his PhD at the Department of Computer and Systems Sciences (DSV), Stockholm University/KTH in Sweden, in the same field, with a focus to service engineering. During 2005-2007 period, Tharaka was actively participated in the INTEROP, an EU/NoE scoped research project on IS interoperability. He is also a lecturer at the Department of Computer Science at the University of Ruhuna, Sri Lanka since 2001.

Elina Kalnina works as a researcher at the Institute of Mathematics and Computer Science, University of Latvia. She is also a PhD student in Computer since. Her area of interest is software development and model driven development (MDD). Mainly she works on topics related to Domain specific languages and Model transformations. She has worked also in area of quantum computing. She has professional experience in web application development and project management. Most recently she has been involved in the ReDSeeDS project financed from the 6th Framework Program for Scientific Research of the European Union. In private she likes figure skating and theatre.

Audris Kalnins holds a Dr. habil. degree in computer science. He is currently a professor at the University of Latvia and leading researcher at the Institute of Mathematics and Computer science (IMCS UL), University of Latvia. Since 1990 he has participated in the research in the area of modelling, metamodelling, UML, business process modelling, modelling tool development and model transformation languages. He is the leader of the transformation language MOLA development team at IMCS UL. He has participated in various modelling tool development projects including GRADE, Generic Modelling Tool and METAclipse. He is teaching courses on modelling, MDD (Model Driven Development) and UML at the Computer science department of University of Latvia. He has published over 65 articles in international journals and conference proceedings. Recently he was the leader of IMCS UL team in the European Union 6th Framework project ReDSeeDS.

Marite Kirikova is a Professor in Information Systems Design at the Department of Systems Theory and Design, Faculty of Computer Science and Information Technology, Riga Technical University, Latvia. She has more than 100 publications on the topics of Requirements Engineering, Business Process Modeling, Knowledge Management, and Systems Development. She has done field work at Stockholm University and Royal Institute of Technology, Sweden, Copenhagen University, Denmark, and Boise State University, USA. Currently in her research she focuses on information systems design in the context of agile and viable systems paradigms.

Marius Lauder received his Master degree in Computer Science in 2008 from the Technische Universität Darmstadt. He is a Ph.D. student and scholarship holder of the Graduate School of Computational Engineering at Technische Universität Darmstadt since November 2008. His research activities are related to Model-Driven Engineering or, more specifically, keeping artefacts of different engineering disciplines in a consistent state by means of bidirectional model transformations. Special research interests are QVT, MOF, compiler, and graph grammars.

Ioan Lazar is Lecturer at the Department of Computer Science, Faculty of Mathematics and Computer Science, Babes-Bolyai University, Cluj-Napoca. He published 7 books and university courses, and more than 30 papers. His current research topics include: object-oriented analysis and design, modeling languages, and programming methodologies.

Ricardo J. Machado is a Faculty member of the Universidade do Minho (Portugal) in the area of Software Engineering and Software Management. He is a member of the Board of Studies of the Ph.D. Program in Information Systems and Technology (PDTSI), and of the Board of Studies of the M.Sc. Program in Information Systems Engineering and Management (MEGSI). He is also the Program Director of the Specialization Course (Post-Graduation) in Software Process Management and Quality (CFE-GQPS). His research focuses on Software Engineering, namely on model-driven development, requirements engineering and software quality. His current research projects focus on the development of multistage approaches in software product lines and on the integration of multistandard models in software process high maturity levels. He holds Ph.D. and M.Sc. degrees in Informatics and Computer Engineering (both from the Universidade do Minho), and a D.Eng. degree in Electronics and Computer Engineering from the Universidade do Porto (Portugal). Ricardo J. Machado is a senior member of IEEE, founding member of the IEEE-IES TCEDU, member of the IEEE-CS EAB, and the former coordinator of IEEE Computer Society Chapters and Student Chapters in Region 8 (Europe, Middle East and Africa). He is also a founding member of the IFIP WG10.2 and the Portuguese representative in the IFIP Technical Committee in Computer Systems Technology (TC10). He is one of the founders of the international workshop series MOMPES (International Workshops on Model-Driven Methodologies for Pervasive and Embedded Software).

Ana Moreira is an Associate Professor at Universidade Nova de Lisboa. She leads the Software Engineering group at Universidade Nova de Lisboa since 2006. Her main research topics are software engineering, software architecture and design, aspect-orientation, model-driven development, software product lines and trade-off analysis. She is a member of the editorial board of the journals "Transactions on AOSD" and "Software and Systems Modeling" and also a member of the Steering Committee for MODELS and AOSD. She has been, and is, involved, as organizer and program committee member, in several conferences, such as ECOOP, CAiSE, UML, MODELS and AOSD and many workshops. She is co-founder of two international movements: Early Aspects (www.early-aspect.net) and pUML (preciseUML, www.cs.york.ac.uk/puml/). She was Conference Chair for UML/MODELS 2004 and Program Committee Chair for AOSD 2009 and JISBD 2008. She publishes regularly in major international conferences and journals. More information can be found at http://www-ctp.di.fct.unl.pt/~amm/.

Simona Claudia Motogna (b. September 24, 1967) received his M.Sc. in Computer Science (1991) and PhD in Computer Science (2000) from Babeş-Bolyai University of Cluj-Napoca, Romania. Now she is Associate Professor at the Department of Computer Science, Faculty of Mathematics and Computer Science, Babes-Bolyai University of Cluj-Napoca, Romania. Her current research interests include component-based software development, model-driven architecture, and formal methods. She has (co-)

authored 6 books and more than 30 papers, 16 conferences participation, member in International Program Committee of 3 conferences and workshops, and reviewer for 2 international journals.

Wiktor Nowakowski works as an assistant lecturer in the Chair of Theory of Electrical Engineering and Applied Informatics, Department of Electrical Engineering of the Warsaw University of Technology. His area of interest is software engineering, mainly in the topics related to the methods of object modeling using UML (Unified Modeling Language), meta-modeling, issues of MDA (Model Driven Development), as well as requirements engineering. Most recently he has been involved in the ReDSeeDS project financed from the 6th Framework Program for Scientific Research of the European Union. In the past he took part in commercial projects in the field of insurance and business impact analysis. He is a passionate rock climber.

Eila Ovaska obtained the MSc degree in 1995 and the PhD degree in 2000 in information processing science from the University of Oulu, Finland. She worked 15 years as a software engineer of embedded systems and from 1995 as a senior research scientist in the Embedded Software research area at VTT. Since 2001 she has been working as a research professor at VTT and since 2002 also as an adjunct professor of software architectures at the University of Oulu. She has acted as a reviewer for a number of scientific journals and as a member of conference program committees. Quality driven architecture design, quality evaluation, model driven service architectures, and ontology oriented design are her main research topics. She has published more than 100 scientific publications and is a member of the IEEE and the IEEE Computer Society.

Bazil Parv (b. September 27, 1953) received his M.Sc. in Computer Science (1977) and PhD in Mathematics (1990) from Babes-Bolyai University of Cluj-Napoca, Romania. Now he is full professor at the Department of Computer Science, Faculty of Mathematics and Computer Science, Babes-Bolyai University of Cluj-Napoca, Romania and chair of Programming Languages and Methods. His current research interests include software engineering, programming paradigms, component-based sofware development, mathematical modeling in experimental sciences, and computer algebra. He has (co-)authored 7 books and more than 120 papers, more than 85 participations in scientific conferences and workshops; member in International Program Committees of more than 15 conferences and workshops.

Hugo Ribeiro manages the Innovation department at Primavera Business Software Solutions since 2002. This department is part of Primavera's software factory and is responsible for the development of application frameworks, R&D projects and technology evaluation. In 1996 he received his diploma from the Computer Science department of the Universidade do Minho (Portugal).

Sebastian Rose received his Master degree in Computer Science at Technische Universität Darmstadt in 2008 for his work about software engineering and security issues. He currently works as a research assistant at the Real-Time System chair of the Electrical Engineering and Information Technology Department of the Technische Universität Darmstadt. He received a Bachelor in Computer Science at Universität Mainz in 2006. Before starting studies at Universität Mainz in 2003 he worked as a software developer for the Computer Science Cooperation (CSC). His research interests are software engineering in general, model driven development and modeling in the large topics like inter-model relationships.

Nilabja Roy is a doctoral candidate in Computer Science in Vanderbilt University. His research interestr include modeling, performance optimization, component placement and profiling of large scale component based distributed systems. His thesis work towards QoS assurance of large scale component based distributed systems through intelligent deployment of application components over multiple nodes. The solution uses profiling, performance modeling and bin packing to assure QoS properties. Previous to joining Vanderbilt, he was involved in software development in the telecom field, designing a distributed mediation application communicating over large geographical distances, which required extensive benchmarking and astute designing skills to maintain reliability, performance for the end-users.

Michael Schlereth received his Diploma in Electrical Engineering in 1992 from the Universität Erlangen. He is currently working in a research and development department for Motion Control Systems and Industry Automation Software at Siemens AG, Nürnberg/Erlangen. His research interests are: engineering of production machine and machine tools, mechatronic engineering, motion control, programmable logic controllers, model driven development and graph grammars.

Douglas C. Schmidt is a Professor of Computer Science and Associate Chair of the Computer Science and Engineering program at Vanderbilt University. He has published 9 books and over 450 papers that cover a range of topics, including patterns, optimization techniques, and empirical analyses of software frameworks and domain-specific modeling environments that facilitate the development of distributed real-time and embedded (DRE) middleware and applications. Dr. Schmidt has served as a Deputy Office Director and a Program Manager at DARPA, where he led the national R&D effort on middleware for DRE systems. In addition to his academic research and government service, Dr. Schmidt has over fifteen years of experience leading the development of ACE, TAO, CIAO, and CoSMIC, which are open-source middleware frameworks and model-driven tools that implement patterns and product-line architectures for high-performance DRE systems.

Andy Schürr holds the Real-Time System chair of the Electrical Engineering and Information Technology Department of the Technische Universität Darmstadt Since July 2002. From 1996 to 2002 he was an Associate Professor at the Institute of Software Technology of the German Armed Forces University, Munich. Andy Schürr received his Master degree in Computer Science in 1986 from the University of Technology Munich and his Ph.D. degree in Computer Science in 1991 from the University of Technology Aachen (RWTH Aachen). Andy Schürr's main research interests are model-driven development of embedded real-time systems with a special emphasis on the application domains of Automotive Software Development and Automation Engineering. Furthermore, Andy Schürr is a member of the steering committees of the European Conference on Model Driven Architecture (ECMDA), the International Conference on Graph Transformations (ICGT), the International IEEE Symposium on Visual Languages and Human-Centric Computing (VL/HCC) and the International ACM/IEEE Conference MODELS.

Michał Śmiałek holds a habilitation (higher PhD) degree in informatics. He is currently an Associate Professor at the Warsaw University of Technology. In the past he has also taught at the Carlos III University in Madrid. Since 1991 he has gained experience in software engineering as a developer, expert consultant and teacher. He has conducted more than 150 editions of various courses in the area of software engineering for major Polish banks, telecoms, insurance companies, software houses and others. He has published over 60 articles in national and international journals and in conference proceedings.

He is the author of "Understanding UML 2.0. Methods of object modelling" (in Polish) published by Helion publishers. He was the Technical Director of the international ReDSeeDS project.

Tomasz Straszak works as an assistant lecturer in the Chair of Theory of Electrical Engineering and Applied Informatics, Department of Electrical Engineering of the Warsaw University of Technology. His area of interest, is software engineering and requirements engineering. He has professional experience in the field of telecommunication and financial sector in software modeling and meta-modeling (mostly with UML - Unified Modeling Language, and MOF - Meta Object Facility), issues of MDA (Model Driven Development), as well as software programming and testing. Most recently he has been involved in the ReDSeeDS project financed from the 6th Framework Program for Scientific Research of the European Union. In private he plays electric guitar and takes a lot of photos.

Yu Sun is a Ph.D. candidate in the Department of Computer and Information Sciences at the University of Alabama at Birmingham (UAB) and member of the SoftCom Laboratory. His research interests include domain-specific modeling, domain-specific languages and model transformation techniques. He received his BS in Computer Science from Zhengzhou University, China and MS in Computer Science from UAB. He is a student member of the ACM.

Lech Tuzinkiewicz received MSc degree and PhD degree in Computer Science in 1976 and 1982 respectively, both from the Wroclaw University of Technology, Poland. His PhD dissertation was associated with the Automation of the design process of Industrial Electrical Networks and Electrical Equipments - formalization issues. Since 1983 he has been working as a professor assistant at the Institute of Informatics, Wroclaw University of Technology. His main scientific interests include, but are not limited to databases, data warehouses, data modeling, software development processes, modeling languages, model driven development, model transformations, and quality of the software products. Lech Tuzinkiewicz has over 70 publications in international journals and conference proceedings from different areas of software engineering.

Jules White is an Assistant Professor in the Bradley Department of Electrical and Computer Engineering at Virginia Tech. He received his BA in Computer Science from Brown University, his MS and PhD from Vanderbilt University. His research focuses on applying search-based optimization techniques to the configuration of distributed, real-time and embedded systems. In conjunction with Siemens AG, Lockheed Martin, IBM and others, he has developed scalable constraint and heuristic techniques for software deployment and configuration. He is the Project-Lead of the Eclipse Foundation's Generic Eclipse Modeling System (GEMS http://www.eclipse.org/gmt/gems).

Sunny Wong is a Ph.D. student in the Computer Science Department at Drexel University. His research interests include software architecture and design modeling, and techniques for automated modularity analysis of design structures. He received his BS in Computer Science from Drexel University. He is a student member of the ACM and the IEEE.

Tao Xie is an Assistant Professor in the Department of Computer Science at North Carolina State University. His research interests include software engineering with a focus on automated software testing and mining software engineering data. He received a Ph.D. in Computer Science from the University of Washington. He is a member of the ACM and the IEEE.

Jelena Zdravkovic has a PhD in the field of process modeling and integration. After the doctorate, she has continued research in the field, with a focus on business and process integration with e-services. In recent years, Jelena has participated in several national and European research projects. She is a PC member / co-organizer of few international conferences and workshops. In addition, Jelena holds the MBA degree in e-business. Besides academic qualifications, Jelena has few years experience as a consultant in systems modeling. Jelena is now working as senior lecturer and researcher at the Department of Computer and Systems Sciences (DSV), Stockholm University/KTH in Sweden.

Index

A

action languages (AL) 254, 255, 258, 259, 262, 263, 268

adaptable systems 310

allocation based configuration exploration technique (ASCENT) 125, 126, 127, 128, 129, 131, 134

Amazon 137, 139, 146, 151, 152, 153

Amazon EC2 (Elastic Compute Cloud) 137, 139, 151, 152, 153

Another Neat Tool (ANT) 335, 337, 341, 345, 346

application programming interfaces (API) 312, 378

Ascent Modeling Platform (AMP) 115, 126, 127, 128, 129, 130, 131

assembly line diagram 71

ATLAS Transformation Language (ATL) 312, 332

augmented constraint networks (ACN) 286, 287, 288, 289, 290, 294, 295, 296, 299, 303

Automatically Tuned Linear Algebra Software (ATLAS) 347

B

bandwidth 360

black-box notation 371

Bluetooth 359, 360

business concepts 232

business knowledge 41, 64

business modeling 41, 45, 61, 62, 317, 319, 320, 321, 322, 330, 331

business model ontologies 234

business model perspectives 34

business models 40, 41, 42, 43, 45, 54, 60, 64, 202, 233, 234, 235, 236, 237, 238, 239, 240, 241, 242, 248, 249, 250, 253

business object-oriented modeling (BOOM) 70

business ontologies 234

business processes 40, 41, 43, 45, 49, 51, 52, 53, 54, 60

business process modeling (BPM) 45

business process modeling notation (BPMN) 7, 45, 63

business scenarios 233

business value modeling 234

business value models 234, 238, 239, 242, 248, 253

C

C++ 117, 122, 126, 128, 160, 163, 165, 166, 167, 170, 171, 172, 311, 335, 360, 418

cause-and-effect relations 20, 21, 23, 26, 29, 34, 35, 36, 38, 39

change management 276, 277, 281, 399, 400

civil engineering 3

class modeling 67

clipboards 193

cloud administrative interfaces 136

cloud applications 139

cloud computing 136, 137, 138, 139, 140, 142, 143, 150, 151, 152, 155

cloud computing services 139

cloud error detection 136

cluster sets (CS) 287

colored petri nets (CPN) 17

commercial-off-the-shelf (COTS) components 115, 116, 117, 131, 134, 135 commercial-off-the-shelf (COTS) hardware 116

Common Warehouse Metamodel (CWM) 208, 227

completeness 65, 69, 70, 73, 87

completeness checking 69

compliance 65, 67, 73, 76, 80, 89

Component Definition, Validation, and Composition (ComDeValCo) 255, 257, 259, 265, 270, 272

component object models (COM) 257

computation independent model (CIM) 65, 66, 67, 76, 86, 88

computation independent models (CIM) 4, 6, 7, 10, 11, 12, 14, 40, 41, 42, 43, 44, 45, 47, 54, 58, 59, 60, 61, 62, 63, 64, 91, 96, 178, 179, 184, 186, 190, 193, 196, 199, 203, 206, 207, 209, 210, 211, 212, 213, 214, 215, 219, 221, 232, 233, 235, 236, 237, 238, 239, 240, 241, 242, 243, 244, 245, 247, 248, 249, 250, 252, 389, 392, 395, 396, 397, 399, 400, 403, 407, 411, 413, 414, 430, 431, 432, 436

computation independent performance modeling (CIPM) 413

computer-aided design (CAD) 3

computer-aided manufacturing (CAM) 3

Concurrent Model-Driven Automation Engineering (CMDAE) 91, 92, 93, 94, 95, 96, 97, 98, 107, 108, 109

Concurrent Model-Driven Automation Engineering (CMDAE) Hypercube 91, 92, 93, 94, 95, 97, 98, 108, 109

constraint logic programming (CLP) 120

constraint satisfaction problems (CSP) 120, 124, 125, 131, 340, 341, 342

Constraints Optimization System (CONST) 336, 337, 338, 339, 342, 343, 344, 347

create-read-update-delete (CRUD) operations 186

cycle structures 15, 23, 27, 31

D

data access objects (DAO) 186

database management systems (DBMS) 209, 210

data-centric publish/subscribe (DCPS) 159

data distribution service (DDS) benchmarking environment (DBE) 162, 163, 164, 165, 166, 167, 168, 170, 171, 172, 173, 174

data distribution services (DDS) 159, 160, 161, 162, 163, 164, 165, 166, 170, 171, 172, 173, 175

data models 201, 204, 208, 209, 210, 220, 221, 222, 223, 224, 230

data transfer objects (DTO) 186, 187, 189

design development 164

design quality 164

design structure matrix (DSM) 285, 287, 288, 289, 296

diesel engines 31

digraph 73, 74

distributed quality-of-service (QoS) modeling languages (DQML) 156, 157, 158, 159, 161, 162, 163, 164, 165, 166, 168, 170, 171, 172, 173, 174

distributed real-time embedded (DRE) systems 115, 116, 117, 118, 119, 120, 121, 122, 123, 124, 125, 126, 127, 128, 129, 130, 131, 134

distribution services platforms 351, 364

domain engineering 277, 278

domain modeling 1, 14, 388, 389, 391, 392, 393, 395, 398, 399, 400, 401

domain models 40, 41, 43, 389, 390, 391, 393, 394, 395, 397, 400, 401

domain-specific development constraints 156

Domain Specific Languages (DSL) 373

domain specific modeling (DSM) 8, 275, 277, 278, 285, 300

domain specific modeling languages (DSML) 156, 157, 158, 159, 161, 164, 166, 173, 174, 278, 279, 285, 342

dynamic execution environments 254, 263, 265, 269, 270

dynamic modeling 67

E

Eclipse framework 194

Eclipse Modeling Framework (EMF) 141, 153

economic values 232, 233, 234, 235, 236, 250, 253

electrical engineering 90, 93, 94, 95, 96, 98
engineering models 15
engineering sciences 3
enterprise application resources (EAR) 345
enterprise architect (EA) 196
enterprise architecture modeling (EAM) 399, 400
Enterprise Java Beans (EJB) 139, 140, 141, 145, 336, 342, 347
enterprise knowledge development methodology (EKD) 390, 394, 400
enterprise modeling 388, 389, 391, 394, 396, 398, 399, 400
enterprise models (EM) 390, 391, 392, 393, 394, 395, 401
e-services 232, 233, 237, 238, 247, 248, 250, 253
Extensible Markup Language (XML) 139, 203, 335, 345
external quality models 203, 204, 207, 209, 211, 218, 219, 227
extreme programming (XP) 3

F

Facebook 407
Feature Description Language (FDL) 373
FeatureMapper 375, 385
feature modeling 334, 335, 338, 339, 342
Filtered Cartesian Flattening (FCF) 124, 125
fingerprint scanners 377
FireAnt 335, 341, 342, 343, 344, 345, 346, 347, 350
foundational unified modeling language (fUML) 254, 255, 256, 259, 262, 263, 265, 270, 271, 272, 273
Four-Layer Architecture 304, 305, 306, 317, 318
free-format textual representations 371
functional requirements 65, 66, 67, 68, 69, 70, 71, 72, 75, 76, 77, 78, 79, 81

G

Gang of Four (GoF), the 307, 308, 311, 326, 327, 328

Generic Eclipse Modeling System (GEMS) 342
Generic Modeling Environment (GME) 122, 123, 124, 126, 127, 128, 129, 131, 134, 159, 161, 166, 285, 301
GMeta 122, 123
GModel 122
goal-based approaches 69, 71, 72, 73
graph-based models 376
graph-based representations 371
graph grammars 90, 93, 94, 103, 109

H

hardware configurations 334
holistic domain models 395
hot spots 355
human machine interfaces (HMI) 90

I

IBM 283, 290, 301, 390, 398, 399, 402, 405
IMDb 408
implementation development 164
information and communication technologies (ICT) 232, 233, 234
information capturing 68
information processing 41, 42, 63
information systems (IS) engineering 388, 389, 392, 393, 398, 400, 401, 403, 404
injected component (iComponent) 254, 255, 263, 264, 265, 266, 269, 270, 271
Institute of Electrical and Electronics Engineers (IEEE) 31, 32, 37, 38, 281, 301, 302, 353, 365, 366, 367
Institut National de Recherche en Informatique et en Automatique (INRIA) 92, 110
interactive systems 310
Interface Definition Language (IDL) 159, 160
International Electrotechnical Commission (IEC) 202, 203, 204, 205, 206, 208, 209, 210, 213, 214, 227, 229, 230, 231
International Organization for Standardization (ISO) 202, 203, 204, 205, 206, 207, 208, 209, 210, 213, 214, 227, 228, 229, 230, 231
Internet users 232

J

Java 117, 122, 127, 128, 129, 139, 141, 153, 159, 160, 163, 176, 189, 196, 309, 311, 328, 332, 335, 336, 343, 348, 349, 359, 360, 363, 407, 422, 425, 433
JavaScript Object Notation (JSON) 140, 141, 153

K

Knapsack Problem (KP) 124

L

Language Extended Lexicon (LEL) 45
Linux 160
local area networks (LAN) 137

M

machine engineering 93
man-made systems 31
many-to-one mapping 76
mathematical models 40, 41, 61
mechanical engineering 90, 93, 94
mechatronic engineering 90, 91, 94, 98, 108
megamodeling 92
MetaEdit+ 285, 302
meta-metamodels 278, 279, 285
metamodeling tools 122, 123
metamodels 117, 120, 122, 123, 124, 126, 127, 128, 130, 131, 132, 134, 278, 279, 281, 285, 286, 294, 296, 356, 357, 358, 369, 370, 379, 382, 383
meta-object facility (MOF) 34, 35, 37, 279, 285, 302
middleware services 351, 352, 359, 363, 364
MobileMedia 281, 286, 287, 288, 290, 291, 292, 293, 295, 296, 298
model driven architecture (MDA) 1, 4, 5, 6, 7, 8, 10, 12, 13, 14, 40, 41, 45, 46, 60, 61, 62, 63, 65, 66, 87, 88, 91, 115, 116, 117, 120, 122, 127, 131, 132, 178, 179, 180, 184, 198, 199, 201, 202, 203, 206, 207, 208, 209, 210, 213, 226, 227, 228, 229, 230, 231, 232, 233, 236, 237, 238, 243, 248, 250, 252, 254, 255, 256, 257, 258, 263, 265, 267, 268, 269, 270, 271, 272,

273, 334, 335, 338, 341, 342, 343, 346, 347, 348, 350, 388, 389, 392, 393, 395, 396, 397, 398, 399, 400, 404, 405, 407, 409, 410, 411, 412, 413, 418, 420, 424, 428, 429, 430, 431, 432, 433
model driven development (MDD) 178, 179, 184, 190, 256, 268, 305, 307, 312, 313, 370, 372, 374, 378, 382, 383, 384
model driven engineering (MDE) 8, 139, 142, 151, 152, 156, 157, 163, 174, 256, 277, 278, 279, 283, 284, 299, 303
model-driven methods 369, 370
model-driven requirements 369, 370, 371, 384
model driven software development 389
model fragments 370, 374, 375, 377, 381
modeling infrastructures 304, 305, 306, 307, 308, 309, 312, 313, 314, 315, 316, 318, 320, 321, 323, 325, 327, 330, 331
modeling languages 136, 155, 257, 258
modeling platforms 40
modeling tools 115, 116, 117, 120, 122, 126, 130
model transformation by demonstration (MTBD) 138, 143, 144, 145, 146, 150, 151, 152
model transformations 369, 370, 386
model-view-controller (MVC) 186, 286
Multi-Dimensional Knapsack Problem (MDKP) 124
multi-dimensional knapsack problems (MMKP) 124, 125, 128, 129, 130, 134
Multiple-Choice Knapsack Problem (MCKP) 124
MySpace 407

N

natural language 371, 372
negative application conditions (NAC) 379
North Atlantic Treaty Organization (NATO) 4

O

Object Constraint Language (OCL) 123, 132
Object Management Group, The (OMG) 40, 62, 64, 90, 91, 92, 95, 96, 97, 98, 100, 107, 111, 159, 179, 199, 233, 252, 256, 257, 259, 267, 269, 271, 272, 279, 285,

304, 305, 306, 307, 312, 313, 314, 315,
316, 318, 320, 321, 323, 325, 327, 330,
331, 332, 353, 355, 367, 370, 371, 376,
383, 385, 386, 409, 411, 414, 417, 418,
435

object-modeling techniques (OMT) 4
object-oriented analysis (OOA) 66, 67, 77
object-oriented software development (OOSD)
66
one-to-one mapping 76
operating systems (OS) 139, 140, 145, 360
Oracle 407

P

pair-wise dependence relation (PWDR) 287,
288, 289
parallelism 371
parametrization 354
Pattern-Oriented Software Architecture (POSA)
310, 311
platform independent models (PIM) 4, 6, 7,
40, 41, 43, 45, 63, 91, 96, 116, 177, 178,
179, 184, 186, 187, 188, 189, 190, 191,
192, 193, 196, 197, 199, 203, 206, 207,
208, 209, 210, 212, 213, 219, 221, 222,
232, 233, 236, 237, 238, 243, 244, 245,
246, 247, 248, 249, 250, 252, 258, 260,
395, 396, 397, 398, 400, 403, 407, 409,
410, 411, 412, 413, 414, 415, 416, 417,
424, 430, 431, 432, 436, 437
platform specific models (PSM) 4, 6, 7, 11, 40,
91, 96, 116, 117, 123, 130, 177, 178, 184,
186, 187, 188, 189, 190, 191, 193, 196,
197, 199, 203, 206, 207, 208, 209, 210,
212, 213, 219, 220, 221, 224, 228, 229,
233, 247, 248, 258, 260, 395, 396, 397,
398, 400, 407, 409, 410, 411, 413, 417,
418, 424, 430, 432, 437
plurality 71
product data management (PDM) 93, 108
product line architecture design 351
product-line architectures (PLA) 334, 335,
336, 337, 338, 339, 341, 342, 343, 344,
345, 346, 347, 351, 352, 353, 354, 355,
360, 362, 363, 364, 366, 368

programmable logic controllers (PLC) 90, 94,
95
programming languages 360
publish/subscribe applied to distributed resource scheduling (PADRES) 159

Q

quality evaluation processes (QEP) 212, 213,
214, 218, 219, 221, 222, 224, 225, 226
quality models 203, 204, 205, 206, 207, 209,
211, 212, 213, 218, 219, 220, 221, 227,
228, 230, 231
quality-of-service (QoS) 115, 116, 124, 131,
134, 156, 157, 158, 159, 160, 161, 162,
163, 164, 165, 166, 168, 169, 170, 171,
172, 173, 174, 175, 176, 337, 349, 408,
427, 428, 429, 430, 432
query/view/transformation (QVT) 312

R

Rational Unified Process (RUP) 233, 304, 313,
314, 317, 318, 320, 321, 322, 323, 324,
326, 328, 329, 330
requirements engineering 389, 392, 393, 399,
400, 401, 403, 404
requirements specification language (RSL)
177, 178, 179, 180, 181, 182, 183, 184,
186, 187, 188, 189, 190, 191, 193, 194,
196, 197, 198
requirements specifications 369, 370, 371, 372,
374, 376, 377, 381, 383, 384, 386
resource-event-agent (REA) 234, 235, 238,
239, 240, 241, 242, 250, 252, 253
retina scanners 377
RightScale 139

S

scope, commonality, and variability (SCV)
335, 336, 338, 342, 344
Semantics for Business Rules and Business
Vocabulary (SBVR) 45
semantic standards 232
semantic transformation layers (STL) 141, 142
service level agreements (SLA) 413, 432
service oriented architecture (SOA) 43

service-oriented component models 254, 255, 270

service-oriented components 254, 263, 265, 269

service-oriented frameworks 254

software assets 275, 276

software development 1, 2, 3, 4, 5, 6, 7, 8, 9, 10, 11, 12, 13, 15, 16, 18, 31, 32, 38, 41, 43, 63, 136, 154, 201, 202, 204, 205, 206, 208, 226, 228, 229, 230, 231, 275, 276, 278, 281, 282, 283, 300, 304, 305, 306, 307, 309, 310, 311, 312, 313, 314, 315, 316, 318, 320, 321, 322, 324, 326, 327, 328, 329, 330, 331, 333, 388, 389, 390, 394, 398, 399, 401, 402, 403, 407, 409, 411, 430, 431, 432, 435, 436

software development lifecycles 407

software development processes 201, 202, 204, 205, 226, 230

software engineering 1, 2, 3, 4, 5, 6, 7, 8, 9, 10, 12, 13, 14, 15, 16, 17, 90, 91, 93, 110, 202, 304, 306, 308, 309, 313, 314, 315, 316, 317, 320, 322, 323, 324, 326, 327, 328, 329, 330, 331

Software Engineering Institute, 277, 302

software engineering method and theory (SE-MAT) 9, 14

software engineers 275

software lifecycles 276, 282

software patterns 304, 305, 306, 314, 326, 329, 330, 333

Software Performance Model Driven Architecture (SPMDA) 412

Software Productivity Research LLC (SPR) 2

software product lines (SPL) 120, 121, 276, 277, 278, 279, 282, 283, 285, 286, 288, 291, 294, 298, 299, 300, 303, 351, 352, 362, 364, 368, 369, 370, 371, 372, 373, 374, 375, 376, 377, 380, 381, 382, 383, 384, 386

software product quality requirements and evaluation (SQuaRE) 205, 227, 228

software solutions 307, 312, 314, 321, 326

software systems 202, 226

software testing 275

solution-oriented 67

SourceForge.net 198, 199

stakeholders 276, 278, 300, 351, 353, 361, 367, 368, 370, 372, 374, 386

state handling 309

strategic scope 72

SVO sentences 181, 182, 184, 186, 187, 189, 196

system requirements models 393

system scope 72

systems development 388, 389, 393, 394, 395, 397, 398

systems engineering 322, 323, 331

T

technical systems 23, 31

TGraph 196, 198

theory driven architecture (TDA) 8

third-generation languages 136

time dimensions 21

topological functioning model 65, 67, 73, 76, 79, 89

topological functioning models (TFM) 9, 10, 11, 12, 13, 15, 17, 26, 27, 28, 29, 32, 33, 34, 35, 36, 38, 40, 41, 45, 46, 47, 48, 49, 50, 51, 52, 53, 57, 58, 59, 60, 61

topological model 73, 74, 78

topological modeling 1, 16, 17, 18, 19, 31, 34, 35, 36

topological models 16, 17, 19, 20, 21, 22, 23, 25, 26, 27, 28, 29, 30, 31, 34, 35, 36, 37, 38

topological properties 15, 23, 30

traceability 65, 67, 71, 73

transformation algorithms 188

transformation engines 136

triple graph grammars (TGG) 92, 93, 100, 101, 102, 103, 104, 105, 106, 107, 108, 109

U

unified modeling language (UML) 4, 7, 12, 16, 158, 178, 179, 181, 184, 186, 188, 189, 196, 198, 199, 206, 208, 210, 226, 228, 229, 230, 232, 233, 236, 237, 241-256, 258, 259, 261, 263-273, 276, 277, 278, 279, 284, 288, 290, 291, 294, 295, 296, 298, 299, 300, 306, 316, 318, 331, 332,

335, 348, 350-367, 373, 374, 376, 378, 379, 381, 382, 385, 389, 390, 394, 405, 411, 412, 414, 415, 417, 418, 425, 432, 435
unified process (UP) 70, 71
uniform resource identifiers (URI) 141, 142
use case 67, 68, 69, 70, 71, 72, 75, 76, 78, 81, 82, 83, 84, 85, 86, 87, 88, 89
use case modeling 67

V

Variability Modeling Language for Requirements (VML4RE) 369, 371, 375, 376, 377, 378, 379, 381, 382, 383
variant management 309
variation points 370, 372

verification and validation (V&V) 257, 270
vide CIM level language (VCLL) 45
video streams 360
virtual machines (VM) 137, 139, 140

W

Web application portals 407, 408, 409, 411, 412, 424, 425, 426, 428, 429, 430, 431, 432
Web applications 232, 233, 407, 408, 409, 410, 411, 412, 413, 418, 419, 420, 421, 424, 425, 426, 427, 428, 429, 430, 431, 432
Web services 232, 233, 247, 250, 252
WordNet 178, 181, 182, 183, 184, 191, 194, 198